Quantrill and the Border Wars

By

WILLIAM ELSEY CONNELLEY

Author of "Doniphan's Expedition, Mexican War,"
"Memoirs of John James Ingalls," "Wyandot Folk-Lore,"
"The Heckewelder Narrative," "The Provisional
Government of Nebraska Territory," etc.

Introduction

by

HOMER CROY

PAGEANT BOOK COMPANY

NEW YORK

1956

Published by Pageant Book Company

59 Fourth Avenue, New York 3, N. Y.

Library of Congress Catalog Card Number: 56-8736

Printed in U.S.A. by
NOBLE OFFSET PRINTERS, Inc.
400 Lafayette Street
New York 3, N. Y.

INTRODUCTION

By

HOMER CROY

One night, in Kansas City, a friend invited me to go with him to a meeting of the Quantrill Club. I had never been there; I didn't dream what would happen to me. During the course of the evening I chirped up and said that Quantrill was the bloodiest man who had ever lived in America. Right then and there I had my horse shot out from under me, for all of them (it seemed to me it was *all*) said that Bloody Bill Anderson and Jesse James were twice as bloody. I said they weren't any such thing. Down went another horse. The way the men rallied around Quantrill astonished me; and they meant it, too. And they all knew what they were talking about, for they were, one and all, specialists in this field. Two of them I want to pay my respects to, here and now. I consider them the greatest Quantrill authorities in America: B. J. George, 3 East 65th Terrace, Kansas City 13, Missouri, and Martin E. Ismert, 51 West 53rd Street Terrace, Kansas City 12. In fact, Mr. George's father rode with Quantrill and B. J. George has collected Quantrill material for thirty years.

I had known something about Quantrill and had him down as a blood-thirsty killer. But not these men. To them he was a quiet, sober, sedate, home-loving body who wouldn't harm a kitten — a credit to the Southern Cause. I could hardly believe my ears, but there it was and there I was, and soon I was as full of holes as a sharecropper's screen door. They said, in essence, that Quantrill was a vastly misunderstood man and that historians had not treated him fairly. They said that William Elsey Connelley was the dog in the manger. At mention of Connelley there was (I'm almost certain) a hiss, so bitterly did these people hate the name of the great historian.

I tried to defend myself, but I didn't know much about Quantrill; I had about the chance a farm boy has who has walked into a bumble-bee's nest. I slapped for a while, then tore for the house as fast as I could go.

When the thing was over, I got my hands on a Connelley book. I had gone through it some years before, but now I really put down my subsoiler (a farm expression you city folks won't know). I re-read the book, and I think it is the most remarkable crime history ever produced in the United States. I realize that is taking in a lot of territory, especially when you think of the fine histories that have been written in this country. But there is none — none at all — like Connelley's. He didn't undertake to depict an era, as our historians do today; or a Great Cause, or a Lost Cause, or a section of the country in travail. He just took out after one man, got him by the breeches and held on till he had him in his power. He wasn't aloofly fair to him; he hated the man and he didn't care who knew it. As a result he produced a book that no one can read without having his emotions stirred; you either hate Quantrill, too, or you say, "The man is not fair to Quantrill" and then begin to hate Connelley. No fence-sitting, here. You are either pro-Connelley, or you want to plant poison ivy on his grave.

His book is badly constructed, at least compared to the way the matter is managed today. He begins with Quantrill in the grave. Usually a book dealing with a man's life begins with the cradle and ends with him in the grave. But Connelley couldn't wait to get him in the grave at the end of the book; so he tossed him in in the first chapter. He tells half of the book backward, but he tells it so breathlessly that you follow him like a bee after honey.

No yawns, no tuning in on television for a change. You are right there in Bleeding Kansas.

About the politest term Connelley applies to Quantrill is "gory monster"; after that he gets personal. Here's one sentence from Connelley: "Because of Quantrill, widows wailed, orphans cried, maidens wept." That's gettin' right in there and pitching. No one could say that Connelley was impersonal; he hated Quantrill and he was going to belt his bones around.

One extremely bad thing (from a technical side) is his free-hand sowing of footnotes; in fact, the man has three times as much space devoted to footnotes as he has to text. If you, today, took a manuscript like that in to a publisher, the publisher would hand you your hat before you got your knees crossed.

And he jumps geographically. Sometimes you don't know whether you're in Kansas, Missouri, or knocking around in Kentucky. But you're with him all the way. Faults! It has more faults than a mother-in-law. But interest — depiction of time and place — the man's marvelous. I don't believe there is a historian today who does the job as well. (Now I'll get Hail Columbia for this. But it's the way I feel and I have to say what I think.)

Connelley opens by telling where and how Quantrill was buried; then the author says that he has three of Quantrill's bones. What an opening! And his statement was exactly true. What a way to approach history! I wrote a book about Jesse James and one about

Cole Younger — but never a bone. But it gives me an idea. The next time I tackle a historical character, I'm going to see if I can't have a go at his bones.

To make sure I wasn't making a wild statement for this Introduction, I wrote to Mrs. Lela Barnes, of the Kansas State Historical Society, and asked her if she knew about the Quantrill-Connelley bones. She did. She wrote, "Our Society has three arm bones and two shin bones, all said to belong to Quantrill." Now that's the way a state historical society should be run. Let them bones rise again.

Connelley got his information from the horse's mouth. He interviewed old-timers, men who were "for" Quantrill, and men who would liked to have applied a buffalo skinning knife to him. Both sides. He went to no end of trouble to run down information about Quantrill. He went to Canal Dover, in Ohio, where Quantrill had been born, and trailed him like an Indian tracker. And he told what he thought of Quantrill in words that smoked. And when Connelley takes up the Morgan Walker incident, he tears into Quantrill with a bull whip. As a result a good many people in the Border Belt feel that Connelley is unfair to Quantrill, and resent it. But allowing for a certain amount of loaded dice, Connelley gives an amazing picture of the man and the times. He takes no aloof point of view, but gets right down there in the grave, holds up Yorrick's skull and says, "*Alas!* poor Yorrick! I knew him, Horatio, a fellow of infinite cussedness."

In poking through the book I became interested in the man behind it, and I found out some interesting things. One was that he was a Southerner, Kentucky-born. He moved to Missouri where he ran a lumber yard. Then he moved to Kansas and became a historian, which would seem to show what that state will do to a person.

He engaged in two strange affairs — affairs about as far apart as you could imagine. One was that he started a movement in Kansas against the great and powerful Standard Oil Company and I'll be dog-goned if he wasn't instrumental in dissolving the company as a trust! It seems impossible, but it's the truth and the lumber yard historian was the man who did it.

The thing he did that was so sharply in contrast with this was that he became interested in the Wyandot Indians and I'll declare if he didn't tag them around till he made out a dictionary of their language; it's still the only one.

Quantrill told a monstrous lie about where he had come from and why he was fighting for the Southern Cause, when he was as Yankee as pot-roast, and a million people believed it. Connelley went quietly out with his spade and dug up the truth. The old guerrillas who had ridden under Quantrill wanted to throw Connelley into the Kaw. But Connelley had the facts and never lowered his mizzenmast, or whatever it is they never lower when the enemy is coming over the side of the ship.

Connelley was a character, himself, His name was Conley, but he decided he didn't like this spelling and so changed it to Connelley. His brother (Henry C. H. Conley) continued his spelling as long as he lived. W. E. was president of the Kansas Historical Society and it was while holding this post that he wrote his amazing book. It was published by The Torch Press, Cedar Rapids, Iowa, in 1910. It was the custom at this time for small printing and publishing companies to print important regional and sectional books. The New York papers, at this time, didn't pay too much attention to the books of small out-of-town publishing companies, and so the Connelley book did not attract much attention. Normally it would have died before frost, but instead it kept kicking and is still kicking and will, I think, fling about for years to come, for there is, as I've said, no other book in America like it.

One thing about Connelley surprises me. Generally he told the truth and in CAPS, but he hid the name of Quantrill's mistress. He called her Kate Clarke, oddly enough calling her by his mother's maiden name. Her name was not Clarke at all, but Kate King. The name Connelley used has passed into history and nothing can be done about it. If you want to, you can turn to the index and see what happened to "Kate Clarke" — you'll be shocked. And a Missouri girl, too!

I had always believed that, at the sacking of Lawrence, Quantrill had fewer than 400 men; the number is usually quoted at 350. And that he was at full strength there and that he never mustered more than 400. I find this is quite wrong. Martin E. Ismert, whom I've already quoted, has been for years drawing up a muster roll of the men who, one time or another, fought under Quantrill. He has 800 names and expects to add to this number. Some were killed, some deserted, some joined the regular Southern army, and some — of all things — joined the North. It just shows how things were going at the time of the bloody warfare between Kansas and Missouri.

One of the things that has touched me is how loyal Quantrill's men were to him. His ex-guerrillas held their first reunion in 1888 and after that met regularly each summer, usually at Wallace Grove, a couple of jumps from Kansas City. They even met during the turmoil of the First World War. But, as the years advanced, fewer and fewer responded to roll-call. Finally the last reunion was in September, 1920, and it met, as the others did, with a large framed portrait of Quantrill on display in the group — a kind of rallying point for the grizzled old veterans. During their first meetings they always gave the Rebel Yell, as terrifying a sound as ever issued from human lips. It sounded like a cross between present-day radio static and the baying of the Hound of the Baskervilles. No one who heard it could ever forget it. If I had to put it on paper it would go something like this —

Yip-yip-yaw—aw-aw.

This shows how useless it is for the feeble letters of the alphabet to try to give the sub-human sounds of the Rebel Yell.

A word as to what happened to the Quantrill collection that Connelley accumulated: On his death, in 1930, his daughter removed most of it from the state historical archives in Topeka, and sold parts of the collection, from time to time, to private collectors. As an example, the original of his library on the Wyandot Indian language is owned by the Public Library, in Kansas City, Kansas.

And now I suppose I should try to show how important this Kansas-born, Iowa-nursed book is. Well, in its field there is nothing like it.

PREFACE

THE border wars must be taken to constitute a phase of that critical period in American history when two antagonistic fundamentals of government contended for supremacy. The devotion of adherents to respective principles was fanatical and fierce, and unusual animosities were engendered.

By stormy conventions the two ideas of the destiny of our common country were reconciled in our growth to the Mississippi. Newly bound and hedged about, they were flung upon the soil of Missouri. But the compromise of a principle is a crime, and the feeble barriers set by time-serving statesmen became tense and strained. The advance-guard of a higher national life burst them asunder and emerged upon the Great Plains. There the contest to maintain itself became a grapple for the existence of the government, and ended in civil war.

The story of the border is the history of preliminary forays and the shock of army upon army in the national contest. It covers ten years. In wealth of romantic incidents, stirring adventures, hair-breadth escapes, sanguinary ambuscades, deadly encounters, individual vengeance, relentless desolation of towns and communities, and bloody murder, no other part of America can compare with it. Some future Scott will make himself immortal by telling this wonderful story.

This is the first effort, it is believed, to make any serious study of the conditions prevailing on the border. The state of society about Lawrence as shown in the year 1860 may be accepted as representative of the general conditions found in Kansas up to the Civil War, and no attempt to describe them has been found. The state of disorder in Missouri was the result in some degree of the reaction upon itself of its course in Kansas. The time has not yet come when a dispassionate study of the conditions which existed in Missouri will be acceptable to all the people of that great commonwealth. But the position that the Missourian suffered most from his brother Missourian is founded on facts and will be sustained by future writers.

Nothing has been written in a sensational way. The simple statement of what occurred is sensational enough, and the old idea that truth is stranger than fiction is demonstrated.

Except the men at the heads of the respective governments, and some of the leading generals, Quantrill is the most widely-known man connected with the Civil War. His place in the public estimation of the South was based upon a misapprehension of his life and motives. He voluntarily imposed himself on the South. He told little of his prior life, and that which he did tell was wholly untrue. It is due to the South that his life be revealed as it actually was. That done, his character and his motives stand clearly outlined. Heretofore there has been nothing on which to base a reason for many incidents in the warfare of the border.

It is one of the strange decrees of fate that the normal man is rarely mentioned in history or literature. The citizen who labors diligently to support his family, to build up his city, to sustain his state, gets little or no notice in the annals of his time. It is the abnormal man, the man in desperate extremity, who is portrayed for the amusement or instruction of mankind.

This work could never have been written fully but for the preliminary labors of the late W. W. Scott, editor of the *Iron Valley Reporter*, Canal Dover, Ohio. He grew up with Quantrill, and it was his desire to write an account of the life of the noted guerrilla. He secured from Mrs. Quantrill the letters written her by her son. He traveled extensively to secure facts. He located the grave and removed the body. Mrs. Quantrill stipulated that the story of her son should not be written in her lifetime. But she outlived Mr. Scott, and he never got beyond the point of gathering material. After his death the author bought his papers.

Many of the most stirring events of the border wars do not properly fall within the scope of this work. It is the intention of the author to publish another book in which will appear adequate accounts of the transactions and doings in the Border Wars of Atchison, Lane, Brown, Robinson, Thayer, Shelby, Jennison, Hoyt, Bill Anderson, Clements, the Youngers, the James boys, George Todd, Senator Steven B. Elkins, Captain William H. Gregg, and the operations generally of Free-State pioneers, border-ruffians, Red Legs, Guerrillas, and Jayhawkers in the disorders on the border.

The author realizes that there may be some objection to the repetition of the statement in the notes that documents cited as authority may be found in his Collection. But long and persistent effort failed to devise a better plan.

This is not designed to be a "Life" of Quantrill, but an account of those incidents of the Border Wars in which he and his men were the leading characters. All that could be learned of the famous outlaw and his family has been set down. It was necessary that this work should be written. Little of the story has ever been told. There has been no definite information. All has been myth, doubt, assertion, beautiful generalization, conjecture. In a general way it has been known that banditti infested the border, that ruthless hands were red with blood, that many a night flared red with burning homes and sacked towns. But of the family and parentage of Quantrill, his life in Illinois, Indiana, Kansas — of his trip to Utah and Pike's Peak, his school, his life at Lawrence, and the Morgan Walker raid—of the organization of his band of guerrillas, its operations in Missouri, Kansas, Texas, and what is now Oklahoma, of his expulsion therefrom and the disintegration thereof — of his life with Kate Clarke, his expedition to Kentucky and his operations there — of his death, burial, and exhumation — of these things no man has been able to speak with confidence, for knowledge of them was not at hand. And the importance of this information is realized when we remember that it embraces much of the history of four states in the Civil War and portrays the bloodiest man known to the annals of America.

There is no good portrait of Quantrill. He had a tin-type

made at the beginning of the war. It was lost in the yard of one Fields, in Jackson county, who found it and preserved it until Thomson Quantrill came to Missouri. He demanded the picture and it was given to him, but it was first photographed. The photographs made from this tin-type, which had lain in the ground some time, are all the portraits known of Quantrill. Some one supposed he wore a mustache, and with a brush supplied one. E. P. DeHart had the portrait painted in Confederate uniform in company with a character known as "Indian Jim," no copy of which has been found. A. M. Winner, Kansas City, Mo., had it painted in Confederate uniform, rank of Colonel, prints of which are common.

William E. Connelley

816 Lincoln Street
    Topeka, Kansas
        July 3, 1909

The last roll-call of the Quantrill Guerrillas, September, 1920. They always put Quantrill's picture in the middle. The man on the front row, on the right, is Jesse James, Junior, a guest; and so is the man on the left, front row (Harry C. Hoffman). The man immediately behind Jesse James, Jr., is "Uncle Simmie" Whitsett, famous leader of the men. The original of this picture is owned by Mrs. Forrest T. Gillam, Maryville, Missouri — "Uncle Simmie's" niece.

MAPS AND ILLUSTRATIONS

TABLE OF CONTENTS

CHAPTER I

THE QUANTRILL FAMILY

HAGERSTOWN, Maryland, seems to have been the seat of the Quantrill family in America. No effort to trace its origin has been made, but from what information there is to be had on the subject and from a study of the Christian names, it would appear that the family is of English extraction. And Captain Thomas Quantrill boasted that his ancestors came from England to Maryland, and that they were pure English.

Thomas Quantrill was the captain of a company raised at Hagerstown for service in the War of 1812. It is of record that he was a brave soldier, and that he was wounded at the battle of North Point, as were two of his men, Lazarus B. Wilson and his brother Samuel. And a number were killed.[1]

Captain Thomas Quantrill was a blacksmith at Hagerstown. He married Miss Judith Heiser, a sister of William Heiser, a man of high character, for many years the president of a bank at Hagerstown, and a man of wealth.[2]

---

[1] Letter of Oliver M. Wilson, Kansas City, Kansas, April 2, 1898, to W. W. Scott, now in the Collection of the author. Wilson was the son of the soldier, Lazarus B. Wilson. He mentions a history and roster of Captain Thomas Quantrill's Company as being in his possession.

[2] Thomas Quantrill quit his trade and became a horse-trader.

He was a blacksmith and married Judy Heiser, sister of William Heiser, for a great many years president of the Hagerstown bank and one of the wealthiest men in the locality and of high character. Probably the wealth of his brother-in-law fired the ambition of Mr. Thomas Quantrill to make riches faster than over the anvil. For he gave up blacksmithing and turned horse trader. Our informant recalls yet more than one instance that got abroad of Mr. Quantrill's sharp practices in horse-dealing. He was a handsome man, dressed well, lived fast, and merely gained the reputation of a sharp operator who was to be watched in a business transaction; he didn't forfeit his standing in the community beyond this notoriety for sharp-dealing. — Clipping from the Keokuk, Iowa, *Gate City*, August 17, 1882, now in the Collection of the author.

The Quantrill blood was evidently bad, the grandfather of the raider

A number of children were born to Captain Thomas Quantrill at Hagerstown, among them William (so named for his Uncle William Heiser), Archibald, Thomas Henry, and Jesse Duncan. The last named died when eight or nine years old, and William's name was changed to Jesse Duncan. There were other sons, the names of whom are not remembered. One of them, it is said, became a pirate on the high seas, operating many years on the Gulf of Mexico between Galveston Island and the mouth of the Sabine; but this may have been a brother of Captain Thomas Quantrill.

Captain Thomas Quantrill often visited his son Thomas Henry, in Canal Dover, where he was regarded as a man of fine appearance.[3] He moved to Washington City, where he died of apoplexy. He was stricken in front of the Treasury building and died suddenly.

Jesse Duncan Quantrill was sent to New York City to attend school. He returned to Hagerstown with two accomplishments — boxing and great skill with a pen. He was his father's favorite, was indulged, and grew up in idleness and mischief. He was a sort of fop or dandy with criminal instincts and tendencies, a dashing, handsome man, wholly devoid of moral char-

---

was a professional gambler. I knew him pretty well, having been introduced to him by his son, Thomas H. Quantrill, at Dover, and met him afterwards, occasionally in this city. A brother of Thomas H. Quantrill was what would now be called a confidence man; he traveled through the Southern States, locating in some city where he would engage himself to the Belle of the place and buy all the jewelry, watches, carriages, etc., he could get credit for and just about the time the bills would come due, would skip to some other place and go through the same performance. He was finally arrested, tried and convicted, and sentenced to states prison for twenty years. — *Letter of John W. Harmon, 1237 Dean Street, Brooklyn, N. Y., December 19, 1900, to W. W. Scott*, now in the Collection of the author.

John W. Harmon was a traveling salesman who lived many years in Canal Dover, Ohio, and who moved to Brooklyn. He was a man of excellent character, as the author is informed by Mrs. Frances Beeson Thompson, daughter of H. V. Beeson, who knew him until the Beeson family came to Kansas.

It will be noted that Captain Thomas Quantrill visited Brooklyn. Perhaps he did so in his vocation of professional gambler.

[3] I have seen old Mr. Quantrill the father of Thos. in Canal Dover frequently, a tall 6 foot portly old Gent., quite respectfull looking. — *From letter of H. V. Beeson, Paola, Kansas, June 5, 1880, to W. W. Scott*, now in the Collection of the author.

acter. Mary Lane, daughter of Seth Lane, said to have been one
of the foremost citizens of Hagerstown, became infatuated with
him, and they were clandestinely married. She was to inherit
a considerable sum of money at a certain age which she had not
attained by a year when married. By making a very full and
sweeping relinquishment he secured this money from the bank
in which it had been deposited, and which, it was affirmed, belonged in part to Seth Lane and his son. When his wife had
attained her majority he endeavored to collect the money again,
alleging that the bank had no legal right to pay the money at
the time it had been paid.

With the money of his wife he had engaged in the grocery
business at Williamsport, Md. This business was a failure, and
the money was lost. He then determined to engage in larger
operations. He went to New York City, where he represented
himself to be the son of a wealthy Virginia merchant well known
there, and purchased on credit a large stock of goods, which he
caused to be shipped to himself at Baltimore. This swindle was
discovered by the merchants in time to stop a portion of the
shipment and save some of the goods. But he succeeded in disposing of a part of the merchandise in a way which baffled all
attempts to trace it. To avoid the consequences of this transaction he availed himself of the benefit of the law for bankrupts,
but as his action was based on fraud he was cast into prison.
For six months his beautiful wife shared his cell. He finally secured an acquittal and was released. While in prison he had
read law under directions from William Price, one of the leading lawyers of Western Maryland.

From Maryland Jesse D. Quantrill went to St. Louis, Mo.,
where he was soon in trouble and in jail, securing his release
finally through the efforts of his wife, who still clung to him.
Upon his release he took boat for Cincinnati, and while on board
committed a forgery which seems to have been discovered at
once, and for which he escaped punishment. From Cincinnati
he went to New Orleans, where he became dissipated and began
to neglect and abuse his wife. She fell ill, and her condition
appeared to work a change in him. He started by boat to take
her home to Maryland; but while the boat was yet on the Mis-

sissippi river he committed a forgery on a Cincinnati bank. He
was soon detected in this crime, was taken to Cincinnati and
thrown into jail. After a confinement in prison of seven months
his wife succeeded in securing him bail, which he forfeited by
not appearing for trial, deserting his wife at that place. She
next heard of him at Hagerstown, where he was in trouble for
a forgery he committed there, but for which he escaped conviction. He then went to Pennsylvania, where he was sentenced
to a term of imprisonment in the penitentiary for forgery, and
he served three years. While serving this sentence his wife secured a divorce from him, it is said, by the act of the Maryland
Legislature. When he heard of her action in procuring the
divorce he made many savage threats against her life. But upon
his release from prison he married a Pennsylvania lady, and
was soon thereafter arrested for another forgery, for which he
was sentenced to a term of seven years in the penitentiary.

Meanwhile, Mrs. Quantrill had married Mr. A. Cowton,
proprietor of the United States Hotel, Cumberland, Maryland,
with whom she was living happily. Quantrill was released from
the Pennsylvania penitentiary in 1848. In March, 1849, he appeared in Cumberland. On the fifth of that month Mrs. Cowton
was in her apartments, when a servant showed up a gentleman
who had just arrived in the city. He dismissed the servant, and
closed and locked the door. He then turned to Mrs. Cowton,
who was horrified to behold Quantrill, her former husband. There
was murder in his looks, and she screamed for help. He told
her that her hour had come, caught her by the throat, threw
her to the floor, placed his knee upon her breast, and snapped a
pistol in her face. When the pistol missed fire, and just as he
was drawing a long knife, several persons who had been attracted
by her screams, broke down the door and rescued Mrs. Cowton.
For this attempt to murder he was sentenced to a term of imprisonment. He must have possessed a fascinating personality,
for he soon obtained an unaccountable influence over the prison
officials and was allowed considerable freedom, even acting as
guard over other prisoners. In 1851 he was pardoned upon condition that he would leave the state and never return.

When Jesse D. Quantrill left Maryland he went to Canal

Dover, Ohio, where his brother Thomas Henry then lived. There he was engaged for a time as jockey and horse-dealer, for or in connection with his father. And it is quite probable that the resident brother was interested in the business. The horses were purchased and prepared for the markets in the cities to the east. The tails of the horses were scored on the under side and then tied up in an elevated position to heal, usually suspended for a time from an over-head beam. This was a cruel process, resorted to for the purpose of causing the horse's tail when healed to stand away from the body, giving it a graceful carriage, greatly improving the general appearance of the animal. After a year or two spent in this business at Canal Dover, Jesse D. Quantrill disappeared and never returned there, though intelligence of him and his doings reached the village for years afterwards. It was known that he assumed various names, one of which was Dr. Hayne; he was also known as Jesse Elliott and Jesse Elliott Quantrill. He married and deserted six women.[4]

There has been much said of a John Quantrill who was believed to have become a guerrilla in the West during the Civil War. It was supposed that he was in Missouri, from whence he

---

[4] Thomas Quantrill and myself at one time had a conversation about this Jesse E. Quantrill, he was a Dead beat and confidence man Mr. Quantrill informed me that he took the name of Elliott for his middle name unlawfully & for some reason he thought strange he also informed me Jesse E. went to Philadelphia and bought up Horses, stages &c. to start opposition lines of stages from Philadelphia & Baltimore against the great contractor Reeside that the Stage Co Bought him off at a Big Price He also informed me that he, Jesse E. went by the name of Doctor Hayne that he had been in about every Penitentiary in Penn., Maryland, Virginia & Kentucky and Perhaps Ohio. My impression was that he was a Bro or Cousin of the Mr. Thos Quantrill. — *From letter of H. V. Beeson, Paola, Kansas, June 5, 1880, to W. W. Scott,* now in the Collection of the author.

This account of Jesse D. Quantrill is taken from various sources, principally from articles in newspapers, the most important of which were published in the Philadelphia *Times* in 1884, in the New York *Graphic*, by "Gath" (George Alfred Townsend) in 1881, and in the Keokuk, Iowa, *Gate City*, August 17, 1882. There is much error and confusion in these and all other articles examined on the subject, most of them supposing Jessed D. Quantrill to have been the guerrilla, William C. Quantrill. "Gath" makes William C. Quantrill the son of Jesse D. But there is much that is true and accurately stated in them. The career of Jesse D. Quantrill as set out here may be relied upon as correct. By his first wife he had a son, named Lawrence Quantrill.

found his way to Texas, where he was befriended by a brother Freemason named Imboden. He is credited with having been a dead shot, and with having killed thirty-eight men in one battle. It is asserted that he died in New Orleans of wounds, of which he received many. There is nothing positively known of this John Quantrill, and it is probable that he originated in the vague conjectures as to the identity of William C. Quantrill.

Archibald Quantill was a printer and was at one time a compositor on the *National Intelligencer*, Washington City. He must have been among the younger children of Captain Thomas Quantrill, for he married Miss Mary A. Sands, whose age is given as thirty-two in 1862. Mrs. Mary A. Quantrill was a staunch and loyal supporter of the Union during the Civil War. Her brother, George W. Sands, was a member of the Maryland Legislature and was U. S. collector of internal revenue under President Lincoln. In September, 1862, Stonewall Jackson parted from General Lee at Frederick, Maryland, on his way to besiege Harper's Ferry. As Jackson passed through Frederick Mrs. Quantrill and her daughter Virginia, afterwards Mrs. Perry Brown, were standing at their gate waving a number of flags — the Stars and Stripes. The soldiers angrily ordered them to throw down the flags, and a lieutenant, with his sword, cut a flag from the hands of Virginia Quantrill. But she continued to wave Old Glory, and it was again cut from her hands by the lieutenant's sword. Mrs. Quantrill then took up a large flag which she waved aloft until the army had passed through the town. Many of the Confederate officers and some of the soldiers applauded her, an officer saying with a salute and marked courtesy, "To you, madam, not to your flag." Archibald Quantrill was in Washington City at the time at work at his trade. For this brave and patriotic act these women have not had proper credit. Indeed, they have been robbed of the fame of the deed by a great poet, and a decrepit and bed-ridden lady of Frederick given the honor for something she did not do.[5]

5 This incident inspired the beautiful and patriotic poem of Whittier, entitled *Barbara Frietchie*. Barbara lived some distance from the line of march, and it is not probable that she saw any of the soldiers who marched through Frederick that day. She was loyal and brave, it has been claimed,

Thomas Henry Quantrill was born at Hagerstown, Md., February 19, 1813. He was a tinker by trade.[6] He afterwards became a tinner. He had relatives, the Heisers, living at Chambersburg, Pa., whom he visited, perhaps in the strolling vocation of tinker. With one of these he learned the tinner trade. While there he met Miss Caroline Cornelia Clarke (or Clark) and became engaged to marry her. Some relative had persuaded him that it would be to his advantage to settle at Canal Dover, Ohio, and he had determined to go there for that purpose in the fall of 1836. Several Hagerstown people were settling at Canal Dover about that time. It was his wish that Miss Clarke should accompany him as his wife, and they were married at

Quantrill's Father

6 Statement of Mrs. Caroline Clarke Quantrill, his widow, published in the Chicago *Herald*, March 4, 1894.

There is some reason to believe that the name of Thomas Henry Quantrill was in fact Thomas Hart Quantrill, or that it had been at one time. In the family Bible it is written Thomas Henry, but the Quantrills seem to have been addicted to the habit of changing their names. His son, the guerrilla, assumed the name of Charley Hart in Kansas to conceal his identity, and it has been said that he used the name *Hart* because it had belonged to his father. He always went by the name of Charley Quantrill in Missouri. For the purposes of treachery he often pretended to be a Federal Captain Clarke, and he was known as Captain Clarke in Kentucky in the spring of 1865, and he gave that as his name at first when mortally wounded.

and would have waved her flag in the face of General Jackson himself if she had been given an opportunity. Her house is still standing, on the banks of Carroll creek, in Frederick. Whittier stated that he secured his information of this matter from Mrs. E. D. E. N. Southworth, the novelist.

There is now doubt as to the loyalty of Barbara Frietchie. Prof. E. Haworth, of the Kansas University, informs me that she was a staunch supporter of the Southern Confederacy. This information he had from her relatives. The poem is as follows:

BARBARA FRIETCHIE

["This poem," says Mr. Whittier, "was written in strict conformity to the account of the incident as I had it from respectable and trustworthy

Chambersburg, October 11, 1836. A little later he secured a contract to do some tin work in Canal Dover for Louis L. Lee, and as this work was to be done at once, the young people set out immediately. The contract was secured towards the latter part of November. They drove overland in their own buggy and arrived in December, stopping at first at the public house or tavern, where they remained but a short time, going to housekeeping in what was locally known as the "Tom West house" with S. Scott and wife.[7] This was a small one-story frame house near the corner of Factory and Fourth streets. It was afterwards in the Quantrill family, seemingly the property of Captain Thomas Quantrill,

House, in Canal Dover, Ohio, where Quantrill was born

---

[7] Memo. made by W. W. Scott, now in the Collection of the author.

---

sources. It has since been the subject of a good deal of conflicting testimony, and the story was probably incorrect in some of its details. It is admitted by all that Barbara Frietchie was no myth, but a worthy and highly esteemed gentle-woman intensely loyal and a hater of the Slavery Rebellion, holding her Union flag sacred and keeping it with her Bible; that when the Confederates halted before her house, and entered her dooryard, she denounced them in vigorous language, shook her cane in their faces, and drove them out; and when General Burnside's troops followed close upon Jackson's, she waved her flag and cheered them. It is stated that May Quantrill, a brave and loyal lady in another part of the city, did wave her flag in sight of the Confederates. It is possible that there has been a blending of the two incidents."]

Up from the meadows rich with corn,
Clear in the cool September morn,

The clustered spires of Frederick stand
Green-walled by the hills of Maryland.

Round about them orchards sweep,
Apple and peach tree fruited deep,

Fair as the garden of the Lord
To the eyes of the famished rebel horde,

On that pleasant morn of the early fall
When Lee marched over the mountain-wall;

Over the mountains winding down
Horse and foot, into Frederick town.

and, later, of Mrs. Caroline C. Quantrill, probably by deed from her father-in-law. It was the home of the Quantrills in Canal Dover until sold by Mrs. Quantrill about the year 1885.

Soon after his marriage Thomas Henry Quantrill wrote and

Forty flags with their silver stars,
Forty flags with their crimson bars,

Flapped in the morning wind: the sun
Of noon looked down, and saw not one.

Up rose old Barbara Frietchie then,
Bowed with her fourscore years and ten;

Bravest of all in Frederick town,
She took up the flag the men hauled down;

In her attic window the staff she set,
To show that one heart was loyal yet.

Up the street came the rebel tread,
Stonewall Jackson riding ahead.

Under his slouched hat left and right
He glanced; the old flag met his sight.

"Halt!" — the dust-brown ranks stood fast.
"Fire!" — out blazed the rifle-blast.

It shivered the window, pane and sash;
It rent the banner with seam and gash.

Quick, as it fell, from the broken staff
Dame Barbara snatched the silken scarf.

She leaned far out on the window-sill,
And shook it forth with a royal will.

"Shoot, if you must, this old gray head,
But spare your country's flag," she said.

A shade of sadness, a blush of shame,
Over the face of the leader came;

The nobler nature within him stirred
To life at that woman's deed and word;

"Who touches a hair of yon gray head
Dies like a dog! March on!" he said.

All day long through Frederick street
Sounded the tread of marching feet;

All day long that free flag tost
Over the heads of the rebel host.

published a "Lightning Calculator." He was by instinct a
mathematician, and one of high order, and for several years he
traveled about and sold his "Calculator." He finally opened
a tin-shop in Canal Dover. He wrote a book called the "Tin-

Ever its torn folds rose and fell
On the loyal winds that loved it well;

And through the hill-gaps sunset light
Shone over it with a warm good-night.

Barbara Frietchie's work is o'er,
And the Rebel rides on his raids no more.

Honor to her! and let a tear
Fall, for her sake, on Stonewall's bier.

Over Barbara Frietchie's grave,
Flag of Freedom and Union, wave!

Peace and order and beauty draw
Round thy symbol of light and law;

And ever the stars above look down
On the stars below in Frederick town!

In the Collection of the author there is a newspaper-clipping which
is an account of this incident. There is nothing to show where or when
the paper from which it was cut was published, but it is given here:

"FREDERICK TOWN."

A HISTORIC OLD PLACE — BABARA FRIETCHIE'S HOME — THE REAL
HEORINE — THE BATTLE OF THE MONOCACY.

It matters little for the purposes of patriotic history that Whittier,
in his immortal poem, has credited that ancient and worthy dame, Barbara
Frietchie, with a deed which she, dear old soul, was physically incapable of
accomplishing. We know too well that on that September morning of 1862,
when Jackson parted from Lee in Frederick, on his way to besiege Harper's
Ferry, Stonewall Jackson and his gray legions passed to the west by a
route which did not take them within two blocks of the now-demolished
dwelling on West Patrick street, wherein old Barbara, hopelessly bed-
ridden, was peacefully slumbering. But the aged lady was herself truly
loyal. She would have waved the Stars and Stripes in the face of Lee's
whole army, or of Jefferson Davis himself. Her humble grave in the
Reformed Cemetery at Frederick would look incomplete without the Star-
Spangled Banner drooping regretfully over it. In a life which wanted but
four years of a century, old Barbara must have

SEEN, FELT AND THOUGHT MUCH.

The banks of Carroll Creek are favorable to meditation, and it is fair to

man's Guide" or the "Tinner's Guide," embellished with drawings showing designs for various articles of tinware and such as could be made from sheet-iron — pans, pipes, cups, elbows, etc. This book was published with money belonging to the

---

infer that the historic stream was more picturesque and less odoriferous in her days than now, when the tanyards of Frederick pollute it with their mingled abominations. From the spot beneath the weeping willow, a hundred yards below her home, near the City Spring, Barbara must have often looked on the ruinous and picturesque shanty, here depicted and still standing, in which the Father of his Country had his headquarters with Gen. Braddock and Benjamin Franklin when the ill-fated expedition to Fort Duquesne passed through Frederick in 1755. The place is now occupied by two colored families, and its dingy rooms suggest a startling mental contrast of the state of things then and now. We know that Washington, though fitted to grace with his majestic presence the Courts of the proudest Empire in the world, retained after his election to the Presidency the Spartan simplicity of taste which distinguished him during his military career. He may have thought — nay he must have thought — when the world did homage at his feet, of the hours spent in that simple cottage on the banks of Carroll Creek.

THE TRUE HEROINE.

But to return to the ancient and neglected Barbara. She was born in Lancaster, Pa., in 1766, and died in Frederick on Dec. 18, 1862, three months after the episode with which her name is falsely but forever associated. The true honor of the waving of the flag has been shown in the light of facts to belong to Mrs. Mary A. Quantrill. The story, as told by Joseph Walker, of Washington, D. C., a son-in-law of Mrs. Quantrill, is as follows, and contains enough elements of romance to cause no regret at the spoiling of Whittier's poem, except in the involuntary and unintentional injustice done by the distinguished poet to Mrs. Quantrill herself.

Mrs. Quantrill was at the time a handsome woman, about 32 years of age. Her husband was employed as a compositor on *The National Intelligencer* in Washington, while she lived at Frederick with her children.

On the day when Jackson passed through the Mountain City Mrs. Quantrill and her daughter Virgie, afterwards Mrs. Perry Brown, were standing at their gate. They had several Union flags, which they waved as the troops of Jackson passed by. Virgie was waving a flag when several rebel soldiers angrily called to her to throw it down; and, as she persisted, a Lieutenant drew his sword and cut the flag from her hand. Still she persisted, and once more it was cut down. Then Mrs. Quantrill displayed a larger flag, and continued to wave it till the ranks had passed by. They were not further molested. Many of the rebel officers and soldiers murmured applause at their courage and treated them with marked courtesy, one officer saluting Mrs. Quantrill as he remarked, "To you, madam, not to your flag."

Whittier says that he derived his information as to Barbara from Mrs. E. D. E. N. Southworth, the well-known novelist. This may well have been, but it is very clear that he did not get at the facts.

MRS. QUANTRILL

appears to have been a woman of superior intelligence. She was for many years a teacher in Frederick, and was a frequent contributor to the *Evening*

school-fund of the village, perhaps before the organization of the Union School. Quantrill was one of the trustees having this money in charge. By collusion with one of his colleagues the money was used to pay for printing the "Guide." In some way H. V. Beeson discovered the misuse of the school-funds and called public attention to the matter. This angered Quantrill, and he threatened to kill Beeson, which, no doubt, he intended to do. One evening, late in autumn, he entered Beeson's house with a cocked derringer in his hand. Beeson, at the time, was sitting before his fire heating the point of a large iron poker, which, when hot, he intended to plunge into a cup of cider which he held in his hand, preparatory to drinking, a very common method of that day for the treatment of cider and other liquors. When Quantrill entered, Beeson rose suddenly and struck him on the head with the poker before he could shoot, laying him unconscious on the floor with a long gash in his scalp. Neighbors came in and carried Quantrill to his own house, where he was some time recovering from the blow.

It was about that time that Quantrill had a difficulty with Mrs. Roscoe, the wife of a Frenchman who lived in Canal Dover. She gave lessons in painting and was a bright, vivacious woman. Quantrill made remarks derogatory to her character. These remarks were persisently repeated by him about the village and finally came to the ears of Mrs. Roscoe. She armed herself with an old-style "cowhide," sought Quantrill on the streets, found him talking to a group of men in a public place, and there administered to him a sound whipping or "cowhiding."

The Canal Dover Union School was organized in 1849. In 1850-51 Quantrill was an assistant to the principal. In the 1851-52 term he was the principal, in which capacity he was continued until his death, December 7, 1854. He died of con-

Herald of York, Pa. She was a Miss Sands, and her brother, George W. Sands, was a member of the Maryland Legislature, and U. S. Collector of Internal Revenue under President Lincoln. The troubles between the Government and Collector Sands are a matter of recent history. Mrs. Quantrill died about six years ago. It is said that she always felt keenly the injustice Whittier had done her. A niece and namesake of Mrs. Quantrill was afterwards a clerk in the Treasury Department.

sumption. He was a good teacher and was much beloved by his pupils.[8]

The records in the Quantrill family Bible are as follows:

MARRIAGES

Thomas Henry Quantrill and Caroline Cornelia Clarke, October 11, 1836.

BIRTHS

William Clarke Quantrill — born July 31, 1837.
Mary Quantrill — born September 24, 1838.
Franklin Quantrill — born November 12, 1840.
MacLindley Quantrill — born December 18, 1841.
Cornelia Lisette Quantrill — born June 20, 1843.
Thomson Quantrill — born October 3, 1844.
Clarke Quantrill — born September 5, 1847.
Archibald Rollin Quantrill — born September 27, 1850.

DEATHS

MacLindley Quantrill — died August 26, 1842.
Cornelia Lisette Quantrill — died July 28, 1844.
Clarke Quantrill — died March —, 1848.
Archibald Rollin Quantrill — died March 2, 1851.[9]

---

[8] Of Thomas Henry Quantrill, Abraham Ellis says, in the Topeka *Weekly Capital*, February 3, 1882:

His father [Thomas Henry Quantrill, father of William C. Quantrill of whom he was speaking] was for many years a teacher in the High School in that place [Canal Dover]; and I never heard anything against his character; but two of his brothers died in state prison. One was a highwayman and the other a sea pirate.

The pirate may have been his uncle. See *ante*.

Speaking of the wickedness and depravity of W. C. Quantrill, Ellis, in the same article, says, "It was in the bone."

[9] Copied from the Louisville *Courier-Journal*, May 13, 1888. Mrs. Quantrill exhibited the Bible, saying:

We had eight children in all, but four of them died in their infancy. Here, in the old Bible in which the records were kept, you see the names and dates. The records were all made by my husband, and I have never written a line in the old Bible since his death, which accounts for the balance not being in. Only one of my children is still alive. Thomson lives in Montana, where he has a family and is doing well. My daughter Mary died in 1863. She was never married. My son Franklin died six years ago, leaving his wife and four daughters, two of whom are now grown. One is a teacher at Canal Dover.

Mary Quantrill suffered most of her life from curvature of the spine. She was a sweet-tempered girl of excellent character and followed dressmaking to help support her mother and the family. Her sufferings were great but she did not complain, and she worked faithfully and patiently until her death.

Franklin Quantrill was afflicted with a white swelling in one of his knees, which made him a cripple for life. He followed the business of fur-dresser, and perhaps bought and sold furs. Nothing whatever appears against his character.

Thomson Quantrill was a vile, base, worthless, despicable but petty scoundrel. In 1879 or 1880 he visited the former haunts of his brother William. For some time he was in Jackson county, Mo., and aided William H. Gregg to plant his crop of corn. He stopped with others of Quantrill's old command and left impressions every time that he was a scurvy cur.[10] He visited the Torreys at Paola, Kansas, and stole the pony of their daughter Lillie and the revolver of the hired man.[11]

---

[10] His roving brother was here a few days ago, and took dinner with me, he was dead broke. He had eyes like Q. and some of his movements remind me of Q. — *From letter of Charles F. Taylor ("Fletch" Taylor) to W. W. Scott.* Dated Joplin, Mo., May 4, 1879. Letter in the Collection of the author.

[11] Thompson Quantrill, youngest brother of William, visited us in 1869 or 1870, and put up at Mr. Wagstaff's, nee Torrey, and one day borrowed Lillie's Pony and [the] hired man's revolver, and has as yet forgotten to return them. —*From letter of John S. Beeson, of Beeson & Baker, Attorneys-at-Law, Paola, Kansas, Nov. 27, 1878, to W. W. Scott,* now in the Collection of the author.

Beeson was the son of H. V. Beeson. Thomson Quantrill rode the pony to Independence, Mo., though he was some days making the trip, and Judge Wagstaff had written there to make inquiry about the pony. When shown Wagstaff's letter Quantrill said he would return to Paola and restore the pony and revolver. He rode out of town and disappeared and was never seen again at either Paola or Independence. The account of this is as follows:

Shortly after the close of the war a man arrived at Judge Wagstaff's house and announced himself as Thompson Quantrill, brother of the guerilla chief. He had been sent by Mrs. Quantrill to inquire after her son's fate, which was then a mystery. Judge Wagstaff gave him all the information he possessed and finally gave him a letter of introduction to the late lamented Judge Woodson of Independence, who, he believed, knew many facts regarding Quantrill. Before leaving, Thompson Quantrill borrowed a pistol from Judge Wagstaff and borrowed a fine pony from his daughter, with a bridle and saddle. Quantrill not appearing for several

Thomson Quantrill became a vagabond rover, a tramp, a hobo, in the West. Letters from him show that he was at or near Tucson, Arizona, from February 10, 1888, to April 23, 1888.

Quantrill's Mother

His mother, in the *Courier-Journal* interview, May 13, 1888, said: "Thomson lives in Montana where he has a family and is doing well." She must have made that statement knowing it was not true, for some of the letters above mentioned were written to her, and she received them and turned them over to W. W. Scott.[12]

The maiden-name of Quantrill's mother was Caroline Cornelia Clarke. The little we know of her early life she told to newspaper writers. In an interview printed in the *Courier-Journal*, May 13, 1888, she said she was born in Somerset county, Pa., April 7, 1819, and

days, Judge Wagstaff wrote to Judge Woodson asking [him] to look out for Quantrill, and inform him if he saw him that he was using his (Wagstaff's) property without leave and that he would like to have him return it. Judge Woodson had scarcely finished reading the letter when Quantrill rode up in a careless, easy style and made known his errand. Judge Woodson gave him all the information he possessed and then called his attention to Judge Wagstaff's letter. "I didn't mean to keep it," he replied, "but while I was out riding I thought I would ride up here." He departed, and from that time neither Judge Woodson nor Judge Wagstaff ever saw him again. He disappeared as mysteriously as if swallowed up by the earth. There are many surmises regarding his fate, but the most plausible one is that some of the old enemies of his brother became aware of his presence in the country and his brotherhood to the great chief and killed him on his way back to Paola. — *Kansas City Times, November 2, 1881*. Clipping in Quantrill Collection, Library of the Kansas State Historical Society.

12 The letters are now in the Collection of the author. They are frivolous and indicate depravity, and exhibit shocking illiteracy. In 1890 he was at Austin, Texas, from which city he wrote his mother a letter which is here reproduced. It is written on the stationery of J. R. Hudson & Co., General Merchandise, Burnet, Texas, from which point he probably went to Austin. The letter is in fact dated at Burnet, but it was posted at Austin, as shown by the postmark:

Austin   Burnet, Texas, Feb 17 1890
Mrs Caroline Quantrell
        Dear Mother
    i Take The Pleasure of Droping you a fiew Lines To Let you know That i am Well and hope you are Well also i Think of you day and night and Will Send for you in The Spring I have Left that Part of The Country

"after my birth in Somerset county my father moved to Chambersburg, Pa., where I was reared and educated." In a statement to W. W. Scott she contradicted the above so far as it relates to her father, saying that "her father & mother died when she was an infant, both [at the] same time, of an epidemic, at Stoyestown, Pa." [13]

Stoyestown is a small village, on Stony Creek, a tributary of the Conemaugh, in Somerset county, some twenty miles south of Johnstown. In the article above mentioned it was said by the reporter that Mrs. Quantrill had "bright light golden hair, blue eyes of most intelligent expression, a round face that must once have been beautiful, and in which the features of her noted son may be traced." [14] She was below the medium height, of good form without any approach to obesity, and a catlike manner which left the impression that her character was based upon treachery and cruelty.

In an interview printed in the Kansas City, Mo., *Journal*, May 12, 1888, she fixed the date of her birth as April 7, 1820, "in Pennsylvania." That she lived at Chambersburg there is no doubt, for there Thomas Henry Quantrill met and married her, but the circumstances under which she was reared, edu-

i Was in and am goying To The Capital i Think i Can Catch on to Something There The Peopel is Verry kind to me We have PLenty of friends out here Every Body is Shaking hant With me i have to Do Something Before Spring Did You Receive my Last Letter Dont Worry aBout me i Will Try and have Money By Spring Texas is my State to Live in it is a fine CLimate Would You Like to Live on The Cost The Peopel say i Look Brave Like William most all of The Young Ladies fall in Love With me BeCause They say i am so hansome i Was at a Big Gathering Lately and We had a Big time They Preachiate us highly and Would Like verry much to see you i have Something in View i may make it if so i Will have PLenty of money if i Win i Will CLise for the Preasant Right soon and tell me all of The News i Will Right more the Next time give my RespeCts to The friends if There is eny
Yours as Ever an affectinate Son
Thomas Quantrell address at austin Tranit Co Texas
By By YCT

[13] Memo. made by Scott on an envelope of a letter of Ann Vandersost to him dated December 3, 1888. The letter was an inquiry concerning Mrs. Quantrill's family, saying that it was possible that some relation existed through the Clarkes, which proved to be not the case. The letter and envelope are in the Collection of the author.

[14] Her hair was brown — a dark brown. The red hair of the family came from the father. Thomas Henry Quantrill had bright red hair — very red. He was a tall slim man, thin-breasted and stoop-shouldered.

cated, and was living there are not known.[15] She said in the
Courier-Journal interview already referred to, that Thomas
Henry Quantrill had relatives living at Chambersburg, and that
it was while visiting them that he met her. They had been
engaged for some time before their wedding, starting for Canal
Dover something more than a month later.[16]

In Mrs. Quantrill's life at Canal Dover there was nothing
which is of much interest to this work. She was a good house-
wife.[17] After the death of her husband she found it very diffi-

---

[15] Being left an orphan when but six months old she was reared in
the family of an Uncle, Judge Thompson. — *Clipping from* ....
Democrat, date unknown, in the Collection of the author.

Judge Alexander Thompson — Scotch-Irish, brother Mrs. Q.'s moth.
Judge of Somerset and Bedford Cos. Mrs. Q. fath. & Moth. died of epidemic
when year old had sict died young. Mrs. Q. born at Stoyestown, Pa.
same year as Queen Victoria. — *Memo. of W. W. Scott*, no date, now in
the Collection of the author.

[16] Married Oct. 11, 1836. Start for Dover in Nov. 1836, and arrived
here in December. In their own buggy overland. He had contract [with]
Louis L. Lee to do tin work. There were a number of Hagerstown people
here. Mrs. Q. was Miss Caroline Clark, of Chambersburg, Pa., — 20 miles
of Hagerstown. Stop at hotel and went to Housekeeping in Tom West
house with S. Scott & wife. Thomas Quantrill's mother was of a wealthy
German family near Hagerstown, named Heiser. His father was probably
of French descent. — *Memo. of W. W. Scott*, no date, now in the Collection
of the author.

The Quant. family all went to Washington [from Hagerstown].
Quant. claimed [to] be of English descent. — old Thos. Quant.

Quant's sister married John D. Otto. Mary Ann — bad. Sister
Eliza. Cornelia visit Dover. Cornelia married Earnshaw, Harper's Ferry;
buried Wash't. City.

Thomas Heiser Q. Bro. Archie, Jesse oldest. Archibald Gov't Printer.
married twice, 2 boys Thos. Joe. Mary Ann, 1st wife; 3 girls by 2nd wife.
Archibald's 2nd wife was a Miss Sands, a cousin of his first wife,
who was Miss Mary ....

Old man Thos. Quantrill was 1812 soldier — thinks Capt. Claimed
[to] be of English descent. Born Hagerstown, Md. & probably a blacksmith. His sons were Jesse Q. and Thomas Heiser Q. Latter came to
Dover to work for Louis L. Lee, who had been a schoolmate at Hagerstown.
The father had married Miss Judy Heiser, daughter in a prominent German
family. Thomas H. Quantrill had learned the tinning business at Chambersburg, Pa., with his cousin, William Heiser. There he became acquainted
with a young lady named Caroline Clark, and they were married in 1836
— about. She was born at ...., Pa., and her parents both
dying of some epidemic when quite young, she was taken to live with her
uncle, Judge Thompson, of Chambersburg. Drove out to Dover with their
own horse and buggy in 7 days; 1836.

Mrs. Quantrill told me foregoing on train betw. Cincin. & Louisville
Dec. 87. — *Memo. of W. W. Scott*, now in the Collection of the author.

[17] Mrs. Quantrill was a good cook and housekeeper, and that to get
his victuals properly cooked seemed about all Thomas H. Quantrill cared

cult to support herself and her children. On this account she pushed her eldest son out into the world hoping that he would meet with success which would better the condition of all. Her temperament was brooding and full of jealousy and malice, and the hardships which fell upon her had already embittered her life before she was familiar with the criminal career of her son in the West. His leaving home was in effect an abandonment of his mother. He wrote occasional letters to her for two or three years, but he never sent her a cent of money in his life. At his death he left his money to be applied to the erection of a monument to himself, and to a former mistress with which to start a house of ill fame in St. Louis — left nothing to his mother. She never heard from him after the Civil War began, except indirectly through the newspapers. "I never knew such unbounded surprise," she said, "as when I began to hear of his war exploits. I received full accounts, the Ohio people who knew me as his mother never failing to send me Northern papers with their accounts of what my son William had done." This statement cannot be reconciled with others she made on the subject. She was familiar with the scalawag character of some of the Quantrills, and perhaps she pretended to believe the deeds committed by her son were those of some of his relatives.[18]

Some time after the war W. W. Scott, of Canal Dover, a schoolmate, began to investigate the career of W. C. Quantrill. Inquiry of the people at Paola, Kansas, with whom he had left Canal Dover and gone West, soon convinced him of the true identity of the guerrilla chieftain. It was the evidence which he obtained there which convinced Mrs. Quantrill. When sure that the guerrilla was her son she wished to visit the place where he had been killed and see the people who knew him in his last

---

for. Mrs. Quantrill had brown hair — not red or auburn hair. She was of a solitary turn, of a brooding disposition, never going to visit her neighbors, but sometimes attending the Presbyterian church. — *Statement of Mrs. Frances Beeson Thompson to author*, August 30, 1907, now in the Collection of the author.

[18] His mother never heard of him after the war began and gave him up for dead. She could not believe, or at least would not believe, that the infamous guerilla was her son. Not until 1887 would she accept the truth, and then the proof of it was convincing. — *Truth*, October 17, 1898; clipping in the Collection of the author.

days. She went to Nelson and Spencer counties in Kentucky, and visited the people there with whom he had stopped while a bushwhacker in the state, also some of those who served under him.[19] In that atmosphere she was soon proud of the course

[19] The trip was made with W. W. Scott. Scott made two trips to Louisville to investigate the death of Quantrill, and Mrs. Quantrill accompanied him on the second. The following notes were made by Scott in reference to his first trip:

Found grave of W. C. Quantrill on this visit, and the entry of death in the Portland Cemetery (Catholic) Louisville, Ky. Talked with Mr. Scally, the sexton, and Bridget Scally his wife. Both were there when Quantrill was buried; with 10 steps of the Cemetery lodge, where they lived. Rev. Powers ordered that no mound be raised over the grave, but that the ground be kept level, and that they should throw their dish-water and other slops over the spot, so as to obliterate it as much as possible to keep the body from being stolen. Quantrill had given Powers $800 in gold and directed his burial. — *Memo. of W. W. Scott*, no date, now in the Collection of the author.

Scott left a full account of his doings at Louisville on his second trip, and it is here set out:

On Wednesday Dec. 7, 1887, I visited the St. Johns Catholic Cemetery (formerly called Portland), Louisville, Ky., and called on Mrs. Bridget Scally, the widow in charge. I had called on herself and husband in the spring of 1884, when I was trying to find out what had become of the body of Wm. Clark Quantrill (the guerrilla), who died in Louisville, June 6, '65. Her husband was then confined to his bed, but both told me that they were present when the body was buried; had been in charge of the cemetery all the time, and Mrs. Scally pointed out to me the spot; although there were no signs of a grave.

At this second call I found the husband had died, but Mrs. Scally was still in charge. I told her that now I had Mrs. Quantrill with me in the city, that she was anxious to see the grave and to talk with her about her son; and that if she could not remove the bones and place them in the family cemetery in Ohio, she would like to have them taken up and placed in a zinc lined box.

I took Mrs. Q. out from the hotel, and herself and Mrs. Scally talked matters over, and Mrs. Scally agreed that the grave might be opened so Mrs. Q. could see condition of affairs. Next day, Thursday, Dec. 8, 1887, I went out after dinner and had grave opened. It was a cloudy, drizzly day and uncomfortable, and Louis Wertz, the employe, did not like to do the work, but I gave Mrs. Scally $2.50 for the privilege, and Wertz a dollar extra. It was 3 p. m. Mrs. Scally pointed out the place, and by spading around a little, the outlines were soon found, and the bones were reached in an hour. They lay in natural position, except top of skull was uppermost, instead of lying on back part. Every vestige of coffin had disappeared except a rotten piece

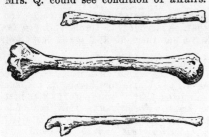

Bones of Quantrill's Right Arm now in Collection of author

pursued by her son and came to believe him a hero and patriot. She remained with Captain A. D. Pence, sheriff of Nelson county, and his wife, all winter. But she made short sojourns with other men who had been in her son's command. At first the people made quite a great-to-do over her, but in a few weeks their enthusiasm cooled. She settled down to the rôle of a heroine and expected due reverence, and the people had to show that they hoped she would soon move on. She wrote to Scott that Captain Pence seemed to have lost interest in her business and that the ladies would soon want to clean house, and urging him to take her to Missouri, where she hoped for a more lasting welcome.[20] She visited the Wakefield farm where

size of a man's hand. His hair had slipped off in a half circle around the skull, and was of a bleached yellow color. A small part of a Government army sock was about the foot bones; and some shirt-buttons were found. A part of the backbone and ribs were so decayed that they crumbled to pieces, but most of the other bones were in a fair state of preservation.

As Mrs. Quantrill could not come out on account of weather, I had the bones put in a small box and put back in the grave, near top, and covered over, and by permission of Mrs. Scally took the skull wrapped in newspaper with me to hotel to show Mrs. Q. Next morning I showed it to Mrs. Q., and she was much affected; and she identified a previously described chipped side tooth in lower jaw on right side. She would not consent to having skull taken back; as she must have it buried beside his father and brothers in Ohio; and that she would manage in some way to get the other parts of the body.

So the skull was carefully wrapped and put in a basket, and left at hotel check room, while I went with her to Samuels Depot, a station ...... miles south, that she might see Doany Pence, Robert Hall and others of her son's band. We left same day (9th Dec.) and arrived at Pence's. Mr. and Mrs. Pence pressed her to remain the winter with them; so she prevailed on me to go to Louisville and get remainder of bones on pretext of having them put in zinc box for re-burial; and that I should take them to Ohio and bury them beside her husband; and that she would see Mrs. Scally before she came back, and smooth the matter over; and arrange for the selling of the cemetery lot.

I did not approve of the deception, but she said that she could not go home without his remains; and that on account of forms and proofs, and red tape, she might not be able to get them at all; or at least not without much trouble.

I stopped, secured them and brought them home and placed them where agreed upon. Mrs. Q. told me that she called on Mrs. Scally some months afterward, and that by putting all the blame for the act on me, she finally reconciled her; and that she admitted that it was perhaps the best way to accomplish it, and with the least notoriety, and that the ends probably justified the means; but that the secrecy should be maintained for the good of all concerned. Mrs. Q. afterwards had the lot sold and received the money. — *Statement of W. W. Scott,* now in the Collection of the author.

[20] Her letters written during her visit to Kentucky and Missouri are

Quantrill was mortally wounded and talked with the people there who knew him in his last days of crime.

Scott consented to take Mrs. Quantrill tc Missouri. On May 7, 1888, she went from Samuels's Depot to Louisville to meet Scott, and on the 8th they left Louisville together for Jackson county, Mo., arriving at Independence on the 10th. There she was well received. The old guerrillas entertained her in their homes and furnished her with money. She made ineffectual efforts to secure some money from a Mrs. Cooper, of Lee's Summit, alleging that Quantrill had left it with her. Mrs. Cooper denounced her as a fraud and paid over no money. Mrs. Quantrill remained in Jackson county more than a year and became so imbued with the greatness of her son William that she regarded her former friends as enemies and people of no consequence. Scott, her ever true friend, said she became a "hellcat" in Missouri. Her letters abuse him soundly and accuse him of the effort to connect himself with her and her son for the purpose of making money. She denounces all "Northern people" for their crimes against the South.[21]

---

in the Collection of the author. They reveal the peculiarities and treachery of her nature. She harbored a bitter hatred for her grand-daughters, the daughters of her son Franklin. She accuses them in these letters of spying upon her actions to the extent of feloniously securing and opening her letters.

[21] Extracts from some of the letters of Mrs. Quantrill are given here. They were all written to W. W. Scott, Canal Dover, from Independence, Mo., or vicinity:

Independence Mo. May 20th 188.

. . . No doubt yo thought because they were my Sons friends, they were of no account. But you are much mistaken if you think so for they are much respected here. I have met many friends here, more than I ever expected, in fact every one here is a friend of my Dear lost son. Now I dont care what the foalks think or say of me or my lost Son, I know how he stands here with the very best. . . . By the way, I saw the Lady who sent me the letter when at blue springs, she called on me before I had time to find her. She saw in the papers that I was in town. I spent one day with her She told me of the bad treatment she received at the hands of the Kansas Fiends she was burned out three times & her life in danger every day. I had no idea they did treat Women as they did. it was perfectly dreadful, & yet to hear the Union men tell they never did any thing bad. Oh, no, it was all the South. they were driven to do what they did. Who would not protect their homes and friends They may say what they please out there about my son. he never did as bad as some of Kansas men did, he alwais respected Woman wherever he met them.

But Mrs. Quantrill finally wore out her welcome in Missouri.
Her former enthusiastic friends tired of her presence and came
to regard her as a mild sort of nuisance, and, later, a real active
nuisance. She was compelled to turn again to Scott and return
to Canal Dover. No Missouri or Kentucky people ever wrote

Blue Springs 1888 July 1st

. . . You say some one has written a long letter to a St. Louis
newspaper about me & my Son & you, saying I am not the mother of Wm
Quantrill . . . The man who wrote that is no friend nothing but a *low-
lifed Black Republican* I have no more respect for that class of people,
they are the lowest of Gods Creation

Independence Mo Oct 17th 1888.

. . . You say there are some foalks there who dont like me, would
like to have hard things said of me, for what reason I cannot tell. I
know there is a dreadful Low class of people there who delight in slandering
& telling Lies, I think if God ever makes another Hell He aught to make it
there, Sink it in the bottomless Pit & put all the Liars in it. It would
not be any too large for all Dover liars.

Independence Mo Feb 24th 1889

. . . Now I will tell you something of your Self The foalks in
These parts did not have any confidence in you from the fact of your
being a Yankey Man They could not depend on your word They didn't
know but you were a Son of Some Old Yankey hunting up something
to make money out off. . . . It was you I had reference to as a Professed friend who was not true. . . . I cannot understand what you mean
By saying you were such a great friend to me in my dark days when I
nieded one, and always took my part and defended me. I dont know of
any very dark days I ever had. . . . You are the chief one who has been,
and is yet agitateing The whole buisness. You may as well give up writing
History of my Dear lost Boy, for You never will get any Thing correct.
no one but His Men & friends and Myself could get up a coreect History
of him. His Men never will Enlighten The Yankeys on The Subject. So
what They gather up will be mostly Lies.

Much more could be quoted showing the disposition of Mrs. Quantrill
towards Scott. Her particular grievance in these letters was the action
of Scott in furnishing Eliza Archard material for an article on Quantrill
and his raid on Lawrence. That he gave her the photographs of the
Quantrill family was particularly aggravating, and Mrs. Quantrill always
refers to Mrs. Archard as ''that Low-Lifed woman'' and ''that nasty
low-Lifed Woman.'' The Archard article was written for the American
Press Association and published broadcast August 26, 1888. Scott really
did Mrs. Quantrill a favor in that matter, and his letter on the subject
reveals that he was in fact the partisan of Quantrill and intended to
write an account which would conceal as much of the bad as possible.
He induced the lady to leave out of her article everything which would
be disagreeable to Mrs. Quantrill. In his letter to her, dated Jan. 29, 1889,
he says:

I told you that there was a woman here to make inquiry about your
family; and that she had seen some people who were not friendly to you;

to her. At Canal Dover she soon met with an accident and suffered a fractured arm and shoulder, becoming an object of charity. Scott, good man and good friend that he was, circulated a subscription paper and secured $120 for her.[22]

In March, 1898, through the efforts of Scott, the Confederate Veteran Association of Kentucky appropriated funds for

and had written up a lot of stuff they had told her. I told her that if she would not publish that stuff, I would let her have a copy of your picture and Mr. Quantrill's. She agreed, and that is the way she got the pictures; and she did not publish the stuff they had told her.

In the previous September Scott had written her about this article, saying:

There was a woman here two or three months ago hunting up something, and some one took her around to different places. Some folks who didn't like you, told her some ugly things. I saw her afterwards and she said if I would let her have your picture and Mr. Quantrill's, she would leave those things out of her article. I did so, and she left them out. There are people here yet who would like to see all the bad published that they could. You know very well that I have always tried to show up for the good side of his [W. C. Quantrill's] life, and make things as smooth for you as I could.

This letter is valuable as showing that Scott was intending to write as favorably of Quantrill as he possibly could.

The "dark days" letter to which Mrs. Quantrill referred was dated Feb. 6, 1889, and the following extract is taken from it:

Mrs. Quantrill, I dont see why you have written me one or two such letters as you have since I left you. I had been your friend in many dark days when you needed one; and I always took your part and defended you. After I came home, you wrote me a very unkind letter, accusing me of having photographed the men at Blue Springs, and sending the photographs to the Police Gazette to be ridiculed. I wrote you back at once that I had not one of their photographs! had not taken any, and had never written a line to the Police Gazette or any other paper; and to prove it all, I got a copy of the Police Gazette and sent it to you. I thought that would convince you that you was mistaken, but you never answered the letter.

When that woman came here to write a piece about your son, she went to several parties and got all the news she could. Finally she came to me, and I found that somebody had told her things that would make you feel bad to see in print; told her likely by some enemy of yours. I made a special request of her to leave those things out; and I told her as good and as straight a narrative as I could.

Notwithstanding her course toward him, Scott continued to be her staunch friend to the end of his life. He got her into "Homes" and "Hospitals" and furnished her clothing. She was not backward in asking that he provide for her, as her letters show.

[22] This paper with the names of the subscribers and the amount each paid is in the Collection of the author.

the maintenance of Mrs. Quantrill in the "Home for the Friend-less" in Lexington, Kentucky.[23]

Mrs. Quantrill remained in the "Home" some months, when she became dissatisfied and returned to Canal Dover. She was very quarrelsome and disagreeable as her years increased. When she returned from Lexington she was placed in the Tuscarawas County Infirmary (Poorhouse) and became a public charge. Her husband had been a member of the order of Odd Fellows in Canal Dover. This fact, long forgotten, was established by Scott. He secured her admission to the Odd Fellows Home at Springfield, Ohio. Her letters from that institution to Scott, almost illegible, are full of gratitude. She sometimes wrote him for money, the receipt of which from him she acknowledges. She depended upon him for a part of her clothing, which he furnished. She died at the Odd Fellows Home, Springfield, in the year 1903.

The Quantrills exhibit the usual characteristics of a family deficient in sound moral fiber developing in a community where there is little restraint of personal inclinations and where con-demnation by public conscience is fitful and feeble. Under such circumstances society is prone to leniency and forgiveness. There were, perhaps, patriotism and manliness of character in Captain Thomas Quantrill, though he became a professional gambler. His son, Thomas Henry Quantrill, loved and labored to support his wife and children, though none too scrupulous as to where he obtained the money for his enterprises. His last years show no false steps. He should not be held to account for the actions of his brothers. But the loose threads and slack twist of his moral man begot in his son the seed-ground for tares which

---

[23] It has always appeared in the newspapers that she was in a Con-federate Home in Kentucky, but the correspondence leading to her going to Lexington is in the Collection of the author, and it clearly shows that she was placed in the Home for the Friendless. She made various statements as to why she did not remain there, one being that her "benefactor" had lost his fortune and could no longer maintain her in the Home. This "Home" seems to have been called "St. Joseph's Hospital." In the *Morning Herald*, Lexington, Ky., March 27, 1898, is the following:

The bringing of Mrs. Caroline Clark Quantrill to St. Joseph's Hos-pital in this city last week," etc., etc. The clipping from the *Herald* is in the Collection of the author.

kindled a conflagration on the border and drenched a land in blood. The broadest possible mantle of charity should enfold the memory of Mrs. Caroline Clarke Quantrill. She comes upon the stage a mother true to her offspring — with a love for him that was stronger than death. She seeks to shield and defend a child. This quality, instinct, in the mother is the hope of civilization. But the union of this couple produced him that shed blood like water, a fiend wasteful and reckless of human life. They endowed him with depravity, bestowed upon him the portion of degeneracy. In cruelty and a thirst for blood he towered above the men of his time. Somewhere of old his ancestors ate the sour grapes which set his teeth on edge. In him was exemplified the terrible and immutable law of heredity. He grew into the gory monster whose baleful shadow falls upon all who share the kindred blood. He made his name a Cain's mark and a curse to those condemned to bear it. The blight of it must fall upon remote generations, those yet unborn and innocent, so inexorable are the decrees of fate and nature. Because of him widows wailed, orphans cried, maidens wept, as they lifted the lifeless forms of loved ones from bloody fields and bore them reeking to untimely graves.

CHAPTER II

EARLY LIFE OF QUANTRILL

WILLIAM Clarke Quantrill was born at Canal Dover, Ohio, July 31, 1837.[1] Of his childhood very little is known. But something of his school-boy life has come down to us. He had few friends, for there was little in common between him and other boys of his age. He was solitary, wandering in the woods with firearms when quite young. There he shot small game and maimed domestic animals for amusement.[2] He would often nail a snake to a tree and let it remain there in torture until it died. He carried small snakes in his pockets, and these he would throw on his sister and other girls at school and laugh heartily at their terror. He would stick a knife into a cow by the roadside, or stab a horse. He often tortured dogs and cats to enjoy their cries of distress. Pain in any other person or in any animal gave him pleasure, delight.[3] He was an expert in the use of the rifle and could throw stones

---

[1] It is believed necessary to make this fact prominent, and it is repeated here.

[2] There was nothing about him to indicate his subsequent career, except that he would occasionally shoot a pig through the tip of the ear to make it run and squeal, and then would laugh immoderately at its antics. Such things in illiterate persons might be attributed to thoughtlessness; but in a young man of his intelligence it looked like a vein of cruelty. In no other way did he ever exhibit an evil disposition. He was strictly temperate and honest.—*W. W. Scott, in Joplin, Mo., Morning Herald, April 29, 1881.* Clipping in the Collection of the author.

Mr. Scott was the friend of Quantrill and his family, and it was his avowed intention to rescue his name from infamy. Attention is called to many of the expressions of Mr. Scott quoted in this work. They establish this friendship and this intention. Many other forms of cruelty practiced by Quantrill in his boyhood are known, and they indicate a depraved nature.

[3] This information was secured from a number of persons who knew Quantrill as a school-boy, among them, members of the Beeson family. There is some evidence that Franklin Quantrill did the same things, chasing cows on his crutches to stab them.

with much force and velocity and with unerring accuracy. He was not of a contentious turn and seldom quarreled. Consciousness of some guilt seemed ever present with him, causing a sort of hang-dog expression of countenance and an inclination to avoid a conflict, but when forced to battle he fought desperately with any thing he could lay hands upon.

Quantrill was a strong boy, but never robust. He suffered from a throat trouble which was expected to develop consumption, a family malady of which his father died. He suffered a rupture when very young, but this never became a serious matter with him. His face was round and full, with piercing blue-grey eyes of a strange tint, the upper lids of which fell too low, imparting a peculiar expression which became very marked when he was in a rage. His forehead was high, his hair almost white (of the "tow-head" variety), and his nose was curved and sinister. His appearance as a whole indicated strong individuality. With some people he was in great good repute, while others despised him from first sight without being able to explain why. He was the favorite of his mother, no other child ever finding the place in her heart which she gave her first-born. She was his champion when he was confronted with the consequences of his evil-doing, always bringing him off without punishment if possible. There was no love between Quantrill and his father.

As an instance of the depravity of Quantrill even as a boy, the following circumstance is related. In Canal Dover the Catholic church stood apart from the village, and the public road ran by its door. The pasture for town-cows lay beyond, and Quantrill drove the family-cow to and from it. Once the priest was called away upon emergency and left the housekeeper, a girl in her teens, alone. She went up into the belfry to ring the evening chimes. This belfry was ascended by steep and winding stairs. It was entered through a door with a heavy shutter which was secured by an enormous lock turned with a ponderous iron key. Passing with the cow, Quantrill saw the belfry door standing open, and, hearing the clanging of the bell, he knew the girl was aloft there and alone. He quietly closed and locked the door, and, taking the key, he went on and threw it into the deep water of Sugar creek. The girl was kept a pris-

oner in the belfry nearly twenty-four hours without food or
water. When released she was prostrated from fright and want,
and so indignant were the members of the church that they
offered a reward of one hundred dollars for the apprehension
of the criminal.⁴

In school Quantrill was a bright pupil. But he gave the
teacher much trouble, especially his father when the latter was
principal of the Union School. He had to be punished often.
One day his father took him out and whipped him soundly. A
young lady ⁵ saw him return to the room, pale, tearless, trembling, and with the look of a demon. There was murder in every
gleam of his strange glittering eyes.

At the age of sixteen Quantrill was employed as a teacher
in the Union School at Canal Dover. Why he was not retained
in that position is not known. It would seem that if he had
given satisfaction or had been regarded as a person suitable for
the place he should have been allowed to remain after his father's
death, his mother being a widow with a large family to support.
But the winter of his father's death (1854-55) he taught a country school in Tuscarawas county, not far from Canal Dover.

From the age of eighteen years there is some record of Quantrill and his actions. In 1855 he first ventured into the world
to try his powers and seek his fortune. The Clapp family, an
old and respected one at Canal Dover, moved to La Salle county,
Illinois. Miss Mary Clapp was a teacher in the Canal Dover

---

4 Quantrill did not admit this crime until after he came to Kansas.
There, when the Beeson and Torrey children met to play, they talked of the
old home at Canal Dover, often expressing a strong desire to return and
sometimes weeping because they could not go. One Sunday afternoon
these young people were strolling along the banks of the Marais des Cygnes,
one of the young ladies in tears from memories of the old Ohio home.
Quantrill was one of the party and asked her why she did not return. She
said she had no money and that she could not return since her family then
lived in Kansas. ''I can tell you how to get the money,'' he said. ''I
locked the Catholic belfry, and if you will inform the church you can get
the one hundred dollars reward offered for the person who did it. I locked
the door and threw the key into deep water in Sugar Creek.'' He laughed
immoderately at the thought of his heartless act and seemed to think it a
fine joke.

5 Now Mrs. Frances Beeson Thompson, of Topeka.

Union School.[6] In the summer of 1855 she went to Mendota,
Illinois, and Mrs. Quantrill prevailed upon her to allow her son
William to go along. Some account of the journey and of Quantrill's impression of that country, as well as of his employment
there, can be found in the following letter written by him to
his mother.[7]

Wednesday August 8th 1855
Mendota La Salle Co
Illinois

Dear Mother.

I arrived here about half past two o.clock this afternoon safe
& sound. My box is not here but I expect it tomorrow. We
traveled day & night ever since we started not having stopped
half an hour at one place. Tomorrow I am going to hunt something to do. We are both well except that Mary was looking
out of the window of the car while we were going along the shore
of Lake Michigan when a spark of fire flew in her eye & made
it a little sore. But that will be well in a day or so. We did not
have any trouble with our trunks at all. I have $6 of my money
left & maybe the next time I write I will send a little along. I
am about 600 miles from home.

This country is a great deal different from Ohio for miles
around I can see nothing but tall grass. There is not much
Fruit here although I have seen ripe peaches at the cars for sale:
but corn, potatoes, cabbage are plenty. We have stopped at
Marys Aunts Mrs Cross but I wont stay here but a day or so.
There are two schools here probably I can get one of them.
Well I believe that is all this time the next time I will write
more

Yours With Respect
William Quantrill

P. S.   Direct to me Mendota La Salle Co Illinois

A manly letter, and it arouses sympathy! Those who have
stood alone and friendless for the first time on a strange shore
will find only indications of honesty of purpose in it. If only
some good influence could have taken possession of him then

---

6 See page 98, *Reminiscences of Dover*, by William W. Scott, Canal
Dover, Ohio, 1879. Miss Clapp was a teacher in the winters of 1852-53
and 1853-54. There it is said: ''Miss Clapp married a prominent Illinois
farmer, and lives at Mendota.'' William C. Quantrill was employed in the
winter of 1853-54, his father dying the following December.

7 Letter of W. C. Quantrill to his mother, now in the Collection of
the author.

and there the latent powers of his character for evil might never have developed. If some sympathetic hand had been extended from the coldness and strangeness of his new world this boy might have anchored at last in a haven of honor and respect! But the world is cold, indifferent. A little kindness might often change the destiny of a soul!

On the 18th of September Quantrill wrote a letter to his mother in answer to one he had received from her. This letter is as follows: [8]

Mendota Sept 18th 1855

Dear Mother.

I received your letter yesterday & was very glad to hear that you are well & I am glad to tell you that I am the same. Well I guess I will teach school this winter, but I was very sorry to hear that you could not find those Texas papers but I want you to look again for them for if you find them I can make some money this winter. I wrote you a letter before I received your last one I suppose you have got it by this time you must be sure to send me those tinners books all of them as soon as you can for those six that I brought with me I sold in one town & I could of sold more if I had them for $2.00 a piece which just paid my board. be sure & send them for I can sell 50 in Chicago there are so many tin shops there. If you send them I can send you some money in a week I have only $8 dollars now. As soon as you send them books in a week I will send you $20 certain. be sure to send them by express You had better try to borrow a little money of Dr. Brashear or Dr. Winnul until I can get those books. for you know I wont get my pay for teaching only every three months. I get $25 a month & boarded. I would like to have those texas papers very much. You had better write to Grandfather & ask him if he has got them & tell him I can do well with them. And I would ask him to help me a little. I think I shall write to him for I guess he dont know I am out here. well I must bring my letter to a close dont forget those books. Send them by express.

Yours With Respect
Your Son
W. Quantrill

I want you to answer this letter a little sooner if you can the man that wants to get that land in texas wants to know pretty soon whether I can get the papers or not

---

[8] Letter of W. C. Quantrill to his mother, now in the Collection of the author.

A number of men from Ohio fought in the Texan patriot army for the independence of the Lone Star Republic, and the Texas papers he requested may have been a warrant for land for military service in the patriot forces. Some of the roving brothers of his father may have served in the Texan army. One of them, or an uncle, was a pirate on the Texan coast, and he may have lived to cast his lot with the Texans. The "tinners books" referred to were copies of the work written and published by his father. It is very probable that his mother sent him some of them, but he did not send her any money. He never sent her a penny in the world. This letter indicates that he had gained confidence in himself.

The next letter written by Quantrill was dated on the 2d of October, and was to Edward T. Kellam, Canal Dover, and is as follows: [9]

> Mendota
> Oct 2ᵈ 1855

Friend Edward.

I suppose you think or had begun to, that I had forgotten you entirely; but not so. I have threatened to write to you, several times, but neglected it. Well I will attend to it a little better if you answer this one.

I live about 80 miles south of Chicago in a little town by the name of Mendota. It is scarcely two years old & yet it contains nearly 1500 inhabitants The reason of its rapid growth, is, that four railroads center here; it will be a large place in a few years if it continues. we have four passenger & eight freight trains every day & night, so now you can judge of the business done here it goes ahead of Dover, for we have a paper printed here. I want you to send me one of the county papers once [letter cut away here] our paper. [Letter cut away here] this is the country for farming, it beats Ohio all to pieces. A man can raise a crop of corn & wheat in one year that will pay for the farm & all the expences of fencing & ploughing. that is. well enough I think; all the objection I have to it, is, that there is not enough of timber which makes wood very high $5,00 a cord only.

This too is the country for hunting & it pays well. Here a man that understands the business can shoot from 50 to 60 prairie chickens every day & get $1.50 per dozen [for] all he

---

9 Letter of W. C. Quantrill to Edward T. Kellam, now in the Collection of the author.

can shoot.   There is a place 16 miles from here called inlet pond,
where there are thousands of ducks and geese.   I was up last
Saturday & I killed 2 geese and 11 ducks, but the fellow that was
with me killed 9 geese and 32 ducks.   we got 50 cts apiece for
the geese & 25 cts for the ducks.   if you was here we would go
every day.   You had better come out here & buy a farm you
cant do better I know.   I guess I must bring my letter to a close.
when you write tell me the news & the fun.   Give my respects
to all the boys and girls

                              [Signature cut away]
when you write address me.
                    Mendota
                        La Salle Co
                            Illinois

   The signature of this letter has been cut off, probably by W.
W. Scott to send to some newspaper.   This letter makes no mention of his school, but it tells us that he had turned pot-hunter.

   On the 17th of November Quantrill again wrote to his
mother, as follows: [10]

                                        Nov 17 1855
My Dear Mother.
   I would have written to you before this but I did not get
that box you sent me untill a few days ago.   I thought I would
not write to you untill I got it for then you would have thought
it was lost, but I have got it, and every thing was safe.   The
boots came a little too late for I had bought me a pair about two
or three weeks before.   I will not need them this winter but I
will keep them in my trunk so that they will be safe.   I have not
had any time yet to get off to sell some books but next [week] I
will have a little time & I think the next time I write you may
expect some money by express as that is the only safe way to
send it.
   Well I must tell you one thing & that is that I am tired
of the west already, and I do not think I shall stay in it very
much longer than I can help; I must stay as long as my school
lasts & that is all.   You may expect me home early in the spring,
for I was a dunce to go away for I could have done just as well
at home as out here & then I would have been at home.   I have
learned one good lesson that I would never have learned at home
& when I get there again (which will not be long) I will turn
over a new leaf entirely   You said the children had the ague;
you must try and cure them if possible & this is the last winter

_____
   [10] Letter of W. C. Quantrill to his mother, now in the Collection of
the author.

you will ever have to keep boarders if I keep my health. I feel that I have done wrong in going from home & hope you will forgive me for it. I must bring my letter to a close.

Yours with respect
Your son
William C. Quantrill

He had received the books but had sold none, he said. She sent him a pair of boots, though her children were sick and she was keeping boarders for bread! What will a mother not do! In this letter a change in Quantrill is quite evident. He made but indirect reference to teaching, and it is possible that he did not teach at all. W. W. Scott says Quantrill worked in a lumber yard; also, that he unloaded lumber from cars at Mendota and taught in the Mendota schools later, which he may have done.[11] There is evidence in the letter that he was sliding rapidly down the moral scale, and he wrote a promise to reform. He made a number of such promises to his mother, none of which he ever kept.

At Mendota there came a crisis in the life of Quantrill. His mother did not hear from him after the 17th of November, 1855, until in February, 1856, his letter bearing date of the 21st of that month. It was written from Fort Wayne, Indiana, and is as follows:[12]

Ft Wane, February 21st 1856

My Dear Mother

I suppose you thought I was dead but not so, for I had and still continue to have, better health than I ever had at home. I suppose that you think that something has happened to me, and you think right; for if it had not been so you would have heard from me before this. I think I will not tell you in this letter what it was as this is the first one I have wrote you since it happened. The last letter I wrote you was then. You will not think so hard of me when you know all. I hope you will forgive me then for not writing.

I am now in Indiana near Fort Wayne teaching a school, and a very good one I have. I have from 35 to 40 schollars every

11 Statement of W. W. Scott, in the Collection of the author. See, also, letter from Columbus, Ohio, to the Cincinnati *Times-Star*, by F. B. Glessner, in 1886, exact date not on clipping in the Collection of the author.

12 Letter of W. C. Quantrill to his mother, now in the Collection of the author.

day. I have got in a good neighborhood, and they say I am the best teacher they ever had. I get 20 dollars a month and boarded. I took up school for three months and my time is half out now.

Well mother I have concluded to come home in the spring when school is out if you are willing, not that I have not fared so well since I left, because I have good clothes, and I have not had to miss one meals victuals. But this is the reason why I think of coming home, it is because I can make just as much money there as any place else, and save a great deal more, and also I think I done wrong in going from home and leaving you by yourself, and let you earn your own living I have earned enough if I had been at home to keep us all comfortably So in the spring I will come home not to seek an asylum, but rather to make one. I suppose if Grandfather is there he has scolded me completely but when he knows all he will think different.

One thing I will tell you this trip I have had has done me more good and I have learned more than I would in three years steady schooling. What I have learned will be of more benefit to me than any thing I now know of I would be willing to stay away another year, if it was not for you and the children, if I thought I could be benefitted as much as I have been the few months I have been gone. I have been studying book keeping this winter and I think I will try that in the spring if I am spared that long. I think I can make more money at it, and it will be better for my health.

I have found a great many people that I am acquainted with, for instance two of Sam Fertig's sisters live in the district I am teaching in. and George Scott lives about 20 miles from here. I saw him once in town he is a different boy from what he was in Dover. he has been making one dollar a day and boarded all winter and that he never done at home and never would in Dover if he had lived there ever so long. when my school is out I am going to see them.

It has been very cold here. two weeks ago the snow in the woods is about 30 inches deep and it bids fair to be still deeper. Two weeks ago last Tuesday the thermometer stood at 30 degrees below zero at day break and at noon was 19 degrees below. both Tuesday and Wednesday it was the same and for five days it did not go above zero. I suppose it has not been so cold there. There was one man here had 160 head of sheep froze in one night and most every body had their pigs and calves froze, and people have had their toes froze so bad that they think they will drop off. among the rest I had my toes and ears froze but not very bad. Every body here most has got the ague, and a great many have died with the typhoid fever. This country is a low

flat swampy unhealthy place, and covered with very heavy timber, more than in Ohio. Almost every body lives in log houses
and to take it all around I would not advise any one to buy a
farm in the state, for really I would hardly live here one year
for a good farm. almost every body here wants to sell out and
leave the country.

I would just as soon be at home as any place else for a
while. I suppose the furnace has been going all winter and
Dover is a little more lively than it was. I suppose some of the
boys have got situations in it by this time. Well mother I am
tedious I suppose with such a long letter. Give my respects to
all my friends & especially the boys & tell them I will write
soon. Tell them I am well and doing well. The next time I
will tell you all about what has happened. But I want you to
never tell any body else whoever it may be for my sake. When
you answer this direct to Fort Wayne Indiana.

I still remain yours Respectfully
Your Son
William Quantrill

Mrs. Caroline C. Quantrill

There is no certain knowledge of what "happened" to
Quantrill at Mendota. W. W. Scott probably knew but concealed it.[13] He left a memorandum written on the fragment of
a letter-head of S. S. Scott, manufacturer of the Scott Fountain
Pen, Chicago. It is the only written evidence of what occurred
at Mendota and is as follows:

Did you ever know that Quantrill kept books for a lumber
firm in Ottawa or Mendota Ill & that while there he shot &
killed a man whom he said knocked him down with the intention
of robbing him.

There is nothing whatever to show who wrote this. A rumor
that Quantrill had killed a man at Mendota reached Canal Dover
in the winter of 1855-56. Quantrill seemingly referred to that
rumor when he said he supposed that his grandfather had scolded

---

[13] That Scott intended to hide the bad in the life of Quantrill up to
the time he came to Kansas, and to put as good a face as possible on his
actions in Kansas and Missouri is evidenced by memoranda left by him
and which is in the Collection of the author. In all the writings of Scott
he shields Quantrill and refuses to believe that he was bad. When forced
to admit that he was bad, the treatment he received in Kansas made him
bad. Much to that effect is in the Collection of the author.

him completely. Rumor made two versions of the affair. One was to the effect that Quantrill was sleeping in the office of the lumber yard when attacked and that he shot his assailant dead. Another version was, that this killing was in the day time and that Quantrill was found behind a pile of lumber standing over a dead man with a smoking pistol in his hand. The man was a stranger. There was no witness, and Quantrill said the man had attempted to rob him. The authorities held Quantrill some time, but as nothing could be found to contradict him, and he being but a boy in appearance, he was allowed to go free. There is nothing positive to be had on the subject, however.[14]

Whatever this crime (it could have been nothing less, from Quantrill's letter and action), Quantrill was a changed man afterwards. While still hoping that he might be forgiven at home, he desired that nothing be said about the matter. His letter speaking of the occurrence was in a bold and confident tone, indicating that he was getting used to the world and stood in little fear of it.

The next letter from Quantrill was dated at Fort Wayne. But a fragment of it has been preserved. He evidently changed his mind about returning home in the spring, for the letter was written in July.[15]

Fort Wayne July 14/56

Dear Mother.

Well mother I am going to write one more letter to you & it is the last one untill I receive an answer   this is the fourth one without an answer yet & the last one.

I am & have been well since I left home with the exceptions of a few shakes of the ague 3 I think I am going to school in this city. I study Chemistry, Physiology Latin & Plane Trigonometry school will be out in 3 weeks I am again going to work again probably in this place but I will teach again in the winter . . . .

---

[14] Mrs. Frances Beeson Thompson, now of Topeka, was living then at Canal Dover, and she remembers these rumors. W. W. Scott told F. B. Glessner that "It is said that he [Quantrill] left his school at Mendota in the middle of the term owing to some trouble or scandal." See a previous note for mention of Glessner and his article in the Cincinnati *Times-Star*.

[15] Letter from W. C. Quantrill to his mother, now in the Collection of the author.

He had made up his mind to remain at Fort Wayne over another winter, but it is quite probable that he returned home shortly after the above letter was written. The tendency to sudden and unexpected actions seemed to be taking a hold on him, and this became characteristic of him in later life. The following winter he taught school in the country, near his native town.[16]

Mrs. Frances Beeson Thompson believes this last school was in a district near Urichsville. He left Ohio without paying his board-bill in the district. Quantrill left his native land never to return. The inexorable tide of events swept him westward to a destiny dark, infamous.[17]

---

[16] W. C. Quantrill taught Dover Union School winter of 1853-54 when 16 yrs. old. He afterwards taught in the Geo. Riker district below N. Philadelphia, and also in the Blicktown Dist. below Dover. — *Memo of W. W. Scott*, no date, now in the Collection of the author.

Quantrill taught two terms of school in country districts in Tuscarawas county, Ohio (his native county), but in which of the two districts mentioned by Scott he taught his last term is not known; it was taught in the winter of 1856-57, and was perhaps not completed, for he left Ohio for Kansas early in March of 1857.

[17] In Kansas H. V. Beeson received a letter from a party to whom the board-bill was due, saying that it was unpaid and making inquiry as to the possibility of collecting it from Quantrill in Kansas. It was in telling the author of this circumstance that Mrs. Frances Beeson Thompson said she believed the school was taught near Urichsville, it being her best recollection that the letter came from some one living near that town.

CHAPTER III

FROM OHIO TO KANSAS

HARMON V. BEESON and Colonel Henry Torrey had lived at Canal Dover, Ohio, several years prior to the year 1857. They found themselves with growing families and in debt. New countries have ever held hope for men in such condition. The total indebtedness of Beeson was five hundred dollars, which sum he owed to Jesse Deardorf. He had considerable property and could have paid the debt, but knowing that it would require money to begin life in a new country, he arranged with Deardorf to have his indebtedness stand over until he could get on his feet in Kansas. Beeson was able to make such terms because it was known that he was a good business man and thoroughly honest.[1]

---

[1] Harmon Vedder Beeson was born in Schenectady county, New York, January 15, 1809; died at Paola, Kansas, May 28, 1886. He was a Civil Engineer and went to Canal Dover, Ohio, to work in that capacity on the Ohio Canal about the year 1827, exact date unknown. He married at Canal Dover, about 1830, Rachel C. Rutt (pronounced *Root*), who was born at Hagerstown, Maryland, June 16, 1812. They had the following children:

Catherine, born March 23, 1833. Married Isaac N. Sparks.

Frances, born October 27, 1836. Married George Thompson; lives in Topeka.

Phoebe, born February 1, 1838. Married G. A. Colton.

Richard, born about 1840. Was in the First Kansas Regiment, Civil War; died at Vicksburg, Miss., unmarried. Died during siege of Vicksburg.

John S., born about 1844; was in a Kansas regiment in Civil War; married, first, Dorinda Parrott; second, ...

Jesse, born about 1846; was in a Kansas regiment in the Civil War; married, first, Clara Rischey; second, ...

Charity, born the day President Zachary Taylor died, July 9, 1850; married William Freeman.

Upon the completion of the Ohio Canal, Beeson was appointed col-

Colonel Torrey could not make satisfactory terms with his creditors. He was an honest man, but he was much involved. When he learned that Beeson was going to Kansas he wished to go with him, and the two men formed a sort of partnership, Torrey saying that he could secure some money from relatives of his wife at White Plains, New York. The two men agreed to meet in Terre Haute, Indiana, but later this point was changed to St. Louis, Mo.

Beeson and Torrey did not bring their families to Kansas with them. Richard Beeson accompanied his father. This caused W. C. Quantrill to wish to be one of the party, young Beeson being a friend of his. Mrs. Quantrill was anxious to have him go, hoping that he might secure a farm upon which could be made a home for herself and children, and she urged Mr. Beeson to take him along. Beeson consulted Colonel Torrey as to what should be done. It was the wish of both to do any thing possible to aid Mrs. Quantrill, and while neither had any confidence in her son, it was decided to take him to Kansas and try to induce him to abandon his roving, idle habits and settle himself to some steady occupation. It was agreed that Beeson should pay his way to the point where Colonel Torrey was to meet him, and that Colonel Torrey should pay it from there to Kansas. This fare was to be an advance to Quantrill, which was to be deducted from his wages, for it was agreed that they would give him employment for some months after their arrival, should he desire them to do so. And this sum was in that way returned to Beeson and Torrey by Quantrill.[2]

---

lector of customs for the State at Canal Dover and constructed a large warehouse. Later he was employed as teacher in the city schools of the town. He accumulated property and became one of the principal citizens of the place. He was attracted to Kansas by the controversy over slavery, and believing it a country of fine resources he moved there hoping to better his condition, settling in Franklin county, March 22, 1857. He was county surveyor of Franklin county and a member of the legislature. In the fall of 1863 he moved to Paola, Kansas, where he engaged in the grocery business, and where he lived until his death, a substantial and much respected citizen. At the time of his death he was the oldest Freemason in the State.

[2] This is what Beeson and his family have always said of this matter. See quotation from letter of Beeson in Note 1, Chapter IV. In his letter

Mr. Beeson, his son Richard, and Quantrill set out for Kansas. They went to the Ohio river and took boat for St. Louis, Mo. There they waited two days for Colonel Torrey to arrive, a circumstance which shows that the contention of Mrs. Torrey-Wagstaff that Colonel Torrey met Beeson and Quantrill in St.

---

to his mother Quantrill says he had enough money to carry him through. He may have referred to his personal expenses and not to fare on boats or railroads. In a letter to Captain W. O. Hubble, dated at Paola, Kansas, January 17, 1884, and published in the Lawrence, Kansas, *Herald and Tribune*, April 15, 1855, Mrs. M. J. Wagstaff (formerly Mrs. Torrey) said, ''Early in the spring of 1857 Col. H. Yancy [msiprint for Torrey], my late husband, left Dover for the City of New York; from there intending to come direct to Kansas. At St. Louis, on his way to Kansas, he met, by accident, H. V. Beeson and W. C. Quantrill, and from that point they came to Kansas and located in the spring of 1857, near Stanton, then in Lykins, now Miami county.''

When Mrs. Frances Beeson Thompson was shown this letter she declared its statements untrue and that the facts are as set out herein.

Writing to his paper, the *True Republican and Sentinel*, Sycamore, Ills., from Paola, Kansas, August 15, 1863, C. M. Chase said:

Paola was once the home of the notorious bushwhacker and outlaw, Quantrell. Here he once lived in harmony with those he would now plunder and murder. Our landlord, Col. Torrey, brought him here from Ohio, when but a lad. He raised him, but says he never taught him the art of bushwhacking.

The Torreys were ever the friends and champions of Quantrill after he arrived in Kansas, especially Mrs. Torrey, who was the real head of the Torrey household. They wined him and dined him while he was in the jail at Paola and were always ready with some defense of him during all his war exploits. The Torreys were pro-slavery in sentiment and also in practice so far as they could be in Kansas. Mrs. Torrey's sister married a Missouri slave-owner who went into the Confederate army and was there killed.

Mrs. Torrey was a Miss Redfield. She was a great horse-woman, and would race through Canal Dover on horseback scattering citizens, geese, children, and pigs as she went. Colonel Torrey was a widower when he married her. Previous to this marriage Miss Redfield had gone to Cleveland, where, with a note for one thousand dollars, having her mother's name to it, she purchased a stock of millinery. She brought this millinery to Canal Dover and induced H. V. Beeson to let her have the front room of his dwelling for a shop. There she opened a millinery shop and disposed of her stock.

Colonel Henry Torrey was a soldier in the Mexican War, and a colonel of an Ohio or New York regiment, it is said. He was a mild-mannered, easy-going, spiritless, hopeless man who drifted through life.

Louis by accident, and came on to Kansas with them cannot be admitted, and that Colonel Torrey was to meet Beeson at some point on the way, as Beeson and his family always claimed. Quantrill carried with him some of the tinner-books published by his father, intending to sell them in towns where the boats might stop. He did not sell them all, having a number on hand when he arrived in Kansas. The first letter he wrote to his mother after he left home was written on a Missouri river steamboat.[3]

Missouri River
March 8. 1857.

My Dear Mother.

I neglected writing to you at St. Louis although we were there two days before Mr. Torry came. We are all well as usual except Richard who has a little cold. We have been on the river since last Wednesday the 4. & we have 296 miles to go yet so that we will not be there for about 3 or 4 days yet we have been delayed very much on account of the bad state of the river. I did not make as much money in St. Louis as I anticipated but still I have enough to carry me through. I will write you another letter at Leavenworth city before we start into the country. There are a great many going to Kansas at present and among them 220 soldiers to keep peace amongst us. Mr. Torry bought a shot gun & two revolvers so that we are pretty well armed. We did not buy much provision for we can get it just as cheap up the river. The boat we are on is pretty well crowded & we have to sleep on the floor. I have not had my clothes off but once since I left & that was to put on a clean shirt so that we are getting used to it allready   Your Son

W. C. Quantrill

He was a thoroughly honest, good man, and was always greatly respected by the people where he lived. When Mrs. Torrey arrived in Kansas she was much disappointed and desired to return to Ohio, but the colonel was not able to take her back. She revolted against her life in Kansas on a squatter's claim in a log cabin. Colonel Torrey sold his land as soon as he could and bought a building in Paola, where he kept a hotel as long as he lived.

Torrey did not return to Canal Dover for his family, but had Beeson bring his wife and children out to Kansas when he went to get his own family. After the death of Colonel Torrey and her marriage to Judge W. R. Wagstaff, Mrs. Torrey became a lawyer and her two daughters became lawyers.

3 Letter of W. C. Quantrill to his mother, now in the Collection of the author.

The intention to go to Leavenworth was abandoned because of the long time it had taken the boat to ascend the Missouri river. The party left the boat at Independence, Mo.[4] Quantrill wrote to his mother from that place, March 15, 1857, saying that they had intended to keep on the river to Leavenworth, but that low water had already delayed them nine days.[5]

At Independence they purchased two ox-teams and outfitted for the rough life in the new country to which they were bound, buying bacon, flour, beans, salt, and other articles. They arrived on the Marais des Cygnes, in Franklin county, Kansas, near Stanton, which is in Miami (then Lykins) county, on the 22d day of March, 1857.

At the time of his arrival in Kansas Quantrill was nearly twenty, lacking only about four months of having attained that age. He was boyish in appearance and seemed no more than sixteen or seventeen. His hair was still very light, almost white, not taking on the red tinge until later. He was rather slim and spare, though not lean. He was well formed, and when seen at a distance too great to distinguish each separate feature he was regarded as fine looking. His carriage was good, though men have been known to take a deep dislike to him at first sight when he was walking about; there was something cat-like and treacherous in his very movement. Following is a review of his life up to the time he came to Kansas:

Quantrill was cruel and heartless as a boy. And his inclination was to be idle and worthless. He was considered "peculiar," to use no harsher term. He was self-contained, self-confident. He was of a reflective turn of mind, brooding over those things which affected him personally. He came to unnatural conclusions from a course of reasoning which others could not comprehend. He was obstinate, often defiant. His chief characteristic was treachery. Kindness did not appeal to him, and he bore malice, cherishing any real or imaginary wrong

---

[4] Rather, at Wayne City, the name of the Independence landing.

[5] This letter is probably lost. Mention of it is made by W. W. Scott in a short sketch he wrote of Quantrill and which is in the Collection of the author. Scott quoted from the letter and must have had it before him as he wrote.

and biding his time. There was no forgiveness in his nature;
any manifestation of gratitude shown by him was but an exception dictated usually by policy. He was calculating and far-
seeing; he had patience and he did not forget. Mentally he was
above the average. He reasoned rapidly and rarely changed his
mind, once he had reached a conclusion. Many of his characteristics were feminine, and he was secretive by nature. He was
sensitive, and no compensation could be made him for an offense;
he might pretend to be satisfied with apology or reparation, but
the matter remained with him and rankled in him. He had
persistency in a marked degree, and he was bold and dogged in
the execution of any design once formed. He had no moral per-
ceptions, being in this respect depraved — a degenerate. Of
physical courage he had enough, though as a boy he was counted
a coward. As a boy, no one could understand him, and to the
end of his life he was a deepening mystery. He was not a
favorite in company, being seemingly pre-occupied and given to
strange remarks. Walking along the bank of the Marais des
Cygnes one day he observed a large branch growing straight out
over the road. He was in the company of a young lady and remarked, "I could hang six men on that limb." The conversation had not been upon hanging men, and from that day the
parents of the young lady refused to allow her to be in his company. Many of these characteristics were still latent in Quantrill when he arrived in Kansas. Under normal conditions they
might not have developed fully. In ordinary times he would
have been a disagreeable neighbor, venting his malice by maiming
a horse or poisoning cattle. Under what he might have considered strong provocation he would have shot his adversary from
ambush or cut him to pieces in the dark. He would have sought
occasions to have acted apparently on the defensive, when he was
the real aggressor.

From the first he was ambitious to acquire property and
have money. But he was lazy. He abhorred labor. He was incapable of continued exertion in any particular direction. Restraint of any kind he would not stand. When at work for another he was impatient of ordinary directions. He wished to
arrive at fortune by some great stroke not well defined in his

own mind, some good luck, favorable circumstance, intrigue. This made him dishonest, and all his life he was a thief. He was devoid of natural affection.[6]

6 His admirers always tell of his deep abiding love for his mother. He had no such affection. After he left home he never contributed a cent to her support, though through theft and robbery he had thousands upon thousands of dollars. At his death he left her nothing, but he did leave his mistress money with which to start a bagnio in St. Louis, Mo. This is established by several witnesses, one of whom is quoted. John Harmon was a traveling salesman who lived long in Canal Dover. Scott, in the *Iron Valley Reporter*, cast some reflections on him and his failure in business at Wooster, Ohio. In answer to the insinuations of Scott, Harmon wrote him a letter dated, 1237 Dean Street, Brooklyn, N. Y., Decembre 19, 1900, in which he says:

After Quantrell was wounded in the skirmish he had with the Federal troops down in Kentucky, the Sisters took him in and sent for a Catholic Priest, to whom he gave the sum of two thousand dollars, being about half the money he had with him, and who granted him absolution; and the other half he gave to a young woman who used occasionally to accompany him in some of his raids. After his death she went to Saint Louis, where White says he called on her and she told him that she furnished her house with the money that ''Billy'' left her.

The question that interests me most just now is this: Will the absolution obtained through the kind offices of the Sisters and the Priest, for which he paid two thousand dollars or more, avail him? Is he now walking the golden streets of the New Jerusalem, singing the Psalms of David, or has ferryman Charon put him on the boat destined for hades, where unfortunately, he may meet some of his many victims who were not so fortunate as to have the absolution of a priest before their sudden taking off at the hands of this bloody murderer? How much nobler to have given this money to his old mother, who was compelled to live in the Poor House for the last few years. No one but a blood-thirsty murderer would have treated his mother as Quantrell has treated his.

The man, White, referred to in the above quotation was at one time with Quantrill. I find the following in reference to him in Harmon's letter:

Several years after the war, the firm I was with hired a young man by the name of White, as a salesman. White told the writer that when Quantrell first organized his company of Missourians, which was for the ostensible purpose of protecting their property against the Kansas Jayhawkers, that he, White, joined it, but soon found out that Quantrell would commit murder on the slightest excuse and at once left him and went to Texas, taking his father's horses and mules with him and remained there until after the war. At the same time that Quantrell was at the head of this Missouri company, he was also at the head of a company of Kansas Jayhawkers for the assumed purpose of protecting their property against Missouri raiders.

As a further confirmation of the fact that Quantrell never sent his mother any money, there is a list of questions written by W. W. Scott for Mrs. Quantrill to answer. This list is in the Collection of the author.

One of the questions is, ''Did he [W. C. Quantrill] ever send any thing home?'' The answer, written after the question, by Scott, is ''Never.'' Scott evidently took his questions to Mrs. Quantrill and wrote down the answers to them from her own lips.

CHAPTER IV

THE first care of Beeson and Torrey upon their arrival on the Marais des Cygnes was to secure farms. The lands were all held by squatters pending the completion of surveys and sales of land by the government. The squatter might sell his "claim," and he often did so. This claim was only possession and the right to preëmpt the land and purchase it from the United States at public outcry. Beeson bought the squatter right to the northwest quarter of Section 34, Township 17, Range 21, and Torrey purchased a similar right to the northeast quarter of the same section. Both claims were in Franklin county, but the corner of Torrey's claim was only a half mile south and the same distance west of the village of Stanton, in Lykins, now Miami, county. The east line of Torrey's claim was the line between the counties. Torrey also bought a claim for Quantrill to hold for him. Quantrill was a minor and could not lawfully hold a claim for himself or any one else, but such irregularities were common at the time. The claim held by Quantrill is the northeast quarter of Section 21, Township 17, Range 21, and something like two miles north of the claims of Beeson and Torrey. He never pretended that he held this claim for himself, never thought of having any ownership or title in the land, assertions of his admirers to the contrary notwithstanding. Beeson and Torrey each paid $500 for his claim, and Torrey paid $250 for the claim held by Quantrill. For holding this claim, bidding it in at the land-sales, and assigning the certificate of sale to Torrey, Quantrill was to be paid $60. He did so hold the claim, did bid it in, and did assign the certificate of sale to Torrey.[1]

---

[1] They arrived in Lykins County, and settled near Stanton on the 22d of March, each one of the three taking a claim, or rather buying a preemption right of a squatter, Beeson and Torrey each paying $500 for

Upon the claim purchased by Torrey stood an old log cabin of small dimensions. Across the back part of it there was a sort of platform which served as a bedstead and upon which Torrey and Beeson slept. Quantrill and Richard Beeson slept on blankets spread before the fire on the floor. The spring nights were cold, and when the fire would burn down the room became uncomfortable. Quantrill would then roll himself in the blankets and leave young Beeson to freeze, and the remonstrances of Beeson and Torrey did not cause him to quit the practice. One night Beeson said, "Richard, you sleep with Colonel Torrey, and I will sleep with Bill," (by Ohio associates Quantrill was usually called "Bill"). The change in bedfellows was accordingly made.

Colonel Torrey had brought from Mexico a dagger with a blade some twelve inches in length, a finely proportioned and beautiful weapon which he had in his trunk in the cabin. In the night while sleeping Beeson was seized with an apprehension of immediate danger, and with difficulty forced himself awake. By the dim light of the fire he saw Quantrill standing over him

---

their claims, and also paying $250 for the claim standing in Quantrill's name. — *Andreas's History of Kansas*, p. 877.

Mr. Torrey and myself and my oldest son Richard and Wm C Quantrell Left Canal Dover on the 26th February 1857 Mr. Torrey going to New York to collect some money there and the Bal [the others] for Kansas with the understanding to meet in St. Louis. Left St. Louis on the 4th of March & Landed at Wayne City Landing on the 13th (Independence Jackson Co. Mo) Bought our outfits and started for Kansas Landed at Stanton on the 22nd of March and Bought 3 claims or quarters of land Wm C. Quantrell holding a timber claim for Mr Torrey and Bidding it in for him on or about the 26 June or Perhaps 28 for and assigning the certificate of sale to Mr. Torrey he Paying the money to U S Commissioner Mr Walker at the Land Sales at Paola (and stands so to day on the government Record of said Sales) — *From letter of H. V. Beeson to W. W. Scott*, dated Paola, Kansas, June 5, 1880. Letter now in the Collection of the author.

The records in the United States land office at Topeka show that William C. Quantrill bid in the northeast quarter of Section 21, Township 17, Range 21, at the sale of public lands held in Paola on the 29th day of June, 1857, paying therefor $2.25 per acre, or $360 for the quarter section.

Some accounts say that Torrey paid Quantrill $200 to hold the claim and bid it in for him. Mrs. Frances Beeson Thompson thinks the amount was $200. Most people say that he was paid $60. The exact amount may never be known.

in the act of plunging the Mexican dagger into his heart. He
called to Quantrill to know what he was doing there, and Quantrill hesitated. Torrey was by this time awake, and Beeson told
him to make Quantrill put the dagger back into the trunk, which
was standing open. This Torrey did. Beeson got up and went
out of the house. He returned with a good hickory switch or
small club which he laid on until Quantrill cried for mercy.[2]

Quantrill wrote home frequently. A copy of the letter to
his mother written May 16 is preserved. It shows that he
wished to have her move to Kansas.[3] The letter is given below:

Stanton Kansas Ter. May 16,1857.
My dear Mother.

I have not received a letter from you since I left home, but
I have heard that you are all well, which kept me satisfied; but
I will not be so any longer until I receive a letter from you. And
I shall continue to write until I receive a letter from you "in
your own hand write" as the Irishman said. We are all well
as usual. I have just finished a hard job of rolling logs at a
clearing around our cabin, which we are going to put in potatoes.
Yesterday we just finished planting a Ten-acre field of corn on
the prairie, which Mr. Torrey & I plowed. Next week we are
going to commence a 20 acre field, so that we will have corn
enough for next winter at least.

We have had a very backward spring here; but from what
news we get they have had a worse time in Ohio and all of the
eastern states. Although the trees are all green here, and the
prairie looks like a field of wheat. I suppose by the time you
receive this letter Granfather will be there if he is not there
already. If he is there or not, I want you if possible to sell out
there and let me have part of the money out here to procure a
home for us all, consisting of 160 acres of land; either prairie
or timber, or half of each, or almost any proportion of each one
would wish to have. If you can do this by any possible means
do so and we can move here this fall & be much more comfortably
situated than in Dover, or any place else east of Kansas. Older
heads than mine may try to persuade you that this is not the
case, but it is so, for all is peace and quietness here now, & it
will remain so without doubt. Why, not less than 50,000 people
from the North have come into the Territory this spring so that

---

[2] Told me by Mrs. Frances Beeson Thompson.

[3] This copy was made by W. W. Scott. It is in the Collection of
the author. What became of the original is not known.

Kansas will soon be a State among States & able to maintain her own rights.

If you can persuade Grandfather to let us sell out root & branch it will be undoubtedly the best thing you could do. Then we will all be square with the world & able to say our soul is our own without being contradicted. Is not this worth sacrificing something for? I think it is and so you will, I know. If we cannot do this I will not stay here longer than fall, for I can make more money in the States at teaching than by hard work here. I am here now as an agent to get a home for us all, which I can do if there is not too much opposition. I have thought over the matter, and Mr. Torrey says it is the best I can do. Do not let anybody persuade you out of this until they produce better grounds for not doing as I have said than I have for doing so. It is the best we can do, and everybody will say so who reasons the case well.

If you can have such good luck as to dispose of the property, you can take out letters of administration yourself. If not, Grandfather or some one in whom you can confide. If the thing can be done, do it as soon as you can for it will be all the better.

I will tell you now how we get along here. We live on side meat — bacon about four inches thick; corn cakes, beans, few dried apples occasionally, & fish & squirrels when we can get them which we have pretty good luck doing. Our house is built of round logs with a fire place made partly of stone; a floor made of puncheon — that is split boards about 3 inches thick. Our furniture consists of 2 stools made out of puncheon, 3 trunks & a table made when we wish to use it by putting a board (which we found in the river) across the 2 trunks. Our walls are decorated with guns, boots, side meat, skillets, surveying chain &c. The only job that we have to do that we all dislike, is dishwashing which Mr. Beeson is doing now. We have to take turn about at it; no one will do it more than twice in succession. Our stock consists of 3 yoke of cattle, six pigs & about 2 dozen chickens. We will have by fall 3 times as much stock if we have good luck. All I want is for the rest of you to be here, and we will live twice as fast.

The letter ends abruptly, and there is no signature on the copy. It is probable that the whole letter was not copied.

Although Quantrill was paid to work he was a very unsatisfactory hand. He prowled through the timber of the river bottoms with a gun most of the time, and every day he visited the claim he was holding for Torrey. He would not be brought to see that he should apply himself steadily to the employment for which he was paid, and on his mother's account he was not discharged. After he had bid in the land for Torrey and received his pay therefor, he began to stay much of the time at the house of one John Bennings.[4] Bennings was in full sympathy with the pro-slavery element, though he pretended to be a Free-State man. He persuaded Quantrill to believe that he had been swindled by Torrey and Beeson. Quantrill demanded $90 in addition to what had been paid him. Rather than have a diffi-

---

[4] In an interview had by the author with Martin Van Buren Jackson, father of Hon. Fred S. Jackson, attorney general of Kansas, March 13, 1908, the following information about the Bennings family was obtained. Mr. Jackson was one of the earliest settlers at Stanton, and his son Fred was born in the old blockhouse there:

John Bennings was born in Pike county, Mo., as Mr. Jackson believed. It is certain that he lived there at one time, for in the Andreas History of Kansas it is stated that his two sons were born there. Bennings was a tall thin-breasted man, afflicted with the old lingering consumption. His children were all tall and thin-breasted, and they all seemed to have consumption. They died in early life, soon after they were grown up. The children were:

John Bennings,
Adolphus Y. Bennings,
Albert Bennings,
"Bud" Bennings, (James?)
"Sis" Bennings.

They are all dead. John Bennings, the father, was a frontiersman. He went to California from Pike county, Mo., in 1849, taking his family. He went from California to Texas. He came to Kansas Territory from Texas, and took a claim on the Marais des Cygnes, near Stanton. He was a hunter and trapper. He had a long, heavy rifle, of large caliber, with which to kill buffaloes, which he called "Betsey" or "Old Betsey." He had a very large shot-gun, and other rifles, pistols and knives, also many traps in which to capture wild animals. His only occupation was hunting and trapping in the heavy timber along the Marais des Cygnes.

Quantrill liked Bennings and his shiftless ways of living — liked the haphazard, irresponsible life led by Bennings. Quantrill loved to roam and tramp idly and aimlessly. These traits bound Quantrill and the Bennings family. Bennings was a strong pro-slavery man, and the first bent of Quantrill in favor of the border-ruffians came from his association with the Bennings family.

Adolphus Y. Bennings told James Hanway that he was with Quantrill on his trip across the Plains, and they were probably in Utah together, returning by way of Pike's Peak. The card of Hanway with this information is in the Collection of the author.

culty with him it was agreed, through the efforts of E. P. Hicks, that he should be paid $63 in two deferred installments — one of $33 and one of $30.[5]

[5] There has been much said and little known of this settlement. As good an authority as the *Andreas History of Kansas* (Herd Book) says this claim was submitted to a ''squatter's court'':

Some time afterwards Quantrill desired to sell out his interest in the claim; and as he and Mr. Torrey could not agree as to what was rightly due Quantrill, the matter was submitted to a ''squatter's court'' for arbitration. The court decided that Beeson and Torrey owed Quantrill $63. The financial relations between Messrs. Beeson and Torrey were such that the understanding was reached between them that the latter should pay Quantrill the $63. Torrey had no money to pay with, and in order for him to raise the money it was necessary for him to go to Lecompton to sell some land warrants he held. On account of sickness he was unable to go to Lecompton. — *Andreas's History of Kansas*, p. 877.

While the settlement was by arbitration it was a small matter and made no stir in the community. It has been confused with the settlement of the business relations between Beeson and Torrey. Even the children of Beeson make this mistake. The ''squatter's court'' was convened to adjust the matters between Beeson and Torrey, and it consisted of a number of settlers, among them Joab Toney, J. B. Hobson, Josiah Bundy, Charles Rice, and perhaps S. A. Hester. Hobson acted as secretary and it required several days to make a satisfactory settlement. Mrs. Frances Beeson Thompson remembers carrying meals to the arbitrators, who held their court in an old log cabin on the river below Beeson's. Mr. Hobson writes the author as follows:

Paola, Kansas, Oct. 22, 1907.

I was not sec. of the board of arbitration between Quantrill, Beeson and Torrey. Their differences were adjusted by E. P. Hicks, the father of Mrs. David Overmyer of Topeka.

I was one of the arbitrators that settled the partnership business between Torrey and Beeson with which Quantrill had nothing to do.

My recollection is that Torrey and Beeson and Quantrill had a business dispute and Quantrill took a yoke of oxen belonging to Torrey and Beeson and hid them in the brush for the purpose of forcing a settlement as he Q. claimed. All three of the parties came to Stanton and selected E. P. Hicks to arbitrate their differences which he did and the oxen were returned. I dont remember what Hick's findings were.

The last payment made to Quantrill on his award was made in October, 1857. The receipt for this final payment is now in the library of the Kansas State Historical Society and is as follows:

30,00 Recd Stanton Oct 22d 1857 of George Torrey thirty dollars for bal. due on settlement by arbitration with Torrey & Beeson
(Signed) W. C. Quantrill

The receipt is No. 1288, Kansas State Historical Society Collections. It was furnished the Society by John Speer, September 30, 1878. Speer seems to have secured it from Mrs. Wagstaff. It is endorsed: ''W. C. Quantrill Receipt 30,00.''

After settlement and before payments had been made on the award Quantrill became clamorous for his money, perhaps at the instigation of Bennings. The amount was due from Torrey and not from Beeson. To force payment Quantrill stole a yoke of oxen from Beeson and some fine blankets and a brace of revolvers from Torrey. Beeson looked the country over for his cattle, thinking at first that they had strayed. Not finding them and being unable to hear anything of them, he concluded that Quantrill had stolen them. Meeting Quantrill, he accused him of the theft, told him if the cattle were not pointed out to him he would shoot him down like a dog, reminding Quantrill of his ingratitude and dishonesty. He ordered Quantrill to step into the path before him and lead the way to the cattle on pain of instant death. Quantrill stepped into the path as directed, and Beeson put the muzzle of his gun against Quantrill's back and told him to lead on. Quantrill led the way into a dense thicket in the river bottom, and there stood the oxen, yoked, chained to a tree, and so weak from starvation that they could scarcely stand. They were famished for water, and had to be fed and watered a day or two before they were strong enough to be driven home.[6]

It is not probable that Beeson saw much of Quantrill subsequent to the settlement made at the instigation of Bennings, for

---

[6] The *Andreas History* says: In consequence of this delay Quantrill became impatient, and in order to get his pay, stole a yoke of cattle belonging to Mr. Beeson. Some few days thereafter Beeson met Quantrill about sunrise on the prairie. Quantrill turned to avoid Beeson, when the latter, bringing his rifle to bear upon the former, who was about ten rods distant, hailed him with, "Bill, stop! I want to see you." Quantrill turned towards Beeson, when the latter again commanded, "Lay your gun down in the grass!" This order was also obeyed, when Beeson said, "You must bring my oxen back by three o'clock this afternoon, or I shall shoot you on sight!" Quantrill promised to return the oxen, and did so about four o'clock that day. — *Andreas's History of Kansas*, p. 877.

For Pay of $60.00 he stole a Yoke of Oxen from me and kept them hid in the Brush until compelled to return them at muzzel of Rifle He stole from Mr. Torrey 1 Pr of Mackinaw Blankets and a Pair of Navy Revolvers the Last he was made to return and the Blankets were found rotten in a hollow Log some time afterwards. — *Letter of H. V. Beeson to W. W. Scott, dated Paola, Kansas, June 5, 1880.* The letter is in the Collection of the author.

The account written in the text was secured from the children of Beeson, and it does not fully agree with the account given by Andreas, and it is possible that it differs from that written by Beeson himself.

he was engaged in building a house on his claim. Quantrill, though, still continued to live at the Torrey cabin a part of the time.[7]

Quantrill wrote his mother a letter in July, a part of which has been copied and preserved.[8] It contains little that can be of value in the study of his life, but it does show that he was of an observing turn of mind and capable of the enjoyment of the beauties of nature. And it reveals the fact that he was restless, solitary and unhappy, a condition, which, if not relieved, was sure sooner or later to become unbearable and cause abandonment of all restraints imposed by society and revels in wild excesses. In a character constituted as was Quantrill's such a condition of mind, if not remedied, was certain to result, as it did later, in a carnival of crime. The extract is as follows:

> Stanton, Kansas, July 9th, 1857.
> It is too dry now to work at the corn; this is why I have this leisure time to write during the week. I have taken my atlas and went to the bank of the river in the shade, to write. Everything feels and looks happy; the wood is full of birds of every kind, seeing which can sing best and sweetest. The fish are playing in the water of the river, which is clear as crystal; and the squirrel bounds from tree to tree, till seing me he stops, and after eyeing me curiously, then scampers on again till I almost envy him his happiness. I have but one wish, and that is that you were here, for I cannot be happy here all alone; and it seems that I am the only person or thing that is not happy along this beautiful stream. But I must close my letter, or I will make you sad; and in caring for three helpless children you have cares enough without my adding to them.

Such characters are always strangers to that happiness — the only source of happiness — which comes from a sense of duty performed, from the knowledge of an honest purpose in life, from right action towards fellow-men. Quantrill was at

---

[7] There was some mysterious tie or connection between Quantrill and the Torreys. This relation survived the Civil War and cannot be explained. The Torreys were always staunch defenders of Quantrill and his memory. It is one of the mysteries connected with Quantrill's life.

[8] This extract was copied by W. W. Scott from the original letter, evidently. The letter is not known to be in existence. The copy is in the Collection of the author.

the time a boy, young man, longing for happiness, yet daily violating the laws of happiness, doing the very things which would make happiness impossible, constantly forfeiting the confidence and respect of his friends and neighbors by indulging in crime. He still believed that despite all these things he should have been happy. He came finally to be against all men, believing them enemies, believing them to be unreasonably antagonistic to him, purposely preventing his attainment of contentment and happiness, seeking revenge upon society for an imaginary wrong — for something amiss within himself, a malady which affected only his own soul. This condition becomes more and more apparent in him, as revealed by his letters, especially those written by him at a subsequent date while teaching.

Beeson returned to Canal Dover early in August to bring his family to Kansas. Quantrill was still enthusiastic about his mother's moving to Kansas. Beeson carried a letter to him from his mother, which he says is the first he had received from her. In his reply he said he would go on a claim and that he intended soon to leave Torrey's. He told of the dissatisfaction of the families of Beeson and Torrey with their new homes in Kansas.[9] His mother must have warned him against an early marriage, and he gave her an assurance that he was "too smart for that." The letter is set out below:

Stanton Kansas Territory
August 23^d 1857

My Dear Mother.

I received your letter by Mr Beeson & it was the first I have received but I hope not the last. The folks all arrived here safely; But they have the blues now awfully there is not enough of city here for them. I am going to [go] on a claim in a few weeks, & I will probably leave Mr. Torrey this week. I wrote a letter to Grandfather to day & I wrote to him about Frank coming out here & a fine letter about Kansas.

I think I shall yet try to get a farm. Do not be afraid of me getting married in a hurry I am to[o] smart for that. I dont think I will see Beesons very often for I am going to do for myself now. I cannot write you a long letter this time but

---

9 This is a beautifully written letter. It is in the Collection of the author.

I will write you another in a week I cannot write any longer
& I must close.

I am Well & hope you may be the same.

Yours Truly
Your Son
W. C. Quantrill

The next letter you write Direct to Stanton Kansas Territory

At a later date he wrote a letter to his brother Franklin,
which is now in the library of the Kansas State Historical
Society.[10] At that time he was evidently expecting to return to
Canal Dover, as the letter will show:

Franklin I have never answered those few lines of yours
yet but will try to do so now. I am glad to hear that you are
well except your leg. You say you and Thomson are going to
school. You ought soon to be able to teach school I think and
when I come home I think I will have you try it. I suppose
Thomson has grown to be quite a large boy and when I come
home I have something in view for him to do if he has attended
well to his book tell him to study hard for he ought to beat me
almost now that I have been so long amongst the indians

Your brother
W. C. Quantrill

The return of Beeson to Canal Dover for the purpose of
taking his family to Kansas created interest, in that village, in
Kansas Territory. Some time in the following fall (1857) a
number of Canal Dover young men went to Kansas. They were
all acquaintances and friends of the Beeson and Torrey families,
and among them were John Diehl, Alexander McCartney,
Charles Wood, and George Hildt. They were all schoolmates of

---

10 This letter has no date. It seems to have been written on a part
of the paper of a letter to some one else, probably his mother, and to have
been torn off afterwards. W. W. Scott gave it to the Society. Perhaps
he tore it off the letter to which it was attached. Or Quantrill may have
written it on a scrap and sent it with a letter to some other member of
the family. It is written on both sides of a scrap some two inches wide
torn from the bottom of a sheet of note paper. It is quite well written,
the penmanship being delicate and regular, much resembling that of a
woman of refinement, and it is superior to any other writing of his, though
there is no mistaking it for the writing of any other person. Quantrill
wrote it.

Quantrill. They settled on adjoining claims in what is now McCamish township, Johnson county, Kansas.[11] Quantrill went there with them and took a claim. They built a cabin on one of the claims in which they all lived, and on each claim they erected a pen or put up a few logs to hold possession until they could break the land in the spring. In memory of their old Ohio home they called their settlement Tuscarora Lake. In January Quantrill wrote a letter to W. W. Scott, who lived in Canal Dover.[12] There are a number of vulgar allusions in the letter, such as are found in none of his other letters, and which may be accounted for by remembering that it was written to a young man with whom he was on familiar terms. He was at that time seemingly in earnest about getting a farm for himself, and urged others to come out and take claims:

Tuscarora Lake
Jan, 22^d 1858

Friend William.

I have come to the conclusion to write to you again. You wrote to me last summer & I answered it shortly afterward; but, not having received one afterwards, I came to the conclusion that you had never received it; for at that time letters frequently were mislaid & lost.

But when one does sit down to write here, he hardly knows what to say; for situated as we are, (that is keeping Bach,) & away from any town we are at more of a loss for news &c. than you gentlemen in the city there.

I have left Col Torreys & now live with the rest of the Dover boys here. George Hildt is in Dover ere this & if you see him tell him we are all well & that the claim North of mine was jumped last Monday by a young fellow from Ind.

About the last election here is this 10,126 votes against the Lecompton swindle & 6000 for it, of which 3000 if not more were illegal. I saw the Ohio Democrat here yesterday which had some what I call D——n lies about Kansas & I would like to tell the editor so to his face. He said Jim Lane, (as good a man as

---

[11] From information given the author by Mrs. Frances Beeson Thompson and Mrs. Isaac N. Sparks, daughters of Beeson. To their best recollection these claims were taken about the first of December, 1857.

[12] Letter of W. C. Quantrill to W. W. Scott, now in the Collection of the author. It is carelessly written in a coarse sprawling hand, and must have been written hurriedly.

we have here) was fighting with U. S. Troops at Fort Scott, he was there but did no fighting; his presence is enough to frighten 100 Missourians. The settlers shot two men & wounded 4 or 5 but in self défence, it is a pity they had not shot every Missourian that was there. The democrats here are the worst men we have for they are all rascals, for no one can be a democrat here without being one; but the day of their death is fast approaching & they will be like the jews be scattered to the four winds of the earth & a guilty look which will always betray them.

If you are in the printing office yet tell the editor if he wants any subscribers in Kansas he must do a little better than he has done, for the boys here will hardly use it when they go back of the house.

If you know where George Scott is tell him to write to me or if he wants to get a farm of [for] nothing to come here as soon as he can; for there are good chances here now, tell him I am safe for 160 acres of land & that I will insure the same to him if he comes here in 8 or 10 weeks; & you too Billy $40 will Bring him here yes 30 if he is economical & I will insure any one $1.50 a day if he wants to work, & Friend William if you want land here is the only place to get it cheap & you had better come if you want any. Tell George if he wants to come, to come by railroad to Jefferson city, Mo. & then shoulder his carpet sack & foot it to Independence & from there to Little Santa Fe. & then to Olathe Johnson County K. T. which is six day walk, if you see any Boys around dover who want to come tell them what I have written.

We have the finest weather imaginable well to tell you the truth the grass has been growing on the prairie all winter or during the season we call winter & we have no rainy or wet weather either.

Last week I helped to kill a deer & since I have been here I have killed myself 2 antelope & one deer & about 25 Wild Turkeys & geese & before you see me in Ohio I will have killed buffalo for they are plenty about 100 miles west of us now & those who have killed them say it is fine sport at least if I keep my health I will try it. This is the place to hunt there is more game to be seen in one day here than in a whole year there.

About the girls I cannot say as much as you could but this is certain a man can have his choice for we have all kinds & colors here Black White & Red But to tell you which I like the best is a mixture of the two latter colors if properly brought up for they are both rich and good looking & I think go ahead of your Dover gals far enough. Em Walton would pass very well for a squaw if she was better looking but I think from present

appearances John Diehl will squaw her about next fall or winter
& that will bleach her a little probably. When you write tell
me all about the girls & especially yours & my fair one that used
to be in years past, if she is around yet. You and the rest of the
boys there must attend to the girls well while we are here in Kansas, & tell them we are all going to marry squaws & when they
die we are coming to old Dover for our second wives so that
they must not despair.

I must close. Now write soon give me all the news my love
to the boys & girls & oblige

Your obedient S.

W. C. Quantrill

These young men always spent Sunday at the house of
Beeson, going there on Saturday evening. Quantrill went with
them, and usually went on to the house of Bennings; at other
times he stopped with the Torreys. This continued until well
along into the spring of 1858, when the others came down one
Saturday evening without Quantrill. They had driven him out
of their camp for stealing. When the weather became mild in
the spring they began to miss their blankets. Some one was
stealing their provisions also. Quantrill had been loudest in
his condemnation of the thieves and had even played detective
and accused some settlers on Cedar creek. But his actions
brought suspicion upon himself. The boys said nothing at the
time, but kept watch. They soon caught Quantrill stealing
some provisions, clothing, and a pistol. They made inquiry of
other settlers and found their blankets, and the settlers said
they had been buying provisions from Quantrill all winter and
had bought the blankets from him in the spring. The boys were
so disgusted with him that they forced him to leave the camp,
not wishing to punish him because of his mother and his having
grown up with them. He was gone two or three weeks, when he
returned to Stanton and again took up his abode with Bennings.
But he was in bad repute and soon went to Fort Leavenworth.
There he attached himself to a provision train bound for Utah
with supplies for the army taken out the previous summer to
subdue the Mormons. He claimed to have accompanied this
train in the capacity of a herder or teamster. If he had any
position at all it must have been in some roustabout capacity.

QUANTRILL IN KANSAS AND UTAH

R. M. Peck, in *The National Tribune*, September 22, 1904, says he was a hanger-on following the army, and that he was one of the most reckless and successful gamblers in the camp at Fort Bridger.[13] The particulars of Quantrill's trip across the Plains

---

[13] He was then known as Charley Hart. R. M. Peck, now (1909) of Whittier, California, saw Quantrill at Fort Bridger and witnessed one of his gambling exploits, which he believes was in June, 1858:

I was a soldier in one of the two companies of 1st Cav. that formed a part of the command of Lieut. Col. Wm. Hoffman, 6th Inf., which command was sent out from Fort Leavenworth early in the spring of '58 to escort several trains — some mule teams and some of oxen — loaded with supplies for the command of Brvt. Brig. Gen. Albert Sidney Johnston, Commanding the Mormon Expedition, who had been snowed in all winter at Fort Bridger, or Camp Scott, as it was officially designated.

We arrived at Camp Scott in the first days of June. A paymaster who had followed us arrived about the same time and paid the soldiers off. As there were few ways of spending the money outside of Judge Carter's sutler store, where prices were outrageously high, during the few days that intervened between our arrival at Fort Bridger and the departure of Gen. Johnston's forces for Salt Lake City, gambling was rife throughout the camp, and, as usually happens, in a short time, a few sharpers had nearly all the soldiers' money.

Amony the celebrites of the camp I had frequently heard the name of Charley Hart mentioned, whose notoriety seemed to be derived from his reckless bettings and phenomenal winnings. I heard it stated that he had come out from Kansas with Gen. Johnston's troops the previous fall, working as a teamster in one of the six-mule trains.

While sauntering through a big gambling tent a day or so after payday, watching the fluctuations of fortune at the various tables where chance games were being operated, I heard some one remark, "There comes Charley Hart", and having heard his fame as a wild plunger in gambling, I took a good look at him. I could see nothing heroic in his appearance, but considerable of the rowdy, as I now recall the impression I then got of him.

He was apparently about twenty-two or twenty-three years of age; about five feet ten inches in height; with an ungraceful, slouchy walk; and by no means prepossessing in features. He had evidently been patronizing Judge Carter's store, since he "struck it rich," for his clothes all seemed new. A pair of high-heeled calf-skin boots of small size; bottoms of trousers tucked into boot-tops; a navy pistol swinging from his waist belt; a fancy blue flannel shirt; no coat; a colored silk handkerchief tied loosely around his neck; yellow hair hanging nearly to the shoulders; topped out by the inevitable cow-boy hat. This is the picture of Charley Hart as my memory presents him now.

As he entered the tent he carried in his left hand a colored silk handkerchief, gathered by the four corners, which apparently contained coin. Advancing to one of the tables where the operator, or banker, as the dealer of a chance game is usually called, was dealing "Monte", he set the handkerchief on the table and opened it out, showing the contents to be gold coins, and seemingly in bulk about equal to the stacks of gold coins tiered up on the table in front of the banker.

Hart then asked, "Take a tap, pard?" meaning would the banker accept a bet of Hart's pile against the dealer's, on the turn of a card. The

are not known. Whether he went directly from Fort Leavenworth to Utah, or whether he loitered in the camps along the
California Trail to ply his profession of gambler until late in
the summer, and then crossed over to Utah, we do not know.
We know from his letters that he was at South Pass on the third
day of September, 1858, and that he went on to Utah and was
there until the spring of 1859. All of this year 1858, after he
left Stanton (about the first of May), was spent in Utah or on
the road thither. He arrived at Salt Lake City about the first

---

banker accepted the challenge, shuffled the cards, passed the deck to Hart
to cut, then threw out the "lay-out" of six cards, in a "column-of-twos"
style. Hart then set his handkerchief of gold on a card, at the same time
drawing his pistol, "Just to insure fair play," he remarked, seeing that
the banker had his gun lying on the table convenient to his right hand.
Keeping his eye on the banker's hands, to make sure that the deal was
done "on the square", Hart said, "Now deal."

Turning the deck face up the banker drew the cards off successively.
Hart's card won. As the dealer looked up with a muttered oath he found
himself looking into the muzzle of Hart's pistol.

"Back out", said Hart quietly. "Don't even touch your pistol. I'll
give it back to you when I rake in the pot."

The banker did as directed, while Hart, without showing any nervous-
ness, still holding his pistol in one hand, reached across the table and with
the other arm swept the banker's money and pistol over to him. Picking
out the twenties, tens, fives and two-and-a-half pieces, he tossed them into
his handkerchief. There still remained on the table about a double handfull of small silver, (there were very few silver dollars in circulation then,
the little one-dollar gold pieces being largely used in their stead), and a
handfull of gold dollars. Sweeping this small stuff into his hands, Hart
said, "I don't carry such chicken feed as that," as he tossed the small
coins up in the air and let the crowd scramble for them.

Then handing the dejected looking banker his pistol and a twenty-
dollar gold piece, he said: "There, pard, is a stake for you," and gathering up his plethoric handkerchief, he meandered on seeking new banks to
"bust."

The next day, so I was told, Hart's marvelous luck deserted him, and
he lost every dollar he had; and after trying in vain to "strike it up
again", he became discouraged and disgusted with gambling, joined some
outfit going back to the states, and went back to Kansas dead broke.

I never heard the name Quantrill used till the summer of '61, when
his depredations along the borders of Missouri and Kansas were bringing
the name into unpleasant notoriety. I then heard that Quantrill, the
bloody-handed guerrilla leader, and Charley Hart, the reckless gambler of
Fort Bridger, were identical.

This letter is dated, Whittier, California, November 6, 1907, and
is addressed to the author, and is now in his Collection. In a later letter
to the author, Mr. Peck says that it was in June that he first saw Charley
Hart at Fort Bridger in 1858. This is possibly an error; it may have been
later. Mr. Peck served in the Union army along the border of Missouri
and Kansas during the Civil War.

of October, and he wrote from that point to his mother on the 15th.[14] It was his intention to go on to the Colville gold mines in Canada in the spring of 1859, but this he did not do. The letter to his mother is as follows:

Great Salt Lake City.
Oct. 15th 1858

My Dear Mother.

I have wrote to you several times since I started across the plains, but I never have had a letter yet, but I do not care so much if you know where I am and know that I am well and doing well. I arrived here about two weeks ago, and I was never so surprised in my life as I was to find a people living here in large cities and towns and farming the lands here, which, without their untiring labor, would be a desert producing neither grass nor timber, nothing but a few stunted weeds; but they have converted it into fine farms and gardens, by ditching from the mountain streams and watering the whole country. You go in their towns and cities and you find the purest and clearest of spring water coming from the snow capped mountains, and running on either side of the streets and through their lots in small but rapid streams, carrying off the filth & keeping every thing fresh as it was when spring first opened. They are an industrious people and all hold to their religion in a manner which shows no hypocrisy, and I think their morals are as good as any people I have met with in my travels.

I have not seen Brigham Young yet, as he has to keep indoors since the war on account of some of the threats made by some of the Mormons & Gentiles and of course they have no religious services & therefore I have had no chance to learn much of their religion. But there is this about it I believe they are not half so bad as they want to make out, at least there is very little of it shown now, & I have been in about 12 or 15 of their towns and cities, they are scattered for 300 miles south of Salt Lake in the valley, in towns, from 10 to 15 miles apart. They settle in this way to defend themselves from the Indians. They held an agricultural fair since I have been here, in the city, and I was never so agreeably surprised, for it equaled any of our county fairs in every thing except fine horses, and cattle, and peaches, apples, plums, grapes, & indeed all kinds of fruits and vegetables equaled and in some instances far surpassed any thing in the east that ever I had seen; especially the vegetables. onions as large as a saucer, potatoes, beets, radishes, carrots,

---

[14] The original of this letter is lost. W. W. Scott made a copy of it, which is in the Collection of the author.

parsnips, &c., were larger than any I had ever seen; and then the needle work was very fine, and the picture gallery was splendid & the specimens of their manufactures were very fine indeed, & then a very fine brass band & string band entertained us an hour or so every half day very agreeably, & indeed I am so well pleased that I shall stay with them this winter at least. I am going to apply for a school and I think I can obtain one, they pay from $50 to $60 per month & I think that will pay for one winter at least.

The soldiers are camped about 45 miles from the city in Cedar Valley, they are having some trouble with the Indians but none in the least with the Mormons.

I am going in the spring to the Colville gold mines in Canada, north of Oregon Territory which they say are equal to the California; at least so says a friend of mine whom I knew in the States & who has been there but had to cease operations on account of the Indians; but Government will send troops there early in the spring, and are hiring men to go with them now so as to be all ready when spring opens.

There has been no cold weather in the valley yet, but it has snowed considerable in the mountains for a month back, and indeed I was caught in a severe snow-storm on the South Pass in the Rocky Mountains on the 3rd day of September; & it snowed hard all day, and froze ice from an inch to two inches thick in our buckets for a week afterwards. There has been no frost in the valley yet; or, indeed, they never have dew or frost, but when it comes cold it commences to snow, and for that reason it is very healthy.

You need not expect me home till you see me there, but bear in mind that I will do what is right, take care of myself, try to make a fortune honestly, which I think I can do in a year or two. I will always let you know where I am & how I am doing & by the next mail I will send you my picture as I appeared in camp coming out here, and also a letter. I have given up long ago thinking my Grandfather will help me, & that is why I am here to make my fortune for the poorest laborer can command $40 per month & I think I can do more. I have not missed a meals victuals since I left Kansas, and I weighed when I came to the city 171 lbs., so that you may not be afraid of my losing my health. I have got rid of that trouble in my throat. I am not thinking of getting married yet, although every man here has from 5 to 8 wives, & the rich have from 12 to 20 & Brigham has at present 43. I will send you some of the Mormon papers when I can obtain them. Adieu

Your Son

W. C. Quantrill

Direct to
          Great Salt Lake City
              Utah Territory
                              Mrs. C. C. Quantrill

In this letter Quantrill was evidently deceiving his mother, writing to her as a green country boy on a trip to his county seat might write. He was living one life and giving her the impression that he was living another. The reckless gambling, the rough language, the proficiency with the revolver were none of them mentioned. His companions were neither mentioned nor described. Adolphus Y. Bennings was with him. Upton Hays, later associated with Quantrill in the guerrilla warfare along the border, and other young men from western Missouri who rode by the moon with him along the Blue and the Sni, bent on blood, roistered and gambled with him along the Oregon Trail and in the valleys of the Saints.

Quantrill suffered from an attack of mountain fever, which he described in a letter to his mother.[15] He told her he was to go to work as a clerk for the quartermaster of the army at $50 per month, and that he would not return home without some money.

                              Great Salt Lake City
                                  Dec 1st 1858.
My Dear Mother.
I am again seated to write a few lines, which I should have done some time ago, but it was not in my power to do so any sooner on account of my having been very sick for about 3 weeks with what is called mountain fever a dangerous disease, which debilitates a person very soon. but once having broke the disease a person gains very rapidly. for the last two weeks I have had such an appetite as hardly could be satisfied but I am very careful not to eat too much I feel very well at present. the Mormons here have treated me very well much better than I could have expected after their disturbance with what they call the Gentiles. Next week I am going to clerk for the Quarter Master in the army at $50 per month which is no more than 25 at home I am so nervous that I can not write worth a cent.

---

15 Letter of Quantrill to his mother. This letter is in the Collection of the author. It is poorly written and shows that he was suffering from the effects of the disease at the time.

I can't tell when I will be home.   I am not coming home without some money.   I will take care of myself.   Give my love to all. If any thing is done with our property you take my share
Your Son
W. C. Quantrill

Direct to Salt Lake City
Utah Territory

It is more than probable that he had no intention of going to work for the quartermaster, and in his next letter he said that he had lost the place through his own fault, and that he was employed as cook for a mess of twenty-five men.[16]   He wrote from Camp Floyd, and if he was cooking at all it was most likely for some mess of hangers-on like himself:

Camp Floyd
Jan 9th 1859.

My Dear Mother.
I again sit down to write a few lines to you without having yet had a letter from you since I have been here.   the last letter I wrote to you was immediately after I had got up from a sick bed but now I am as well & hearty as ever, if not more so.   I had rather a hard time of it then but it was all my own fault That throwed me out of employment in the dead of winter in one of the worst countries in the world for a case like mine   I have been cooking for a mess of about 25 men for some time untill I can get a situation in government, which I have good recome[n]-dations for (as soon as a vacancy occurs,) from some of the head men in the camp.   do not greeve any more than possible about me for I will surprise you some of these days which will be worth something dont fear.   I have a notion to marry 4 or 5 women here if I can for here is the only place I will ever have a chance I expect, the Mormons have from 3 to 8 on an average. They are a very ignorant set of people generally & generally great rogues & rascals thinking nothing to be to[o] bad to do to a gentile as they call us & I must say that the gentiles are generally the same way.   It is drawing to what is called tattoo in camp that is when all lights are put out & they go to bed & the sentinel does not let any one pass him after that time.   Now I must close give my love to all & do not dispair.
Your Son
W. C. Quantrill

Direct to Salt Lake city

---

16 This letter of Quantrill to his mother is in the Collection of the author.   It is carelessly and hurriedly written and is brief.

After this letter nothing was heard of Quantrill for more than six months. Some part of his adventures during that time is referred to in a letter to his mother written from Lawrence, Kansas, 30th July, 1859.[17] He had made another one of his erratic moves, one of his unexpected and lightning-like changes. He was drifting aimlessly about with no plans. The old rumors of a man murdered, perhaps more than one, on this trip followed him back from the cañons across the Plains and would not down. And pinned to his next letter, in the handwriting of W. W. Scott, is the following note:

The incident mentioned in this letter, furnished Quantrill with the foundation for the yarn he gave the Confederate side as his excuse for betraying his three comrades Morrison, Lipsey and [Ball] to their death, and his flopping from a Union man to a rebel. He told the Southern side that he was on his way thro Kans to Pike's Peak with his brother and team; and that the Kans Jayhawkers surprised them, murdered his brother, shot him thro the leg, and took the team and outfit.

When he would deceive a community as to his motives, when bloody-handed and guilty, thrice guilty, of murder, he stood in the presence of strangers who could not comprehend his traitorous action, he turned to his adventures on the Plains, and from them evolved a lie as black as midnight which he hoped would save his guilty neck and slander a people, a State.

Lawrence July 30th/59.
My Dear Mother.
It has been some time since I wrote to you, and I am now a long ways distant from the place I last wrote to you. I have seen some pretty hard & scaly times, both from cold weather & starvation & the Indians & I am one of 7 out of a party of 19 who started from Salt Lake city for the Gold Mines of Pikes Peak, which are talked of all over the country & undoubtedly *the* Humbug of all Humbugs; I say so because I spent two months in the Gold region haveing my own experience & that of a number with whom I was acquainted to prove it conclusively.

---

[17] The original letter is in the Collection of the author. It is fairly well written, though not so full as we could wish. He could have made the work of the historian so much more satisfactory by lifting the veil just a little more.

there is more or less gold scattered over a country about 40 [miles] in width runing from the mountains east & about 200 [miles] long running with the mountains but not in quantities paying of 1.00 per day in the best diggings. I dug out $54.34 & worked 47 days which money hardly paid my board and expenses.

I am now in Lawrence after having spent over $300 & many a day & night when I expected either to be killed or freeze to death & at last when nearly in the settlements to have my horse and all taken from me & a companion of mine shot in 3 different places & left for dead & all that saved my head was I was out hunting away from the camp about a mile and a half & hearing the firing hurried to camp in time to see the indians driving off our horses & my friend lying on the ground apparently dead but still breathing with difficulty having been shot 3 times, his leg broke below the knee shot in the thigh with 7 iron slugs & last shot through the body with an arrow which I first thought would kill him but he lives yet & if taken care of properly will be as well as ever in 6 or 8 weeks. I hardly know what to do at present nor where to go but in my next letter I will be able to tell you some more I think my friend & myself will make government pay us for our losses by the Indians if possible when he gets well You would hardly know me if you were to see me I am so weather beaten & rough looking that every body says I am about 25 years of age I expect every body thinks & talks hard about [me] but I cannot help it now it will be all straight before another winter passes. I must bring my letter to a close by saying that I am well, & my love to all.

Your Son
W. C. Quantrill

Direct to Osawatomie
        Lykins Co
            K. T.

Nothing has developed to indicate who was his companion. Taking his own statement, twelve of his compaions died from some cause, and the odor of murder came in from the Rocky Mountains with him. He felt that his mother knew the estimation in which he was held and the hard talk afloat about him and said he could not help it then. Whether he killed a man or men in the Pike's Peak gold regions may never be known. In his later letters he described some of his adventures in mining for gold. That is all that can be positively charged to him now

— all that can be known at this time of that most mysterious life in those dim days in the snowy gulches and on the hazy plains sweeping up to the foot of the Rocky Mountains.

Quantrill returned to the vicinity of his first haunts in Kansas. He requested that his mail be directed to Osawatomie. When he went there is not known. What he did there, if any thing, before the following winter, there is nothing to tell. He may have joined in raids into Missouri to free slaves and carry out loot and plunder, and he probably did that. About this time he began to play detective both for his own interests and for hire. At Osawatomie it is said that he raided Kansas as well as Missouri, robbing wherever the opportunity offered, living a sort of double life, a border-ruffian in Missouri and a Jayhawker in Kansas. There he made the acquaintance of Jennison and the Snyders and other radical anti-slavery men. Some of these were ranging up and down the Marias des Cygnes, occasionally preying on the pro-slavery settlers and sometimes shooting or hanging them, and it must be said that some of them needed shooting or hanging very much, while others of them were splendid men, good settlers earnestly striving to build homes for themselves and families; these were rarely molested. They remained in Kansas; some of them went into the Union army; many of them came to take an active interest in building the State when the war was over and are to-day among its foremost citizens.

More than two years before he had arrived in Kansas with opportunities equal to any other young man in the rising new territory. But he accomplished nothing. If he brought in a good name with him he had forfeited it. He was branded as a thief and robber, and the rumors of murder committed by him would not be silenced. He was a vagrant. He had no occupation, no visible means of support. He would not apply himself, was given to sudden and unexpected changes, mysterious appearances and disappearances. He was sliding rapidly down the scale of morality to the inevitable consequences of his course — total depravity.[18]

[The author attended the reunion of the guerrillas who served under Quantrill held at Independence, Mo., August

---

[18] The character of helpers, teamsters, herders, roustabouts, and hang-

20-21, 1909. There he formed the acquaintance of J. B. Forbis, a young man who lives in the town. Mr. Forbis said there was a man living in Independence named Chiles who was an army contractor at Fort Leavenworth in 1858. Mr. Chiles had to deliver eighteen hundred cattle at Fort Laramie that spring. While hiring herders three men were turned over to him by some one. They wanted work, and he hired

---

ers-on who went out to Utah in the summer of 1858 may be found fully described in *Five Years a Dragoon*, by P. G. Lowe, beginning at page 302:

The conditions of Colonel Johnston's army were such that the Government saw the necessity of moving other commands to the front as promptly as possible. Great numbers of horses and mules were purchased at Fort Leavenworth, many of the latter unbroken, and the task of organizing and breaking in trains fit to transport supplies for troops in the field was no small matter.

At Two Mile Creek, below the fort, were located extensive corrals and a "catching-out" crew under experienced "mule tamers", and here all mules were first hitched to wagons and sent to camp some place within a few miles of the post.

Mr. Levi Wilson, general superintendent of transportation at Fort Leavenworth, was the most efficient man I ever saw in the Government transportation line, but his services were required inspecting horses and mules from the middle of March to the last of May, 1858.

I was notified to wind up the feeding business, and bring over mules from Platte the first of April, which I did. Three trains had been organized and camped in Salt Creek Valley. The news that many men would be needed brought them from every direction; some, enterprising young men from the country, ambitious to better their condition or work their way to the Pacific Coast; but there seemed an over-supply of the off-scourings of the slums — men leaving their country for their country's good. The variety and makeup of these fellows, many of them fleeing from justice, the arms they carried and their outfits generally, were curious enough.

I was instructed to take charge of the trains. Many complaints had come to Mr. Wilson against a train in the Valley, and he requested me to see to it and do whatever seemed best. I rode out and found a drunken mob — mules scattered, harness in the mud, etc. The wagonmaster was asleep. A mouthy fellow called him "Captain," and he finally crawled out. In a few minutes I saw the utter uslessness of wasting time. He had come with a railroad gang from North Missouri, the most blear-eyed, God-forsaken looking set I ever saw. I told him that he and his men were wanted at the quartermaster's office; that they should take all their be-were numerous, but I quietly cut them off, and in half an hour they were strung out, poor wretches, with the "Captain" in the lead. I promised to meet them at the quartermaster's office, and then rode down the creek a mile to another train, and asked the wagonmaster to give me his assistant, a fine young fellow (Green Dorsey), and loan me half of his men. With them I returned to the drunken train, told Dorsey to take charge as wagonmaster, hire any man that came who suited him, and I would send him more, but not to hire any of the old gang, and galloped to the post in time to see them paid off. It was remarked at the office that such an outfit had never before been seen there. I called the "Captain" and his

them. One of these was Quantrill. He wore a flaming red woolen shirt, from which circumstance he was named "Red Shirt" by his companion herders, and he went by that name while in the service of Mr. Chiles. As Mr. Chiles was absent from home to be gone some weeks it was impossible to get further facts relating to the matter. Mr. Forbis could not recall the names of the two men hired with Quantrill.]

longings with them, because they would not return to this train. Inquiries men aside and advised them to seek employment elsewhere; that they had mistaken their calling, and were unfit for the plains, and assured them that not one would ever find employment here. The rain and scarcity of whiskey had sobered them some, and they started for the Rialto Ferry and Weston.

This incident spread among the trains and camps on the reservation, and I told every wagonmaster not to hire bad men — we did not want to be bothered with them; and it was soon understood that thieves, thugs and worthless characters generally might as well move on. Many of these found employment in ox trains belonging to Government contractors, and were the cause of strikes, mutinies and loss to their employers. Of course, there was no civil law applicable to the management of men on the plains. In a military command the officer in charge was all-powerful, as he must be everywhere within his jurisdiction. Necessity knows no law, and while all well disposed men would perform their duties without friction, the lawless element, sure to crop out from time to time, stood so much in awe of the military power that they did little harm to their fellows or the Government. Where there was no military command the same restraint did not exist, and discontented spirits, schemers and rebellion breeders often caused trouble. . . . I recall many instances of mutiny — teamsters in rebellion against their wagonmasters, in some cases possibly with a grievance, and in others through homesickness or the spirit of rebellion that recognizes no authority, always ready to make trouble, delighting in the opportunity to become leaders for more pay, or to show their power when their services were most needed. . . . By the first of June more than six hundred six-mule teams, one-half of the mules never before handled, were organized into trains of about twenty-six wagons each, and about five hundred and fifty of them sent out with columns of troops en route to Utah. The whole months of April and May were exceedingly wet, no bridges in the country, and to move the first one hundred and fifty miles west from Fort Leavenworth was something terrible.

CHAPTER V

QUANTRILL AS A KANSAS TEACHER

QUANTRILL taught one term of school in Kansas — no more, no less. Vague and indefinite stories about Quantrill as a Kansas teacher have been abroad for more than forty years.[1] Many of them are ridiculous.

Some time after Quantrill returned to Stanton (he did not live at Osawatomie, but boarded at the house of Bennings) he decided to teach a school the following winter — the winter of 1859-1860. The neighbors had put up a rude log school-house in the Judge Roberts district. This school-house stood on the northwest corner of the southwest quarter of Section 33, Township 17, Range 22, and almost half a mile from the Judge Roberts dwelling, which is yet standing in a good state of preservation. The school-house was torn down long ago. It was heated by fires in an old fashioned fireplace. The furniture was primitive in the extreme, the seats being made by splitting

---

[1] *Andreas's History of Kansas*, p. 877, says:

In the winter of 1857-58, he taught school in Judge Roberts's district in Stanton township, and in the following spring went to Salt Lake City.

On the same page Andreas has a letter written by Quantrill in his school-house, describing his school, and dated at Stanton, Kansas Territory, February 8, 1860. Andreas was usually accurate, and it is difficult to understand his carelessness in this instance.

In a paper filed in the library of the Kansas State Historical Society, Mrs. Sarah T. D. Robinson says:

He taught two or three terms in the Stanton district and gave satisfaction to the patrons of the school. In the year 1858 he joined the John Brown band operating along the Kansas border living off their robberies in Missouri.

He taught but one term, of six months. In 1858 he was in Utah and not with the John Brown band. Quantrill took no part in Kansas affairs until after John Brown had left the State, and very little until after John Brown was dead. But malice outruns truth, and in this case it refutes itself and becomes ridiculous.

small logs and putting pegs in the round side of the slabs, and
they were so high that, being without backs, it was very tire-
some and uncomfortable to sit on them, especially for the children whose feet did not reach the floor. It was a subscription
school — a private school. The term was six months, divided
into two sections of three months each for the purpose of com-
puting the tuition, which was $2.50 per scholar for three months.
It was the agreement that Quantrill was to "board around,"
remaining with each family or patron two weeks. But he remained with some longer than with others, being two months at
the house of Judge Roberts.[2]

---

[2] In a letter now in the Collection of the author, from Judge Thomas
Roberts to H. V. Beeson, dated at Paola, May 16, 1881, Roberts says:

In answer to your Enquiries of my acquaintance with Wm C. Quantrell In reply would state that I became personally acquainted with him
in the fall of 1858. He taught the School in my neighborhood the winter
of 58 & 59 and boarded at my house about two months of that time, in
the spring of 59 he left that neighborhood. afterwards I saw him in the
early summer of 1861 he was confined in the County Jail of Miami
county.

The judge's memory was at fault as to the winter in which the
school was taught. He could not have become acquainted with Quantrill
in the fall of 1858, for Quantrill's own letters show that he was at that
time in Utah or on his way there, and that he was in Utah all of the
winter of 1858-59, the time Judge Roberts says he was teaching school in
his district. The judge puts the winter just a year too early, for Quantrill taught in his district in the winter of 1859-1860, as he himself says
and as his letters conclusively prove.

On the 19th day of October, 1907, the author, in company with his
friend of long standing, Major J. B. Remington, of Osawatomie, and Mrs.
Remington, visited the people living in the vicinity of where Quantrill
taught the school. Many people live there who as children attended that
school, or as parents, patronized it. They all said he was a good teacher,
and that he had no trouble whatever in his school. Among those who at-
tended were Thomas F. Roberts and his wife, Roxey Troxel Roberts,
George Hill Troxel, Harrison Troxel, George Shearer, H. Shearer, Delama
Shearer, Belle Roberts, Eliza Roberts, Flora Roberts, Mark Updegraff,
Augustus Updegraff, David Updegraff, Drusilla Updegraff, Mary Updegraff,
Martha Updegraff, Elzena Williams, Amanda Williams, Jefferson Williams,
Polk Williams, Roger Williams, Wesley Baker, Hester Baker, Adolphus Y.
Bennings, and James Bennings.

William Stockwell did not attend the school, but he lived near it
and had helped to build the school-house; he attended "spelling-school"
Friday nights. Mr. Stockwell came from Michigan to Osawatomie, and

The first letter written by Quantrill after beginning his school, which has been preserved, was to his mother.[3] In it he

took the claim on which he now lives on the 13th of March, 1857. He said that Quantrill talked for the Free-State side but took no part in affairs while teaching; that he was very quiet; told of having been across the plains; dressed neatly, and seemed very particular and careful as to his dress; had peculiar eyes which were blue, though at times they were a strange undefinable color, and the upper lids had a queer look; complexion light; hair light but not red — not even a sandy color; no beard; no mustache; said Quantrill always stayed at the Bennings home Saturdays and Sundays.

Mrs. Roxey Troxel Roberts is the daughter of the late Frederick Troxel, a Kentuckian who moved to Illinois, then to Iowa, then to Kansas, arriving in Osawatomie in 1855; owned a part of the land now owned by Major Remington, on which he lived when Quantrill taught the school; Quantrill boarded with him two weeks. She says Quantrill was a good teacher; had large light-blue eyes, a Roman nose, light complexion, light hair. She spoke of his peculiar eyes, saying they were like no other eyes she ever say — upper lids heavy. Says school began in the fall, rather late, and continued until the next spring; school-house heated by fireplace in which was kept a roaring fire; slabs for benches; Quantrill talked for the Free-State side, but so far as she ever heard he took no part in affairs; dressed neatly; stayed at Bennings's Saturdays and Sundays; a very quiet man, secretive and peculiar; "no one knew how to take him."

The author talked with many others, and they all told practically the same story, agreeing with those given above. It was the opinion of all that Quantrill could not have been engaged while teaching in any of the raids into Missouri, for he was making his home with Bennings, a pro-slavery man and friend to the Missourians. They could not say as to the charge that he was acting as a "detective" for the Missourians and spying on the Kansas settlers during that period.

In the letter written to W. W. Scott by H. V. Beeson, dated Paola, Kansas, June 5, 1880, Beeson says:

He hung around Stanton some time [after he had been driven out of the camp at Tuscarora Lake by the Canal Dover young men for stealing] and then disappeared for some time and when he came Back he taught school in the neighborhood of Judge Roberts winter 1859, our Probate Judge, he stated to his Friends that he had been out west to Utah under Col or Gen Johnston (who was afterwards, if I am not mistaken, killed at Pittsburg Landing on the Rebel side) he also stated to me that he was Employed in the Quartermasters department, in Utah.

It will be seen that Mr. Beeson has the correct date of Quantrill's school-teaching. Also, that Quantrill lied to him about having been employed in the department of the quartermaster; he was not so employed.

3 Letter of W. C. Quantrill to his mother, now in the Collection of the author. It is quite well written.

says that he had written a letter a short time before, sufficient time not having elapsed for an answer to arrive:

Stanton, Kansas Terri.
Jan. 26th 1860.

My Dear Mother.

I again seat myself down to pen you a few lines, hoping that they may cheer you in a measure, and if so it is all I can do at this time.

I have not yet received an answer to the one I wrote you before this, for the reason that it has not had time to reach here; but I expect to have one by the time you receive this.

In my last letter I said we had quite fine weather here; but I can now look out of the window at my school-house and see every thing clad in snow & ice, which was put on but last night, and now seems to hold every thing in its cold embrace; indeed so sudden has been the change, that it seems not only to have caught the forest & prairie napping in the sunshine but the people also, for I feel it myself and seem to shudder when I look out upon the snowcovered ground, & hear the cold wind whistle around & through the forest; and it brings to my recollection scenes which I passed through in the mountains but a short time ago; it makes me think of what one of the party said; (a German,) when we were lost at night in the mountains, and he had looked in vain for the trail, he said, "well boys my heart is almost broke when I think that we may all die here tonight." We laughed at him then, (for we may as well laugh as cry at that time for neither done any good,) but when I have thought of it afterwards & could see what danger we had been exposed to, I feel thankful for having got off as well as I did. But I have slipped through it all comparatively easy and I now begin to realize my situation, and see how much easier I have been dealt with than most of my traveling companions were, and I often think that there must have been something else for me to do, that I was spared; for my companions were all strong healthy men & endured no more hardship than myself, still the greater part of them have seen their friends for the last time on this earth; all of this has had a tendency to rouse me & let me see what I have been doing.

It is now noon and I again write, for I had to stop when it was time for school to begin. The weather has changed some little since, and ever and anon the sun bursts through the clouds, melting the snow on the roof, and causes the ice clad forest to sparkle & shine like silver, and the storm is gradually passing away, and it seems it has been only a frown which has passed over the heavens, which are now being lit up with glad smiles, and soon all will be pleasant again. And when I look out upon the snow it reminds me again of my mountain trip; and the excruciating pain we suffered from snowblindness, caused by looking all day on the bright snow; none of us were exempt from this, the sensation is that of having your eyes badly smoked, which lasted for several days, the eyes become inflamed & swollen causing very much pain.

There is no news now I believe at present, all is peace and quietness in the country, and all seems to move on smoothly, but times are hard, and the people complain of the taxes which they have to pay, and indeed they are enormous for such a new country, and under the present form of government are not apt to cease.

You have undoubtedly heard of the wrongs committed in this territory by the southern people, or proslavery party, but when one once knows the facts they can easily see that it has been the opposite party that have been the main movers in the troubles & by far the most lawless set of people in the country. They all sympathize for old J. Brown, who should have been hung years ago, indeed hanging was too good for him. May I never see a more contemptible people than those who sympathize for him. A murderer and a robber, made a martyr of; just think of it.

When you write let me know all that you have time to write about, for I feel anxious to know something about home and the village of my boyhood more than I have been heretofore and I cannot really say why it is so, but I think of it more, and have lately visited it in my dreams, which was quite rare before; it may be because my mind has become more settled, and my mind must be employed in some way, and I suppose that is the most natural. I wish to know all that has happened of note lately, and I would like well to be there and I think I will be, (if I live) in the course of the summer. At least I have made up my mind to that point I suppose all the people about there think I am never coming back again, and that also that I have done wrong in going away at all; this I will acknowledge, but who could have made me believe it at that time, I think no one, for my brain ran so with wild thoughts that I was blind to every thing else. I think that I am not the only one, of that failing; only it has, probably been carried to a greater extent in my case than others, and my situation has been different from theirs.

Though I have been quite foolish in my notions of the last three or four years, still I have been taught many a good lesson by them, and think I shall not regret it in after life so much as I do now, for it is now that I feel it the keenest, and can see

the whole picture of my doings in one broad sheet, which may
be rolled up and laid by to look upon in after life. I have seen
a little of the world I know how others manage to keep moving
in the vast crowd which is moving ahead; I have seen the means
used by different communities to keep body and soul together,
I have compared them with each other and find in the end they
all amount to the same, with only this difference, that their situations are different, and the ends accomplished are adapted to
their situations. this (is all) a good comfortable living, which
any person of good health & mind can procure in any country
for theirself and two or three others & still have plenty of time
for amusement; and this is all we can have in this world.

Well I must bid you good by; for my sheet is about full,
and when I receive an answer to my first one I will write again,
Hoping that this may find you and all in fine health as the
writer is. My love to you all - - - - - -

Your Son

W. C. Quantrill,

Kansas.

Here is the first evidence that Quantrill was changing political faith. In his letter written two years before from Tuscarora
Lake he said every Missourian should have been shot and that
all Democrats were rascals. His association with the rough
characters following in the wake of the army across the Plains,
most of them from Missouri, had wrought the change. The influence he was under at the home of Bennings was bearing fruit.
Those now living, who knew him while teaching, say he talked
in favor of the Free-State people. But he was at that very
time, as this letter conclusively proves, secretly against them
and had gone over to their enemies. He was, among them, a
wolf in sheep's clothing, a hypocrite, a spy, a traitor. This letter is the explanation of the actions of all his subsequent life.
He lived nearly a year longer in Kansas, but he had made up his
mind to cast his lot with the enemies of Kansas. There may
have been times in his life of crime the remainder of
his days in Kansas when he had thoughts of remaining, but they
were fleeting if he had them. He had deliberately made up his
mind to go over to the Missourians, and the time he remained in
Kansas was spent in seeking an opportunity to do Kansas as
much injury as possible in making the change. For a year he

lived a border-ruffian in Kansas, false to every associate, to every principle he professed. And it is well to remember that he had no cause from any settler of Kansas to make this change. The settlers had been lenient with him and borne with him in his crimes, not even arresting him for any of them. Only a man who has reached the depths of moral degradation is capable of such action — capable of such a life.

And the friends of John Brown should be glad that this letter has been preserved. No man has been so persistently slandered and traduced as has John Brown in recent years by those jealous of the place he made for himself in history, especially in Kansas history. Petty and insignificant souls, dollar-bent, saw a great commonwealth rise here upon the broadest possible foundation of liberty, to which they contributed little. It grew in spite of the frenzied finance they practiced in the administration of its revenues. Some of the loot so obtained has been used to hire unprincipled characters to write coarse and vulgar slanders of John Brown. Other sources having been exhausted without effect, they have recently asserted that Quantrill and John Brown operated together in Kansas. True, there was never a syllable of authority for such assertion, but slander is never based on any authority.

This is a good place to state the facts in this matter. Quantrill came to Kansas in the spring of 1857. Then the most important events of the Territorial troubles were passed. The Wakarusa War, the sacking of Lawrence, the battle of Black Jack, the battle of Osawatomie, the killing of Dutch Bill and his dupes on the Pottawatomie — all these had occurred before Quantrill came to Kansas. From the time of his coming in 1857 to the time he was driven from the camp at Tuscarora Lake certainly the most bitter enemy of John Brown would not say that they had acted together. In the spring of 1858 Quantrill went to Utah and did not return until the last of July, 1859. John Brown had been gone from Kansas six months when Quantrill came back to Kansas. Brown was in Virginia, and he never returned to Kansas. And his men were with him. The only time John Brown and Quantrill were in Kansas at the same time was in November, 1857, and then for less than a month.

Brown was at Lawrence and Topeka. He had come to take his men out to have them drilled for the Virginia campaign. It is safe to say that Quantrill never saw John Brown — never saw any of John Brown's men, and that neither Brown nor a single one of his men ever saw Quantrill. Because of the action of Forbes, John Brown had to postpone his Virginia campaign a year, and he returned to Kansas, arriving at Lawrence on the 25th of June, 1858. Reference to P. G. Lowe's excellent work, *Five Years a Dragoon,* will show that all the trains had left Fort Leavenworth for Utah long before the arrival of John Brown in Kansas in 1858, and as Quantrill went out with one of these trains, it is impossible that he saw Brown at that time. The few days that John Brown and Quantrill were even in Kansas Territory at the same time was in November, 1857, and Quantrill was then a petty thief stealing provisions from his comrades at Tuscarora Lake.

Quantrill's best letters were written while teaching this term of school in Kansas. On the 8th of February he wrote a long letter to his mother.⁴ He was in a pensive mood at the time. Perhaps if he could have reformed without effort — by some miracle in the execution of which he had no part, he would have welcomed the change. Man is cursed with such repentance as that. He sees the gleaming mountain-tops of a better land and longs to enter an ideal life there, but the call back to life as it is and has been breaks the spell. Strength to rouse from the lethargy of the old life and turn about and flee from it as from very death to the hills from whence cometh help is wanting. The better self is called back and stifled. The old burden is taken up to be borne by stumbling feet over sinks and quagmires while anxious eyes behold the star of hope fall below the rugged line of the dark mountain to be replaced by *ignis-fatui* kindled of vanities and temptations by the devil:

----

4 The original of this letter is lost. It is published in *Andreas's History of Kansas,* as a part of the history of Miami county. There is a copy of the letter in the Collection of the author, also the correspondence between Andreas and W. W. Scott leading up to its publication. As published, it would seem that there were omissions made by the printer, but the copy made by Scott corresponds with the letter as published.

Stanton, Kansas Territory,
Feb. 8, 1860

My Dear Mother.

It is a pleasant morning, this; the sun is just rising, its light causing the trees, bushes and grass to glitter like brilliants, while the hanging sheets of frost drop from them, announcing his warmth, then silently melting away. I stood in my schoolhouse door, and viewing this it made me feel a new life, and merry as the birds. But these feelings and thoughts are soon changed and forgotten, by the arrival of eight or ten of my scholars, who come laughing and tripping along as though their lives would always be like this beautiful morning, calm and serene. And I wish that I could always be as these children. But I have been so no doubt, and I have no reason to expect it a second time. Every year brings its changes and no two are alike.

School is now closed for the day, and I am again left alone with my thoughts. I am thinking of home and all the happy days I spent there; and then of the unhappy days I have spent since and those you have spent. In a few days it will be three years, though it only seems like a few months. The sun is shedding its last rays, and the chill air of evening still declares that summer has not yet arrived. Every now and then a blast from the north holds all nature in check, in spite of the warming influences of the sun to revive it.

How different now to me it is from one year ago, when I was amidst the snow covered mountains of Utah. It seemed that a summer of sunshine would not be sufficient to break the icy fetters of winter. We should have died of *ennui* in the Mormon society if it had not been for the excitement attendant upon a camp of soldiers.

You perceive, I suppose, that I am writing at different times between my school hours, which causes my letter to be somewhat broken.

It is now noon, and the sun shines warm, with a pleasant south wind; and my scholars are enjoying themselves as scholars did when I was one. And they, like all children, are enjoying more happiness now than they will at any other period of their lives. I sometimes wish that I was again a scholar in the old brick schoolhouse at Dover; and again with my companions on the playground. But scholars and companions are all far from me now, and I am left alone to contemplate. It all seems to me but a dream, a very little of which I ever realized; or, more like a sheet of paper on the first page of which there are a few signs, showing that something has been commenced, and then all the rest left blank, telling you not what was the purpose of the writer, and leaving you to surmise; though if it had been continued it might have been of benefit to some one. Thus my mind is ever recalling the past, and my conscience tells me that if something noble is not done in the future to fill up this blank, then it had better be destroyed, so that none may take it for an example.

But as this is leap year, I think it advisable for those who intend to turn over a new leaf, to take their leap with the year, and then keep moving with it, and then probably they may have something more than a blank. I think I can insure it if there is a firm resolution.

I can now see more clearly than ever in my life before, that I have been striving and working really without any end in view. And now since I am satisfied that such a course must end in nothing, it must be changed, and that soon, or it will be too late. All the benefit that I can see I have derived from my past course, is that I have improved my health materially, which was none of the best when I came here. I have also learned to do almost any kind of outdoor work, which experience will serve in future to preserve my health, and also enable me to get along much better than if I was only fitted for the schoolroom or other indoor business.

When my school is finished, I will be able to tell you better what my plans are for the coming year. One thing is certain: I am done roving around seeking a fortune, for I have found where it may be obtained by being steady and industrious. And now that I have sown wild oats so long, I think it is time to begin harvesting; which will only be accomplished by putting in a different crop in different soil.

There is no news here but hard times, and harder still coming, for I see their shadows; and "coming events cast their shadows before," is an old proverb. But I do not fear that my destiny is fixed in this country, nor do I wish to be compelled to stay in it any longer than possible, for the devil has got unlimited sway over this territory, and will hold it until we have a better set of men and society generally. The only cry is, "What is best for ourselves and our dear friends."

I suppose Dover has changed a great deal since I was there, but not more than I have, and probably not as much; for I think there are few there who would know me if I were to come unexpectedly. I suppose the boys have grown to be almost men, and likely I should hardly recognize them if I were to see them any place but at home. Well, surely I have changed around a great deal in the last three years, and have seen a great many people and countries, and enough incidents to make a novel of adventures.

When I get a letter from you, and some of the others, I will write again, but now I must close, by hoping that this bit of scribbling may find you in as good health as the one who is writing. My love to you all, and respects to those who inquire of me.   Your Son,

                                        W. C. Quantrill.

To Mrs. Caroline Quantrill,
        Dover, Tuscarawas County Ohio.

These sentiments appear all through the letters written by Quantrill while teaching in Kansas. The journey across the Plains comes up before him. There is no doubt but that he stood in the very presence of death in those stormy days. Perhaps memories came to him which he bid depart — memories in the presence of which he stood aghast, memories which would fade away only when overwhelmed and crushed by some act far exceeding in ferocity and wickedness that from which they sprang. What a flood engulfs him with bloody hands and a mind demoralized! A man may ride such a tide as it roars through gorges over sunken rocks, but he is flung at last into that black lake where he shall cry out for death and it will mock him and flee far away.

The next letter of Quantrill was written to his sister Mary. She was visiting her grandfather Quantrill in Washington City.[5] By all accounts she was a sweet good girl upon whose life there dawned no hope of higher things in this world than she found within the walls of the poor cottage of her mother. She did the lowly duties of the life of a sewing-girl to get bread for those she loved. She wasted with consumption, but no complaint rose to her lips. She sang ''The Song of the Shirt'' nightly, but no bitterness entered her heart. How unworthy are the best of men of the love of a good woman! How shall we express the base ingratitude, the utter unworthiness of Quantrill of the lovely life of his sister Mary, whose name he blackened by his inhuman crimes!

                        Stanton, Kansas T. Mar 23, 1860.

My dear Sister.

        I received your kind letter on the 17th, with much pleasure

---

[5] The original of this letter is lost. W. W. Scott made a copy of it and this copy is in the Collection of the author.

& not a little surprise. I am glad to hear that you are well and in such good spirits, for then I know you are happy. You say you like to live in the city [Washington, where she was on a visit], and that you have enjoyed yourself very much since you have been there. Then you have surpassed me, for I have not enjoyed myself much or felt very happy since I left home; for happiness depends on contentment, and that has not fell to my lot, and it seems to me never will.

I would like very much to see you and the rest of the family, and I will (if I keep my health and have no bad luck) sometime this summer. The weather is very fine here, and has been for the last month, causing the flowers to spring up and the grass to carpet the prairie in green; also causing the forest to be set with green sheets, soon to form a screen for the merry songsters and shelter them from the noonday sun of midsummer. The pleasant whistle of the Bob White and red bird, have caused the plowboy to join in with them while he turns over the warm soil, for the reception of the golden seed. What a contrast! One year ago I was amid snow and desolation in the Rocky Mountains, where nothing was to be seen but snow & sky; no signs of life except in our little company. Some of us strove to be merry, & occasionally would start some song, which would be broken off by some one calling for help to get some poor animal out of the snow. Or by the time one verse would be sung then his merriment would be ended. But when night came and we were about to lie down to rest, and nothing but the snow to make a bed upon, it was enough to make any one have cool thoughts.

You people of the crowded city can form no idea of what men go through & how they have to struggle to keep from the grasp of grim death, which apparently stares them in the face as they move along.

I will give you a little sketch of myself as I appeared in camp, and the way we passed our time. My dress consisted of a complete suit of buckskin; pants, coat, moccasins, a red woollen shirt, a fur cap, a large leather belt in which is a large pistol and knife; and then mounted on an Indian pony, with my rifle laying across the saddle, ready for use in a moment's warning. We look rough enough, for we do not shave or cut our hair, and to a person not used to such sights, we look like ruffians. When we camped, & the horses and mules were turned out to graze, and one or two of the company to watch them while the rest attended to camp, make a fire, bring water and cook our camp meal, which is composed of biscuit or cakes, coffee, and venison or buffalo steak; and sometimes by way of a treat, some bacon, and beans, usually on Sunday; and occasionally a grouse or rabbit or duck, & then to finish with, a relish for this never felt by those of the city or town.   After supper the animals were brought to camp and picketed close by; we spread our blankets on the ground and with the heavens for a canopy & the howling of the wolves we are lulled to sleep with more satisfaction than I ever felt any place else.   Some watch while the others sleep, & by sunrise the next morning we are again on the road.

You think this is quite an unpleasant way to spend time, but we can see some pleasure, but persons not acquainted with such times cannot realize that there can be any satisfaction at all. There are hundreds of persons going to the gold regions this spring again; but I shall not go for I want to come home and see the folks once more any how.   I suppose you will be at home when I get there, and then we will all be together again, if we live.   Tell Thomas Leckron that I would like to see him, and maybe he would like to come and see some of the West after seeing so much of the East.   If I knew his directions I would write to him and also to Grandfather.

You will perceive this letter has not all been written on the same day, for I write before and after school occasionally, and therefore it will appear somewhat broken.   You say you are glad that I am not married; but I might take a notion to bring some pretty Kansas girl along home when I come, and let you see that there are a few pretty ones here as well as there.   I have a couple of interesting ladies coming to school now.   I have seen a great many pretty girls since I have been away from home, and have had considerable sport sometimes; but as to marrying any of them, I have not had any serious thoughts yet.

I suppose a good many girls of Dover have been married since I left, and all of the small ones have grown up to be young ladies.   I expect Dover and the people have changed a great deal since I was there, but not more than I have.

I wonder if the weather is as fine with you as it is here, for it is most delightful here.   The prairie looks as green and fresh, and then so many flowers peeping up as though half afraid Jack Frost was somewhere near.   And then the songs of so many merry little birds make one wish he were as happy as all around him; but that cannot be; as this earth is not a heaven for man; for we at the happiest day feel a burden of sorrow which we cannot throw off here.   I will put a couple of flowers in this letter that you may see some of the beauties of Kansas.   And now

I must close my letter, hoping that it may find you and all in as good health as myself.   Give my love to all, and a kiss for yourself

Your Brother.
W. C. Quantrill

Direct your answer
to Lawrence
         K T.

When Quantrill wrote the next letter to his mother he stood on the threshold of a new era in his life.   This period was to be brief — to continue less than a year.   He declared that he had determined to rove no more, but it is not certain that he did not return immediately to the Pike's Peak gold region, nor is it known positively that he did so.[6]

---

6 There is some evidence that Quantrill crossed the Plains twice.   If so, he set out on his second trip immediately after his school closed.   For he certainly did not return to Kansas before going into the gold region after his trip to Utah, but went with a party from Utah to the Pike's Peak region, and from there he returned to Kansas in the summer of 1859.

The following postal card, written by James Hanway to W. W. Scott, would seem to be conclusive evidence that Quantrill crossed the Plains twice:

Lane, Franklin Co. Kansas — April 13, 1879

Dear Sir —
Yesterday I came across a man of the name of Adolphus Y. Bennings, Lane P office, who crossed the Plains twice with Quantrill — & he tells me that Q — boarded at his fathers house, near Stanton, Miami Co — after Q —had left Beesons & Torrey — and he was with Quantrill after the Walker affair and was arrested & placed in the Paola Jail — He evidently could give you some incidents about Q — life in Kansas.   But there may be some difficulty in opening up a correspondence with him — He is a poor scribe, & has evidently been a pro-slavery man, at the time of the troubles. He says he will propound any questions you may ask — better send him a letter — He has moved from Stanton & now lives a few miles from Lane —
James Hanway.

This card is in the Collection of the author.   It is addressed to "Mr. W. W. Scott

"Canal Dover
"Ohio"

The postmark is as follows: "Lane, Franklin County, Kansas.   D. L. Welsh, P. M."

There is a letter in the Collection of the author, from Colonel Sam Walker, of Lawrence, saying that if Quantrill went out with the Parsons party, which left Lawrence May 21, 1858, he had not known it until he received Scott's letter.   An account of the trip made by that party is given by William B. Parsons, a member of it, in *The Kansas Magazine,*

During the time he was teaching, if there is any reliance to be placed in what he wrote to his mother, he had seen a kindly hand beckon him to a new life and felt inclined to follow in the hope that he might find there a remedy for his unhappiness. But, in the light of his later course and actions, what he wrote to his mother must be taken with great allowance; for, in Kansas he lived one life and wrote his mother of one he did not live. By his letters she was to see that he was a poor, meek boy struggling to get board and clothing. That was to avoid sending her any assistance, if his after life is to be considered. He was in fact a thief from the first in Kansas, and long before he wrote these poetic letters to his mother and sister he was a wild and reckless gambler. The letters bear an air of insincerity and dissimulation. He wrote "against time," filling his letters with sentiments about spring and flowers — abstract flights of fancy and stories of discontent and unhappiness, never asking how his mother was managing to live and support his brothers and sisters, never sending her aid, but always talking of the ideal climate, the green prairies and forests, the merry songsters, the whistling of the Bob White (in March), and harping about his disquieting state of mind. In his letters he was Dr. Jekyl; in Kansas he was Mr. Hyde.

Quantrill had sown the wind. If any better things had appealed to him he turned away and set his face hard against them. His decision was finally reached, his mind made up. The die was cast, and he told his mother to direct her letters to Lawrence. He would continue to sow the wind.

Stanton. Kansas.
Mar. 25th. 1860

My Dear Mother.

I again seat myself to write you a few words to let you know that I am still among the living and healthy for this coun-

---

Vol. I, p. 552, *et seq.* If Quantrill went out with that party he did not return with it, but fell in with the trains going to Utah and went on to that country. It is very improbable that he went with that party. It is almost a certainty that he went to Fort Leavenworth and started from that point to Utah.

Scott must have believed that the Lawrence party left for Pike's Peak in the spring of 1860 — two years later than it actually did leave.

try; and if these few words find you in the same situation will be all I can wish for at present. I have not received an answer to my last letter yet; although I received one from Mary two weeks ago; and answered it last week. She said she was enjoying good health, and passing her time quite pleasantly.

The weather is quite pleasant here, and has been for a month back. The prairie has a carpet of green, variegated with innumerable flowers, peeping half afraid through the green blades as though they were afraid of Jack Frost, but they show a change from the cold frown of winter to the glad smiles of spring. The forests too show a change, for every branch is set with shoots of tender green, soon to screen the earth's naked breast and afford a shelter from the noonday sun for the merry songsters now congregating there; and hailing the golden sun with their joyous notes, as he shows himself on the distant prairie, and continuing their songs the livelong day, delighting the ears of the woodsman & inspiring new life in the emigrant; for the nights are cool and put somewhat of a damper on their spirits; for you must know these people have to be exposed, and therefore cannot realize the return of spring, as we who are situated comfortably. And then the crowing of the grouse, the whistle of the Bob White, enliven the farmer & he joins with them as he turns over the rich loose soil, from which he is to reap his harvest for the support of his family. Every thing, and every body around me seems to be happy; but I am not because I am not contented & there lies the chief source of happiness on this earth. As I sit in my schoolroom and contemplate these scenes, in their beauty; I cannot but contrast them with the scenes of a twelve month ago, when all around me was desolation, nothing to be seen but snow and sky; and no animated objects but our little company, and they struggling hard to be merry and full of joy; but still little more life remained than in the huge drifts of snow around us; but every thing here appears rife with life, the forests, the prairies the river and lakes, and the air, all teeming with animation or imparting it to surrounding objects causing the husbandman, the mechanic, the merchant, and all mankind, to have fine dreams of the future, and building up their prospects on what they seem to see in the future. I think every thing and every body around me is happy and I alone am miserable, it seems man is doomed to aspire after happiness; but never in reality to obtain it; for God intended that this earth should *be earth* and not *heaven* for mortal man.

How I would like to be in Dover again and once again to see the scenes and to call up recollections of the past, in my happy schoolboy days. And then to visit the old school house, the playing ground; and most of all my own dear home and its occupants, then at least for a short time I would be happy as also those around me. I should hardly know some of the places about there; and people; and I doubt if there is any one there would know me now if I were to arrive there or meet any one of them here, well I will put it to a test this summer; and then I shall know for·myself. Now do not think that I will disappoint you in coming home, for if I keep my health I will be there as soon as possible. But it will not be before the middle of the summer. I would .like to know that ladie's name you have picked out for me for I am afraid some of the ladies here will win my affections unless I have some one else to guard them for me. But do not be alarmed about my getting married soon, unless something turns up favorable beyond expectation. You must excuse this short letter for I have had no answer to my last one and I hardly know what to write about. I must close. My school will be out in a few days; and the next letter you write you may direct it to Lawrence. Give my love to all and a kiss for yourself. Good by

[Your son
W. C. Quantrill.] 7

---

7 This letter is in the Collection of the author. The signature is cut off, which was done by W. W. Scott, as is shown by his writing in copying in the sentences cut away with the signature. He probably sent the signature to some newspaper with an article on Quantrill. The penmanship of the letter is delicate and good.

CHAPTER VI

QUANTRILL must have gone to Lawrence immediately after his school closed. On the 25th of March, 1860, he wrote his mother that his school would close in a few days, directing her to address him at Lawrence. He must have gone early in April. He remained in the vicinity of Lawrence, making that his home, or "headquarters," until the following December.[1]

---

[1] Henry S. Clarke, of Lawrence (died about January 1, 1908), says in an article written for the Kansas Historical Society, published in the Seventh Volume of the Collections of the Society, that he saw Quantrill at Lawrence first in June, 1858. Mr. Clarke was mistaken as to the year. In June, 1858, Quantrill was at Fort Bridger, as the letter of R. M. Peck, Whittier, California, dated December 28, 1907, and in the Collection of the author, says. Mr. Peck saw him there at that time and describes his reckless gambling in the camp at that place. It was evidently in 1859 that Mr. Clarke first saw Quantrill at Lawrence, for he says that Quantrill then told him of having been to Utah "as a teamster with a government expedition against the Mormons; that the weather turned bad and the expedition wintered at Fort Bridger; that when the grass started in the spring he started back East, as he did not like the job."

This is important, as it shows that Quantrill got back to Lawrence from the Utah and Pike's Peak expedition in June, 1859, though he did not write to his mother until July 30, 1859. See his letter, *ante*, page 81. The scene described by Quantrill in that letter, of his partner having been shot, and which Scott says was the foundation for the lying account told by him to the Missourians at Morgan Walker's, was probably wholly untrue. It was suggested, in all probability, by the occurrence described by Mr. Clarke, though it was in 1859 instead of 1858, as Mr. Clarke has it:

My first real acquaintance with him was on the 4th day of July, 1858. The people of Lawrence held a celebration on that day across the Kansas river on the Delaware reserve. John C. Vaughan, then living at Leavenworth, came over and made the address of the day. While the Judge was speaking, there was an outcry a little distance off in the brush, and

When Quantrill returned from Pike's Peak to Lawrence
(in 1859) he went to live with the Delaware Indians, in their
Reservation on the north side of the Kansas river, and which extended up the river to the west of Lawrence. As he had an acquaintance with the Indians as the result of his previous residence among them, he went there to live at the expiration of his
school, and this acquaintanceship may have been the sole cause
of his going to Lawrence to live in the spring of 1860.[2]

Quantrill made his home with John Sarcoxie, son of Sarcoxie, chief of the Delawares. John Sarcoxie lived on Mud
creek, about four miles northeast of Lawrence. Quantrill had no
occupation among the Delawares, and he did not work at any
thing while he lived with them. He told other people that he
was the detective for the Delaware Nation. He spent his time
riding about the country mounted on an Indian pony, often visiting Lawrence. He soon began to frequent the north ferry
landing. The ferry was established by John Baldwin and was
the first ferry at Lawrence. In the spring of 1860 it was still

several of us ran out to see the cause. There we found a white man lying
on the ground in an unconscious condition, with his head badly cut and
hacked up by an Indian tomahawk, apparently. Quantrell was one of the
first to arrive on the spot. He said he knew the Indian who committed
the assault, and went on to say that the man had enticed the Indian's
wife away, and this was done for revenge. Quantrell assisted for an hour
or more in caring for the man, while the doctor was giving restoratives,
dressing the wounds, etc., during which time he told me that he started
for Salt Lake the fall before as a teamster with a government expedition
against the Mormons. . . . He also went on to say that he was living at
that time with Henry Bascom, a Delaware Indian, out about three miles
from Lawrence. Later in the summer I saw him again, and he said he
was living with George Sarcoxie, another Delaware Indian, about five miles
out from Lawrence, on the reserve.

In a letter written by Mr. Clarke to W. W. Scott, dated Lawrence,
Kansas, April 7, 1898, now in the Collection of the author, he says:

I think the first I saw of Quantrell was in 1859. He claimed, at
that time, to have been across the plains with an army supply train, that
accompanied the government expedition against the Mormons just previous
to that time. I think he claimed to have driven a team for the government on that expedition.

[2] S. S. Herd, of Lawrence, knew Quantrill during his residence there.
In a long statement to the author, made November 4, 1907, Mr. Herd says
Quantrill made his appearance at Lawrence about the middle of April or
first of May, 1860, coming from the Indian settlements in the Delaware
Reserve, where he then lived. The statement is in the Collection of the
author.

owned by Baldwin and operated by his nephew John Baldwin
and S. S. Herd, whom he employed for that purpose. Quantrill
would make his appearance at the north landing about nine in
the morning. He would hitch the pony in the brush and then
go down to the landing; and he usually remained there until
near night, when he would remount the pony and return to the
home of Sarcoxie.

The ferry was the loafing-place of a very disreputable gang
of border-ruffians. They were thieves, murderers, kidnappers,
negro-stealers. Most of them lived about Lawrence, and they
were in close communication with the ruffians who lived in Missouri and raided the Free-State settlements of Kansas, which
circumstance did not prevent the Kansas ruffian from invading
and plundering Missouri. Among these lawless characters were
the McGees, who came to Kansas from Pennsylvania. There were
Old Man McGee and his two sons, Jacob and Thomas, called
Jake and Tom. There was a cousin to these, a very hard character, who, because of the marital calamity which befell him very
frequently, was called "Cuckold Tom" McGee. The McGees
had a claim on the Kansas river about two miles east of Lawrence, in the timber, surrounded by almost impenetrable brakes
and thickets; and, in a little clearing they had there, they had
built a cabin in which they lived. Living with them was another
cousin, named Henry McLaughlin, of character equally base and
vicious. A constant associate of these men was Esau Sager, a
border-ruffian, and as tough a character as lived in Kansas Territory. There were Jack Elliott, John Stropp, Jay Vince, and
Frank Baldwin, all of whom would make raids into Missouri to
get slaves or live stock, kidnap a free negro in Kansas, or plunder people of property anywhere.[3] They acted with the pro-

---

[3] G. W. W. Yates, Topeka, Kansas, is the son of the late William
Yates, one of the first settlers of Douglas county, Kansas. William Yates
was the captain of one of the Free-State companies in Territorial times.
In his company were Jake McGee and Tom McGee. So, it seems that the
McGees were playing a double game, aiding both the Free-State and pro-
slavery sides. Their attitude may have suggested that course to Quantrill.
G. W. W. Yates was a boy in Territorial days, and can scarcely believe
that the McGees were so bad. He did not know they had acted with the
border-ruffians. Colonel O. E. Learnard, an early settler at Lawrence, told

slavery party in Kansas and rejoiced in turmoil and anarchy.
The above list is by no means complete; there were many others.
All these were in a slight degree subject to Jacob or "Jake"
Herd. Herd was the terror of the Free-State people, and he
gloried in the name, "Jake Herd, the Border-Ruffian." He
waylaid and captured Dr. John Doy and his party on the
"underground railway" in 1859, and carried them to Platte
City, Mo., and cast them into jail. He was at the head of the
lawless bands inhabiting the regions about Lawrence — tough
citizens, border-ruffians, thieves, highway robbers, kidnappers,
drunken carousers, rioters, brawlers, reckless of human life.[4]

---

the author that there were worse characters in Kansas than the McGees,
and that the McGees had served under him in the service of the Free-State
party.

The author would not knowingly place any one in a wrong light. He
wishes to be perfectly fair, and state facts only. The information here
set out was secured from S. S. Herd, H. S. Clarke, and others, and is
believed to be reliable and accurate.

[4] Herd's father came to Kansas from Pennsylvania about 1855 and
settled with his family about four miles southeast of Lecompton. There
is a biographical sketch of Sidney S. Herd in the Seventh Volume of the
Kansas Historical Collections; he is now a well-to-do and respected citizen
of Lawrence. He served throughout the Civil War in the Union army, and
he was a gallant soldier. Jake Herd soon became notorious for his devotion
to the cause of the rough element which invaded Kansas from Missouri
from political motives and for the purpose of plunder. He was not in
favor of a "free white state," as has been claimed, but was a partisan of
the pro-slavery element which had its root in the Blue Lodges in Missouri.
He was a kidnapper of free negroes who came to Kansas, selling them
"down South," and many crimes were laid at his door. But having the
protection of the Federal government, he escaped the consequences of his
crimes. As showing the character of the times and the part played in
them by Jake Herd, see the little book written by Dr. John Doy, the statements in which no attempt was ever made to refute, and from which the
following quotation is made:

During the winter of 1858-9, several attempts were made by a gang
of unprincipled fellows, living in and around Lawrence and Lecompton, to
kidnap a number of colored persons from the city of Lawrence and its
neighborhood, with the intention of selling them into slavery in Missouri.

The first attempt discovered, was made upon Charles Fisher, a light
mulatto, who kept a barber's shop in Lawrence. He was seized and put
into a carriage; jumping out was chased and shot at, but managed to evade
the ruffians. On the next evening, another colored man, William Riley,
was seized and carried off; but he, also, succeeded in escaping from the
room in which he was bound and confined, in the house of a man named

These were the acquaintances made by Quantrill at the ferry. He would sport with them on the broad sand-bars, running foot-races, jumping, wrestling, drinking occasionally, shooting, gambling. In a short time he was regarded as one of the gang and began to cross the river, spending some of his time at

---

Corel, about two miles from Lawrence, and got back to that "city of refuge."

Much feeling was excited among the citizens by these attempts, and two men named Fry and Goss, the former an old resident of Lawrence, the latter a stranger, were arrested and examined before a justice of the Peace, upon the charge of kidnapping. Sufficient proof of their complicity was shown, to cause them to be committed to answer at the U. S. District Court, but they were released under a writ of *habaes corpus*, issued by Judge Elmore, an appointee of the Administration, and the largest slave holder in Kansas. This was in October, 1858. . . . During the Autumn and Winter, the attempts at kidnapping became more and more frequent, and were sometimes successful. At last the colored people in Lawrence, finding themselves in constant danger, applied to the citizens for protection. In consequence of this application, a meeting was held in the Court House, on or about the 18th of January, 1859, to take the matter into consideration. As no adequate protection against the insidious attempts of the kidnappers could be assured to the colored people if they remained in Lawrence, a removal to Iowa was agreed upon, and some money raised to defray the expenses.

I was solicited to convey these people as far as Holton, in Calhoun County, as I had just returned from a tour through that section of Kansas, and, being well acquainted with the roads and the people along the route, was considered the person best fitted for the task. Holton is on the direct northern route traveled by the Free State emigrants in 1856.

I complied with the request, and agreed to undertake the trip with my own wagon and horses, to be driven by my eldest son Charles, then twenty-five years of age. As my wagon would not contain all the passengers, another wagon and pair of horses were obtained, and Mr. Clough, a young man who lived near Lawrence, engaged to drive them. All necessary preparations were made for the journey; beds, bedding, camp utensils, provisions and some arms were packed into the wagons, for the convenience of camping out, and for defence. The passengers were eight men, three women, and two children. All the adults, except two, showed my son their free papers. All had them except these two, whom we knew to be free men; one, Wilson Hays, from Cincinnati, Ohio, the other, Charles Smith, from Brownsville, Penn. They had both been employed as cooks, at the Eldredge House, in Lawrence. Our entire party numbered sixteen.

We started early in the morning of the 25th of January, I being on horseback, and the men walking behind the wagons, which contained the stores with the women and children; crossed the Kansas River at Lawrence, and traveled through the Delaware Reservation towards Oscaloosa. When about twelve miles from Lawrence, and eight from Oscaloosa, having ascertained, as I supposed, that the road was clear, I requested the men to get into the wagons, as we had quite a long descent before us, and would go down at a brisk pace. They did so, and then, excepting myself, all the party were in the wagons, which were covered and thus effectually prevented them from seeing what occurred immediately afterwards, and from defending themselves.

the McGee cabin, and doing his full share to perpetuate the reproach expressed in the *sobriquet* of "Cuckold Tom." His ideal was Jake Herd, possibly the most daring border-ruffian that ever lived in Kansas. At Lecompton, Herd was the right-arm of the rough element, the "terror-raiser" of the pro-slavery

At the bottom of the hill, on the right of the road, is a bluff; from behind this, as we turned it, came out a body of some twenty, or more, armed and mounted men. Eleven of them approached with leveled rifles and ordered us to halt; they keeping, however, at a safe distance from our revolvers. My son, with Wilson Hays, the colored man from Cincinnati, sprang out of my wagon, which was ahead, and shouted: "Father, we're stopped: shall we shoot?"

Dismounting, I ran round to the off side of the wagon, telling them to hold on till I ascertained who the men were and what they wanted. As I advanced towards the latter, demanding their business, some of them cried out, "Shoot him! shoot him!" and aimed their guns at me. I told them to shoot me if they wanted to, but not to fire at the wagons, as there were women and children in them.

I felt perfectly reckless, seeing that we were overpowered, and that, hampered as the party were in the wagons, we could do nothing, while I anticipated the fate in store for our poor passengers; for I now recognized five of the assailants: two young men named McGee, living near Franklin; a fellow named Whitley, living in Lawrence; Dr. Garvin, the modern Democratic postmaster of that city; and a notorious ruffian and kidnapper, Jake Hurd, who lived about four miles from Lecompton. These were all Northern men by birth, the first two being from Illinois, Whitley from Ohio, Hurd from Pennsylvania, and Garvin from Indiana or Ills.

I spoke to these men separately, asking if they had any process against us, that they stopped us on the highway. The only replies were oaths, threats, and revolvers thrust in our face.

Turning to Whitley I said, "What? You here, Whitley? A Free State man! Where's your process?"

"Here it is," the brute replied, putting the muzzle of his revolver to my head.

"You will have to pay for this," was my answer.

I then asked the others if they had any papers to show that any of the colored people were claimed as slaves, or if their professed owners were present. The only replies were bitter denunciations of "nigger thieves," and finally an offer of five hundred dollars, from a man who was a stranger to me, if I would drive the colored people to the Rialto Ferry, on the Missouri River, opposite Weston.

I told him no teams of mine should ever be used to carry a human being into slavery with my consent.

"You shall go any how, d—n you. We don't mean to let you go back and bring an infernal gang of G—d d—d abolitionists on us."

"That's your business," said I. "I should not go if I could help it."

A portion of the party then dismounted and went towards the wagons, the rest keeping their rifles leveled upon us. The men and women were ordered out and tied, one by one, as they descended from the wagons.

My son had a gun in his hands which he discharged into the air, finding that resistance was useless. At the same time Jake Hurd came near shooting himself as he tried to draw a gun out of the wagon. The hammer caught in some bedding, and the contents of the barrel passed

party in Kansas. He was known in every town on the border
as being "sound on the goose," a holy terror, violent, quick and
deadly with the revolver, fearless and daring, and a man who
would risk his life to capture a negro, either free or a runaway
slave. Quantrill's admiration for Herd was unbounded. They
differed in that Herd was open, bold, loud of tongue, drunken,
relying alone upon his force and courage for success, while Quantrill was silent, sober, unpretending, scheming, depending more
upon cunning, deceit, and intrigue than courage or force in
reaching his ends.

Upon what circumstances Quantrill adopted the name Charley Hart we do not know. He assumed it when he started to
Utah with the expedition to succor General Johnston in 1858.[5]

---

between his arm and body. [Deflected by a button on his overcoat. — The
author.]

"I wish to the Lord it had shot you through the heart, Jake!" I
exclaimed involuntarily.

Hurd foamed out, "I'll shoot you, G—d d—n you."

"Do so," I replied, "and I'll give you the best horse I own."

After the colored people were all secured, three of the gang seized
me and attempted to tie my hands behind my back, but seeing that my
son's arms were already tied, I broke away from them and went up to
Hurd, asking him to loose him. He would not, and I untied the rope
myself. Hurd threatened to shoot me, but I paid no attention to his
threats.

Finding that we valued life cheaper than they supposed, they consented that Charles and I should go unbound, provided we would go
quietly, urging at the same time the necessity of keeping us till they were
beyond the reach of pursuit, and promising that, when we reached the
Rialto Ferry, our property should be restored to us and we be free to
return, with good pay for our time and trouble. Of course we had no
choice but to submit.

Shortly afterwards, seeing the two colored men before named with
their arms tied, I proceeded to loose them also, telling the kidnappers that
I knew they were free men.

Our captors were much angered by our reckless acts and speech, and
held a consultation as to what should be done with us. Jake Hurd and
the McGees advised our murder, saying, "Dead men tell no tales." Others
advised a hasty retreat, as they thought that an armed escort might be
expected from Lawrence.   This startled them; I was ordered to get on my
horse, the rest were hurried into wagons; then, with a man on each side
whipping the teams, we drove furiously towards Leavenworth. Camped
two miles from Leavenworth. About midnight drove on to Rialto Ferry
opposite Weston. Large bonfire and many armed men there — Taken to
Weston. Then to Platte City and put in jail January 28th.

5 The description given by R. M. Peck of Quantrill at Fort Bridger
(see note, *ante*, page 75) is a good one. Peck states that he was then

He was known by no other name on that trip, and he gave no
other name in Lawrence in either 1859 or 1860.   S. S. Herd says
he knew Quantrill only as Charley Hart and did not hear the
name Quantrill until it became notorious along the border at a
later day; and neither did H. S. Clarke.   Judge Samuel A. Riggs
prosecuted him at Lawrence in 1860 for burglary and larceny,
for arson and kidnapping, under the name of Charley Hart.[6]
Mr. Holland Wheeler, of Lawrence, knew him at this time.   He
describes Quantrill as he appeared there about June, 1860.   He
stopped at the hotel owned by Nathan Stone and registered as
Charley Hart.   Stone was in his confidence and knew his name
to be William C. Quantrill, having that fact of record on the last
page of his hotel register.[7]

---

and there known as Charley Hart. His description agrees with that given
by Mr. Clarke in the article before referred to, which is as follows:

I first saw Quantrill in June, 1858 (1859).   He was about twenty-one
years old, and, as I remember him, was about five feet ten inches tall,
rather slight of stature, weighing, perhaps, 150 pounds, walked with an easy,
slouchy gait, head bent a little forward, eyes cast downward, hair of a
yellowish-brown color, cut straight around the neck about even with the
lower part of the ear, the end of the hair turned under towards the neck.
He wore a drab corduroy suit, with pants tucked into tops of his high-
heeled boots: also a drab slouch hat.

Mr. Clarke was a man much respected in Lawrence for his worth as a
citizen and for his upright life.   There is a biographical sketch of him in
the Seventh Volume, *Kansas Historical Collections*.

6 See the statement of Judge Riggs, in the Seventh Volume, *Kansas
Historical Collections*, where there is, also, a biographical sketch of the
judge.   He is a lawyer of ability and served long as judge of the district
court in his district.   He is an upright man and is highly regarded by
the people of Lawrence, where he has lived for half a century.

7 See account written by Wheeler, published in the Seventh Volume,
Kansas Historical Collections.   His description of Quantrill is as follows:

I came to Kansas in 1858.   Have resided at Lawrence most of the
time since; in the spring of 1860 was at the old Whitney House, kept by
Nathan Stone.   One day, perhaps in June, there came a lone footman
across the ferry.   He was dressed with corduroy pants tucked into his
boots, woolen shirt, slouch hat, and carried an oilcloth grip.   He was about
five feet nine inches in height, bow-legged, weight about 150 or 160 pounds,
sandy hair, rather hooked nose, and had a peculiar droop to his eyelids.
He walked into the hotel office, deposited the grip, and registered as
Charles Hart.   He left the next morning, leaving the grip for his bill.
Some days after he returned.   Mr. Stone, calling me to the desk, opened
the day-book and showed me on the back page the name Wm. C. Quantrill,
remarking, ''That is Hart's real name.   He is a detective for the Delaware
Indians.''   Quantrill was at the hotel at times from this on up to quite
late in the fall.   He usually had the same room with myself.   During

All the time Quantrill lived in and about Lawrence he was known as Charley Hart. Very few people there knew that he had any other name. His true name was known about Osawatomie and Stanton, and it became known there that he was living at Lawrence under the assumed name of Charley Hart. So, the people of Lykins (Miami) county were never deceived as to his identity.

Charley Hart and William C. Quantrill have herein now been shown to have been identical. There never was any man named Charley Hart in Kansas. William C. Quantrill falsely represented himself to be Charley Hart, and he did so because of the criminal life he intended to lead and did lead. As there never can be any question as to his identity, Quantrill will be spoken of by his true name hereinafter. But it must be remembered that to the people of Lawrence he was Charley Hart. Few of them knew he was Quantrill until after he became a bushwhacker in Missouri. And this name "Charley" stuck to him to his death. In Missouri he was known as "Charley" Quantrill, and he is so known to this day by his followers there. In most books by Missourians in which he is mentioned his name is given as Charles William Quantrill.[8]

the very warm nights we frequently slept on the roof of the veranda. (Often I borrowed a pistol to put under my pillow. Why? Well, I don't know myself.)

Quantrill told me of his trip to New Mexico (Utah) a short time before. He called Paola his home. His most usual companions were the Miller brothers and one Baldwin. He also was about Dean's shop. Had a lady friend who was in town at times. Saw him riding with her in a carriage several times. He told me about her; all of which I forget. Quantrill and myself frequently went down on the river bank to practice pistol shooting. He was very friendly with me.

8 A. M. Winner, Esq., Kansas City, Mo., has Quantrill's watch. Quantrill lost this watch in an orchard in Jackson county during the war. More than thirty years after it was lost there the orchard was cut down and the ground plowed up, when the watch was found. The finder of the watch gave it to Mr. Winner, who has shown it to the author. On the inside of the back lid or cover of the case is cut with some sharp instrument the name, "Charley Quantrill." Quantrill called attention to the loss of his watch a few minutes after it disappeared and searched for it for an hour or more. He and his men got their dinner at the home of the man who owned the orchard, and whose name the author does not now recall. He was a prominent citizen of Jackson county, and Quantrill requested

him to keep the matter in mind and find the watch if he could, which he did many years afterward.

In the *Kansas City Times*, Dec. 1, 1894, appears the following account of the finding of the watch:

A very interesting relic, interesting from the historic relations of the man who once owned it, was found on the farm of Ink Hicklin at Greenwood, near Lee's Summit, a few weeks ago. It is the watch once carried by the famous renegade, Charles Quantrell, and lost by him on Mr. Hicklin's farm thirty-two years ago. Quantrell and his band were riding through the country, pursued by the federal troops at the time the watch was lost, and while hunting for it Quantrell barely escaped being captured. The day after it was lost Quantrell returned, and with Mr. Ink Hicklin, now living on the farm upon which the watch was lost, hunted for it, but failed to find it. The watch lay there for thirty-two years and was picked up by the man who had helped its owner look for it, when the owner's bones had been dust for many years and his daring and heartless deeds almost forgotten, save for the blot on the scroll of history.

Why Quantrell should risk being captured to search for the watch is a puzzling question, certainly not because of its intrinsic value, as the case is of brass, at one time gold plated. It is a hunting case, and closed together well, for the wheels are almost intact after all the years it has been exposed to the elements.

The name "Charles Quantrell" is rudely cut on the inner side of the back cover of the case, and looks as if it had been done with a pocket knife. That the watch is genuine, Daniel Williams of Greenwood will swear, for he saw Quantrell cut the name on the case. The watch belongs to Jack Atkins, a jeweler at Greenwood, and it was when he poured some acid on it to find what it was made of that the name was made legible. Mr. Atkins sent the watch to The Star for inspection, and it is undoubtedly genuine. All the old settlers in the neighborhood where it was lost and found remember the circumstance of Quantrell losing his watch.

In the Collection of the author there are some letters from Samuel Walker, long a resident of Lawrence, to W. W. Scott. In one of these letters, dated Lawrence, Kansas, April 14, 1889, Walker says:

He never went by any other name here than Hart. I never heard the name Quantrill until after he went to Mo.

Mr. Walker was Sheriff of Douglas county and knew Hart well, having made repeated efforts to arrest him for crimes committed there.

CHAPTER VII

QUANTRILL AS CHARLEY HART — A BORDER-RUFFIAN
AT LAWRENCE

Q UANTRILL took part in the expeditions and forays of
the kidnappers and ruffians as soon as he was well enough
known to have their confidence, which must have been
within a month or two from the time he took up his abode again
with the Delawares. These forays and thieving excursions did
not occupy all the time of the ruffians. They transacted their
business much as robbers and highwaymen transact theirs to-day
— by making a raid and disposing of their plunder secured, then
lounging and loafing about liquor-shops and skulking through
thickets with fallen women for a time before again taking to the
road. Associating with fallen women was Quantrill's greatest
weakness; his other forms of dissipation were few, gambling
being one of them. Herd says that his living among the Indians
first caused the McGees to think there might be something in
Quantrill that would make him one of their band.[1] While Quan-

---

[1] There is a little discrepancy in Herd's statements, that published
in the *Kansas Historical Collection*, differing somewhat from what he told
the author. The published statement is the first public utterance he made
on the subject, and he was in making it naturally cautious, having been
to some extent associated with Quantrill. But there is substantial agreement in all he has said — the differences being caused by the evident fact
that he has not yet told the whole story of what he knows of Quantrill's
actions. Here is his account of Quantrill's first appearance and of his
becoming acquainted with the characters at Lawrence, taken from the
Kansas Historical Collections:

During the summer of 1858, and for a year or two thereafter, I was
much of the time employed with the Baldwin boys operating the old rope
ferry across the Kansas river at this point, connecting Lawrence with the
Delaware Indian reserve.

It was here at the ferry where I first met W. C. Quantrill, then under
the assumed name of Charles Hart. Hart claimed then to be stopping with
a son of Sarcoxie, a Delaware chief, a few miles out on the reserve, and
he frequently crossed the river with us going to and from Lawrence. At

trill became as reckless as any of the gang of which he was a part, he ever tried to remain out of the public eye. And he was, while a border-ruffian, trying to act with the radical anti-slavery people at Lawrence. He could not be true to any cause, for, of moral character, the foundation of devotion, he was devoid. Being false at heart and governed by self-interest solely, it was natural that he should be two-faced, untrue to everything and everybody, governed entirely by what he believed would make him the most money. His old trait of sudden disappearances and reappearances was observed by his associates at Lawrence.

One day a negro came out of the woods on the old Indian trail leading through the Delaware Reserve to the ferry at Lawrence. He was young and strong, but he seemed worn and weary from running. Herd was at work on the ferry-boat, and the negro inquired of him the way to the house of James H. Lane, saying he desired to go there. Herd put him across the river. Quantrill and Frank Baldwin were loafing at the south landing. Herd told them where the negro desired to go and turned him over to them, telling him they would take him to Lane's house. They said they would take him to Lane's house, certainly they would. Then they told him to "come along." The negro went with Quantrill and Baldwin, and, believing that he was with friends, he answered their questions freely. He had escaped from his owner, a widow named Gaines, who lived at Platte City, Mo. He had come through Leavenworth and the Delaware Reserve, believing that if he could get to Lane's house

---

first Quantrill appeared to be rather reticent, but after a time, crossing frequently as he did, he appeared to become more sociable, and often stopped and chatted with the boys, and after a time became more chummy, often spending a half hour or longer with us when we were not busy, practicing jumping with the boys, running short foot-races, etc. He did not strike me as having any braggadocio or desire to make any display in any way. If he had any money, to amount to anything, no one knew it but himself. He did not appear to have any business or means of support, so far as I knew. I don't think he had any very positive convictions on questions that were agitating the territory at that time; if he did, he certainly kept them to himself. One thing is certain, he was always willing to go into anything that turned up that had a dollar in it for Charley Hart.

During my acquaintance with Quantrill, he did not appear to be permanently located in any place, and would frequently leave without any warning to any one of us, and be gone for days, and sometimes weeks, and then turn up again as unexpectedly as he had departed.

he would be safe — and so he would have been. They took him to McGee's.

That night Quantrill, Jake McGee and Frank Baldwin tied the negro on a horse and took him to Westport, stopping in the woods near the town. There McGee left the negro to be guarded by Quantrill and Baldwin, while he rode to Platte City to arrange with the widow for as large a reward as could be wrung from her for the slave's return. She agreed to pay five hundred dollars for his return, though the statutory reward was but two hundred dollars. McGee went back to Westport, and the next day they took the negro to Platte City and received the sum agreed upon — all in new twenty-dollar bills of some Missouri bank. The widow asked the slave why he had run away, and he said the keeper of the livery stable had induced him to do it. When Quantrill and associates returned to Lawrence they gave Herd one hundred dollars of the money they had received for taking the negro back to Missouri.[2]

---

[2] When the author heard this story from Herd he wrote to Hon. R. P. C. Wilson, of Platte City, to secure verification of it. At first Mr. Wilson could find no evidence of such an occurrence, and so wrote me. Later, he secured the evidence, when he wrote me the following letter, which fully confirms Herd's account:

Platte City, Mo., Nov. 27, 1907.

Dear Mr. Connelley:

I have just had a conversation with an aged negro, now known here as "Old Milt" Paxton — having belonged to our old friend, Mr. W. M. Paxton — who told me that just before the breaking out of the war, "Ike" Gaines, a slave belonging to Joanna Gaines, widow of R. P. Gaines, was persuaded off, went, or was taken to Kansas, and then brought back bound with ropes across the Missouri, delivered to his owner, who paid the statutory reward — maybe more than that sum; — that Miles Harrington, a wealthy man here, the son-in-law of Mrs. Gaines, transacted all the business pertaining to the recovery of "Ike." Ike, the old negro thinks, lives now in Wathena, Kansas. Harrington and his whole family are, I think, now dead.

There is, then, no doubt that there was a Mrs. Gaines living here at the time indicated; that her slave, Ike, ran or was enticed away, and was brought back "in ropes" and returned to his mistress (Widow Gaines) — who paid a substantial reward — how much is not positively known. Old Milt says that sort of thing was going on right along then. I think now Q. was in the game — and your informant was probably correct in his statement.

Yours truly,
R. P. C. Wilson.

Reference to *Annals of Platte County, Missouri*, by W. M. Paxton,

Soon after his arrival at Lawrence from returning "Ike" Gaines to bondage Quantrill suddenly disappeared. He was gone some time — two or three weeks — when he suddenly made his appearance riding a race-horse, a sorrel with white feet and legs, and called "White Stockings." Quantrill claimed to have bought the horse at or near Paola; it was his intention to win some money with the racer. William Mulkey, one of the famous pioneers of Kansas City, Mo., was at that time (and long afterwards) a breeder and trainer of race-horses. He then had a horse with a reputation for speed on the track, known as "Mulkey's Colt" throughout western Missouri and Kansas. Quantrill believed that White Stockings could beat Mulkey's Colt. He, Herd and Frank Baldwin took Quantrill's horse to Westport to arrange for a race. Mulkey was a shrewd man and a good judge of horses. Fearing that Mulkey would not bet much on his colt after having seen White Stockings, Quantrill put on his horse a high-horned heavy saddle and brought him out muddy and unkempt generally. Mulkey was deceived and bet one hundred and fifty dollars on his colt. Baldwin rode White Stockings in the race, and Mulkey's Colt was badly beaten. The party remained about Westport two or three weeks, but finding no further opportunity for a race they left town. Quantrill and Baldwin took the horse south along the state line and were gone a week or two, when they returned without the horse. They were among the Indians — perhaps the Cherokees. This was in the early part of the summer of 1860.[3]

the most complete history ever written of any county in the United States, shows the following, page 187:

RICHARD P. GAINES, b. in 1789; d. Sept. 6, 1854; m'd in Kentucky, Joanna Tinder, who survived him. He came to Platte City in 1842, and purchased of J. V. Cockrell the frame hotel on the southeast corner of what is now the public square. He was a fat and jolly landlord, and highly esteemed.

It was the widow of Richard P. Gaines who had to redeem her slave "Ike" from Quantrill and his gang, and they wrung from her more than twice the lawful reward.

[3] In his published account, Herd says of this horse:

In the summer of 1860 he suddenly disappeared, and after an absence of some time he as suddenly returned with a running horse, named "White Stockings," which he claimed he had bought in the neighborhood of Paola, Kansas. On this occasion he insisted that Frank Baldwin and myself

It is believed that it was on the trip to dispose of the race-horse that Quantrill conceived the idea of bartering with the Missourians and preying upon them through treachery. There was much feeling in Jackson county (and other border counties) against Captain John E. Stewart, who lived about four miles south of Lawrence, whose claim was in the heavily wooded bottom of the Wakarusa, where the creek makes a sort of horse-shoe bend. Stewart had built a strong fort on his claim.[4] He

should accompany him to Jackson County, Missouri, and assist him in making some races, more particularly with the "Mulkey colt," that had quite a reputation as a runner. Baldwin and I went on that trip, and were gone about three weeks with him. Seeing no chance for further sport in that community, Baldwin and I decided to come back to Lawrence, and Quantrill said he was going to start south, down, perhaps, as far as Fort Scott, Kan., with his horse. We left him at McGees and returned to Lawrence.

Herd says both he and Baldwin returned, leaving Quantrill at McGee's which must be an error, for the McGees lived within two miles of Lawrence. The account in the text was given by Herd to the author. But this may mean that they left him at the hotel of Milton McGee, in Kansas City, Mo.

4 Stewart's claim is the present Douglas County "Poor Farm." It is the northwest quarter of Section twenty, Township thirteen, Range twenty. It was surrounded by timber and thickets of brush, in a secluded and inaccessible place.

In a clipping from the *Lawrence Tribune*, no date, now in the Collection of the author, is the following concerning John E. Stewart:

He [Quantrill] professed to be an ardent and very radical Abolitionist, and soon became intimately acquainted with the leading men of that class, among whom John E. Stewart was a leading spirit, and an acknowledged chief. Stewart had been a Methodist minister in good standing and repute before coming to Kansas, and had preached to good acceptance at Salem, N. H., for a considerable time. He lived in 1859-60 on a farm claim about four miles Southeast of Lawrence on what is now the "Douglas County Poor Farm" and his house was a common rendezvous of a certain class of extreme "Free State" men and of slaves escaping from Missouri. Among others who are remembered as frequenting at Stewart's may be mentioned John H. Kagi and young Coppic, who afterwards went with old John Brown on his Harper's Ferry enterprise. Quantrell alias "Charley Hart" soon became extremely intimate with Stewart, and when he was not at the City Hotel it was commonly supposed that he might be found at Stewart's; though in point of fact he was known to have made several trips into Missouri, sometimes in company with Stewart — and he also scoured the country on horseback in various directions from Lawrence. Stewart had already won the nickname of the "Fighting Preacher," and had been actively engaged with old John Brown and Col. James Montgomery during the troubles in Linn and Bourbon Counties, and had taken part in bringing slaves out of Missouri. He was beginning to be suspected of entertaining loose notions with regard to property in horses as well as negroes, but his burning zeal in behalf of the Free State cause and the

was a preacher and very active in securing slaves from Missouri to take out over the underground railroad.   He made many raids into Missouri and always brought out slaves — perhaps other property.   The State of Missouri set a price on his head, as did some counties and individuals.   Quantrill would willingly have betrayed him into the hands of the Missourians for these rewards. After the Morgan Walker affair Stewart said Quantrill had been trying all summer to get him to go on that trip, but that he would not go with Quantrill as he did not trust him fully.[5]

That Quantrill and Stewart were close friends for a time there is no doubt.   Quantrill and a man named Sinclair made a raid into Salt Creek Valley, in Leavenworth county, and stole more than eighty head of cattle from pro-slavery settlers there. They drove the cattle to Lawrence, crossing at the ferry, and took them to Captain Stewart's fort.   The owners of the cattle followed them, and, securing the services of the sheriff of Douglas county, recovered all but two, and these were being butchered at Stewart's before the officers arrived.[6]

freedom of the colored race caused his irregularities to be winked at to some extent, by those who became aware of them and his excesses to be excused.

Most people only know him as ''The Fighting Preacher,'' the friend of John Brown, the pronounced Abolitionist, and the man ever ready to harbor and defend fugitives from slavery.

[5] In the published statement of S. S. Herd, it is said:

At the time we made this trip to Jackson county, Missouri, with Quantrill, there was much excitement among the people over the depredations committed by some of the ''abolition leaders,'' and a very bitter feeling existed toward Captain John E. Stewart and others, and I have always had my suspicions that it was during this trip, and after he left us with his racing-horse, that he conceived the idea and perhaps laid his plans to deliver Captain Stewart over to the authorities of Jackson county, which finally resulted in the episode at Walker's house, later in the season.

[6] Letters of Samuel Walker to W. W. Scott, now in the Collection of the author.   There are two of these letters, one dated January 28, 1883, and one dated April 14, 1889.   Both were written from Lawrence, Walker's home.   Walker was the sheriff.   He was one of the first settlers of Lawrence.   He was a very conscientious man and an excellent citizen, but entertained strong prejudices.   There are contradictions in the statements made in these letters.   In the first he says that ''Hart and Coppock'' stole the cattle.   In the second, he says they were stolen by Hart and Sinclair. Barclay Coppoc returned to Kansas after the Harper's Ferry raid, and he lived at that time with John Dean at Lawrence.   But it was Sinclair who was on this raid into Salt Creek Valley with Quantrill.   And this valley

While Quantrill would flee to the protecting walls of Stewart's fort with cattle and horses stolen from pro-slavery settlers in Kansas, he did not hesitate to attack Stewart and attempt to storm his fort if he saw a dollar in it for himself for doing so. During the summer of 1860 Captain Stewart received and concealed for transportation over the underground railroad some slaves who had escaped from their masters in Missouri. Before the slaves could be forwarded their owners appeared in pursuit of them. They enlisted, to help them recover the slaves, Jake Herd, Jake McGee, Tom McGee, "Cuckold Tom" McGee, Henry McLaughlin, Esau Sager, and Quantrill. They went to Stewart's fort and demanded the slaves. Quantrill remained in the background so as not to be seen by Stewart. Stewart had armed

---

was one of the favorite raiding grounds of Quantrill; he stole many horses and cattle from settlers in Atchison and Leavenworth counties, taking them usually from pro-slavery men, driving them to Stewart's fort, from which point they were disposed of in the country south of the Kansas river. Of the identity of Sinclair nothing is known for certain, but he must have been Walt Sinclair, afterwards a Red Leg and murderer under Jennison. In one of the letters Walker says he recovered more than eighty head of cattle; in the other, he says he recovered fifty head. The following quotation is from the last letter:

Hart & Sinclair came across the Kansas River at Lawrence from Salt Creek Valley . . . with 80 odd head of cattle. . . . Hart & Sinclair were alone. they took the cattle to Stuarts fort. ` I found the cattle at Stuarts, and found Stuart, Buchannon, St. Clair & Hart playing cards & some men skinning two of the steers in the yard. the cattle were taken from pro-slavery men that lived in Kansas. . . . I was Sheriff of Douglas County & lived at Lawrence. the owners came to me & stated that they had lost the cattle & tracked them to the river. I was at the river in the morning & saw the cattle cross & Hart & St. Clair was driving them. I knew at once they were taking them to Stewarts fort 5 miles south of town. Hart was indicted for stealing horses in the U. S. Court and I as Deputy U. S. Marshal tried to arrest him.

In the same letter, Walker describes his first meeting with Quantrill, as follows:

My first acquaintance with Charley Hart was in Paola in this State. I met him with Capt. John Stewart. he introduced him to me as an Ohio boy & I being from that state I had a long talk with him. I was Badly impressed with him then & never got over it. he did not deceive me one bit.

In the first letter, Walker says:

I will be plain with you. I had thought that no one but A Democrat or Rebel would try to Excuse Charley Hart, as I saw you had done in Several Articles you had written. he was a Monster of the worst kind. when any one tells me that he could not control his men they simply say they

the negroes, and he refused to surrender them.   A battle ensued, and the kidnappers were repulsed after securing but one slave; they claimed that the others were so badly wounded as to be worthless, but as Stewart led the fight and was not injured, it is not to be supposed that any of the negroes were seriously hurt. They were probably all able to go out on the next train over the underground railroad.   Quantrill had given the information to his ruffian partners of the presence of the slaves at Stewart's fort, and he was planning to kidnap them and sell them or take them to Missouri for the rewards offered for them when the

---

are not Posted. I could tell many things about Hart that came under my observations, at that time, as I was Sheriff and Deputy Marshal, that would not be flattering to his Mother.

It will be observed in the above that when Hart was operating with the Free-State men he claimed to be from Ohio. When he went to Missouri he claimed to have been born in Maryland. At the time spoken of by Walker, Quantrill was associated with the ultra wing of the anti-slavery party and also with the border-ruffians. With him it was any person or party that would afford him an opportunity to steal. He had no choice — no principle — no moral sense.

In the clipping from the *Lawrence Tribune* already quoted from is the following account of the cattle stolen by Quantrill:

Charley Hart is supposed to have paid his bills at Stone's Hotel in a satisfactory manner, though it was not easy to see how he could get the money for that purpose. Some suspicion was at length entertained that he occasionally indulged in horse stealing, and some time in the fall of 1860 he was seen with another young man driving a herd of fine steers across the Kansas river, through Lawrence in the direction of Stewart's farm. He made no great secret of the fact that he had taken the cattle without buying them; told an acquaintance as he passed through Lawrence that he had ''jayhawked'' them and went on his way in peace. Not many hours afterwards some men from the neighborhood of Kickapoo, in Leavenworth County, came following on the trail of the cattle, crossed the river near where the Lawrence bridge now is, talked with Capt. Sam Walker then sheriff of Douglas county, learned where the cattle were likely to be found, took Sheriff Walker with them and went direct to Stewart's farm. They found the cattle in a large corral, except two that had been killed and were then hung up to cool. Stewart claimed that he had bought the two steers he had slaughtered from two men who had passed on to the south, and who would return in a day or two for the cattle left in his keeping. But there sat Quantrell alias ''Hart'' with the other man who had assisted him in driving the cattle through Lawrence and Walker knew that Stewart's story was a bare-faced lie. Quantrell made no claim to the cattle and said not a word about them. Stewart claimed only the two he had killed, and Walker delivered the others over to their owners who drove them quietly home again to Kickapoo.

owners appeared in pursuit. This was what he called his
"detective work."

There were not wanting accusations that Quantrill was ply-
ing his vocation of murderer even in the town of Lawrence, and
that murders were frequently committed by him there little
doubt can now remain. The *Lawrence Tribune* has the following on this head:

Sometime after this incident Quantrell came to Sheriff
Walker and told him that two men had come up from Missouri
on the hunt for some runaway slaves and had put up at Stone's
Hotel. That two well known citizens of Lawrence had taken
them in charge promising to guide them to where their slaves
were secreted; had taken them down to the banks of the Kansas
river below where the bridge now stands and had there KILLED
THEM, tied their bodies together with cords and thrown them
into the river. To convince Walker of the truth of his story,
Quantrell offered to show him where the horses were which the
two Missourians had rode, and accordingly he took Walker across
the river to a spot near where Moak's elevator now stands, then
covered with a dense growth of timber and showed him two
horses which appeared to have been kept there for several days.
Sheriff Walker took the horses in charge and advertised them,
but they were never claimed or called for.

There was not the slightest reason for believing that the two
men accused of murder by Quantrell were guilty of such a deed;
they laughed the story to scorn; but nevertheless the murders
were undoubtedly committed by some persons, for within ten
or twelve days from the time that Walker took possession of the
horses, the bodies of two men were found floating in the river
near Eudora, tied together with a rope, as described by Quantrell, and were taken out and buried at some place not far from
Eudora.

There can be no shadow of doubt that Quantrell himself
either alone or with the help of a confederate, murdered those
two men from Missouri in cold blood for the purpose of obtaining
the money they had on their persons, and perhaps for the further
object of showing some of his more reckless associates that he was
ready to go all lengths against "Negro Hunters."

Very possibly there was another reason for killing these
men. It was then suspected and is now well known that Quantrell was playing a dangerous double game, that of Abolitionist and Slave Liberator in Kansas, and that of an extreme
Pro-Slavery man in Missouri, professing to slave-holders there
that he was acting the part of a spy, detective, and slave-catcher

in Kansas. He was aiding and persuading slaves to escape from their masters into Kansas, and then betraying them by disclosing their place of refuge to those same masters for a reward. Whether he ever actually assisted in kidnapping or capturing escaped slaves and taking them back to bondage is not clear. Such devil's work was done by others here if not by him, and it is hardly probable that he would allow such a rich mine of hellishness and infamy to be worked by others, while he took no share in it. Assuming that this was so, we may readily imagine that these two men fresh from Missouri on the hunt for runaway slaves, had become masters of the dangerous secret of his two-faced career, and that Quantrill thought it his safest course to dispose of them, remembering the trite saying, that "dead men tell no tales."

Additional evidence that Quantrill was never actuated by any principle or convictions, but solely by his innate love for lawlessness, robbery, and plunder, may be found in the following incident. Late in the fall of 1860 he made up a party at Lawrence for the purpose of raiding into Missouri to steal horses, mules, and cattle. This raid was made into Cass county. Quantrill had carefully gone over the roads there and had marked the farms from which stock was to be taken. The party secured a large amount of live stock and started to return to Kansas. Quantrill slipped away from his companions and alarmed the people where the stock had been stolen, gathered a number of them together, and led them against his own band of thieves, who were overtaken before they had reached the State-line. A battle was fought in which the robbers resisted fiercely and succeeded in escaping with most of their spoil, which they sold along the route home. Quantrill contracted with the Missourians to find and identify the live stock at so much per head, and he secured the return of much of it from those who had purchased it from the robbers. When he returned to Lawrence he claimed that he had become bewildered in the dark, had lost his way to the camp, had been set upon by enraged owners of the cattle and horses and nearly lost his life, but finally escaped by making a long detour to the south. He claimed his portion of the money the live stock had been sold for, and it was paid over to him. But his associates were not satisfied with his explanations, and they would not follow him any more. After that he operated almost entirely with the ultra wing of the anti-slavery people.

Such duplicity is amazing. A character capable of such baseness is incomprehensible. Depravity in such a form and carried to such an extent bewilders, becomes a mystery.[7]

While engaged in this carnival of crime Quantrill wrote his mother a letter — the last word she ever heard from him. He did not leave even a word for her in the mouth of the priest who shrived him at death for his gold. The letter is dated at Law-

---

[7] This was a famous raid, and memory of it still exists among the old residents along the border. The author has had many indefinite accounts of it, most of the details having been forgotten. Hon. William Higgins, now of Bartlesville, Oklahoma, furnished information that was valuable in securing an adequate account of it. Mr. Higgins lived at that time at Paola, Kansas. This is believed to have been the raid referred to by S. S. Herd, in his printed statement, in the Seventh Volume, *Kansas Historical Collections*, as follows:

The next, and in fact the last, time I saw Quantrill was in the spring of 1861. I received word from some of the boys to be out at John Stropp's on a certain evening. (Stropp lived about a mile and a half east of town, in a double log-house, surrounded by timber and brush.) At the appointed time I went there, and found Quantrill (who did not dare to be seen in Lawrence at that time), Stropp, Jay Vince, Jack Elliott (a brother-in-law of Frank Baldwin), and Frank Baldwin. Quantrill said he wanted to raise some men to go down on the border, a little way over the line in Missouri, and make a trip down through that country, and get some stock. He said there was fine stock in that section, and he knew the country well. The other boys that were present all agreed to go, and they got another man or two to go with them, but I do not now remember what their names were. They made the trip, being gone, to the best of my recollection, about ten days, when they all returned to Lawrence with the exception of Quantrill. The boys said they had a good time, and got lots of stock, and were getting out nicely till they got near the Kansas line, when they were partially surrounded and attacked by about thirty of the Missourians, and had a brisk fight, but managed to escape that night and get into Kansas with most of their plunder. Much of the stock they traded off to the farmers in that vicinity and along the road from there to Lawrence. This was undoubtedly the stock that Quantrill afterwards engaged to locate or return to its proper owners for so much per head.

The raid described by Herd may not have been the same as that described in the text, but the probability is that they are identical. Herd says it was in the spring of 1861, which would be impossible, for after the Morgan Walker raid Quantrill did not operate from Lawrence, and that raid was made in December, 1860. The date of the raid described was November, 1860, but just what time in the month it was made can not now be determined.

rence, June 23, 1860. In this letter he again promised to send
her some money, a promise he did not keep. It is known that
he had money — that he received considerable sums as the results
of his kidnappings and robberies. And he deceived her by saying he had sent her some money in previous letters — which she
never received and which he never sent. Perhaps the world has
seen few men who would deliberately lie to their mothers to
avoid sending a few dollars to aid them to feed and clothe their
orphan children. It may be that Quantrill stands in a class
alone in this respect. His mother was a widow with a large
family of almost helpless children to support. She did not forget him, but sent him once a pair of boots and frequently sent
him small presents the first year he was in Kansas — sent them
by friends who came from Canal Dover to the Territory. Yet,
when he had plenty of money as the result of the criminal lawless life he was living, he did not send her a penny, and he deliberately broke off correspondence with her rather than keep his
promise made in this last letter to send her a few dollars. For,
had he written again he would have been compelled to send her
the money he promised or to have invented some lying excuse for
not doing so. He chose deliberately to abandon her, and she
never again heard from him.

Quantrill probably had some thought of returning to Ohio
when he wrote this letter. He intended to run when it became
too hot for him in Kansas, and he had calculated that September
would bring that condition of affairs. But he remained as long
as he could — until December — then ran only to Missouri. By
that time he had grown much in the science of villainy, and he
saw immense possibilities in that line along the border during
the continuance of the war that was then on the land.

In his letter he claimed to have been surveying lands in the
Delaware Indian Reservation, making this assertion to cause
his mother to believe he was leading an industrious and honest
life.[8]

---

[8] Letter of W. C. Quantrill to his mother, now in the Collection of
the author. It was the last word his mother ever received from him, the
last time she ever heard from him except indirectly and by chance through
newspaper reports.

Lawrence, Kansas
June 23. 1860.

My Dear Mother.

I seat myself again to write to you without having received an answer to my last two letters, and from the delay suppose you have not received them. If you did not I shall be quite disappointed for in one of the[m] I enclosed five dollars & the other ten knowing that you needed it and if I knew you had received them I would in this one send more. You spoke about havi[n]g to put a new roof on the house; well answer this immediately and I will send the means in the form of a check & then there can be no loss. I would like to come with it, but I cannot get away yet a while. I am expecting to get some money from a man who has brought suit against Government & has had judgment rendered in his favor but without that, I can send you fifty dollars as soon as you answer this letter. I received a letter from Mary dated June 1st Washn only two days ago and as she said she would probably start home about the middle of the month I will not answer it at present until I hear from you

It has been very dry here in this section of the country causing the crops to be backwar[d] and times rather dull. People a[re] generally healthy. I had a slight chill and fever the other day but none since. I think it was owing to having exposed myself too much for a couple of weeks. I have been out with a surveying party on the Delaware Indian lands & was obliged to camp out under rather unfavorable circumstances. I wish you a merry fourth of July. I intend spending mine near where I kept school last winter if nothing happens When you write tell me all the news for I never hear any thing from there only what you write. You must excuse my short and badly written letters, for I stop at taverns & never can feel at home enough to collect my thoughts & write an interesting letter. Tell me something about Grandfather for I have a desire to hear from him & would write If I knew where to direct to. If you have only received my two last letters is all that I wish at present, but let me know about it as soon as possible for I have money in my pocket now for you & will send it as soon as you write & probably sooner should I go to Leavenworth city for there I can get a check

Give my respects to my friends & my love to you all, hoping that soon I will see you all again.

Your Son
W. C. Quantrill——

P. S. I will here say that I will be home any how as soon as the 1st of September & probably sooner   by that time I will be done with Kansas.   W. C. Q.——

Lawrence Kansas
June 25. 1860.

My Dear Mother.

I seat myself again to write
to you without having received an answer
to my last two letters, and from the delay
suppose you have not received them. If
you did not I shall be quite disappointed
for in one of the I enclosed five dollars &
the other ten, knowing that you needed it
and if I knew you had received them I would
in this one send more. You spoke about having
to put a new roof on the house; well answer
this immedeately and I will send the means
in the form of a check & then there can be
no loss. I would like to come with it, but
I cannot get away yet a while, I am
expecting to get some money from a man
why had brought a suit against goverment
& has had judgment rendered in his favor
but without that, I can send you fifty dollars
as soon as you answer this letter. I received
a letter from Mary dated June 1st Mushan
only two days ago, & and as she said she would
probably start home about the middle of the
month, I will not answer it at present
untill I hear from you

Your Son
W. C. Quantrill

Written in pencil by W. W. Scott, is the following: "Closing paragraph of last letter Mrs. Quantrill ever received." This endorsement was made for the reason that the last paragraph and the postscript are written on a fragment of a sheet of paper about one-third the size of the sheet on which the letter is written.

On this same fragment is the following endorsement written in pencil in a hand unlike any other writing about the letter: "Belongs to letter dated Lawrence, Kans., June 23, 1860, last any one in Ohio ever received from him."

In the fall of 1860 one Heath put in a foundation for a stone house near Kanwaka, a village some four miles southeast of Lecompton. Cold weather coming on, the house could not be completed at that time, so, joists were put in, and on these joists prairie hay was stacked to keep out the rain and snow and to keep the walls dry. Some underground railroad enthusiast hid a runaway negro under this hay and boasted that Jake Herd could not find him. Some school children found him and told Jake of his whereabouts. Herd took Quantrill and some others and went to the house and got the negro. In taking him out the hay was burned and the people were attracted to the place. The walls of the building were ruined by the fire. A sort of pitched battle took place between the friends of the negro and Herd and his followers, but they got away with the negro and took him to Missouri and sold him. This was very late in the fall.

For this crime he was prosecuted by Hon. Samuel A. Riggs, then county attorney of Douglas county. Quantrill had also broken into the powder storage house of Ridenour & Baker and stolen a large amount of powder; he was indicted for it. He was indicted for kidnapping, and there was an indictment against him in the Federal Court for horse-stealing.[9]

---

[9] In a statement published in the Seventh Volume, *Kansas Historical Collections*, Judge Riggs says:

During the years 1860 and 1861 I was county attorney of Douglas county. During the year 1860 Quantrill was living and operating in the vicinity of Lawrence under the name of Charley Hart. By that name I prosecuted him in this county, during the summer and fall of 1860, for burglary and larceny, in breaking open and stealing from a powder-house of Ridenour & Baker; for arson, in setting fire to a barn in Kanwaka

The following incidents will show that Quantrill had trouble with the Delaware Indians and robbed them, though they had given him a home — had sheltered him and had fed him. In his published statement, Henry S. Clarke says:

One little incident that occurred in the summer of 1860, that others who are now living here witnessed besides myself, I will relate.

About half a dozen Delaware Indians came riding into Lawrence one day very much excited, and soon had a large group of people around them inquiring what was up, etc. White Turkey, a young Delaware, who talked pretty good English, and always sported an eagle's feather dangling from his hat, was telling the crowd about several of their ponies being stolen, and said they had traced them to the Kansas river near Lawrence, and that Charley Hart (as Quantrill called himself then) was one of the men seen with the ponies. Quantrill, who was in the rear of the crowd, heard the remark, and stepped forward with a big bluff, warning White Turkey that that kind of talk did not go, and made a motion toward his revolver. White Turkey whipped out his gun and had him covered in less than a second. Quantrill had his pistol out of the holster, but dared not attempt to elevate it, but backed out of the crowd with his pistol pointing toward the ground, as White Turkey slowly advanced toward him, until he (Quantrill) saw a chance to give his adversary the slip, which he was by no means too proud or reckless to do at the first opportunity.

The following is from the published statement of Holland Wheeler, already referred to:

At one time an Indian woman came into the hotel and told Quantrill she wanted seven dollars or her saddle. He got the saddle for her. "Now," she says, "where are my ponies?" He said: "I don't know anything about your ponies." "Well," she says, "they will be back by to-morrow, or you will have trouble."

Quantrill had stolen this poor Indian woman's saddle and riding ponies. She made him produce the saddle and return it. Whether she recovered her ponies is not known. The evidence is conclusive that Quantrill would rob anybody, man or woman.

township this county, and for kidnapping. These charges were all pending against him when he disappeared from this county, to turn up here again on the fateful 21st of August, 1863. He was an outlaw when he took to the bush.

When Sheriff Walker attempted to arrest him for his many crimes, Quantrill fled and took refuge in the wagon-shop of John Dean, closing a heavy door as he ran in. Before Walker could batter down the door, Dean had concealed the criminal. From that day Quantrill did not show himself in the streets of Lawrence. He forsook, in great measure, the ruffians, and cast his lot with Dean, Stewart and the other abolitionists about Lawrence.

Samuel Walker

The *Lawrence Tribune* says of the attempt of Sheriff Walker to capture Quantrill f o r horse-stealing, and his escape:

A warrant for his arrest was placed in the hands of Sheriff Walker, but not until Quantrell had by some means learned of the indictment, and declared that he would never be arrested on the warrant. Sheriff Walker, calling George Earl to assist him, soon found Quantrell on Massachusetts street, but as soon as Quantrell saw him approaching, he started down the street upon the run, and bolted into the wagon shop of John Dean, closing and barring the door behind him. Walker was not long in smashing the door, but Quantrell had disappeared, and Walker never set eyes upon him afterwards. Stone's City Hotel was carefully searched from top to bottom, and every other place in town where it was thought likely he could be found, but in vain.

Years afterward Walker learned from John Dean that Quantrell spent the night following his attempted arrest at the house of a man named Reed, the owner of a wholesale liquor store on the east side of Massachusetts street, near where the Grange Store now is, known as the "Checkered Front" store. Reed's dwelling house was a brick building, a little north of where the Lawrence House now stands, on Vermont street. That house was burned at the time of the "raid," and was never rebuilt. In that house Quantrell passed the night, with the Ex-Reverend John E. Stewart for a bed fellow.

There is no reason to suppose that Reed had any suspicion whatever of the true character of his guest, but Stewart knew that he was a bad man on general principles.

Quantrill's career at Lawrence to this period can be sum-

9

marized as follows: He was a desperate character, steeped in crime. He played a double rôle with the people in his vicinity — was a border-ruffian and an ultra, rabid abolitionist. He was also playing a double rôle between his ruffian associates and the people of Missouri whom they robbed. And he was playing still another double rôle — between Kansas and Missouri.

Quantrill was making progress on his way to a bloody destiny.

CHAPTER VIII

WHEN Quantrill fled to Dean's wagon-shop to escape arrest for his many crimes, he, in large measure, severed his relations with the local border-ruffians. He had played out the game. He was under suspicion. His comrades in crime had not come quite to a realization of his treachery, for in that event he would have been led into the brush and promptly shot. Quantrill was cunning and knew exactly how far he could carry his double-dealing with the ruffians. He had been under suspicion before, but was always able to satisfy his ruffian associates that he hung about the abolitionists only in the capacity of detective — to find out what they were doing, that their work might be undone. As he had given his gang information often that enabled them to kidnap a free negro or rescue a runaway slave from the conductors of the underground railroad, his explanation seemed plausible and was accepted. But his excuse for deserting them in Missouri on the last raid was not well received. They would not follow him again, and he knew that he would have to turn to the abolitionists for protection. Walker had made ineffectual attempts to arrest Quantrill all summer and fall, and the criminal had saved himself by flight and quick dodging. Dean had saved him more than once, and he fled to Stewart's fort upon more than one occasion. Long before the last raid into Missouri Quantrill was an outlaw, a skulking fugitive from justice, and he realized that it would be impossible for him to remain much longer at Lawrence in any capacity. He lingered only to consummate the plans he had been developing all summer for his master-stroke, then he would cast his lot with the border-ruffians of Missouri and make a new deal and prey upon the people of Kansas exclusively. These were his plans, and he hoped they would materialize. His intention was to take some very prominent man to Missouri and

betray him to death in order that he might bound into promi-
nence and become a hero.   But he saw that this would be impossible when he fled to Dean's wagon-shop.   He gave up Captain
Stewart and went to work to get any one he could — and as
many as possible.

It was said that Quantrill had planned to assassinate a number of his associates at Lawrence, then flee to Missouri.   Failing
in this, he planned to take them to Missouri on a predatory foray
and there have them killed — the conception which finally developed into the Morgan Walker Raid.   There is some documentary
evidence to sustain this.[1]

Quantrill was well known to Dean.   Indeed, Dean says
Quantrill brought letters of introduction to him from people
living about Stanton and Osawatomie, so the acquaintance must
have dated from the arrival of Quantrill at Lawrence in the
spring of 1860.[2]

---

[1] In addition to the foregoing statement, the Kansas Historical Society has among its manuscripts seven different letters, in all about forty-
eight pages, from John M. Dean to Joseph Savage, dated Waukon, Allamakee county, Iowa, written during the year 1879.   Under date of June
8, 1879, in a four-page letter to Savage, is the following:

About that time, August, 1860, Ridenour & Baker's powder-house,
that stood on the bank of the river, was robbed by some one who lifted
one corner of the roof.   [Samuel A. Riggs, page 234, 7th volume, says he
prosecuted Quantrill, alias Hart, for this.]   In talking the thing over,
Quantrill said he knew where that powder was stored under a haystack
down at Jake McGee's, and the intention was to use it when the collision
came, and use it for the Southern interest, and that he (Quantrill) would
be only too glad to see the stack burned and the powder destroyed, and
would go with us any night and do the job.   Without telling him, we went
down there one night and inspected every stack, by taking steel ramrods to
muskets and probing through every stack, but found nothing.   The next day
Quantrill was in my shop talking about it, and I asked him many questions, and finally told him he was mistaken, for I had been there, searched
well, and found nothing.   He said he was not mistaken, had seen the powder
in its place of deposit, and would be only too glad to take me and the
boys there and prove the thing.   To end the controversy, I agreed to go
with him that night, and eight of us did get ready but did not go.   After
Walker's raid, I learned the fact that, if we had gone, few, if any, of us
would have escaped, for there was a heavy ambushing party waiting to
receive us, of which Quantrill was one. — *Kansas Historical Collections*,
Vol. VIII, p. 329.

[2] Dean came to Kansas from Iowa.   Little is known of him.   He had
a wagon-shop in Lawrence and was an earnest anti-slavery man of the impracticable and visionary type.   He was bombastic, theoretical, bigoted,

While Quantrill usually boarded at the hotel kept by Nathan Stone when in Lawrence, he lived for a time in the home of Dean. When Dean would question him concerning his associating with Jake Herd and the McGees, Quantrill would declare that he was doing so in the capacity of detective — that he was trying to discover their plans that he might thwart them. The

---

self-important. He was shallow, and he believed he was accomplishing great things at Lawrence in 1860. He contributed nothing to the cause of freedom in Kansas, but he left the state and returned to Iowa honestly thinking that he had contrived and executed much of the work of saving Kansas. Dean was a braggart and a boaster, and he was an arrant coward. A number of his labored, heavy, windy, ridiculous letters are in the Collection of the author. In one of them he asserts that Governor Claiborne F. Jackson, of Missouri, had offered a reward of $5,000 in gold for his head — something wholly improbable. But where he had knowledge of a matter his statements bear the stamp of truth, and I regard his letters as good authority, though they are embellished with fanaticism and egotism. There is, also, in the Collection of the author a paper entitled, ''John Dean's Statement to W. W. Scott of Canal Dover in Reply to Interrogatories,'' typewritten from an original now in the library of the Kansas Historical Society. In this paper Dean says:

I first met William C. Quantrill in Lawrence in the early spring of 1860. He was introduced to me by one Ingersoll, a lawyer. My interview with him in Ingersoll's office was of about two hour's duration. He showed me many recommends, etc.; said he had been teaching school all the past winter in Lykins county; said he had often heard of me as a strong anti-slavery man that was running off slaves from Missouri, and wanted to unite himself with me in that business and do all he could to help along the cause.

My first impression of Quantrill under those conditions was not favorable, and I said so to him at the time. Still he insisted upon proving himself ''by work'' true to the anti-slavery cause.

He made Lawrence, Kansas, his ''headquarters'' from early spring of 1860 until November of same year, having no particular legitimate business and doing nothing but mixing and meddling with the slavery question upon both sides. When asked why he associated so much with the other side, his reply was, to learn their secrets. He was continually trying to complete some ''plot'' that would ''work all right.''

While in Lawrence he was a very frequent visitor to my workshop, and was persistent in his efforts to gain my confidence and knowledge of my plans and doings.

In a letter to W. W. Scott, dated Waukon, Allamakee county, Iowa, Jan. 26, 1879, now in the Collection of the author, Dean says:

I met *Quantrell* as a *now* known spie and *assassin*, working in connection with *many others* for *reward of Earth*. He was a *sensitive, falsely polerized*, or polerized to *Evil* Your description of him was fair but not positively correct or sharply drawn. He was some *taller* not less than 5-10 we have stood back to back & compared. I am 5-10½ strong and he

rôle of detective was a favorite one with Quantrill. He made it hide his participation in many crimes.

There are of record few incidents in which Dean and Quantrill were associated. Dean says (in a letter) that he knew of but one raid which Quantrill made into Missouri — the Morgan Walker Raid. This shows how little Dean really knew of Quantrill's actions. But Dean and Quantrill acted together in the Allen Pinks affair.

Allen Pinks was a free negro who came to Missouri from Pittsburg, Pa. He was a mulatto of less than one-half negro blood, his grandmother having been, as he claimed, a German woman. He was a barber and a cook on a steamboat in 1859. He was discharged at St. Joseph, and, in company with some

---

less than ½ inch shorter. I never knew of his having a *picture* taken his eyes were *uncommonly large* and *full.* he was quite *talkative* at times. Very *pleasant* as a studied rule, laughing & joking, not a loud boisterous laugh, but a rolling, rippling, quiet laugh. He was *acting* the spie in his connection with me and of course much of his seeming character was ''put on.''

There was a reward of $5000. in gold on my life at that time, offered by Gov Clabe Jackson of Mo. for I was doing all I could then on the Under ground R R. or freeing slaves. *he bought* his introduction to me through one professed rabid Anti slavery Lawyer by the name of Ingersoll at the time showing me letters & recommends from men then residing in Lykins Co. I will say to you that he *never* had *my* full confidence. I was always on my guard and many of his *plots* misscarried in consequence. What time he was spending around Lawrence was in *one* way active he was very temperate as I now remember, but did at last, or about 1861 begin to have his little times of a drink or two, did not use tobacco in any way as I remember, but was given to the worship of women somewhat. his time was spent much with those lawless and reckless neer do *wells* that abound in such times and places. When asked *why* he *did* associate with such characters, he claimed to be spieing *their* plans, with the intention of doing good and was often telling of some scheme of theirs to kidnap colored people to sell again, and in the carrying out of one of these plots he got himself and his pro-slavery friends indicted by the Grand jury of Lawrence and I escaped the snair that was laid in the plot.

In a letter to Samuel Walker, dated Waukon, Allamakee county, Iowa, July 3, 1879, now in the Collection of the author, Dean says of Quantrill:

Quantrells occupation while living at and near Lawrence, was that of a ''spie'' or detective in the interests of Slavery, and it may possibly be of the then Gov't. One of the Coppic boys that was at ''Harpers Ferry'' with old John Brown, was in ''Kansas'', and some with me about that time, and the U. S. Gov't was looking for *him*. After the mask had been removed and the light of *truth* let in to those heretofore uncertain matters, there could be no other conclusion than that Quantrell was acting the part of detective or spie in the pay or interests of the South, and put his time in in the *best* way to ''make'', not always governed in his actions by the plumb line of ''right''.

white man, he set out to walk to Leavenworth, but was appre-
hended at the Rialto Ferry and carried to Platte City, Mo.,
and cast into jail. He finally made his escape and went to
Lawrence.[3]

---

[3] Dr. John Doy found Allen Pinks in jail at Platte City and left this
of record concerning him, in Chapter XII of his little book:

He was quite a light colored mulatto, of about twenty years of age,
born at Pittsburg, in Pennsylvania; his grandmother being a German woman, as he informed me. He had been cook and head waiter on board of
steamboats on the Mississippi and Missouri Rivers, and had last been paid
off at St. Joseph, Missouri. From there he started for Leavenworth, walking down the Missouri bank of the river with a white man, who had been
on board the steamboat with him. At the Rialto Ferry, he was stopped
by the Ferryman on suspicion of being a fugitive slave, and lodged in
Weston calaboose till he was transferred to Platte City jail.

Thinking his free papers were wearing out, he had left them with a
free colored wagon-builder at Independence, Missouri. As it was for the
interest of those concerned in detaining him, that he should not prove himself free, he could get no one to send to Independence, though only thirty
miles distant, and ascertain whether his assertions were true or false. . . .

To finish Pinks' story, I will state that, after my rescue from the
hands of the Missourians, expecting an attempt to recapture me, I was
fortified at Mr. Stearns' brick block, in the centre of Lawrence, for nearly
a month.

One morning about five o'clock, I was called by Mr. Stearns, who informed me that a rough-looking man, who said he was from Platte City, was
asking for Dr. Doy at the front door. I looked out from my upper window
and whom should I see but Allen Pinks. He was nearly naked, having
nothing on but shirt and trowsers, and those almost torn to pieces. When
let in, he accounted for his dilapidated appearance, by saying that he had
traveled a bee line from Platte City, and having been in somewhat of a
hurry, had not paid sufficient respect to the thorns and briers he met with.
He had swum the Missouri River above Leavenworth and come into
Lawrence through the Delaware Reserve — begged a passage over Kaw
River, and finally arrived in safety at the city of refuge.

We bound up and healed his cut and swollen legs and feet, and sent
to Pittsburg, Penn., for his free papers. They reached us 14th September,
1859, and were supported by the affidavits of Mr. Wm. McArthur and Dr.
F. G. Gallaher, of Pittsburg, who had known Pinks from birth. When they
came, I said to him, "Pinks, I've got something for you."

"What is it, doctor!"

"Your free papers."

"Oh!"

"You don't seem to care much: aren't you glad?"

"Why should I be? What good will they do me? Haven't we seen
plenty of free papers torn up and burnt in Platte City jail?"

And Pinks was right. A colored man's free papers are not worth one
red cent to him in the border towns of Missouri, even if he carries them
with him and has them registered in every town on the river in which he
works. . . . Free-born men are kidnapped and sold into hopeless slavery.

Allen Pinks is now employed in the Johnson House at Lawrence, is
considered one of the best and steadiest hands there, but says he had had
sufficient experience of the blessings of freedom for colored men in this

There was a kidnapper living in Lawrence by the name of Bob Wilson. Wilson was operating with Dean, Stewart, and others having in charge the underground railroad, though like Quantrill, he had the full confidence of Jake Herd and the McGees and often joined them in kidnapping forays. It is a strange thing that most of the ruffians and kidnappers living in Kansas would join the underground railroad agents in raids into Missouri to get slaves for freedom, but often they would kidnap these same slaves after they had assisted in bringing them into Kansas, then return them to their owners for the reward or sell them again into slavery.

Allen Pinks came finally to turn against his own people. This was probably at the instance of Wilson and Quantrill who used him in their business of kidnapping. Pinks began to act as a decoy to run free negroes and fugitive slaves into the clutches of Quantrill, Jake Herd, and Wilson. The real abolitionists, such as Stewart and Dean, when they were satisfied that Pinks had turned traitor to them and to the negro people, decided that he must be put to death. Quantrill and Wilson were assigned to the work of killing him. These worthies saw rank waste in murdering him, when the same end might be accomplished by kidnapping him and selling him into slavery. They decided to kidnap Pinks and carry him to some slave market. Pinks was then running a barber-shop in Lawrence. Wilson lived about where the present Santa Fé passenger station is now located. That part of Lawrence was then covered with a thick growth of hazel brush and tangled vines, through which were cut narrow lanes. Wilson lived in a small one-story frame house of two rooms. He went to Pinks and engaged him to go to his house to dress his wife's hair, pretending that she was sick, or had been sick, and was unable to attend to her hair.

Union, especially in the state of Missouri. That state did indeed, keep him for three months without any charge for rent or board, but as, if he had stayed one month more, he would have been sold at the auction block like a beast, he prefers not to try her hospitality again.

In the statement of Holland Wheeler, referred to before, it is stated that Allen Pinks was shot by an enraged mob of his own people at Leavenworth. He turned kidnapper himself, and caused many free negroes to be kidnapped and sold into slavery.

It took some persuasion to get Pinks to go, for he was guilty and scary. When Pinks went into the house, a hack or closed carriage drove up, two kidnappers alighted from it, and they went one of them to each of the doors of the room where Pinks was beginning work on Mrs. Wilson's hair. Pinks knew in a moment what was up, for he had devised traps for negroes himself. He ran into the next room, pursued by Wilson, and escaped from the house by a small window and got into the thickets of hazel brush. He was searched for but not found.

Dean was much chagrined when he found that Pinks was not murdered, as he supposed he would be by Quantrill and Wilson, and he may have entertained suspicions of their good faith in the matter. In any event, he decided to take no further chances; he determined to kill Pinks himself. It is claimed that Dean had been associated in some matters with Pinks for which he was liable to be prosecuted and wished him put out of the way at once, which was an additional motive for Dean's action. There was a public well in Lawrence, and one day when Pinks was drinking from the bucket on the curb of this well, Dean, from concealment, shot him in the back of the head with a small rifle. The thickness of the negro's skull saved his life. The rifle-ball glanced on the skull and ran around just under the skin and lodged in his forehead. Seeing that he had failed to kill Pinks, in the excitement Dean escaped and fled to Stewart's fort and acquainted Stewart with the facts in the case, and it was given out there that Dean had been in the fort nearly all day and was not in Lawrence when Pinks was shot.

Concerning the opinion held by some that Dean and Quantrill tried to kill Pinks to prevent him from appearing against them as witness in kidnapping cases, it is enough to say that Quantrill did not wish to kill him, but to kidnap him and sell him, while Dean would not have taken any part in a kidnapping. In his fanaticism for abolitionism he could have killed Pinks for being a traitor to the negro people and the holy cause, but there is no evidence whatever that Dean was a kidnapper. He was a true abolitionist and an enthusiastic agent of the underground railroad.

Dean was afterward, at his own solicitation, arrested and

thrown into jail at Lawrence for the attempt to murder Pinks.

There were many other incidents in the life of Quantrill at Lawrence as Charley Hart of the same nature as those set out herein. But the details are very difficult to secure and verify. Enough has been shown to reveal his true character. The climax of his criminal career in Kansas was reached in December, 1860, in the Morgan Walker raid.[4]

---

[4] Among the newspaper clippings in the Collection of the author, relating to Quantrill and his career, is one from the *Kansas City Journal*, written by the Lawrence correspondent of that paper. Unfortunately, the date of the publication of this article is lost. It, however, gives the facts in the matter of the residence of Quantrill at Lawrence and his relations to the people there during the time, and it is given here:

Quantrell first came to Lawrence in 1858 and remained until 1861, and from the time he came till he left he boarded at what was then the Whitney House, kept by Mr. Stone, now known as the Derfee House. Mr. Stone, the proprietor, and Quantrell became fast friends and were together a good deal. During his stay here he was treated with kindness by the citizens, who never at any time offered him any violence, although it was a notorious fact that, together with two or three others, he was in the habit of going to some slave-holding state to steal slaves, which were brought to this county and kept at a rendezvous at a place near where the poor farm is now located. When the owners of the stolen slaves would offer rewards for their return, Quantrell and his associates would take them back and secure the rewards. . . . It was not till January of 1861 that he took his departure. In that month the grand jury had been having a session at Lecompton, and among other indictments had found a true bill against Quantrell for stealing horses from the Kickapoo Indians. Stone, his friend, of the Whitney House, was a member of the grand jury which found the bill against him. Col. Walker was United States Marshal at the time, and the warrants for the arrest of Quantrell were placed in his hands. Old man Stone told Quantrell that warrants were out for his arrest, and the latter prepared himself to make resistance. He went into Duncan's hardware store, where he procured a couple of pistols and loaded them, in anticipation of an attempt to arrest him. He appeared to be greatly excited, and stepping out to the edge of the sidewalk, with both pistols drawn, he swore several good round oaths that he would not be taken. Col. Walker at that time was not a man to be easily intimidated, so, in company with a little man named Geo. Earle, he approached Quantrell to serve his warrants. The latter, not appearing to relish a fight as much as one would have supposed from his violence, turned and incontinently fled, without firing a shot. Walker and Earle followed close after, firing several shots, but missing him, till at last he ran into a wagon shop kept by John Deane, on what is now a vacant lot next to Apitz's harness shop. Deane was also a friend of his, and therefore shut the door and locked it in the marshal's face. It was broken down, however, but not before Quantrell had had time to escape from the back door. Search was diligently made at the Whitney House, but to no purpose, and it was afterwards learned that he had been secreted in a brick house not far from there, where he also had friends. The remaining facts of his departure were learned from a letter written by Deane to Col. Walker after several years had passed. The next night after the circumstances related above had transpired, old Stone furnished a wagon, and Deane and four other young men went along with Quantrell to pilot and protect him through the state and over the line into Missouri. The next evening they camped in the woods near Independence, worn and hungry, with their long day's ride. Here it was decided that Quantrell should go to the house of Judge Walker, which was in the neighborhood, and steal some eggs for supper. Instead of doing this he went to Judge Walker and others, relating the pretended robberies which these men had committed, and offering to betray their hiding place. In this act the devil in his nature cropped out with greater distinctness than ever before. With the full knowledge of the hardships which these young men had undergone with the sole purpose of befriending him, he led a posse of men upon them, and with his own hands blew out the brains of two who had never done him aught but kindness. Two others were killed by the posse, but Deane, though shot in the heel, managed to escape, though not till he had been an eye witness of the villainous murder by Quantrell of his two friends. This is the true story of his departure from Lawrence. Deane afterwards returned to Lawrence, where he was immediately arrested by Col. Walker for assisting Quantrell to escape, and was confined in the jail here until the war broke out in earnest, when he was, together with the other inmates of the jail, enlisted in Col. Walker's company.

Quantrell was regarded by all who knew him while in Lawrence as a consummate coward and perfectly unprincipled. He never looked a man square in the eye, nearly always going with his eyes bent toward the ground, and always lowering his head when he saw any one look him in the face. The statement that he raided Lawrence because his brother was killed here, or that he was mistreated by the citizens, bears not a word of truth. No brother of his ever lived here or in the state. On the morning he arrived on his errand of death one of his first inquiries was: "Where does Col. Sam Walker live?" His motive for his raid through Kansas was simply plunder, with perhaps some personal spite.

The details of the trip to Morgan Walker's are not properly set out in this article. Old man Stone did furnish Deane with a wagon to drive to the house of Walker in Jackson county, but William Partridge had taken his wagon and carried the men of the party to Osawatomie, from which point it was intended to go into the Cherokee Nation and bring out some slaves to be taken to Canada over the underground railroad. At Osawatomie the Cherokee trip was abandoned, largely through the influence of Captain Ely Snyder, and then the trip to Jackson county to rob Walker was planned by Quantrill. Some of the party would not go on the Walker trip, and it was necessary to rearrange all the plans of the expedition. As Partridge had gone away with his wagon and none could be had at Osawatomie, Captain Snyder refusing to furnish his, Deane returned to Lawrence and secured Stone's wagon and drove it to the Walker farm to meet and aid Quantrill and the others to get away with the slaves. The whole story will be found in the following chapters.

CHAPTER IX

IT IS necessary to introduce the characters of this fatal expedition in detail. They were principally members of a settlement of Quakers from Springdale, Iowa, at Pardee, in Atchison county, Kansas.[1]

Charles Ball was born at Salem, Ohio, in 1837. He moved with his parents to Springdale, Iowa, in 1852. The family was poor and suffered the hardships and privations common to a new

Charles Ball

country. Ball attended the common schools, and for a time he was at Penn College, at Oskaloosa, Iowa. There, in addition to his other work, he studied drawing, in which he made considerable progress. He moved with his parents to Kansas in 1857. His sister says he was the favorite of the family, affectionate and faithful. His parents were Quakers, and he was a birthright member of the Quaker church. At Pardee, under the powerful ministry of Rev. Pardee Butler, he united with the Christian church. He was a first cousin to the Coppoc brothers who went to Harper's Ferry with John Brown. Ball was an associate of John Dean and made raids into Missouri to liberate

---

[1] Pardee is situated on the southwest quarter of Section 34, Township 6, Range 19, Atchison county. It was named for Pardee Butler, the famous Free-State Christian minister who was mobbed and set adrift on the Missouri at Atchison by the border-ruffians. He lived at Pardee. For an account of him and the prominent part he bore in the territorial days, see *Personal Recollections of Pardee Butler*, Cincinnati, 1889.

slaves for transportation over the underground railroad. It was through Dean that he became acquainted with Quantrill.[2]

Chalkley T. Lipsey was the son of John and Ann Lipsey. He was born at Mt. Pleasant, Jefferson county, Ohio, in 1838. His parents were Quakers, and he had a birthright membership in the Quaker church. In 1844 his parents moved to Columbia county, Ohio. He was educated at the Quaker school at Middle-

Chalkley T. Lipsey

ton and at a college at Mt. Union, Ohio. He attended college but two years. While at Mt. Union he united with the Methodist church. His sister Anna had married A. L. Taylor, who moved with his family to Atchison county, Kansas, in the spring of 1857, settling on a claim one and three-fourths miles southwest of the village of Pardee, on the road leading from Atchison to Topeka by way of Grasshopper Falls. In the summer of 1857 Lipsey went to Kansas, stopping there with his sister. There he united with the Christian church of which Rev. Pardee Butler was pastor. He worked on the farm and taught a school at Pardee. In 1858 he started with a freighting train across the Plains, but became ill and was compelled to return home. In the spring of 1860 he went in company with two brothers named Smith to Pike's Peak to dig gold. This trip was a failure so far as securing gold was concerned, and he and another Pike's Peaker walked back to Atchison county. They were almost famished, had suffered much from cold, being compelled to travel at night to avoid freezing. After his return he went west on a buffalo hunt to the country beyond the Blue river. And when he returned, he went on the fatal raid to Morgan Walker's. He seems never to have been previously in any raid into Missouri to liberate slaves. His sisters say he was never out of Kansas after his arrival in the Territory, except on the Pike's

---

[2] Statement of Rev. J. J. Lutz and letters of R. L. Harris to Lutz now in the Collection of the author. Also article by Lutz in *Midland Monthly*, Des Moines, Iowa, June, 1897.

Peak trip, until he went on the fatal raid with Quantrill. And they did not know of his having lived in the cabin with Harris, Morrison, Ball, and Southwick, though he may have done so. He may have gone to Iowa with a cargo of slaves, but the probability is that he did not do so. His sympathy was with the slaves, and he aided those who passed through Pardee or were assisted to reach that place. There is no evidence that he ever saw Quantrill until he met him to go on the raid which ended at Morgan Walker's. It is not known that he previously knew John Dean, though Dean says Morrison, Ball, and Lipsey were *his* men.[3]

Edwin S. Morrison was born April 16, 1839. His birthplace was either Rutland county, Vermont, or Erie county, New York. His ancestors went from Aberdeen, Scotland, to Londonderry, Ireland, and from thence to Londonderry, N. H. From that point his great-grandfather moved to Rutland county, Vermont, from which place his father moved to Erie county, New York, where it is probable that his son was born. In 1853 the family moved to Springdale, Iowa. He was a birthright member of the Quaker church, his ancestors having been Quakers for generations. He had a common-school education and was industrious, sturdy, faithful, quiet, and honest. He came to Kansas in 1859 in company with his cousin, Albert Southwick, Albert Negus, and his wife Martha. Mrs. Negus was the daughter of Benjamin Ball and sister to Charles Ball. Morrison and Southwick were carpenters, and they built a dwelling for Negus, on his claim, one mile south of Pardee, Atchison county.[4]

Albert Southwick was born in Ohio in 1837. His parents were Quakers, and they moved to Springdale, Iowa, about the year 1852. He came to Kansas with his cousin, Edwin S. Morrison, in the company of Albert Negus, early in 1859. They all settled near Pardee. Southwick started on the raid which ended at Morgan Walker's, but at Osawatomie he was persuaded to

---

3 Letters of R. Anna Taylor and Mrs. Charles L. Trueblood to Rev. J. J. Lutz, dated at Springdale, Iowa, in 1897, now in the Collection of the author. Also article in *Midland Monthly*, by Lutz, June, 1897.

4 Letters of D. B. Morrison, Springdale, Iowa, 1897, to Rev. J. J. Lutz, now in the Collection of the author. Also article by Lutz in the *Midland Monthly*, Des Moines, Iowa, June, 1897.

abandon it, and Elias Snyder believes that he remained there

Albert Southwick

with Captain Ely Snyder until it was known that Quantrill had betrayed his companions to death. He afterward said that he had been at Walker's in the raid, and that he returned there in the capacity of spy to get the particulars of the tragedy. There is little probability that he ever went back to Walker's. It is possible, and even probable, that he slipped away from Snyder to go with Dean in the wagon to aid Quantrill at Morgan Walker's farm. He seems to have been of very limited intelligence and somewhat unbalanced. He served in the 10th Kansas during the Civil War, after which he lived in Salina, Kansas, where he was in the coal business. He moved to Kansas City, Mo., and there died about the year 1893. His statements concerning the Walker raid are incoherent and conflicting.[5]

Ransom L. Harris was born in Addison county, Vermont, in 1842. His parents were Quakers, and they moved to Springdale, Iowa, in 1852. He had a common-school education. Harris says he came to Kansas in March, 1859, for the purpose of liberating slaves to go out over the underground railroad. He settled at Pardee. In Iowa he had known Ball, Morrison, and others who engaged in this business, but became acquainted with Lipsey in Kansas. He was in the 10th Kansas, and in May, 1863, General James H. Lane made him first lieutenant in the First Colored regiment. He was wounded at the battle at Poison Springs, and was discharged for disability. Returning to Iowa, he became a physician.[6]

---

[5] Letters of R. Anna Taylor and Mrs. Charles L. Trueblood to Rev. J. J. Lutz, now in the Collection of the author. Also article by Lutz in the *Midland Monthly*, Des Moines, Iowa, June, 1897.

There is a long statement made by the sisters, Taylor and Trueblood, of what Southwick told them of the raid; this statement is in the Collection of the author.

[6] Letters of R. L. Harris to Rev. J. J. Lutz, dated in 1897, at Audubon, Iowa, now in the Collection of the author. Also the article of Lutz in

In Springdale, Iowa, Charles Ball, Morrison, Lipsey, Southwick, and others were members of a secret lodge which had been
organized to forward the freedom of slaves. In the lodge the
whole subject of operating the underground railroad was constantly under discussion. The members of this lodge were able
to maintain themselves in a high degree of excitement by attending the meetings of another lodge, debating society, or "Congress." In the winter of 1857-58 John Brown stationed his men
at Springdale. He directed that they form a "Congress" in
which to discuss all features of the slavery question. In this
body the whole slave-system, its actions, the attitude of all parties toward it, its probable fate, were discussed with great earn-
estness and considerable eloquence by John Brown's men. Some
of the citizens joined in the debates, and when John Brown was
at Springdale he was always present at the meetings and took
part in the discussions. Stevens, Kagi, Realf, and others were
splendid speakers, and they kept the enthusiasm of the young
men at white heat. This was the real cause of their moving to
Kansas and their settlement at Pardee.[7]

the *Midland Monthly*. Lutz submitted a long list of questions to Harris
concerning the Walker raid, and these were answered by Harris. Questions and answers are now in the Collection of the author. The document
contains conflicting statements and assertions which are at variance from
known facts. Harris says Southwick was in the Morgan Walker raid.

[7] It will be remembered that in the winter of -57 & 8, John Brown and
his men were in rendezvous in Springdale, or near this village. Among
these men were Realf, Cook, Kagi. These three were gifted men with high
attainments and acquirements, and among these were grand oratorical
powers. We had at that time what we termed a mock Legislature, where
all most vital questions of the day were discussed. Among which were the
Mo. Compromise; the fugitive slave laws; the chief Judge Taney decision;
and the outrages perpetrated on the free state men in bleeding Kansas, &c,
&c. These three men became members and took an active part in the debates. The two first were brilliant men and could hold a crowded house
almost spell-bound. They were just from bleeding Kansas and were no
doubt justly inflamed against the Missourians for dreadful outrages perpetrated on the free state men of Kansas. Kagi, though not so brilliant
as the others was in my humble opinion the man of the greatest mental
depth and breadth of all the party, in fact these three men were all the
mental superiors of Old John Brown himself. John Brown impressed me
as a sturdy, honest man with the courage of conviction and made of the
same stuff that martyrs are made of. However these boys listened to
these debates, and the tales of horror related by them of bleeding Kansas,
as they also read of them in the daily papers as they appeared in flaming
headlines. And there and then I make no doubt the lattent fires of their

Immediately upon their arrival in Kansas, Ball, Morrison, and Southwick organized a secret lodge to arrange for the transportation of rescued or escaped slaves over the underground railroad.[8] They lived in a little log cabin, 12 by 14 feet, on the claim of Benjamin Ball, "keeping bach" there. They worked at farming or other occupations during the day, and at night they discussed the ways and means successfully to invade Missouri to secure slaves to take to Canada. There is little doubt that John Dean (who came to Kansas from Iowa) was well known to these young men, and, being blatant and insistent, impressed them as a great champion of human rights. One successful raid was made by them into Missouri under the leadership of Dean and Stewart. Some ten or twelve slaves were secured, and these were delivered over to the "underground" at Springdale, where some of them live to this day — others being taken on to Canada. This raid was made in the summer of 1860, but is not identified, and it is not known from what part of Missouri the slaves were taken.[9]

Harris says that Quantrill visited the cabin where these boys lived — that he came there once during the summer (1860) but that he was absent at the time and did not see him. Mrs.

---

love for justice and humanity were kindled, and they determined to lend a helping hand to make Kansas a free state. I think that most men on the higher planes of thought and feeling recognize at times a conflict between human enactments and that higher law of their being; and so reserve the right to owe their highest allegiance to the higher law, and suffer the human penalties. And I believe these to have been in the main the thoughts and feelings that actuated these young men. — *From letter of D. B. Morrison to Rev. J. J. Lutz, Springdale, Iowa, April 3, 1897*, now in the Collection of the author.

8 Statement of R. L. Harris in a letter to Rev. J. J. Lutz, dated Audubon, Iowa, March 3, 1897, now in the Collection of the author.

9 Statement of Rev. J. J. Lutz now in the Collection of the author. Lutz obtained his information from the family of Ball, which he visited for that purpose. In the list of questions and answers Harris had this raid confused with that to Morgan Walker's, in all probability. The Morrisons question the presence of Harris at the Pardee settlement of Springdale Quakers. But he was there, no doubt. His dates are wholly unreliable and some of his statements are wild, but he pretty well describes the preparations made for the Walker raid, though he has it in May, 1857 — about the time in 1860 that the first raid was made and in which the slaves were secured that were taken to Springdale.

11

Taylor says her brother, Lipsey, spoke of Charley Hart. He must have visited the cabin frequently during the summer of 1860, but the first acquaintance with him was doubtless at Lawrence through Dean. Southwick says it was at Lawrence.[10]

It was necessary for Quantrill to get out of Kansas quickly. He had made up his mind to do so. It was his desire to make a master-stroke in getting out, but the caution of Stewart made it impossible to pilot him to his death at Morgan Walker's. This Walker raid had cost Quantrill much time and pains; he had set his heart on it. It seemed that he must give it up and escape to Missouri in his favorite rôle of detective. But the devil cares for his own, and the fates threw into bloody hands the active anti-slavery members of the Springdale Quaker settlement at Pardee. An expedition for slaves was planned, and its failure gave Quantrill the opportunity he had so long desired and so persistently waited for.

The expedition was planned at Lawrence. Three Cherokee refugee slaves were at Springdale, Iowa. It is not known that they had ever been sent on to Canada, but it is believed they had been, and that they had returned from Canada to Springdale. In any event, they came from Springdale to the Quaker settlement at Pardee. Their object was to secure assistance to enable their relatives who were still slaves in the Cherokee Nation to escape and return with them to Springdale or to Canada. Their appeal to the Quakers at Pardee met with a ready response, and Ball, Morrison, Southwick, and Lipsey went with them to Lawrence. These negroes were William Thompson, John Thompson, his brother, and John Martin.[11]

---

[10] Statement given to Rev. J. J. Lutz by Mrs. Martha Negus, now in the Collection of the author.

[11] These negroes remained at Osawatomie. When the Civil War began the Thompsons went into the Union army at Fort Scott as teamsters. They served until the war closed, part of the time as enlisted men. Martin lived at Osawatomie until about 1890, when he moved to Garnett, where he afterwards died. This information was given me by Elias Snyder, who lives near Osawatomie, and who is the son of Captain Ely Snyder, and who knows the facts. The author visited Mr. Snyder on the 18th day of October, 1907, and secured from him a long statement covering many Territorial subjects. These Cherokee refugees are mentioned also in a

The expedition was carefully planned. It was to go into the Cherokee Nation and rescue and bring out the relatives of Martin and the Thompsons and as many other slaves as possible. Men enough for the purpose could not be secured at Lawrence because of the great distance to be traveled and the danger to be incurred in operating so far away from home. It was supposed that additional men could be had at Osawatomie; the first stage of the invasion ended there with the effort to enlist the men necessary to its success. Those who arrived at Osawatomie from Lawrence were Quantrill, Dean, Morrison, Ball, Southwick, Lipsey, John S. Jones who went under the name of "Mr. Baker,"[12] and the three Cherokee negroes.

Quantrill preceded the others of the party, arriving at Osawatomie some days before they appeared. He registered as Charley Hart at the old hotel kept by Gears, but he was so well known there that he deceived no one. It is remembered that at Osawatomie he was sometimes called "Ed Hart," and he made hs headquarters at the postoffice, where there was a pro-slavery postmaster.

After Quantrill had been gone some days the others of the

letter of Captain Ely Snyder to G. A. Colton, dated Osawatomie, Feb. 14, 1883, now in the Collection of the author.

There is some reason to believe that Quantrill was in hiding when the Pardee party arrived at Lawrence on the way to the Cherokee Nation, and that John Dean, knowing his whereabouts, sent him an invitation to join the party. The following extract from the *Lawrence Tribune* supports this view:

Early the next morning — before the people were astir — Quantrell was furnished with a day's provisions and a bottle of whisky, and got safely out of town to a snug place in the timber, two or three miles northwest from Lawrence, where he kindled a small fire and spent the day alone. That night a party of five young men, all reckless and enthusiastic Abolitionists, took Quantrell into a wagon and started for Missouri. Their object was doubtless to help off some slaves and send them on to freedom in Canada, via Lawrence and Nebraska.

This was the day after Sheriff Walker had attempted to arrest Quantrill and he ran into Dean's shop.

[12] When the Civil War began Jones enlisted in the 5th Kansas under his correct name. He enlisted as a private in Company H, October 13, 1861; discharged at Fort Leavenworth, Dec. 11, 1864. He re-enlisted in the Hancock Corps. Authority: statement of Elias Snyder and the report of the adjutant general of Kansas.

party left Lawrence for Osawatomie, though they said they
were going on a buffalo hunt. They employed William Partridge to haul them in his wagon. They traveled west from
Lawrence two days, then turned south, then went east to Osawatomie. This roundabout course was selected by Dean, who
was the leader of the party, and who doubtless supposed he was
displaying great generalship and fooling people.[13] Still further
to show his genius as slave-stealer, Dean would not recognize
Quantrill when he first arrived with the wagon-party, nor allow
the others of the party to do so, pretending never to have seen
Quantrill before, meeting him as an entire stranegr and gradually working up an acquaintance with him. Dean was known to
Captain Ely Snyder, and after his arrival he laid his whole
scheme before Snyder and others and requested their aid.
Snyder immediately condemned the expedition as impracticable
and refused to have anything to do with it. Dean then took
Quantrill to Snyder, saying that Quantrill believed the invasion
of the Cherokee Nation feasible and had consented to be one of
the invaders. Snyder quickly told Dean that he knew Quantrill

---

[13] I left Lawrence in November, 1860, to build houses on a government contract for the Sac and Fox Indians on the Marais des Cygnes, near
where Quenemo is now situated. After I had been there a few weeks I
was aroused one night by some one calling my name aloud. On going out
I found the caller to be William Partridge, of Lawrence, whom I knew
to be a reliable abolitionist. He wanted to know if he could stop with me
a few days. I told him he could. After the team was cared for, I inquired how long since he left Lawrence, etc. He replied he had been out
some days, and volunteered the statement, ''I would hear something drop
soon,'' and went on to say that Quantrill and John Dean hired him with
his team to take them, Charles Ball, and a man that worked for Dean, and
another man or two I did not know, out on the plains for a buffalo hunt,
and that after traveling west a couple of days they turned south, and
later on, east, and finally turned up in southern Kansas, where there were
known to live some ''reliable parties.'' At this place there was a conference of two or three days, and one or two of the original parties dropped
out and their places filled by others from that community; and he added:
''I delivered my load where they said they wanted to stop, and I pulled
out. I guess they will find transportation home all right.'' I heard
nothing further from the expedition for probably ten days, when the word
came, ''All killed but Dean, and he wounded and missing.'' Dean, however, turned up after a few days with a bullet in his foot, and was lodged
in the Douglas county Jail on some trivial charge made by his friends,
who evidently considered a Kansas jail preferable to one in Missouri.
Soon after this the war commenced, and we held no further communication
with Missouri, and Dean was released. — *H. S. Clarke*, in the Seventh
Volume, *Kansas Historical Collections*, pp. 220, 221.

well and did not trust him at all — that Quantrill's reputation at Osawatomie was bad. Dean was very reluctant to believe this, but Jones (Baker), Southwick, and the negroes were soon convinced and refused to have anything further to do with Quantrill. The Cherokee invasion was abandoned.

When the expedition into the Cherokee Nation was given up Quantrill began to talk of the Morgan Walker raid. He had made up his mind to leave Kansas on that trip. He saw an opportunity to kidnap three lusty refugees and sell them in Missouri. He made extraordinary efforts to induce the negroes to go to Walker's, but they grew more and more suspicious of him and his intentions. He told them that they would be of great benefit in the raid, as they would prevail on Walker's negroes to leave him in a body and to fight if they were pursued.[14]

---

[14] Quantrill had made raids into Missouri from Osawatomie in company with Jennison and others. He borrowed a pistol once of a party who could not go. This pistol he refused to return, saying that he had not been given an equitable portion of the loot secured on the raid. He called himself Hart — sometimes "Ed" Hart and sometimes "Charley" Hart when at Osawatomie. Captain Snyder had been on raids into Missouri with him and had concluded that he was false — a traitor. These raids were into Cass and Bates counties in Missouri. When Quantrill went into Missouri alone he always reported on his return that he had been there in the capacity of a detective — spy. He always told the border-ruffians this same story when questioned as to his association with the Free-State men.

In the Collection of the author are a number of letters written by one W. L. Potter to W. W. Scott. Potter was a border-ruffian, a hanger-on about the offices of pro-slavery officials, often acting as deputy U. S. marshal, deputy sheriff, deputy jailer, deputy constable. In these letters he claimed to have been very intimate with Quantrill, calling him "Bill" Quantrill. Potter was a sort of irregular Confederate soldier — a sort of wandering pirate — roving about from one command to another. These letters are boastful, egotistical, inaccurate as to dates and incidents (they would suit the Robinson partisans of Kansas exactly, as they claim that John Brown was still destroying Missouri in 1861), and they are a dead match for those of Dean for involved construction and far surpassing Dean's in general rambling and complete failure to come to the point. There are streaks of facts in them, however, though mixed with much that, to say the least, is wholly untrue. They were written from Harrison, Ark., in 1895 and 1896. In one about December, 1896, he gives at great length and with many digressions an account of Quantrill's spying on the

Quantrill finally prevailed over Snyder. The raid to Morgan Walker's was determined upon, and hopes almost blasted were finally to be realized. True, he was to have no prominent Kansas characters with him to betray to death, but those he had were to him better than to have none at all to murder.[15]

Free-State men. Potter was living at Paola when the matters he describes occurred:

I will take time to make notes of every thing of importance, that I can remember concerning, the Brave & Gallant Quantrell.

There was no officer in the Trans Miss[iss]ippi Department during the War, that was admired & Honored by the Confederates as W C Quantrell was. . . .

It was in the fall of 1860 That a meeting was held up stairs of the Union Hotel in Paola Kan. I was there as well as every one, then Present by special invitation. None but those who were known to be opposed to the Jay Hawking carried on by Montgomery Jennison & Ossawatomie Brown, or John Brown & their followers, were admitted, or knew of our Meeting. The following citizens of Paola to my certain knowledge were Present some of whom are still living Dr W D Hoover now in Paola & Geo W. Miller Ex circuit Judge of Denver Colorado The rest of the members of that assembly are now Dead, except the writer Their names were Lawyer E. W. White Lawyer Robert White, Lawyer Massey Dr Taylor, Goodwin Taylor a Merchant, Allen T. Ward Merchant, Thomas Kelley, General Seth Clover Indian agent & Col Torrey I think was there & some one or two others that I do not remember — Wm C Quantrell was I introduced him to the citizens He stated to us that he was at Lawrence or Topeka Kansas in Nov 1860 . . . Quantrell said that he wanted to get Jennison in a Place where he could either capture or Lawfully kill him . . . Quantrell stated, at the meeting that the Jayhawkers, while in camp near Ossawatomi had contemplated a Raid on Paola, intending to rob the stores & the Town, and also contemplated the Robbing of the Kansas City, Paola & Fort Scott Stage with the money that was expected to be sent to Gen Clover, The agent for the Miami Indians some $30000

He sent word to Gen Clover to that Effect before the Payment was Made. a company of Infantry under Major Brook, from Leavenworth was sent to escort the money to Paola, & remained in Miami Co until after the Payment was made. I will say here that the Jay hawkers never made an attack on Paola, but then it was often threatened.

After the interview was over Quantrill espressed his willingness to answer any and all questions concerning his connections with Jennison

He also stated that the Jayhawkers, received $60.00 Per head for all the slaves they stole out of Missouri, & delivered to the agents of the Underground Rail Road company

Who forwarded them on to Canada.

[15] In the Collection of the author there is a letter written by Captain Ely Snyder to G. D. Colton, who lived then at Paola. The letter is dated at Osawatomie, Feb. 14, 1883, and says:

in the year 1860 some time in the month of Dec Late one Eve[n]ing 10 men and a two horses wageon with one man the o[w]ner of the Team w[h]ich would make 11 men Stopt at my house in Osawatomie ask me to Stay all Night I Told them that my House was Small that I co[u]ld not accommodate them thay said thay must Stay if thay had to Stay in the

barn they wair all Strangers to me at that time and I thought that thay
might not be on Eny good as thay was one Thousand dollars Reward for
me then in Masurie I had a em[p]ty house a short distance from mine
and give them the key and told them to go in that house w[h]ich thay
did thair was 7 white men and 3 black men besides the teamster w[h]ich
went away the next mor[n]ing the ten Stayed in the house but I seen
thay had Som[e] Object in v[i]ew but did not tell me what it was for
Som[e] days when thay told me that thay Started from Larrance with the
Intention of going toe the Cherekee Nation to bring out Some Slaves and
wanted me to take my team and wageon and go with them as thair Captain I decline and told them it was in the cold winter and it wo[u]ld
take a big sum of Money to Accomplish eny thing and I found out that
thay had Little Money So I perswaded them that thay had better Let
the Job out at presant they then perposed that thay wo[u]ld cut me
Some wood thay all went to wurk but Quantrill and he made his hed
quarters at the Post Office it was then proslavery post office and the plan
of the rade on Wa[l]ker was in my [k]nowing got up in the Post office
at Osawatomie and had it not been for myself perswadeing the 9 men
Quantrill wo[u]ld have got all the party in the Same boat as he did the
three that he persw[a]ded to go with him I went to the Timber wair
theas wair at work and got them all Together and told them that I
k[n]ew that Quantrill wo[u]ld get them in tro[u]ble if thay did go with
him John M. Dean, Albert Southwork and John Jones, William Thomson
John Thomson and John Martin the three Last names are the names of
the three black men thay wair Cherekeys fugitives thay wair Intelligent
black men and So wair all of the white men the Six names that I have
mentioned took my A[d]vice and did not go with Quantrill to Walkers
but the other three got very Indignant at me for thinking that Quantrell
wo[u]ld by Gilty of get[t]ing them in tro[u]ble the name[s] of the three
that wair kill[e]d at Walkers ones name was Charles Ball. the others
Last names I dont remember the thair anechiates wair Charles and Ed-
went and the three went from my House on the morning thay started for
Walkers and Quantrell started from the Post office I walked with them a
short distance and bid them good by and told them that I did not expect
to ever see them again thay went on and met with thair fate it may be
that I can get thair names in future but I will say that John M. Dean
was not at Walkers nun but Quantrell and the 3 that I have mentione[d]

It will be observed that Captain Snyder says that Quantrill came
to his house in the wagon of Partridge, but he is in error. His son, Elias
Snyder, says that Quantrill arrived some days ahead of the others. Captain Snyder also says that the men were all strangers to him when they
arrived in the wagon, but it is well known that both Quantrill and Dean
were well acquainted with Snyder and had been on raids into Missouri
with him. There was a kind of Freemasonry among the men who raided
into Missouri, and it extended to the end of life in many cases, and they
protected one another in all statements given to the public. And for this
reason Snyder says Dean was not at Walker's. And it is just possible that
Snyder did not know that Dean went to Walker's after he left Osawatomie.

On the matters touched on in the letter of Captain Ely Snyder the
text in this chapter follows the statements made by Elias Snyder to the
author at his house on October 18, 1907.

CHAPTER X

QUANTRILL AS CHARLEY HART, THE TRAITOR—
THE MORGAN WALKER RAID

THE men who went from Lawrence to Osawatomie to go into the Cherokee Nation were Quantrill, Dean, Ball, Morrison, Lipsey, Southwick, Jones (Baker), the Thompson brothers — William and John, and John Martin. Of these men, only Quantrill, Ball, Morrison, and Lipsey left Osawatomie to go to Morgan Walker's. The others followed the advice of Captain Snyder to have nothing to do with Quantrill — except Dean.[1]

The men carried for arms only knives and revolvers. Guns in their hands would have aroused suspicion in the country through which they were to pass and might have caused them serious trouble. Morrison left his Sharps's rifle with Elias Snyder.[2] They carried blankets and cooking utensils for use in camping in the woods on the journey. They walked, and they pretended to be on their way to work on the Missouri Pacific railroad, then being graded in Lafayette county, Mo.[3] There

Sharps Rifle carried by Morrison

---

[1] As said before, Southwick must have gone, at the solicitation of Dean, with the wagon which Dean procured and took to Walker's. It was possible for him to have absented himself from Osawatomie a day or two without the knowledge of the Snyders, and he must have done so.

[2] Elias Snyder presented this gun to the author in October, 1908. It is in good condition. It is No. 1113.

[3] In the letter of E. W. Robinson, former probate judge of Miami county, Kansas, to W. W. Scott, dated at Paola, Kansas, May 9, 1881, now in the Collection of the author, it is said:

I was well acquainted with Wm C. Quantrill who came to Kansas in the spring of 1857 with H. V. Beeson & family. I lived in the same neighborhood, at Stanton in this County from March 1857 — to Apr 1868, when I moved to Paola the Co. Seat.

I saw him several times during the time he was teaching School — in the winter of 1858. After his return from Salt Lake I met him in Lawrence, where he was known as ''Charley Hart'' and where I first learned from him, of his trip to Salt Lake. I saw him next while on his

were with Quantrill at the time only two men. Morrison, Ball,
and Lipsey left Osawatomie with him. Where was the third
man? Had he been sent back to Osawatomie secretly to find
Southwick and induce him to go to Walker's with Dean in the
wagon provided by Stone? He must have been, and he must
have succeeded in his mission.

And Dean. What of him? He left Osawatomie before
Quantrill and the Pardee Quakers left that place to go to Morgan Walker's. It is not to be believed that the Pardee Quakers
would have gone with Quantrill had Dean forbidden them.
Neither can we think they would have gone had not Dean assured them that he would meet and coöperate with them at the
critical moment. There was a wagon in waiting near the house
of Morgan Walker on the night of the attack. This wagon and
the team drawing it were taken there by John Dean, though he
says in his letters that he was not at Morgan Walker's.   The
wagon was furnished by Stone, proprietor of the hotel at which
Quantrill lived much of the time. Quantrill must have sent one
of his men to guide Dean to the proper locality. This course
must have been agreed on between Quantrill and Dean. Dean
did not arrive until after dark and after Quantrill had returned
to camp from Walker's house. He drove by the road and waited near the house while Quantrill and the others went across the
fields to Morgan Walker's house.[4]

---

way to Walkers in Jackson Co. Mo. There were with him then two young
men, who he said were going with him to get work on the Mo. Pacific
R. R., then building from Lexington to Kan. City. A few days later we
heard of the Walker Tragedy.

The statement of Judge Robinson that Quantrill taught school in
1858 is erroneous, as is shown by Quantrill's letters, published herein,
which see in chapter on his teaching in Kansas. The judge trusted to his
memory alone in fixing the date.

[4] This is the story which Dean told at Lawrence upon his return with
one of his heels shot away. He told only a few and told them for the
purpose of acquainting them with his reasons for wishing to be arrested
and thrown into jail for the attempted murder of Allen Pinks. Among
those he told of his presence at Walker's were Captain Stewart, Samuel
Walker, and H. S. Clarke. Mr. Clarke so informed the author on November
4, 1907, and he had given the author this information frequently before
that time. He had, in addition to the word of Dean, the statement of
M. J. Burlingame, who was at the time teaching school in the Morgan

The exact date of the attack on Walker's house is not fixed. It was in December, 1860, perhaps late in December. Nor is it certain as to the number of men who went to the house with Quantrill. Dean had not gone alone with the wagon. And it is possible that Quantrill did not know who came with Dean, as their arrival was but a few minutes before the party left the camp to go to the house. Walker's son speaks of Southwick as having been one of the party, and he could not have known that Quantrill had an associate of that name but from Quantrill himself.

Morgan Walker was a Kentuckian who settled near Blue Springs, Jackson county, Mo., in 1834. He was a man of affairs, and he owned nearly two thousand acres of fine land, upon which he lived. His house contained nine large rooms — five below and four in the second story. It was three miles northeast of Blue Springs and nearly seven miles southeast of Independence. He owned some thirty slaves and more than a hundred horses and mules, and he had a large sum in gold in his house. The house was about fifty feet in length and stood north and south, facing east, with a porch along the whole front. In the north end of the porch there was a small room where harness was stored, called the harness-room. The road ran north of the house, and the house was back from the road about a quarter of a mile. It was burned long since. Clustered back of the house were barns, cribs, and negro quarters.[5]

Morgan Walker

Walker district. Notwithstanding his denial, John Dean was at the house of Morgan Walker on the night of the raid.

The adjutant general's report, state of Kansas, shows that Albert Southwick, of Springdale, Iowa, enlisted in company C, Tenth Kansas regiment, October 28, 1861, and was mustered out August 20, 1864. The State Historical Society has a life-size picture of Southwick hanging on the wall, a gift from Eli H. Gregg, first sergeant company C, Tenth Kansas. Gregg was recruited by Barclay Coppoc, and on the way to Kansas when Coppoc was killed by the burning of the Platte river bridge. At least twice in John M. Dean's correspondence, Dean inquires, "Who is Southwick?" — *Kansas Historical Collections*, Vol. VIII, p. 330.

5 In the letter of Andrew J. Walker, son of Morgan Walker, to W. W.

THE MORGAN WALKER RAID

It is supposed that Quantrill and his men, or some of them, had been in camp in the vicinity of the Walker farm several days prior to the day they moved near the house. They must have talked with the slaves and have received satisfactory responses before venturing upon the final stage of the raid. It is certain that the attack was made the night after they got to the farm. Morgan Walker rode to Independence that day, and on the road he met Quantrill and his men. He either did not know Walker or pretended not to know him, for he inquired of him for Morgan Walker and the way to his house. Walker replied: "I am the man." Quantrill seems to have had no business to discuss, and he only asked of Walker if his sons were at home, which shows that he had some knowledge of the family. He probably knew Walker well, even if Walker did not know him.

When the Jayhawkers came within a mile of the house they camped in a thicket in a piece of woodland. Then Quantrill went to the house of Andrew J. Walker, son of Morgan Walker, about a quarter of a mile from the residence of the senior Walker, arriving there about eleven o'clock in the forenoon. He told Andrew J. Walker that some men were coming from Kansas that night to rob his father; that they were lying in wait in the brush and had sent him to reconnoiter the premises. He told all their plans and left it to Walker to take such action as he might deem proper. At the Morgan Walker home that day there were but Mrs. Walker, her daughter Nancy,

---

Scott, dated Lebeck, Mo., Nov. 1889, the house is described and a cut or rude drawing of it made. Says the letter: "The house stood north and south 5 large rooms below and four above porch on the east side about 50 feet in length the little room was in the north end the road was north of the house about a quarter of a mile from the house."

Morgan Walker was an old citizen of Jackson county — a veritable pioneer. He had settled there when the buffalo grazed on the prairies beyond Westport, and when in the soft sands along the inland streams there were wolf and moccasin tracks. Stalwart, hospitable, broad across the back, old-fashioned in his courtesies and his hospitalities, he fed the poor, helped the needy, prayed regularly to the good God, did right by his neighbors and his friends, and only swore occasionally at the Jayhawkers and the Abolitionists. His hands might have been rough and sunbrowned, but they were always open. None were ever turned away from his door hungry. Under the old roof of the homestead — no matter what the pressure was nor how large the demand had been — the last wayfarer got the same comfort as the first — and altogether they got the best. — *Noted Guerrillas, or the Warfare of the Border*, by Major John N. Edwards.

and the negro women. It was agreed that Quantrill should lead his companions to the house, aid in killing them, and then remain with Walker. Andrew J. Walker informed four of the neighbors — John Tatum, Lee Coger, D. C. Williams, and one whose name is now lost. They armed themselves with double-barreled shot guns heavily charged with buck-shot and repaired to the house of Morgan Walker. On the porch near the little room at the north end Mrs. Walker had her loom. Andrew J. Walker put three of his men in the little room, and he and the other one concealed themselves behind the loom. It was agreed that Quantrill and his men should go into the house to talk to Morgan Walker about taking away his slaves and other property, and that Quantrill should remain in the house. When the others came out to gather up the slaves they were to be fired on while they were yet on the porch in the light streaming through the door.

Morgan Walker came home from Independence about ten minutes before Quantrill and his victims arrived there. He was hastily acquainted with the posture of affairs. At first he could scarcely comprehend the situation. It was sudden and unexpected. He swore that all should be killed, Quantrill and the

Front View Walker House

others together, but with the aid of his wife, the son was able to bring him to acquiesce in the agreements which had been entered into. Quantrill and his men arrived about seven o'clock — at that season, long after darkness had set in. Morrison was left a guard on the porch. Dean and perhaps others were stationed in the yard near the porch. Quantrill had desired all to come into the house with him, but this the men would not agree to, and he, Lipsey, and Ball went into the house. After a brief greeting Ball said he might as well state their business at once, and then he told Walker that they had come to take his slaves to Kansas; that they would also take his horses and mules; that they would take what money there was in the house. Walker asked Ball if he had talked with the slaves and was told that the slaves had been consulted. Walker told him to go and get them, but that if any of them objected to going to Kansas they were to be left at home — that he did not see any good reason why those who did not wish to go should be compelled to leave him. He also believed that if his slaves were taken he should be allowed to retain his money and live-stock. Quantrill then told

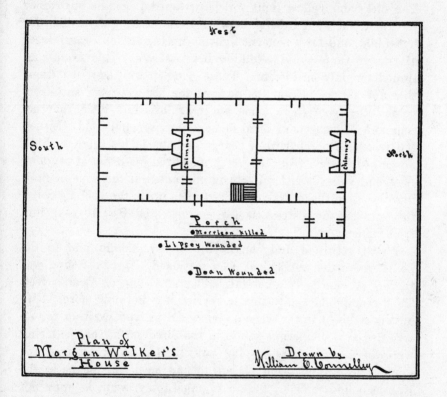

Ball to go out and gather up the slaves — that he would remain in the house and "take care of the old folks," intending that Ball should understand that he would guard Walker and his wife. As no other persons had been seen by the robbers, Ball must have believed there were no other persons at the house or about the farm. Quantrill remained with Walker and his family, and Ball and his companion opened the door and stepped out upon the porch.

The night had changed — outrider and precursor of doom. It was now intensely dark. Ghostly clouds scudded across the leaden sky. Dashes of rain and sleet beat upon the earth and rattled against the narrow panes and boarded walls of the old farmhouse. A moaning wind had risen and now sighed and wailed through the crevices and about the angles of the rambling homestead. A fitful roar came from the wind-shaken forest. The flickering yellow light which streamed from the open door fell upon the Jayhawkers, showing those along the yard-border but dimly, and for a moment lighting up the anxious, eager faces of two or three timid, skulking negro slaves. This scene continued for only an instant. Those lying in wait saw in it their time for action. From the door of the harness-room and from behind the loom there came an irregular, dull, dead roar accompanied by sheets of lurid flame. Morrison fell dead. Lipsey fell from the porch with a charge of balls in his thigh. Ball, unscathed, leaped from the porch and fired his pistol at random. A second volley was fired into the darkness in the hope of finding those on the outskirts. Then rose upon the sobbing wind the wild cry of distress as Lipsey entreated Ball to bear him from danger.

Ball returned and caught up Lipsey, taking him to the point where the wagon had been stationed. But no wagon was there. A charge of buckshot had struck one of Dean's feet. That redoubtable slave-stealer tarried for nothing more. He hastily hobbled to the wagon, clambered in, and, waiting for no one, fled at a lumbering gallop in the direction of the sheltering walls of Lawrence, oh so far away! Southwick pursued the panic-stricken and fleeing Dean, to find means of escape in the Kansas-bound vehicle. Ball, carrying Lipsey, went, he knew not whither. It was enough to know that he was leaving the house of Walker and the scene of black treachery. He arrived in a woods about a mile north of Walker's house, but not on the Walker farm. In a secluded thicket which he discovered there he stopped and passed the night with his wounded companion as best he could. No doubt he recalled with bitterness the warnings and parting prediction of Captain Ely Snyder which he had so foolishly scorned a few days before.

It does not appear that Walker or his neighbors made any effort to trail those whom they had not killed. They may have supposed all the survivors had escaped in the wagon. The night was wild, the robbers were defeated, and a precious rogue had been recruited for the slavery side — one destined to bring fire and sword and woe upon the land. The dead slave-stealer was stretched flat on his back on the floor of the harness-room. His prowess and ferocity were descanted upon by Quantrill in a way strangely at variance with the youthful look on the Quaker face of him who should now raid again nevermore. He had laid his life on the altar of human liberty, the victim of delusion, knavery, treachery, and nothing did he heed of the slanders of him he had counted friend but an hour ago.[6]

---

[6] The author has sought every source of information on what occurred at the house of Morgan Walker. He has interviewed many of the old citizens of Jackson county. The text is a faithful account of what could be obtained. Most of it is sustained by written evidence, the best of which is found in two letters from Andrew J. Walker to W. W. Scott, now in the Collection of the author, as are others of his letters. He moved from Jackson county to St. Clair county, Mo., his postoffice there having been Lebeck. He moved from that point to Texas, where he died some years since. Under date of February 3, 1883, he writes:

I think I know as much about Quantrill as any man living and am the only man living who can give his coming into Missouri and commencing the War. . . . There were only three men with Quantrill. I can't give the exact date when they came to my father's house, but it was about the middle of December, 1860. The men were all killed, none got away, their names were Charley Ball, Charley Southwick and I have forgotten the others name. My Mother and Father are both dead. Quantrill had a long neck, small Roman nose, rather slim face, blue eyes and never wore long hair. . . . The day they came my father was gone to Independence. Quantrill met him and asked him the way to Morgan Walker's. He told him he was the man. Quantrill then asked him if his sons were at home, he told him he guessed they were. He accordingly came to my house, I lived a quarter of a mile from my fathers and told me his story, that there were some men from Kansas coming to rob my father that night, that they were living in the brush and had sent him to reconnoiter the premises. He told me all their plans and left it to me to do as I pleased. I went and got four men each with a double barrel shot gun well loaded with buck shot. There was a long porch in front of the house with a little room at one end. My mother had a loom in the same end of the porch as this little room. I put three of my men in this little room and myself and one man got behind the loom and the understanding was to let the men go into the house My father got home about ten minutes before they came. Quantrill and two others went into the house and one man stood sentinel. Our understanding was to let them come and Ball told my father they had as well tell their business. They told my father they were going to take his slaves, he had thirty two slaves. They told him they would take his slaves, his horses, his mules and his money. There were about 100 horses and mules. My father asked Ball if he had talked with the negroes and whether they wanted to go or not. He said he had, he told him to go and get them then, but that if there were any that did not want to go to let them stay. Quantrill said he would take care of the old folks and they could go and get the negroes. They came out and we fired on them, one of my men fired too soon. One man was killed dead on the porch and another wounded in the thigh, Ball got away without a scratch. The night was very dark.

In his letter dated February 22, 1883, Walker says:

I had never met Quantrill before he made the raid on my fathers house. It was about eleven o'clock in the morning when Quantrill came to my house, and to my fathers house about seven o'clock at night. Southwick stood guard. We supposed they had made their escape.

Andrew J. Walker also made a statement at a reunion of Quantrill's men held at Blue Springs, May 11, 1888, which was published in the *Kansas City Journal* the following day. This statement does not agree exactly with his letters, but this may be the fault of the reporter. In the statement he says:

I first saw Quantrill in the latter part of November, 1860. He came upon the farm of my father, Morgan Walker, which consisted of 1,900 acres and was located three miles northeast of Blue Springs, one afternoon in that month. My father had 26 niggers, and 100 horses and mules; he also had about $2000 in the house. I was in the field shucking corn at the time. He told my father that he was with a party of three men who had come over from Kansas to rob us of our money, horses and mules, and run off our niggers. He said he would aid us in thwarting their design. We got several men together between that time and dark. I got down behind a loom, and my father, John Tatum, Lee Coger, and D. C. Williams were hidden in the harness room and other parts of the house. We had it all arranged that when the robbers came to the door a lighted candle was to be placed in one of the windows. That was the signal for the fun to begin. Quantrill, Charles Southwick, Charles Ball, and Lipsey came upon the porch. Quantrill stepped inside and said: "We have come to take your niggers with us to Kansas. We also want your hosses and mules and what money you have in the house." My father replied that if his niggers wanted to go to Kansas they were at liberty to do so, but he did not see any reason why those who did not want to go should be compelled to leave him, and he thought he ought to have his stock and money left him. The other three were standing outside the door, which was then shut; a candle was put in the window and the other lights turned out. We then opened fire on the three companions of Quantrill. Lipsey was killed, but Southwick and Ball got away. Southwick was wounded, however.

It will be observed that in this account, Andrew J. Walker has his father in the harness-room and also in the main room of the house talking to Quantrill, an impossibility. In this statement there was careless reporting or reckless talk. His letters are by far the best authority.

Dean has left accounts of the Morgan Walker raid. They are not the whole truth, for he denies his own participation in it, and it is known that he was a late arrival on the ground with a wagon, and that possibly he was accompanied by Southwick. Dean's accounts are set out here. In a letter to Colonel Samuel Walker, dated at Waukon, Allamakee county, Iowa, July 31, 1879, now in the Collection of the author, he says:

Those young men that he betrayed to their death at Morgan Walkers, were, as I knew them Gods noblemen, the sons of Quakers, full of that spirit of Liberty that cheerfully gave such a sacrifice soon after. They in no sense as *I* knew them, loved the *conflict*, but was *filled* with love for the cause of Liberty deep in their natures, abhorred the dark and damning stain upon the Escuthion of America. had no real love for the *work* of "abrasion" that must "rub it off" but would not hold aloof from such "*work*" They were Iowa men. their names were Charles Ball, Edwin Morrison, Harry Lipsey I was not one of the party, but the particulars of the affair, as I will give you, you can rely upon as nothing but the truth. Need I tell you that I did not rest or stop untill I had learned the facts. Need I tell you that I had "blood in my eye" and at that time thought that there was such a thing as "retributive justice" and that it was good

The party that left Osawatomie for Walkers numbered four men. the three Iowa men above given and Quantrill. I was there at the time on "*business*" and had the confidence and love of those Iowa men The evening before they left I had a long and serious talk on "*business*" matters with Chas Ball the acknowledged leader of the party. We freely talked about Quantrell, his "fitness" for the work Ball thought he might *do*, and seemed to have more confidence than I in *his* frequent declarations that all he wanted was a chance to prove by "*work*" his honesty. My counsil to Ball was *caution*. Quick, sharp, decisive action. give every man his place and duty and see that they kept their place and done their duty. with only a very limited measure of confidence in Quantrill, untill he had *proved* worthy. I did not believe at that time that Quantrill knew the destination of the party

The four, left O 'e, supplied with necessary blankets, provisions, arms, spy glass &c &c and made a hasty camp near Walkers in the woods, and proceeded to look the ground over, and arrange the plan of attack, which was decided upon and to be made just at dusk of evening. Quantrell made a visit to the house and gave Walker the notice of the intended raid that evening, and arranged how *he* should be *known*, by moving away from the party, to the oblique, while approaching the house. Walker arranged a *reception* and when the party approached the house, Quantrill moved away as arranged. Ball suspecting something, spoke sharp to him and when Walkers volley came into the party from the house, Ball and Quantrell exchanged shots, with no harm to either in the dusk of the evening. Ed Morrison was instantly killed and was the only one of the three that could be found that night.

In the Collection of the author there is a statement which has been typewritten by the Kansas State Historical Society from an original, perhaps in the library of the Society. It was made to W. W. Scott in reply to interrogatories. In it he describes the Morgan Walker raid, and the following is taken from that statement:

The party that made that attempt left Osawatomie about the middle of December, 1860, numbering four persons, three Iowa young men and Quantrill. The three Iowa young men were sons of Quakers and loved the cause of liberty, not the combat which must ever exist between the despotism that demands servitude without just reward, and the spirit of free-

11

dom, but they loved liberty, and their lives were devoted to the attempt to make it universal. The oldest of the three, and acknowledged leader, was Charley Ball; the next Ed and Harry, while Quantrill went along as helper. Before starting Charley Ball and myself had a long and serious talk about the trustworthiness of Quantrill. I did not endorse or recommend but left everything to Ball, he promising to be very watchful and guarded, and not too confiding in him. The party started on foot, well armed with revolvers, and well supplied with blankets and provisions. They arrived safely and camped very near Walker's in the timber, waiting for the dusk of evening. Quantrill left the camp upon some excuse and notified Walker of the intended raid and how he would dispose of himself by stepping on one side when the party advanced so as not to be shot. Walker called in the neighbors and when the party was advancing Quantrill moved away from them to the left rear and they were about to shoot him, fearing his movement spoke treachery, when the volley came from the house into them, and Quantrill and Ball exchanged shots. The volley killed Ed and badly wounded Harry, but when Walker searched the ground he could find only the dead Ed.

Dean either never knew what occurred at the house or made these erroneous statements about the matter. That he was present there is no doubt. But he may have been where he could not see what occurred at the porch or the house — in the house. His theory in his accounts is that the men never entered the house, but were killed as they approached it. His statement as to the leadership is balderdash. Quantrill was the leader, and the leader with Dean's knowledge and demand. The idea that Quantrill should not know the destination or object of the expedition, when Stewart said Quantrill had been urging him to go to Walker's all summer! Captain Snyder knew whom the leader was and made every effort to prevent the Quaker boys from going with Quantrill.

Dean made his statements to try to shift and evade responsibility. Captain Stewart afterwards told H. S. Clarke that Dean was in the raid to Morgan Walker's and there got the bullet in his heel, and that with his blundering in a matter for which he was not fitted, it was a wonder that he was not killed.

Southwick told a story not greatly different from that told by Dean. The improbable part of his story is that which takes him back to Walker's in a few days in the capacity of a spy. It is most likely that he had slipped away from Osawatomie for a day or two at the instance of Dean, and had gone with that heroic abolitionist in a wagon to aid the others at Morgan Walker's. There he was scared to death — almost. His mind was a wreck ever after. If there was any place in all the world he never could have been forced or cajoled into visiting that place was the house of Morgan Walker after the raid; but he says he went back there and had dinner. He knew Quantrill was there. Is his story probable?

Major John N. Edwards, in his efforts to deify Quantrill, in splendid rhetoric, in his *Noted Guerillas*, sheds many tears and wastes much genuine sympathy for a Quantrill who never lived — a poor, honest, injured, imposed-upon, outraged, innocent, guileless Maryland boy who fell victim to the rough mercies of the leading Free-State men! Excuse can be made for Major

Edwards, in that he did not know the truth about Quantrill — none of the Missourians knew it. Quantrill told them a story wholly false. Major Edwards secured most of his information from Frank and Jesse James while they were hiding from justice in Louisiana. They wrote letters to him all of one summer. They were the poorest authority for historical statements on earth, the most wretched imaginable in a matter of this kind. His account of the Morgan Walker raid is as follows:

There came also from the East about this time some sort of a disease known as the club mania. Those afflicted with it — and it attacked well nigh the entire population — had a hot fever described as the enrollment fever. Organizations of all sorts sprang up — Free soil Clubs, Avengers, Men of Equal Rights, Sons of Liberty, John Brown's Body Guard, Destroying Angels, Lane's Loyal Leaguers, and what not — and every one made haste to get his name signed to both constitution and by-laws. Lawrence especially affected the Liberator Club, whose undivided mission was to find freedom for all the slaves in Missouri. Quantrell took its latitude and longitude with the calm, cold eyes of a political philosopher and joined it among the first. As it well might have been, he soon became its vitalizing influence and its master. The immense energy of the man — making fertile with resources a mind bent to the accomplishment of a certain fixed purpose — suggested at once to the club the necessity of practical work if it meant to make any negroes free or punish any slave-holders. He knew how an entire family of negroes might be rescued. The risk was not much. The distance was not great. The time was opportune. How many would volunteer for the enterprise? At first the Club argued indirectly that it was a Club sentimental — not a Club militant. It would pray devoutly for the liberation of all the slaves in the world, but it would not fight for them. What profit would the individual members receive if, after gaining all Africa, they lost their own scalps? Quantrell persevered, however, and finally induced seven of the Liberators to co-operate with him. His plan was to enter Jackson county, Missouri, with three days' cooked rations, and ride the first night to within striking distance of the premises it was intended to plunder. There — hidden completely in the brush and vigilant without being seen or heard — wait again for the darkness of the second night. This delay of a day would also enable the horses to get a good rest and the negroes to prepare for their hurried journey. Afterwards a bold push and a steady gallop must bring them all back safe to the harbor of Lawrence. Perhaps the plan really was a daring one, and the execution extremely dangerous; but seven Liberators out of eighty-four volunteered to accompany Quantrell, and in a week everything was ready for the enterprise. . . .

Between the time the Liberators had made every preparation for the foray and the time the eight men actually started for Morgan Walker's house, there was the space of a week. Afterwards those most interested remembered that Quantrell had not been seen during all that period either in Lawrence or at the headquarters of his regiment.

Everything opened auspiciously. Well mounted and armed, the little detachment left Lawrence quietly, rode two by two and far apart, until the point of the first rendezvous was reached — a clump of timber at a ford on Indian Creek. It was the evening of the second day when they arrived, and they tarried long enough to rest their horses and eat a hearty supper. Before daylight the next morning the entire party were hidden in some heavy timber two miles to the west of Walker's house. From this safe retreat none of them stirred except Quantrell. Several times during the day, however, he went backwards and forwards ostensibly to the fields where the negroes were at work, and whenever he returned he always brought something either for the horses or the men to eat.

Morgan Walker had two sons — true scions of the same stock — and before it was yet night these two boys and also the father might have been seen cleaning up and putting in excellent order their double-barrel shot-guns. A little later three neighbors, likewise carrying double-barrel shot-guns, rode up to the house, dismounted, and entered in. Quantrell, who brought note of many other things to his comrades, brought no note of this. If he saw it he made no sign.

The night was dark. It had rained a little during the day, and the most of the light of the stars had been put out by the clouds, when Quantrell arranged his men for the dangerous venture. They were to proceed first to the house, gain possession of it, capture the male members of the family, put them under guard, assemble the negroes, bid them hitch up all the wagons and teams possible, and then make a rapid gallop for Kansas.

Fifty yards from the main gate the eight men dismounted and fastened their horses. Arms were looked to, and the stealthy march to the house began. Quantrell led. He was very cool, and seemed to see everything. The balance of the marauders had their revolvers in their hands; his were in his belt. Not a dog barked. If any there had been aught save city bred, this, together with the ominous silence, would have demanded a reconnoissance. None heeded the surroundings, however, and Quantrell knocked loudly and boldly at the oaken panels of Morgan Walker's door. No answer. He knocked again and stood perceptibly to one side. Suddenly, and as though it had neither bolts nor bars, locks, nor hinges, the door flared open and Quantrell leaped into the hall with a bound like a red deer. 'Twas best so. A livid sheet of flame burst out from the darkness where he had disappeared — as though an explosion had happened there — followed by another as the second barrels of the guns were discharged, and the tragedy was over. Six fell where they stood, riddled with buck-shot. One staggered to the garden, bleeding fearfully, and died there. The seventh, hard hit and unable to mount his horse, dragged his crippled limbs to a patch of timber and waited for the dawn. They tracked him by his blood upon the leaves and found him early. Would he surrender? No! Another volley, and the last Liberator was liberated. Walker and his two sons, assisted by three of his stalwart and obliging neighbors, had done a clean night's work and a righteous one. Those who had taken the sword had perished by it.

The errors in the foregoing quotation are many, glaring, and plain to be seen. The party did not go directly from Lawrence, but indirectly, going first to Osawatomie. It was designed to go to the Cherokee Nation, not to Morgan Walker's, when it left Lawrence. There was no such club or organization as Major Edwards describes. The men were not mounted, but went to Walker's on foot. Four only left Osawatomie to go on the foray, and these were reinforced by Dean and perhaps another, possibly Southwick. Andrew J. Walker did not know of this reinforcement, for it arrived late — after Quantrill had left the house. Perhaps if Quantrill had known of the presence of this reinforcement he would not have acquainted Walker with the fact, for it might have deterred Walker from making a stand against the raiders. The manner of approaching the house is erroneously stated, and the number of men killed too many by more than half. The men were shot, not from the door of the house, but from the harness-room and behind the loom.

It is a great pity that so beautiful a description as that written by Major Edwards should have so little foundation in the facts as they occurred.

Morgan Townley Mattox, one of Quantrill's men, told the author, at Bartlesville, Oklahoma, April 29, 1909, that Dr. Riley Slaughter, the divorced husband of Anna Walker, was at the house of Morgan Walker the night that Quantrill betrayed his companions to death. Slaughter told Mattox so, and described the whole affair. He was the fourth man in the squad raised to kill the Jayhawkers. Mattox says it was generally known in Missouri that Quantrill killed his companions. His proposition to Walker was that he must kill the Kansans himself — that he would not have revenge otherwise, and that he would not ask the Walkers to take the burden of killing these men.

May 15, 1906, at Independence, Mo., "Babe" Hudspeth told the author that Quantrill sometimes boasted of having killed the wounded man at Morgan Walker's. He said the other ran and Morgan Walker shot him in the head with a musket.

During the war, Cyrus Leland, Jr., was often in the Walker neighborhood, and the people told him Quantrill killed his companions.

A man named Campbell lived near Walker. He was one of the men who went with Quantrill and Walker to the brush to kill Ball and Lipsey. He said Ball was wounded and fell helpless. Lipsey was already helpless. Quantrill shot both of them while they were begging for their lives. Campbell had a claim in Douglas county, Kansas, near Fort Saunders, which he kept until after the war and lived on it part of the time. It was while living there that he told the editor of the *Lawrence Tribune* of Quantrill's killing his helpless companions.

In a letter of C. F. (Fletch) Taylor in the Collection of the author it is said:

He came with the men for the purpose of robbing Walker and stealing slaves, when Quantrill betrayed them, and all were killed, one instantly, and the other two next day. One was killed by Quantrill, who ran up to him and shot him dead, so we only had his story for the cause, which was so far as I could find out then, and even to this day I know of no other cause.

CHAPTER XI

IT WAS necessary that Quantrill should give to the people of Missouri some excuse for his treachery. They were grateful for his aid in preventing robbery, but they could not forget that he came among them and made himself known to them as a member of a band of marauders who stole into Missouri to despoil Morgan Walker not alone of slaves, but of horses, mules, and money. There were many — some in Missouri — who could have forgiven the raid had it been for the sole purpose of restoring liberty to enslaved men and women, but they saw neither unselfish sacrifice nor devotion to high ideals when horses, mules, and money were demanded as booty. Quantrill knew all this as well as any man in the world, and he had fortified himself against that time when he might feel a rope about his neck or gaze into the muzzle of a navy pistol. And this is the story he told the Missourians:

That he was born at Hagerstown, Maryland; that he had an elder brother; that his brother lived in Kansas and sent for him to come on and go with him to California; that he had come out as requested; that they had outfitted, each with a wagon and four fine mules, provisions for the way and a free negrò to cook and tend camp and mules; that they had started out over the Old Santa Fé Trail; that they had reached the Cottonwood and there camped one night; that in the night James Montgomery and a body of Jayhawkers numbering thirty, came upon them, slew his brother, wounded him in the left leg and breast, robbed him and the dead body of his brother, took teams, wagons, and supplies, as well as the negro, and left him naked, starving, and helpless on the plain; that he watched by his brother's dead body, defending it from buzzards by day and from wolves by night; that he was dying from thirst and starvation when an old Shawnee Indian named Golightly Spiebuck who lived near Leavenworth (the Shawnees lived south of the Kansas river and nowhere near Leavenworth) came along and buried his brother and carried him to his home and nursed him back to health; that, vowing vengeance against the Kansas people, he had joined some military organization (usually said to have been one commanded by James H. Lane — the preposterous idea of joining Lane's command to have an opportunity to take vengeance on Montgomery's men seems not to have struck the Missourians); that he had found in his company the men who had murdered his brother and wounded himself; that they were his companions in arms under Lane (how they came to be under Montgomery when they found him on the Cottonwood is not explained); that from time to time he had slain man after man of those who had attacked him and killed his brother until now only those with him at Morgan Walker's were left; that in the death of those his vengeance would be completely glutted and his thirst for blood satiated.[1]

---

[1] Quantrill may or may not have gone into these details to Andrew J. Walker when making arrangements to betray his comrades to death, but he told the main part of the story, at least. In a letter written by Andrew J. Walker to W. W. Scott, dated Feb. 22, 1883, now in the Collection of the author, Walker says:

Quantrill had been living in Kansas up to the time he came on that slave stealing expedition. His statement was that he and an older brother had started to Pikes Peak in Colorado, with a four mule wagon, a negro man and equipments for mining and that this same band that was with him, robbed them of all they had, killed his brother and he himself escaped wounded through the leg. After he got well he went and joined them under the name of Charley Hart, in order to wreak vengeance. He also stated the band consisted of sixty men, headed by a man by the name of Montgomery. Their headquarters was at Osawatomie, Kansas, and were to get one hundred dollars for every negro delivered at that place. He said they run them around to New Orleans and there sold them.

Captain William H. Gregg, formerly deputy sheriff of Jackson county, Mo., served under Quantrill until about January, 1864. He has written a long account of his services for the author, now in the Collection of the author, in which he says:

Quantrill told this story to his men. I was born in Hagerstown, Maryland, in 1836. Me and my older brother, a negro boy, wagon and team, started for Pike's Peak, arriving at Lawrence, Kansas, then but a village. We stopped to make some purchases, leaving sometime in the afternoon, camped near the Kaw River, where sometime in the night we were attacked by Montgomery's band of Jayhawkers. My brother was killed, I wounded and left for dead, the negro, wagon and team, with our plunder appropriated. After keeping vigil for twenty-four hours amidst

Quantrill's holy life of hardship and devotion to the South
(as told by him) grew in Missouri with the lapse of time. It,
together with his guerrilla outrages and inhuman massacres, became a deification. His fame as a martyr and saint in Missouri
reached its zenith in the days when Major John N. Edwards
strove so gallantly and wrote so eloquently for the press of that
State. Major Edwards believed what he wrote, for he was an
honest man. He had no correct information upon the subject
of the life of Quantrill in Kansas, and much that he wrote he
obtained from Frank and Jesse James long after the war and
when they were in hiding, outlaws for highway robbery and

the hideous howlings of hundreds of coyotes, becoming almost famished for
water, I managed to crawl to the Kaw River, and quench my thirst, after
which I espied a canoe at the opposite bank, and soon after an Indian
approached the canoe, to whom I halloed, asking him to come over, which
he did, and, after hearing my story, buried my dead brother, when he and
his wife nursed me to health.

Soon after I was restored to health, I sought Montgomery and joined
his band, under the name of Charley Hart. I had not been with Montgomery long when I found that I had the confidence of all the officers and
men. I then, in a systematic way, obtained the names of all the men who
took part in the killing of my brother, &c. I had joined Montgomery for
the purpose of getting revenge, managing to get one at a time away from
camp. I never allowed one to get back alive, until, when the war came
on, there were only two left.

The above story was somewhat shaken, however, when a woman
purporting to be Quantrill's mother together with a Mr. Scott, both from
Canal Dover, O., appeared in Jackson County, Missouri, about 1884, both
of whom told the same story. Mrs. Quantrill said, My son William had no
older brother, he had a younger brother ''Thompson.'' William was my
oldest child, hence the story which you relate cannot be true, besides, says
she, my children were all born and raised at Canal Dover, Ohio. Mr. Scott,
who claimed to be a bosom friend and schoolmate of William Clark Quantrill, voiced what Mrs. Quantrill said, and further said that he was very
much surprised at the course taken by Quantrill, for, said he, he was raised
an ''abolitionist.''

Whether Quantrill was a deception thus far or not, rests with the
truth or falsity of the latter statement.

At a later date Quantrill told the women with whom he associated in
Missouri the same story with many additions. In a letter written by Mrs.
Olivia D. Cooper to W. W. Scott, dated Lee's Summit, Jackson county, Mo.,
May 9, 1881, now in the Collection of the author, is the following:

The man I knew as W. C. Quantrill always said he was born and
raised in Hagerstown, Md., When he became such a noted rebel partisan
chieftain his mother had to leave home went to Virginia was there when he
was wounded and died in Louisville, Ky., he wrote to her all the time he
was in the state he told me a few days before he was wounded about his
relatives said he had three brothers one was killed in Kansas when they
were on their way to Colorado while they were in camp one night the Jay-

murder; they told him what they had heard from Quantrill and only that. They knew nothing more; no one in Missouri knew more. As the work of Edwards is the most pretentious on the subject, and as it contains such ridiculous statements and bald untruths, some of its assertions are noticed here:

Major Edwards begins by saying that Quantrill was born at Hagerstown, Md., July 20, 1836, and that he lived there until he was sixteen years of age, a devoted and affectionate son, helping his widowed mother. In his sixteenth year he was taken to Cleveland, Ohio, by an old friend of the family, a Colonel Toler (Torrey?), and there given an excellent English education. He never saw his mother again. He had an only brother in Kansas long before 1855, older by several years than himself. This older brother is represented to have been a father to him and the mainstay of his widowed mother, "still fighting the uncertain battles of life heroically and alone." Quantrill's brother wrote for him to come to Kansas to go with him to California, as "the brother in Kansas would not go without the brother in Ohio," and about the middle of the summer of 1856 both brothers began the overland journey, each having a wagon loaded with provisions, four good mules each, and "more or less money between them." They took a negro along to do the cooking and to care for the teams.

"The three were together when that unprovoked tragedy occurred which was to darken and blacken the whole subsequent current of the younger brother's life, and link his name forever

hawkers as they were afterwards called came on them in the night killed his brother shot him breaking his leg left him for dead took their outfit and negro man they had and left his second brother killed fiting under the gallant Stone Wall Jackson in Virginia his other brother a lad twelve years old was a cripple at home with his Mother and Sister about eighteen years of age. you say he was born at Canal Dover Ohio is why I think there must have [been] two men of the same name the young man that was here gave his name as Thompson Quantrill so I cannot give any information concerning the [one] you speak of the one I knew was true to the cause for which he fought and [a] son that any Mother might be proud off as to the questions you ask I could never think of writing not being much of a hand at letter writing as you see when you read this I know brave deeds and hair bredth escapes of him and his brave company but dates I cannot remember he was a true catholic this Thompson said they were all Prebyterians the Priest name was Powers but I have heard that he died about a year ago. Capt. Quantrill was buried in the Catholic grave yard between Louisville & Portland Ky. I have his photograph but I can not send it from the fact it is not at home at present tis a good likeness of him.

with some of the savagest episodes of some of the most savage guerrilla history ever recorded.'' This orderly and brotherly company camped one night on the Cottonwood, *en route* to California, (in 1856, mind you — a year before Quantrill came to Kansas), when thirty armed men ''rode deliberately up to the wagons where the Quantrells were and opened fire at point-blank range upon the occupants.'' The elder brother was killed instantly, and Quantrill was badly wounded in the left leg and right breast and left to die. As the wagons were driven off the negro requested that food be left the wounded man, which was refused. The pockets of the Quantrills were robbed. Then Quantrill fought buzzards by day and wolves by night to keep them from devouring the dead body of his brother. Fever consumed him and he rolled himself down to the stream to drink, some ''fifty good steps'' distant, and rolled himself up again, staunching his wounds with grass. He lived by force of will to avenge his wrongs.

Early in the morning of the third day the old Shawnee Indian, Golightly Spiebuck, came along and found this wounded man in his deplorable condition. He buried the dead brother. Spiebuck is said to have told this story often, but the Indian is noted for truthfulness, and there was probably no such man, though Edwards says he died in 1868. It required four hours for him to dig a grave for the dead Quantrill. ''Quantrell watched the corpse until the earth covered it, and then he hobbled to his knees and turned his dry eyes to where he believed God to be. Did he pray? Yes!''

Quantrill taught a school the remainder of 1856 and paid Spiebuck liberally for saving him, and on the 15th day of August, 1857, went to Leavenworth and took the name Charley Hart. There he became intimate with Lane, who, in this remarkable story, is said to have been in command of a regiment with headquarters at Lawrence, a statement which is preposterous. Quantrill went from Leavenworth to Lawrence and enrolled (in 1857, mind you), in the ''company to which belonged all but two of the men who did the deadly work at the Cottonwood River.'' There he became a fine soldier in that company and was in constant service, scouting from the Kaw to the Boston Mountains.

One day he was sent to Wyandotte to aid Jack Winn, "a somewhat noted horsethief," to get some slaves out of Missouri.
One of the men who went with Quantrill failed to return with
him and he was found near a creek some days later with a round
smooth bullet-hole in the center of his forehead. Winn was also
shot just inside a cornfield there and found with the "same
round hole in the forehead."

Then Quantrill's company was ordered to Fort Scott, together with three other companies. This force was to expel
hordes of border-ruffians who had invaded Kansas and overrun
some counties in those parts. Much fighting was done by the
Free-State men, and "Quantrill was first in every adventurous
enterprise and the last to leave upon the skirmish line." Sixty
men were lost by the Kansas forces — killed. Forty-two were
killed by the border-ruffians and eighteen by Quantrill — eighteen. They had "the same round, smooth hole in the middle of
the forehead." After the return of the forces to Lawrence a
sentinel was found dead at his post every week. "The men began to whisper one to another and to cast about for the cavalry
Jonah who was in the midst of them. One company alone, that
of Captain Pickens — the company to which Quantrill belonged
— had lost thirteen men between October, 1857, and March, 1858.
Another company had lost two, and three one each. A second
Underground Railroad conductor named Rogers had been shot
through the forehead, and two scouts from Montgomery's command named Stephens and Tarwater."

Quantrill was made a lieutenant in the company of Captain
Pickens. He and the captain became intimate. One night Pickens told exultingly of having raided the camp of two emigrants
on the Cottonwood, "and the artistic execution of the raid which
left neither the dead man a shroud nor the wounded man a
blanket." Pickens told, too, how the plunder was divided, the
mules sold, and the money put in a heap and gambled for.
"Three days thereafter Pickens and two of his most reliable men
were found dead on Bull creek, shot like the balance in the middle of the forehead."

Then there was a panic among the soldiers, but finally the
matter was forgotten in the daily routine of the camp. But

Quantrill bought the finest horse in the Territory and two navy revolvers. To test the matter as to whether he was suspected, Quantrill had a long talk with Lane, the colonel of the regiment, and concluded that he was not under suspicion. Two months later Quantrill was ordered to take his own company and details from two others, in all one hundred and fourteen men, and scout out to the extreme west end of the Territory, which, at that time, was the top of the main chain of the Rocky Mountains. No Indians were seen, but thirteen men were missing — three shot through the forehead. Then an orderly was missing, and, later, a member of Lane's staff. The last man killed by Quantrill while in this regiment was this orderly, who had boasted that he killed the elder Quantrill at the Cottonwood. And in this remarkable story the next incident is the Morgan Walker raid, taking Quantrill over to the Missourians.

The whole tale is false. There is no truth in any part of it. Quantrill was not born at Hagerstown, Maryland; he had no older brother — he was the first-born. He never started to Pike's Peak or California with any one, but did stop at Pike's Peak on his return from Utah. He never owned a wagon. He was not set upon by any body of Kansas men on the Cottonwood, nor at any other point. There was no such military organization in Kansas as that described. The Free-State forces were the settlers who assembled at the call of a captain selected by themselves, and when the border-ruffians were expelled they returned to their claims and cabins. Quantrill never belonged to any military organization in Kansas. He was a member of a band of robbers in 1860, most of the time skulking through the brush to escape the strong hand of Sheriff Walker. There was no Captain Pickens, no Jack Winn, no Stephens, no Tarwater. All these characters and incidents originated in the mind of Major Edwards or some informant who ignorantly or maliciously told him a string of falsehoods.

In 1856 Quantrill was yet in Ohio — had not come to Kansas, but this story puts him then on the road to California and in a massacre on the Cottonwood, where his brother met death at the hands of the Free-State men. He is made to enlist in a regiment of Kansas settlers at Leavenworth August 15, 1857. At that time he was in Miami (Lykins) county stealing oxen

from Beeson and blankets and pistols from Torrey. He is made
to do military service in a regiment which never existed, in the
winter of 1857-58, while the truth is that he was at that time
sponging his board from his friends and stealing their food and
blankets at Tuscarora Lake, Johnson county, Kansas. In the
fall of 1858 Edwards has Quantrill shooting Jack Winn at Wyandotte, when in fact he was in Utah cooking for a mess of soldiers. He is made to assassinate the men in the company of
Captain Pickens somewhere between the fall of 1858 and the
Morgan Walker raid, and finally to murder Captain Pickens
himself, when the truth is that most of that time he was a principal character in as disreputable a band of cut-throats, kidnappers,
highway robbers, murderers and border-ruffians as ever went
unhung, and he did his full share of the work engaged in by the
banditti. He robbed indiscriminately — Missouri or Kansas,
Lawrence or Independence, Osawatomie or Harrisonville — border-ruffians or Free-State men. He was a kidnapper and a
Quaker, a slave-stealer and a negro-driver, a blackmailer and the
humble disciple of the "Fighting Parson," a Puritan and the
reproach of "Cuckold Tom." When Major Edwards would have
him slaying Free-State men by the score, he was in fact stealing
cattle from the pro-slavery settlers in the Salt Creek Valley.
When his worshipers would have us believe he was an innocent,
injured Maryland boy in the cabin of the Shawnee, he was a
roistering gambler at Fort Bridger.

Quantrill had no convictions, stood for no principles, was
in favor of no State or party, had no choice of communities,
could not comprehend honesty, was an utter stranger to loyalty,
and did not know such a thing as friendship.

As to murder and assassination. Major Edwards says he
killed at least twenty-eight men while he lived in Kansas. That
is probably the only statement in this story in which Major Edwards strikes the absolute truth. He no doubt killed many
more. And there were Illinois, Indiana, Utah, and the Pike's
Peak country, in all of which he spilled blood before he had a
beard. Still, he was deified by Major Edwards and was worshiped in Missouri. He made widows and orphans by the
hundred, plundered Puritan and Cavalier, slew his foes and betrayed and murdered his friends and drenched a border in blood.

CHAPTER XII

AFTERMATH OF THE MORGAN WALKER RAID

THERE was great excitement in that part of Jackson county about Blue Springs when word of what had been done at Morgan Walker's spread abroad. Men armed themselves and rode to Walker's house by the dozen and by the score. The body of the dead Jayhawker, "straightened for the grave," was laid out to be gazed upon. Many were the surmises of his reckless daring and ferocious temper. Several men were certain he had visited their separate neighborhoods and carried away slaves. Some had met him on lonesome roads — were sure of it — and had then marked him for an abolitionist and Jayhawker. Quantrill was questioned closely and repeated his manufactured tale about his brother's death, always increasing the brutality and savagery of the Jayhawkers and his awful sufferings at their hands. Most of the men believed he was lying, and quite a number favored hanging him then and there.

At the solicitation of Walker's wife and other women Morrison was buried late in the day after he was killed. In those days there was a family burying-ground on almost every farm, that on the Walker farm being quite extensive. But Morrison was not buried in it. He was carried to a different part of the place and buried near the road in a rude coffin made by one of the slaves from native lumber. The crowds dispersed and every man betook himself to his own domicile convinced that his slaves were in danger and that desperate steps would have to be taken to protect them.

It was supposed that Morrison was the only raider who would be secured — that the others had made good their escape. Two or three days after the attack the slave of a neighbor to Walker was hunting hogs in the woods and found Ball and Lipsey in their camp in the thicket. They entreated him to go with them to Kansas and aid in getting the wounded man back to his home, assuring him of his freedom if he should do so. He was directed to say nothing of the camp of the Jayhawkers, to secure what cooked food he could lay hands upon, and come with a wagon and team in which they would all go to Lawrence, thence to Pardee, from which place the negro would be taken to Iowa and Canada. He agreed to do all that was required of him, no doubt expecting to perform his promises at the time he was making them. But his stupidity and the instinct of his people in their servitude made him decide upon loyalty to his master and treachery to those in distress who would give him liberty. He went straight home and told of finding the camp and described its occupants and what they had said to him. He said they had already stolen a horse upon which to ride out of Missouri, and that it was tied to a sapling near the camp. Ball had killed one of the very hogs he had missed and gone to hunt, and this was furnishing them meat. He had also extracted a quantity of buck-shot from Lipsey's wounds, which were severe and highly inflamed, and he was treating them with applications of heated leaves and water.

The neighbor went at once to the house of Walker and told what the slave had said. The men at Walker's, accompanied by the neighbor and two or three other residents there, armed themselves and set forth to find the raiders and kill them. All had heavily-charged shot-guns except Morgan Walker and Quantrill, the latter having only his pistol and Walker a heavy musket or buffalo-gun, perhaps a Hawkins rifle. Dean and Southwick always said that Ball saw them coming, and, knowing that the game was up, stood over Lipsey waving his revolver and challenging Quantrill to step out and fight to the death with him.[1]

---

[1] In the letter of Dean already quoted from, addressed to Samuel Walker, it is stated:

A day or two after one of Walkers slaves found the other two in the woods, while looking up a missing horse, and found the horse tied with them. Ball was seemingly ''all right'' and had a small camp fire, was making a poultace of bark for Harry, who was *dying* of his wounds The slave left the horse with them and promised not to betray them, but did immediately go and tell Walker, who summoned his ''army'' and guided by the negro, surrounded the ''camp.'' when Ball saw them approaching he at once knew that he was ''lost'' and singling out Quantrell who stood beside Walker, dared him to come near enough to give him a fair chance. Ball stood over his dying comrade and shook his pistol at the attacking

The Missourians say that Ball started to run when Walker and his posse appeared, and that Morgan Walker shot him in the back of the head with his heavy gun, killing him instantly. And they say that Lipsey was killed by a volley fired by the whole Walker force. Andrew J. Walker says that only the Walkers and Quantrill went to the camp to kill Ball and Lipsey, and that a volley fired by them killed both men, and that Quantrill did not fire and did not kill either of the men.[2]

party Walker himself, being armed with a long range rifle, shot Ball in the forehead and killed him instantly. When Ball fell, Quantrell ran up, looked at Harry and Ball, put his revolver into Harrys mouth and fired, and there was no one of the party to tell Walker any different story than Quantrells.

In the statement made by Dean to Scott in response to interrogatories, before quoted partly, is the following account of this part of the affair:

The second day after the attack one of Walker's negroes reported at the house that in hunting up stray stock, he had found in the woods the other two men, that the small one (Harry) was badly wounded in the hip and helpless, while Ball had obtained a horse and cooked up some herbs, made a poultice for Harry's wounds and was getting ready to carry the wounded man away. Walker loaded up his rifle and all the guns on the place as quick as possible, and with the many neighbors that were there seeking the wonderful, they all started, led to the place by the negro who made the discovery, Quantrill and Walker walking together. When they arrived at the place they spread out in a semicircle and advanced to rifle range, under Quantrill's caution to keep away from Ball's revolver. When Ball saw them and then knew that the negro had betrayed him, he stood over his wounded comrade and shaking his revolver at Quantrill, dared him to come out in fair sight and range, and as he thus stood, Walker with his rifle shot him square in the center of the forehead. The instant Ball fell Quantrill ran up to him and putting his revolver into the mouth of Harry, who lay helpless, fired, killing him.

[2] In the letter of Andrew J. Walker dated February 3, 1883, already referred to and quoted from is the following:

Two days later a negro man saw them in the woods and told his master who told my father. My father, brother, Quantrill and myself went out where they were. They drew their pistols and my father and myself fired on them killing them both. Quantrill did not kill either of them. Southwick was so badly wounded that he could not stand. They had stolen a horse the night before and had it tied in the brush near by. They were to leave that night.

The statements of Andrew J. Walker do not always agree. In his interview printed in the *Kansas City Journal*, May 12, 1888, heretofore noticed herein, is the following on this matter:

A negro servant of my father saw them in the brush a few days later. My father and I shouldered our guns, loaded with buckshot and went after them, and they were buried right there. Ball jumped up and Southwick raised himself on his elbows. He laid down immediately and did not rise any more. Quantrill was along, but he did not shoot at Ball or Southwick.

Walker supposed that Lipsey was Southwick. As to Quantrill's shooting Ball and Lipsey, see text and notes *ante*.

May 15, 1906, the author was at Independence, Mo., and saw there some of Quantrill's men, among them "Babe" Hudspeth, A. J. Liddill, and Warren Welch. Hudspeth said Quantrill always boasted of having killed the wounded man, justifying the act by claiming that Lipsey had helped to plunder him and his brother on the Cottonwood, and had fired with the party that killed his brother and wounded himself, but Hudspeth did not know the name of the wounded man was Lipsey. There was at that time in Judge Liddill's office a man named James Harris. Harris said he was a boy about ten years old when Quantrill came to Morgan Walker's and betrayed his comrades. Harris said his father lived about a mile from the house of Morgan Walker. He said that Walker shot the man who started to run — shot him with a big gun in the back of the head and killed him instantly. He also said that Quantrill ran up and shot the wounded man in the head, and the wounded man died at once. It was supposed that Quantrill wished to prevent Lipsey from talking, fearing that he would tell some truths that would give the Walkers a true insight into his character. Harris described the scene which occurred at the house of Morgan Walker when he got back from Independence and was told of the robbery that would be attempted in a few minutes. Walker wanted to shoot or hang Quantrill the night of the raid — thought it would be best to kill all the raiders. and that others present believed the same thing. Andrew J. Walker, however, insisted that Quantrill be saved, as his promise was to that effect, and he finally prevailed.

Ball and Lipsey were buried where they were killed, and without coffins. Physicians or "doctors" came, in a day or two, and carried away all the bodies for dissection.[3]

While the people of Walker's neighborhood were satisfied

[3] Dean and Southwick insisted always that Morgan Walker turned the bodies over to "doctors" before burial, but Andrew J. Walker says in the letters before referred to that the bodies were decently buried. Old residents of Jackson county have told the author that the bodies were buried — that they were present and saw them buried, and that neither Walker nor his family were responsible for the exhumation of the bodies. They said that public sentiment was such that no effective protest could be made, and that it could not be prevented. Residents in the country have a horror of desecrated graves, and to take a body for the purpose of

12

with the termination of the raid, the county authorities believed
it should be investigated.   The sheriff went to Walker's, arrested

James Younger

Quantrill, and took him to Independence.
There he threw the prisoner into jail.
Andrew J. Walker went to Independence
with the sheriff.   There was no formal
charge against Quantrill, and Walker
prevailed on the sheriff to release him.
That night Walker and Quantrill slept
in the same room in an Independence tavern.   On the following day the town was
full of people from the surrounding country, and excitement ran high.   There was
generally no correct understanding of the
affair.   People believed that all the Jayhawkers should have been killed; they
could not comprehend the reason for Quantrill's escape.   Quantrill's statement was reduced to writing, and in it he gave as
the place of his birth, Hagerstown, Md.[4]   Walker saw that feeling was running high against Quantrill, and at noon he realized
that it was near the danger point.   He went to the livery stable
and mounted his horse with the intention of taking Quantrill
home with him.   When he reached the public square arrangements were in progress there for the hanging of Quantrill, who

"'cutting it up'' is regarded as the height of wickedness, heartlessness, and
depravity.   It is not probable that any of the country-folk approved the
course of the ''doctors.''   Who these ''doctors'' were is not now known.

4 To the article of H. S. Clarke, published in the Seventh Volume,
Kansas Historical Collections, is added the following foot-note:

"Memoirs of a Missourian,'' by John W. Henry, in the *Kansas City
Star*, September 22, 1901, says: "In 1860 Quantrill came to Morgan
Walker, a farmer, near Blue Springs, and informed him of a plot of four
Kansas desperadoes to run off his negroes, giving the precise date at which
they would make their raid.   They came at the time designated and were
killed.   After the attempt to run off Walker's negroes, Walker came to
Independence with Quantrill, then known as William Clark, and a self-
constituted committee met them in the court-house, and I was requested
to reduce to writing Quantrill's statement, which I did, and kept it for
several years, but do not recollect what became of it. . . . When under
examination as above mentioned, I have forgotten whether he gave his true
name or not, but am inclined to think that he did not, because I wrote to
the clerk of the court, at Hagerstown, for information in regard to him,
and he wrote that he never knew such a man.   Yet I have no doubt that
he came from Hagerstown or that vicinity.''

seems then to have been with Walker. Walker was able to turn the crowd from its purpose, but he had to stand firmly against it and say that Quantrill could be secured only over his dead body. When the tide was turned he went to a store and bought Quantrill a suit of clothes made of blue jeans, and then carried him back to Morgan Walker's. The following day Morgan Walker gave Quantrill a horse, bridle and saddle, and fifty dollars in cash, with the understanding that Quantrill was to leave his house for the time being. A justice of the peace, "Squire Lobb," gave him ten dollars. Walker feared that if Quantrill remained with him his farm would be raided by parties from Kansas to revenge the death of those who came with him.

Stopping with different farmers in the neighborhood of Morgan Walker, Quantrill spent the winter of 1860-61. He was often at Walker's house. Most of his time was spent at the hospitable home of Mark Gill, where he became a great favorite. Dreading publicity and fearing recognition, he did not visit Independence, but kept always to the rural districts. He made two or three trips to Kansas, going to Paola and remaining there some days an honored guest at the tavern of Torrey, fêted and caressed by the family. He was made a hero by Potter and other pro-slavery people living then in that town.

Quantrill was restless and uneasy. He longed to be engaged in active operations against his former associates in Kansas. He found it difficult to organize forays. Times were changing. Kansas was a State, and the people felt free and confident when they had escaped from the domination of the Buchanan government. When the State was lost to the South, many Missourians favored a cessation of hostilities. And in the excitement preceding secession the people of Jackson county thought more about getting their slaves safely to Texas than of preying longer upon the lean pioneer homes and towns of bleeding Kansas. By the light of the moon Quantrill rode constantly. It was necessary for him to get on a familiar and confidential footing with men in his new environment. His trips to Kansas were in search of something attractive enough to induce his new associates to again cross the border. In the one last undertaken, he ventured beyond Paola and deep into the Jayhawker settlements in the hope of finding there some adventure which would aid him to rouse the waning enthusiasm along the Sni and the Little Blue. He promised Andrew J. Walker, then the most hopeful of his new converts, that he would be gone a few days only.[5]

---

[5] The best evidence is to the effect that Morgan Walker gave Quantrill a black mare of the Morgan stock, and that he called her "Black Bess." But Mr. George W. Thompson, son-in-law of H. V. Beeson, thinks it was a horse. The animal had lost an eye by some accident, but was a thoroughbred of fine form and splendid qualities, and was a swift runner. Mrs. Thompson remembers having seen Quantrill dressed in his new suit when he rode by the Thompson home on his way to the house of Bennings, and it was made of blue jeans.

In the letter of Andrew J. Walker, dated February 3, 1883, it is said:

The sheriff came and took Quantrill to Independence and put him in jail. I went with him to that place and got the Sheriff to let him out that night. I took him to the Hotel and we slept in the same room. A great many people were in town the next day and the excitement ran very high. In the afternoon I thought it time to start home and·went to the stable to get my horse. When I arrived on the public square, I found a great crowd gathered about. I rode up to them to see what it meant and learned that they were going to hang Quantrill. I told them they must not do it; but some of them seemed inclined to be stubborn about it. I told them if they did, they would do it over my dead body and they gave it up. I then went with Quantrill and bought him a suit of clothes of which he was badly in need and we went home. The next day my father gave him a horse, bridle and saddle and $50.00 in money with the understanding that he was to leave, as it was thought best. He left for Kansas; but told me he would be back in a few days and he was. He made two or three trips into Kansas. He was caught once and put in jail at Aubrey, I think.

In his letter dated February 22, 1883, Walker says:

The Sheriff had no warrant for his arrest when he came and took him to Independence. When he got there he put him in jail. I asked him why he put him in jail, when he answered, for his own safety and would take him out as soon as the excitement was over and true to his word turned him out about eight o'clock that night. The next day the town was crowded with people and all sorts of rumors were afloat and a great deal of excitement prevailed. The people had not got to fairly understand the matter and they hardly knew themselves what they were going to hang him for, only for the fact that he was in bad company and there was naturally a prejudice against Kansas men, as there had been a great deal of trouble between Kansas and Missouri. The crowd was mostly pro-slavery men. The reason we thought it best for Quantrill to leave my father's house, was this; we thought the remainder of the gang would hunt him up and kill him if possible, or if he staid there they would burn my father's house or do him some other great harm. He was not in danger of being molested by the neighbors, for that matter had all been settled. We all felt under obligations to him for saving my father's life and property. He never taught school in Missouri.

CHAPTER XIII

QUANTRILL'S RETURN TO KANSAS — HIS ESCAPE

QUANTRILL did not venture to Lawrence, but went to Stanton and lodged with his old-time pro-slavery friend, Bennings, knowing that he could there secure accurate information of people and conditions in Kansas. He had played double so long that he was bold and thought he might thus far penetrate his first Kansas haunts without danger. It is said that he had a lady friend in that vicinity whom he often visited — one whom he met and formed some acquaintance with while teaching there. She is said to have been fascinated with him and devoted to his interests and enterprises, but that her parents strongly objected to his attentions to her. From her he knew he could secure reliable information of his former companions.[1]

On the 25th day of March, 1861, Quantrill entered the Stanton settlement in great glee, singing as he rode "Black Bess" along the banks of the Marais des Cygnes. He passed the Beeson home, where Thompson, the husband of Beeson's daughter, was then living. He rode back of the house near the kitchen door, laughed a sneering insult and passed on down the river in the direction of the home of Bennings. Mrs. Thompson did not see him and asked her husband who had passed. He replied, "some one you ought to remember." She looked out and saw Quantrill, who was gayly dressed in his new suit of blue jeans. She observed that Quantrill had been seen by a neighbor, for William Strong hurriedly mounted his horse and rode towards Osawatomie. She knew of the feeling in the community against Quantrill, and she believed Strong went to notify Captain Snyder of his presence.

---

[1] This information was given the author by Hon. William Higgins, of Bartlesville, Oklahoma, who says the young lady was well known to him, as were her parents, and that she was a Catholic. This was the last visit Quantrill made to Stanton or Kansas before the Civil War.

This visit of Quantrill was the third he had made to the home of Bennings after the Morgan Walker raid. He must have had more than one object in these visits. Dean says, in one of his letters, that Quantrill made inquiry of the stage driver to learn where he (Dean) was. Dean believed that Quantrill desired to find and murder him. He may have intended to assassinate other Free-State men with whom he had been associated. Captain Snyder had heard of the flying visits of Quantrill to the house of Bennings, and he had decided to kill him if possible when he should come again. Snyder had provided means of having notice of the next visit of Quantrill — the one he was then making. William Strong and a German boy named Peter Hauser each rode to Osawatomie with the intelligence of the presence of Quantrill on the Marais des Cygnes. Two parties left Osawatomie to capture Quantrill.

It was from Peter Hauser that Captain Snyder had word that Quantrill was at the house of Bennings. His father, Samuel Hauser, was justice of the peace at Stanton. Young Hauser did not find Captain Snyder when he first arrived at Osawatomie, and he finally told Elias Snyder what message he bore. Elias Snyder immediately informed John S. Jones and W. M. Martin, and the three armed themselves and went to the house of Bennings, where they stationed themselves in such position that Quantrill could not escape them. It was their intention to arrest Quantrill and take him to Lawrence and turn him over to Sheriff Walker who had warrants for his arrest on the charges of horse-stealing, burglary, and kidnapping. They intended to kill him if he gave them excuse or favorable opportunity.

Later, Peter Hauser found Captain Snyder and delivered his message. Snyder desired to kill Quantrill for his treachery at Morgan Walker's, but he wished to kill him under some color of justification. He supposed Quantrill would resist arrest, and he went to Stanton where he secured from Hauser a warrant based upon Quantrill's crimes at Lawrence. He had with him a number of desperate men. The justice obstructed Snyder in his plans, prevailing upon him to allow one Jurd, the constable, to have the warrant and make the arrest, to be supported by Captain Snyder and his men as a *posse*. Upon their arrival at the house of Bennings they found Elias Snyder, Jones, and Martin, whom they added to the *posse*. It was then almost daylight. Quantrill was aroused. He stood at bay. He at once realized that his chances for life were worth very little just then. He said he would fight to the death, and Captain Snyder believed that he meant to do it. A long parley ensued between Quantrill and Bennings on the one side and Snyder and his men on the other side. The constable was finally admitted to the house for a conference with Quantrill, it being agreed that Snyder and his men were to remain at a distance during the negotiations. The constable agreed that Quantrill should have protection if he would submit to arrest and go to the office of the justice, an arrangement against which Snyder strongly protested. When they came out of the house the constable held up Quantrill's pistol to show that he had disarmed the prisoner, but Bennings had slipped another heavy pistol to Quantrill.

Upon the appearance of Quantrill, Adolphus, the son of Bennings, was seen to hurry to the stable and take therefrom Quantrill's black mare, saddle and mount her and ride like the wind in the direction of Paola. On the way to Stanton every opportunity was sought to have Quantrill do something which would serve as an excuse for killing him, but without success. Captain Snyder saw that he would have to act without having a pretext, and raised his gun. As he was in the act of firing some one knocked up the muzzle of his gun and saved Quantrill's life. The office of the justice was over the store of T. R. Wilkerson at Stanton, and Quantrill and his guards went into this store where the justice was when they arrived. Quantrill objected to being sent to Lawrence, saying he would die before he would go there. The justice wished to send him to Lawrence, and it is probable that he had sent a courier to bring the sheriff or his deputy to Stanton to take Quantrill to Lawrence. Quantrill knew he would never live to reach Lawrence. There was much talk. At one time Quantrill believed Captain Snyder would kill him, and he slunk behind the counter and cowered below it. He proposed that he be armed and given a position where he could fight it out with his captors, saying that he did not like to be shot down like a dog. Captain Snyder's gun was pushed from Quantrill's body more than once. The justice finally decided to commit Quantrill to the Paola jail. While the commitment was being made out John S. Jones seated himself on the counter where but one man was between himself and Quantrill, who was also sitting on the counter. Jones all the time fumbled at the lock of his Sharps's rifle, pretending that it was out of order. Getting his gun across the lap of his neighbor with the muzzle against Quantrill, whose attention was attracted elsewhere, he suddenly cocked it and attempted to shoot, but the gun missed fire, and Quantrill had again escaped death.[2]

----

[2] This account of the capture of Quantrill at the house of Bennings is the result of what the author secured from different parties who saw the whole affair. The accounts do not agree as to detail. Following is what George W. Thompson told the author, Jan. 14, 1906. Mr. Thompson lives at No. 1030 Morris Avenue, Topeka, and married Frances, daughter of H. V. Beeson. He was one of the *posse*, and the author wrote his account for his Collection, as follows:

George W. Thompson told of the capture of Quantrill. His account differs from that of Shearer. He says that Ely Snyder, the blacksmith, of Osawatomie, and his men often made raids into Missouri to get slaves and other property, and that Quantrill was frequently with them. On one occasion he had no gun or revolver, and as one of the band did not go Quantrill took his arms. The raid was successful, and the plunder was divided in Osawatomie. Quantrill was not satisfied with the portion falling to him and would not give up the arms of the party who could not go, but kept them, saying they would just about make him even. He may have kept a horse, also, thus angering Snyder, after which he remained at Paola much of the time. One day he came from Paola to the house of John Bennings, about a mile south of Stanton. As he passed the house of William Strong he was recognized, and Strong went to Osawatomie to notify Snyder and his men. The next morning some eight or ten of them went to the house of Bennings, and Thompson thinks they went there to kill Quantrill. Quantrill believed that Snyder and his men would kill him and refused to come out of the house, saying that he would fight if they came in. They claimed they wanted a settlement on the plunder which they had fallen out about. Seeing that Quantrill would not come out, they sent one of their party to Samuel Hauser, justice of the peace at Stanton and secured a warrant for the arrest of Quantrill for horse-stealing. The constable, one Jurd, came to serve the warrant. Quantrill asked him to protect his life and Jurd agreed to do so. Then Quantrill came out and surrendered to the constable, who summoned, first, however, some half a dozen men to defend him, among them Thompson. They took him to the office of the justice of the peace, which was over the store of T. R. Wilkerson, in Stanton. The justice had sent to Paola for the Sheriff to come out as quickly as possible and bring a *posse* to protect Quantrill and take him to Paola. When the men arrived at Wilkerson's store Quantrill was put inside and a man placed at each door to keep Snyder and his men out until the arrival of the Sheriff. Snyder and his men did not know the Sheriff had been sent for. Thompson was placed at the back door of the store.

The foregoing account of the capture of Quantrill at the home of Bennings may not embrace all that occurred on that occasion. Captain Ely Snyder says that he become suspicious of Jurd, and that he then broke down the door and captured Quantrill. That he did this is more than probable, for he was a

He heard the click of a gun as it was cocked behind him; he put out his hand and knocked the barrel of the gun to one side, and it was jerked outside before he could learn who had attempted to shoot Quantrill. The Sheriff came and put Quantrill into his buggy and drove away with him and put him in jail at Paola. The justice had the papers ready when the Sheriff arrived. Thompson says Quantrill did not go up stairs at all. He does not remember that Robert Shearer was there at all. Wilkerson was a loyal man.

The account of Quantrill's riding by Thompson's house was given the author by Mrs. Thompson, August 30, 1907.

In the letter written by Captain Ely Snyder to G. A. Colton, dated at Osawatomie, Feb. 14, 1883, now in the Collection of the author, he gives his version of the affair, as follows:

Erly in the spring of 61 I do not now remember the day of the month or the month at this time but can get the date of the time to the day Late in the Evening Squire Hauser Sent me a message that Quantrill was at Bennings I got 5 men to go with me and captive the outlaw and bring him to Justice with a inch roap when we came near to Benings I left the party and in the woods and went to Hausers House and Hauser Advised me to make the arest under the shade of Law as I did not think best but Mr Hauser was at the time Justice of the Peace and I gave way to his Plan and he Apointed me Constable and then reconsidered it and thought best to give the papers in the hand of the Constable which was Jurd said that Jurd would be all right Jurd proved to be a friend to Quantrell and spoiled the hole Bisness he Jurd told me that he would go in and being acquainted with Benings that he had warrant for Quantrell to have him run out at the back door and then we could get him but Jurd did not do that. he told Quantrell that I had a posse of men out side and for him not to go out or I would get him so Jurd made me fals prommas and kept me waiting until almost daylight when [I] hured the thing up by bursting open the door and stept in the house Quantrell was standing in the middle door with a Revolver in each hand Quantrell atempted to rais and bring them to range on me when I spoke to [him] and said bill drop them revolvers or I will kill you I had my Revolver in range of the place wair he Lived he Obaid quick I then told [him] to hand them Revolvers to Jurd wich he did he then was taken to Squire Hausers office and Jurd and Bening sent to Paola for Millar and White and Potter theas three Proslaves came and waved examination and he would go to Jail So the Constable Jurd took him to Jail Shortly after that I got a order from Sheriff and [he] depetised me [and] ordered me to Bring Wm Quantrell to Larrance and turn him over to the athorities of Do[u]glis Co   I shoed my papers to H. H. Williams and my demand he would have to give up the Prisner [He] said he could not go to Paola for 2 hours but would send my depety wich was Jim Cree to see that Quantrell was not taken out of Jail before we got over and Cree said that Williams told him to go to White and tell White that Snyder had a order to take him [Quantrill] to Larance and when Williams and Myself came in paola Quantrell was Left

fearless man. He was also a truthful man, and he would not
have made any claims not fully justified. The only feature in
his description that seems improbable is his failing to kill Quantrill when he had the drop on him when he broke down the door

---

out of Jail and on the horse that Walker giv Him for his Sirvis of Geting
Some of the Kansas Abilishens kild.

The Rev. Robert Shearer, of Miami county, Kansas, in a letter to the
author, dated August 30, 1903, now in the Collection of the author, gives
an account of this affair. He has the date a year too late, saying it was
in the spring of 1862, when it was in the spring of 1861. There are other
things in the letter that contradict what others say, as follows:

Wm C. Quantrell was in Stanton in 1857 & 1858 in 1859 He went
to Pikes Peak and returned same year. He lived at Lawrence for some
time but returned to Stanton in 1861 in the early spring of 1862 he was
living near Stanton with a man by the name of Bening I was in the
Kansas Militia doing service on the Kan. line it was about the first of
April 1862 I came home on a short furlow leaving my Horse at Home I
went to Stanton telling my wife I would be back in one or 2 Hours   I
carried my Revolver with me as I walked up to the only Store in the
town Quantrell and a man by the name of Jurd a Constable was standing
about 30 feet from the Store House I shook Hands with them I saw
five men Walking very fast coming in our direction about 20 yards off they
Had Sharps Rifles slung over their Shoulders Mr. Jurd said to me I
depotise you to Protect Quantrell from those men I knew 2 of them One
of them Was Elias Snyder the other was called Buckskin as they came
near one of them drew his gun to shoot Quantrell I knocked the gun up
and drew my Revolver and said whats up Quantrell said they are going
to kill me I said what for he said he did not know Quantrell was very
Pale and Excited I said if there is any shooting I would take a Hand
in it and ordered Quantrell to go into the Store thoes men had their guns
cocked and trying to get a shot at him I kept my Pistol Presented in
their direction saying I would shoot the man that fired the first shot.
When Quantrell got in the store I held the door there was a ladder
standing in the center of the Floor reaching to the Sealing I ordered
Quantrell to enter a square Hole in cealing When he was up I walked
in and Started up the Ladder saying that the first man that stuck his head
above the trap door I would kill there was one bed up there I found
Quantrell sitting on it. They ordered me to come down or they would
shoot through the floor but they did not know just where we were then
they said they would burn the house the Store Keeper to save his building
tried to get us to come down Quantrell said to me to give him my pistol
and for me to go down and he would sell his life to the best advantage
I told him he was my prisoner and that I would turn him over to the
Sheriff I had told Jurd to send some one after the Sheriff and Possey to
Paola He sent a man by the name of John Billings on Quantrells Horse
it was 10 miles in less than three hours the Sheriff came with 4 good man
I turned Quantrell over to them next day they send a Man out to My
Place for me to Come to Paola I went in they wanted to know why I
had Quantrell under arest I was in the Jail talking with Quantrell and
the Sheriff I stated that I had taken him to save his life. In less than
20 Minutes he was out and gone He went straight for Missouri and took
the Bush.

and entered Bennings's house. His mistake seems to have been in consulting with Squire Hauser. The officer did his duty and saved the life of Quantrill, who stood on the verge of the grave a number of times before the gates of the old jail at Paola closed upon him.

The son of Bennings arrived at Paola early in the morning bearing a note from Quantrill to the border-ruffian Potter or some of the pro-slavery people with whom Quantrill was on intimate terms. It is possible that Squire Hauser had sent messengers to hasten the sheriff. Very soon after the intelligence of the posture of affairs arrived at Paola wheeled vehicles left that town at flying speed loaded with border-ruffians and pro-slavery friends of Quantrill. It was enough to know that an accomplice was in trouble and needed help. Potter claims to have led the chase, and the whole *posse* descended upon Stanton with that brazen assurance, loud profanity, and vulgar swagger then common to the border-ruffians in their attitude and intercourse with the Free-State settlers.[3] They found the commit-

3 In his rambling way Potter has a long account of this matter in the letters written by him and now in the Collection of the author. In that dated, Harrison, Arkansas, Jan. 20, 1896, he says:

A few weeks after this meeting Hon George W. Miller, called to me as I was passing Col Torreys Hotel, one morning early and handed me a letter from Quantrell stating that he was at Mr Bannings House, & Surrounded by some 14 Jayhawkers, who were trying to take him a Prisoner on a Fic[ti]tious charge

I after reading the letter I told Mr. Miller that there was but one thing to do & that was to Raise 14 other men & go over there & take him from them and Protect him

He wanted to know if I could get the men, & how long it would take. I replied that I will be ready in 15 Minutes with armed men, & will you go for one. he replied certainly

I sent to the Livery stable & got a Team & three seated Hack I called on Lawyer E. W. White Lawyer Robert White Lawyer Massey, Dr. W. D. Hoover, Tom Kelley, Goodwin Taylor merchant Lon Light, and several others whose names I do not now remember. We went there in a sweeping trot in Hacks, Buggies & on Horeseback. no one else in Town knew where we were going or any thing about our business, until we came back with Quantrell in triumph. We were all armed with Revolvers, Rifles, & shot guns, & Plenty of amunition

I was the first to arrive in the Little Town of Stanton. I went direct to the store of Tom Wilkerson, where Quantrell was in custody of the constable The store was filled with the 14 Jayhawkers under Capt Snyder I walked direct to Quantrell shook hands with him, & said How do you do Bill. What are you driving at now? stealing Horses?

Quantrell. Well they charge me with it.

Potter: Oh certainly they are all honest men that prefer the charge

ment papers ready and the justice anxious to have Quantrill off his hands alive. He delivered papers and prisoner to the sheriff or his representative and bade the ruffians be off, for he could restrain the men of Captain Snyder no longer. Quantrill was hurried to Paola, where he was caressed by the Torreys

against you I suppose. They know nothing about stealing Horses & Niggers, Robing & Burning Houses, & murdering citizens, from one end of the Land to the other.

Eli Snyder was standing a few feet from us & heard every word I said as I wanted him to. He winced & walked a few steps toward the door. I stooped down & whispered to Quantrell & said, Bill dont be uneasy. I have plenty of men coming. He replied I am not one bit afraid, and the same Pleasant & cheerful smile appeared on his lips, that allways accompanied him when in danger. Not one sign of fear did he show, either by word or act. His Lawyers called for a Private consultation, which the Justice granted in the store Room up stairs. When it was decided to Wave his examination & demand a commitment to the county jail It was well understood by us that the Justice who was a Jayhawker sympathizer & an enemy of Quantrell would prolong the examination by summoning one witness after another until reinforcements of Jayhawkers could collect & out number & over power us & then take Quantrell out & hang him.

I went to Judd the constable who had Quantrell in charge & asked him what he meant by summoning such men as Snyder, & his followers as a Posse comitattus, to assist to make an arrest of a citizen accused of crime? he replied well Potter I will tell you how it occurred at midnight a messenger come to my House & told me the Justice of the Peace wanted me. I went there. that Snyder & his men were all there with Arms & that they would assist in making the arrest, & save the trouble of disturbing the Neighbors. I replied. yes you are all very fraid of disturbing the country you ought to be ashamed of yourself for selecting such men a Possey commitattus

He handed me the Warrant & affidavit, & said. here Potter take these Papers. I will turn the matter over to you. I do not want to have any thing more to do with it.

I took the papers & told him to Dismiss his Jayhawkers & tell them he had no further use for them.

I went to Quantrell & his Lawyers told them what I had done Some of our Party were affraid of an attackt on our road to Paola. I told Quantrell that I would bring him safe & well to Paola, or never go back their alive

I wrote out the commitment to the county Jail & finally the Justice signed it.

On January 22nd Potter wrote another letter to W. W. Scott in which he continues his boasting account. The reader is requested to note with what pride he tells of his connection with Quantrill; how he shook hands with him and called him "Bill," etc. His additional account is as follows:

I went down stairs in the store & bought 2 lbs of Buck shot 1 Box of Water Proof caps & 2 lbs of Rifle Powder, recapped every gun that needed it, distributed amunition to all, with orders to use it & take good aim in case they made the attack

I will state here that Justice of the Peace very reluctantly, consented

and sympathized with by most of the inhabitants. He was feasted at the Torrey hotel until night, when he was "accompanied" to the jail, and was secretly given a heavy navy revolver. He was also furnished with a large knife with which he later assaulted the jailer, and he was assured that he would be pro-

---

to Permit Quantrell to wave his examination E. W. White & G W Miller his attorneys showed him the law in the case & told him very plainly that it was his duty to do so, & had no power or authority to prevent it. But even then he went down in the store & held a consultation with Eli Snyder in low tone of voice.   I over heard Snyder remark to him, the Justice of the Peace well, it is the only thing that we can do, some other time.

I frequently interrupted their secret conversation, by telling Mr Jurd that we were waiting on him & had no time to waste. Then Jurd finally went up stairs, & consented to the waiving of the examination He then wanted to go to his office & look up the Form to write out the commitment. I handed him a form of commitment which I had allready written out. all ready for his Signature. Jurd read it over & finally signed it. In the mean time, one of the Jayhawkers, below stated out loud in the store below, that we had sent over to Missouri for a Reinforcement of Two hundred Border Ruffians who were then, as he said on their way to Paola to Liberate Quantrell, and that Quantrell should never leave there alive & go back to Paola. I looked him in the face and told him Plainly that Quantrell was going to Paola, according to Law and that I would take him there or else, I would strew the road, between here & Paola with dead men, no farther threats were made.

I also summoned, a Deputy Sheriff by the name of Cree, as one of my Posse commitatus to Preserve the Peace & assist in guarding Quantrell to Paola I also summoned some two others who refused to act. one was a Doctor living in Stanton. I do not now remember his name.

Constable Judd, was sent up stairs, to ask me to search Quantrell for a Pistol that he was supposed to have.

I went to Quantrell, told him that the Snyder gang, wanted him searched, & to give me his Revolver if he had one. he immediately drew it from his Breast, & handed it to me, before Judd, got up in the Room. I put it in my breast under my vest. Turning to Jurd I said, Bill they think you are armed. let Mr Judd search you then they will be satisfied. he Judd done so & remarked, no he has no Weapons went on down before us & told them so. as soon as Judd's back was turned I handed Quantrell his Revolver, & told him that if they fired one shot, that I would shoot Snyder in the face & keep shooting, as long as there was one left, & for him to do the same I gave orders for all others to do I came down stairs in the Store with Goodwin Taylor & Quantrell & the rest of my Posse following me. with my Double barrell shot gun in my left hand, & my navy six in my right hand. I commanded the Peace I ordered the mob to disperse

The mob opened & some went out in the street & stood around & looked at us, but made no move to attack us.

The three seated Hack was at the door. Quantrell & G. Taylor occupied the Middle seat. three others were in the Hack Lon Light drove his Hack. Lawyer E. W. White & Lawyer Massey, rode in Mr. Whites Buggy They all started out of town Dr Hoover, Tom Kelley & my self were the last ones to leave town. no farther threats were made

Mr Cree, the constable of Ossawatomie Township, & one of the Dep-

tected, the foremost lawyers of the town being "retained" for him, or perhaps they volunteered their services in his behalf. Quantrill was regarded by Paola as a guest of honor. But it was then a border-ruffian town, as were Fort Scott and Leavenworth in the early territorial days. Many disloyal people remained there until the Civil War was well under way, but by the conclusion of that struggle it was a loyal Kansas town and has ever remained such; the border-ruffians disappeared.

Quantrill remained in jail for a few days. His friends were active in his behalf. They secured a writ of *habeas corpus*. Judge Thomas Roberts issued the writ. When Quantrill was produced before him, the judge gave him his liberty.⁴ There was great rejoicing in the town and Quantrill was again banquetted at Colonel Torrey's tavern, after which he was loaded with delicacies and caresses and escorted to the door, where he found "Black Bess" equipped to bear him to Missouri. He mounted the nag just as Captain Ely Snyder and H. H. Will-

---

uties of Mr Williams who was sheriff of Lykins County at that time since changed to its present name Miami County, were each members of the Republican party. Mr. Cree, by his honorable conduct in this case received the commendations, of the Honorable Republicans in his party as well as the Democrats, for there was a great many members of the Republican Party in Kansas, that were bitterly opposed to the Jayhawkers & their way of doing business. H. H. Williams the sheriff of Lycans County, was according to Quantrell's story, a Frequent visitor in Jennison's camp and often consulted, with him & he was well known at that time to be a Jayhawking Sympathizer In fact after the commencement of the civil War, that Desolated our loved country, H. H. Williams this same sheriff of Miami county in May or June 1861 organized a company of Jayhawkers at Ossawatomie, led them in Missouri went to, the Little town of West Point on the Border, & with his hands in open daylight, Broke down the door of the first store that was Robbed by the Kansas Jayhawkers, at the commencement of the war in the state of Missouri. The solid facts of History will accord him that high Honor. he was afterwards a colonel of a colored, Regiment of Kansas, Troops, & in 1866, under the Reconstruction acts he was sheriff of Jackson Co Missouri, for one Term.

⁴ In the Collection of the author there is a letter written by Thomas Roberts to H. V. Beeson. It is dated, Paola, May 16, 1881, and says:

Afterwards I saw him [Quantrill] in the early summer of 1861 he was confined in the County Jail of Miami County (then Lykins Co) Kansas. I was then acting as Probate Judge of said County. He was taken out and brought before me on a Writ of Habeas Corpus, and by me was released from Custody their being no legal cause for his confinement. after his release he left Paola going North and that was the last time I ever saw him I am confident it was the same W. C. Quantrell that led the gang of Bushwhackers that committed so many Atrocities in Kansas and Missouri for instance the Lawrence raid.

iams entered the town with a *posse* to take him to Lawrence
upon writs issued by the courts there. Quantrill put his thumbs
to his nose and made a defiant gesture, and then, leaning forward in his saddle, patting himself in a still more defiant, vulgar, and insulting gesture, put spurs to his beast and bade a final
farewell to Kansas. This was the third day of April, 1861, and
he never returned again except as a spy, murderer, or assassin
under the cloak of a soldier in the Rebellion.[5]

---

[5] In his letter dated Jan. 22, 1896, already referred to, Potter tells
with many a proud boast of the reception tendered Quantrill at Paola, and
quotations therefrom are made here:

We got to Paola took supper at Col Torreys Hotel. after supper I
accompanied Quantrell to the county Jail. I took his Pistol, & after Tom
Akers, the Jailer searched him, I went in his cell to talk to him, & then
gave him his Revolver again, & some caps & amunition I told him in case
the jail was attackted, to remain, back in his cell, & make every shot tell
I told him that as soon as I heard one shot that I would be among them
with some thirty or more armed men and would commence firing on any
mob, that would attempt to take him out of Jail to mob him he remained
there some three days before E. W. White, G. W. Miller & my self had him
brought out of jail on a writ of Habeas corpus, before Mr Roberts, the
Probate judge who was a Republican, but a man that was strictly Honest,
& Honorable who Examined the evidence against W. C. Quantrell. He
asked Tom Akers if he had any farther Evidence against W. C. Quantrell
or any other authority for Holding W. C. Quantrell a Prisoner. He replied
that he had not. Turning to Quantrell he said to him, you are discharged
from custody & at Liberty to go where you pleas. W. C. Quantrell &
Myself immediately went to the Hotel, which was kept by Col Torrey.
where, a hasty Lunch, of cake, Bread & butter, & sandwich's, was hastily
Prepared by the Ladies of the Hotel & col Torrey. While hurriedly filling
his over coat Pocket with them said to W. C. Quantrell you well know that
you are always welcome, & that we are allways glad to see you. But you
see, What danger you have incurred.   What trouble you have got your
friends in to in assisting you. and now do not come back here any more
until this matter is, all settled & come here no more, until You can come
with out danger to your self & Friends. he promised to follow his advice.
I had his fine Black Hors fed, saddled & Bridled & wating for him.
I gave him directions which road to take to avoid meeting Snyders men,
who were guarding the Road to West Point Missouri Expecting to, meet
him & Recapture him on his way to Missouri W. C. Quantrell mounted
his horse, & went out of town in a Lope, Waving his Revolver over his
head & was soon lost to view He arrived at Squiresville some 14 Miles
distant in less than two hours after, leaving Town & went [to] Little
Santa Fee & Missouri the same evening

Following is a certified transcript of the records of Miami county in
this proceeding against Quantrill:

A.

STATE OF KANSAS   ⎫
                  ⎬ ss.
COUNTY OF LYKINS ⎭

        To any Constable of Stanton Township in said County Greeting:
Whereas W. C. Quantrill has this day been brought before me on a

warrant issued from my office this 26th day of March 1861, charged with the crime of Larceny on the Oath of Eli Snyder, and whereas the Defendant W. C. Quantrill this day waives his examination before me this 26th day of March 1861.

These are therefore to command you to take the Body of the said W. C. Quantrill and him safely keep and deliver him forthwith without delay to the Keeper of the County Jail in the City of Paola, there to remain until discharged by due course of Law.

Witness my hand and seal this 26th day of March 1861.

Samuel H. Houser
Justice of Peace

I, Samuel H. Houser, a Justice of the Peace, certify that the above warrant is a true copy of an original one filed in my office, this April 2, 1861.

Samuel H. Houser
Justice of Peace

STATE OF KANSAS } ss.
LYKINS COUNTY

Before me, Samuel H. Houser a Justice of the Peace for said County personally came Eli Snyder who being duly sworn according to law deposeth and saith that on or about the March 1st 1861 that there was a horse stolen near Sumner in this State, also one horse stolen near Atchison in this State, and different other crimes have been committed, and this deponent says or does verily believe that one Quantrill is guilty of the facts charged, and further this deponent saith that according to good authority and report, the Sheriff of Lykins County has a writ at this time for the above named Quantrill.

Sworn to and subscribed before me this 26th day of March 1861.

Samuel H. Houser
Justice of Peace

Eli Snyder.

I, Samuel H. Houser, a Justice of the Peace, certify that the above Affidavit is a true copy of an original one filed in my office April 2, 1861.

Samuel H. Houser
Justice of Peace

A.

STATE OF KANSAS } ss.
COUNTY OF LYKINS

TO ANY CONSTABLE OF SAID COUNTY.

Whereas complaint has been made before me, Samuel H. Houser, Justice of the Peace, in and for the County of Lykins upon the oath of Eli Snyder that one Quantrill, late of the County of Lykins, did on or about March 1st 1861 steal and take from the owner near Sumner in this State, one horse, and different other crimes that are alleged to the charge of said Quantrill, and according to good report, the Sheriff of this County has at this time a writ for said Quantrill. These are therefore to command you to take the said Quantrill, if he can be found in your State and take and safely keep the said Quantrill, so that you have his body forth with before me to answer the said complaint according to Law.

Given under my hand this 26th day of March 1861.

Samuel H. Houser
Justice of Peace

I, S. H. Houser, a Justice of the Peace, certify that the within committment is a true copy of the original.

April 2, 1861.   Samuel H. Houser J. P.

Cost.

docket	$	10
oath		10
warrant		50
3 papers		30
trying		75
order		35
mittim.		35
docket		25

$2.70

State of Kansas ⎰ Criminal Action.
Against Quantrill ⎱
Eli Snyder for State.
Before me, Samuel H. Houser a Justice of the Peace
for said Lykins County, personally came Eli Snyder
who being duly sworn according to law says there
was a warrant issued to Constable E. B. Jurd on
26th day of March 1861. Warrant served on prisoner in custody.

E. B. Jurd Const.

Const. Cost
Mileage to

Bennings	20
Ser. warrant	50
Sum. 13 mentto	
take Quantril	3.25
Taken to Jail	50
Sum. 3 men	75
copy	10
Milage	1.10

$6.40

March 26th 1861
Case called. Prisoner waived the right of examination and was committed to jail in the custody of
E. B. Jurd Constable to await further trial according to Law.

Samuel H. Houser
Justice of Peace

March 30, 1861. Mittimus Returned. Prisoner delivered to the jailer, also a copy of Mittimus. Given
under my hand this 1st day of April, 1861.

S. H. Houser
Justice of Peace

I, Samuel H. Houser, a Justice of the Peace, certify that the within
a true copy of an original transcript of my docket. April 2nd 1861.

Samuel H. Houser
Just. Peace.

TO THE HONORABLE THOMAS ROBERTS PROBATE JUDGE WITH-
IN AND FOR LYKINS COUNTY, STATE OF KANSAS, GREET-
ING:

Your petitioner W. C. Quantrill would most respectfully represent to
your Honor that he is unlawfully imprisoned or restrained of his liberty by
Thomas Akers, Jailer in the jail in the City of Paola, County and State
first above mentioned, and your petitioner W. C. Quantrill further avers
that on or about the 26th day of March A. D. 1861 upon the oath of one
Eli Snyder before S. H. Houser, a Justice in Stanton Township, County
and State aforesaid, your petitioner was arrested and brought before the
said Houser on a charge of horse stealing and other crimes alleged to have
been committed on or about of March A. D. 1861 at or near Sumner and
Atchison in this State. Your petitioner further states that the said arrest
was malicious, false and illegal, and in proof of this would state First.
That the places designated in said Affidavit are not in the bounds of this,
Lykins County. Second, That the said Justice of the Peace, S. H. Houser
had no right to hear an examination, and commit the said Quantrill, not
having jurisdiction in this said case. Third. That the said Justice had
no power to waive an examination. Fourth. That the said Justice erred
in not fixing bail in the said case. Fifth. That the said Affidavit does not
charge your petitioner with having stolen any particular horse nor from
whom stolen, nor whether there was property or ownership in the said
property. Sixth. And for other good and sufficient reasons set forth by
the papers here to attached marked (A) and made a part of this petition,
the same being copies of the Affidavit, Warrant and other papers in the
case under the hand of the said S. H. Houser J. P. Wherefore your petitioner prays that he may be released from said confinement, and restored

13

to his liberty by your Honor. Seventh. And that he further states that on the day set apart for his examination before the said S. H. Houser, Justice of the Peace, that the reason of his waiving his right to investigation and examination, that an armed body of men surrounded the said prisoner and the Court, and that he was under duress and great bodily harm, and even death itself was threatened. Eighth. The Affidavit in the above entitled cause sets forth no sufficient cause for a warrant to issue against the said Petitioner. All of which he respectfully submits.

W. C. Quantrill

The affiant W. C. Quantrill being duly sworn says that the facts set forth in the foregoing petition is true to the best of his knowledge and belief.

W. C. Quantrill

Sworn to before me and subscribed in my presence this 2nd day of April A. D. 1861.

Seal

Thomas Roberts
Probate Judge.

Now on this 3rd day of April A. D. 1861 comes W. C. Quantrill and files his petition for a writ of Habeas Corpus to reclaim the body of the said W. C. Quantrill from the custody of Thomas Akers, jailer of said Lykins County, State of Kansas, for the reason that the said W. C. Quantrill is illegally detained by the said jailer, and restrained of his liberty contrary to law. Whereupon a writ of Habeas Corpus was duly issued to said jailer and W. L. Potter authorized to serve the same. Now comes Thomas Akers, jailer of Lykins County and returns the above writ with the body of the above W. C. Quantrill. It appearing to the Court the offence for which the said W. C. Quantrill was committed to the custody of the said jailer was one of which the said Samuel H. Houser, Justice of the Peace of said County had no jurisdiction. The jurisdiction being in a Justice of County where said offence was alleged to have been committed. Ordered and adjudged that the said W. C. Quantrill be discharged from further custody of the jailer of said Lykins County, and he is hereby discharged from the same.

Thomas Roberts
Probate Judge.

STATE OF KANSAS ⎱
LYKINS COUNTY ⎰ ss.

To Thomas Akers, jailer of said County, You are hereby commanded to have the body of W. C. Quantrill, now imprisoned and restrained of his liberty by you, by virtue of a Mittamus issued by one Samuel H. Houser, a Justice of the Peace in and for said County, in the State of Kansas, together with the time and cause of said imprisonment and detention before me the undersigned Judge of the Probate Court in and for the County of Lykins and State of Kansas without delay to do and receive what shall then and there be considered concerning the person imprisoned.

In testimony whereof I, Thomas Roberts, Judge of the Probate Court in and for said County of Lykins, and State of Kansas have hereunto set my hand and affixed my official seal at Paola this 3rd day of April A. D. 1861.

Thomas Roberts
Probate Judge.

Seal

I hereby authorize W. L. Potter to serve the within process.

Thomas Roberts
Probate Judge.

Received the within writ by delivering it to Thos. Akers at 15 minutes past ten o'clock A. M. of the 2nd day of April 1861.

W. L. Potter Ms.

Received the within writ at 17 minutes past ten o'clock A. M. of the 2nd day of April 1861. Executed by bringing the prisoner W. C. Quantrill into the custody of the Court.

Thos. Akers

Jailer

THE STATE OF KANSAS ⎱
COUNTY OF MIAMI ⎰ ss. PROBATE COURT.

I, Thos. Hodges, sole Judge and ex-officio Clerk of the Probate Court, within and for the County aforesaid, do hereby certify the foregoing to be a true Copy of Habeas Corpus proceedings in the matter of the State of Kansas vs W. C. Quantrill, as the same appears from the records of said Court

IN TESTIMONY WHEREOF, I, have hereunto set my hand and affixed the Seal of said Court at Paola Kansas this 11th day of March A. D. 1908.

Probate Judge
SEAL
Miami County, Kansas

Thos. Hodges,
Probate Judge and
ex-officio Clerk.

THE STATE OF KANSAS ⎱
COUNTY OF MIAMI ⎰ ss.

I, Thos. Hodges, sole Judge of the Probate Court, within and for said County, the same being a Court of Law and Record, hereby certify that the signature attached to the above certificate, purporting to be that of Thos. Hodges is his genuine signature, and that he was at the time thereof ex-officio Clerk of said Probate Court, and as such full faith and credit are due his acts, and that the attestation of said clerk is in due form of law, and by the proper officer.

WITNESS my hand and the seal of said Court, at Paola, Kansas, this 11th day of March, 1908.

Probate Judge
SEAL
Miami County, Kansas.

Thos. Hodges,
Probate Judge.

CHAPTER XIV

QUANTRILL returned to Jackson county much discouraged. Those who saw him in those distressed days say he was despondent. His efforts to stimulate business had terminated disastrously. He realized that he was lucky to escape from Captain Snyder with his life, and for this great good fortune he was duly thankful. In his revengeful heart, however, he treasured his humiliation to another day when he might exact a bloody retribution. His experience had demonstrated that his future field could not be in Kansas unless he crossed the border with an adequate force. But his operations had been conducted hitherto with few men. Skulking like a craven about cow-pens, horse-corrals, and isolated negro-quarters along the skirts of Missouri had been his ideal life, and the possibility of a command had not occurred to him. The future appeared black, barren, fruitless. From Kansas he seemed shut out forever, and he could no longer prey upon the Missourians. If he should steal slaves could he escape with them? In this dilemma he had no intention of going about any honest work, and it began to appear that in exchanging Kansas for Missouri he had made a poor bargain, even though the blood of three men cried from the ground in his exultant ears as the result of it.

Such characters can only live and thrive in troublous times, in disrupted conditions, in a disturbed state, in a disordered society. While the times were out of joint indeed, so novel and unusual were they that the possibilities in his lines did not reveal themselves sufficiently for him to perceive them. Missouri was just entering on that vacillating course which made her ridiculous in the eyes of both the North and the South and ended in humiliation. From the pleasant pursuit of pushing slavery into other countries she was compelled to bestir herself to save the ignominious institution within her own bounds. Atchison and other leaders of border-ruffian hordes headed slave caravans to Texas and Louisiana. From crusaders for the extension of human slavery they became exiles for a forlorn hope.

In such times petty characters are swept aside and forgotten. Quantrill was stranded and overlooked. Realizing his insignificance, he cast about him to see if perchance there might not appear some safe port, be it ever so foul and disreputable, where he could furl his sail and outride the storm. He renewed his visits to the home of Morgan Walker. In his extremity there was an attraction there which he could not resist and upon which he fixed his hopes — a daughter who had been divorced from her husband because of her own shortcomings.[1] Indeed, some have believed that it was on account of Nannie (or Anna) Walker Slaughter that Quantrill planned and executed the

---

[1] In relation to Quantrill and the daughter of Morgan Walker, it develops that Walker had a daughter named Nannie (or Anna). She married a very respectable and good man named Slaughter, who was a merchant at Blue Springs. He is also said to have been a physician. She was a fine-looking woman. But for her nose, which was crooked and gross, giving her a sensual look, she would have been beautiful. Her form is said to have been fine. There was a doctor boarding with Slaughter. There came a very cold spell of weather one winter. In the room of the physician there was no fireplace, and she made a bed upon the floor in the room of herself and husband where there was a fire in which the doctor was to sleep until the weather moderated. One night Slaughter was awakened by his wife's getting back into bed with him, and his suspicions were aroused; but he said nothing. The following night he feigned sleep, and his wife left his bed and lay down upon that occupied by the physician, remaining there a long time. Slaughter, when convinced of his wife's infidelity, arose to kill the doctor, but that worthy escaped. He at once obtained a divorce from his wife, and she returned to the home of her father. This was a short time before the raid on Morgan Walker's home by Quantrill and his companions. She had a number of lovers, among them George Todd and Quantrill. In April, 1862, Joe Vaughan married her. He took her to Clay county, or to some place north of the Missouri river, and kept her there until after the close of the war. He was never again with Quantrill nor with the Confederate army. Morgan Walker died about the close of the war, and his daughter inherited her part of his land, which she sold, and with the proceeds set up a bawdy house at Baxter Springs. After receiving her money she told Vaughan she had no further use for him and made him leave. She was a woman after Quantrill's own heart, and it may be that some acquaintance with her caused him to plan the Morgan Walker raid as a means of winning her to himself.

treacherous plot to betray his companions to death. She was to become heir to a large tract of land, slaves, and money, and these things appealed to Quantrill. To his mind, the consummation of such betrayal would make him a hero in the eyes of women, and with this particular woman he may have been correct in his judgment. But even this debasing design failed him and came to naught.

In the spring of 1861 Gill moved to Texas, and Quantrill, in desperation and overflowing with resentment for what he termed the ingratitude of the Missourians, went there with him. That country, however, did not seem to please him, and he soon left it and went to the Cherokee Nation. The irresponsible life of the Indian suited Quantrill. In the land of the Cherokees he lived with Joel Mayes, a thrifty and prosperous man of only part Cherokee blood, and who, many years after the war, was elected Head Chief of the Nation. Mayes espoused the cause of the Confederacy and was captain of a company or band of Cherokees who followed General Ben. McCulloch to Missouri. Quantrill was with this company, but it is not known that he was a member of it, though he always claimed to have fought with it at the battle of Wilson Creek. The Indian mode of warfare had a great charm for Quantrill, and later he copied it almost entirely, even to the custom of scalping the dead. At Wilson Creek the Indians hung about the skirts of the battle and gathered all manner of plunder and army-drift, including not a few scalps, in all of which Quantrill participated.

Quantrill deserted his Indian friends after the battle of Wilson Creek and followed General Price north to the Missouri river. Why he did this can only be conjectured, for the Indian life was to his liking. It can be accounted for, perhaps, by remembering his infatuation for the fallen daughter of Morgan Walker. Women of such character ever had great influence over him, even where there was no property consideration involved. And the tightening of army rules and the enforcement of discipline as General Price's army assumed a higher organization served to dispel the Indian forces which had operated with it, and while he did not relish the strict routine of the life of the regular soldier, Quantrill saw in it numerous possibilities in the line of his inclinations. Unlimited license attracted him. The unsettling of society along the border, due to the war, and which he now began to perceive, held illimitable charms for him, a foretaste of which he had enjoyed in the capacities of Jayhawker and border-ruffian.

Quantrill is identified in the battle of the Drywood, east of Fort Scott, September 2, 1861. Colonel Moonlight there made a daring attack on the Confederate main body, the audacity of it alone saving him from destruction, for the enemy supposed he was supported by the whole Union force. Turning sharply to the north out of a deep ravine in pursuit of scattered pickets or scouts, he suddenly rode out on the prairie in front of the enemy's army. He hurried forward a small cannon he had with him and commanded it to open fire upon the batteries of the Confederates. The gunner made two shots, neither one effective. In disgust Moonlight sprang from his horse, wheeled the gun about, aimed it himself, and fired. The shot struck a Confederate gun which was pouring out grape, dismounting it and sending it turning end over end several yards into the ranks marshaled behind. Then, before the astonished enemy could recover from the surprise of the whole proceeding, Moonlight turned and marched his company away unmolested. Quantrill was near this dismounted gun and afterwards described the occurrence to a captive Union soldier, one who had stood by Moonlight at the time.[2]

2 Lieutenant Reuben A. Randlett, Company A, Fifth Kansas, who lives, 1908, in Topeka. Randlett described the action of Colonel Moonlight to the author. He was standing near the gun and saw it aimed by Moonlight and witnessed the destruction of the enemy's gun by the shot. Randlett was afterwards captured by Quantrill at Aubry and retained by him for several weeks, being finally released, an account of which will appear later in this volume.

In a conversation with Cyrus Leland, Jr., the author was told that Colonel Moonlight had been an artillery officer in the regular army. At Osceola, Moonlight and Colonel Wear sat discussing the merits of artillery. The court-house was in plain view of them. Moonlight pointed to a small howitzer and said that with it he could put a ball between two windows in the building, which he designated. Colonel Wear doubted it and Moonlight wheeled the gun into position and fired it, hitting the mark. Colonel Wear said it was an accident. Moonlight designated two other windows

Quantrill was with Price as a nondescript at the siege and battles of Lexington. He is described as having worn there at the siege a red shirt and a waving black plume, inspired, doubtless, by his association with the Indians. At Lexington energy and bravery have been attributed to him.[3]

In the retreat of the Confederate troops, Quantrill, it is said, followed General Price as far south as the Osage, where his taste for the life of a soldier in the regular service seems to have vanished altogether. He turned back and soon arrived once more in Jackson county. Having been cast and schooled in petty villainies, he could not comprehend the broad principles for which the Confederacy contended. To him warfare was nothing without opportunity for assassination and plunder. He again assumed the rôle of detective and soon reported to Morgan Walker that some people from Kansas were robbing citizens in what was then known as the Stone neighborhood, four miles north of Blue Springs. Andrew J. Walker (or "Andy" Walker, as he was called) raised eleven men, of whom Quantrill was one, and went to find the marauders, who were traced to the house of a citizen named De Witt, which they had just left when their pursuers arrived. They were followed to the farm of Strawder Stone, where they had robbed the house, in doing which one of them had struck Mrs. Stone on the head with a pistol for her sharp and righteous reproof. Walker and his party came up with them as they were coming out of the house of one Thompson, a quarter of a mile beyond Stone's, mounting to depart.

---

between which he would put a ball, which, when he did, convinced Colonel Wear of his splendid ability as an artillery officer.

3 In his *Noted Guerrillas*, Major Edwards has the following:

As a private he served with conspicuous daring in the battles of Carthage, Wilson's Creek, and Lexington, but especially at the latter place did his operations in presence of the enemy attract attention. Mounted there on a splendid horse, armed with a Sharpe's carbine and four navy revolvers, for uniform a red shirt, and for oriflame a sweeping black plume, he advanced with the farthest, fell back with the last, and was always cool, deadly, and omnipresent. General Price — himself notorious for being superbly indifferent under fire — remarked his bearing and caused mention to me made of it most favorably.

General Price made no mention of Quantrill in his official report of the battle of Lexington. The notice above referred to has not been found.

Quantrill was not in the battle of Carthage. When it was fought he was yet in Texas or the Cherokee Nation.

Walker and his party there charged them, killing the man who had struck Mrs. Stone, and wounding two others, both of whom died at Independence later. Walker says these marauders burned the houses of both Stone and Thompson, but this is not confirmed. They must have been acting under authority, for the civil officers took note of the matter, and both Stone and Thompson were arrested for murder and arraigned before Judge Hightower. Quantrill appeared before the justice and made affidavit that he had himself done the killing, and that neither Stone nor Thompson were guilty, and they were released; but it does not appear that Quantrill was detained in custody. The soldier killed by Quantrill at Stone's was the first Federal soldier killed in Jackson county, Mo., in the Civil War.

This occurrence seems to have put Quantrill forward materially. He became the ruling spirit of the *nebula* which developed later into his guerrilla band. A deserter from Price's army named Searcy arrived in Jackson county about Christmas, 1861, and began to rob citizens. Quantrill and his men captured him, though not because of the robberies of which he was guilty, but because he had attempted to shoot Quantrill. The band took Searcy to the Little Blue and there hung him. From long practice and its frequent perpetration murder was becoming easy to Quantrill, and he foresaw a rich harvest in that field for the future.[4]

Probably the first real contest with an armed force engaged

---

[4] The statements of Andrew J. Walker are the principal authority for the account of Quantrill's operations after deserting Price at the Osage and his return to Jackson county. In his letter of February 3, 1883, already referred to, he says:

He stayed a part of the balance of the winter at Mark Gill's, was back and forth to my father's several times during the winter. He went with Gill to Texas in the spring of 1861; but in the summer returned to the Cherokee Nation and stayed a time with a Cherokee named Joel Mayes. He staid there until the battle of Springfield, Mo., between Generals Lyon and McCulloch. Sometime after that he returned to my fathers. I think it was about the first of October, 1861. Shortly after he returned, some Kansas men came into the neighborhood robbing. I got 11 men together, Quantrill with me and we started on the hunt of them. Coming onto them we fired into them. It was near old Mr. Thompson's house and they accused Thompson and Stone of the affair. They burned their houses and taking them prisoners were going to kill them; but Quantrill to save them from death went to a Justice of the Peace and made oath that it was he who did it and that neither Thompson or Stone knew any thing of it.

in by Quantrill and his men was in Independence. It occurred
shortly after the Strawder Stone affair. In the Rush Bottom
there was organized a band of Homeguards. These were in
Independence one day, and Quantrill and his men rode into the

The Union troops then attempted to catch him.   He then began his
Guerilla warfare and became chief of the band.
    In his letter dated Feb. 22, 1883, Walker says:
    The time I spoke of firing on those Kansas men, it was in Missouri
about three miles from where I lived. Stone and Thompson were both old
settlers in Missouri. I was not with Quantrill all the time during the war.
I went south shortly after we fired into that squad near Thompson's and
returned in the latter part of the summer of '61 [He means 1862, for
it was late in the fall of 1861 when he fired on the Kansas men at
Thompson's. — W. E. C.] and he went south the same fall. I staid with
Capt. Todd who was leading officer that winter. Quantrill returned in the
spring of '63 and I staid with him till March of '64; but he went to
Texas with his men in the fall of '63 where he stayed all winter on Red
River. Early in 1864 he started north for Missouri. Myself and others
went to Old Mexico and I never saw him again.
    In the *Kansas City Journal*, May 12, 1888, there is printed an inter-
view with Walker, in which he says:
    He stopped with Marcus Gill, father of Judge Turner A. Gill. Early
in the spring of 1861 he went to Texas, but he did not stay there long.
He went into the Cherokee Nation, where he put up with Joe Mays, the
present chief.   He went with a company of Cherokees, of which Mays
was Captain, to Springfield, and took part in the battle at that place, in
which General Lyon was killed. He returned to Jackson County soon after
General Price captured General Mulligan at Lexington. A week later he
reported to my father that some Kansas men were robbing people down in
what is called the Stone neighborhood, which is four miles north of Blue
Springs. I got eleven men together that day and evening. Quantrill and
my younger brother Zach were away, but they returned next morning. We
then got on our horses and went after the robbers. They had gone from
De Witt's house to Strawder Stone's farm, where they plundered his residence. Mrs. Stone got angry at them and talked pretty sharp to them,
and one of them struck her on the head with his pistol. We overtook them
just as they were coming out of Mr. Thompson's house, a quarter of a mile
from Mr. Stone's house. They had just mounted their horses. We put
spurs to our horses when we saw them, and as we neared them, fired,
killing the man who struck Mrs. Stone with his pistol. Two others were
wounded, both of whom, it was reported, died at Independence subsequently.
We then dispersed. The next day Stone and Thompson were taken to
Independence, and 'Squire Hightower investigated the death of the man
killed. Quantrill went before the justice and informed him that Stone and
Thompson had nothing to do with the killing, and that he and others were
responsible. The result was that they were exonerated. Then the Federals
in Independence wanted Quantrill, but he kept out of their way. I give
you these details because I want the public to know just how Quantrill
began his celebrated career as a guerrilla and bushwhacker. He was at
that time just like the rest of us. He was content to be one of the
privates. I was, in fact, during the fight at Stone's farm, the leader.
About Christmas of that year George Searcy came into Jackson County and

town also. The Homeguards took refuge in the court house. There was much shooting back and forth; the Homeguards running out of the building to shoot at the guerrillas as they went around a corner. In one of these sorties, Bill Haller captured a Homeguard named Smiley after he (Haller) had shot out every

began robbing Union men of their horses and mules. Quantrill had by that time become the leading spirit among the guerrillas. I had, in obedience to the advice of my father, returned to the farm, and given up bushwhacking. Quantrill and his men captured Searcy, and took him to a point on the Little Blue River and hanged him. I was not a member of the band then, but I went along and helped hang Searcy. He was a rebel soldier, who had been with Price in every battle up to the time he left the command. A short time before his death he waylaid Quantrill and attempted to shoot him.

I went to Arkansas in February, 1862. I got back just before the fight at Independence in the summer of that year. In the winter of 1862 I went to Colonel Burris at Wyandotte, and surrendered to him. He gave me protection papers. But Colonel Penick arrested me in Independence and put me in prison there. It was all my Union friends could do to keep him from hanging me. In order to get out of prison I joined the Federal army. I was given a furlough of ten days, but I never returned. The ninth day I was going to Captain George Todd's camp. I met Mathew Scott, a Union man who had protected me. He asked me where I was going. I told him I was going to join Captain Todd's bushwhackers. He said: "You are joking, ain't you?" I said, "No." "Well", said he, "I'm going to town and they will ask me about you, what shall I tell Colonel Penick?" "Tell him to go to h—l", I replied. I went to Captain Todd's camp. He told me to go back home and fix up quarters in the brush and stay there all winter. John Koger, William Cox, Alf Ketchum and myself fixed up a board shanty in the brush. Colonel Penick was determined to capture me. He searched every house in the neighborhood. The second night we were in our shanty it snowed about four inches. Next day the Federal scouts saw our smoke and that night Penick came with eighty men and surrounded us. I was stripped to my underclothing and was barefooted. Ketchum ran out of the shanty and was shot down. I was the next man out, and I went too fast for the bullets. Koger was badly wounded and was captured. Cox escaped. I went one mile barefooted in the snow to my own house. I had no clothes there to put on. As it happened there was an old pair of pants that had been left by Fletch Taylor, one of Quantrill's most noted men. They only reached to my knees. I put them on. I also put on a boy's hat, a negro woman's shoes and a bed blanket. I then bade my wife and child good-by, and told the colored woman to scatter corn, when she fed the hogs, in my tracks so that they would be blotted out in the snow. I took the big road to within two miles of Independence. Two days later I joined Captain Todd. He then had ten men. We staid all winter in the Lake hills, near Lake City.

Judge A. J. Liddil, of Independence, in the *Kansas City Star*, Jan. 5, 1905, describes Quantrill's recovery of some cattle about this time. He also says that Quantrill's father was suspected of having been a counterfeiter, and he may have handled counterfeit money in his strolling capacity of tinker and book-peddler. Judge Liddil, in this article, says that he

load in his pistols. He pretended that his pistols were loaded and commanded Smiley to surrender, and he did so. Quantrill could not dislodge the Homeguards and got three or four of his men wounded, among them Bennett Wood.

Times began to improve for Quantrill. From this date they became more and more to his liking. Disorders followed imme-

---

was the first leader of the Quantrill band, a claim others do not admit. He says:

Quantrill had come to Independence some time before I was directed by General Price and Governor Jackson to do what I could to restore order. All we knew of him was that he had some reputation as a fighter and his own statement to me that his family had been compelled to leave one of the states because his father was suspected of being a counterfeiter.

There had been a great deal of horse and cattle stealing going on about Independence in those troublesome times, and I had information that caused me to strongly suspect a gang of renegades from Kansas. Just as I was preparing to start in pursuit of them, Quantrill asked that he be allowed to join my party. I consented and he became one of us, being probably about the ninth to join. We captured the leader of the gang of thieves, with more than a hundred horses and a large number of cattle. The thief we held court on, I acting as judge advocate, and we condemned him to death and executed the sentence. The horses and cattle were returned to their owners, those who could afford it being required to pay $10 a head for the return of the horses.

This affair led to the belief, or pretended belief, on the part of Union soldiers stationed in Kansas City that I and my men were in league with the horse thieves, and merely returned the stolen property as a ruse for extorting money from our neighbors. As a consequence, we were made the object of an attack some time later, during which I had a narrow escape from capture, being shot at, I think, at least 500 times. . . . Because of my family, I was compelled to be away from the company a good deal, and it was decided to elect a leader who should have direct command and plan our movements. The men offered me the place, but I declined it, and their next choice was Quantrill.

The errors of Major Edwards must be still further refuted. He says:

In May, 1861, Quantrell enlisted in Captain Stewart's company of cavalry, an organization composed of hardy settlers from what was then known as the Kansas Neutral Lands.

As already shown, Quantrill went to Texas early in 1861 with Marcus Gill and did not return until he drifted in behind General Price's army. So, this statement of Major Edwards is not true.

The description of the hanging of Searcy is given by Edwards:

One Searcy, claiming to be a Southern man, was stealing all over Jackson county and using violence here and there when he could not succeed through persuasion. Quantrell swooped down upon him one afternoon, tried him that night, and hung him the next morning. Before they pulled him up, he essayed to say something. He commenced: "Not so fast, gentlemen! It's awful to die until red hands have had a chance to wash them-

diately upon the beginning of hostilities, and where there were disorder and relaxation of the operation of law Quantrill could prosper. His course began to define itself. The lowering of the dark clouds of war and strife was really the lifting of the mists for Quantrill. His problem, as he read it, consisted in making the Missouri people believe that he was devoted to their cause from principle, hence, he was born in Maryland and was a Southerner by birth. To this fiction was added still another older brother, one who was serving in Lee's Army of Virginia. Quantrill worked the elder-brothers business on the Missourians very successfully. These mythical brothers stood him in good stead many times. Knowledge of them always came through women to whom he paid attentions. When men made inquiry of him he observed a studied silence. It was easy to deceive a devoted woman, and as a means of spreading intelligence an enthusiastic woman can never be surpassed.

Then, too, Quantrill's experience in Kansas had convinced him that he could no longer deal doubly — that he must now be one thing or the other, else he would soon front a file of grim guerrillas lined up to produce a subject for a short quick funeral. So he gave his entire energy and talents to the insidious warfare in which he engaged.

selves.'' Here his voice was strangled like the voice of a man who has no saliva in his mouth. Four Guerrillas dragged on the rope. There seemed to be — as his body rested at last from its contortions — the noise as of the waving of wings. Could it be that Searcy's soul was taking its flight? Seventy-five head of horses were found in the dead man's possession, all belonging to citizens of the county, and any number of title deeds to lands, notes, mortgages, and private accounts. All were returned.

It will be noted that Searcy was a member of General Price's army. It is very strange that that admission is made. According to all rules he should have been charged up to Kansas.

Searcy was the man of whom Judge Liddil gave an account in the quotation from the *Kansas City Star*. It will be observed that Judge Liddil *does* charge him up to Kansas.

CHAPTER XV

TO UNDERSTAND properly the events which transpired in Missouri after the Civil War began something of the political conditions existing there must be set down here. By the commencement of the year 1862 matters pertaining to the war had found permanent alignment in Missouri. He that was then for the Union remained so, and he that was for the Confederacy stood for it to the end. The division was sharp, often cutting quite through families — father from son, brother from brother. Feeling reached a higher point than in any other state. There was deeper and more lasting bitterness between the people of Missouri than existed in any other part of the land. Neighbors with no cause for quarrel beyond Union and dis-Union became enemies relentless and cruel as death. They pursued and harried one another with sword and torch. Assassination was rampant for years. And for why? The Missourian is kind, hospitable, generous, tolerant, open-hearted. He is charitable above all others. He will ride through heat or snow or storm to relieve distress. Bred on a generous soil, he is broad of shoulder, a man of affairs, and more generally of liberal fortune than the people of other States. General intelligence was always of a high order in Missouri. Missouri is the mother of the West. Her people are a thinking people, independent and self-reliant. They are now and have been from the first the most conservative body of people in the Union. They adhere to the simple principles proclaimed by our fathers with more unanimity and greater tenacity than the people of any other State. They are sane and safe, and they are as progressive as the most theoretical could desire. They have less demagogy in public life than can be found in any other country of equal size in the world. And as soldiers they have never been surpassed on earth.

It was these very qualities of her people that made the Civil

War a carnival of blood in Missouri. Every man stood upon his own convictions, and he stood immovable. He laid his life and all his possessions upon the altar of his devotion. Such a man may be ruined, despoiled, slain, but he will not be false to his sense of right and justice.

The people of Missouri were for the Union by an overwhelming majority every day of the Civil War, and they demonstrated that fact by enlisting in the Federal army. Including militia, nearly one hundred and fifty thousand soldiers were furnished the Union by Missouri. And, all told, the Confederacy did not get fifty thousand. The man with the farm of medium or small size, the merchant, the business man, and the dwellers in cities were generally for the Union. The man with a plantation and slaves was for the Confederacy. These were the main divisions, and they carried their different influences to the uttermost bounds of society. There were many exceptions in both divisions.

The secessionists were influential in all the walks of life in Missouri. Back of them were pride of ancestry and achievement and traditions which exerted vast influence on the life of the people. They were aggressive and bold. For the Confederacy they became intolerant and dictatorial. Their devotion to the traditions of the South was fanatical, and as slavery had been kept at the forefront of Southern institutions the secessionists of Missouri made it their shibboleth, their political god, their rallying-cry from the passing of the Kansas-Nebraska bill to the close of the Rebellion. The contention of Major Edwards and other partisan writers that the actions of Union soldiers in Missouri, whether from Kansas or elsewhere, were responsible for the bloody nature of the war there is wholly and completely refuted by the record.[1] Quantrill and his men, and Bill Ander-

---

[1] See all through the *Rebellion Records*. No better evidence can be cited. See also the work of Colonel William Monks of West Plains, recently published — *A History of Southern Missouri and Northern Arkansas*. See even the histories of Missouri counties written and published by themselves. They are filled with outrages of Missourians upon Missourians inspired by political conditions alone. There were undoubtedly many instances of brutal conduct on the part of Federal soldiers in Missouri, and some of the worst were by Kansas soldiers. But they were not frequent

son, Todd, Gordon, Hildebrand, Porter, and many others perpetrated deeds in Missouri upon Missourians as brutal as any
others did and as inhuman as could have been conceived by the
savage Indians of the Plains in their wildest and bloodiest days.
And their only justification for such a course was that their
brother Missourians stood for the Union.   Major Edwards himself knew this to be true, and he all but admitted it:

Chaos had now pretty well come again.   In the wake of a
civil war which permitted always the impossible to the strongest,
beggars got upon horseback and began driving every decent
thing before them to the devil.   In the universal upheaval
lean people saw how they might become fat, and paupers how
they might become kings.   To the surface of the cauldron —
because of the tremendous heat beneath it — there came things
mean, cowardly, parasitical, crouching, contemptible, bad.   Beasts
of prey became numerous, and birds of ill-omen flew hither and
thither.   The law — it was the sword; the process — it was the
bayonet; the constitution — it was hung upon the gibbet; the
right — the

> "Good old rule — the simple plan,
> That they should take who have the power,
> And they should keep who can."

Much has been said of the course of the Federal troops
enlisted in Kansas and their actions in Missouri.   Also, of the
brigandage practiced there by irregular troops from Kansas, and
even persons not in any way connected with the Federal military forces.   The burning of Osceola by General James H. Lane
was much complained of, and the destruction of private property in that town by him must be condemned.   But the action
of Lane was not of the vicious predatory nature practiced later
by guerrillas in Kansas.   Non-combatants were not killed.   Public records were preserved.   The Federal troops went there
because ordered by the Federal government to do so, and this
order was given for the reason that Osceola was the supply-base
for General Sterling Price for operations in Missouri.   To capture the town and destroy the military stores belonging to the
Confederate government there was legitimate procedure under

---

or widespread, and for barbarity and savagery did not approach the actions of the Missourians towards one another.

the rules governing the awful condition of society called Civil War.[2]

As to the course of Colonel Jennison in Missouri very little in justification can be said. Jennison was a bad man, certainly. He committed outrages and crimes in Missouri. There is no doubt that the people of Missouri had just cause of complaint against him. And this fact makes it impossible that Missourians could be justified for doing in Kansas what Jennison did in Missouri. But the service of Jennison was cut short by the Federal government. It must be remembered that he was appointed and commissioned by Governor Robinson of Kansas, and that after a campaign of about ninety days in Missouri he was ordered out by the Federal government and resigned. And it should not be forgotten that General Lane at that time usually decided what the Federal government did in military matters in Kansas. Jennison did not have the approval of the government in his course in Missouri, nor did Quantrill have the approval of the Confederate government for his course in Kansas. The course of Jennison was not approved by any great

---

[2] It was charged that General Price was much enraged by the destruction of his stores at Osceola, and that he counseled the sacking of Kansas towns and murder of innocent people in retaliation. Quantrill asserted this at Lawrence. The author has found little to support this charge. General Price was a humane man and an honorable soldier, and it is not probable that he advised any such course. In a letter written by C. M. Chase from Humboldt, Kansas, to his paper, the *True Republican and Sentinel*, Sycamore, Illinois, August 19, 1863, it is said that

In 1861 the rebel Colonels Williams and Matthews visited the town with a small force, and sacked nearly every house and store. The next year immediately after Lane burned Osceola, General Price sent Colonel Talbot to retaliate on Humboldt, which he did effectually, leaving but one or two houses standing around the square. The citizens have had their share of the evils of rebellion. Col. Talbot not only sacked and burned, but killed some four or five of the citizens who attempted to defend their property.

The author can not believe that this was done at the instance of a soldier with the delicate sense of honor known to have actuated General Price. And there were many Kansas towns much nearer the border and more easily reached than Humboldt, and these would probably have been chosen for destruction had General Price wished to assume the rôle of freebooter.

14

number of Kansas citizens, nor was that of Quantrill in Kansas approved by the people of Missouri.

That the irregular forces — guerrillas — resulted from conditions existing in Missouri must be admitted. That the actions of Federal soldiers aggravated these conditions and became in some measure responsible for the guerrillas and their actions must also be admitted. But that this cause could be held to justify what the irregular forces did in Missouri can not be maintained. In crushing the rebellion against the government in Missouri the guerrillas would have been just what they were had all the Federal troops sent there been from New York or Ohio. In fact, most of these troops were native Missourians. Guerrilla warfare always originates spontaneously from such conditions as existed in Missouri in Kansas Territorial times and the Civil War. It would have existed in Missouri in those times if there had not lived a single soul in what is now Kansas.

As showing the actions of the Missourians favoring the Confederacy towards their neighbors and friends when the war began, the case of Colonel William Monks, of West Plains, Mo., may be cited. An instance from that part of Missouri is selected for the reason that it is adjoining the state of Arkansas and was wholly out of the range and influence of the Kansas Territorial troubles, and it is the desire that no injustice be done Missouri or a single citizen of that state. Colonel Monks was born in Alabama, on the Tennessee river. His father moved to Northern Arkansas in 1844 — Fulton county. Monks grew up in that part of Arkansas and in Southern Missouri. At the commencement of the Civil War he lived at West Plains. He was intensely loyal to the Union and so remained throughout. General McBride — Confederate — was at that time judge of the Eighteenth Judicial Circuit Court of Missouri, which included West Plains. He was mad on the subject of "Southern Rights." He took the lead against the Union men of Southern Missouri:

As the organization of the Confederates proceeded they grew more bitter against the Union men and declared, by meeting and passing resolutions, that every Union man should show his colors in favor of the South or be hung as high as Haman.[3]

---

[3] *A History of Southern Missouri and Northern Arkansas*, p. 46. This work will be referred to hereafter simply as the Work of Colonel Monks.

One day a neighbor came to Colonel Monks and told him of an order issued by General McBride "requiring all Union men to come in and take the oath, and unless they do they are going to be hung as high as Haman." McBride soon issued another order, directing that all arms, ammunition, and horses be seized, and that the country be given over to the leading rebels who resided in it, and who immediately gave notice that all who refused to take the oath would be either arrested, imprisoned, or forced into the Confederate army to fight, and their leading men hung. Then they began to capture the Union men, who had to flee to the woods and hills:

After they had completely disarmed them and forced many to join the Confederate service, had taken most of their horses, cattle and hogs for the use of the army, the leading rebels in the county claimed that they had organized for the purpose of ridding the country of all Union men who had refused to join the Confederate forces; and that when McBride moved west he was going to leave the whole matter in their hands, and they intended to string up the Union men to limbs and shoot them, so they would soon be rid of that class of men who were friends of the lop-eared Dutch and were nigger lovers.

Small bunches of rebel troops came in from Arkansas and joined the bands that were raiding the country, and the Union men were hunted like wild beasts. Then set in the darkest days that ever any class of patriots true to their government, had to confront.[4]

Prior to his march to join General Sterling Price, McBride issued another order, directing that "they arrest and seize every Union man possible" and saying that after he had marched, the committee which had been organized "would at once exterminate every Union man who had failed to take the oath or join the Confederate army." Many Union men joined the Confederate army to save their lives and their families from destruction. But the great majority chose to take their chances and if need be suffer death rather than fight against their convictions for the Confederacy. Monks was one of these. On the 7th of July, 1861, he was arrested under the order promulgated by McBride. As he was taken to McBride's camp he was warned as follows:

---

4 The Work of Colonel Monks, p. 51.

Listen! Do you hear the drums and the fife? That is General McBride's command moving west to kill them lop-eared Dutch that you Union men have brought into the state of Missouri. Do you know what we are going to do with such men as you are? Those of you that we don't hang, the first fight that we get into with the lop-eared Dutch, we will make breastworks out of to keep the bullets off of good men.[5]

As Colonel Monks was being taken past an Oregon county company its captain said, "Why have you brought a Union man in here alive? If my company had possession of him, he could not live ten minutes." When his guard reached their own company with him the captain asked, "Why have you brought him in here alive?" Some of them said Monks was their neighbor and they hated to kill him. The captain replied: "When I saw him at West Plains at the speaking when he got up and contended that there was a Union and the government ought to be preserved, I wanted to shoot his black heart out of him and I feel the same way yet." In discussing what disposition should be made of him many said "Hang him outright." Others thought that too harsh for a neighbor, but favored putting him in the Arkansas penitentiary until the war was over. This plan was objected to as "too easy for a man who was in favor of the lop-eared Dutch; that we are in favor of taking all like him right into the army and making them fight and if they won't fight the first engagement we get into, pile them up and make breastworks out of them, so that they will catch the bullets off of good men."

Later, Monks was traded off for a beef-cow, and the gang that got him told him to run, expecting to shoot him for trying to escape. He refused to run. Then a man came with a rope and said, "Monks, you have half a minute to say you will join the army and fight, or go to hell, just which you please." Monks appealed to the captain for protection, and the captain replied: "I have been shooting and wounding some of these black Republicans who are friends of the lop-eared Dutch, but I intend to shoot the balance of them dead." The appeal to the captain secured Monks a short reprieve. At Yellville he was put with some other prisoners. "As usual, the abuse that had been con-

---

5 The Work of Colonel Monks, p. 58.

tinually heaped upon the prisoners during the march was renewed and in a short time a man who was said to be from one of the counties north of Rolla, Mo., commenced making a speech and inciting and encouraging the soldiers to mob the prisoners at once; that he had disguised himself and entered the camps of the lop-eared Dutch at Rolla, and that to his own personal knowledge they had men's wives and daughters inside their camps, committing all manner of offenses possible, and that they were heathens; didn't resemble American people at all and that he would not guard nor feed any man who was a friend of them; that they ought to be killed outright."[6]

Colonel Monks escaped from McBride at Eureka Springs, and thus escaped death. He describes the pitiable condition of the Union men in Southern Missouri after the battle of Wilson Creek:

The rebels being encouraged by the late victory, determined to rid the country of all Union men at once. About that time about 350 men, mostly from Oregon county, commanded by two very prominent men, made a scout into Ozark county, Mo. On reaching the North Fork of White River they went into camp at what was known as Jesse James' mill. The owner, a man of about 55 or 60 years of age, as good a man as resided in Ozark county, was charged with grinding corn for Union men and their families; at the time he and a man by the name of Brown were cutting saw logs about two miles from home in the pinery. They went out and arrested them, arrested an old man by the name of Russell and several others, carried them to a man's house, who was a Union man, and had fled to prevent arrest. They took Brown and James about 300 yards from the house, procured a rope, hunted a long limb of a tree, rolled a big rock up to the tree where the first rope was tied to the limb, placed the noose about James' neck, stood him on the rock, rolled the rock out from under him and left him swinging, rolled the rock to the next rope, stood Brown on it, placed the noose around his neck, rolled the rock out and left Brown swinging in the air, went to the third rope, placed Russell on the rock, and just as they aimed to adjust the noose, word came that the home guards

6 Read also *Parson Brownlow's Book*. It describes many murders and outrages committed on Union men in Eastern Tennessee, the sole cause of these outrages having been inflicted upon the Union men and their families because they clung to the Union.

and Federals were right upon them in considerable force. They fled, leaving Russell standing upon the rock and both Brown and James dangling in the air.

Every Union man now having fled in fear of his life, the next day the wives of Brown and James, with the help of a few other women, buried them as best they could. They dug graves underneath the swinging bodies, laid bed clothing in the graves and cut them loose. The bodies fell into the coffinless graves and the earth was replaced. So the author is satisfied that the bones of these men still remain in the lonely earth underneath where they met their untimely death with no charge against them except that they had been feeding Union men, with no one to bury them but their wives and a few other women who aided.

Some of the men who were in the scout and present when the hanging was done are still living in the counties of Howell and Oregon.

A short time after this hanging there was a man by the name of Rhodes, who resided at the head of Bennett's Bayou in Howell County. He was about eighty years of age and had been a soldier under General Jackson. His head was perfectly white and he was very feeble. When he heard of the hanging of Brown and James he said openly that there was no civil war in that, and that the men who did it were guilty of murder.

Some two weeks from the date of the hanging of Brown and James, about twenty-five men, hearing of what he had said, organized themselves and commanded by Dr. Nunly and William Sapp, proceeded to the house of Rhodes, where he and his aged wife resided alone, calling him out and told him they wanted him to go with them. His aged wife came out, and being acquainted with a part of the men, and knowing that they had participated in the hanging and shooting of a number of Union men, talked with them and asked: "You are not going to hurt my old man?" They said: "We just want him to go a piece with us over here." Ordering the old man to come along, they went over to a point about a quarter of a mile from the house and informed him of what he had said. There they shot him, cut his ears off and his heart out. Dr. Nunly remarked that he was going to take the heart home with him, pickle it and keep it so people could see how a black Republican's heart looked.

In the meantime, Rhodes not having returned home, and not a single Union man left in the country that Mrs. Rhodes could get to look after him, and having heard when they reached Joseph Spears' that the old man was not with them, although very feeble, she still continued the search; on the second day, about fifty yards from the road and about a quarter of a mile from home, she heard hogs squealing and grunting as though they were eating something. She proceeded to the place and found the hogs were just about to commence eating the remains of her husband. The Union men having fled, she notified some of the neighbors, and the women came in and helped dress the body and buried him the best they could.

There never was a man arrested by the Confederate authorities, or a single word of condemnation uttered, but as far as could be heard there was general approval. It was said that the means were desperate, but that was the only way to get rid of the men and strike terror to them so they could neither give aid nor countenance to the lop-eared Dutch.

In a few days following they proceeded to arrest Benjamin Alsup, residing in Hutton Valley, who was a strong Union man, took him to Little Rock, placed him in the state penitentiary, and kept him there until after Little Rock fell into the hands of the Federals, when they exchanged him with other prisoners. While they had him in prison they worked him in a bark mill by the side of an old mule, with a strap around his breast and two leather hand holes. He pulled so much in the mill that his little finger was calloused and he almost entirely lost the use of it.

After they had hung, shot, and captured and driven from the country all of the Union men, they called a public meeting for the purpose of taking into consideration what should be done with the families of the Union men, which meeting had a number of preachers in it. After discussing the premises, they arrived at the conclusion that if they let the families of the Union men, who had escaped and gone into the Federal lines, remain, they would return and bring in the lop-eared Dutch. They didn't believe that both parties could ever live together, and as they now had the country completely rid of the Union men, they would force their families to leave. They at once appointed men, among whom were several preachers, to go to each one of the Union families and notify them that they would not be allowed to remain; because if they let them stay, their men would be trying to come back, and they didn't believe both parties could live together. They stated at the same time that they were really sorry for the women and children, but nobody was to blame but their husbands and sons, who had cast their lot with the lop-eared Dutch. Also, as they had taken up arms against the Confederate States, all the property they had, both real and personal, was subject to confiscation and belonged to the Confederate authorities; but they would allow them to take enough of their property to carry them inside of the lines of the lop-eared Dutch, where they supposed their men were and where they could care for them.

They said they might have a reasonable time to make preparations to leave the coutnry, and if they didn't leave, they would be forced to do so, if they had to arrest them and carry them out.

The wildest excitement then prevailed among the women and children. They had no men to transact their business and make preparations to leave. Little had they thought, while they were chasing, arresting, hanging and shooting their men, that they, too, would become victims of the rebel hatred and be forced to leave house and home, not knowing where their men were or whether they were dead or alive. All they knew of their whereabouts was, that those who escaped arrest had left their homes, aiming to reach the nearest Federal lines.

Women were at once dispatched to reach the nearest Federal lines, if possible, and inform them of the Confederate order, and procure help to take them out. Their homes and houses were being continually raided by small bands of Confederates roaming over the country, claiming that they were hunting Union men, taking all classes of property that they might see proper to take, without any restraint whatever.

The suffering that followed the women and children is indescribable. They had to drive their own teams, take care of the little ones, travel through the storms, exposed to it all without a man to help them, nor could they hear a single word of comfort spoken by husband, son or friend. On reaching the Federal lines, all vacant houses and places of shelter were soon filled, and they were known and styled as refugees. Many of them went into soldier huts, where the soldiers had wintered and covered the tops of their huts with earth. They had to leave home with a small amount of rations, and on the road the rebels would stop them and make them divide up the little they had started with, and reaching the Federal lines they would be almost destitute of food and many of them very scantily clothed.

They would at once commence inquiring for their husbands and sons. Numbers of them never found them, as they had been captured, killed and imprisoned while attempting to reach the Federal lines. O! The untold misery that then confronted them! After they had traveled and half starved and suffered from cold and exposure, promising themselves that when they reached the Federal lines they would again meet their loved ones who could again care for them, they were doomed to disappointment, in a large number of instances.

Those who did meet their husbands and sons were also disappointed; they had either joined the service or been employed by the government as guides and scouts, and the small amount of pay they received from the government, wouldn't provide food and raiment for their families. They were compelled to still be absent from their families, although they were suffering greatly for all of the necessaries of life and for clothing and shelter. The women's task of caring for and looking after the family and the little ones was just as great after they had reached the Federal lines as before. . . . . . Winter came on and they underwent untold sufferings; disease set in from exposure, besides the contagious diseases of small pox and measles, and hundreds of them died for want of proper attention, while their men were in the lines of the service of the government.[7]

---

[7] Colonel Monks relates one incident in which it appears that a squad of the "lop-eared" Dutch took a moderate revenge upon one of these fire-eaters of Southern Missouri, and as it is perhaps the only instance of the kind which can be found, it is set out here.

The author remembers one incident that occurred during the stay at West Plains. A man named Lusk, who was constable of Howell township, and resided in West Plains, was a strong Union man at the beginning of the war; when the general order was made that every man who had been a Union man had to join the Confederate service and show his colors or be hung, Lusk enlisted in the Confederate army and went out with McBride's command.

Three or four days after the capture of the author by the rebels, Lusk came up to him in a braggadocio manner and says, "You ought to have your black heart shot out of you." Lusk had taken the oath and had been released before the author reached West Plains. The author met him in West Plains and remarked to him: "Hallo, Lusk! How are you getting along? And what are you doing here?" He replied that he had taken the oath; that he was tired of fighting. The author asked him if he felt like he did when he wanted to shoot his black heart out. Lusk replied: "Captain, I am sorry for what I did, and Captain Emmons so maltreated me the other day that I could scarcely sit in my saddle." The author remarked to him: "I will just give your face three good slaps with my hand." After giving him three raps, the author let him pass.

Soon meeting Captain Emmons, who belonged to the 6th Missouri Cavalry, had asked him what the trouble was between him and Lusk. He said that while he was prisoner Lusk came to him with his big knife belted around him, and said that he was just equal to ten lop-eared Dutch and he had that knife for the purpose of taking ten Dutch scalps before he returned home, and otherwise abused him for being a Union man and a friend of the Dutch.

On the arrival of the troops in West Plains he inquired of the citizens if Lusk had returned home. They informed him that he had and was residing on Spring Creek, about six miles from town. About half of Emmons' company were Germans. He went immediately to his company, ordered the Orderly Sergeant to make detail of ten men and he wanted them all to be Germans. He ordered them to be mounted and ready for a scout at once. Taking charge of them in person he proceeded to the house of Lusk, about six miles west of West Plains at the head of Spring Creek, rode up to the house and halloed. Lusk immediately came out into the yard and recognized Dr. Emmons and said "O! Doctor! Is that you? I am proud to see you." The Doctor said to him, "I am proud to see you, too." The Doctor at once informed him of what he had said to him

In further proof that it is preposterous to charge all the robbery and outrage committed in Missouri on those not in sympathy with the Southern Confederacy, I quote from the letter of Thomas C. Reynolds, Confederate Governor of Missouri, printed under his signature in the Marshall (Texas) *Republican*, and published at pp. 467-474, *Shelby and His Men*, by Major John N. Edwards. The robberies and outrages were committed, Gov-

---

when he was a prisoner in regard to being equal to ten lop-eared Dutchmen and how he had his knife prepared to take that number of scalps before he came back home, and wanted to know if he got the scalps before he came back home. Lusk replied that if he killed a single Dutchman he didn't know it and that he got all the fighting that he wanted, didn't want to fight any more.

The Doctor wanted to know if he ever saw any lop-eared Dutch and Lusk replied that he "didn't know that he had." The Doctor replied, "I have selected ten of the smallest sized of the full stock and I want you to step over the fence and view them." He then ordered the scouts to dismount and form in line. Lusk told the Doctor he didn't want anything to do with them whatever. After they had formed a line the Doctor made him step in front and view them; asked him what he thought of them. He said "They are good-looking men." The Doctor said to him, "If you didn't get the chance when you were out in the service to fight ten of them, and you say you didn't get any scalps, I have brought these ten down and intend that you shall fight them." Lusk pleaded with the Doctor that he didn't want to fight them and for God's sake not to let them hurt him. Emmons said to him "Why Lusk! you said you were equal to ten of them and intended to bring back ten of their scalps and there will be nothing unfair about this fight. I intend to give you a fair show." He ordered Lusk to get his horse and get onto it and get ready to march.

There were some four-foot clapboards stacked up near Lusk's house, and Emmons ordered six of the Germans to get a board apiece. They were all soon mounted and moving towards West Plains, soon coming to a "horsen" log. Emmons ordered them to dismount and form a line, placing the men about ten paces from Lusk, then said to Lusk, "Now, prepare yourself, and if you can whip these ten lop-eared Dutch I will let you go back home and give you a chromo." Lusk pleaded pitifully to not let the Dutch abuse him. Emmons ordered the six who had the clapboards to move one pace in the rear, leaving four of the number to attack Lusk; he then ordered the four men to seize Lusk, take him to the "horsen" log and take down his clothes. Two of them were to take him by the hands and two by the legs and buck him tight against the log; if they succeeded, the six would proceed, one at a time, and strike him three licks across that part of the body that generally used for sitting on.

He then turned to Lusk, saying, "Prepare to meet them; if you are a better man than they are, down them and pile them up." At the command of Capt. Emmons, the four men advanced on Lusk, who did not attempt to move, seized him by the arms, led him to the log, bucked him over it, two holding him by the arms and two by the legs, ordered the six men to advance, one at a time, strike three licks with the flat side of the board, march on a few paces and give room for the next.

After the performance had been completely carried out as commanded,

ernor Reynolds charges, by the soldiers under General Price, in
his invasion of Missouri in 1864. Major Edwards admits the
truth of these charges in publishing them, and he expressly admits them, in addition:

It would take a volume to describe the acts of outrage;
neither station, age nor sex was any protection; Southern men
and women were as little spared as Unionists; the elegant mansion of General Robert E. Lee's accomplished niece and the cabin
of the negro were alike ransacked; John Deane, the first civilian
ever made a State prisoner by Mr. Lincoln's Government, had
his watch and money robbed from his person, in the open street
of Potosi, in broad day, as unceremoniously as the German merchant at Fredrickstown was forced, a pistol at his ear, to surrender his concealed greenbacks. As the citizens of Arkansas
and Northern Texas have seen in the goods unblushingly offered them for sale, the clothes of the poor man's infant were as
attractive spoil as the merchant's silk and calico or the curtain
taken from the rich man's parlor; ribbons and trumpery geegaws were stolen from milliners, and jeweled rings forced from
the fingers of delicate maidens whose brothers were fighting in
Georgia in Cockrell's Confederate Missouri Brigade.

the Captain declared that he could have heard Lusk halloing a mile distant every time the clapboard hit him.

After he had received the boarding, Emmons said that Lusk was
blistered where the boards hit him, and that he never saw ten Germans
enjoy themselves as much in his life. He then asked Lusk, in their
presence, how he felt now in regard to fighting lop-eared Dutch. Lusk
declared that he had nothing against the Dutch and that he never would
want to fight another one as long as he lived, and he hoped that Dr.
Emmons would not let them do him any more harm. He dressed himself,
they were all mounted, formed a line, and Lusk was brought into West
Plains and took the oath, under the promise that he would never fight
another lop-eared Dutchman.

So, the excuses made for Quantrill and others who led guerrillas
and bands of outlaws and murderers fall to the ground upon investigation.
The actions of these bands were not inspired by the treatment Missouri
received from Union soldiers. There was no reason whatever why the
Confederacy should permit the existence of such bands. The story told by
Colonel Monks is the story of all Missouri, the story of Eastern Kentucky,
Eastern Tennessee, and all the border. It may be safely said that a great
majority of the outrages committed in the South by Union men resulted
from the brutal treatment they, their wives, and children had been compelled to suffer at the hands of brigands and the inhuman banditti with
which they were surrounded, and this bad element was but a small portion
of the population.

CHAPTER XVI

U P TO the beginning of the year 1862 the guerrillas acted
as a mob. They had no organization and were but
bunches of men skulking through the brush and over
the rough hills in defiance of authority either civil or military.
They were taking revenge personally for such wrongs as they
pretended to believe themselves or the country subjected to. A
man might appear or not to go on any guerrilla service. There
was no responsibility, no one to exercise any power, no one to
enforce such rude discipline and primitive conventionalities as
even guerrillas must recognize. Such authority as they might
voluntarily bow to was lying in the bush or in the highway unused. Quantrill seized it, having first recognized it by reason
of his long career as a Jayhawker and border-ruffian, his experiences in Kansas giving him great advantage over his new-found
associates in Missouri. In some loose way he in a manner succeeded Upton Hays, who had acted upon some sort of roving
commission as chief of "Partisan Rangers" between the Osage
and Missouri rivers in Western Missouri. The succession was
accomplished by the departure of Hays and the voluntary occupation of the field by Quantrill. No "orders" have been found
that in any way relate to the matter; perhaps there were none.

The material for the guerrilla or bushwhacker force was being created day by day by the organization of the armies of the
Union and of the Confederacy. Some were forced to an independent course by circumstances they could not control. To
secure protection some who favored the Confederacy joined the
Union army. Sometimes these found life and service in the
Union army impossible to them, and their hatred of the Union
was so intensified that they deserted. They were afraid to enlist
in the Confederate army, for if captured and recognized they

would be shot for deserters and traitors. They invariably became guerrillas. A goodly number of the men who followed Quantrill and Anderson were such deserters. Many citizens of Missouri could not make up their mind to join the Confederate army, though favoring the cause. These remained at home in sullen rebellion against the Union, and were sympathizers with the Confederacy. They harbored and encouraged the guerrillas, and became spies for them and furnished intelligence of what was transpiring at Federal posts which they visited. Many of this class loudly proclaimed that they were Union men better to hide their real position and secure protection. The outrages committed by occasional bands of lawless Union troops so enraged those suffering therefrom that they joined the guerrillas in hope of being able to wreak vengeance upon any and all Union partisans and sympathizers — to do to their neighbors of a different political belief those very things they complained had been done to themselves. The irresponsible nature of the service of the guerrillas attracted the worst elements of society and afforded them opportunities for robbery and a freedom from restraint in the indulgence of their worst passions. All this nondescript material existed, awaiting only the hand of some master of villainy to give it shape and fashion it into form and thus create a force vicious, brutal, without responsibility to any power, bent on revenge — to despoil, ravage, pillage, lay waste, and rejoice in the destruction of human life.

By Christmas, 1861, Quantrill had gathered about him some seven men. They were William Hallar, George Todd, Joseph Gilchrist, Perry Hoy, John Little, James Little, and Joe Vaughan. About Christmas day William H. Gregg, James A. Hendricks, and John W. Koger joined Quantrill. They rode together in search of him, finding him and his seven men at the farm of Mrs. Samuel Crump, on the public road leading from Independence to Blue Springs. The band was not in camp there, but the men were found sitting on their horses in the road in front of the farm-house. This may be said to have been the beginning of Quantrill's band as an entity — as a separate and distinct organization with a recognized leader.

At the Crump farm Quantrill disbanded his company for a

month. Each man was to use the time in preparation for active work as soon as the weather would permit. No opportunity to secure other men was to be overlooked. At this time Jennison was stationed at Blue Springs.[1]

The first skirmish mentioned by Gregg was on the 27th of January, 1862, and was between seventeen of Jennison's men and three of Quantrill's men, at the house of Noah McAlexander, in Sni-a-Bar township, Jackson county. Gregg, Hallar, and one other were the Quantrill men. Crocket Ralston, John Frisby, and John Barnhill, three unarmed citizens, were also in the house. The armed men determined to fight, and the citizens were to go out first and remain between the Union men and the Quantrill men. Ralston and Frisby struck out for themselves as soon as they cleared the door, and both were captured and shot. Barnhill followed Gregg's party. One of the Quantrill men was shot, but Gregg, Hallar, and Barnhill escaped. None of Jennison's men were injured, so far as is known.

The first mention of Quantrill in the official records falls on February 3, 1862.[2] This mention is brief and it is as follows:

General: I have just returned from an expedition which I

---

[1] Manuscript of William H. Gregg, now in the Collection of the author. This manuscript was written by Gregg, who was an officer under Quantrill until the winter of 1863-64. Gregg was quite young when he joined Quantrill. He was driven out of the band by the cut-throats at or near Sherman, Texas, early in 1864, when he joined Shelby and was made a captain in Shanks's Brigade. Or, rather, the band became so reckless of life that the men began to kill one another, and Gregg left in disgust. The manuscript will be referred to hereafter as the *Gregg Manuscript*. It is faithfully written and very accurate to have been written from memory alone. Some incidents are set down out of their order, but the accounts are modest and truthful, and they are entirely devoid of that spirit of boast and brag found so prominent in the works of Edwards. Captain Gregg has been (1908) deputy sheriff of Jackson county, Missouri, for many years under Republican officials, and he is a good officer and a worthy citizen. When the war was over it was over forever with Captain Gregg, and he immediately returned to his farm and took up the pursuits of peace, which he ever after cherished and followed.

[2] *Rebellion Records*, Series I, Vol. VIII, p. 57. Report of Captain William S. Oliver, Seventh Missouri Infantry, to Brig.-Gen. Pope, dated Independence, Mo., February 3, 1862.

was compelled to undertake in search of the notorious Quantrill
and his gang of robbers in the vicinity of Blue Springs. Without mounted men at my disposal, despite numerous applications
to various points, I have seen this infamous scoundrel rob mails,
steal the coaches and horses, and commit other similar outrages
upon society even within sight of this city.. Mounted on the
best horses of the country, he has defied pursuit, making his
camp in the bottoms of the ———— and Blue, and roving over
a circuit of 30 miles. I mounted a company of my command and
went to Blue Springs. The first night there myself, with 5 men,
were ambushed by him and fired upon. We killed 2 of his men
(of which he had 18 or 20) and wounded a third. The next day
we killed four more of the worst of the gang, and before we left
succeeded in dispersing them. . . . .
     Quantrill will not leave this section unless he is chastised
and driven from it. I hear of him tonight 15 miles from here,
with new recruits, committing outrages on Union men, a large
body of whom have come in tonight, driven out by him. Families of Union men are coming into the city tonight asking of me
escorts to bring in their goods and chattels, which I duly
furnished. I had 1 man killed and 2 wounded, during the expedition.

     February 22, 1862, Quantrill, with some fifteen men, rode
to Independence, supposing no Union troops were there. Doubleday's Ohio Cavalry had just passed through the town, and when
Quantrill arrived the stragglers galloped out and informed the
regiment, which immediately returned, entering the public
square at the southwest corner. Quantrill and his men were at
the northeast corner and saw the Ohioans come in on the dead
run in platoons. The day was dark and foggy, and it was impossible to distinguish uniforms at a distance of fifty yards.
The Union men were armed with holster pistols and sabres —
Quantrill's with navy revolvers, shot-guns and Sharps's rifles.
Quantrill's forces fired at point blank range and retreated on the
Spring Branch road, closely pursued by the Ohioans, who shot
out their pistols and drew their sabres. Near the public spring
Gabriel George and Hop Wood, guerrillas, were killed. A Union
soldier rode beside Gregg, in the fog mistaking him for a comrade. Gregg snapped his pistol three times within a few inches
of the Ohioan's ear, but the weapon missed fire. The trooper
seeing his mistake, drew his sabre and slashed at Gregg, who

received several strokes on his arms. Quantrill and his men ran away from their pursuers and were soon lost in the mists, with several wounded. The Ohioans lost none. In this skirmish Quantrill was wounded, and his horse killed, about half a mile from Independence. He climbed up a steep bank or bluff, between the rocks, and was not pursued. He attended the funeral of George, a day or two later, walking with a cane.

The sacking of Aubry, in Johnson county, Kansas, was on the 7th of March, 1862.[3] *Andreas's History of Kansas*, usu-

-----

[3] In the *Gregg Manuscript* this event is placed after the affair at the Tate house. Gregg has the exact date of the attack upon Quantrill at the Tate house. But official reports are correct as to dates and all other authorities must give way to them. Gregg informed the author that he saved Lieutenant Randlett from death at Aubry that he might be exchanged for Perry Hoy, who had been captured at the Tate house. The official report was made from Fort Leavenworth, March 19, and says intelligence of the affair had been received on the 10th, which would allow sufficient time after the 7th for it to reach Fort Leavenworth.

Randlett must have been spared for some other than the assigned cause, or Hoy was captured before the affair at the Tate house. On the 25th of February, 1908, the author discussed this matter with Mr. Randlett at his home, 706 Jefferson street, Topeka. He believes the man he was saved to be exchanged for had been captured at Independence by Doubleday's Second Ohio, on the 22nd of February, and that this man's name was Brady.

In a letter to the author, dated Kansas City, Mo., February 27, 1908, Captain Gregg says:

No, we never had a man named Brady. One or two of Parker's men were captured by the Ohioans at the time of which you speak, but none of ours, and Parker had no man by that name. I have never heard of any one denying that Hoy was captured at the Tate House. The fact is, I know that Hoy was captured there, and, notwithstanding dates to the contrary, I know that Randlett was captured after the Tate House affair. And all the circumstances go to prove that I am correct. I have perused war records to considerable extent myself, and have found many dates, as well as narratives, wrong.

Captain Gregg is relying upon his memory alone, and he is in error as to this date and the order in which these events occurred. He must do like all good soldiers when surrounded and no chance of escape is seen — surrender. And he must also give up the idea that it was Hoy for whom Lieutenant Randlett was saved for exchange, for it was a man named Brady.

In his interview with Randlett, as set out above, the author urged

ally so complete and accurate, gives no date. It mentions the matter indefinitely, saying that ''Five newly arrived citizens, who went out one evening to gather honey, promising their wives to return early, were murdered by Quantrill's men, and the place of their burial is not known. Greenbury Trekle, a Mr. Whitaker, Washington Tullis, —— Ellis and John Cody, all were killed by border-ruffians.'' There is nothing here to connect the men named with the affair of the men who were slain while in search for honey, nor is it said that they were killed at the sacking of the town.

Reuben A. Randlett was second lieutenant of Company A, Fifth Kansas. He was sent home on sick-leave in the winter of 1861-62. While yet suffering from the ague he started to return to his command, which was then at Barnesville, Kansas. The weather was still cold. He left Kansas City, Mo., the morning of the 6th of March. Night coming upon him at Aubry, he stopped at the village tavern. There he was given a room with a man named Ellis, a stranger to him. At daylight the following morning the landlord knocked loudly at the door of their room, advising that they get up at once, as the guerrillas were coming into town. Randlett remarked that such means to get them up early was outrageous. But the landlord soon returned to inform them that the guerrillas were surrounding the house. The

---

him to make diligent search for an old diary he said he had kept at that time. He believed he had the diary, but had failed to find it after more than one long search. After a part of this chapter was written Randlett found the diary and with it a letter written to him by Colonel McNeil, commandant of the post at Kansas City, and he has exhibited both the diary and the letter to the author. They are old and musty, but in a good state of preservation. The diary fixes the date beyond dispute as the 7th day of March, 1862. And this agrees with the date as given by Abraham Ellis, which will appear in his letters published, *post.*

Entries in the diary are as follows:

Thursday, March 6th, 62.

Left Kansas City. Took dinner at Shawneetown. Had a shake and stopped at Aubrey.

Friday, 7th.

Taken prisoner by Capt. Quantrell.

The diary shows that it was a man named Brady for whom Randlett was saved for exchange.

15

night had been cold, and the window panes were covered with frost, except on narrow margins next to the sash, which the warmth of the wood had kept clear. Randlett dressed himself and looked out of the window, but could see no one; then he went into another room, from the window of which he saw a number of guerrillas, and he heard shots and shouts in the streets. A man, partly dressed, wanted to fight the guerrillas, but when Randlett found that all the house had but three pistols in the way of arms with which to fight forty men he advised against it. He said to the others that he would go down and surrender.

Lieut. Reuben A. Randlett

He went into the tavern office and handed his revolver to a guerrilla he found there, saying that he was a Union soldier and demanded the treatment due a soldier who surrendered. He was led out on the porch and turned over to two guerrillas found there. They swore horribly, one thrusting the muzzle of his pistol into Randlett's mouth (this was Joe Young, after the war a printer at Kansas City) and the other holding a revolver at his ear. Then a man came by, believed by Randlett to have been Quantrill, but Captain Gregg says it was himself, and ordered Young and his companion not to injure Randlett as he wanted him for a certain purpose. He was taken into the office and questioned by Quantrill, who asked him if he had a horse. Randlett replied that he had a good mare in the tavern stables. Quantrill at once ordered it saddled and brought out. Just then Ellis came into the office with his face all covered with blood. Quantrill recognized him at once and said, "Why, Ellis, is that you?" Ellis replied that it was himself and that Quantrill had shot him. It seems that Ellis had been looking out of the window, with his face near the sash where there was no frost. Quantrill saw him and fired, the ball going through the top of one sash and the bottom of the other where they joined in the middle of the window before it struck Ellis in the forehead; the sash saved his life. Randlett did not know then that the bullet had gone through the sash before striking Ellis, and supposed it had gone into his head instead of flattening against his skull, and expected to see him fall down dead. Ellis had known Quantrill in Lykins (Miami) county, having been superintendent of schools there, where he examined the guerrilla for a certificate to teach. Quantrill talked with Ellis for some time, and told him to hitch up his team and go on his way and he should not be molested. Randlett wiped the blood from Ellis's face. Ellis was fastening the lines to the bits as Quantrill and Randlett rode away, and Randlett saw him fall backward and supposed he had fallen dead from his wound.[4] The

---

[4] In the Collection of the author are two letters from Ellis to W. W. Scott. Ellis ran a newspaper at Elk City, Montgomery county, Kansas, after the war. In the Kansas legislature of 1863 he was engrossing clerk in the House, and not a member as his letter would lead one to believe. He had a large depression in his forehead, caused by the wound inflicted by Quantrill, and was known as ''Bullet-Hole'' Ellis; this name always stuck to him. His letters contain some errors, also much of value, and they are here reproduced in part:

Elk City Montgomery Co — Kan Jan 5th 1879
MR. W. W. Scott — Dear Sir

My first acquaintance with William C. Quantrell was in the winter of 1858 & 1859 — [Error; it was in the winter of 1859-60; see Quantrill's letters, ante.] he was then teaching school near Stanton in Miami County & I was Superintendent — I visited his school, & put up, at his boarding house — I found him an interesting well educated man — we slept together & talked until after 2 P. M. The next thing I heard of him he had turned Abolitionist & was acting as a conductor on the under ground Railroad & assisting Negroes from Missouri to Canada — But he was not prompted by conscience, or pure unadulterated religion — as he was never known to assist any Negro unless the Negro first assisted him to steal a horse or mule — The stock was Quantrells & the Negro passed North through Iowa to Canada. . . . And my next interview with Quantrill was on the 7th of March, 1862 I stopped for the night at Aubrey in Johnson county, Kan — Not anticipating any trouble — But at daylight I was awoke by the cry — The cut throats are coming — But before I could dress the house was surrounded & they were yelling & screaming & swearing like Devils — and five men who were in the lower rooms started to run across the fields But were soon overtaken & butchered there were five of us up stairs (all travelers) & about thirty of them were riddling the house with bullets while these men were being butchered in the field & I was carelessly looking out at the window up stairs & Quantrell saw me through the window & gave me a dip — he made a good shot — (or as he afterwards expressed it, a dam'd good shot) I was struck in the center of the forehead where the brains of most men are supposed to be located — I fell & was supposed to be dead — the others then went down stairs & surrendered & in a few moments Quantrell & two others of the gads hill Band Came up stairs — each had a revolver in his hand — with the hammer raised They were trembling

proprietor of the tavern and two hired hands found working for him were chased into a field in which dry cornstalks were standing and there killed by Quantrill and his men.

Randlett was with Quantrill from the 7th to the 18th of March. He was released before the affair at the Tate house. Whether it was for Perry Hoy or some other member of his band that Quantrill desired to exchange him, there is no doubt of the fact that he was saved alive to be exchanged. Quantrill wrote several letters to the commandant at Fort Leavenworth requesting an exchange of his man for Randlett, but he received no reply, as he and his men were considered to be outlaws and not soldiers, making communication with them impossible from a military standpoint. Quantrill had Randlett write requesting that the exchange be made, which he did, but he received no answer to his letter.

While Randlett was with Quantrill a man came to the camp

---

like criminals & Swearing like Devils & to give an idea of their interesting language — I will give a few detached sentences — I was lieing on a mattress at the head of the stairs & they had been told by the prisoners that there was only one man up stairs & he was probably dead — So Quantrell and two others started up stairs & as soon as they got within about four feet of me they all pointed their revolvers at my head, with their fingers on the trigger — at last one of them balled out — If you have any money God damn you give it to me in a minute or I'll blow you to *Hell* and as I had no hankering after [that] place — I passed over the checks — (or in other words) I handed him $250.00 they then passed on & searched the rooms & I heard one of them say, that he had found a pocket book & that it was a dam-d fat one — They then ordered me down stairs & said that I was not dead by a dam-d sight — I then crawled down stairs & was helped into a chair & in a few minutes Quantrell came down stairs & then recognized me & got a cloth and some water & washed my face & said he did it himself & was dam-d sorry for it — as I 'was one of the Kansas men he *did not* want to hurt — I then told him of my team & about fifty dollars worth of groceries that were there in the house he said that he was glad that I had told him, as he was sorry for what he had already done & said that not one thing more of mine should be touched & if I had then thought of my money it is possible that that he might have given it back to me — But I was too far gone to think of money & soon after I fainted away & lay on the frozen ground about four hours senseless & motionless & to all appearances dead & all who saw me pronounced me dead. I was really supposed to [be] dead by all who saw me & if any of my Ohio friends are anxious to see my likeness & the bullet & portions of my skull bones all they have to do, is to call at the army Medicinal Museum in Washington City — D. C. I am a native Buckeye — was born and raised in Green County, Ohio — But the only redeeming traits I ever saw in Quantrell was that he showed by his kindness to me, after I was wounded that he was not entirely a Demon — But history will record him a desperately bad man — a highway robber, of the darkest shade & a desperate

one day and said the Red Legs were burning houses and robbing people in Cass county. The order to "saddle up" rang through the guerrilla camp at once, and in a few minutes the whole band took the road. Three houses were found on fire. The Red Legs retreated when they saw Quantrill coming, and there was a long and exciting chase towards the Kansas line. At a point near the State line, about east of Paola, but in Missouri. Quantrill overhauled the marauders. A brisk skirmish ensued in which some of the Red Legs were wounded, but none killed. Randlett's guard took him up on a high place where he could see the engagement.

One Saturday night while Quantrill was camped somewhere in Johnson county, Mo., there broke upon the air the sounds of hoof-beats rapidly approaching. The guerrillas were stopping with two farmers, their friends, one living on one road and the other on another road; these roads joined about a half mile from the farm-houses. The running horses rapidly approached, and soon a voice was heard crying out, "Don't shoot! don't shoot!" Two horsemen came down at a dead run and were captured. They claimed to be deserters from the Union army looking for Confederate soldiers to join. They were put under guard in a room at one of the houses and questioned. Randlett was at one of the houses under guard, and the prisoners were taken to the other house. Quantrill went to Randlett

leader of a set of the most desperate Demons that ever disgraced the name of man — infinitely worse than he was. None of them with bravery enough to meet an enemy — But they took every advantage of the surroundings — by treachery to drench the earth with blood & carnage —
Abraham Ellis

In this letter Ellis says Quantrill's Brother Masons helped him escape from jail at Paola.

There has been much controversy as to whether or not Quantrill was a Free Mason. It is not probable that he was. Captain Gregg was a Mason during his service under Quantrill, and he told the author that if Quantrill was a Mason he never made the fact known to him. It may be safely said that he never was a member of the Masonic order.

Following are extracts from the second letter of Ellis:
Elk City Kan Jan 18th 1879 —

Mr. W. W. Scott — My Dear Sir —

I received yours of Jan 13th a day of two ago, & I will endeavor to comply with your request — But it would be impossible for me to describe any man minutely at this date, with whom I never had but a limited ac-

and asked him if he would like to see the prisoners, and Randlett said he should like to visit them.   They seemed to know
that Randlett was with Quantrill, and they had advised Quantrill
that Randlett be "strung up" without delay; this was reported
to Randlett by Quantrill.   Quantrill and Randlett went over to
the house together.   Before going in Randlett changed coats
with the guard, and the prisoners supposed he was one of Quantrill's men.   They told Randlett that the Yankee prisoner ought
to be hanged at once.   When Randlett came out Quantrill asked
him what he thought of the prisoners.   Randlett said he believed
they were thieves or spies.   Shortly after Randlett arrived again
at the house where he was stopping he heard a volley; he never
saw the prisoners again; no one ever mentioned them after
that; Randlett had no doubt about their having been shot, and
very little doubt but that they deserved it.

As nothing could be heard from the Federal authorities
about the exchange, Quantrill proposed to parole Randlett for
a period of ten days and send him to Fort Leavenworth to see
if he could effect the exchange.   This being agreeable to Randlett, Quantrill marched to Independence.   It was a rainy winter

quaintance, But he was a well built man light hair blue eyes — round face,
pleasant countenance, with little or no beard (at the time he was teaching
school at Stanton) & in my opinion he would not weigh more than 140
or 45 lbs — But when I saw him at Aubrey — he had changed in appearance — he had Mustash & Side whiskers & both had a red tinge & at that
time, he had assumed the appearance of a desperado — yet he could be
pleasant at times — He talked kindly to me a few minutes after he recognized me & promised not to disturb any more of my property & when he
was about to leave, he discovered that one of my horses had been taken &
he inquired who took it & was told — he immediately ordered one of his
men to go & tell him to bring that horse back immediately or it would be
the last time that he would disobey orders   This conversation was heard
by the women — I was lieing on the ground near them, at that time but
had quit *hearing things* — the horse was returned   At the time I was
wounded I was post Quartermaster & stationed at Barnesville — a small
town on the eastern border of Kansas about eighty miles south of Kansas
City, Mo.   I was stationed there in Sept — 1861 — I had served as a member of the first State Legislature that closed its labors June 20th 1861 —
& after I was wounded in March I laid in the shade until about the last
of August. . . . My residence at the time I was wounded was near New
Lancaster — a small village on the eastern border of Miami Co, Kan. . . .
                                                                    A. Ellis.

Randlett says Quantrill did not touch Ellis, and did not wash the
blood from his face as Ellis claims, after he came down stairs. And
Randlett says Quantrill did not go up stairs at all.

day. On the road a man stopped the band and said he had
something for the men. He produced from a capacious bag
swung to his saddle-horn a corpulent jug of apple-jack and gave
each man a liberal drink. Quantrill told him to give Randlett
some. This, it seems, he had entertained no notion of doing,
but upon being directed to do so, replied, "Yes, I will give the
―――― ―――― ―――― some," and handed Randlett a stiff drink,
which was relished greatly. At Independence Quantrill left
Randlett in a hotel at the northeast corner of the public square.
Before he went out he wrote on a sheet of paper secured from
the hotel table the necessary papers for Randlett to take with
him to Leavenworth in the matter of his exchange. Having done
this, Quantrill and his men rode out of town and were gone
several hours.

The rain had dripped from Randlett's overcoat and soaked
his shoes, making his feet cold. As he sat at a stove trying to
warm himself Randlett noticed that men began to gather at the
hotel to see the "prisoner." They drank whiskey at the hotel
bar and soon became boisterous. Whoops and yells could be
heard in the streets, and Randlett heard threats made there to go
in and kill the prisoner. It was necessary for Randlett to get
out of the way, and he determined to leave the hotel at once, let
the consequences be what they might. He got up and walked
to the interior of the house-lobby or general room, in doing which
his attention was called to a man leaning on the bar. He was
an old man, and said nothing, but pointed to a dooor which Randlett entered and found himself in the dining-room. The old
man came in soon and told Randlett he was in great danger,
and said, "I am the friend of any soldier." He went to the
doors of the room and after a little while told Randlett that the
coast was clear for a minute, and led him into an alley, then
through several alleys, and finally to a large stable just off the
northeast corner of the public square. There he told Randlett
to get into a manger, and after Randlett had done so, he filled it
with hay, saying that if any one came he should pull the hay up
over him and conceal himself — that the horse would be eating
the hay but would not injure him. In a short time he brought
the postmaster to see Randlett. The postmaster handed Rand-

lett a letter from the military authorities in Kansas City. Randlett inquired why it had not been delivered to him. The postmaster told him that he had heard the letter read by the colonel who wrote it and he knew that its delivery meant the death of Randlett.[5]

When Quantrill returned with his men to Independence, Mr. Perry (the old man who had been Randlett's friend all day) hunted him up and told him where Randlett was and how he came to be there. Quantrill and this old man were friends, though Perry was openly a Union man. He carried letters to Kansas City for Quantrill and was useful to the guerrilla in many other ways. Quantrill thanked him for his care and discretion and requested him to see Randlett safely off for Kansas City the next morning. Perry had a large tavern building, in which he lived, but which he was allowing to remain idle, having closed out his business. But he and his wife lived in the building, and Perry was running a stable which was attached to the tavern building. Quantrill remained with Perry till late in the night, and Mrs. Perry prepared a good supper for her husband, Quantrill, and Randlett. Quantrill left the house about ten o'clock at night and marched his band out of town.

The next morning at three o'clock Randlett was called up

---

[5] This was on Tuesday, the 18th day of March, 1862. The entry in Randlett's diary for that date reads:

Tuesday, March 18, '62.
Released at Independence on Parole of honor for 10 days.

The letter was discovered by Randlett in his search for his diary, mentioned before in this chapter, and is as follows:

Kansas City, March 17/62
Lieut. R. A. Randlett,
        Sir:
            Yours of this date is received. I would say in answer that the communications of the Bandit Quantrell is whose hands you have unfortunately fallen was forwarded to Colonel Weer at Wyandotte and referred to General Hunter and by the Colonel sent to Leavenworth. I have received no answer but I can assure you that you will soon be liberated and if the party who holds you dares harm a hair of your head they will one and all be hung when taken which is now only a matter of time and that time short.
        Yours very Respectfully,
          John McNeil,
            Colonel.

Colonel McNeil was then commanding the post at Kansas City.

by Perry and found a good breakfast ready for him and his mare saddled. He and Perry rode to Kansas City together. There Perry left him, and he went at once to Colonel McNeil's office, on Union avenue. When Randlett reported to the colonel and made himself known McNeil abused Quantrill, but said he was busy, and requested that Randlett return at eight o'clock. When Randlett returned to the office he found the colonel and a captain standing before a big map which was hanging on the wall. The colonel said as Randlett entered, "Here he is now." Then he told Randlett that the captain was to be sent out with a company to destroy Quantrill, and that Randlett was to go along as guide. Randlett said he would not go; that he was in honor bound to carry out his agreement with Quantrill and would not go with the captain. Words rose high and Randlett said to the colonel: "I will not go, and d——n you, you can't make me go," and with that he left the room in haste and descended a stairway so hurriedly that he ran against Colonel Weer and knocked him off the sidewalk. Randlett had started to find the colonel and was glad to find him so easily; he immediately related his story. Colonel Weer told Randlett that orders had just arrived for McNeil to turn over the command to some other officer, and he would not have anything more to say in the matter. Randlett was allowed to proceed to Leavenworth, where he went over his case with General Sturgis, but found his position the same as that of Colonel McNeil — he would have nothing to do with Quantrill and would hold no communication with him, as he was an outlaw. Randlett was permitted to do as he pleased, but advised not to return to Quantrill. But Randlett considered himself in honor bound to go back to him and report the facts as he found them. When he arrived at Independence he found twelve hundred Union soldiers quartered in the town. No one could tell him where to find Quantrill. Just such an emergency had been provided for, and Randlett had been told to whom he should report if Quantrill could not be found. This he did, and then returned to Kansas City. He never saw Quantrill again.[6]

_____
6 The following is taken from the *Gregg Manuscript*:
Soon after the affair at the Tate House Quantrill made a raid on

It is probable that Randlett at first told Quantrill his name was Brown. When captured by the border-ruffians in May, 1856, he gave his name as R. A. Brown. The *Gregg Manuscript* says that Quantrill released Randlett after his return from Fort Leavenworth. The entries in Randlett's diary would bear out his statement that he never again saw Quantrill after leaving Independence to go to Fort Leavenworth, two of these entries being as follows:

Monday, March 24.—Arrived at Fort Leavenworth but could do nothing in regard to the release or exchange of Brady.

Friday, March 28.—At Kansas City — Went to Independence and returned.

The official report of the affair at Aubry is as follows: [7]

Sir:

I have the honor to report that on the 10th instant I received intelligence that the rebel Quantrill had with his band entered Johnson County, in this State, and murdered several citizens at Aubrey, in said county, and carried away quite an amount of property. I was instructed from Headquarters of the then Department of Kansas to take such steps as were necessary to protect the citizens of the exposed region. I accordingly sent orders to Capt. John Greelish, Company E, Eighth Regiment Kansas Volunteers, to move his command immediately from Olathe, Kansas, to Aubrey, and to take such measures as he deemed best to defend the citizens of that locality. Two days after a skirmish took place near Aubrey between about 30 men

---

Aubry, Kansas, seven or eight miles south from Santa Fe, for the purpose of securing horses to remount the men. We arrived there about sunrise, and captured a number of good horses. We captured, also, a Lieutenant belonging to a Kansas cavalry regiment; his name was Brown, and we held him to exchange for Perry Hoy, who was then held a prisoner at Fort Leavenworth. We kept this Lieutenant three or four weeks. He was a splendid fellow, and we all became much attached to him. We allowed him the liberty of the camp and lines, and his uniform alone distinguished him from one of our men. During his detention Quantrill wrote the commanding officer at Fort Leavenworth proposing to exchange Lieutenant Brown for private Perry Hoy; but he received no reply. Finally after waiting some days, Quantrill paroled the Lieutenant and sent him to Fort Leavenworth to effect the exchange. Within a week or ten days he returned and informed Quantrill that the commander at the Fort refused to make the exchange.

7 *Rebellion Records*, Series I, Vol. VIII, p. 335. Report of Colonel Robert H. Graham, Eighth Kansas Infantry, to Major General H. W. Halleck, Commanding the Department of the Mississippi, dated, Headquarters Eighth Regiment, Kans. Vols., Leavenworth, March 19, 1862.

of his company, under First Lieutenant Rose and a portion of Quantrill's band. From the official report [not found, the editors say] of Captain Greelish I learn that it resulted in the retreat of Quantrill, with a loss of 2 killed and several wounded. Several horses were also killed. On his retreat Quantrill drove a family from their home and burned their house.

On our side none killed, and but 1 wounded — private Charles Cooney, severely in the foot. ......

I am fully satisfied that I cannot as provost-marshal-general, protect the state from guerrilla parties from without and the depredations of the horde of jayhawkers within in the present scattered condition of my regiment without several companies of cavalry.

CHAPTER XVII

BY ALL the rules of civilized warfare Quantrill and his men were subject to outlawry, and early in March, 1862, the Federal authorities formally declared them outlaws. The order was issued by General Halleck, Commander of the Department of the Mississippi.[1] Quantrill first learned of the

---

[1] This order has not been found. General Totten, commanding at Jefferson City, issued orders outlawing the guerrillas, set out here. Found in *Rebellion Records*, Series II, Vol. III, p. 468:

Special Orders, No. 47. } Headqrs. District of Central Missouri.

Jefferson City, Mo., April 21, 1862.

I. It is represented on reliable authority at these headquarters that bands of Jayhawkers, guerrillas, marauders, murderers and every species of outlaw are infesting to an alarming extent all the southwestern portion of Jackson County, and that persons of influence and wealth in these vicinities are knowingly harboring and thus encouraging (if not more culpably connected with) these bands of desperadoes. A prairie known as the "Doctor Lee Prairie," its borders and surroundings, are mentioned as the haunts of these outlaws and the farmers generally in these neighborhoods are said to be knowing to and encouraging the lawless acts of these guerrillas, etc., as mentioned above. Murders and robberies have been committed; Union men threatened and driven from their homes; the U. S. mails have been stopped; farmers have been prohibited planting by the proclamation of a well-known and desperate leader of these outlaws by the name of Quantrill, and the whole country designated reduced to a state of anarchy. This state of things must be terminated and the guilty punished. All those found in arms and open opposition to the laws and legitimate authorities, who are known familiarly as guerrillas, jayhawkers, murderers, marauders, and horse-thieves, will be shot down by the military upon the spot when found perpetrating their foul acts. All who have knowingly harbored or encouraged these outlaws in their lawless deeds will be arrested and tried by a military commission for their offenses, and those who have harbored and fed such miscreants as guerrillas, etc., but against whom clear proof cannot be obtained and who profess ignorance of having done these wrongs will be put under heavy bonds and security for their future good conduct or confined until they give such bonds, etc.

II. In order to correct the evils mentioned in the preceding paragraph and insure the passage of the mails regularly, Lieut. E. B. Brown, Seventh Missouri Volunteers, commanding the counties of Jackson and Cass will station one company of cavalry about five miles north of Pleasant Hill on the southern and one company on the northern border of the "Doctor

issuance of this order on the night of the 19th of March, 1862, while he and sixty of his men were quartered in the little Blue Baptist church, about twelve miles southeast of Independence.[2] This intelligence came through the medium of the *Missouri Republican.* After Quantrill had read the order he mounted his men and read it to them, carefully explaining to them that they were all deprived of the benefits of the civil or military laws, that from that day no quarter would be given them, and that Federal soldiers would hang or shoot them at once, wherever captured or found. He gave his men an opportunity to remain with him or not as they might wish, for men choosing outlawry must make the choice freely and voluntarily if anything worth while is to be accomplished by them. There were twenty men from Johnson county, Mo., in the force, and these rode out, abandoned him, and rode home. But by so doing they had not improved their condition. They were still outlaws, and when this fact impressed itself upon them, they returned to Quantrill after the absence of a month. Many young men of Jackson county, already in the brush, now joined Quantrill, and by the 22d of March, 1862, his command numbered more than a hundred men.

Quantrill could not let his men remain inactive. If he could not keep them constantly employed his band would disintegrate and disappear. After reading the order of outlawry to his men he immediately left the Little Blue church and marched

Lee Prairie'' to punish these guerrillas and escort the mail in safety whenever necessary.

III. Major Carley, commanding post at Warrensburg, will send one company First Iowa Cavalry to proceed to Pleasant Hill and escort the mail now there through to Independence, when it will return again to its present post.

By order of Brig. Gen. James Totten, commanding district.

Lucien J. Barnes,
Captain and Assistant Adjutant-General.

[2] F. Luther Wayman, Muskogee, Oklahoma, told the author, in April, 1909, that this was an old log church, ''eight-cornered'' or octagonal in form. He also said that when Quantrill had read the order over to himself and reflected on it a few minutes, he stood on a bench and explained it to his men. Then he said to the prisoner, Lieutenant Randlett, ''What do you think of that, lieutenant?'' Randlett replied: ''I could not blame you for shooting me, now.'' After some joking, Quantrill said, ''Not a hair of your head shall be harmed.''

to the house of Captain Deering, four miles south of Independence, and camped. This movement was in consequence of information which he had received to the effect that Independence was held by a force of but seventy-five Union soldiers. He believed he could defeat that force and that he might possibly capture it, in which event he would see what the Federal authorities might think of what an outlaw could do in the line of retaliation. But when Captain Deering arrived at home from Independence he told Quantrill that three hundred additional troops had been sent to the town. Quantrill did not dare attack so many, and he was inactive until the morning of the 22d of March. On that day he decided to sweep about the south skirts of Kansas City in search of adventure. At Pitcher's Mill he struck the Westport road. From that point a small scouting party was sent in advance. This party captured a Federal sergeant at the Big Blue bridge, now known as Twenty-seventh Street bridge. The sergeant was disarmed and dismounted just as Quantrill came up with the main body of his men. Fully to impress them with the condition in which they found themselves as the result of the order of outlawry, as well as to set an example which should be followed faithfully by them all in the future, Quantrill drew his pistol and shot the sergeant dead. Then facing his command, he flourished his smoking revolver aloft and cried in a loud voice:

"Boys, Halleck issued the order, but we draw the first blood!"

While the blood of the sergeant was still running red upon the ground an old man and his son, a small boy, came out of the city upon the highway leading across this bridge. The man was seized, accused of being a spy and informer, given a brief trial, convicted and immediately shot in the presence of the child. Then the bridge was burned, the command mounted and marched away from its victory, leaving a dead soldier, a dead citizen, a terrorized orphan boy weeping by the corpse of his murdered father.

It was still early in the day, and the guerrilla band rode to the Majors farm, eighteen miles southeast of Kansas City, in time for dinner. Here Quantrill lingered until near night, when he took his men to the house of David Tate, near the State-line, and near the station now known as Red Bridge, about three miles south of Little Santa Fé. Quantrill and twenty of his men stopped with Tate. Gregg and Todd, with ten men, stopped at the Wyatt farm, a mile south of the Tate house. Hallar, with a squad, went south beyond the Wyatt homestead to find lodging with a friendly farmer, and Kerr went still south of Hallar.

Quantrill and his men believed that some one living near the Tate house went to the Union troops and notified them of their presence at Tate's farm. Tate was already under suspicion at headquarters in Kansas City. He had been aiding Quantrill, if not actually a member of his band occasionally, and this was not the first time he had harbored a guerrilla band. Plans for his capture had been under consideration for some time before this date. When it was known in Kansas City that Quantrill had burned the Big Blue bridge and turned southwestward it was believed that he would go to the vicinity of the Tate house. Major Banzhaf, First Battalion Missouri Cavalry, notified Colonel Robert B. Mitchell, Second Kansas Cavalry, of the movements of Quantrill, and requested him to come to his assistance with troops. Colonel Mitchell left Kansas city at 6:30 P. M., of the 22d, and arrived at Little Santa Fé about ten o'clock the same evening. He immediately made a detail from Company D, to be commanded by Captain Amaziah Moore, and one from Company E, to be commanded by Lieutenant Elias S. Stover. He put this detachment under the command of Major James M. Pomeroy (Second Kansas) and sent it to capture and bring in David Tate.

When Major Pomeroy reached the Tate house he demanded admittance. The response to this demand was a shot fired through the door, doing no harm. He then called on the inmates to surrender, to which no answer was made. He then ordered them to send out their women and children, if any were in the house. Nothing was said in answer to this demand, but revolver-shots were fired from the windows. Quantrill was stacking furniture and bedding against the doors and windows all this time. Major Pomeroy ordered his men to fire a volley into the house.

This resulted in the cries of women and children, and he ordered the firing to cease. The women and children came out of the house and were sent to a place of safety, and both sides began firing. At this point two men came out through a window and surrendered, stating that Quantrill and twenty-six men were in the house. Major Pomeroy then notified the inmates that he would burn the house unless they surrendered at once. Upon their refusal to surrender an attempt was made to set the house on fire, but the part against which the fire was kindled was of logs, and it did not take fire until the light material was burned up. In this attempt to fire the house Major Pomeroy and a private were shot. The wound of Major Pomeroy disabled him, and Captain Moore took command and sent to Colonel Mitchell for reinforcements. He gave the inmates notice that the house would be fired unless they surrendered immediately, and as there was no response the house was set on fire and burned rapidly.

Quantrill had expected the house to be set on fire, and his movements had been directed to finding a means to escape. Nothing to further this design had presented itself. Now he saw

William Hulse

that he must leave without delay. Perhaps the red blood spilled at Big Blue bridge that morning did not cry from the ground with enough force to influence him. There was already too much on his hands for that of two men to make any material addition. He was cool and collected. In searching the lower portions of the house for a means of exit he came upon a part of the wall made only of weatherboarding. Marshaling his men in this room, he broke down the wall with some article of furniture and made a breach large enough to admit him and his men. They tumbled out helter-skelter and dashed into the thick brush and timber growing near-by and were lost in the darkness. As they ran from the house two of them were shot down, one killed and one mortally wounded; he died the following day. When the prisoners came out of the window they reported that four or five guerrillas were wounded, and Colonel Mitchell could plainly see five bodies in the burning building when he arrived. Colonel Mitchell says he took six prisoners, so the loss of Quantrill must have been at least seven men killed and six prisoners, thirteen all told. The two men killed outside the house were brothers named Rollen.

The Union loss was Major Pomeroy wounded, and private William Wills dangerously wounded in the right arm near the shoulder with a minnie ball and in the groin with buck-shot, dying afterwards. The guerrillas lost their horses and all their horse-equipments.

Colonel Mitchell led his men to an attack upon the Wyatt homestead, leaving the Tate house at 6:30 A. M. Upon his approach the men there fled to the timber, which was near the house. He dismounted some of his men and sent them into the woods in pursuit, and they captured two of the guerrillas.

Few commanders would have escaped from this burning building with any of their men. Quantrill's actions there showed courage and ability. But he was fighting for his life, as was every man with him. They knew they were outlaws. They had accepted the challenge and had shed the first blood under the new order. Their lives were forfeited. Surrender meant death. Knowing this, they believed they might as well die fighting. All the desperate courage of these guerrillas came from the position in which the order of outlawry placed them. The old excuse originated by Major Edwards, that each man had a private personal grievance, was never anything but an excuse. It stated no fact. Men in the regular and volunteer service lost fathers and brothers and property, but they did not become blood-mad because of it. Many of the events named as the causes of desperate deeds by guerrillas occurred long after the bloody actions they were made to justify at a later date.

Some parts of the official report of Colonel Mitchell are given here that the truth may be compared with the fiction of Major Edwards.[3]

---

[3] *Rebellion Records*, Series I, Vol. VIII, pp. 346-47. Report of Colonel Robert B. Mitchell, Second Kansas Cavalry, to Major W. E. Blair, Com'd'g, Leavenworth, Kansas.

Hdqrs, Second Regiment Kansas Volunteers,
Camp Blair, March 24, 1862.

Major:

I have the honor to report that on the night of the 22d, in accordance with a request from Major Banzhaf, commanding First Battalion Missouri Cavalry, and also in pursuance of a plan that I had been maturing for some time, I left camp with a detachment detailed from all the companies in this command, the detachment about 300 in number, with Majors Fisk and Pomeroy.

Quantrill, with a part of his gang, had burned the bridge between Kansas City and Independence, and it was contemplated by Major Banzhaf to march from Kansas City, and in conjunction with Colonel Weer, Fourth Kansas, to surround and entrap Quantrill.

I left camp about 6:30 p. m. of the 22nd inst, reached Little Santa Fe about 10 o'clock that night, and sent Major Pomeroy about 3 miles from the town, with instructions to arrest one David Tate, whom I had reason to believe was connected with Quantrill. Major Pomeroy had with him a detachment of Companies D and E, under command of Captain Moore and Lieutenant Stover. When Major Pomeroy reached the house he demanded entrance, and a gun was immediately fired through the door. He then called upon them to surrender, and to send out their women and children if they had any in the house. After waiting some time, while shots were fired from the house, he ordered a volley to be fired into the house. The cries of women were then heard, when he ordered the men to cease firing. The women and children then came out and the firing was resumed on both sides. Two of the men then came out of one of the windows and surrendered. They stated to Major Pomeroy that Quantrill was in the house with 26 men. Major Pomeroy then threatened to fire the house, and upon their continued refusal to surrender he ordered the house to be fired, and an attempt was made to fire it, but without success. Major Pomeroy and private Wills of Company D, were at this time shot. Major Pomeroy becoming disabled, Captain Moore took command, and sent back to me requesting reinforcements so as not to let any of the men escape. Captain Moore having threatened, in case of the enemy not surrendering, to set fire to the house and they still refusing to do so, he ordered the house to be again set on fire, and this time the flames rapidly enveloped the house. The men in the house who were not wounded then burst out the weatherboarding at the back of the house and ran for the timber immediately in the rear. Two were shot down as they ran — 1 killed instantly and 1 mortally wounded, who died about 3 o'clock in the afternoon. The others escaped, and though the woods were carefully scoured, no traces of them were found. While the firing was taking place several men were seen to fall in the house, and the prisoners stated when they were first taken that there were 4 or 5 wounded. Five bodies could be distinctly seen in the flames at the time I reached the spot with that part of the command which was left behind. I caused all the horses and horse equipments of the enemy to be gathered together and guarded and remained at the house until 6:30 o'clock in the morning, when I started for the house of one Wyatt. As we neared the house 6 or 7 men were seen to break from it into the brush immediately adjoining the premises. I immediately dismounted some of my men and sent them into the brush, but succeeded in capturing only 2. ....

Our loss was as follows: Major Pomeroy, severely wounded with a minnie ball in the right thigh near the femoral artery; Private William Wills, of Company D, since died, with a minnie ball in the right arm near the shoulder, and also with buck-shot in the groin and abdomen. We also lost two horses in the fight. The Jayhawks' loss was 5 killed or wounded and burned up in the house, 2 killed outside, and 6 prisoners. We took 25 horses, some of which have been already identified as belonging to parties in this state, from whom they were stolen, and about 20 sets of horse equipments. The 2 men killed outside the house were named Rollen (brothers). The names of those killed and burned up in the house I am unable to ascertain. ....

Particular attention is called to the fact that Colonel Mitchell here calls Quantrill and his men Jayhawks — Jayhawkers. Of this matter something will be said at the end of this chapter.

As against the official report of Colonel Mitchell the fanciful account written by Major Edwards is here set out. The exaggerations of Edwards in this account are duplicated in every account of a battle he describes. His object was to make heroes of Quantrill and his men:

The house was surrounded! To the men within-side this meant, unless they could get out, death by fire and sword. Quantrell was trapped, he who had been accorded the fox's cunning and the panther's activity. He glided to the window and looked out cautiously. The cold stars shone, and the blue figures under them and on every hand seemed colossal. The fist of a heavy man struck the door hard, and a deep voice commanded: "Make a light." There had been no firing as yet save the shot of the sentinel and its answering volley. Quantrell went quietly to all who were still asleep and bade them get up and get ready. It was the moment when death had to be looked in the face. Not a word was spoken. The heavy fist was still hammering at the door. Quantrell crept to it on tip-toe, listened a second at the sounds outside, and fired. "Oh!" and a stalwart Federal fell prone across the porch, dying. "You asked for a light, and you've got it, d——n you," Quantrell ejaculated, cooler than his pistol barrel. Afterwards there was no more bravado. "Bar the doors and barricade the windows!" he shouted; "quick, men!" Beds were freely used and applicable furniture. Little and Shepherd stood by one door; Jarrette, Younger, Toler, and Hoy barricaded the other and made the windows bullet-proof. Outside the Federal fusilade was incessant. Mistaking Tate's house for a frame house when it was built of brick, the commander of the enemy could be heard encouraging his men to shoot low and riddle the dwelling. Presently there was a lull. Neither party fired for the space of several minutes, and Quantrell spoke to his people: "Boys, we are in a tight place. We can't stay here, and I do not mean to surrender. All who want to follow me out can say so; all who prefer to give up without a rush can also say so. I will do the best I can for them." Four concluded to appeal to the Federals for protection; seventeen to follow Quantrell to the death. He called a parley and informed the Federal commander that four of his followers wanted to surrender. "Let them come out," was the order. Out they went and the fight began again. Too eager to see what manner of men their prisoners were, the Federals holding the west front of the house huddled about them eagerly. Ten guerillas from the upper story fired at the crowd and brought down six. A roar followed this, and a rush back again to cover at the double quick. It was hot work now. Quantrell, supported by James Little, Cole Younger, Hoy, and Stephen Shores, held the upper story, while Jarrette, Toler, George Shepherd, and others held the lower. Every shot told. The proprietor of the house, Major Tate, was a Southern hero, grey-headed but Roman. He went about laughing. "Help me to get my family out, boys," he said, "and I will help you to hold the house. It's as good a time for me to die, I reckon, as any other, if so be that God wills it. But the old woman is only a woman." Another parley. Would the Federal commander let the women and children out? Yes, gladly, and the old man, too. There was eagerness for this, and much of veritable cunning. The family occupied an ell of the mansion with which there was no communication from the main building where Quantrell and his men were save by way of a door which opened upon a porch, and this porch was under the concentrated fire

of the assailants. After the family moved out the attacking
party would throw skirmishers in, and then — the torch. Quantrell understood it in a moment, and spoke up to the father of
the family: "Go out, Major. It is your duty to be with your
wife and children." The old man went, protesting. Perhaps
for forty years the blood had not coursed so pleasantly and so
rapidly through his veins. Giving ample time for the family to
get safely beyond the range of fire of the besieged, Quantrell
went back to his post and looked out. He saw two Federals
standing together beyond revolver range. "Is there a shot-gun
here?" he asked. Cole Younger brought him one loaded with
buck-shot. Thrusting half his body out the nearest window,
and receiving as many volleys as there were sentinels, he fired
the two barrels of his gun so near together that they sounded
as one barrel. Both Federals fell, one dead, the other mortally
wounded. There followed this daring and conspicuous feat a
yell so piercing and exultant that even the horses, hitched in the
timber fifty yards away, reared in their fright and snorted with
terror. Black columns of smoke blew past the windows where
the Guerillas were, and a bright red flame leaped up toward the
sky on the wings of the wind. The ell of the house had been
fired, and was burning fiercely. Quantrell's face — just a little
paler than usual — had a set look that was not good to see.
The tiger was at bay. Many of the men's revolvers were empty,
and in order to gain time to load them, another parley was had.
The talk was of surrender. The Federal commander demanded
immediate submission, and Shepherd, with a voice heard above
the rage and roar of the flames, pleaded for twenty minutes.
No. Ten? No. Five? No. Then the commander cried out in
a voice not a whit inferior to Shepherd's in compass: "You
have one minute. If, at its expiration, you have not surrendered,
not a single man of you shall escape alive." "Thank you,"
said Cole Younger, *sotto voce*, "catching comes before hanging."
"Count sixty then, and be d——d to you," Shepherd shouted
as a parting volley, and then a strange silence fell upon these
desperate men face to face with imminent death. When every
man was ready, Quantrell said briefly: "Shot-guns to the front."
Six, loaded heavily with buck-shot, were borne there, and he put
himself at the head of the six who carried them. Behind these
were those having only revolvers. In single file, the charging
column was formed in the main room of the building. The glare
of the burning ell lit it up as though the sun was shining there.
Some tightened their pistol belts. One fell upon his knees and
prayed. Nobody scoffed at him, for God was in that room. He
is everywhere when heroes confess. There were seventeen who
were about to receive the fire of three hundred.

Ready! Quantrell flung the door wide open and leaped out. The shot-gun men — Jarrette, Younger, Shepherd, Toler, Little and Hoy were hard behind him. Right and left from the thin short column a fierce fire beat into the very faces of the Federals, who recoiled in some confusion, shooting, however, from every side. There was a yell and a grand rush, and when the end had come and all the fixed realities figured up, the enemy had eighteen killed, twenty-nine badly wounded, and five prisoners, and the captured horses of the Guerillas. Not a man of Quantrell's command was touched.

Thus it always is in the work of Major Edwards. Quantrill escapes without loss, or with an insignificant loss, when he retreats. And he always inflicts immense loss on the Union soldiers. Here he is credited with having killed eighteen and wounded twenty-nine. The truth is, as shown by the official report, that the Union loss was two wounded, one of whom died. At the Big Blue bridge Quantrill shot down thirteen Union soldiers, according to Edwards. But, as we have seen, he shot but a sergeant and a citizen, and the authority for that statement is the *Gregg Manuscript*, written by one of Quantrill's men who was present, and who is known to be truthful and reliable. And, according to Edwards, every skirmish and battle fought by Quantrill resulted in a victory for him, though he records it often that he had to run for it, and frequently had to scatter his men to avoid destruction. The average reader wonders why it was necessary to flee for life and scatter like birds after a victory had been won. According to Edwards, Quantrill and his men must have killed several thousand Union soldiers during the war. The truth is, that the number of soldiers killed by Quantrill and his men was insignificant, and those killed were mainly shot from ambush.

The work of Major Edwards is the standard authority on Quantrill and his men, and this is why it is necessary often to call attention to its exaggerations.

JAYHAWKERS

In going through the *Rebellion Records* the author finds that the name "Jayhawkers" was applied indiscriminately to irregular bands on both sides in Kansas and Missouri and to both

Kansans and Missourians. It did not, during the war, certainly not in the first years of the war, have any more application to Kansas people than to any other people.

When and how the name "Jayhawkers" came to be applied to Kansans in their forays for depredation does not appear. And how the Kansas people came to be generally called Jayhawkers has so far not had any satisfactory explanation. The Pat Devlin fiction perpetrated in *Andreas's History of Kansas* was never worth any serious consideration. Even the origin of the word "jayhawker" has not been satisfactorily traced. It is known that some Forty-niners who survived the terrible ordeal of crossing Death Valley called themselves Jayhawkers, but they themselves did not know why. One of them claims that the word originated with them, but his explanation of its origin is as ridiculous as that given by Pat Devlin. And the other members of the company made no such claim, and intimate that the name was in use long before the party reached the Platte, where the member of the party who claims it originated with them says it was "coined." The word did not originate with this party — that is certain.

It has been said to have originated in the patriot army of Texas fighting for the Independence of the Lone Star State against Mexico, under General Houston.

CHAPTER XVIII

FROM the Tate house Quantrill made his way on foot to the house of David Wilson, on the head waters of the Little Blue. He was almost exhausted when he arrived there. He waited at Wilson's for the gathering of his men, for he had sent couriers to notify those at the Wyatt homestead and other places that the rendezvous had been fixed on the head waters of the Little Blue. Quantrill, however, did not remain at the house of Wilson until all his men arrived, fearing the Union forces. In two or three days he moved to the house of John Flannery, where he remained until Hallar and his other followers came in. When all had assembled he gave them directions for again coming together and then disbanded his men long enough to allow those who had lost their horses to secure new mounts. All were to report within a few days at a designated point on the Sni. By the last of March the command had reassembled, and the men were eager to be on the trail.

Quantrill soon made his camp at the farm of Samuel C. Clark, near Pink Hill, which is about nineteen miles southwest from Independence. Here he was attacked on Sunday, the 30th of March, 1862, by Captain Albert P. Peabody, commanding Company D, First Missouri Cavalry. Captain Peabody was in command of a detachment of sixty-five men, and he was searching for Quantrill, having heard that he was at Pink Hill. When nearing that point he had divided his force, placing thirty-five men under command of Lieutenant White of Company C, and retaining thirty men commanded by Second Lieutenant Gurnee, of Company D. With these two detachments he began to scour the country for the purpose of routing Quantrill from his hiding-place. Captain Peabody discovered his camp at the Clark farm and charged upon it. Quantrill was taken by surprise. Koger had just arrived from a visit to an acquaintance in the neighborhood, and was hitching his horse to the rail fence in front of the house when the firing commenced; he was slightly wounded by the first shot fired. Gregg was acting barber, cutting a comrade's hair in the front yard. All the guerrillas got to cover at once and made preparations for a bold stand.

Quantrill had with him about thirty men, though the official reports credit him with twice that number at the beginning of the fight and say that he received reinforcements from neighboring farmers and at the conclusion had one hundred and fifty men, a thing not at all probable. The battle was fought between the sixty-five Federals and about half that number of guerrillas.

Quantrill, with eight men, fought from the lower story of the Clark dwelling, and Todd, with eight men, fought from the upper story. Gregg, with eight men, fought from the negro cabins. The dwelling and negro cabins were built of logs, from between which the chinking was knocked to make port holes through which to fire. Quantrill's horses were in the barn about two hundred feet from the dwelling.

Captain Peabody sent a courier to bring up Lieutenant White, and as soon as the detachment arrived he charged the dwelling. This charge convinced Quantrill that he could not hold the premises; perhaps he had no intention of doing so longer than was necessary to secure his horses, from which he was cut off. The charge caused him to determine to escape at once. He divided his men equally between himself and Todd and left Todd to hold the house. He started to the barn, but had not reached it when Captain Peabody came down in another charge. This scared Todd, and he called loudly for Quantrill to return, which he did. Peabody was now closing in upon the guerrillas, and Quantrill ordered his men to follow him from the house, and the whole band fled to the rough timberland at the back of the house, losing all their horses.

The official reports [1] state the losses as follows: Union, three wounded — two slightly, one severely; killed, none; three

---

[1] *Rebellion Records*, Series I, Vol. VIII, p. 358. Report of Major Charles Banzhaf, First Missouri Cavalry, to Maj.-Gen. H. W. Halleck, Commanding Department of the Mississippi. Dated, Kansas City, Mo., April 5, 1862.

horses shot dead. Guerrillas, six killed; wounded carried away and nothing known of the number; twenty horses and equipments. As usual, Edwards has a large number of Union soldiers killed — twenty-seven at one volley, as well as their horses.

It is doubtful whether the guerrillas had any killed or wounded. The *Gregg Manuscript* says the slight wound sustained by Koger was their only damage, except the loss of the horses.

Captain Peabody had sent to Pink Hill for reinforcements, and these were promptly started — fifty-one men under Captain Murphy. In his retreat Quantrill went to the Sni ford by which these reinforcements would have to cross to reach the Clark homestead. He took a position on a high bluff with a steep face which commanded the ford. Captain Murphy found Quantrill there and attacked him, though at much disadvantage. The guerrillas poured in a vigorous fire until Captain Peabody, having now burned all the buildings at the Clark homestead and started to follow, came up on their trail and struck their rear. Then they retired. Losses in this engagement, as stated in the official reports,[2] were as follows: Union; two wounded, one mortally; two horses killed. Guerrillas; five killed, six wounded, and one taken prisoner. As Captain Kaiser could have no means of ascertaining the number of guerrillas wounded, the accuracy of his statement of the losses of Quantrill is open to question.[3]

The guerrillas were again dismounted, and a period of inactivity lasting a few days was necessary in order to secure horses for the men. The rendezvous was at the house of Reuben Harris, ten miles south of Independence. There Quantrill

---

[2] *Rebellion Records*, Series I, Vol. VIII, p. 360. Report of Captain John B. Kaiser, Boonville Battalion, Missouri Cavalry (Militia), to Col. John D. Stevenson. Dated, Pink Hill, Mo., April 1, 1862.

[3] Brig.-Gen. James Totten, U. S. Army, made a report of this affair, which can be found in *Rebellion Records*, Series I, Vol. VIII, p. 359, in which he uses the following: "——————— of a skirmish which took place between his command and some bands of Quantrill's and Parker's Jayhawkers."

Captain Kaiser, in the report cited above, uses the term — "Parker's and Quantrill's Jayhawkers."

These instances are here mentioned to illustrate further what the author said on the subject of "Jayhawkers," *ante.*

planned to capture Harrisonville, county-seat of Cass county, and to this end moved to the house of Job Crabtree, eight miles east of Independence, on the Little Blue. The report of the activity of Captain Peabody caused Quantrill to abandon his design to capture Harrisonville, and he moved from Crabtree's to an abandoned house, known as the Jordan Lowe house, twelve miles southwest from Independence, and not far from Little Santa Fé. He and his men slept in the timber near the house.

The Union troops were actively looking for Quantrill. Lieut.-Col. Brown, of the Seventh Missouri Cavalry, had been trailing him for five days. Having arranged with a scout to be at Ray Point (Jackson county) at midnight of the 15th of April, 1862, with definite information as to Quantrill's camp, he sent a detachment of thirty men of the First Missouri Cavalry, commanded by Lieutenant G. W. Nash, to capture him. The scout was successful, and he met Lieutenant Nash at Ray Point with the desired information. The night was very dark. A heavy thunderstorm raged until four o'clock, A. M., of the 16th, and rain fell in torrents, the darkness and rain completely concealing the movements of Nash's force. The heavy rain drove Quantrill and his men from the timber to the house. They posted no guard, supposing that no troops would be out in such a night. The door was barred, and the men went to sleep, some of them in the loft. Their horses were hitched to the fence at the rear of the house.

Just at dawn and while the men were yet asleep, Lieutenant Nash arrived at the Lowe house and quietly secured the horses of the guerrillas. He then threw his men about the house and opened fire. The surprise was complete. But Quantrill had no thought of surrendering. He determined to escape from the house at once and called on all the men to follow him. Todd, Blunt, and Gilchrist were firing from the loft and did not hear the order to abandon the house. When the guerrillas had almost reached the timber Cole Younger noticed that

Dick Maddox

Todd was still firing from the loft, and he returned to bring him off. He succeeded in getting Todd away, but the others were captured. A new recruit, an Irish boy, was killed, as was William Carr. Gilchrist was killed, and Blunt was wounded.[4]

It has always been represented by the Missouri biographers of Quantrill that he was engaged in protecting the Southern sympathizers and was engaged in a righteous and holy defensive warfare in Missouri against invading hordes from Kansas, molesting no man not in arms, conducting his irregular warfare in great simplicity and good faith, with the good of the people at heart — a sort of Francis Marion — a patriot of pure character, the champion of innocent and helpless people, never doing anything wrong.

In the official report of Captain John B. Kaiser, before cited, it is said:

The Union people here are suffering greatly from the bands of these ruffians. They are daily driven from their homes and many of them are caught and either hung or shot. No Union man is safe one mile from camp unless a force is with him. Parker's and Quantrill's bands now number nearly two hundred men, as nearly as I can learn. The peaceable citizens are very anxious that I remain.

And attention is called to the fact that the official reports make it plain that it was not the Kansas troops that were stationed along the border, but in almost every instance these troops were Missourians who had enlisted in the Union army. So far, it does not appear that any Kansas troops were in any battle with Quantrill and his men. Nor does it appear that they were stationed in Jackson county. And these reports show that Quantrill had to contend with Missouri troops, was chased and

---

4 The official report of this affair is found in *Rebellion Records*, Series I, Vol. XIII, p. 58. Report of E. B. Brown, Lieutenant-Colonel, Commanding Seventh Missouri Infantry, to Captain Lucien J. Barnes, A. A. Gen., Jefferson City. Dated, Independence, Mo., April 16, 1862. This report fixes the loss of the guerrillas at four killed, four wounded, and five prisoners, horses, clothing, and other property. The *Gregg Manuscript* says Gilchrist was killed and Blunt wounded after they were captured. It makes no mention of the Irish boy nor of William Carr. No loss reported by the Union troops.

attacked by Union troops from Missouri and not from Kansas. And all this confirms the position taken in a former chapter — that the Missouri people were hopelessly divided in the war, and that most of the outrages committed in that State were committed by Missourians upon Missourians. There can be no doubt that troops enlisted in other States committed crimes in Missouri, and that some of the worst of these crimes were committed by Kansas troops under Jennison. But these things were not countenanced by the Kansas people any more than were the acts of Quantrill by the Missouri people; and Jennison was discredited and resigned.

Official reports usually show a very different state of affairs from rumors and general talk and gossip.

CHAPTER XIX

QUANTRILL IN THE SUMMER OF 1862

IT IS probable that in May, 1862, Quantrill's ammunition was exhausted and that he was unable to procure a supply. He had usually been successful in having the women of Jackson county who sympathized with him get pistol caps, lead and powder from Kansas City. This resource had now failed him. His operations could not go on without ammunition, and as all his efforts to replenish his store had failed, he determined to go himself and procure a supply. Two plug horses were provided. On these Quantrill and Todd rode to Hannibal, Missouri. There they sold the horses. In three or four days they succeeded in buying about fifty thousand pistol-caps without arousing the suspicions of the military authorities there. They returned by the way of St. Joseph, going to that point by rail. From St. Joseph they returned to their haunts, riding from Platte City to Harlem, Clay county, in a hack or closed carriage. There a sentinel challenged the driver, and while he was questioning the gentleman of the reins and whip, Todd and Quantrill escaped from the conveyance by the door on the side from the sentinel. They went down the north bank of the Missouri River seeking means to cross. Fortunately they came upon Andrew Blunt and William Bledsoe, who were fishing from a skiff — "jugging for catfish in the shutes of the Missouri." The meeting was a surprise to both parties, for the guerrillas did not know where their chief had gone, and Quantrill did not expect to find any of his men so near to Kansas City.[1]

Quantrill was active in a small way, only, during the month

---

[1] The hairbreadth escapes and thrilling adventures of Quantrill and Todd in Federal camps, dressed in the uniforms of Federal officers, as set forth by Major Edwards, are all pure fiction, so far as the author has been able to learn. Careful research fails to find any verification of the account. Edwards has them remain three days in St. Joseph, at the headquarters of the Union troops, pretending to be majors in the army.

of June, 1862. He seems to have remained away from the vicinity of Independence, and to have avoided the Union troops. Only occasional glimpses are caught of him in the official reports, and indirect mention of his presence here and there. He was evidently riding industriously and undoubtedly harrassing Union citizens, no doubt hanging, shooting, and robbing them frequently. But the war was growing in volume and intensity, and many minor matters escaped notice.[2]

The return of Colonel Upton S. Hays to Jackson county for the purpose of recruiting a regiment for the Confederacy was the beginning of a season of activity for Quantrill and his men. He arrived about the middle of June and immediately sought Quantrill and requested his assistance. Quantrill agreed to help. They planned to change the field of operations to some point away from Jackson county, hoping to lead the Union troops a fruitless chase; and when the country was clear Hays would return and enlist his men without molestation. With this end in view they led the guerrilla bands to the south some eighty miles, to the north part of Henry county. They camped on Walnut creek in a vacant farm-house, where they were attacked the following morning, wounding and capturing one of the Union men.

When it was certain that the Union forces knew of the appearance of the guerrillas to the south, and their absence from their usual haunts, Hays became impatient to begin his recruiting. He asked Quantrill for a body-guard with which to return to Jackson county. Quantrill gave him Todd and thirty men. Hays departed early in July, leaving Quantrill with sixty-five men. Even then the Union forces were closing in on Quantrill. Major James O. Gower, First Iowa Cavalry, heard of him on the 8th on Sugar creek, near Wadesburg, Cass county, and sent out Lieutenant Reynolds, Company A, First Iowa, with ninety men to search for him. This detachment then returned to Clinton.

---

[2] *Rebellion Records*, Series I, Vol. XIII, pp. 120, 131, 132, 156, 157, mention Quantrill at this period. He was in the vicinity of Pink Hill, in the edges of Cass and Johnson counties, and perhaps he hovered sometimes along the State-line.

Major Gower sent dispatches to Butler and Warrensburg directing details of men to meet him at the Lotspiech farm, Cass county. At five A. M., on the 10th, Major Gower marched for the rendezvous with seventy-five men, arriving at eleven o'clock, where he found Captain William H. Ankey with sixty-five of the First Iowa, and Captain William A. Martin with sixty-five men of the Seventh Missouri. Shortly afterward sixty men of the First Missouri Cavalry under Captain M. Kehoe and Lieutenant White, came up, making a total force of two hundred and sixty-five men.

Quantrill's trail was struck at Lincoln Ford on Big creek by Captain Kehoe, he having left his camp on Sugar creek at four o'clock P. M., of the 9th. The trail was followed east of Rose Hill, Johnson county, then up Big creek to the Hornsby farm, where the guerrillas had taken dinner. Having marched his men fifty miles, Major Gower camped there, and it was agreed that all should start the next morning, Friday the 11th, at daybreak.

At the appointed time Captain Kehoe's command was in the saddle, and notice was sent to Major Gower that it was ready to move. Not receiving a response, and supposing that the Iowa troops would follow immediately, Captain Kehoe marched slowly in the direction of the guerrilla camp. About four miles west of Pleasant Hill he encountered Quantrill's pickets, and he at once sent word to Major Gower that he was about to engage the enemy, and calling for reinforcements. Half a mile beyond the picket station Captain Kehoe found Quantrill's command at the house of one Sears (Searancy?), a Union man, making preparations to burn the house. He charged the enemy, supposing it to be a part of the body, but finding it to be the main command.

There had been a heavy rain toward night the day before, and the guerrillas were thoroughly soaked. The morning was bright and warm. They had hung their blankets and other effects on the fences to dry. When the pickets were fired on Quantrill called the usual command — "Saddle up." The horses were at once equipped and hitched in a ravine back of the horse-lot. The men were ordered to the front and concealed behind the lot fence and ordered not to fire before the word was given.

Six of Captain Kehoe's men charged down upon this position. When they were within thirty yards of the gate Quantrill ordered his men to fire, and the six Union soldiers fell from their saddles dead, and nine of those following were wounded. Quantrill opened the gate to the lot at the suggestion of Gregg, and the horses of the dead Federals came in at full speed. The arms of the dead men were secured, and the guerrillas again concealed themselves, but no further charges were made. Some additional troops had joined Captain Kehoe, and fire was opened on the enemy at long range, killing John Hampton and wounding George Mattox and William Tucker. Quantrill charged the Union troops, killing two. After sending away his wounded he led his men to a ravine half a mile away surrounded with dense thickets of rough brush. The banks of the ravine were from five to seven feet high and from thirty to sixty feet apart. Captain Martin was the first to attack Quantrill at this ravine. He dismounted his men and began a charge when twenty of them were in line. Their fire was reserved until the brink of the ravine was reached. After delivering his fire he threw his men forward into the defile among the guerrillas, who charge

Lee McMurtry

that this was recklessness caused by the men being drunk. A hand-to-hand struggle, bloody and terrible, ensued. It was again Missourian against Missourian. The guerrillas were driven from the ravine and forced to the opposite side of the thicket. Major Gower had, however, sent a force to that side of the timber, and Quantrill and his men ran at full head against it. A fierce volley and charge drove them back through the weaker line of Captain Martin, who followed them back to the ravine and again renewed the hand-to-hand grapple, and the guerrillas were again forced out. They took a position in another branch of the defile in the same thicket. Here they were again attacked by Captain Martin, who had received some reinforcements, and the struggle was renewed. The guerrillas held their ground well,

17

and Captain Martin charged them several times. Quantrill was wounded in the thigh. His men were without ammunition and had resorted to throwing stones, and he saw that he should be unable to remain longer in the ravine. Many of his men were dismounted. He ordered those having horses to mount and try to escape, and Gregg led them out — twenty-one men. Quantrill led out the dismounted men, taking a direction opposite to that by which the horsemen departed, but still remaining in the timber on the rough ground.

This battle raged an hour and a half and was the hardest yet fought with the guerrillas — one of the hardest ever fought with them. The heavy foliage of the brush made it impossible to see ten feet in any direction there. The cries of the men, the sharp and steady cracking of carbine and revolver, the flash of the fire in the dark woods, the fierce grapple when sabre-stroke was parried with clubbed gun, the shouting of the officers, the groans of the wounded trampled under foot as the battle rolled back and forth through the tangled thickets, were terrifying and made a scene rarely equaled in the warfare of the border.[3]

---

3 *Rebellion Records*, Series I, Vol. XIII, pp. 154, 155. Report of Major James O. Gower, First Iowa Cavalry, to Colonel Fitz Henry Warren, Commanding Sub-District, Butler, Bates County, Mo. Dated, Clinton, Henry County, Mo., July 13, 1862.

Also, report of Captain Henry J. Stierlin, Company A, First Missouri Cavalry, to Brig.-Gen. James Totten, Commanding Central Division, Missouri. Dated, Warrensburg, Mo., July 12, 1862.

Also, report of Captain William A. Martin, Company C, Seventh Missouri Cavalry, to Major A. H. Linder, Commanding Detachment Seventh Missouri Cavalry. Dated, Harrisonville, Mo., July 12, 1862.

The *Gregg Manuscript* has a good account of this battle, and claims a loss of four dead, only. The official reports state the losses as follows: Union loss; eleven killed and twenty-one wounded. Guerrillas; fourteen known to have been killed — probably eighteen killed and twenty-five to thirty wounded. This is the report of Major Gower.

At the ravine Captain Martin had one killed and one wounded. He captured thirty horses and a large number of saddles, blankets, coats, guns, and other equipments. Captured the equipments, overcoat and spyglass of Quantrill.

CHAPTER XX

INDEPENDENCE was in 1862 in the military district commanded by General Totten, with headquarters at Jefferson City. June 7, 1862, he assigned Lieutenant-Colonel James T. Buel to the command of the post at Independence. Buel established a camp about half a mile west of the public square, on the south side of Lexington street. The camp was in a depression or piece of low land used as a pasture; there were no buildings in or near it, and the troops were sheltered with tents.

Colonel Buel had about five hundred men in his command. There were three companies of the Seventh Missouri Cavalry, commanded by Captain Breckenridge; two companies of Neugent's Second Battalion, Missouri Provisional Militia, commanded by Captain Jacob Axline and Captain Aaron Thomas; and a company of the Sixth Missouri Enrolled Militia, under command of Captain W. H. Rodewald, which was temporarily attached to the Seventh Missouri. Captain Jacob Axline was ordered to report to Colonel Buel from Kansas City, which he did on Sunday, August 10th.

The disposition of the troops of the command was the worst that could have been made at all. Colonel Buel had his headquarters in the Southern Bank building (now known as the McCoy Bank) on the south side of Lexington street, just off the southwest corner of the public square. His guards, under Captain Rodewald, were quartered in buildings on the opposite side of the street. The provost-marshal (acting) was Lieutenant Charles W. Meryhew, of the Seventh Missouri. He was stationed at the county jail, on North Main street, one block from the public square. The three companies of the Seventh Missouri and the two companies of Neugent's Battalion were camped in the pasture a full half mile from headquarters, with no means of maintaining communication with the commander in case of an attack. This proved to be the fatal defect of position when the battle came to be fought.

When Quantrill and his men fled from the battlefield at the ravines they went to the head waters of the Little Blue. Quantrill was hidden away nursing his wound and a case of erysipelas which it brought on. Most of his men had returned and were aiding Colonel Hays to recruit his regiment.

After the battle of Pea Ridge the Missouri State Guard was reorganized, and that part which entered the Confederate service was sent east of the Mississippi. Those who did not enter that service straggled back to Missouri during the summer and became guerrillas. It was to gather up and enlist these stragglers, or some of them, that Upton Hays had returned to Missouri. After he left Quantrill in Henry county he went directly to Jackson county and began to recruit his regiment, in which work he did not have the success he desired, having secured only about three hundred men prior to the battle of Independence.

About the first of August, 1862, Colonel John T. Hughes arrived in Jackson county from Arkansas. He had with him about seventy-five men. It was his design to recruit a brigade for the Confederate army, and he had been commissioned a brigadier-general. Hughes was a good soldier. He at once thoroughly informed himself of the disposition of the Federal forces in Western Missouri. He intended to recruit his brigade in the country north of the Missouri river, and he did not believe he could get it out after he had enlisted it with Buel in possession of Independence. And he believed the men of that section would be of that opinion, which would make it difficult to induce them to enlist. He decided to stop for a time in Jackson county, and went into camp at the Charles Cowherd farm near Lee's Summit. There he raised a Confederate flag on a tall pole and established a recruiting station. This flag could be seen from the court-house at Independence. Colonel Hughes intended to attack Colonel Buel and capture him or drive him from Independence as soon as he could muster enough men to do it. That was a part of his plan for raising and taking out his brigade.

If he could go into North Missouri after a brilliant victory at Independence he could quickly raise the forces he desired and could get them out before troops could assemble to prevent it. It was in this condition and from this necessity confronting Colonel Hughes that the battle of Independence originated.

When Colonel Hughes found it difficult to secure recruits in Jackson county and that he would not be able to attack Colonel Buel for a long time, he decided to ask Colonel Hays and Quantrill to aid him. Hays and Quantrill must have been camped in the vicinity of Blue Springs, and some of their bands were probably on the Sni. Hays gathered his men, about three hundred, and marched to join Hughes. This was on Sunday, the 10th of August, 1862. A Mrs. Wilson saw them march past her house, about three miles north of Blue Springs, at ten o'clock that night. She was a loyal woman, and she immediately mounted a horse and rode to Independence. She reported to Colonel Buel, and in the presence of Captain Rodewald, that she had seen these men march by her house and had heard they were to attack Independence that night. She supposed there were a thousand of them. And she had heard of another body of men, on the Sni, perhaps Quantrill's, who would march against Independence that night, also. Buel treated Mrs. Wilson rudely, and the information which she had been at such pains to bring him he treated with contempt. Even after Colonel Samuel D.

Colonel Upton Hays

Lucas had vouched for the honesty and general good character of Mrs. Wilson he refused to credit the information she gave and declared that he knew how to take care of himself and wished that people would stop bringing in such reports. It was generally known in Independence on Sunday that the town would be attacked on Monday morning. Indeed it had been known before that, and some people had gone to Kansas City almost a week before the battle came, to be out of it. Buel took no precautions for the defense of the town, left his forces scattered about and officers away from their commands, and he snored in stupid (imagined) security at his headquarters.[1]

It is said that Colonel Buel intended to attack the camp of Hughes on Monday, and that on Sunday he searched Independence and seized all arms and ammunition found. That no preparation of his forces for such an attack appears would indicate that he had abandoned that design.

The attack on Independence was planned by Colonel Hughes and the battle was fought on plans laid out by him. Until his death he was in command. Hays had about three hundred men, Hughes one hundred, and Quantrill about twenty-five. Colonel Gid. W. Thompson was one of the officers, but he had no troops of his own to command. In assigning the officers their parts Colonel Hughes gave Quantrill two things to do — one, to cut off Buel from his men; the other, to picket the town after it was taken. He said to Quantrill: "You will be well supported. In fact, I shall be right behind you when you enter the public square."[2]

---

[1] The incident of Mrs. Wilson's ride to try to save the Union troops is found in *The Civil War on the Border*, Vol. I, p. 316. This work is by Wiley Britton, who was a Union soldier, and it is one of the best authorities ever written on the Civil War. Mr. Britton gives a splendid account of the battle of Independence and the preliminary movements of the troops.

[2] Morgan T. Mattox, one of Quantrill's men, gave the author the following concerning the battle of Independence:

On the Saturday before the battle of Independence Mattox was sent to the town as a spy. He carried a supply of onions and pies which he sold to Buel's men. He observed the whole situation and returned to Quantrill. On his way out he went to the place at which he had left the command, but it was gone. He soon met Arch Rockwell who took him to Quantrill, to whom he reported. Quantrill had gone to the camp of Hays and Hughes on Saturday night.

To reach Independence *all* the forces went by the Spring Branch Road. They found the Federal pickets at Mr. Burford's gate, about one hundred and fifty yards east of the Spring at the east edge of Independence. The Quantrill men ran on the pickets and shot them down. Then Quantrill rushed his men to the square.

Colonel Hughes was right behind Quantrill and he did not stop in the town, but rushed on to the camp of the Federals west of town. He was killed at the gate of the field in which the Federals were camped. Kit Chiles was killed right at the bank.

Before this battle Jim Knowles, of Independence, had piloted Buel into the Blue Cut neighborhood. At the Blue Cut, Buel met George Todd, Ed Koger, and John Little, and killed Koger and Little. Todd got away. This gave the Quantrill men a grudge against Knowles, who was City

It was the plan of Colonel Hughes to get into the town and take possession of it, with the main part of his force between Buel and his men, without firing a gun or raising an alarm. Quantrill entered the town by Spring street, the pickets east of the town on the Spring Branch road being found dead the next day. He entered the public square and waited for Hughes, who entered with the main body, on the Lexington road, just a minute later. Hughes dismounted a part of his force and the horses were hitched about the public square. Quantrill then formed his men into platoons and rode out of the public square west on Lexington street at a sharp gait, closely followed by Hughes and the main force. It was half past four o'clock and not yet daylight. The guard at Captain Rodewald's quarters commanded a halt and fired his gun to alarm his comrades. He rushed into the guard-room and found the men there gettting to arms. The street was soon filled with Confederate soldiers. A few shots were fired into them from a second-story window, when some one there cried out: "For God's sake don't fire; it's your own men." Believing this and not being able to see in the darkness, Captain Rodewald led his men down stairs and out into the street, where he saw a Confederate soldier well known to him, whom he took prisoner. He called to his men that the force in the street were rebels, and ordered them to form into line, which they did, cutting off some of the moving column of Confederates. He ordered his men to fire into the receding ranks, the rear of which was yet in range, and they did so, killing Colonel Kit Chiles. Captain Rodewald retained his position an hour and a half, repulsing three attacks of the enemy, two from the public square and one from the west. In the last he mortally wounded Major Hart and captured a lieutenant and eleven privates.

Marshal of Independence. One day he killed an old Irishman who was drunk and "cutting up" a little. For this he was put in jail, and was in jail when the battle was fought.

Bill Bassham had been a stage driver on the Old Santa Fe Trail, but had quit and come home to Independence about the time Knowles killed the Irishman. He had not been connected with the war in any way at that time, but some one preferred the charge that he was a Quantrill man, and he was locked up in jail.

Quantrill's men broke into the jail and released Bassham, who then and there joined them. George Todd then shot and killed Jim Knowles.

Colonel Buel did not leave his headquarters and put himself at the head of Captain Rodewald's men and make an effort to reach his main camp as a brave and capable officer would have done. He ordered them to leave the street, where they were fighting bravely and maintaining themselves well, and come into his headquarters, the most stupid action he could have taken. The enemy surrounded him at once, and Quantrill was sent into a store-building on the opposite side of the street, the second story of which commanded the front windows of Buel's rooms in the bank building. He poured in a perfect hail of shot until after nine o'clock, when Buel surrendered.

Colonel Buel did nothing to save the day. He did not hoist his flag until a few minutes before he surrendered. In fact, the flag was not at his headquarters but at Captain Rodewald's quarters. It was brought over by a bugler, a barefooted boy of sixteen, who volunteered to fetch it. He crossed the street, secured the flag, and re-crossed the street through showers of balls fired at him, and came off unhurt. There was not even a flag-staff, and two of Captain Rodewald's men who were sent up to fasten it to the chimney were instantly killed on the roof by Quantrill's men. Then the Confederate lieutenant and one of his men, captured in the last charge of Captain Rodewald, were required to fasten the flag to the chimney, and by going on the roof and making themselves known were allowed by Quantrill to do so.

The troops at the camp and at the jail had been obliged to rely upon themselves. Lieutenant Meryhew, at the jail, fired one volley and then abandoned his post and fled through the woods to Kansas City, where he arrived with fourteen men late in the afternoon.[3]

The real fighting of the day was done by Captain Axline and the men he was able to rally around him. The Confederates struck the camp just at daylight. There seems to have been no

---

[3] By some it is claimed that the volley fired from the jail wounded Major Hart. The author has followed Britton, who says Hart was wounded in the last charge upon Captain Rodewald. Webb, in *Battles and Biographies of Missourians*, has a good description of the battle of Independence.

guards or pickets on duty anywhere. The Confederates fired
a deliberate volley from a line not a hundred feet from the tents
in which the Union soldiers were sleeping. This fire killed
many. Those uninjured rushed to arms. The sudden attack
and surprise either frightened Captain Breckenridge or else
the charge that he had conspired to surrender the men into the
hands of the enemy was true. Immediately after the first fire
he called out in a loud voice: "Boys, we are completely surrounded, and we had better surrender." His call to surrender
was the first order heard by the troops from any officer. It was
successfully offset by Captain Axline, who cried in a voice heard
above the roar of battle: "Boys, get your guns and ammunition and rally behind the rock-fence." This was a stone wall or
fence half a mile long, running east and west along the south
side of the camp. As the men emerged from their tents they
fired with spirit, and, directing their fire to the east and southeast, they were able to check the enemy long enough to gain
the wall. Many of them, in retreating, were pushed west beyond
the wall, and they retreated out of range. Some of them did
not stop until they reached Kansas City. Their retreat would
have been disastrous had it been followed up, and they escaped,
possibly, only because after the first volley many of the Confederates ceased fighting and began to plunder the abandoned
tents of the Union troops.

Captain Axline was exposed to a heavy fire from front and
rear, some of the Confederates being far enough south to enfilade
the south side of the wall. He retreated along the wall until he
came to a gully three or four feet deep which it crossed. Here
he made a stand, and he could not be driven out. In a charge
upon the right of Captain Axline's position here, in an attempt
to flank it, Colonel John T. Hughes was shot in the forehead and
instantly killed.

Lieutenant Herrington, of the Missouri State Militia, soon
came to the aid of Captain Axline, who was then able to cover
three-fourths of the camp with his fire. His position was
impregnable, and but for the cowardice of Captain Breckenridge he would have held out and saved the day. Shortly after
getting into his favorable position and as his men were beginning

to have confidence in their ability to hold the field, some one called attention to a white flag hoisted on the wall to the west. Axline directed Lieutenant Herrington to see what the flag meant, while he went himself to gather up the many stragglers he saw in that direction, leaving Sergeant Blake in command of the firing-line. He met Captain Breckenridge with a white flag tied to a ramrod, who asked if he should hoist it and was told —"certainly not," and that "he put it up at his peril."

Captain Axline discovered that there were a number of men half a mile west, collected in a house, and he sent Lieutenant Herrington to take them and charge up the street on the north of the camp and clear it of the enemy, which was successfully done. Twenty nen were sent in charge of a sergeant to clear the ground and corn-patches in front and to the south, which was quickly done. Captain Axline then returned to his main position, which was bravely held by Blake, who had been severely wounded in the foot. Two thousand rounds of ammunition were served to the men and preparations made to move forward to the public square in three detachments, a movement which would have been successfully carried out and snatched victory from defeat had not messengers arrived from Colonel Buel with a white flag and orders to surrender. Axline was not in favor of complying with this order, but Captain Breckenridge and Adjutant Preble urged him to do so. He consented with much reluctance, though at the time he had but seventy-five men. The real hero of the battle of Independence was Captain Jacob Axline, able, brave, self-reliant, patriotic.

After the death of Colonel Hughes, Colonel Thompson took command of the Confederate forces. He also made a charge on the Federal right, but was repulsed, as Colonel Hughes had been, and was severely wounded in one of his legs. Hays then took command, but prudently avoided a grapple with Axline, and contented himself with sharp-shooting from protected places. He was soon wounded in the foot.

Colonel Buel insisted, as one of the conditions of surrender, that none of his men should be murdered by Quantrill or his men after they became prisoners, and this provision was enforced by Colonel Thompson, who, though suffering from his wound, paroled the prisoners after the battle was over.

The Federal loss was twenty-six killed and seventy-four wounded; eleven of the wounded died. About one hundred and fifty surrendered. The Confederates left on the field twenty-three dead men, of whom ten were officers. They also left nine men mortally wounded. Many wounded had been sent to their homes in the neighborhood, as were some of the dead. The rage of the Confederates against the Germans was vented upon Captain Thomas. He was killed in his room, his body horribly mangled and kicked down stairs.[4]

The victory at Independence was not worth what it cost the Confederates. They secured enough arms and ammunition to arm the slim regiment of Hays, and they carried away camp-plunder to the amount of twenty or more wagon-loads, after burning much and allowing Quantrill to hide a quantity which he could not take with him at the time. But their ablest officer, one of the ablest in Missouri, was killed, and most other officers either killed or wounded. They marched out of Independence towards the camp of Hays, in the direction of Blue Springs, about five o'clock in the afternoon, scattered and disappeared.

Buel and his men, paroled, were left at Independence, where they remained a few days, when they marched to Kansas City, and later were sent to St. Louis and quartered in Benton Barracks. They were mustered out of the service. Buel and Breckenridge were both tried for conspiracy and cowardice, but as they were to be mustered out at once no strenuous efforts were made to convict them and they escaped justice.

Quantrill and his men claimed credit for the victory, and there is merit in this claim. They made the attack on the bank building so fierce and effective that Buel surrendered. The entry of the Confederate army into the town without causing an alarm was due to their familiarity with the country, the town, the disposition of the Federal troops — and, not least, the deaths

---

[4] *Leavenworth Conservative*, August 13, 1862. Files in library of the Kansas State Historical Society. Britton says Captain Thomas was killed while endeavoring to reach the camp from a hotel, and says nothing of mutilation.

of the outlying pickets. They were active in all parts of the battle. Captain Gregg broke down the doors of the jail and released Southern sympathizers imprisoned there. James Knowles, charged with killing a Southern man, was shot in his cell.[5]

5 *Rebellion Records*, Series I, Vol. XIII, pp. 226, 227, show the official reports of Colonel Buel and Captain Axline.

CHAPTER XXI

QUANTRILL A CONFEDERATE CAPTAIN

FROM the victorious field of Independence Quantrill moved his men to the Morgan Walker farm, where he remained until late in the day of the 12th of August. Then he marched to the Ingraham farm, six miles west of Lone Jack. There the fourth day after the battle of Independence, he and his men were regularly mustered into the Confederate service.

From the fifteenth day of August, 1862, the Confederate government was responsible for all the acts of Quantrill and his men. From that day they were regular Confederate soldiers, properly enrolled, with officers regularly commissioned. Quantrill was commissioned captain. One hundred and fifty men were mustered under him. A military organization was effected, as follows:

Arch Clements

Captain, William Clarke Quantrill.
First Lieutenant, William Hallar.
Second Lieutenant, George Todd.
Third Lieutenant, William H. Gregg.

On the morning of the 16th of August Quantrill took ninety of his men to Independence to carry out camp-plunder stored there by him after the battle was over. He thus avoided the battle of Lone Jack, which was fought on that day. It has been charged that he was not pleased with the presence of the larger lights and greater personages of the Confederacy then appearing in Jackson county, and that he purposely absented himself that day to avoid helping them win a victory. He left sixty of his men in camp at the Adams farm with peremptory orders to Hallar, whom he left in command, not to move under any circumstances without orders from

him, unless attacked and driven away by the enemy. He knew
the enemy was in the vicinity. He had decided to let these
"big guns" fight their own battle. He resented their invasion
of his territory. They brought soldierly rules and permitted no
murder of prisoners. He made war in no such feminine fashion.
If mawkish sentiment was to prevail upon the gory field he would
be absent and employ himself in lugging off the loot of a former
action.

Quantrill must have started early to Independence, for at
eight o'clock a messenger from Hays arrived at the Adams farm
with a dispatch requesting his aid. Hallar refused to go. Late
in the afternoon another arrived with a more urgent message.
Gregg persuaded Hallar to heed this request, though he knew
it was in disobedience to express orders. The men were mounted
and put upon the road, going in on the dead run. But the battle
was over. They gathered in the straggling fugitives found trying to escape to the number of one hundred and fifty.

After the battle of Lone Jack, Quantrill established a camp
three miles east of Lee's Summit on the east branch of the Little
Blue. Colonel Hays lingered in Jackson county some ten days
after the battle of Lone Jack. When he was ready to leave
for Arkansas he turned over to Quantrill, Lieutenant Copeland,
of Neugent's regiment, whom he had captured at the battle
of Lone Jack. He knew that Quantrill would have him shot,
and turned him over for that reason. The execution of Copeland
is thus described in the *Gregg Manuscript*:

On the evening of August 28, 1862, Charles Cowherd and
William Howard came to our camp, bringing with them a copy
of the *Missouri Republican*. Quantrill was seated by a table
reading this paper. Gregg was sitting by the table waiting to
see the paper. Suddenly I saw a change come over Quantrill's
countenance; he dropped the paper and drew a blank-book and
pencil from his pocket. He wrote a note and handed it to Gregg,
telling him to give it to Blunt. Being anxious to know what
was up, I opened the note and read:

"Take Lieutenant Copeland out and shoot him. Go to
Woodsmall's camp, get two prisoners from his camp, shoot them,
and return as quickly as possible."

Perry Hoy, who, it will be remembered, was captured from
our command at the Tate House, and for whom we had tried

to exchange the Kansas Lieutenant, had been shot at Fort Leavenworth. When Blunt returned from the execution of the prisoners we were ordered to saddle up and prepare to move. On inquiry I learned from Quantrill that he was going to Kansas to kill ten men for Perry Hoy. We moved to the vicinity of Red Bridge, near the Kansas line, where we remained until the next afternoon, when we marched on Olathe, the county-seat of Johnson County, Kansas. However, before we reached Olathe we had killed ten men, most of whom were known to our men. But we had started to take the town and persisted in that purpose. When we arrived near the place, Quantrill ordered Lieutenant Gregg to advance with sixty men and throw a cordon about the town that no one might escape, which was accomplished. Quantrill with the remaining men marched to the center of the town. On their arrival at Court Square they found one hundred and twenty-five Federal soldiers drawn up on the sidewalk on the south side of the square. It was determined to capture these men without bloodshed. Quantrill ordered his men to hitch their horses to the courtyard fence in close order, and when this was done, to form in the rear of the horses. This completed, they drew their revolvers and ordered the Federals to surrender, which they did without firing a shot. One man refused to give up his gun and was shot and killed. So, we had killed fourteen men for Perry Hoy!

We remained in Olathe until morning, when we marched our prisoners out on the prairie about two miles from town, paroled them, and turned them loose.

It will be seen from this account that the raid on Olathe was for the purpose of avenging the execution of Perry Hoy. But Captain Gregg has the date wrong. The guerrillas entered the town the afternoon of the 6th of September and remained until the 7th.[1] They numbered one hundred and forty men. Frank Cook, John J. Juaɔ, and his brother, James B. Judy, all of whom had enlisted in the Twelfth Kansas a short time before, were killed just before the town was entered. Hiram Blanchard, of Spring Hill, was in Olathe at the time; he protested against the action of the guerrillas in stealing his horse and tried to prevent

[1] *Andreas's History of Kansas* gives the date as the 6th. Wilder's *Annals of Kansas* fixes the date on the 7th. Both are right, as Quantrill was there both days — came in on the 6th and left on the 7th.

it, and was shot and killed. Josiah Skinner and Phillip Wiggins were both shot and killed; they were citizens and not soldiers.[2]

Quantrill was very proud of his official position with the Confederate government. He carried with him his commission as captain in the Confederate service, and he exhibited it to those he wished to impress with the dignity of his office and his importance and standing. While walking about the public square, reviewing the citizens of the town, all of whom were bunched there and held under guard, he recognized Judge E. W. Robinson, then and now a citizen of Paola. He called Robinson out to the fence, which surrounded the square, and upon which they seated themselves and talked for more than an hour. Quantrill repudiated the familiar name of "Bill" by which he was known in Paola and requested Robinson to address him as "Captain Quantrill," producing at the same time his commission as captain for the judge's inspection.[3]

Quantrill robbed stores and dwellings. All the people were plundered. Horses and wagons were stolen and loaded with loot from the sacked town. On the 7th of September Quantrill

---

[2] In *Rebellion Records*, Series I, Vol. XIII, p. 803, will be found the letter of Dr. Thomas Hamil, dated Leavenworth City, November 6, 1862, to Major General Curtis, a portion of which is here set out:

I have been living in Johnson County, Kansas, for four years. I was in Olathe when Quantrill came there; he took everything of wearing apparel and all the horses that he could get; he took all of my clothes, a good horse, and a fine gold watch; but we did not care for being robbed, if he had not killed our citizens in cold blood, taking our best citizens from the bosom of their families and shooting them down like so many hogs. It is horrible to relate. . . . Nearly all the families have left between us and the line.

[3] Letter of E. W. Robinson to W. W. Scott, dated, Paola, Kansas, May 9, 1881, now in the Collection of the author. Robinson was probate judge of Miami county when the letter was written. This letter has been quoted from, *ante*, in relation to the Morgan Walker raid. Concerning his capture at Olathe, Judge Robinson says:

I saw no more of him until September, 1862 — when he sacked Olathe. He had with him at that time 220 men. Quantrill recognized me among the prisoners, invited me outside the corral, to a seat beside him surrounding the public square, where we talked for more than an hour. During the conversation I addressed him once as "Bill" — he very politely requested me to address him as "Captain Quantrill," and took from his pocket and showed me what he claimed was a commission from the Confederate Government, but I did not read it, — being an old acquaintance, and having no grudge against me, he treated me kindly. Not more than a dozen persons were killed on this raid, the object being plunder.

marched his prisoners out of the town and paroled them. Then he took his way over the prairies back to Missouri, his band burdened to its full capacity and staggering under the spoil of Kansas citizens.

From Olathe Quantrill went to Johnson county, Mo. Colonel John T. Burris was sent to capture him or disperse his command. He found the guerrillas near Columbus, Johnson county. They were driven to Lafayette county, where they camped on the farm of Harvey Gleaves. A party was sent out on the Texas prairie to gather provisions. This party was fallen upon by a squad of militia from Lexington and narrowly escaped capture. Hastening to camp and securing reinforcements the guerrillas followed the militia, coming up with them at Wellington, driving them from the town to the bridge over the Sni, where a stand was made. The guerrillas charged across the bridge and scattered the militia, killing some of them, and having one man, Lieutenant Ferd Scott, wounded in the side. The guerrillas returned to their camp and the whole command marched to the village of Mecklin, where supper was had. Colonel Burris was in close pursuit. The guerrillas camped three miles north of Mecklin, moved at daylight to Bone Hill, where they were discovered at breakfast and routed. Colonel Burris followed them all day, and at four o'clock in the afternoon came up with them on the high prairie four miles north of Pleasant Hill. There they were defeated in a short sharp battle and lost some killed and wounded, among the former, Young Simmons, of Westport. They fled to the timber and scattered, preventing further pursuit.

The guerrillas assembled again in a week. Colonel Penick, then in command at Independence, sent Captain David with his company to look for them. David camped at the Morgan Walker farm the night of the 5th of October, and on the 6th he discovered Quantrill's camp between Sibley and Big Hill — about a mile from Sibley. Quantrill broke camp and moved along the Lexington and Independence road to the Garrison farm where the Sibley road came in. There an ambush was prepared for Captain David, and Colonel Dick Chiles was put in command of it. Captain David found this ambush in an old log house at a sharp turn in the road. The house was surrounded by a high

18

rail fence enclosing a patch of half an acre. In the first charge of Captain David, Colonel Chiles was shot through the lungs, dying from that wound soon after the war closed. Another guerrilla was wounded. Quantrill had not wished to trust Chiles, but had been induced to do so by Gregg and Todd. Seeing that the fight was lost, Quantrill retreated to the brush. Captain David lost one man killed, one mortally wounded, and one slightly wounded.

The following day Captain David continued the pursuit of Quantrill, and at night the guerrillas scattered to avoid being chased longer, having scattered and assembled a number of times during the day.[4]

Quantrill soon planned another raid into Kansas and selected Shawneetown, a village in Johnson county, near the Missouri line, and doomed it to the torch. He reached the town on the 17th of October. Just before he arrived at the town he came upon a wagon-train passing over the Santa Fé Trail, guarded by an infantry escort. This escort had stopped to rest. Most of the men were asleep. No guard had been posted. The guerrillas pounced upon this somnolent escort and slew one-half of it — about fifteen men — and scattered the remainder. This whetted their appetites for blood, and the guerrillas dashed into Shawneetown and murdered seven citizens there. The brand was applied and the village reduced to ashes. A Mr. Stiles and a Mr. Becker were killed in the town, and James Warfield, a Shawnee Indian, and three others were chased out and killed in the fields and highways. The stores were robbed, and horses and household goods were taken back to Missouri.[5]

---

4 *Rebellion Records*, Series I, Vol. XIII, p. 312. Report of Captain Daniel H. David, Fifth Missouri Cavalry (Militia) to Colonel W. R. Penick. Dated, Independence, Mo., October 8, 1862.

5 Still the excuse for sacking Lawrence was that Kansas troops robbed the citizens of Missouri and killed them! Fourteen men are admitted to have been killed by Quantrill in the Olathe raid; perhaps many more were killed. Seven citizens were killed in the Shawneetown raid — twenty-one Kansas citizens killed on Kansas soil minding their own affairs. And this in a little more than two months. And two towns sacked, one of them destroyed by the torch! And hundreds of Missouri citizens in Missouri in the same time butchered in their own homes! How preposterous the

The leaves were down, the trees were stripped, the thickets on the Sni, the Little Blue, and the Grand were bare. All the hiding-places were uncovered, and the disloyal element in Missouri began to move and show signs of uneasiness. The guerrillas and their abettors ran together in bunches and skulked in heavily timbered bottoms and along naked hillsides. Thoughts of security inside the Confederate lines in Arkansas filled their minds. A rendezvous was fixed by Quantrill on Big Creek, Cass county, near the field where Captain Martin had beset the guerrillas and smote them so sorely. The location of this camp was sent broadcast, and it was noised abroad that all who wished to go inside the Confederate lines would be welcomed and carried there in safety. Many responded.

The march south was commenced on the 3d day of November. Quantrill had one hundred and fifty guerrillas, and many fugitives. Cole Younger, Joe Lea, and Dick Yager each remained in Missouri with a small squad. Hallar had left Quantrill because of a disagreement with Todd and had gone into a squad commanded by one Harrison, whose men went south with Quantrill.

On the day that Quantrill began his march south Colonel Edwin C. Catherwood, Sixth Missouri Cavalry, started a train of thirteen empty wagons back from Harrisonville to Sedalia, with an escort of twenty-one men commanded by Lieutenant W. M. Newby, Company G, Sixth Missouri. About four o'clock in the afternoon Lieutenant Demuel Campbell reported that he had seen Quantrill's command marching down the divide between

---

excuses that have been made for the actions of Quantrill! The falsity and hypocrisy of these excuses have been shown to this point. The excuses for the actions following will be shown to have been more ridiculous.

William Laurie was captured by the guerrillas in this raid. In Kansas City he had refused to aid in the hoisting of rebel flags and was threatened with death. Fearing to remain in Kansas City, he moved to Shawneetown and engaged in photography. When the guerrillas entered the town his partner was shot, but not killed, and he was captured and stripped of his clothing except his underwear. He was put to loading a wagon which the guerrillas took back to Missouri. After dark a lamp was furnished him to work by, and when the wind blew it out he ran into a field and escaped. He and his brother were murdered by the guerrillas at Lawrence.

Harrisonville and Rose Hill. This made Colonel Catherwood apprehensive for the safety of his train, and he took one hundred and fifty men and started out to protect it. But he was too late. Gregg had been given forty men and ordered to attack the train, which he did, capturing it and scattering the escort, killing four soldiers and six teamsters, and wounding two soldiers and one teamster. Lieutenant Newby was captured, also some privates. At the first sight of the guerrillas he had corralled his wagons and made an effort to get his men inside, but the guerrillas were down upon him before this could be done. The night came on cloudy and dark, but Colonel Catherwood pursued the enemy, coming upon him in camp two miles south of the battlefield. He attacked the guerrillas and recovered Lieutenant Newby and one private, killing six and wounding twenty-one of the enemy.[6]

Quantrill met Colonel Warner Lewis a short distance north of Lamar. Lewis had three hundred men. He induced Quantrill to undertake the capture of the Union garrison at Lamar. Quantrill, when told that the Union troops were quartered in the court-house, a brick building, was not sanguine of success. The attack was to be made at ten o'clock at night, and Quantrill was to come in from the south, while Lewis was to enter the town from the north. Quantrill was on time and drove in the pickets. Lewis did not make his appearance at all, but Quantrill attacked the force in the court-house and fought there two hours, accomplishing nothing, but losing two men killed, Peter Burton and James Donohoe. He burned a portion of the town, the fire destroying the court-house. The attack was on the night of the 5th of November 1862.[7]

---

6 *Rebellion Records*, Series I, Vol. XIII, p. 347. Report of Colonel Edwin C. Catherwood, Sixth Missouri Cavalry (Militia) to Brig.-Gen. Ben. Loan, Commanding Central District of Missouri. Dated, Harrisonville, Mo., November 5, 1862.

7 *Rebellion Records*, Series I, Vol. XIII, p. 796. Report of Brig.-Gen. E. B. Brown to Brig.-Gen. John M. Schofield, Commanding Army of the Frontier. Dated, Springfield, Mo., November 16, 1862.

Also, Report of Major Benjamin S. Henry, Third Wisconsin Cavalry, to Brig.-Gen. James G. Blunt. Dated, Fort Scott, Kansas, November 11, 1862.

When Quantrill drew off his men at Lamar he continued on his way to the southward, causing some alarms by the way. He went to Fort Smith, passing down the old Fort Scott and Fort Gibson road. Upon his arrival in the Confederate lines his band was attached to the command of General Shelby.

CHAPTER XXII

QUANTRILL GOES TO RICHMOND, VIRGINIA

WHILE Quantrill's company was attached to the command of General J. O. Shelby when it reached the Confederate lines in Arkansas, Quantrill himself did not remain with it. Gregg was then his first lieutenant, and Quantrill turned the company over to him, and set out for Richmond, Virginia, to secure permission to enlist a regiment under the Confederate Partisan Ranger Act. It was his ambition to be the colonel of a regiment. For this strange being, this mysterious person who was not surfeited with the stream of blood he had caused to flow in Kansas and Missouri since the year 1859, had ambition to rise in the Confederate world. And we shall see that he had marked out bloody lines along which he hoped to advance — along which he had dreamed he might even lead the Confederacy. If he was not blood-mad, insane, he was a monster, the most gory, blood-thirsty and horrible character in American history. And the actions of his whole life would indicate that he was degenerate and depraved rather than insane — that he loved to kill — delighted in murder and rapine.

Quantrill must have departed from Richmond very soon after reaching the Confederate lines, for General Shelby began his invasion of Missouri before the end of November, and the guerrilla command took part in all the battles of that campaign, beginning with Cane Hill, which was fought on the 28th of November. Quantrill took with him Blunt and Higbee. He accomplished little at Richmond. His program for conducting the course of the Confederacy did not favorably appeal to the War Office. To his surprise and chagrin his plan for a general massacre and the hoisting of the black flag by the Confederacy was rejected. It is said by some that he received no commission, and by others that he did receive one. It is known that he insisted that he was a colonel, and that he secured a Confed-

erate colonel's uniform and had himself photographed with it
on.   And he signed the official report of the Baxter Springs massacre as "Colonel."   It is very probable that he was given the
commission he sought and sent back to Missouri with a promotion
as to rank but the refusal of permission to recruit himself a regiment.   But there is nothing certainly known on this subject.[1]

---

[1] All that we know of what passed between Quantrill and the officials
of the Confederacy is contained in the statement of General Louis T.
Wigfall, then a Senator from Texas, who was present when Quantrill
presented his plan.   The only account of this interview seen by the
author is that given by Major Edwards.   It is embellished by him, no
doubt, and is embodied in his florid rhetoric, and it is given here for what
it may prove to be worth:

His interview at Richmond with the Confederate Secretary of War
was a memorable one.   Gen. Louis T. Wigfall, then a Senator from
Texas, was present and described it afterwards in his rapid, vivid, picturesque way.   Quantrell asked to be commissioned as a Colonel under the
Partisan Ranger Act, and to be so recognized by the Department as to
have accorded to him whatever protection the Confederate government
might be in a condition to exercise.   Never mind the question of men, he
would have the complement required in a month after he reached Western
Missouri.   The warfare was desperate, he knew, the service desperate,
everything connected with it was desperate; but the Southern people to
succeed had to fight a desperate fight.   The Secretary suggested that war
had its amenities and its refinements, and that in the nineteenth century
it was simple barbarism to talk of a black flag.

"*Barbarism!*" and Quantrell's blue eyes blazed, and his whole
manner and attitude underwent a transformation, "barbarism, Mr. Secretary, means war and war means barbarism.   Since you have touched upon
this subject, let us discuss it a little.   Times have their crimes as well as
men.   For twenty years this cloud has been gathering; for twenty years
— inch by inch and little by little those people called the Abolitionists have
been on the track of slavery; for twenty years the people of the South
have been robbed, here of a negro and there of a negro [many of these
negroes stolen from the South by Quantrill — W. E. C.]; for twenty years
hates have been engendered and wrathful things laid up against the day
of wrath.   The cloud has burst.   Do not condemn the thunderbolt."

The War Secretary bowed his head.   Quantrell, leaving his own seat,
and standing over him as it were and above him, went on.

"Who are these people you call Confederates?   Rebels, unless they
succeed, outcasts, traitors, food for hemp and gunpowder.   There were no
great statesmen in the South, or this war would have happened ten years
ago; no inspired men, or it would have happened fifteen years ago.   Today
the odds are desperate.   The world hates slavery; the world is fighting you.
The ocean belongs to the Union navy.   There is a recruiting officer in every
foreign port.   I have captured and killed many who did not know the
English tongue.   Mile by mile the cordon is being drawn about the
granaries of the South, Missouri will go first, next Kentucky, next Tennessee, by and by Mississippi and Arkansas, and then what?   That we must

Quantrill's men, or a part of them, were in the campaigns in Northwestern Arkansas and Southwestern Missouri during the winter of 1862-63. They were in the battles of Cane Hill, Prairie Grove, Springfield, and Hartville. Todd, however, was not pleased with regular warfare. He deserted two hours before the battle of Cane Hill began, and, with seven other desperate guerrillas, returned to Missouri. A fair field and honorable battle did not suit him. The opportunities for murder and plunder were not sufficient to attract him. And we shall see that Todd

---

put gloves on our hands, and honey in our mouths, and fight this war as Christ fought the wickedness of the world?''

The War Secretary did not speak. Quantrell, perhaps, did not desire that he should. ''You ask an impossible thing, Mr. Secretary. This secession, or revolution, or whatever you call it cannot conquer without violence, nor can those who hate it and hope to stifle it, resist without vindictiveness. Every struggle has its philosophy, but this is not the hour for philosophers. Your young Confederacy wants victory, and champions who are not judges. Men must be killed. To impel the people to passion there must be some slight illusion mingled with the truth; to arouse them to enthusiasm something out of nature must occur. That illusion should be a crusade in the name of conquest, and that something out of nature should be the black flag. Woe be unto all of you if the Federals come with an oath of loyalty in one hand and a torch in the other. I have seen Missouri bound hand and foot by this Christless thing called Conservatism, and where to-day she should have two hundred thousand heroes fighting for liberty, beneath her banners there are scarcely twenty thousand.''

''What would *you* do, Captain Quantrell, were your's the power and the opportunity?''

''Do, Mr. Secretary? Why I would wage such a war and have such a war waged by land and sea as to make surrender forever impossible. I would cover the armies of the Confederacy all over with blood. I would invade. I would reward audacity. I would exterminate. I would break up foreign enlistments by indiscriminate massacre. I would win the independence of my people or I would find them graves.''

''And our prisoners, what of them?''

''Nothing of them; there would be no prisoners. Do they take any prisoners from me? Surrounded, I do not surrender; surprised, I do not give way to panic; outnumbered, I rely upon common sense and stubborn fighting; proscribed, I answer proclamation with proclamation; outlawed, I feel through it my power; hunted, I hunt my hunters in turn; hated and made blacker than a dozen devils, I add to my hoofs the swiftness of the horse, and to my horns the terrors of a savage following. Kansas should be laid waste at once. Meet the torch with the torch, pillage with pillage, slaughter with slaughter, subjugation with extermination. You have my ideas of war, Mr. Secretary, and I am sorry they do not accord with your own, nor the ideas of the government you have the honor to represent so well.'' And Quantrell, without his commission as a Partisan Ranger, or without any authorization to raise a regiment of Partisan Rangers, bowed himself away from the presence of the Secretary and away from Richmond.

was even then a rising star, keenly jealous of Quantrill, and that he finally usurped the prestige and power of the guerrilla chieftain and drove him out of the service.   Quantrill's fear of the growing power of Todd was one reason why he sought more power and authority in Richmond.

After the battle of Hartville the command of Quantrill was still further depleted.   General John S. Marmaduke sent Gregg, John Ross, John Koger, and Bennett Wood to Missouri to recruit men for his command.   They arrived in Jackson county, January 19, 1863, having marched more than two hundred miles over rough roads and in a strange country.   Gregg captured and paroled nearly two hundred militia on the trip.   When he turned over the command of the guerrillas to Lieutenant Scott to go to Missouri there were but twenty-five men in it.

Quantrill returned from Richmond through Mississippi.   He stopped two or three days at the camp of some Missouri troops on Black River twelve miles east of Vicksburg.[2]   He arrived at the camp of his followers much crestfallen and discouraged.   He was ambitious.   Through his distorted vision he saw promotions in store for him and honors heaped upon him.   He believed he had earned them, and well earned them.   But he had found the world larger than he believed it, and he was surprised and vexed to find that the eyes of the whole Confederacy were not fixed upon him and his achievements.   He pined to be a hero, and was hurt to think he was not so regarded.   He had not been wined and dined in Richmond.   His discouragement was augmented when he saw the dilapidated condition of his band, the mere skeleton which remained of it.   He carried his woe to General Sterling Price, who cheered him up as best he could.   General Price promised him great things and insisted that he stop his bushwhacking and horse-stealing, insisting that there was yet time and chance for promotion.   Indeed, Price may have given him the colonel's commission, for this was a common procedure in the Confederate service west of the Mississippi.   And Price had fared little better at the hands of the Richmond officials

---

[2] Told the author by T. C. Caldwell, Esq., of Independence, Mo., May 15, 1906.   Mr. Caldwell saw Quantrill at the camp on Black River, but does not recall that any one was traveling with him.

than had Quantrill. President Davis held General Price in supreme contempt.[3] With his men Quantrill put on a bold face for a short time and talked of regular warfare. This was the worst possible course he could have taken with his men, especially with his officers. They in a manner deserted him and formed bands of their own. Each of these bands operated independently of all the others. Quantrill was recognized as a sort of head officer, and the lesser chieftains paid him a sort of homage and co-operated with him in the guerrilla warfare he engaged in during the summer of 1863.[4]

Quantrill's captains were very busy during the summer of 1863, but Quantrill himself did little except to plan and execute the Lawrence raid. He fell again into despondency, to alleviate which he had recourse to his favorite dissipation. He kidnapped a girl named Kate Clarke and made her his mistress, and he spent most of his time with her in the brush.[5]

---

[3] See *The Battle of Westport*, by Paul B. Jenkins, pp. 22, 23.

[4] The arrangement between Quantrill and General Price is fully set out in *Rebellion Records*, Series I, Vol. XXIII, p. 320, Report of Walter King, Lieutenant-Colonel, Fourth Missouri State Militia Cavalry, dated, Lexington, Mo., May 5, 1863. It is as follows:

An hour has elapsed since penning the foregoing paragraph, spent in interview with "John DeCourcy," my most trusted spy, who reached here, and I gather the following: Quantrill is here; he came from Price to conscript; he came with 40 men; he has joined Reid's, Jarrett's, Todd's, Younger's, and Clifton's gangs to his own, which give him from 125 to 150 men; he disbanded his force on Sunday night, with orders to rendezvous on Thursday night on the Big Sni, precise place not definitely learned; has orders from Price to stop bushwhacking and horse stealing. Price is to invade Southeast Missouri, and Quantrill is to annoy Kansas and Western Missouri; intends to conscript all of military age; has secret notice among Southern men to come to his camp and get property taken by mistake; came here to stay, not to take away any recruits; seems to be rather elevated in his purposes by his six or eight months' experience with the regular forces.

[5] Letter of Charles F. Taylor ("Fletch" Taylor) to W. W. Scott, now in the Collection of the author. Taylor wrote very interesting letters. He saw deeper into Quantrill and his motives than any of his men. Quantrill took this Kate Clarke to Howard county with him in the summer of 1864 and did almost no fighting.   Nothing of the parentage of Kate Clarke has been learned. Quantrill became much attached to her, and at his death left her two thousand dollars in gold, with which she established a house of ill fame in St. Louis. This house became notorious. Scott wrote the Clarke woman there, but his letter was returned and is now in the Collection of the author. Scott must have been informed that Quantrill

The rumors and flying reports of the great activity of Quantrill in the summer of 1863 were rumors only. The activity and actions of all his captains were laid at his door. The *Rebellion Records* have little to say about that summer, and the *Gregg Manuscript* contains accounts of the movements of the captains only during that period. He was nominally in command and the captains yielded him certain allegiance, but the guerrilla deeds that summer up to the Lawrence raid were principally their deeds, and they will appear in the notices of the captains respectively. It is not meant to say here that he did nothing in the summer of 1863. He did much, but nothing to compare with what he did in the summer of 1862. He still had much influence over all the guerrillas, and he realized that his power was waning long before his men thought of that matter.

---

had married Kate Clarke, for he asked her that question in the letter. Extracts from the letters of Taylor are given here:

Q. was a good commander and a brave man and all the men had confidence in him. Don't think he was cowardly, although I never saw him in a close place, as the men preferred to go in the lead, and let him manage, as we did not wish to lose him.

He took Kate Clarke in the summer of 1863, and she went willingly, as he borrowed my Gray mare for her to ride on to a place some five miles from camp. I don't know whether Walker gave him anything or not, but his girl was Quantrill's mistress for some time after I joined; she has since married a man by name of Woods.

Others say he kidnapped this girl and that it took her some time to become reconciled to the life to which he doomed her, but that she became infatuated with him, even wearing a man's clothing and riding in the ranks to be near him.

CHAPTER XXIII

THE LAWRENCE MASSACRE

I.

THE genesis of the Lawrence Massacre lies back seven years. The roots of this bloody and inhuman deed were sunk deep in the political compost of the affairs of Territorial Kansas and Missouri border-ruffianism. It was the consummation of the unrelenting purpose of the spirit of slavery which ran riot along the border in 1856. There were subsequent causes, to be sure, but they were subordinate and local.[1]

Lawrence was founded in the spirit of human liberty. It had its inception in the idea that slavery should not be one of the institutions of Kansas. When the Emigrant Aid Company made the town its headquarters in Kansas the forces of slavery on the border decreed its destruction. This Emigrant Aid Company caused deeper and more lasting bitterness in Missouri than all other incidents in the history of Kansas. Nothing else so enraged the South. And Lawrence was the town of the "Aid Company." It stood as the embodiment of the anti-slavery sentiment of the North — abolitionism, if you will — final de-

---

[1] Other raids were for plunder, the Lawrence raid was for slaughter. That some of the raiders should assign retaliation as the motive was to be expected. It was the nearest motive at hand and made a plausible excuse. That some of the raiders had suffered personal wrongs and were inspired with feelings of revenge, we can well believe. But this could not have been the inspiration of the attack, nor the cause of its excessive brutality. These things show that it had its roots deeper than this. Its roots ran back into the old pro-slavery hate of six years before. . . . Its inspiration and its venom flowed from the same source and sentiments whence the earlier invasions came. It sprang from the same sentiment which had three times before assailed Lawrence and been foiled. . . . The movement sprang from the same soil which produced the Wakarusa War and the troubles of 1856. It was the same conflict on a larger scale. The same principles were at stake, and the same parties confronted each other. The same feelings inspired either side. The same hate sought to gratify itself under the new conditions.

The border ruffians of 1856 became the bushwhackers of 1863. — Dr. Richard Cordley, in his *History of Lawrence*, pp. 196, 197.

struction of the institution of slavery. Perhaps some of the
founders of Lawrence repudiated 'the term " abolitionist," but
it was well understood in all quarters that if slavery was defeated
in Kansas it could not survive in the Union. The man who
claimed that he was simply anti-slavery and not an abolitionist
insisted upon a distinction without a difference. The man who
labored to make Kansas a free State labored for national abolitionism whether he admitted it or not. This was perfectly understood in the South, and a careful study of the debates in the
Congressional sessions of those times will clearly show that it
was equally well understood in the North. The repeal of the
Missouri Compromise had made any other interpretation of the
Kansas strugle impossible. The Missourian believed that in
fighting Lawrence he was battling against national abolitionism,
and that in her destruction the evil day for his favorite institution might be postponed, if even complete victory should not be
attained. To him Lawrence was Kansas, and he sought every
means to destroy it in the interest of the government and civilization he was trying to establish there. It became the object of
deep and bitter hatred in Missouri, and, while in 1863 no one
there was so mad as to believe its destruction could have any influence on the result of the war, there lingered in the mind of
every secessionist and every Confederate in Missouri a malignant
hatred of Lawrence. And it remained for Quantrill, a man who
cared nothing for slavery as an institution, nothing for the abolition of slavery, nothing for the North, nothing for the South,
to seize upon this feeling and make it a means to gratify his
thirst for blood and greed for spoil and plunder.

In enumerating some of the instances showing the results of
this feeling in Missouri in the Territorial days of Kansas the
author again disclaims all desire to revive bitterness between
sister States. Kansas has her history, and that history cannot be
spoken of without mention of the various incidents of it; and as
Missouri assumed the right to make Kansas history and shape
Kansas institutions, many of her people were parties to these
incidents. In Kansas there has been no feeling on this matter
for forty years. And it is believed there is none in Missouri.
These two States are more closely identified in business matters

and all material interests than any other two States in the Union. Goodfellowship is universal, and recounting historical facts which occurred in other times under conditions which all rejoice to know are gone never to return should not be taken as any desire to disturb it. To a proper understanding of the conditions in Western Missouri which made the Lawrence Massacre possible it is necessary that these times be reviewed.

When Kansas was made a Territory the slave-party was in power at Washington, and the Washington government stood behind all the acts of the border-ruffians in Kansas. The invasions of Kansas were upheld there and even applauded. To carry the first election in Kansas, Missourians came over by hundreds and by thousands. They took possession of the polls, thrust aside the lawful judges at the muzzle of the revolver, voted, certified to the accuracy and legality of the poll-books, packed them up and carried them away. These actions were performed by direction of the leading men of the border counties. General David R. Atchison, long United States Senator from Missouri, was the chief mover in the matter. He was at the bottom of all the agitation. William C. Price, of Springfield, Mo., once told the author that Atchison acted at his suggestion, and that he himself represented in Missouri the ultra-wing of the slave power.

For condemning the people of Missouri for going to Kansas to vote, the *Luminary*, published at Parkville, Mo., was destroyed and the presses and type thrown into the Missouri river. This act was approved in all the border counties by public assemblies. The mob held a meeting at the conclusion of its work and decided to reassemble at the same place in three weeks. It adopted the following resolution touching the proprietors of the paper: "And if we find G. S. Parks or W. J. Patterson in this town then or at any subsequent time, we will throw them into the Missouri River, and if they go to Kansas to reside, we pledge our honor as men to follow and hang them whenever we can take them."

William A. Phillips, a lawyer at Leavenworth, favored the Free-State cause in Kansas. For this he was kidnapped, carried to Weston, Mo., where one side of his head was shaved; he was tarred, feathered, and ridden on a rail about two miles, and then sold at auction for one dollar, a negro slave being forced to cry him off to the highest bidder.

On the 25th of October, 1855, Charles W. Dow, a Free-State settler in Douglas county, was murdered by Franklin N. Coleman, a pro-slavery settler. Out of this murder grew the Wakarusa War. Fifteen hundred Missourians gathered at Franklin, about four miles east of Lawrence, for the avowed purpose of destroying the town. A treaty of peace was signed by Lane, Robinson, and Governor Shannon, and this turned the Missourians homeward, but they plundered Free-State settlers wherever found. During this war Thomas W. Barber, a Free-State settler, was shot and killed in cold blood by either George W. Clark or James N. Burnes, border ruffians.

In May, 1856, the *Herald of Freedom* and the *Kansas Free-State,* newspapers, and the Eldridge House, all at Lawrence, were decreed nuisances by the Federal grand jury and ordered abated. Acting under this authority, General Atchison gathered about six hundred Missourians and invaded Kansas. Lawrence was sacked. The newspapers and the Eldridge House were destroyed. The people were driven from their homes and the stores and dwellings pillaged. The dwelling of Governor Robinson was burned. In his exultation General Atchison made a speech to his men as they began their work in which he said:

Boys, this day I am a Kickapoo Ranger, by God. This day we have entered Lawrence, "Southern Rights" inscribed on our banners, and not one damned abolitionist has dared to fire a gun. No, by God, not one! This, boys, is the happiest day of my whole life. We have entered the damned city, and to-night the abolitionists will learn a Southern lesson that they will remember to the day of their death. And now, boys, we will go in with our highly honorable Jones, and test the strength of that damned Free-State Hotel, and learn the Emigrant Aid Society that Kansas shall be ours. Boys, ladies should be, and I trust will be, respected by all gentlemen; but, by God, when a woman takes on herself the garb of a soldier by carrying a Sharps's rifle, then she is no longer a woman, and, by God, treat her for what you find her, and trample her underfoot as you would a snake. By God, come on boys! Now to your duties to yourselves and your Southern friends! Your duty I know you will do; and if a man or woman dare to stand before you, blow them to hell with a chunk of cold lead!

A few days later John Brown and a party slew five pro-slavery men on Pottawatomie creek. These men had terrified the Free-State settlers, ordered them to leave the Territory, and had insulted their wives and daughters; it had come to the point where one party or the other had to leave the country or fight. John Brown chose to fight. General Jo O. Shelby, a few weeks before his death, told the author that John Brown was the only Free-State man with the true conception of the conditions which prevailed at the time, saying:

"I was in Kansas at the head of an armed force about that time. I was there to kill Free-State men. I did kill them. I am now ashamed of myself for having done so, but then times were different from what they are now, and that is what I went there for. We Missourians all went there for that purpose if it should be found necessary to do so to carry out our designs. I had no business there. No Missourian had any business there with arms in his hands. The policy that sent us there was damnable, and the trouble we started on the border bore fruit for ten years. I ought to have been shot there, and John Brown was the only man who knew it and would have done it. I say John Brown was right. I knew the men he killed. I condemn his killing of the younger Doyles, but the others got only what they deserved. After that I had great respect for Old John Brown. He did in his country what I should have done in mine under like circumstances. Those were days when slavery was in the balance, and the violence engendered made men irresponsible. I now see I was so myself." Brave words from one of the bravest men and best soldiers that ever shouldered a musket in America! Only a brave man — and great man — can bring himself to make such a confession.[2]

---

[2] In the last years of his life General Shelby was United States Marshal for the western district of Missouri. His office was at Kansas City. This was during the last administration of Grover Cleveland. General Shelby died while yet in office.

General Shelby was a Kentuckian, as I am. I lived then in Kansas City, Kansas, and I often visited him at his office to talk over olden times and historical events. We often discussed the Territorial times of Kansas

John Brown fell upon a band of some thirty ruffians at Black Jack, near the present town of Baldwin, in Douglas county. He had less than a dozen men, but he captured the Missourians. In this battle there was a young Missourian named Jacob Cantrel who fought under John Brown, or who rendered him signal aid and service. He had the misfortune to be captured by a band of his countrymen a few days later: As these were returning home they camped one night on Cedar creek, west of Olathe. There they tried Cantrel for "treason to Missouri," convicted him, and led him out of camp and shot him to death.

The demoralization was terrible. An act committed at Leavenworth confirms this. It is described by Dr. John H. Gihon, private secretary to Governor Geary, in his splendid work, *Geary and Kansas*:

On the 17th, a shocking affair occurred in the neighborhood of Leavenworth. Two ruffians sat at a table in a low groggery, imbibing potations of bad whiskey. One of them, named Fugert, belonging to Atchison's band, bet his companion six dollars against a pair of boots, that he would go out, and in less than two hours bring in the scalp of an abolitionist. He went into the road, and meeting a Mr. Hoppe, who was in his carriage just

---

and the border troubles. General Shelby always denounced Quantrill in the severest terms. He had outlived and outgrown the bitterness of border times. He was a very just, earnest, sincere man. He told me without reserve of the raids he had made into Kansas during the troubles in Kansas Territorial days. He repented his actions and reproached himself that he had ever done these things. He said he was wrong, that he had no business in Kansas on any such errands, that the policy of the South which sent him there was damnable, that John Brown was the only Kansas man who had the right idea of the conditions existing there and the only man who had the courage to resist Missourians at the muzzle of the rifle. He believed John Brown was right. I have heard General Shelby say more than once that Virginia would some day erect a great monument to John Brown. He was an admirer of John Brown and often said that Brown was the bravest man who ever stood upon a scaffold. He said Brown would have shot him had he found him harrowing Kansas settlers, and that it would have been just and right. That in so doing Brown would have done no more in Kansas than he, Shelby, would have done in Missouri.

The words in the text are as nearly what General Shelby said as I could write them after our interview. He expressed the sentiments of the text to me many times.

19

returning to Leavenworth from a visit to Lawrence, where he had conveyed his wife, Fugert deliberately shot him; then taking out his bowie-knife whilst his victim was still alive, he cut and tore off the scalp from his quivering head. Leaving the body of Hoppe lying in the road, he elevated his bloody trophy upon a pole, and paraded it through the streets of Leavenworth, amid the shouts of the "law and order" militia, and the plaudits of some who are denominated the noblest specimens of "southern chivalry," and regarded as men of respectability. On the same day a teamster, who was approaching Leavenworth, was murdered and scalped by another human monster.

A poor German, when the scalp of Hoppe was brought into Leavenworth, was imprudent enough to express his horror of the shocking deed, when he was ordered to run for his life, in attempting which a number of bullets sped after him, and he fell dead in the street. The pro-slavery men aided Fugert to escape from the territory by sending him down the river, and furnishing him with money. He wore, upon his departure, the boots he so nobly won:

Quoting still further from Dr. Gihon, it will be seen that robbery was one of the objects of Missourians in the invasion of Kansas:

On the 7th, Reid, with one hundred and seventy men, marched into Osawatomie, and without resistance, entered each house, robbing it of everything of value. There were but few men in the town, and the women and children were treated with the utmost brutality. Stores and dwellings were alike entered and pillaged. Trunks, boxes, and desks were broken open, and their contents appropriated or destroyed. Even rings were rudely pulled from the ears and fingers of the women, and some of the apparel from their persons. The liquor found was freely drunk, and served to incite the plunderers to increased violence in the prosecution of their mischevous work. Having completely stripped the town, they set fire to several houses, then beat a rapid retreat, carrying off a number of horses, and loudly urging each other to greater haste, as "the d——d abolitionists were coming!"

This was Captain John W. Reid, who, under Colonel Doniphan, had done so nobly at the battle of Sacramento. Under the demoralization brought on by the battle in Kansas for slavery he degenerated into a robber and murderer. He returned later to Osawatomie and killed several men and burned the town.

Thomas H. Gladstone, correspondent for the *London Times*, visited Kansas in 1856. At Kansas City he met the border-ruffians returning from the sacking of Lawrence. They were loaded with property stolen at Lawrence, the value of which he fixed at one hundred and fifty thousand dollars. He was a shorthand writer and noted down the conversation of some of the leaders, extracts from which are quoted here:

The day following the attack upon Lawrence being that of my own arrival in the territory, I am able to supply its later history from personal observation, and will endeavor to illustrate the condition of Kansas at that excited time by the narrative of things seen and heard during the period of my visit.

The border-ruffian forces employed in the siege and sack of Lawrence, being disbanded, were to be seen on the following day spreading over the roads towards the east, carrying fury and violence wherever they went. Having once been taught that robbery and outrage, if committed in the service of the South, were to be regarded as deeds of loyalty and obedience, these ministers of a self-styled "law and order" were slow to unlearn a doctrine so acceptable. The day, like the preceding, was extremely hot, the thermometer standing at above ninety degrees; their thirst knew no bounds; and when a barrel of Bourbon, or Monongahela, or Double Rectified was accessible, they forgot even in some instances to ask the politics of its possessor. Thus through the day they sustained their turbulent fury, and when night came, it found them prepared for any excesses.

It was on that night that I first came in contact with the Missourian patriots. I had just arrived in Kansas City, and shall never forget the appearance of the lawless mob that poured into the place, inflamed with drink, glutted with the indulgence of the vilest passions, displaying with loud boasts the "plunder" they had taken from the inhabitants, and thirsting for the opportunity of repeating the sack of Lawrence in some other offending place. Men, for the most part of large frame, with red flannel shirts and immense boots worn outside their trousers, their faces unwashed and unshaven, still reeking with the dust and smoke of Lawrence, wearing the most savage looks, and giving utterance to the most horrible imprecations and blasphemies; armed, moreover, to the teeth with rifles and revolvers, cutlasses and bowie-knives, — such were the men I saw around me. Some displayed a grotesque intermixture in their dress, having crossed their native red rough shirt with the satin vest or narrow dress-coat pillaged from the wardrobe of some Lawrence Yankee, or having girded themselves with the cords and tassels which the

day before had ornamented the curtains of the Free-State Hotel.
Looking around at these groups of drunken, bellowing, blood-
thirsty demons, who crowded around the bar of the hotel, shouting for drink, or vented their furious noise on the levee without,
I felt that all my former experiences of border men and Missourians bore faint comparison with the spectacle presented by
this wretched crew, who appeared only the more terrifying from
the darkness of the surrounding night.   The hotel in Kansas
City where we were, was the next, they said, that should fall;
the attack was being planned that night, and such, they declared,
should be the end of every place which was built by Free-State
men, or that harbored "those rascally abolitionists."   Happily
this threat was not fulfilled.

A number of these men became my companions for the night,
as I went up by one of the Missouri steamboats from Kansas City
to Leavenworth. . . . . A general rush to the bar ensued.
Already maddened with whiskey, each would treat his fellow
in arms:—

"Step up, and liquor here, you sir.   A heap finer this stuff
than that there rot-gut ashore.   Here, you sir; don't be askeared.
One of our boys, I reckon?   All right on the goose, eh?   No
high-falutin' airs here, you know.   Keep that for them Yankee
Blue-Bellies down East. If there's any of that sort here, I reckon
they'd better make tracks mighty quick, and that's a fact, while
I'se on board, unless they want to make a quicker road out than
they came in.   Yes, sir, this yere tool of mine [handling a pis-
tol], it isn't the first time it has seen a Blue-belly.   If there's any
of that 'ere sort aboard, I say the'd better clear out, that's sar-
tin.   We ain't agoin' to stand them coming here, we ain't.   Isn't
their own place down East big enough for them, I should like
to know?   We ain't agoin' to stand their comin' and dictatin'
to us with their ———— nigger-worshipping, we ain't.   I reckon
we'll make the place hot enough for them soon, that's a fact.
Here, boys, drink.   Liquors, captain, for the crowd.   Step up
this way, old hoss, and liquor."

This respectable merchant was surrounded, as he stood in
the cabin of the boat, by a circle, which I joined.   Out of a side-
pocket protruded the head of a pistol; in his hand he brandished
another, loaded, as he told us, and ready for action.   With
threatening aspect and attitude, he poured forth, amid many
oaths, the following language addressed to us all:

"I am bound to bring down some one before I'm done; I
tell you, by —— I am.   I'll teach those infernal nigger-stealing
Freesoilers a lesson right peartly, that's a fact.   If there's a dog-
gauned Abolitionist aboard, I should like to see him, *that* I

should. I'm the man to put a chunk o' lead into his woolly head, right off; yes, *sir,* that's what I'll do.''

Then looking around at each of us, ''I reckon I can raise the top off the head of ere a one of you with this hyere tool. Speak the word, and, by ——, I'm your man. That's so. I should like to see the first Freesoiler that opens his mouth; that I should. I'd send him to hell pretty quick, afore he know'd what he was about; that's what I'd do. I'm a might ce-urious customer, I am.''

And so thought, probably, one of his hearers, for he said to the curious customer, ''Come, old hoss, won't you have some breakfast?'' The old horse was not to be so easily diverted, however.

''Breakfast! think I'd be after breakfast when I've got my duty before me? No, *sir,* exercise is the thing for me — not eating. I tell you I'm bound to drop some one afore I'm done — that I am. I've got to fight for the liberties of my country and our glorious constitution, and rid the place of those cowardly Blue-bellied Yankees. Yes, *sir,* that's what I've got to do. I should like to know what they've to do in this hyere place, with their snarlin', sneakin', whittlin'-o'-nothin' ways. I tell you there's not a man amongst them as knows how to fight. I should like to see the first one as 'll open his mouth here, — that's what I should like to see. I tell you I'm a ce-urious customer. Yes, sir-ree; my dog knows that,'' pointing to a large dog that seemed prepared to stand by his master for better or worse. Then, ''I should like to sot my eyes on the man as would touch that 'ere dog of mine. I'd lay him dead in a moment, *that* I would. Just see me.''

None of us felt inclined to touch the dog, and the respectable merchant returned to his politics and patriotism.

''No Northern nigger-stealers here. I'll fix 'em up mighty smart, I will. I ain't here for nothing, and that you'll see, just about as soon as anything. Yes, *sir,* I only want to see the first Freesoiler here. I'll drop the first one of you that opens his mouth for abolition cusses; I be dog-gauned if I don't.''

Mr. Gladstone gives us the language of but one of the ruffians. All the others were as bad; there was but one spirit actuating all of them. There was then promulgated and taught as justice and righteousness the principle that governed the ruffians of the border until after the close of the Civil War. Gladstone thus expressed this principle:

''*Having once been taught that robbery and outrage, if com-*

*mitted in the service of the South, were to be regarded as deeds
of loyalty and obedience, these ministers of a self-styled 'law and
order' were slow to unlearn a doctrine so acceptable."*

The violence of those times is now inconceivable.   In a
speech at St. Joseph, March 26, 1855, Benjamin F. Stringfellow
said:

I tell you to mark every scoundrel among you that is in the
least tainted with free-soilism or abolitionism and exterminate
him.   Neither give nor take quarter from the damned rascals.
I propose to mark them in this house, and on the present occasion,
so you may crush them out.   To those who have qualms of conscience as to violating laws, state or national, the crisis has arrived when such impositions must be disregarded, as your rights
and property are in danger, and I advise one and all to enter
every election district in Kansas, in defiance of Reeder and his
vile myrmidons, and vote at the point of the bowie-knife and the
revolver.   Neither give nor take quarter, as our cause demands
it.   It is enough that the slaveholding interest wills it, from
which there is no appeal.   What right has Governor Reeder to
rule Missourians in Kansas?   His proclamation and prescribed
oath must be prohibited.   It is to your interest to do so.   Mind
that slavery is established where it is not prohibited.

Robert S. Kelly was a typical border-ruffian.   He swore he
could not rest or die happy until he had killed an abolitionist.
"If," said he, "I can't kill a man, I'll kill a woman; and if I
can't kill a woman, I'll kill a child."

Dr. Gihon gives us a general description of the times, as
follows:

There are hundreds of well authenticated accounts of the
cruelties practiced by this horde of ruffians, some of them too
shocking and disgusting to relate, or to be accredited if told.
The tears and shrieks of terrified women, folded in their foul
embrace, failed to touch a chord of mercy in their brutal hearts,
and the mutilated bodies of murdered men, hanging upon the
trees, or left to rot upon the prairies or in the deep ravines, or
furnish food for vultures and wild beasts, told frightful stories
of brutal ferocity from which the wildest savages might have
shrunk with horror.

In these actions and conditions, and in the spirit which they made the code of justice and morality along the border the Lawrence Massacre had its origin.

May 19, 1858, Dr. Hamelton and twenty-four other border-ruffians planned and executed an indiscriminate massacre of Kansas citizens. This is known as the Marais des Cygnes Massacre. They arrested eleven citizens of Linn county, Kansas, marched them to a ravine, formed them in line there, and fired until every man fell. The murdered numbered five and the wounded five. One escaped unhurt; he and the wounded escaped by feigning death. The bodies were robbed and left weltering in their blood, and the murderers returned to Missouri; they were never molested or called to account.

The burning of Osceola by General James H. Lane has been generally cited by Missouri writers as a justification for the Lawrence Massacre by Quantrill. On this subject George W. Martin, Secretary of the Kansas State Historical Society, said in a recent address:

James H. Lane, in command of the United States troops, on the 22nd day of September, 1861, destroyed the town of Osceola, St. Clair county, Missouri. This is generally stated as the excuse for the Lawrence Massacre of August 21, 1863. Lane went to Osceola on a legitimate errand of warfare — to destroy certain supplies of the enemy — Sterling Price at this time having captured Colonel Mulligan at Lexington. Lane was fired on from ambush, and in returning the fire killed one man. Lane's men helped the women get their personal effects from their houses. Lane took the records from the court-house before applying the torch, and returned them at the close of the war. Lawrence was destroyed or besieged three times — in December, 1855, May 21, 1856, and September 15, 1856. This third time Governor Geary arrived with United States troops to turn back to Missouri the 2,700 invaders. Osawatomie was raided and robbed by 150 Missourians June 6, and destroyed by 500 Missourians August 30, 1856. The Marais des Cygnes Massacre, May 18, 1858, was planned at Papinsville, Bates county, Missouri, and put into lawful execution on the 19th. Thus there were six raids from Missouri into Kansas before John Brown made the first raid from Kansas into Missouri, December, 1858, when he brought out eleven negroes. The second raid from Kansas into Missouri was by James B. Abbott and party, July 23, 1859, who rescued John Doy from jail in St. Joseph. Lane's march upon Osceola was five months after the assault upon Fort

Sumter, and prior to it there was the seizure of Camp Jackson, the Platte Bridge Massacre, the battle of Wilson Creek, the siege of Lexington, and the battle of Morristown.

With all these things Quantrill was familiar. He had arrived in Kansas too late to participate in all the wars between the Territory and Missouri. But he was a prominent character in the bands that invaded Missouri for reprisal. How he had been carried over to the side of the Missourians has been told herein. He carried there with him an intense hatred of Kansas, and he added to it all the bitterness he found there as the result of the conflict which arose over slavery. He had no convictions on any subject, but governed his life by personal grievances which came upon him because of his crimes.

When the war came on and the pro-slavery men had cast their lot with the Confederacy, the positions of the Kansans and the Missourians were exactly reversed; the Washington government was behind the Kansans. There were rough characters in Kansas who had been developed in the bloody scenes upon the border. These took occasion to settle old scores over the line. They did, after the war began, what the Missourians had been doing to Kansas since 1854. That some of these Kansas men as soldiers committed excesses and crimes in Missouri has always been admitted. General Schofield, in his official report of the Lawrence Massacre, admits it, and it has never been denied. And in Kansas it was never justified, palliated, nor excused. The perpetrators of these crimes were never in good standing in Kansas. They slunk out of sight and disappeared. They did not engage in general highway robbery and murder after the war. Kansas executed or killed Cleveland or Metz during the war for attempting such a course.

And, as has been pointed out herein, the Missourians had more to complain of from brother Missourians than from any other people. All the immediate causes for the Lawrence Massacre enumerated in the *Gregg Manuscript* are expressly charged in that paper to Colonel Penick and his regiment of Missourians.

And it must be remembered that prior to the Lawrence Massacre Quantrill had raided Aubry and burned it, had raided Shawneetown and burned it, had raided Olathe and murdered and robbed there, and had killed citizens and non-combatants in all these raids. Todd had raided Spring Hill, and Bill Anderson had raided far into Kansas along the Old Santa Fé Trail, burning and murdering.

No, the guerrillas had no sufficient cause for the Lawrence Massacre. It was never the home of Jennison, the Kansan of whom Missourians had most cause to complain. The Massacre had its origin in the hatred slavery bore the town and in the depravity and desperation of Quantrill himself.

CHAPTER XXIV

THE LAWRENCE MASSACRE

II

KANSAS should be laid waste at once.

That is what Quantrill told the Confederate secretary of war at Richmond when he went there seeking authority to raise a regiment of Partisan Rangers.

Kansas should be laid waste at once.

This was the one idea of Quantrill. It was ever present in his mind. The one object of his life was to enter Kansas with an adequate force, and then burn and murder. He would devastate — would become a devouring fire.

And for what? Not that Kansas or any of her citizens had harmed him or injured Missouri. Quantrill cared nothing for Missouri. He cared only for Quantrill. His whole life was predicated on the incomprehensible misanthropy rankling in his own soul. Missouri and Missourians were to him a means to an end — to harrass, murder, burn, rob, destroy, lay waste in Kansas. Only that. Nothing more. He murdered many Missourians. Any man in Missouri who would not aid him to ravage Kansas was a dead man if Quantrill could get his hands upon him. When a man deliberately and with malice wrongs another the act embitters him, recoils upon him, plunges him into excesses. He hopes the cumulative nature of these excesses may in some way work him out a cause — a justification. This self-deception seems to be inherent in man. It had complete control of Quantrill. He had run swiftly in the ways of wickedness, depravity and crime in Kansas. He knew that he should be despised there, abhorred; and knowing this, he believed the people of Kansas held him in loathing, detestation. A soul like Quantrill's reasons that way. He raged against Kansas day and night. He thought of nothing but the humiliation and destruction of her people.

That is why he sought authority in Richmond to raise a regiment of outlaws. For then he could shed blood like water in Kansas. Then would the sky be blackened with the smoke rising from the scourging of Kansas, and the land filled with the lamentations of the orphan and the homeless widow — a sacrifice required, demanded, cried for by the hideous, monstrous, misshapen thing Quantrill called his soul. "Kansas should be laid waste at once." That was his cry, his thought day and night — his life.

While Quantrill had lost favor with his officers, he was still strong with the guerrillas. They worshiped him. According to his tale he had a grievance, a cause for his malevolence, a justification for his desperation. They could understand that matter as long as they believed his story true, and he was careful to talk little of his past life. He knew he lived over a mine always smouldering to the verge of explosion.

Seeing what sympathy and strength a grievance brought to Quantrill, other guerrilla captains sought to establish grievances for themselves. In some instances these grievances were invented for them long after they were dead.

In 1863 General Ewing, in command at Kansas City, had been compelled to arrest and imprison a number of young women living in Jackson county, Missouri. These women were spies, impelled by love for fathers, brothers, or sweethearts in the guerrilla camps. The love and devotion of women can never be told. Woman is a partisan. She will give her life for any cause she may espouse — and give it freely — and all the more freely if maternal love is involved. This principle is the sheet-anchor, the hope of the world.

These women rode into Kansas City almost daily. They saw everything and

Nannie Harris

talked to those who could give them information that would be of benefit to the guerrillas. They secretly bought pistol-caps and other ammunition. When they left the city they rode by many a turn of lane and stream, through thickets and over rough hills, to the safe hiding-places of the guerrillas to report and deliver supplies. Who could blame the guerrillas for worshiping them, for being ever ready and willing to fight to the death for them? No one. It is to their credit that they thus regarded these young women — greatly to their credit. Nor can one find it in his heart to censure much these girls, though their actions forfeited their lives by all military codes. No doubt, General Ewing much regretted the necessity for placing them in confinement, for any harsh measure towards woman grieves every honorable man. He dealt with them very leniently and allowed them great latitude; when they were cut off from communication with the guerrillas his whole object was accomplished.

Among these women were the sisters of Bill Anderson — three sisters, Josephine, Mary, and Jenny. They had been arrested south of Westport, near the State-line, by a detail sent out for that purpose. Their arrest was accomplished with difficulty, for they fought like wildcats and screamed at their highest pitch. But two of them were arrested, the third being but a child. Bill Anderson and a number of guerrillas chanced to be in hearing and came to the rescue. The two men who had discovered the girls were dismounted and marching them along the road — a lane enclosed by high rail fences — when the guerrillas appeared. The captors forced the girls to mount, then they mounted behind the saddles. Seizing the reins they faced the guerrillas, who could not shoot without hitting the captives. It was a desperate situation, and the men told the guerrillas that if either horse or man was wounded the girls would be shot at once. Then these Union soldiers backed their horses along the road in slow retreat from the guerrillas until the other portion of the detail came up, when the girls were brought off easily and taken into the lines. The younger sister, Jenny, came in voluntarily to live with the others.

These women were imprisoned in a cheap, poorly constructed, two-story brick building on Grand avenue between Fourteenth and Fifteenth streets. The rear of the building

extended back into a ravine, where the
walls of the foundation had been built
without excavation, the ground there
being low, and the intention being to fill
about the walls and thus give them earth
support. But this filling had not been
done. The rear room of this building,
in the first story, had never been completed. There was no floor in it, and the
hogs that then ranged at large in Kansas City came there to lie in the shade
and the loose dirt which they rooted up
along the walls. It must be said that
there was negligence in the care of this
building by General Ewing.

Charity Kerr

There were about a dozen of these women in prison. Seventeen, in all, had been arrested. Some time in the summer or
fall of 1863 it was decided to send them to St. Louis where better accommodations could be found for them. In some way they
discovered that they were to be sent away from Kansas City,
and they determined to escape if possible. They dug under the
foundation wall of that part of the building occupied by them,
and in one more night they would have dug their way out and
have been free. But a wind-storm came up and the building col-
lapsed, killing a number of the women and wounding others.
The guerrillas at once charged that the Union military authorities had caused the walls to be undermined for the purpose of
throwing down the house to kill the captives. It is very difficult
to see what motive could have been behind any such action.[1]

_____

[1] There have been many versions of this affair found by the author.
Some of them are very different from that given in the text, and some
could not appear in print. The above account is the best the author
could make up from the conflicting stories. There is no certainty that it
is correct in all its details. This statement the author desires to make,
for he would not do injustice to these girls for the world. They were
unfortunate. They may have been harshly dealt with, though it is the
opinion of the author that they were very leniently dealt with. Where
a woman is concerned in such a matter she must have the benefit and
advantage of every thing that can favor her. The author has found few

Major Edwards drew a very pathetic and touching picture
of the sorrow of Bill Anderson when he saw the dead body of
his sister.   There is no doubt that he suffered deep sorrow, guerrilla though he was, and fiend and murderer.   Major Edwards

people who believe that the building was undermined, or who believe there
was any thing which could have caused the military authorities to desire
that such a thing should be done. It would be very unjust to the memory
of General Ewing to fix such a charge upon him now without incontroverti-
ble proof. All accounts agree that he strained the rules to give them as
much liberty as possible.

Many persons have denied to the author that any evidences of recent
excavations or digging about the walls were found. Hon. Cyrus Leland, Jr.,
was then on General Ewing's staff, and he is of the opinion that the girls
were digging their way out; that is his recollection of the matter now. It
was largely through the efforts of Mr. Leland that Miss Van Ness and
others were liberated.

Whatever grievance appears for the guerrillas must be set down. In
all discussions of these times they must have not only justice but the
benefit of the doubt. Even then their case will be difficult enough. It
is the desire and intention to be absolutely fair and just to all men here.

In an interview in 1887 with Ike Hall and Don Pence at Samuels's
Depot (now Wakefield, Ky.) W. W. Scott was told that General Ewing
captured seventeen girls in Jackson and Cass counties, Mo., and that the
charge was harboring their brothers, which could not have been true, for
some had no brothers nor parents living. Among them were one sister
of Tom Hall and one of John McCorkle. It was told Scott that Bill
Anderson was working on a farm in Kansas, and that his two sisters
were captured there and taken to Kansas City. These girls were arrested
in 1863, and, as said above, the Andersons had been desperate guerrillas
two years then. The story that the house had been undermined was told
Scott by Hall and Pence.

At this same interview it was charged that John Fox, about thirteen
years old, who had a brother with Quantrill, was shot and killed while his
sister and mother had hold of him begging for his life. The charge was
that he fed his brother. James Nicholson, fourteen years old, was killed
because he had two brothers with Price. Hicks George was hung, but not
killed, and joined Quantrill. What he was charged with is not stated.

Don Pence said he joined Quantrill in May or June, 1864. His
brother, Bud Pence, had joined him six months before. Men came to his
father's house, in Clay county, Mo., and put a rope around his father's
neck and threatened to hang him if he did not tell where Bud was. He
did not know. They broke a fiddle over his head and also the stock of
a gun in their persuasions before hanging. These had no effect, and he
was pulled up off his feet two or three times. But no information was

would have us believe that the death of his sister under these circumstances caused Bill Anderson to become a guerrilla. Kneeling beside her he vowed to avenge her death and immediately entered the guerrilla camp. Now, the truth is, that Bill

gained. He was allowed to live, and moved to Liberty to save sending Don to Quantrill, but finally sent him.

Ike Hall said that Joseph Hall and family lived in Cass county, Mo., fifteen miles from Kansas City, when they first heard of Quantrill, in connection with the Morgan Walker raid. They saw Quantrill riding about with a squad after the war broke out. His brother, Joseph Hall, joined him in 1861, and in April or May, 1862, Ike joined him at Blue Springs. Later in that year Bob Hall joined. That left the father, mother, and one sister at home. Jennison, in the winter of 1862, made the mother set fire to her own house. When she cried and put up her hands to wipe away the tears they jerked her hands down and cursed her. They let her take out a part of her things, but made her throw some of them back into the fire. They burned the houses of four neighbors the same day.

The above are probably true accounts. The Memo. of the interview is in the Collection of the author.

In a letter written by C. M. Chase in 1873 from Leavenworth, Kansas, to his paper at Lyndon, Vermont, the following, in relation to Jennison, appears:

This is the home of Jennison, the Kansas Jayhawker, and of his associates. He was a strong slavery man in the '56 times, but when the rebellion broke out the Union side afforded the best opportunities for robbery, and he was nominally a Union man, but really a plunderer of Missouri property. There are miles and miles of Missouri thoroughfare, on the border, on which Jennison and his men burned every house and in many instances slaughtered the people. One old lady tells us her experience: Her husband had been reported a rebel, by some of Jennison's men. In passing his house Jennison called him out, and, without much parleying, ordered his boys to string him up on his own piazza. In spite of the woman's entreaties and crying a rope was fastened to his neck, and, with the other end thrown over a beam, he was jerked several feet into the air. As his neck was not broken, he struggled violently for release, when Jennison ordered two of his men to jump upon him and break his neck. This was done, in the very face of the wife, ''and there,'' said she, ''is the very beam where they hung him.'' This is but one specimen of the numerous cases of out-lawing perpetrated in those times.

The error in this is the statement that Jennison was a slavery man; he never was that.

But to show that such things were not uncommon, and to show that they had existed long, the author will say that Hon. George W. Martin, Secretary of the Kansas State Historical Society, has repeatedly told me that a member of his family saw Sheriff Jones, of Douglas county, Kansas Territory, set on fire the homes of six Free-State settlers one day as he

Anderson was one of the first guerrillas to take to the brush. He was active in 1861. At the time of his sister's death Bill Anderson and his brother had been the most desperate guerrillas and horse-thieves on the border for two years. But it was made an excuse for Bill Anderson's savagery and one of the excuses for the Lawrence Massacre.

ALICE VAN NESS

One of these girls, Alice Van Ness, afterwards achieved fame as an actress. Her stage name was Alice Vane. Before the war her father, then a widower, moved with his children from Mary-

Alice Van Ness

land to St. Joseph, Mo., and there engaged in the wholesale liquor business. He died about the year 1861, leaving a son, then in California, and a daughter — Alice. This daughter was a very beautiful girl; she sympathized with the South. Not much is known of her until the spring of 1863. She often visited at the home of the Torreys, in Paolo. The Torreys were in full sympathy with the South and with Quantrill, and their tavern was always a meeting-place for disloyal people. After a visit there of some weeks in the spring of 1863 Miss Van Ness returned to Kansas City, and was soon arrested by order of General Ewing as a spy and imprisoned in the old house on Grand avenue. She was in the building when it fell down, but escaped unhurt.

The prisoners were placed in the Union Hotel when rescued from the ruins of the Grand avenue building. There they were given the top floor, and guards were set to protect and retain

rode into Lecompton. Sheriff Jones lived in Westport, Mo., but in border-ruffian rule in Kansas was the sheriff of Douglas county. Such men as Jones had practiced murder, robbery, house-burning, town-sacking in Kansas Territory six years before the Civil War began. That did not justify Jennison or any other officer in violation of the rules of civilized warfare in Missouri, however. Jennison should have been hung for his crimes there, no doubt.

them. This hotel was on Main street (east side) about Sixth street.

Lieutenant Cyrus Leland, Jr., then on General Ewing's staff, boarded at this hotel. He was sent to the prison one evening after the Lawrence Massacre, and was there spoken to by Miss Van Ness, whom he had never seen before. She wished to secure a parole and permission to again visit the Torreys, and inquired of Leland how to proceed in the matter. Leland told her to write a letter to General Ewing stating her request. This she did, and Ewing had her brought before him for examination, which ended in her being paroled for ten days with permission to visit the Torreys. She returned to Kansas City at the expiration of her parole and was permitted to live with an old lady, an acquaintance and friend of the family, who lived in McGee's Addition. She was required to report to headquarters at stated periods, and there she often saw Leland. He sometimes called on her at her residence. He had delivered her the papers — parole and permission to visit the Torreys — and she at that time sang a number of songs, playing a guitar as accompaniment. Her father was a Jew and a fine musician, and she had inherited his talent in that line. She always sang when requested by Leland and other young men who called on her, and her musical talent was soon well known.

She desired to be released and to go to work at something for her support. There was no direct evidence against her on the charge of being a spy. She appealed to Leland to aid her, and he said he would do what he could to assist her. At that time the Templeton & Wildman Theatrical Co., was playing an engagement at Long Hall, on the east side of Main street, about Seventh. Leland often went there, and was acquainted with Templeton, whom he told of the musical ability of Miss Van Ness. Together they went to see her, and she sang a number of pieces for them. Templeton said that if she could sing before an audience he would give her a position in the company, but would not pay much salary at first. It was arranged that she should appear in the regular performance two or three days later. Templeton advertised that in the interval between the musical part of the program and the farce with which the performance was

21

closed, a lady living in the city would sing, but did not say who the lady was. Leland desired that she make a success of the effort, and he procured a number of bouquets to be thrown on the stage at the end of the pieces to be sung, and got parties in the proper position to throw them. She was a little nervous, but got through the first piece very well, and when the bouquets were thrown to her she seemed much pleased. She was applauded. In rendering the second piece she did much better than in the first, being then completely recovered and reassured. The audience called for her again, but Templeton had told her she must sing but two pieces, and she was permitted only to appear and bow her acknowledgements. General Ewing and his wife witnessed the performance. Templeton engaged Miss Van Ness to sing regularly.

When General Ewing was given the St. Louis Military District, he issued orders of permanent banishment against a number of people in the Kansas City District. Leland had him issue one against Miss Van Ness, that she could go with the theatrical company. She was required to leave the District in three days. The second night the company played at Atchison, and the third night at St. Joseph, which was outside the lines of the District.

Miss Van Ness later married John Templeton, principal owner of the company, and their daughter, Fay Templeton, is the famous actress. Fay was put on the stage by her parents when but a child, and at the age of eighteen she was the star, and the company was reorganized and called the Templeton Opera Company. For many years Alice Van Ness Templeton played a leading part in the company under the name of Alice Vane. She retained her beauty to late in life. After the death of her husband she married a man of wealth and lives now in Chicago.

Some months after her engagement with the Templeton & Wildman Theatrical Co., it was determined that the company would go to Little Rock to fill an engagement there. Permission to go had to be secured from General Ewing, at St. Louis. The little steamer on which they descended the Mississippi and ascended the Arkansas was captured by Confederate soldiers below Little Rock. When the pillage of the boat began Miss Van Ness bethought her of her banishment papers. She waved them above her head and called for the commander of the troops. When he saw that she had been banished for loyalty to the South she demanded protection for herself and the company, which the commander granted, and no property of Templeton & Wildman was molested.

CHAPTER XXV

III

THAT the Lawrence Massacre was not in retaliation for the destruction of the Confederate warehouses and supplies at Osceola is fully established by Quantrill's statement of the reasons why it should be accomplished. [1] This statement was made to the captains of the various bands of guerrillas who paid him allegiance. He assembled them early in July, 1863, to urge upon them the necessity of destroying Lawrence. Captain William H. Gregg was present, and in his *Manuscript* has preserved a portion of what Quantrill said to his captains in laying the matter before them. And in this relation Gregg says of Quantrill:

"He longed to get even with Kansas. His proposition was to go to Lawrence."

"He longed to get even with Kansas." Do not forget that.

Continuing, Gregg quotes part of the speech of Quantrill to his captains, as follows:

He said in part:

"The Kansan has been murdering and robbing our people for two years or more, and burned their houses by districts, hauled their household plunder, farming implements, etc., to Kansas, driven off their cattle, etc., until forbearance has ceased to be a virtue. Lawrence is the great hot-bed of abolitionism in Kansas. All the plunder (or at least the bulk of it) stolen from Missouri will be found stored away in Lawrence. We can get more revenge and more money there than anywhere else in the State of Kansas."

---

[1] For a full account and discussion of the burning of Osceola, see *Kansas Historical Collections*, Vol. VI, p. 305, *et seq*. The account is by John Speer, who visited Osceola and obtained the facts from the people of the town.

Some said the undertaking was too hazardous. On this point the Chief said:

"I know the hazard this enterprise bears, but if you never risk, you never gain."

So, Quantrill won, though the council was long and spirited, and his victory was secured with difficulty. The deliberations lasted twenty-four hours.

Notice these reasons.

"The Kansan has been murdering and robbing our people for two years or more, and burned their houses by districts, hauled their household plunder, farming implements, etc., to Kansas, driven off their cattle, etc., until forbearance has ceased to be a virtue."

Against this, set Aubry, Olathe, Shawneetown, Spring Hill, Humboldt, which was twice sacked and burned, and the murders and burnings of Bill Anderson along the Old Santa Fé Trail as far west as Council Grove. This during the war. Then set down the Territorial sackings.

"Lawrence is the great hot-bed of abolitionism in Kansas."

Against this we have nothing to place as an offset. It does not require any offset.

"We can get more revenge and more money there than anywhere else in the State of Kansas."

Quantrill had reserved his strongest argument to the last of the debate. Revenge and money. Plunder. Loot. The same old causes which had induced him to invade Missouri and carry out negroes in Territorial times. Revenge was well enough for the others of the band. For himself, money, money. And incidental revenge on individuals who might know too much of his past or with whom he had kidnapped free negroes or runaway slaves. Money and a general and bitter hatred of Kansas on personal grounds. He cared nothing for the array of crimes he first enumerated to his captains. Such things would do for them. For himself, he kept his own counsel. He carried scars they could not see.

Quantrill had sent spies to Lawrence frequently in the summer of 1863. And his guerrillas have told the author that some residents of the town had always kept in communication with

him. Edwards says that Charles T. ("Fletch") Taylor had
been in Lawrence for some time just previous to the raid. In the
Kansas City Star, July 19, 1903, there is a long and excellent
article by Frederic William Hinsey on the events preceding the
Lawrence Massacre. It gives an account of a visit by Quantrill
himself, with two of his guerrillas, to Eudora, a town some eight
miles east of Lawrence. This visit was a few weeks before the
Massacre at Lawrence, and Quantrill was no doubt making a personal examination of the country to refresh his memory as to
roads, and to see what obstacles he would have to contend with.
He was recognized beyond doubt, it would seem from this
account, but not until he and his men were mounted and ready
to depart. Then defiantly announcing that he had that day
"fooled the Dutch" (Eudora was settled by Germans) he rode
away. That he was thoroughly informed concerning Lawrence
and the country around it for some months before the raid there
is no doubt. His men, in conversation with me, have impli-
cated one of the prominent men of Kansas in Quantrill's designs
on Lawrence, saying they had seen letters in the hands of Quantrill from him under a name agreed on by them. John Noland,
a negro, now living in Kansas City, had been sent to Lawrence
as a spy by Quantrill, but he insists that Quantrill had gone on
the raid before he returned.[2]

---

[2] The author has seen Noland, but he would not talk. He seems
afraid he might yet have trouble if he should admit that he saw Quantrill
after he returned from Lawrence and before the raid. That Quantrill had
accurate information of the situation at Lawrence there is no doubt.

The inauguration of the Lawrence Massacre is thus described by
Major Edwards:

Without in the least degree increasing or decreasing the difficulties
of the undertaking, Quantrell laid before his officers his plan for attacking
Lawrence. For a week a man of the command — a cool, bold, plausible,
desperate man — had been in the city — through it, over it, about it, and
around it — and he was here in the midst of them to report. Would
they listen to him? "Let him speak," said Todd, sententiously. Lieutenant Fletcher Taylor came out of the shadow, bowed gravely to the
group, and with the brevity of a soldier who knew better how to fight than
to talk, laid bare the situation. Disguised as a stock trader, or, rather
assuming the *role* of a speculating man, he had boldly entered Lawrence.
Liberal, bountifully supplied with money, keeping open rooms at the
Eldridge House, and agreeable in every way and upon every occasion, he
had seen all that was necessary to see, and learned all that could be of
any possible advantage to the Guerrillas. The city proper was but weakly

The council of captains to make final plans and arrangements for the raid was held about the 10th of August. From this council the captains returned to their camps to set things in order. For some days the guerrillas did little but clean and oil their pistols, mould bullets and mend their war-harness. Every woman who would make the venture was sent to Kansas City to get pistol-caps and powder, and an immense supply was collected.

The general rendezvous of the guerrillas was the farm of Captain Perdee, on the Blackwater, in Johnson county, Mis-

garrisoned; the camp beyond the river was not strong; the idea of a raid by Quantrell was honestly derided; supineness next to belief was the most predominant madness of the people; the streets were broad and good for charging horsemen, and the hour for the venture was near at hand.

"You have heard the report," Quantrell's deep voice broke in, "but before you decide it is proper that you should know it all. The march to Lawrence is a long one; in every little town there are soldiers; we leave soldiers behind us; we march through soldiers; we attack the town garrisoned by soldiers; we retreat through soldiers; and when we would rest and refit after the exhaustive expedition, we have to do the best we can in the midst of a multitude of soldiers. Come, speak out, somebody. What is it, Anderson?" "Lawrence or hell, but with one proviso, that we kill every male thing." "Todd?" "Lawrence, if I knew that not a man would get back alive." "Gregg?" "Lawrence; it is the home of Jim Lane; the foster-mother of Red Legs; the nurse of the Jayhawkers." "Shepherd?" "Lawrence; I know it of old; niggers and white people are just the same there; it's a Boston colony and it should be wiped out." "Jarrette?" "Lawrence, by all means. I've had my eye upon it for a year. The head devil of all this killing and burning in Jackson county, I vote to fight it with fire — to burn it before we leave it." "Dick Maddox?" "Lawrence; an eye for an eye and a tooth for a tooth; God understands better than we do the equilibrium of civil war." "Holt?" "Lawrence; and quick about it." "Yager?" "Where my house once stood there is a heap of ashes. I haven't a neighbor that's got a house — Lawrence and the torch." "Blunt?" "Count me in whenever there's killing. Lawrence first, and then some other Kansas town; the name is nothing." "Have you all voted?" "All." "Then Lawrence it is; saddle up, men!" Thus was the Lawrence Massacre inaugurated.

Major Edwards in attempting to justify the Massacre recites all the murders and outrages that had occurred in Missouri to that date and charges them upon Kansas. He goes all along down the line to Cass, Bates, Vernon, and other counties. He says that in the fifteen days preceding the Lawrence Massacre more than two hundred men had been killed in Missouri by Union soldiers. Of course these were all harmless and innocent! But he forgets that Colonel Penick, a Missourian, was then stationed at Independence, or had been a short time before, and other Missouri troops and commanders at Lexington, Harrisonville, Clinton, and other towns in Western Missouri. General Ewing, an Ohio man, was

souri, about four miles southwest of Columbus, six miles southeast of Chapel Hill, and nine miles east of Lone Jack.   Quantrill's
immediate followers assembled on the Little Sni, in the Cum-
mings settlement, twenty-four miles southeast of Independence,
on the 18th of August.   That night they rode to the farm of

---

in command of the military district including all this territory. These
men who were killed must have been disloyal, and no doubt many of them
were guerrillas who were caught at home. That some were innocent and
harmless, and their execution murder, there is no doubt.

*And the important matter that he omits, and that Captain Gregg
omits, is that there were few Kansas troops then in Jackson county or any
other Western Missouri county. General Blunt was holding the country
from Fort Scott to Fort Smith, where he had some troops from Kansas.
The unfair thing in all these attempts to justify the Lawrence Massacre is
the charging to Kansas and Kansas troops all the outrages committed in
Western Missouri during the war up to that time, when the writers knew
that few Kansas troops were in Missouri after 1861. In writing history
some regard ought to be paid to the facts. Also, to the official records.*

In support of the above, there is copied here the list of garrisons in
the Military District of Central Missouri for the year 1863, taken from
Rebellion Records, Series I, Vol. 23, p. 891. These assignments were made
December 31, 1862:

Butler, Mo.

Second Missouri State Militia Cavalry, Major Frank J. White.

Calhoun, Mo.

Sixth Missouri State Militia Cavalry, Companies B and D, Captain
William Plumb.

Gasconade, Mo.

Twenty-third Missouri, Company A, Lieutenant Ephraim L. Webb.

Harrisonville, Mo.

Fifth Missouri State Militia Cavalry (four companies), Lieutenant
Colonel Philip A. Thompson.

Independence, Mo.

Colonel William R. Penick. Fifth Missouri State Militia Cavalry
(three companies), Major Thomas B. Biggers.
Missouri State Militia Artillery (one battery).

Jefferson City, Mo.

Lieutenant-Colonel H. L. Burns. Fourth Missouri State Militia Cav-
alry, Company I, Captain Hannibal B. Davis.
Fifth Missouri State Militia Cavalry, Company E.
First Missouri State Militia Battery, Captain Albert Wachsman.

Kansas City, Mo.

Fifth Missouri State Militia Cavalry (one company), Major William
Drumhiller.
(Later, Major Preston B. Plumb and some Kansas troops were added
to the garrison at Kansas City).

Captain Perdee. The bands from Lafayette and Johnson counties arrived the same night. Quantrill assembled the captains when they had all arrived, and they discussed the outlook for the contemplated raid. Nothing was found to prevent its continuance, and it was decided to move on Lawrence.

On the morning of the 19th the guerrillas began their march. They spread extensive wings of videttes in every direction and moved slowly. This was a day spent in feeling their way among the Federal troops in the country through which they were passing. The videttes reported every hour — some of them more frequently. The march was in the direction of Lone Jack, and the command was halted at the farm of a Mr. Potter, after hav-

---

Lexington, Mo.

First Missouri State Militia Cavalry (six companies), Colonel James McFerran.

Osage City, Mo.

Twenty-third Missouri, Company D, Captain John W. Moore.

Pleasant Hill, Mo.

Fifth Missouri State Militia Cavalry (one company), Captain John Pinger.

Saint Aubert's, Mo.

Twenty-third Missouri, Company I, Captain Marion Cave.

Sedalia, Mo.

Lieutenant-Colonel Alexanqder M. Woolfolk. First Missouri State Militia Cavalry (four companies), Lieutenant-Colonel Alexander M. Woolfolk. Third Indiana Battery.

Warrensburg, Mo.

Sixth Missouri State Militia Cavalry (six companies), Colonel Edwin C. Catherwood.

There were some changes in these garrisons during the spring and summer of 1863, but in the main they remained as indicated by this assignment. Colonel C. S. Clark, Ninth Kansas, commanded the small border posts south of Kansas City to Trading Post, with headquarters at Coldwater Grove, Mo., but he was a poor soldier and never did any fighting he could possibly avoid.

Colonel W. C. Ransom was brought into the district in the summer with the Sixth Kansas and did hard work and much fighting of guerrillas. A part of his regiment was at Kansas City. There were a few Kansas troops at other points. But the Missourians in Western Missouri had to deal with Missouri troops principally in the spring and summer of 1863.

This is a further confirmation of what was stated in an early chapter of this work. It was Missourian against Missourian, largely, during the entire war. Lane and Jennison were in Missouri in 1861, after which there were very few Kansas troops in Missouri.

ing spent a day in riding ten miles. All the scouts were called in and their reports heard. No enemy had been encountered in any direction. Then it was that the final decision to go on to Lawrence was made. The men were assembled, and Quantrill addressed them, saying, as nearly as Captain Gregg can recall:

You, one and all, will understand that the undertaking we are about to commence is one of extreme hazard. It might be that the entire command will be overwhelmed, the ranks decimated as they have never been before. Hence, I say to one and all, if any refuse to go they will not be censured.

Gregg was at the time a lieutenant and was acting as adjutant and aid to Quantrill. He counted the men and reported to Quantrill that there were two hundred and ninety-four, rank and file, who responded to roll-call.

The preliminary arrangements and movements were completed at the Potter farm. When all was done and every man knew where he was going, the guerrillas were directed to feed their horses and refresh themselves with a light supper, which they did. Then rang out the command—"Saddle up."

The guerrillas were in their saddles almost instantly, the column was formed and the march to Lawrence was commenced in earnest. At seven o'clock the next morning they were on the head of the Middle Fork of Grand river, in Cass county, four miles from the Kansas line. There they halted and remained until three o'clock in the afternoon. Then the guerrillas "saddled up" for the final march to the doomed town. South of the Blue they had met Colonel John D. Holt with one hundred and four men, and he was invited to take his men, new recruits, principally, to Lawrence and have them "christened." To this Colonel Holt consented, and he was then made third in command. He had been to Northern Missouri and was on his way out of Missouri with men he had recruited, and had fallen in with Quantrill by accident.

The guerrilla command was further reinforced while on the Middle Fork of Grand river by the arrival of about fifty men from other parts of the Grand river country and from the Osage.

The total force of Quantrill was made up as follows:

The original force, as reported by Gregg,	294
Holt's command,	104
The Grand river reinforcement,	50
Total, by official count,	448

There were doubtless other accessions, making a total force of guerrillas of not less than four hundred and fifty men.[3]

The guerrillas crossed the State-line at the southeast corner of Johnson county, Kansas, where the Fort Scott Military Road leaves Kansas and enters Missouri, and crosses one of the head branches of Grand river, there flowing some three miles eastward and out of Kansas. At this point a road then branched off and led west, passing one and one-half miles south of Aubry. At Aubry, Captain J. A. Pike, Company K, Ninth Kansas Volunteer Cavalry, was stationed with his company and Company D, Eleventh Kansas Volunteer Cavalry. Each of these companies numbered about fifty men. Captain Pike formed his men in line of battle on the prairie south of his post and watched Quantrill march his guerrillas into Kansas only one and a half miles from his line. He did not offer to attack. He did nothing. His actions were strange, for his home was in Lawrence. He could not have defeated Quantrill, for he was outnumbered four to one. But he knew it was Quantrill, and he could have hung upon the flanks of the guerrilla column; he could have annoyed and retarded it. He could have delayed it a few hours, and that would have saved Lawrence. But he did not even use diligence in notifying the Union commanders of other garrisons. The conduct of Captain Pike was reprehensible in the extreme.[4]

---

[3] See report of General Thomas Ewing, *Rebellion Records*, Series I, Vol. XXIII, p. 580.

[4] The conduct of Captain Pike was severely criticised at the time by General Ewing in his official report of the raid.

Pike tried to shield himself by reporting that Quantrill crossed into Kansas five miles south of Aubry. He realized that he ought to have done something and would be condemned for his inactivity. If he had reported that he saw Quantrill in Kansas, marching west within a mile and a half of his garrison, and that he did nothing, he would have been court-martialed, as he should have been. Perhaps he did not then know it was Quantrill, but it was his business to have known. Captain Gregg's account says that Quantrill marched west only half a mile south of Aubry. Aubry

The inefficiency, stupidity, diffidence, we will not say cowardice, of Captain Pike made up the first of a remarkably strange, untoward, and lamentable series of incidents that left Lawrence without any notice of the black cloud gathering on the border to overwhelm her.

Let us consider this column of guerrillas strung out on the virgin prairies of Kansas, crawling toward Lawrence like a monstrous snake, creeping upon its prey. There were more than four hundred and fifty of them, as can be made out from the official reports, Gregg's count and the statement of Colonel Holt to Hon. H. S. Clarke.[5] Most of them had been in the guerrilla warfare of the border two years. Some of them had been in the old Kansas wars. These, as far back as 1855, had ravaged

Bill Anderson

Kansas settlements by the light of burning homes. Bill Anderson had lived on the Old Santa Fé Trail near Council Grove before the war and had stolen horses and cattle all along the Neosho Valley. His father met a violent death there in connection with a horse-stealing incident. A year before this raid he had carried the torch along the old trail and burned men alive in their homes. He was more savage than a mad wolf, and his men panted for blood. When he was killed he had, so it is said, the scalps of two women on the

is three miles west of the State-line and two miles north of the point where Quantrill entered Kansas. Gregg is in error as to the distance.

5 Edwards says Holt was with Quantrill at the inception of the raid, but this is not probable. He had been to Northern Missouri to recruit men for the Confederate army and was on his way out with them, and was not seeking service with Quantrill nor in Missouri. He fell in with Quantrill after he crossed the Blue, probably about Chapel Hill. Colonel Holt spent most of his time while at Lawrence at the front gate of the premises of H. S. Clarke; there he made his headquarters. He told Mr. Clarke that he had fallen in with Quantrill by accident after crossing the Blue and that Quantrill had invited him to come with him to Lawrence to get his men christened. He saved Mr. Clarke's life. Mr. Clarke had S. W. Brewster, Esq., Chanute, Kansas, publish an account of his experiences on the day of the Massacre, and a copy of the pamphlet is in the Collection of the author.

headstall of his bridle.[7] Some of the guerrillas were not lost to a sense of justice, but being in the warfare felt that they could not afford to be outdone by their rabid comrades. These would spare a life if they could do so without its becoming known to their companions. Many had opposed the raid and saw nothing to be gained by it. Colonel Holt's men had seen little of war, and most of them had committed no outrages and had suffered none. The venomous blood-rioters of the guerrilla band were under Bill Anderson and George Todd; these panted for blood, blood, blood. They lived only to murder. Next to these in ferocity stood the bands of Younger and Jarrette. Frank James had no band — never had one — but was with Younger. Jesse James had not yet joined the guerrillas and was not in the raid.

John Jarrette

These guerrillas were mounted on the best horses the country could produce. It is not probable that many of the guerrillas had horses that they had come by honestly. They were the best horsemen in America at that time, and as a mounted military organization perhaps the world has not surpassed that band of horsemen led by Quantrill to Lawrence.

The dress of the guerrillas was peculiar to themselves. It was entirely original. It was in a sense a uniform. Its distinguishing piece was an over-shirt — called the guerrilla shirt. This was the garment of all times, purposes, and occasions. It was to the guerrilla what the tartan is to the Highlander. It was cut low in front, the slit narrowing to a point above the belt and ending in a ruffle-bunch or rosette. This slit was usually bound or faced with some fabric of light weight and brilliant color, as were the pockets and sometimes the tail. The tails might be or might not be tucked into the trousers. Of pockets there were usually four of generous capacity — one on each breast and one on each side below like those in a coat, but there

7 Border Ruffian Troubles in Kansas, by Charles R. Green, p. 52.

was no strict rule on this point, the matter being determined by the whim of the
owner or the fancy of the maker. The
shirt was made from any cloth of sufficient weight that the guerrilla could lay
his hands upon. Their style admitted
some variety in cut, and in color they
ranged from the brilliant scarlet of red
flannel to the somber, subdued, and dis-
couraging hues of the homespun butter-
nut. They were usually made for the
guerrillas by their wives or sweethearts,
and some of them were elaborately ornamented with fine needlework and otherwise.

Jesse James

At the Lawrence Massacre, Quantrill wore a guerrilla shirt
made of brown woolen goods.

The arms of the guerrillas consisted principally of Colt's
navy revolvers of forty-four caliber. Some of them carried
cavalry carbines which they had captured, a few had Sharps's
rifles, and there were even shot-guns and old muskets among
them. The main reliance of the guerrilla, however, was upon
the revolver. And the guerrilla was usually a dead-shot either
afoot or on horseback. Quantrill became very expert with the
revolver. There has been much said about his teaching his men
to shoot by drilling them and insisting upon compliance with
some certain formula or routine of action. He did nothing of
the kind. He urged constant practice at first, but each man
could shoot as he liked if he shot well. Quantrill required
results in pistol-firing, and the guerrilla understood this art
much better than any other soldier. The powder-charge of the
Union soldier was made up for him and these charges were uniform in size. The guerrilla made up his own charge. He was
compelled to be economical of his ammunition. He discovered
that a small powder-charge enabled him to shoot much more
accurately than he could shoot with a heavy charge. His pistol
did not "bounce" when fired, and the aim was not spoiled.
And the ball ranged as far and penetrated as deeply as did that

fired with a heavy charge. Every guerrilla carried two revolvers, most of them carried four, and many carried six, some even eight. They could fire from a revolver in each hand at the same time. The aim was never by sighting along the pitsolbarrel, but by intuition, judgment. The pistol was brought to the mark and fired instantly, apparently without care, at random. But the ball rarely missed the mark — the center. Many a guerrilla could hit a mark to both the right and the left with shots fired at the same instant from each hand.

No more terrifying object ever came down a street than a mounted guerrilla wild for blood, the bridle-reins between his teeth or over the saddle-horn, the horse running recklessly, the rider yelling like a Comanche, his long unkempt hair flying wildly beyond the brim of his broad hat, and firing both to the right and left with deadly accuracy. When a town was filled with such men bent on death, terror ensued, reason and judgment fled, and hell yawned.[8]

---

8 Theodore Bartles was an early settler in Wyandotte county, Kansas. His father settled on the Leavenworth road in that county and established the "Six Mile House," for many years a famous hostelry. In the Civil War Theodore Bartles was a famous Union scout and a Red Leg. His brother, Jacob H. Bartles, was in the Sixth Kansas; he died at Dewey, Oklahoma, which town he founded. Bartlesville was founded by him and named for him.

The author knew Theodore Bartles many years — until his death. He was a famous shot with a revolver — had defeated Wild Bill (Hickock) in many a contest in markmanship. He and Wild Bill often scouted together.

More than once has the author gone to the woods about Old Quindaro with Bartles. He loved to shoot. He would fire two revolvers apparently at random at a nickel stuck on a tree distant thirty paces. There would be but one report, but in the fragments of the nickel would appear two holes made as though the balls had gone through it side by side and pressing against each other. The mark on the tree where the balls had entered would show similar impressions. With the revolver he could easily kill small song birds on the wing. He never "took aim," but fired instantly, seemingly in the most careless and indifferent manner. He has often related to the author an incident of the war. He was riding out the Leavenworth road one dark rainy night. On the "big fill" he was fired on by persons from below in the deep gulch. He saw the flash of the gun and fired several times, aiming where he had seen it. The next morning he returned there and found pools of blood all about and the tracks of men leading to the Missouri river where a boat had been moored. It seemed that he had killed or severely wounded one, who had been carried to the boat by the others, some of them wounded.

The author taught a term of school at the village of Tiblow, in Wyandotte county, in the winter of 1881-82. The place is now the thriving village of Bonner Springs. There was living near that place at the time an old Quantrill guerrilla under an assumed name. He was far gone with consumption and in deep poverty. The author spent some nights "sitting up" with him when he was bedfast and helpless. He often told of his war experiences and how he could shoot. Once he rallied and regained some of his strength. He rode his old white horse one day to a point where a telegraph pole stood near the public road. Here he produced his Colt's navy and gave the author an exhibition of his skill as a marksman. He would, on his old horse, charge down upon the telegraph pole firing rapidly as he approached it, emptying his revolver. The balls would all be placed exactly in the center of a crack running down the pole (made by the seasoning of the pole) at an equal distance apart. The difficulty of this feat will be better understood by remembering that these "seasoning" cracks follow the grain of the wood and rarely run straight up and down the pole.

He could hit the pole about three shots out of five by firing over his shoulder as his horse ran away from it. This man was at Lawrence. He denied that he did any killing there, and only admitted that he was there after long acquaintance with the author and a promise never to reveal his identy. For strange to say, he was an "Eastern man" and a pioneer in Kansas. What mysterious things may happen in bloody war!

THE REVOLVER

So general was the use of the revolver during the Civil War that a brief sketch of its origin and development may be of interest.

Revolvers were made by many manufacturers, and various styles were furnished, all, however, based on the models designed and patented by Colonel Samuel Colt, the inventor of the revolver idea.

Samuel Colt was born in Hartford, Conn., July 19, 1814; died in 1862. His father was a manufacturer, being largely engaged in spinning and weaving silk. The son worked in the silk mills under the good old New England rule that a boy should work six months of the year and go to school the other six months. But he was enterprising and restless, and while quite young, ran off to sea, shipping for Calcutta as boy before the mast on the *Corlo*. This voyage gave him a general knowledge of the world, and it was while handling the old bell-mouthed, brass-barreled, clubby firearms carried by the ship as a defense against pirates, that he con-

Colonel Samuel Colt,
Inventor of the Revolver

ceived the idea of the revolving cylinder containing chambers to be discharged through a single barrel. He whittled out a rough model, which he brought home with him, hoping to interest his father in the manufacture of the weapon. But in this he was disappointed. His idea was regarded with indifference and something of ridicule, and was believed to be wholly impracticable and useless. His was the fate of all inventors.

But Colt had the persistency of true genius. He was confident of ultimate success. In the years 1835 and 1836 he secured patents covering his invention, and in the latter year organized the ''Patent Arms company,'' which established a factory at Paterson, N. J. Having adopted the newly-discovered percussion cap instead of the old flint-lock, he found it hard to bring his weapon into public favor. The criticisms of his invention proved beneficial, however, and he labored diligently to overcome objections and perfect his models.

Colt's first financial success was in the Seminole War. He took a cargo of his revolvers to Florida, where they were enthusiastically received by the soldiers, and their use carried dismay to the Indian bands. The savages could not understand how so many shots were fired without reloading, and they pronounced the revolver ''big medicine.''

The ending of the war with the Seminoles destroyed the demand for revolvers. In looking about for a market it occurred to Colt that Texas might prove a good field. The surplus stock was sent there and sold, and the patriot army put them to such good use that to this day the Texan and his revolver are the terror of the Mexican. The independence of Texas was due in some considerable degree to the use of Colt's revolver.

On May 16, 1843, it was the principal factor in winning for the Texans a naval victory over the Mexican fleet, in honor of which a new model was designed by Colonel Colt, on the cylinder of which was engraved a representation of the naval battle. This was the

Colt's Navy,
The Deadly Weapon of the Border

origin of the famous ''navy'' pistol, perhaps the most popular and widely-known firearm ever made. It was the model used so generally by the soldiers on both sides in the Civil War. In the warfare of the border it was the principal weapon, and the guerrillas and other irregular forces rarely carried any other arm. Quantrill and his men never used anything but the Colt's navy, and their superior marksmanship came from the mastery and application of its principles. The pride to-day of the survivor of the Civil War is the Colt's navy revolver carried by him through that period of strife. The weapons were so honestly made that almost every one to be found is in good condition and would do good service after nearly fifty years of almost constant use. It can be safely said that no manufacturer ever turned out an article more conscientiously made than the arm made by Colonel Colt, a quality which is still found in all the products of the institution he founded.

Colonel Colt must be reckoned one of the great American inventors. The influence of his genius is felt to-day. The lore of the revolver has been the principal literature of the frontier, and sustains the prediction made by Colonel Colt that his pistol would make all men equal.

CHAPTER XXVI

IV

CAPTAIN PIKE reported that Quantrill crossed the State-line into Kansas five miles south of Aubry. The point is about three miles east and two miles south, following directly east and south courses. The original surveys of the land show an old road or trail leading west from Missouri towards that royal highway, the old Santa Fé Trail. Quantrill followed this old trail, then in constant use, to a point about two and a half miles south of Squiresville. There he halted and had his men feed their horses.[1] This camp must have been made on Section 18, Township 15, Range 24. The halt was made to enable the guerrillas to capture a Colonel Sims, who lived in that vicinity. Sims had been a strong Benton Democrat in Missouri, and he was on the death list carried by Quantrill. His absence from home saved his life, though the squad sent to murder him compelled Mrs. Sims to cook them a supper. The camp was just ten miles, by the trail, from the point where the guerrillas had crossed the State-line.

From this camp, when darkness had settled over the rolling prairies, Quantrill turned southwest and, in about two miles, struck Spring Hill, then a mere village on the trail.[2] There a

---

[1] *The Lawrence Massacre*, by Hovey E. Lowman, p. 42. This agrees with the *Gregg Manuscript*, which says: ''Dusk coming on, we halted, grazed our horses for half an hour, when we resumed our march.''

[2] Lowman, in his *The Lawrence Massacre* says that Quantrill marched from this camp in a northwesterly direction towards Gardner. This is, I think, a statement made without adequate information. *Gregg's Manuscript* says that the guerrillas passed through Spring Hill, and Gregg has often told the author that they went through Spring Hill. In his official report General Ewing says Captain Coleman struck Quantrill's trail at Spring Hill.

few soldiers were seen, but they were not molested, for Quantrill wished to avoid any act which would then alarm the people along the State-line.

From Spring Hill the line of march was almost directly northwest to Gardner, a small town on the Santa Fé Trail. The exact route between these points can not be fixed. It followed one of a number of trails sprawling over the prairies. The distance was about eight miles.

Most recent writers on the Lawrence Massacre speak of the moon as having been full at the time. The full moon would have made a night almost as light as day, for the weather was clear. But there was no full moon. Almanacs for 1863 show that in August there was a new moon on the 14th, a first quarter on the 22d, and a full moon on the 28th. On the night of the 20th the moon went down about 10 o'clock, from which hour until daylight of the 21st there was only starlight. In timber it is intensely dark in summer on such nights.

All accounts agree that it was about eleven o'clock at night when the guerrillas reached Gardner. Gregg says some Union soldiers were seen there, and not molested. The guerrillas were under peremptory orders not to break ranks or straggle, but a few at the rear fell out of the column. They stopped at the well of Mr. G. Rue to get water, where they said they were a part of Major Ransom's command on their way from Fort Scott to Lexington, Mo., though they inquired the way to Leavenworth. When they were well beyond the town a squad of fifteen returned to the village hotel, kept by a Mr. Cramer, and ordered a supper, which they ate, after which they exchanged, at the hotel stables, two of their exhausted horses for two fresh ones, promising to return the next day and get their own.[3]

The guerrillas followed the Santa Fé Trail about three miles west of Gardner to the point where the trail to Lawrence turned from it to the north. There it became necessary to have a guide. Quantrill knew the country, but there is found there a perfect maze of creeks, tributaries of Camp and Captain's creeks, and a false direction followed even a few miles might have involved the guerrillas in ruin. A guide was taken from

---

[3] *The Lawrence Massacre,* by Hovey E. Lowman, p. 43.

the nearest farm-house. In thirty minutes he was recognized as a former Missourian and promptly shot. Gregg says that in marching the next eight miles at least ten guides were shot. If a guerrilla found in any guide a resemblance to some one who had left Missouri he shot him down. And when a guide knew the road no longer he was shot.

The trail of the guerrillas turned north about Section 20, Township 14, Range 22. It crossed the head rivulets of Camp's creek and followed the high land between Camp and Captain's creeks some four or five miles. Captain's creek was crossed on the south part of Section 25, Township 13, Range 21, and then the trail turned sharply to the west, entering Douglas county from the west line of Section 26. From that point it bore to the north to strike the famous Blue-Jacket Crossing on the Wakarusa. There were then few fences and a multiplicity of trails leading in all directions, and an exact location of the trail at this date is impossible. It can be accurately located in certain places, however.[4] It passed the Friends' Meeting-house in the Quaker settlement west of Captain's creek, and its course was by the little settlement of Hesper, still to the west. Beyond the Blue-Jacket Crossing it followed the old and well-worn trail of the border-ruffians through Franklin to Lawrence.

Soon after leaving the Santa Fé Trail west of Gardner they came to the residence of Dr. Shean. He was on the death roll carried by Quantrill. The guerrillas knocked at his door but the quick apprehension by Mrs. Shean of the true character of the callers saved his life. She directed him to leave the house quietly by the rear door, at the same time assuring the bush-whackers that he would be down presently. This he did, concealing himself some distance away in a patch of high weeds. There he was sought by the guerrillas, who came near stepping on him several times.

At the intersection of the roads from Lawrence to Olathe and Gardner to De Soto lived a Mr. Myzee, a refugee from Missouri. He was roused to act as guide. Being almost blind, he

---

4 Lowman says that the only deviations from the main traveled road were across curves where distance could be saved. The roads have now been generally crowded over to section lines, and do not follow their original courses in many localities.

convinced the guerrillas he could not serve them in that capacity. Fortunately he was not recognized by any of the party and was not shot.

William Bentley lived on the east bank of Captain's creek near the crossing. He was a private in the Twelfth Kansas, and was not at home. Two of his comrades, on furlough, returning to their command, were stopping at his house that night. As they were giving final attentions for the night to their horses the guerrillas came up and engaged them in conversation, soon avowing their true character. One of the soldiers instantly ran into the brush and escaped with a wound in the wrist; the other surrendered and was at once murdered.

A mile west of Captain's creek the bushwhackers came to the house of William Bromelsick. Living with him was a Mr. Klingenberg. These Germans were refugees from Missouri, and their lives were forfeit to any guerrilla who might find them. The house was surrounded. The men were ordered to act as guides to Lawrence. They knew their danger. Bromelsick asked permission to tie his shoes, and it was granted. As he stooped for this purpose, he blew out the light in the hands of his wife, and sprang through the door, reaching a cornfield amidst a shower of balls, but uninjured. Klingenberg concealed himself under some rubbish, but was soon found and allowed to dress. A guerrilla took hold of each of his arms and led him into the yard. There, being a man of great size and strength, he shook off his captors and rushed to the friendly cover of the growing corn with no further mishap than several bullets through his clothing.

Captain A. J. Jennings, Company E, Twelfth Kansas Infantry, lived on the road where it is intersected by that leading south from Eudora. He owned a house on each side of the road. At that time he was at Fort Smith, Ark. Mrs. Jennings was not troubled beyond blustering threats and having to furnish vessels for taking water from the well to quench the guerrilla thirst.

In the second house lived Joseph Stone, a refugee from Missouri. In the house was his grown son and a boy named Jacob Rote. Stone's house was surrounded and loud knocking was accompanied by rough demands for admission. A guide to

Lawrence was wanted.   Here the guerrillas told for the last time that they were Union troops.   Mrs. Stone was not deceived by this misrepresentation, and knew that her husband and son would be murdered if once seen by the bushwhackers.   But she opened the door and began to plead excuses for Mr. Stone, saying that the weather was extremely hot and he had worked hard the day before and was in poor health.   She said that young Rote could serve them better, and they were about to accept him and allow Stone to remain at home, when George Todd came over from the Jennings house and ordered him brought out.   Todd recognized Stone as the man who had caused his arrest in Kansas City at the beginning of the war.   This announcement caused the guards to leave the rear door and come into the front yard. Stone's son now escaped from the house by the unguarded door and was soon safely concealed in an adjacent cornfield.

Todd wished to shoot Stone, but Quantrill said that there must be no more shooting, for they were nearing Lawrence and premature alarms must be guarded against.   Todd took Stone about a mile from his home, but finding no means of killing him, he sent back to the house for a rope with which to hang him. No rope being found, the resourceful messenger brought out an antiquated musket.   Todd seized this weapon and with it beat out the brains of the helpless prisoner.

The guerrillas entered the timber growing along the Little Wakarusa immediately after braining Stone.   There Quantrill's knowledge of the country asserted itself and he was suddenly familiar with every feature of it, and the remainder of the distance he led the way himself, but young Jacob Rote was carried mounted behind a guerrilla to be used should any emergency arise.   At the Blue-Jacket Crossing the crowing of cocks and the early notes of the birds admonished the guerrillas that daylight was at hand, and the horses were put to the trot. At Franklin the dawn was riding up the eastern sky and it was light enough to distinguish a citizen from a soldier, several of the latter crossing the street in front of the command, according to Gregg.[5]   The bushwhacker behind whom Rote was mounted

---

[5] Dr. R. L. Williams was living at Franklin. He was up when the guerrillas arrived in the town and saw them ride through it toward Lawrence. He did not know they were guerrillas, but he counted them. They

asked him if he knew in whose custody he was. Replying in the negative, he was told that the command was Quantrill's and that it was going to destroy Lawrence.

Day was rapidly breaking over the Kansas Valley. Some guerrilla was heard to complain that they were late and should "have been in Lawrence an hour ago." Quantrill threw his command into a column of fours and put it to the gallop. Reaching the summit of the rolling elevations between Franklin and Lawrence, Quantrill halted and sent Gregg with five men to feel out an entrance to the doomed city. He gazed down at many a familiar scene. Here he had kidnapped a free negro. There he had burned a house. Yonder he had counseled with his robber companions. Along those streets he had walked and plotted with stupid Dean. At this point he had been hard pressed by Sheriff Walker. Over that glittering river he had brought his stolen cattle. And still beyond lived the trustful Delawares whom he had wronged and robbed. In that court-house were papers which meant prison-terms for his black crimes. Now he was come as master, monster, avenger of his own grievances. A sense of gloating filled him. He grasped his death roll to make it sure. Without awaiting the return of Gregg he signaled the advance. The black cloud gathered there stirred and leaped forward. With shoutings, deep curses, horrible imprecations, demoniac yells, cries of savage exultation it swept down to a carnival of death and a gorge of innocent blood.

---

were in a column of fours, and he counted one hundred of these files of four. There were some scattered along the command, and he estimated the whole force at four hundred and fifty, almost the exact number. He heard a command — "to hurry up; we ought to have been in Lawrence an hour ago. Rush on, boys; it will be daylight before we are there." He noted that many of the guerrillas were attached to their saddles with straps to prevent their falling from their horses when asleep. Gregg says the command was thrown into a column of fours at Franklin and put to a gallop.

CHAPTER XXVII

V

WHY had Lawrence no warning of impending doom? Why came there no intelligence of stirring activity and sudden agitation in the coverts of the Blackwater, the Sni, the Little Blue? And why, after her seven years in the very jaws of death, did Lawrence hide her head under the delusive sands of fancied security and defenceless await the decrees of butchery planned and promulgated by skulking savagery beyond the border?

It was fate! There come times when men will not see, when they will not hear, when the alarm does not rouse them, when danger ceases to hold terror for them. In such times the senses are dulled, warnings are regarded with indifference, ominous incidents viewed with stolid incomprehension.

Early in the summer of 1863 the mayor of Lawrence made application to the military for a permanent garrison for his city. In response some twenty soldiers were sent under command of Lieutenant Hadley. This guard had dwindled to less than fifteen by the time of the raid, and strange to say, had been removed to the north side of the river, under Lieutenant Ellis, where no enemy was expected, and where it could not possibly render aid to Lawrence in case of emergency. Late in July, less than a month before the massacre, General Ewing secured information of the gathering of the guerrillas for the destruction of Lawrence. A small force was sent out to ride through the guerrilla country. It saw nothing and accomplished nothing. The mayor of Lawrence had received the same information, and for a few days some show of concern was manifest.

Lieutenant Hadley's brother, an officer on General Ewing's staff, wrote him that Quantrill would descend upon Lawrence at the time of the full moon in August. After the receipt of this letter the town was picketed and patroled for a short time. Cannon stood grim and threatening at strategic points. Before the coming of the full moon and the guerrillas the town had lapsed into indifference. The mayor assembled the guns at the armory and permitted none carried away by any of the volunteer defenders of the town.

The gathering of guerrilla hordes was reported to one of the border posts on the 15th day of August. A scout said that he had just come from guerrilla camps and that the rendezvous on the Blackwater was active with increasing forces designed for an attack on some Kansas town about the 20th. If this intelligence ever reached headquarters it was wholly disregarded.

We have mentioned the failure of Captain Pike to notify promptly the posts along the border of the presence of Quantrill at his camp and his neglect to take any steps to harrass or hinder the guerrilla band. C. S. Clark, Lieutenant-colonel Ninth Kansas Cavalry, was in command of the troops of the border south of Little Santa Fé (twelve miles north of Aubry), with headquarters at Coldwater Grove, Mo., (thirteen miles south of Aubry). Clark was incompetent, and his report shows that he did nothing in the pursuit of Quantrill and very little indeed to prevent his escape.

It is now known (and it was notorious at the time) that the force under General Ewing was woefully insufficient for the service required of it. It was deficient in men and equipment. These conditions, combined with the incompetency of Clark and Pike, produced a military paralysis in that part of the district where the highest efficiency was needed. The troops that did actually come up with Quantrill saw, while in the public square at Olathe, the smoke rise from the fires consuming Lawrence.

A number of individuals made heroic efforts to notify Lawrence of the approach of Quantrill. Fate stopped them all.

When the guerrillas had gone from her house, Mrs. Jennings determined to send tidings to Lawrence if possible. With her servant girl and children she went to the home of William Guest, who lived half a mile to the north. Guest would not believe her story and she could not prevail on him to go to Lawrence. Henry Thompson, a negro, who was working for Guest, offered to go if Guest would furnish a horse for him to ride. This Guest refused to do. Thompson then set forth afoot to do the best he could for the doomed city, and Mrs. Jennings returned home. Frederick Pilla, a justice of the peace at Eudora, had been down the Lawrence-Olathe trail to perform a marriage ceremony, and, returning long after midnight, came upon Thompson on his way to Eudora. Thompson soon told his story. Pilla hurried to Eudora and cried an alarm. The citizens gathered at the block-house and heard the account of the passing of Quantrill. Volunteers to go to Lawrence were called for, and three responded — David Kraus, the city marshal, Casper Marfelius, and Jerry Reel. Kraus was thrown from his horse before getting beyond the village limits, but, being behind the others, they did not notice his absence. He went no further, and never fully recovered from the injuries of the fall.

Reel and Marfelius rode rapidly in the direction of Lawrence. It was necessary for them to reach the intersection of the Eudora and Franklin roads ahead of Quantrill, and the dawn began to appear. Reel was mounted on a fine Kentucky mare that he called "Crow" as she bore the color of that swift and wary bird. Just as day was breaking the black mare stumbled and fell, her gallant rider under her, crushed and wounded unto death. Marfelius got the mare to her feet, moved the unconscious Reel to the roadside, and hurried to a farm-house for succor for the stricken man. But by the time aid was secured Quantrill was entering Lawrence. Reel died of his injuries the following day.[1]

Perhaps the most heroic effort to save the doomed city was made by a Shawnee Indian named Pelathe.[2] He rode into Kansas City near midnight with the courier of Captain Coleman

[1] This account is taken from the article published by Frederic William Hinsey in the *Kansas City Star*. Hinsey gathered his information carefully, and his article is an excellent one. The author has drawn from it in the account of the advance of Quantrill upon Lawrence, for particular incidents. In a letter of recent date to the author, Oscar G. Richards, of Eudora, says these men did not start to Lawrence until after it was destroyed. Dr. Cordley, in his excellent accounts of the Massacre, says some efforts to warn Lawrence were made, but ended in disaster. He may have had this in mind.

[2] Pĕ-la-thé, the Eagle.

from Little Santa Fé. Theodore Bartles was at General Ewing's headquarters when he arrived. Bartles was one of the most efficient scouts in the service and a famous Red Leg. He heard the story of the courier and said at once that Quantrill was going to Lawrence. Learning that no one had been sent to warn the town, so far as the courier knew, Bartles raged against the

stupidity of the officers of the various posts. He thought seriously of trying to reach Lawrence ahead of Quantrill, but when he remembered that the journey would have to be made on the north side of the Kansas River to avoid the guerrillas, he thought it could not be done. When he determined not to go the Shawnee expressed a desire to try it. Bartles had known him a few months, and knew him to be a good horseman, a daring and hardy man thoroughly familiar with the country through which he would ride.

Pelathe, the Shawnee

Bartles took the Shawnee to the Six Mile House, two miles west of Quindaro. He believed it impossible for the Shawnee to reach Lawrence ahead of Quantrill, but he was willing that he should make the effort. In those days Bartles had the best horses to be found, and he led from the corral a sorrel mare, a Kentucky thoroughbred of speed and bottom. It was past one o'clock when the Shawnee, heavily armed, but garbed as an Indian, mounted to race against fate.

At first the Indian rode leisurely. He knew the prairies and timber-clumps, the streams and where to cross them. He kept to no single beaten way. In an hour he was going at terrific speed. The mare was moving easily in long, regular strides, her neck straightened and her nose thrown well forward.

For another hour the noble animal held her pace, but her breath was coming hard, and he thought best to pull her in for a momentary rest.

The Shawnee dismounted, removed the folded blanket used in lieu of saddle, and, with a large red handkerchief from about his neck, he rubbed dry her limbs, her quivering flanks, her neck, her head. He led her gently along that she might not become stiff or chilled. At a pool in the bed of a stream he cleansed her mouth of foam and allowed her to drink a little water. Leading her to the summit of a prairie swell and finding her rested and much refreshed he replaced the light blanket, mounted, and was away.

The mare soon pushed her speed to the limit. She had found her second wind. She moved freely in the long springy reaches of the perfect racer. The prairie swam by in the soft light of the brilliant summer stars. Miles melted under the steady hoof-beats of the splendid runner. Hours were passing. Rounding a long sweep of the winding trail he saw far to the southwest the black line that marked the broad woodland beyond which lay Lawrence, and he knew that if his faithful mare could but hold her pace another hour he would save the city. But could she do it? Making a long ascent, she fell to a slower gait, and at the top she faltered. Her flanks heaved and her breathing was heavy. She was failing. She had done her best. Her wonderful powers of endurance were spent.

The Shawnee was a man of resource. He was racing with Death. No sacrifice was too great if it would but give him the goal. Perhaps he might yet snatch victory from this desperate extremity. He decided to offer up the noble animal which had served him so faithfully. With his long knife he cruelly gashed her reeking shoulders. Into the wounds he rubbed gunpowder from his pistol-charges. She bounded madly forward for a few miles, plunged violently, stopped suddenly, reared, and, with a cry of protest almost human, pitched forward dead.

The Shawnee leaped from the falling mare and sprang away on the trail. He ran with that swiftness for which his race is famous. As the dawn touched and tinged the sky-line he saw far down the dim forest aisles the cabins of the Delawares. To alarm them he sounded the quavering war-cry. From an enclosure he took an Indian pony and recklessly rode for the Lawrence ferry. As the golden sunshine flooded the land he reached the goal only to hear the rising roar of battle and find the city doomed.

In the race with Death the Shawnee had ridden well but had lost![3]

---

[3] This story I had from Bartles. It was confirmed by some of the Shawnees I knew, among them Chief Charles Blue-Jacket. Bartles saw him at the State-line on the 22nd of August in the pursuit of the guerrillas. He and some fifteen or twenty Delawares under Chief White Turkey crossed over to Lawrence by the first boat, which was when Quantrill began his retreat.   They were among the best of the pursuers, entering Missouri. Mounted on their tough ponies, they acted on their own initiative and cut off many a straggler. And no doubt they scalped every dead guerrilla they found.

Blue-Jacket gave me the story of the Shawnee's death. Soon after the Lawrence Raid he returned to Fort Smith. In the winter of 1863-64 he was sent on many desperate journeys, one of which proved his last. Some of Stand Watie's band followed him two days, finally coming upon him in a rough and hilly part of the Cherokee Nation west of Fayetteville, Ark. In his last stand he killed three Cherokees and wounded a number.

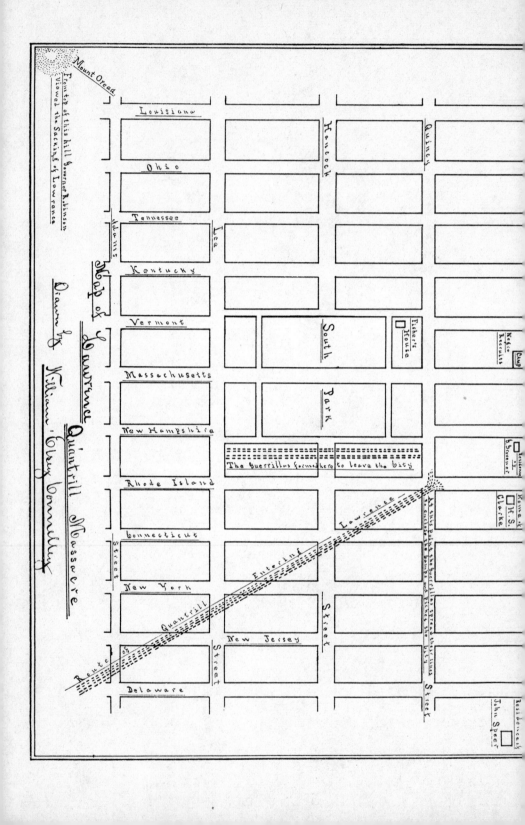

Mount Oread

From top of this hill Governor Robinson Viewed the Sacking of Lawrence

Map of Lawrence

Drawn by

Quantrill Massacre

William Cleary Connelley

Louisiana

Ohio

Tennessee

Kentucky

Vermont

Massachusetts

New Hampshire

Rhode Island

Connecticut

New York

New Jersey

Delaware

Adams

Lea

Street

Street

Street

Hancock

Quincy

South

Park

Street

Quincy

Fisher's House

The Guerrillas formed here to leave the City

Negro Recruits

CAMP

Residence of Governor

Kentucky

Lawrence

Entering

Quantrill

Route of

At this Point the Guerrillas Spread their Lines, one on each side, to Burn and Sack the City

Street

H. S. Clarke

Residence of John Speer

CHAPTER XXVIII

THE LAWRENCE MASSACRE

VI

IN 1863 Lawrence was a city of about two thousand people.[1]
When the guerrillas halted on the elevation overlooking
Lawrence many of them hesitated in their purpose to enter
the town. It must be remembered that there was an element
in the command opposed to the raid and its object, and this
element included some of the captains. Quantrill had ordered
Lieutenant Gregg to take five men and enter the city to ascertain
what force there was to oppose them. Without awaiting the
return of this party Quantrill rode along the ranks and said:

[1] The principal authorities on the Lawrence Massacre are as follows:
Narrative of the Lawrence Massacre; by Hovey E. Lowman, Lawrence, 1864, pamphlet of 96 pp. Very scarce. There is a manuscript copy
in the Collection of the author, who also made a manuscript copy and filed
it in the library of the Kansas State Historical Society. Lowman was
a native of New York, lived in Lawrence, and was editor of the *Lawrence Journal* after the massacre. The work was published in weekly in-
stallments in a newspaper. It ends abruptly and is incomplete. It is said
that for financial reasons the last signature was never printed in form
for the pamphlet. It is fair and temperate in statement, is without
prejudice or feeling, and is a full statement of fact. There are a few
errors in it, but it is by far the best authority on what occurred in the
city that has yet been published.

The Lawrence Massacre; by J. S. Boughton; a small pamphlet of 36
pp., published at Lawrence by the author, without date.

A History of Lawrence, Kansas, to the Close of the Rebellion; by
Rev. Richard Cordley, Lawrence, 1895; contains a good account of the
Massacre.

Pioneer Days in Kansas; by Rev. Richard Cordley, Boston, 1903, also
contains a good account. Mr. Cordley was the Congregational minister at
Lawrence at the time of the Massacre and escaped with his life, but his
house was burned. He was one of the pioneer preachers of Kansas, and
left his impress on the state. He died at Lawrence in 1908.

Reminiscences of Quantrill's Raid upon the City of Lawrence, Kansas;

"You can do as you please. I am going into Lawrence." He spurred forward, and the guerrillas followed him to a man, though one cried aloud: "We are lost!" At the residence of Mr. Hanscom, in the southeast part of the city, two of the horsemen returned to report. Two men were sent along a path leading northwest about a hundred rods, to the house of Rev.

by John C. Shea, Kansas City, Mo., 1879, a pamphlet of 27 pp. It was written as a series of letters to the *Chicago Times* in the summer of 1875, and is exceedingly rare, the copy in the Collection of the author being the only known copy. There is a manuscript copy in the library of the State Historical Society, made and filed there by the author of this work.

Life of Gen. James H. Lane; by John Speer, Garden City, Kansas, 1897; published by the author. It contains a good chapter on the Massacre.

Incidents of Quantrell's Raid on Lawrence; by Hon. Henry S. Clarke, Lawrence, Kansas, 1898; a pamphlet of 17 pp. The work was written by S. W. Brewster, Chanute, Kansas, and describes the remarkable personal experiences of Mr. Clarke the day of the Massacre. It is accurate and very valuable, and is now quite scarce. Mr. Clarke was a pioneer in Lawrence, was sheriff of Douglas county, and a man of force and character. He died in January, 1908. The author knew him well and had many interviews with him, one about a week before his death.

Border Ruffian Troubles in Kansas; by L. D. Bailey, Lyndon, Kansas, 1899. A pamphlet of 101 pp. It is a series of letters written for the *Garden City Sentinel* in 1887, and was published in its present form by Charles R. Green. Judge Bailey was in Lawrence at the time of the Massacre, and his account is valuable.

The Gregg Manuscript; by Captain William H. Gregg, written for the author of this work and now in his Collection. Very valuable. Has never been published. Covers all the Civil War period.

Noted Guerrillas; by Major John N. Edwards. This work is well known. It passed through many editions and was published in various forms. Major Edwards wrote splendidly, but his object was to justify outlawry and glorify outlaws. He was extreme and unfair, and his work was long since repudiated. It was not satisfactory even to the guerrillas. It contains the false statements made by Quantrill to the Missourians, much embellished and enlarged.

The Gun and the Gospel; by Rev. H. D. Fisher, Chicago, 1897. This is the second edition. The escape of Dr. Fisher from the guerrillas was wonderful beyond belief. His book is one of the best authorities on pioneer times in Kansas.

The Kansas Conflict; by Charles Robinson, Lawrence, 1898; contains a page or two on the Massacre. The book was written as a personal defense of the author and to defame all who did not agree with him. It is full of bitterness, malice, abuse, denunciation, and, beyond the docu-

S. S. Snyder, a lieutenant in the Second Colored Regiment. They found him in his cow-yard milking and shot him. He was the first man to fall that day in Lawrence.[2]

At this halt orders were issued by all the captains that women and children were under no circumstances to be molested, and these orders included negro women and children.

There were two camps in Lawrence, that of the white recruits (for the Fourteenth Kansas Regiment) being situated near the center of the block bounded by Warren, Berkeley, Massachusetts, and New Hampshire streets. The camp of the recruits for the Second Colored Regiment, who had been enlisted by Rev. S. S. Snyder, was on the southwest corner of Berkeley and Massachusetts streets.[3] Lieutenant Gregg came upon the

---

ments reprinted in it, has little or no value. As an authority it discredits itself and is wholly unreliable. It puts John Brown, Abraham Lincoln, James H. Lane, P. B. Plumb, and other prominent men in Territorial times and the Civil War, in the same class and sets them down as tricksters, liars, thieves, and blacklegs.

[2] Many of the guerrillas carried lists of the names of men they wished to kill in Lawrence, and there was a list made by the officers. In some instances the lists carried by individuals were copied from the general list. Many citizens heard these lists read off and saw them consulted when the guerrillas were inquiring for certain parties.

[3] The camps were about three hundred feet apart. In the negro camp there were about twenty recruits, most of whom escaped. They had not been armed or uniformed, and they scattered at the first sound of the firing and escaped general slaughter. The location of this camp was given the author by C. L. Edwards and G. Grovenor, May 14, 1909. Mr. Grovenor believes all the colored recruits were killed, but reliable negroes, among them the late Andrew Williams, of Topeka, say that almost all of them escaped. Williams lived in Lawrence at the time and escaped by running into the willow thickets along the river. Some thirty negroes got together in the dense jungle on the river bank two miles east of Lawrence, where they remained until late in the afternoon. Williams was there, and he said about half the colored recruits were there, having run at the sound of the first pistol and the sight of Gregg's party firing on the white camp.

The Methodist church was afterwards built on the site of the colored camp, and it stands to-day, though not used for services now.

The site of the camp of the white recruits was located by G. Grovenor and other pioneers of Lawrence. The citizens of Lawrence have marked the site of this camp with a granite tablet on which is inscribed: "*Here near a Score of Unfortunate Recruits were shot August 21, 1863.*" This

22

camp of the white recruits. Some of them were asleep on the
porches of residences, and on these the guerrillas opened fire
while waiting for the main body to come up. The guerrilla
command rode northwest across lots to the intersection of
Quincy and Rhode Island streets, where files left the ranks to
picket the town, eleven men being sent to the top of Mount
Oread to keep a lookout for pursuing troops. The lines opened
to enclose a clump of residences and the two camps. Before
Quantrill came up with Gregg, a young man (about eighteen,
Gregg says) in full uniform, with a young lady, both on horseback, came by. Gregg saw this young man killed and the woman
turned back into the city.[4]

---

tablet is too far east, being between the sidewalk and curb on the west
side of New Hampshire street, in front of house Nos. 933 and 935. The
camp was west of this about a hundred feet, and was a little more to the
north. H. S. Clarke locates it on the rear of lots 80 and 82, Massachusetts street, which is about the proper place.

    4 Gregg believes this couple to have been Miss Sally Young and her
escort, but it could not have been. It must have been young Collamore,
son of the mayor, who was shot in sight of H. S. Clarke, though Clarke
does not mention that he was accompanied by a young lady. If it was
Collamore, Captain Gregg is mistaken as to his death; he was wounded
and left for dead but recovered. The party of Miss Young consisted of
herself and Steve Horton, and Miss ''Nin'' Beck and John Donnelly.
They had ridden to the Wakarusa, it is said, before daylight, and saw
the guerrillas first near Franklin, but supposed they were Union troops.
There are various accounts of the escape of the young men, one of which
says they entered the town after the ladies had gone in and after the pickets had been placed. They were met by Miss Young and told that the
town was held by Quantrill. She urged them to ride slowly and
carelessly and try to get away, which they did, only one guerrilla
following them a short distance. In other accounts Miss Young
and Donnelly only are mentioned. They saw the guerrillas when
south of the city, and when approached the young lady told Donnelly to
run for his life, which he did, making his escape, though closely pursued.
He told Shea that his horse saved his life, and that he was chased out
of two cornfields, someting not very probable. Miss Young returned to the
city and went boldly among the guerrillas and saved several people from
death. She was suspected of having been in league with the guerrillas,
was arrested and taken to Fort Leavenworth for court-martial, but no
evidence being produced against her, she was discharged. Dr. Cordly does

When the guerrilla command arrived at the camp Gregg
pointed to the tents and fell in beside Quantrill, the two turning

not mention either of these riding parties in his books, a significant omis-
sion.

No information as to what became of Miss Beck has been secured.
It is still believed that she was a spy. No account of her after meeting
the guerrillas has been found. This whole matter got into politics in
after years, and the following broadside was anonymously printed and
openly circulated. As it contains the only known recorded reference to
Miss Beck, it is believed necessary to preserve it. The copy in the Collection of the author is the only one known to be in existence:

VOTERS! READ AND CONSIDER!

Can Lawrence forget the wrongs that were done
By men in her midst when the war had begun?
Shall her envy be buried with her fallen and true,
And pardon be offered for the traitor to blue?
Shall Lawrence forget her block-house and gun,
Planted on her streets, because victory is won?
Shall the men in her midst who favored the grey,
Ever by the loyal be favored to-day?
Shall she give him an office of honor and trust,
Though all of his friends may claim it but just?
Shall she give up her honor and favor a man,
Who fought for slavery, and favored the klan
That murdered her citizens, and burned up her town?
And even to-day looks upon Lawrence with a frown?
Shall Griswold, and Trask, and poor L. L. Jones,
Lying in their graves, have disgrace to their bones,
By electing to office a man who was opposed
To the principles of freedom causing death unto those?
Shall we trust those officials, and elect them again,
Who've acted unfairly in assessing those men,
Which gave them their office of honor and trust,
Believing their assessments would be honest and just?
But assessors have friends the same as had Tweed,
Who help to form rings to fatten their greed;
Yes! Friends are quite plenty, yet WALTER and NACE,
Are trumps that are added to YOUNG who's an ace
With corruption in office, and with rings to elect
The DEMOCRATIC BROTHER, who was along with "NIN" BECK.
SHALL THE MAN WHOSE SISTER DID LEAD THE VILE CREW,
Into Lawrence, to murder the friends of the true,
Be favored with the best which the county affords,
Instead of a man whose ARM with its sword,
Was lost in the south in defending the right?
Shall this be forgot, and so soon lost to sight?
No! let us be free from this dirty mess:
Oh! Give us a clean and unspotted dress:
We fought for the right and victory we won;
Let us not forget till the last rising sun,
The men who opposed, and sought us to slay,
Because, forsooth, we were fighting the grey.

into Massachusetts street. The captains led a charge on the camp. There were twenty-two recruits, all uniformed, but not armed, mostly boys just old enough to enlist. They had not been drilled, and it is said they had just called in their guard, but it is quite probable that they had not placed a guard. The guerrillas rode down the tents, trampling everything to earth, shooting the surprised and bewildered recruits. In three minutes, Gregg says, there was not a tent standing or a soldier alive there. Five escaped as by a miracle.[5] H. S. Clarke saw a guerrilla take the flag which had floated over the camp and tie it to his horse's tail and gallop away, the flag dragging in the dust and being torn to shreds. This man was Larkin Skaggs, killed later in the day.[6] One of the boys from the camp reached Clarke's house; he had been shot at a dozen times. In the street in plain view of Clarke a bullet struck him and brought him to his knees. He called out with his hands held up: "For God's sake don't murder me, men." A brutal and vulgar reply, a pistol shot, and the stripling fell back in the dust dead. Clarke saw another boy running from a bearded guerrilla who was firing at him every bound of his horse. The little fellow reached a house, ran in, and quickly came out on the other side with citizens' clothes on; he walked slowly away and escaped, passing the guerrilla, who was waiting for him to reappear in his blue clothes. Another boy was shot and killed within fifteen feet of Clarke's door.

Quantrill and Gregg galloped up Massachusetts street, Quantrill firing to the left and Gregg firing to the right until they reached the river. Opposite the Eldridge House, as they returned, a man dressed in the uniform of a Federal major appeared in the street. Quantrill said: "Get that major." Gregg charged after him but he ran into the livery stable fronting south on Winthrop street, near Mas-

---

[5] Lowman says but four escaped — eighteen killed. Cordley and Boughton say seventeen were killed. No mention is made of the camp by Shea. Clarke says there were twenty-one recruits and a crippled boy who worked about the camp, and that seventeen, including the cripple, were killed.

[6] There was a high flagstaff at the upper end of Massachusetts street, or in that vicinity, on which was a large flag. This flag was also cut down and tied to the tail of a guerilla's horse and dragged through the streets.

sachusetts street, and closed and barred the door. Gregg did not see him again. Having shot out his pistols, Gregg stopped

in front of the barn, threw his leg over the horn of his saddle and proceeded to reload, and while so engaged the main body of guerrillas arrived in front of the Eldridge House. At the camp, when the tents were prostrate and the recruits dead, there had risen over the roar of battle the cry "On to the hotel," in response to which the column thundered up Massachusetts street, slim files going up New Hampshire and Vermont streets to prevent citizens from escaping from the rear of the business houses on the main thoroughfare.

Captain William H. Gregg

CAPTURE OF THE ELDRIDGE HOUSE

The night before the Massacre there had been a meeting in the Eldridge House in the interest of the Kansas Pacific Railroad. This meeting had brought to Lawrence people from different towns, and the hotel was crowded.

The Eldridge House was built of brick and was four stories high. Iron trimmings adorned the front, giving it a formidable appearance. There the guerrillas expect-
ed resistance. They filled the street in front — dust-begrimed, bearded, clad in the guerrilla shirt, pistols drawn and cocked, growling and muttering oaths and threats as crackling pistol-shots resounded from adjacent streets. There seemed a lack of concert of action, and some indecision. At the sound of the huge gong beaten through the halls to arouse the sleeping guests, they fell away from the building to the opposite sides of the streets, supposing it a signal for the inmates to gather for resistance. At that moment a deadly volley fired from the

Colonel S. W. Eldridge

hotel windows would have saved the town many a life and many a dollar.

Captain Alexander R. Banks was provost marshal of Kansas at the time and was living at the hotel. He was awakened by the firing, and on looking from his window saw the streets filled with guerrillas. He consulted with many of the beleagured guests as to what should be done. Some advised that nothing be done and that events be allowed to take their course. Others believed it would be best to surrender the hotel if the safety of the prisoners could be guaranteed. Knowing the desperate character of the guerrillas, Captain Banks accepted the latter view. Taking a sheet from his bed he waved it from his window in token of surrender, and called for Quantrill.

A spare man making a fine figure on horseback rode forward as the exultant shouts of the guerrillas rose on the wings of the morning. He was magnificently mounted, his horse having been taken from Buel at the battle of Independence, a brown gelding of fine size and proportions. He wore a low-crowned, soft, black hat with a yellow or gold cord around it for a band, cavalry boots, into which gray trousers were stuffed, and a guerrilla shirt of brown woolen, ornamented with fine needlework, and made for him by some devoted daughter of the South. He was sun-beaten and unshaven, but without a beard. In his belt were four Colt's navy pistols, and in holsters at his saddle-bow were more formidable weapons.

That was Quantrill, come now to avenge the fruits of his own crimes on a defenseless town and an innocent people — a community he had disgraced by a career as black as midnight.

He inquired if the display of the white flag meant a surrender of the hotel. When Captain Banks replied that it did if he could have a guarantee for the safety of the prisoners, another shout of triumph rose from the guerrilla ranks. They knew the town was at their mercy.[7] Turning to his men he rose in his stirrups, dismissed the greater part of them to over-

---

[7] C. M. Chase, at that time working on the *True Republican and Sentinel*, at Sycamore, Ills., was making a tour of the West. He arrived at Lawrence on the morning of the 22d, and wrote a letter to his paper describing the Massacre. In this letter he says:

A boarder waved a white flag from the balcony and inquired for Quantrill, who soon appeared, and the following colloquy took place: ''What

spread the city, ending with this order, "Kill! kill! and you will make no mistake! Lawrence should be thoroughly cleansed, and the only way to cleanse it is to kill! kill!"[8]

Quantrill and some of his men came at once into the hotel. He announced that the building would be burned. The guests were assembled and systematically robbed — both men and women. The work of pillaging the hotel began. Guards were set, Quantrill taking station on the second step down the stairway leading from the second floor, upon which were the offices, the street floor being occupied by stores. There he was seen by Judge Bailey, a guest who had just been robbed. A resident of the town, one Spicer, was leaning over a banister, talking to him, recalling better times and reminding him he was Charley Hart then. With a look that chilled further familiarity, he said it mattered not what he was called, and Spicer drew away from danger. Three strangers refused the guerrillas admission to their chamber, and a number of shots were fired through the door; one of them was wounded, and they came out and were robbed.

When the hotel had been plundered and the inmates all robbed, Quantrill stationed a guard on the stairs leading to the second floor and left the building. He secured a white team and a buggy and drove about the town, going to the top of Mount Oread.[9] Guerrillas began to crowd the stairs and express dissatisfaction at the terms accorded the prisoners. They

___

is your object in coming to Lawrence?" (Quantrill) "Plunder." (Balcony). "We are defenseless and at your mercy, the house is surrendered, but we demand protection for the inmates."

Later, Quantrill said he "was surprised that his men were murdering people, but said they had got into the saloons, got drunk and beyond his control. He came to destroy the town and plunder its wealth, in retaliation for Lane burning Osceola."

The statement that Quantrill was surprised that his men were murdering must have been made by Chase on erroneous information, and would seem to cast doubt on the account written by him. Here, too, is the only recorded statement that Quantrill said he was destroying Lawrence in retaliation for the burning of Osceola.

Chase was afterwards local editor of the *Leavenworth Daily Times*.

8 Quoted from the *Gregg Manuscript*.

9 Told the author by the late Frank C. Montgomery, who was a boy and living in Lawrence at the time. He saw Quantrill as he drove about the town in this buggy. Quantrill left the buggy and walked about on Mount Oread, looking over many a familiar scene.

had broken open the liquor shops and many of them were drunk. The scenes of carnage had made them blood-mad. The guard stood true to his orders, but the prisoners began to fear that he could not long afford them protection. The buildings on all sides were on fire. Captain Banks and R. S. Stevens became convinced that the guerrillas would finally murder the prisoners, and they sent for Quantrill. In five minutes he appeared, his whole demeanor changed. It was apparent that he had repented his merciful terms, and that he would not be bound by his agreement. Perhaps his captains had protested against sparing these prisoners. When he entered he demanded to know who had sent for him, when Stevens stepped forward and said he was the man. Stevens had defended him at Lecompton for crimes committed in Douglas county three years before. He soon secured a renewal of the promise of protection. Banks said the building was on fire and the prisoners could not long remain there. Quantrill offered to permit them to go into the street, to which Banks objected, saying that it would be folly for them to go there or any other place without a sufficient guard. Quantrill then said they might go to the City Hotel which he was protecting, but Banks would not lead out the prisoners until guards were detailed. The guerrillas present objected to the disposition made of the prisoners and fired into them, killing one, a half-witted man. George Todd was given charge of the prisoners, and, clearing the way, ordered them to march out.

The City Hotel, sometimes called the Whitney House, was a frame building on New Hampshire street, south of Pinckney street, fronting south and east, and was one block east and almost a block north of the Eldridge House. It was kept by Captain

Nathan Stone, who had often befriended Quantrill when he was both border-ruffian and Jayhawker at Lawrence. He had, at Quantrill's request, furnished Dean and Southwick a wagon in which to drive to Morgan Walker's, and neither team nor wagon ever came back from Missouri.

Stone's Hotel, where the Prisoners were kept

As a member of the grand jury, Stone had told Quantrill of impending indictments, enabling him to conceal himself from the vigilance of Sheriff Walker. When the prisoners were on New Hampshire street a drunken guerrilla rode up and began shooting into their ranks, but was driven off by Todd. Soon Quantrill appeared, riding upon the left, and in a loud voice assured them of protection, ending with the statement *"That Old Man Stone in times past had done him a kindness, and he would be damned to hell if a hair of his head should be injured."* When the prisoners had entered the City Hotel, a guard was thrown around it, and Quantrill established his headquarters there.

CHAPTER XXIX

VII

WHEN the guerrillas were sent from the Eldridge House, upon its surrender, with orders to "Kill! kill!" they burst upon the town a perfect storm of fire and death. A cordon had been thrown about the city and every avenue of escape closed. The survivors of that awful day said that guerrilla guards seemed to rise out of the ground, so quickly and thoroughly were they stationed. The command separated into squads and bands, each under its own captain. Fiery liquors from plundered shops were poured down thirsty throats, and the band became a drunken mob. Demoniac yells rose above the crackling of pistol-shots. Hundreds of flags were secured from a book-store and tied to the tails of horses on which drunken guerrillas rode recklessly through the principal streets firing wildly and shouting in exultation for Quantrill, Jeff Davis, and the Southern Confederacy. Other bands bent on murder went about their business with method and dispatch. Victims were sought in homes, in shops, about the streets, in gardens, ravines, and fields of growing corn. Terror was carried to every heart. Women with disheveled and flowing hair clung desperately to husbands or brothers to shield them from the fury of the bushmen from beyond the border. Sometimes they were rudely flung aside with savage threats to save them injury from the bullet that bereaved them. When the deadly revolver was thrust between husband and wife she was deluged with blood following the muffled report that made her a widow. Fires were kindled in dwellings and shops and flames leaped and roared through all the streets and ways, consuming sometimes the living — often the dead. Shrieks of distress and cries of despair could be heard above the uproar and tumult raging in the city. Hell was loosed and the pent wrath and mad fury nursed for years by border-ruffians against Lawrence ran bloody riot in the pandemonium of that awful day.

Of the personal experiences, miraculous escapes, horrible deaths, effective appeals, touches of human nature, even ludicrous incidents, a volume could be made from what is preserved.

Joseph Savage lived three-quarters of a mile southeast of Lawrence on the road over which the guerrillas came. He says[1] they passed his house at early dawn — "in the gray twilight — a sort of heavy dense atmosphere such as precedes earthquakes — the air seemed ominous and sounds were all audible a long way off — a murky air." He was standing in his yard when he saw them thirty rods away, but supposed them Union troops, and went into the house to bathe his eyes, which were somewhat inflamed. A loud knocking on the front door told him some one desired admittance, but he waited to wipe his eyes. When he reached the door a man on horseback was passing out at the front gate and he joined his comrades just as an order to "double-quick" was given. As he turned into the ranks he was loudly laughed at for his failure to kill Savage, who stood looking at them, and they at him. He describes them thus: "Low-crowned, broad-brimmed hats — all alike nearly — unshaven — stoop-shouldered — all without coats — nearly all wore red flannel shirts much begrimed with camp-grease and dirt —

Joseph Savage

saw only two or three guns." Savage estimated their number at two hundred. They had thrown away their coats, knowing they would get new ones at Lawrence, which they did, making the clerks fit them out from top to toe, and often shooting the clerks after they had done so. Ten minutes after they passed his house Savage saw fires rising about the Eldridge House. When

---

[1] Letter to W. W. Scott, Jan. 22, 1879, now in the Collection of the author. There are other letters written by him to Scott in the Collection, dated Dec. 11, 1878, Jan. 29, 1879, and Feb. 11, 1879, as well as two cards, dated Jan. 25, 1879, and Jan. 16, 1883.

the flames appeared, it dawned on him that it was a guerrilla force he had seen. He harnessed his horse in a hurry, and his wife took her spoons and silk dress, and he took his "horn," as he was a musician, and they started to the country. A mile out they ran into a patrol in the act of shooting his neighbor, he crying piteously, and they damning him for running from them. Savage jumped from the buggy and by crawling, tumbling, sometimes running, he got into a field of growing corn. After shooting the neighbor the guerrillas came to the buggy, and said they did not want spoons or dresses, but wanted money, of which Mrs. Savage had none. They said the "horn" had been playing for Yankees, they expected, and smashed it by beating it over the fence. The hired man, a half-witted German, who had been driven from Texas, was made to get out of the buggy, but he looked so stupid and so appealingly that, at Mrs. Savage's pleading, they spared him, saying he was not worth a load of powder and lead. Savage remained in the cornfield until ten o'clock when he went to a house and got something to eat, after which he went into the city to aid in gathering up the dead. This was the saddest work he ever did. Mourning and wailing filled the streets and those houses left standing. The services at the churches on Sunday were prayers only — no singing or preaching.

Savage believed Quantrill better than his men, saying that it would have been much worse for Lawrence if Quantrill had not been along.

John Laurie and William Laurie, brothers, were killed in the presence of the wife of the latter. They lived on a farm twenty miles from Lawrence, and drove to the town in the afternoon of the 20th to transact some business there on the 21st. Hearing the firing they became panic stricken and ran from point to point only to find every avenue of escape closed. The guerrillas soon wounded them and both lay on the ground unable to rise. The pistols of the ruffians were empty, and as they were reloaded, Mrs. William Laurie begged on her knees with her babe in her arms that the brothers be spared. Seeing that her prayer was to be denied, John Laurie begged that his brother might not be killed. William had escaped murder by the same band at the sacking of Shawneetown and was recognized by one of the guerrillas, who replied to John: "We are not so particular about you, but that fellow, we will put him through." The brothers were shot to death. Turning to Mrs. Laurie, the guerrillas said: "We are fiends from hell; get into the house, or by heavens, we will serve you the same." [2]

The Johnson House stood on the west side of Vermont street just north of Henry street and was kept by a Mr. Pickens. It was built of stone. The guerrillas surrounded it as soon as they came into the city. Some fourteen men were gathered in the house. In demanding the surrender the ruffians said: "All we want is for the men to give themselves up, and we will spare them and burn the house." Some would not believe this, and by secreting themselves finally escaped. The others surrendered. They were robbed, marched out into the street, and murdered — all except two, a Mr. Hampson and James B. Finley. Hampson was shot and wounded but fell with the others as dead, and lay quite still. The hotel and other houses were set on fire and burned rapidly. Mr. Hampson was near them and he was in danger of being burned to death. The guerrillas filled the street, and he dared not move. His wife was watching near-by and discovered that he was alive. In desperation she begged a guerrilla to help her carry her dead husband from the vicinity of the burning buildings, which he did without discovering the truth. Mrs. Hampson put her husband into a hand-cart, covered him with old clothes, and pushed the cart along the street through the charging ruffians.

Finley, quickly seeing that he had made a mistake in surrendering, turned and ran for his life, taking refuge from his pursuers in a well or pit in an unfinished building on Massachusetts street, though severely wounded. As he entered the building a man ran through it and was shot by a guerrilla on the other side. When those in pursuit of Finley came up they asked this guerrilla if he had seen a man, and he replied that

---

[2] Letter and statement of a sister of the murdered brothers, Mrs. Annie Laurie Quinby, to W. W. Scott, dated, Dayton, Ky., October 25, 1888, now in the Collection of the author. The Lauries were well-to-do English people and had recently come to America. In the published lists of the killed the name is sometimes erroneously written *Lawrie*.

he had seen one and had shot him. Believing this their man they pressed the fugitive no further. Finley, from loss of blood, became too weak to climb out of the pit, but was found helpless about noon; he died of his wound six weeks later.

Dr. J. F. Griswold lived on the southeast corner of Indiana and Winthrop streets, and H. W. Baker and wife, J. C. Trask and wife, and S. M. Thorpe and family were boarding with him. Five guerrillas rode to the gate and with oaths and fierce denunciations demanded that the house be surrendered, at the same time bringing their pistols to bear on Mr. Trask, who was standing on the porch roof trying to discover the cause of the tumult in the city. Mr. Trask told them that if they would not shoot into the rooms where the women and children were he and the other men would surrender if they could be protected as prisoners. Protection was promised, and Mr. Trask went into the house and informed the others of his stipulation. Trask, Griswold, and Thorpe went out at once, and Baker followed as soon as he was dressed. The captain demanded their business, which was frankly given. They were then robbed and ordered out of the enclosed yard to be taken to the Eldridge House and placed under guard. Coming into the street they were formed in Indian file, Baker at the head, Griswold next, Trask next, and Thorpe in the rear. A guerrilla rode by each, cursing them for being so slow. They quickened their pace and were immediately fired on. Baker was hit in the neck and stunned; as he fell he received another shot in the wrist. Trask's murderer missed him the first fire, and he ran some twenty yards before the second ball pierced his heart. Griswold was not disabled by the first fire, and ran toward the house and tried to

Dr. J. F. Griswold

Josiah C. Trask

climb over the fence, where he was killed, having been hit several times.   Thorpe was shot through the body and left for dead.

The guerrillas left, supposing the four men dead, but others were constantly riding by on errands of death. When they were far enough away to allow the wounded men to do so they talked of their injuries. Two rode by, one of whom observed that Baker was not dead, and said to his companion: "Fred, one of them d——d nigger-thieving abolitionists aint dead yet; go and kill him." "Fred" rode up to Baker and shot him through the right lung. Later, another guerrilla came wandering by. He rolled Baker over, believing him dead, and thought it

H. W. Baker

well to search him for money. Taking out his knife he inserted it in Baker's pocket and ripped the trousers some eighteen inches, but found nothing. Turning Baker over, he ripped a like gash on the other side. Finding nothing, he took the victim's hat and

S. M. Thorpe

rode away. These men lay bleeding for three hours in the hot sun of a sultry August morning in the very presence of death. When the guerrillas left the city, the wounded men were cared for. Baker recovered, but Thorpe died after two days of dreadful suffering. The guerrillas who shot these four men went into the Griswold residence and plundered it, with fierce and vulgar threats forcing the women to deliver the rings worn on their fingers — wedding rings given by the husbands lying murdered in the street. They were beginning to fire the house, when the appeals of the women touched the heart of one guerrilla, who drove the others out and saved the building.[3]

---

[3] A tablet has been placed to mark the place where these men were shot. It is in the parking, near the alley, and near Winthrop street, lot

General Collamore's residence was a little to the north of the Griswold house. It was surrounded before any of the family had risen, and there was no hope of escape. General Collamore and Patrick Keith, his hired man, descended into the well, which was in a building attached to the dwelling. The guerrillas searched diligently for Collamore, but he was not found. The house was plundered and the women and children robbed. Then the house was set on fire. The ruffians believed the men were concealed about the building, and watched it burn to the ground. The foul gas generated in the well by the fire killed the men hiding there. After the raiders had gone Captain J. G. Lowe went into the well to rescue them, not knowing they were dead. When he reached the deadly gas he fell, and the slim cord about his body broke. He, too, died in the well.

Mayor Geo. W. Collamore

Senator James H. Lane's residence was at the northwest corner of Mississippi and Henry streets. He had been absent from home several days and had returned late on the 20th. It was the intention of the guerrillas to capture Lane and take him to Missouri and publicly hang him in Jackson county.[4] When the raid was

24, Block 6, Lane's First Addition; is of granite, and bears this inscription: "*Here Griswold, Baker, Thorp and Trask were shot Aug. 21, 1863.*" Trask was editor of the *Lawrence Journal.*

[4] The *Gregg Manuscript* contains this statement, and Captain Gregg has often so informed the author.

In the Lexington, Ky., *Morning Herald*, March 27, 1898, there is a long article on Quantrill, in which is quoted a conversation had with him while he was lying wounded at the house of Wakefield. This conversation is based on the recollections of W. L. Davis, a very worthy and truthful man who went to administer to the wants of the wounded guerrilla. Davis asked him if the published reports of the Lawrence Massacre were correct. Quantrill replied: "You want to know why I sacked and burned Lawrence and killed all the male population? Well (and here a look demoniacal in its wickedness overspread his pale face) it was because I wanted to kill Jim Lane, the chief of all the Jayhawkers, and the worst man that was ever born into this world. My scouts had located him in a certain house in Lawrence the night before that awful day. My indetermined on, spies were sent to Lawrence, and they were instructed to report definitely on the whereabouts of Lane, which they did, saying that he was absent from the town, much to the chagrin of the guerrillas. If they had known he was at home they would have planned carefully his capture. At the first appearance of the bushwhackers Lane sprang from bed and wrenched off the plate on his front door. Then, in his night-shirt only, he ran through the house and into a near-by field of growing corn. From this field he crossed a low hill to a deep ravine immediately west of the present residence of Governor Stubbs. At a farm-house he procured a pair of trousers, the property of a very short fat man (Lane was a very lean, spare man, more than six feet high), a battered straw hat, and a pair of old shoes. Of another farmer he got a plow-horse with a "blind" bridle, but no saddle. Thus garbed and mounted he rode southwest and alarmed the people, having eleven men assembled by the time the guerrillas marched out of town. His house with most of the contents was burned. Mrs. Lane requested the guerrillas to help her save the piano, which they consented to do, but, being quite drunk, they could lift little, and soon abandoned the instrument to the flames. Many residents of that part of the town ran into the field of corn to which Senator Lane escaped, and by so doing saved their lives.

In the vicinity of Senator Lane's house a Mr. Cameron shot and wounded a guerrilla, who fell from his horse. The women there carried him water, dressed and bound up his wounds, and did what they could to alleviate his suffering.[5]

Quantrill found Arthur Spicer a prisoner at the Eldridge

structions were to search that house and find Jim Lane, if possible. You know it was just daylight when we got into town. We reached the house where Lane had been, reached the room he had occupied, saw his bed and it was yet warm, but he had flown. Then the command was given to kill and burn, and well did the men do the work. [The command had been given long before that]. You want to know what would have been done with Jim Lane had he been captured?" As Quantrill asked this ques-tion, his eyes flashed fire, it seemed, his nostrils were distended, and although unable to move, he looked the fiend incarnate as he almost hissed the answer between his clenched teeth: "I would have burned him at the stake!"

5 Lowman's *The Lawrence Massacre*, p. 72.

23

House. They had known each other when Quantrill was Charley Hart, the Jayhawker. The guerrilla chief turned Spicer over to a squad of ferocious butchers, telling them to kill him unless he served them faithfully as guide. If he did this he was to be returned to Quantrill, who said he had an account to settle with him. They mounted him and bade him take them to Senator Lane's residence, which he did, but Lane escaped, as we have seen. Spicer came near being shot by the bushwhackers at the house of Mr. Allen, occupied by Mrs. Hoyt as a boarding-house. His story saved the house as he inadvertently said it belonged to her, and Mrs. Hoyt was not molested, as, according to Spicer's information to the bushmen, she was a "poor widow woman who kept boarders." His confusion of the "magazine" and the "armory" would have cost him his life but for the fortunate appearance of George Todd just as the guerrillas had raised their pistols to kill him. Todd sent him under escort to Quantrill, who then had his headquarters at the City Hotel, where he had eaten a good breakfast. Quantrill met him at the curb and ordered him to dismount and go into the hotel, which he did. He sought the first opportunity to escape and did not see Quantrill again, and the settlement, probably the delivery of a pistol-ball, was not made.

George Holt and J. L. Crane were partners in a shoe store in the building of Holt near the Johnson House. When they first looked from the windows of an upper story of their store, Vermont street was filled with galloping, yelling guerrillas, bristling with deadly weapons. Escape was impossible. Their surrender was demanded, to which no response was made, but the squad soon left. Soon a single bushwhacker returned and offered them protection if they would surrender. They accepted the terms, and were at once robbed and turned over to a second bushman who had appeared; he ordered them shot, saying "they have been in Missouri killing our people." Before they could refute that statement they were shot. Crane was killed instantly

John L. Crane

and Holt was very badly wounded.   The building was plundered
and then burned.

At the unfinished residence of Judge Josiah Miller, Captain George W. Bell, county clerk, was killed.   He had seized
his gun and come into town from his residence on Mount Oread.
But nothing could be done in the way of defense, so he threw
away his gun and started home.   It was too late.   The guerrillas
were overflowing the streets from the Eldridge House.   He and
another man ran into Miller's house and climbed up on the joists,
where they were shot at by a bushwhacker, whom Bell soon recognized as an acquaintance and made himself known to him.
The ruffian promised to save them if they would come down,
which they did, but he took them out to his companions, who
cried out, "Shoot them!"   A volley followed.   Bell was killed,
but his companion recovered, though frightfully wounded.

The business part of the town, both sides of Massachusetts
street south to Warren street, was burned, only a few buildings
escaping the torch.   The Eldridge House was burned, as was the
building north of it on the opposite corner used for the court-
house; the county records were destroyed.   South of the
Eldridge House was the large clothing store of Eldridge and
Ford.   James Eldridge and James Perrine, mere boys, clerks,
slept in this store.   The guerrillas were admitted by the boys,
and Eldridge was taken by one of them to Ford's house to get
the key to the safe, which was opened and robbed.   Then the
boys were made to fit out the bushmen with new clothes.   This
done and the place plundered, the boys were butchered and the
store fired.

The bank of Simpson Brothers stood on the corner east from
the Eldridge House.   It was burned, as was the office of the
Lawrence *Journal*, adjoining it on the east.

The office of the *Tribune*, John Speer's paper, stood opposite
the south end of the Eldridge House.   M. M. Murdock, founder
of the Wichita *Eagle*, another printer, and John Speer, Jr., slept
in the *Tribune* office.   When they were alarmed the streets were
full of cursing, raving ruffians shooting at every living person
seen.   Murdock and his companion ran into an adjoining building, in the cellar of which was a deep pit for drainage purposes.

In this pit they hid and escaped death. Young Speer ran out of the back door of the office and got to the corner of Henry and New Hampshire streets, a block from the office. There he met a guerrilla who demanded his money. The boy gave him his pocket-book, saying there was very little money in it but it was all he had. This guerrilla was Rev. Larkin M. Skaggs, of Cass county, Missouri, a Baptist minister who had taken an active part in all the raids into Kansas in Territorial times and had helped Sheriff Jones sack Lawrence, May 21, 1856. When young Speer handed him his money, Skaggs shot him, wounding him badly, and left him for dead. The wounded boy lay helpless within ten feet of a house which was set on fire by three other guerrillas. When the heat became unbearable he implored them to move him and not let him burn alive. In response once of the guerrillas shot him dead and went on. The fire was, later, put out. Robert Speer was seventeen. He and another printer worked in the *Republican* office. The building in which this office was situated was burned, and with it Robert Speer and his companion workman. No trace of the body of either was ever found. In indescribable sorrow and the undying hope of a mother Mrs. Speer placed the dish and chair at his place at the table every meal she ever spread in her home until her death in the vain expectation that he might, through the providence of God, be still alive and come back to her before the meal was finished. William Speer was fifteen. As he went out at the door a guerrilla halted him and asked his name. The boy replied "Billy Smith." The bushman produced a list and examined it, but found no "Billy Smith" marked for slaughter, though every male member of the Speer family was on it. He was allowed to go, but being unable to pass the guards, he hid under a sidewalk. Fearing detection and death there he crawled out, and, as a band alighted to murder a man and burn his house, he advanced and offered to hold their horses, which he was permitted to do. He was shamefully beaten and abused, but finally escaped, later to take vengeance for the death of his elder brother, as we shall see.

John Speer, the father, lived in the extreme east part of town, and was able to get into a field of growing corn before the guerrillas reached his house. This they set on fire and left, and his wife extinguished the flames. He was collector of internal revenue for Kansas at the time, and his office and all records were burned, as was his newspaper building and office. He was a pioneer editor in Kansas and always bold, fearless, and independent. His residence was three times destroyed by border-ruffians.

Judge Louis Carpenter lived on the northwest corner of Berkeley and New Hampshire streets. Several squads of guerrillas visited his house, but he met them so frankly and received them in such genial manner that they did nothing but rob him and plunder his house. Near the time of their leaving a gang rode up quite under the influence of liquor. They came to murder. They desired to know where Carpenter came from to Kansas, and when he told them he came from New York, one of them said, "It's you New York fellers that's doing all the mischief," as he drew his revolver. Carpenter ran into his house, and up the stairs, then down again, the ruffians after him, firing all the time. He finally got to the cellar badly wounded. There he

George W. Maddox

was soon discovered and driven out to the yard where he fell mortally wounded. His wife and her sister threw themselves on him to shield him from the brutal guerrilla. But he was not to be thwarted in his purpose. He pulled the women aside, thrust his pistol against the judge's head where his wife must see, and fired the fatal shot. They fired the house, the marks of which are plainly to be seen to-day. Mrs. Carpenter's sister put out the fire.

Edward P. Fitch lived two blocks from Judge Carpenter. He went down to the door at the command of the ruffians and was shot, falling in his door. After he was down one bushwhacker emptied his pistol into his prostrate form, though he was already dead. The house was then fired and Mrs. Fitch started to drag her husband's corpse from the building, but was forbidden to do it. She was not permitted to take his portrait from the wall. She became horror-stricken by the brutality of the guerrillas and stood dazed and stupefied. She would have been burned in her house had not a ruffian driven her out. She took her three small children a little way and sat down on the grass. While watching the flames eating their way to her husband's body she saw a guerrilla go to it and take the boots from its feet, put them on himself and walk away. Mr. Fitch taught the first school in Lawrence.

Colonel Holt made his headquarters at the house of H. S. Clarke, at what is now No. 1004 Rhode Island street. Mr. Clarke went to Kansas from Jefferson county, New York. On

Henry S. Clarke

January 1, 1860, he was married to Miss H. M. Felt, of Worcester, Mass. At the time of the Massacre he was in the furniture business, his store being in the eight hundred block, on Massachusetts street. His stock was worth about three thousand dollars. On the morning of the Massacre he looked out of an east window of his dwelling house and saw horsemen coming four abreast, and a boy riding towards them. He saw the lines open and take in the boy. When he was fairly surrounded they began to shoot at him and charged toward the town yelling like demons. The boy was the young son of Mayor Collamore. He was not killed, though as many as fifty shots were fired at him. He fell from his horse and lay wounded in the road. He recovered.

Clarke was one of the home military company and had a gun and nine rounds of ammunition. When he saw the force was a guerrilla command, he thought to join his company and make resistance, but at the solicitation of his wife did not leave the house. He saw the camp of recruits attacked and the boys killed.

Two boys, guerrillas, about eighteen years old, knocked at the door. When Clarke opened it they presented carbines, and Clarke said they need not shoot, as he knew what they wanted and was prepared for them. One of them said, "Shell out, then, G— d—— you!" Clark had divided his money, reserving seventy-nine dollars in bills to give to the guerrillas, and giving his wife four hundred dollars to hide. When he handed one boy the money the other stepped up and asked if that was all the money he had, to which Clarke replied that it was. "Every damned cent?" persisted the youthful bandit. Clarke had a few dollars in fractional currency which he delivered. They told Clarke to get his things out of the house, as they would soon return to burn it, but they did not return.

Clarke saw the guerrillas kill Judge Carpenter and then became convinced that he would also be killed. This was just as the flames broke out of the Eldridge House, and he could see his own store burning. Soon a guerrilla came riding deliberately south on a horse which Clarke recognized as having belonged to James Eldridge. He seemed in no hurry and carried a box of cigars in his hand. Clarke determined to make friends with him and hailed him. After some friendly conversation he told Clarke that he was Colonel Holt, of Vernon county, Mo., and that Jennison had burned him out, destroying a twelve-thousand-dollar stock of hardware, after which he joined Price. He had been to North Missouri to recruit, and had raised a company of one hundred and four, mostly boys, and started to join Price. South of the Blue he had fallen in with Quantrill, who had requested him to go to Lawrence and get his boys christened.

Colonel Holt gave Clarke a cigar and was invited to have breakfast, which invitation he accepted, but had the food brought to the gate and ate while sitting on his horse, first requiring Clarke to eat of the food to show it was not poisoned. Soon others came, and all were fed, as many as twenty being at the gate at one time. One arrived after all the food was gone and begged Mrs. Clarke to get him something to eat if possible. She brought out a dish of cold potatoes, and he fell to with a will, saying "O how good they are!"

A swarthy guerrilla with a gray beard reaching almost to his waist came along and aimed a pistol at Clarke, who felt sure he would be shot, but Colonel Holt prevented it. One fellow in response to a jest said they were only killing the Dutch, and seeing William Faxon across the street said, "There's sauerkraut in that fellow,'' and went over to kill him. Fortunately the pistol snapped and Faxon escaped death.

Colonel Holt rode away when the guerrillas began to gather to depart. As he was starting George Todd rode by on a fine prancing horse, dressed in a new Federal uniform taken that morning from Captain Banks who surrendered the Eldridge Hotel. As the guerrillas passed they discussed their work, one saying he had killed eleven, another that he had killed eight, another, five. Two young men to whom Clarke had given water showed him the bright new caps on their revolvers free from powder-smoke and said they had not snapped a cap all day — that they had come to burn and destroy, but not to kill. Two men reported that two of Holt's men had been wounded by the soldiers on the north side of the river and could not ride their horses. Colonel Holt directed that they get an ambulance and put feather beds in it for the wounded guerrillas to ride on and be at the rendezvous quickly. As the colonel rode away he told Clarke's wife and sister to get him into the house for he would be killed if he remained outside.

Another guerrilla came along with a shot-gun and inquired for a colored preacher named Lee. Clarke pointed to a clump of houses, which the guerrilla visited without finding the preacher. As he returned, Mrs. Clarke asked him what success he had, and he replied that he had not found the preacher, saying, "but that d——d nigger belongs to me. I would like to find him.''

Clarke saw Mrs. Riggs, wife of Judge Samuel A. Riggs, clinging to the bridle of a guerrilla's horse, the guerrilla trying to shoot her husband, who was making his escape.

Among the last of the guerrillas to pass was one leading a horse on which was mounted a prisoner, a neighbor to Clarke, who seemed despondent indeed. Two guerrillas were urging the horse forward by striking it with their revolvers. The prisoner said to Clarke that he would never see him again. Clarke said to the captors, "I thought you took no prisoners.'' They replied: "This man has been playing off on us. He has been down in Missouri stealing our niggers. He had his cellar full of niggers.

We are going to make an example of him." Soon a large, well-dressed woman came up the street crying, "Oh, my dear husband! My dear husband! They are going to burn him alive." Clarke tried to quiet her by telling her they would release her husband. She then decided to come into the house and rest, which Mrs. Clarke feared for her to do, as the guerrillas were still passng and might be attracted by the loud wailing of the unhappy woman. At this refusal to entertain her the woman became enraged, and, with vile epithets, threatened to report the Clarkes to the Federal authorities for feeding the guerrillas. The husband escaped and returned home uninjured.

After Colonel Holt had gone, straggling guerrillas stopped at the gate, and Clarke narrowly escaped death, but Mrs. Clarke's tact and courage saved him.

Years afterwards Colonel Holt and Clarke had some correspondence in which they discussed with pleasure the dangerous day when Clarke owed his life to the Missourian's humanity.

The guerrillas went to the house of a German named Albach, who was sick, bedfast. They set the house on fire, and the women carried the sick man into the yard. When the guerrillas came out of the house after robbing it they shot Albach and killed him as he lay there helpless on a mattress.

Houses and lives were saved by accident at the corner of Tennessee and Pinckney streets. The guerrillas went there and took from the stable of J. G. Sands a pet pony. They were followed by another squad, one of whom exclaimed, "Why in h—ll are not these houses burnt?" They dismounted and were in the act of burning the houses when the pet pony galloped by. One of the gang from whom it had escaped called out "Catch that pony." All joined in the pursuit of the pony, and none returned. This saved the lives of Sands, Dr. Fuller, and B. W. Woodward, all of whom lived there and were concealed in their houses.

Gurdon Grovenor lived on the southeast corner of Berkeley and New Hampshire streets. His house was burnt. He saw

Judge Carpenter killed and did not expect to escape himself, but he did.[6]

Rev. H. D. Fisher narrowly escaped with his life. He lived near the northwest corner of South Park, in a brick house. His wife called him up and he got to the door just in time to see Rev. Mr. Snyder shot. He started with his family to Mount Oread as soon as they could dress, but was too weak from a recent illness to run, and he saw the pickets there to intercept him. He and his wife and two children returned to his home, while the two eldest, boys, ten and twelve years resepctively, ran on with a companion named Robin Martin, twelve years old. Robin's mother had made him a suit from a soldier suit

Rev. H. D. Fisher

---

[6] Mr. Grovenor has furnished the author an account of his escape and the part of the Massacre which he saw, and it is set out here:

G. Grovenor

The raid occurred on the morning of Aug. 21st, 1863. It was a clear, warm, still morning, in the midst of one of the hot, dry, dusty spells of weather common in Kansas in the month of August. The guerrillas reached Lawrence just before sunrise after an all night's ride from the border of Missouri. Myself and family were yet in bed and asleep. They passed directly by our house, and we were awakened by their yelling and shouting.

I thought at first that the noise came from a company of colored recruits who were camped just west of our house; thought that they had got to quarrelling among themselves. I got up and went to the window to see what was the matter, and as I drew aside the curtain the sight that met my eyes was one of terror — one that I never shall forget. The bushwhackers were just passing by my house. There were 350 of them, all mounted and heavily armed; they were grim and dirty from their night's ride over the dusty roads and were a reckless and bloodthirsty set of men. It was a sight we had somewhat anticipated, felt that it might come, and one that we had dreaded ever since the commencement of the war. I turned to my wife and said: "The bushwhackers are here." They first made for the main street, passing up as far as the Eldridge House to see if they were going to meet with any opposition, and when they found none they scattered out all over town, killing, stealing and burning. We hastily dressed ourselves and closed up the house tightly

worn by his father, and a guerrilla pursued the boys and shot him, his brains splashing in the face of one of the Fisher boys. The children became separated, were shot at a number of times from a distance, but were not killed.

When Fisher returned to the house he went into the cellar, which did not extend under the whole house. Earth from the cellar had been thrown on the part not excavated, and he crawled behind that. Four guerrillas came to the house and inquired for Fisher. His wife said he had left the house. They insisted that he was about the house and went to the cellar entrance, but it was so dark below that they called for a light. Mrs. Fisher brought a lamp, but they turned the wick down into the bowl of oil, and then told her to fix it so it would light. She said it

as possible and began to talk over what was best to do. My first thought was to get away to some hiding place, but on looking out there seemed no possibility of that as the enemy were everywhere, and I had a feeling that I ought not to leave my family, a young wife and two children, one a babe of three months old, and so we sat down and awaited developments. We saw men shot down and fires shooting up in all directions.

Just on the north of our house, a half a block away and in full view was a camp of recruits twenty-two in all, not yet mustered into service and unarmed. They were awakened by the noise, got up and started to run but were all shot down but five. I saw this wholesale shooting from my window, and it was a sight to strike terror to a stouter heart than mine. But we had not long to wait before our time came. Three of the guerrillas came to the house, stepped up on the front porch, and with the butt of a musket smashed in one of the front windows; my wife opened the door and let them in. They ransacked the house, talked and swore and threatened a good deal, but offered no violence. They set the house on fire above and below, took such things as they fancied, and left. After they had gone I put the fire out below, but above it had got too strong a hold, and I could not put it out.

Not long after a single man rode up to the front gate; he was a villainous looking fellow, and was doubly villainous from too much whiskey. He saw me standing back in the hall of the house, and with a terrible oath he ordered me to come out. I stepped out on the piazza, and he leveled his pistol at me and said: "Are you union or secesh?" It was my time of trial; my wife with her little one in her arms, and our little boy clinging to her side, was standing just a little ways from me. My life seemingly hung on my answer, my position may be imagined but it cannot be described. The thought ran through me like an electric shock, that I could not say that I was a secessionist, and deny my loyalty to my country; that I would rather die than to live and face that disgrace; and so I answered that I was a union man. He snapped his pistol but it failed to fire. I stepped back into the house and he rode around to the north door and met me there, and snapped his pistol at me again, and this time it failed. Was there a providence in this? Just then a party of a half dozen of the raiders came riding towards the horse from the north, and seeing my enemy, hallooed to him "Don't shoot that man." They rode up to the gate and told me to come there;

would take half an hour. They then robbed the house and demanded another lamp, one of them holding the baby while Mrs. Fisher went up-stairs to get it. This they lighted and took into the cellar. They did not think to look behind the heap of dirt by the wall and did not find Fisher, though he was within two or three feet of them. They came up and said "the d——d rascal has escaped." The house was set on fire and one of the

I did so and my would be murderer came up to me and placed the muzzle of his revolver in my ear. It was not a pleasant place to be in, but the leader of the new crowd told him not to shoot, but to let me alone until he could inquire about me, so he asked me if I had ever been down in Missouri stealing niggers or horses; I told him "No that I never had been in Missouri, except to cross the state going and coming from the east." This seemed to be satisfactory so he told my old enemy to let me alone and not to kill me. This seemed to make him very angry, and he cursed me terribly, but I ventured to put my hand up and push away his revolver. The leader of the party then told me if I did not expect to get killed, I must get out of sight, that they were all getting drunk, and would kill everybody they saw; I told him that that was what I had wanted to do all the morning, but I could not; "Well," he says, "you must hide or get killed." And they all rode away. After they had gone I told my wife that I would go into the cellar, and stay until the fire reached me, and if any more of the raiders inquired for me to tell them that I had been taken a prisoner and carried off. Some years ago I read an article in the Sunday School Times, saying that a lie under any circumstances was a sin. I thought then that I should like to see that writer try my experiences at the time of the raid and see what he would think then; I did not feel my lie a sin then and never have since.

The cellar of my house was under the ell and the fire was in the front and in the upper story. There was an outside bulk-head door, where I knew I could get out after the fire had reached the floor above me. I had not been in the cellar long before my wife came and said they had just killed my neighbor across the street.

Soon after the notorious Bill Anderson, passing by the house, saw my wife standing in the yard, stopped and commenced talking with her; told her how many men he had killed that morning, and inquiring where her husband was; she told him that he had been taken prisoner and carried away — was it my wife's duty to tell him the truth, tell him where I was and let him come and shoot me as he would a dog, which he would have done? Awhile after my wife came and said she thought the raiders had all gone, and so I came out of my prison just as the fire was eating through the floor over my head, thankful that I had passed through that dreadful ordeal and was safe.

Such was my experience during those four or five terrible hours. Our home and its contents was in ashes, but so thankful were we that my life was spared that we thought but little of our pecuniary loss. After the raiders had left and the people could get out on the street, a most desolate and sickening sight met their view. The whole business part of the town, except two stores, was in ashes. The bodies of dead men, some of them partly burned away, were laying in all directions. A large number of dwellings were burned to the ground, and the moaning of the grief stricken people was heard from all sides. Gen. Lane, who was in the city at the time, told me that he had been over the battle-party left to see that it burned down. He offered to aid in getting out any furniture Mrs. Fisher might wish to save. She asked him to aid her to put out the fire, but he said it would cost him his life to do that. She then asked him to get on his horse and ride away and she would put it out. He did not go until he supposed the house could not be saved; as he left he told her the house was one that was marked and would surely be

---

ground of Gettysburg a few days before, but the sight was not so sickening as the one which the burned and sacked city of Lawrence presented. The exact number killed was never known, but it was about 150, many of them of the best citizens.

I could relate scores of incidents that came under my personal observation, showing the cruelty of the raiders and the sufferings of our people; but my story is already getting too long — I will only give two. The first thing that I did after the raiders left was to assist in "laying out", preparing for burial, the body of one of my neighbors, Judge Louis Carpenter, who had been killed. Carpenter was a young lawyer, who had been married only a few months, and had just commenced housekeeping with his young wife in a new home which he had built the previous spring. The raiders chased this man through his house, breaking two or three doors, and finally shot him in the cellar, but he got out and fell just outside the bulk-head door. His young wife threw herself on him to protect him, but they raised her up and shot him through the head — it was one of the cruel things of that morning of cruelties.

Before I had finished my unpleasant task at the home of my neighbor, my wife came running to me and called out, "They have killed John — they have killed John". John was her oldest brother. Early in the morning he had been called to his door by one of the guerrillas and shot down as he stood in the doorway. Then they set the house on fire, but his wife dragged his lifeless body into the street and sat down guarding it all those long hours that the work of destruction went on. I found her sitting beside her husband's body in the Methodist church where he had been carried. That church had been cleared of its seats and was being used as a morgue. The dead were carried there until they could be recognized and taken away by their friends. The scene that met me as I went into that church I shall never forget, and I said then that I hoped God would spare me from ever witnessing another like it. Mothers and wives were coming in and as they recognized the lifeless bodies of their sons and husbands, they gave away to their grief and their sighing and moans were most pitiful, and brought tears of sympathy from the most careless. I took the body of my brother and his heart broken wife, to the house of a neighbor, who kindly invited us, and from there we buried him on the following day. A stranger minister who happened to be in town conducted the funeral services. My brother-in-law owned and conducted a boot and shoe store that was totally burned and all its contents; his house and all in it was burned, and all that his widow had left in the world was a calico wrapper, in which she hastily dressed that morning. And such was the experience of many a wife that fatal morning.

That cruel raid with all of its loss of life and property, its widowed wives and fatherless children, its suffering and mourning, was the result of civil war. May God so enlighten and guide us that our beloved country may never see another.

burned. She carried water to the upper chambers and put out the fire. Three other guerrillas, drunk and savage, came to the house. They were furious when they saw the fire had been extinguished, and broke up furniture and piled it in the rooms and set it on fire, saying also that it was one marked to be destroyed and must be burned. Two of them left and one remained to see that the fire was not put out. Mrs. Fisher made heroic efforts to save the house, fighting the flames until the floors were ready to fall in. Then she went to the cellar and called to her husband to come out as he would soon be burned alive if he remained. When he came up she threw one of her dresses over him, took up one edge of the carpet and threw it over him, and told him to stoop as low as possible and walk under the carpet as she pulled it from the house. In this way he got to a bush on which vines had been trailed, under which he crouched while chairs and other household articles were thrown over the carpet concealing him. Four guerrillas sat on their horses not eighty feet away with cocked revolvers as Fisher was dragged from the burning building, but they did not discover him.

Judge Samuel A. Riggs encountered one of the ruffians as he left his house. Mrs. Riggs ran out to aid her husband. The

Samuel A. Riggs

guerrilla lifted his revolver and Riggs knocked it aside and ran. Mrs. Riggs seized the reins of the bridle and held to them until dragged around the house, over a pile of wood, and back into the street. Riggs was not yet out of sight, and the guerrilla raised his revolver to kill him. Again Mrs. Riggs clung to the reins and whirled the horse about until her husband had disappeared, the ruffian cursing her, striking at her and trying to ride her down all the time.

Fred W. Read, brother of Mrs. L. Bullene, lived on Henry street. He took refuge in the upper part of his house and looked out of a small window. A bullet struck within six inches of his right eye. He concealed himself at once and was saved by the indomitable courage of his wife. To no other house did the guerrillas come so often as to his. Seven times they came, and they set the house on fire four times. The fire was put out each time by Mrs. Read. The sixth squad were all drunk and with vulgar oaths swore the house should not escape. One seized Mrs. Read by the wrists and held her while the others broke up furniture and kindled the flames anew. When the house was burning fiercely she was released and told "to put that out if she could." When they left she covered herself with blankets and threw herself against the burning windows, pushing out blazing frame and sash; then she easily extinguished the fire. When they were robbing the house they found some

Fred W. Read

jewelry which had belonged to her baby, dead only a few months. She begged hard for this, but the ruffian who had it angrily replied, "Damn your dead baby, she'll never need them again," and took it. The last gang inquired for her husband, saying, "Where in h—ll is Fred Read?" Mrs. Read told them that he had gone East to buy goods. "Where is your store?" demanded a guerrilla. She pointed to Woodward's drug store, corner of Henry and Massachusetts streets. Consulting a paper, he said: "Yes, some one has gone East for that store;" but it was P. R. Brooks, not Mr. Read. Mrs. Read then said, "You seem to be an officer. Look at this house and that burning store and say if you have not punished us enough." He turned to his men and said, "Go on; tell others not to molest these premises; this family has been punished enough." He remained half an hour on the porch to see that the house was not again molested.

L. Bullene lived on New Hampshire street. He was a pioneer merchant in Lawrence and at the time of the Massacre was in the East buying goods. Mrs. Bullene, her children, and her sister, afterwards the wife of Senator William Warner, of Kansas City, Mo., were at home. Being near the business center of the town, their house was surrounded by guerrillas from the time they came until they left. George Todd made it a sort of headquarters or rendezvous, and ordered breakfast for himself and his men. The women cooked as long as there was anything left. The guerrillas requested them to taste the food to show that no poison had been put into it. One band said the house must be burned, but Mrs. Bullene requested them first to aid her to carry out her sick mother. When they saw the pale and feeble invalid they went away. To another band bent on the same purpose Mrs. Bullene said that Captain Todd had ordered that house to be spared. "In that case we will not burn it; we obey orders," they said, and rode away. William L. Bullene was a lad and did not think of being in danger, and saw much that took place. One guerrilla drew a revolver on him and would have killed him had not his mother grabbed the pistol and pushed the fellow back. He saw the guerrillas kill nine men, among them the son of John Speer. This man had the flag, taken at the camp, tied to the tail of his horse. He saw the officer in charge of the recruiting office escape. This officer first hid under the office, but was routed out by fire. He stripped off his uniform and ran through the street filled with guerrillas, many of whom shot at him. He got into the Bullene house, where young Bullene put him in female attire; he remained there and was not further molested.

The residence of G. H. Sargent was on New Hampshire street between Henry and Winthrop streets. The guerrillas came early to this house and ordered the men into the yard and fired the house, but aided in carrying out the piano. While the house was burning they shot the men — Sargent, Charles Palmer, and a Mr. Young, a printer. Sargent was only wounded. Mrs. Sargent fell on her knees by her husband and tried to shield him, begging for his life, but the guerrilla placed his pistol by her head and fired a ball through the head of her husband. Young fell with the others, supposing himself to be mortally wounded, and unable to roll himself away from the burning building. He was severely burned before the women dragged him away and put him with the dead. He had not been wounded at all.

James F. Legate, a pioneer in Kansas and for more than forty years prominent in State politics, was at Lawrence. He had a thrilling escape from death, of which he often told. He was the first to take the news to Leavenworth, and until his arrival there General Ewing knew nothing of Quantrill's invasion of Kansas.[7]

---

[7] The following account of the experiences of Legate appeared in the *St. Louis Globe-Democrat* shortly before his death:

Special Correspondence of the *Globe-Democrat*, Leavenworth, Kan.

Several articles have appeared recently on "Quantrell's raid on Lawrence," but no one can tell a more thrilling story about it than James F. Legate, the noted Kansas politician, who was a resident of Lawrence at the time. Mr. Legate took a leading part in border ruffian troubles during the early territorial days, has served nine terms in the Kansas Legislature, and has passed through some exciting times, but he considers them tame compared with his marvelous escape from Quantrell's gang. It was Mr. Legate who brought the news to Leavenworth of the sacking and burning of Lawrence, and he told Gen. Ewing, then in command of Fort Leavenworth, the way to head off the guerrillas. Had his advice been acted on the outlaws would have been captured before getting out of the state. Mr. Legate nearly killed three horses in making the trip from Lawrence, and his story contains some historical points about the famous raid never published before.

Mr. Legate is quite old, and is becoming very feeble. He was called on at his home on Fifth avenue by a *Globe-Democrat* reporter, when he consented to tell the story, which follows:

On the night of August 20, 1863, we had a very large meeting at Lawrence, in which the people were very much excited concerning the Union Pacific Railroad. The excitement grew out of the fact that it was asserted that Senator Lane was indorsing the project of building the road about three miles north of town. Everybody was very much excited over it. During the meeting it was announced by Lane that he had information that a rebel spy was in town, but the excitement over the railroad and the charges against Lane led every one to conclude it was one of Lane's tricks. The meeting broke up about 12 o'clock. We all went home, not thinking anything about rebels or Quantrell or any one else excepting the railroad.

On the morning of the 21st, about daybreak, a little colored boy living with me came to my room with much excitement, saying "The rebels are in town." I said to him "Put on my hat and run to the woods." I got up and dressed and walked out of the house. I saw the town full of Quantrell's men, shooting and yelling, giving them the appearance of a great degree of ferocity. I put on my coat and walked right down among them about two blocks from my house. They were killing three men, and I never in my life heard such pleading for a moment of life as came from these men, yet I was so stupified that I was entirely unmoved by their prayers. I did not dare to run, lest I might attract their attention as not being of their number. I turned slowly around, walked up onto the hill where John Speer lived, went into the house of a Swede, which was filled with frightened women, who had gathered there, and they seemed to be of all nationalities. I was asked questions by each in their turn, but made no answer, walking straight through the house into the yard in the rear,

24

General Dietzler was at the residence of Governor Robinson — the last house north on the west side of Massachusetts street, a block from the Eldridge House. He was not molested. Only two guerrillas appeared at the Robinson house and they were fired on by the soldiers on the north side of the river and left.[8]

[8] F. Luther Wayman, living now in Muskogee, Oklahoma, told the author, April 27, 1909, that General Deitzler robbed his father of several horses and mules near the beginning of the war. These were thoroughbred horses, none but one being worth less than two hundred dollars.

where there were four rows of corn planted in the lot. I managed to find the center row, and I walked through to the fence, got over the fence and started on a run like a quarter horse, through the valley to a hemp field. Through fright and nerved to the quick, I performed a feat that $1,000,000 couldn't make me repeat. I made a jump over a ditch about 2 feet wide, over a four-rail fence, into the hemp lot.

About half way through the hemp lot I met John Speer and his deputy coming from his house. I told them rapidly of what I knew, and what I had seen, and turned and ran toward the timber. I ought to have said just as I jumped the fence a bevy of Quantrell's men fired a volley at me, and they seemed to hit everything and everywhere but exactly where I was. After speaking with John Speer I turned toward the timber, the grass was high, and there were little clumps of bushes. As I ran near one of the clumps of bushes I saw a movement and started directly toward the clump to see what it was. As I reached the clump I found Solon O. Thatcher, afterwards Judge Thatcher, hid in that clump of bushes. We were both equally frightened. He cried out "Oh, don't! don't, don't!" I jumped back, apparently very brave, and said, "Who are you, or I'll put a hole through you in a second?" He, recognizing my voice, in plaintive manner said, "Why, it's Solon; why, don't you know Solon?"

We conversed but a moment. I said that I was going to the river, and he followed me. We got down to the river and we heard the clatter of horses' feet coming pellmell toward us. He started back for the brush and I jumped into the river. They were so near to me I didn't dare to go into the river, so I backed up under a stump, under which the water had washed out. They came down, and seeing our footprints, waited but a moment, discussing what to do. Finally one of them discovered the footprints of Judge Thatcher going towards the brush. With a wild yell they all started in that direction.

As soon as they had gone I started to swim across the river. I swam, it seems to me, faster than any steamboat I had ever rode upon to that time. I was two-thirds over the river when they all came back, and they began to shoot at me. Their shots all went wide of the mark. I thought there was too much surface to my back to shoot at. I whirled over and swam on my back so that I could see them. One fellow got off his horse and says: "I can hit that Abolition son of a ——." He rested his musket against a tree — I presume this is imaginary on my part, but it seems entirely real — I imagined that I could see to the very bottom of that gun, and thought that he would certainly hit me. I turned my eye to see whether I should float down the river or strike a sand bar. I looked back before he had fired, and it seemed to me that when he pulled the trigger I could see the muzzle of the gun turn to the right, and I felt perfectly safe. The ball struck about 10 feet to my left, as I lay on my

The actions of Governor Robinson that day are not very clear, though he and others have made explicit statements about them. In the introduction to his *Kansas Conflict*, written by his friend, Isaac T. Goodnow, it is said, "Even in the terrible massacre during the Lawrence raid, and when the Doctor slowly retired from his barn to the brow of Mt. Oread, near where several of Quantrill's men were on guard, they did not molest him." In the same work Robinson himself says: "He [Quantrill] also said, as Robinson, while governor, did what he could to preserve peace on the border, he should not molest him or his property."9

---

9 How peace could be preserved on the border during the Civil War is not explained in this remarkable statement attributed to Quantrill, who, it is intimated here, wanted peace on the border. What steps Robinson took to preserve peace on the border as "War Governor" are not enumerated. If Quantrill desired peace he had a strange way of showing it. He must have appreciated Robinson's actions, whatever they were, for Robinson himself says his life and property were spared by Quantrill on account of them.

back, which convinced me that my sight was correct when I saw the movement of the gun. I had then got near the shore.

As I reached the shore I looked around and a Delaware Indian by the name of Half Moon said to me in Indian, "Give me your hand." I gave him my hand and he pulled me out of the river. He wanted to know who they were. I told him they were Quantrell's men, rebels. "Well," he said, "I'll take one shot at them." He had an old Kentucky rifle. He took one shot at the crowd and one man fell from his saddle. They immediately got off and put the man back in the saddle and slowly moved away toward town again.

I went from there to Old Pechaukee. I found there only the old lady, his wife, and the children. They had a horse and buggy all hitched up. I asked for the use of the horse and buggy. While she could speak English as well as I could, she wouldn't utter a word in English, but said to me in the Delaware language, "No, Pechaukee has gone with the men and has bade me go to the bottoms with the children in the buggy. There is going to be a fight." I said to her, "All right, I want to ride up on the hill to see where the fight is going to be. Will come back again."

I started in the buggy for Leavenworth and made the horse run until he entirely broke down. It was a very hot day.

I rode up to where Mr. McFarland, an old gentleman who formerly lived in Lawrence, was making hay, and he had a very fine-appearing horse hitched to the fence. He said, "Yes, sir, he is one of the finest buggy horses in the territory." I said to him, "I want to try him," and then stripped the harness off of the Indian's horse and put McFarland's horse in the buggy. I did it so quickly the old gentleman was much surprised and somewhat alarmed. I left him on a dead run. His son followed me to Nine-mile Creek. When his son overtook me and I told him the story he said, "All right, go ahead."

That horse broke down, or so near broke down that I rode up to the stage stable. There was a stage stable at Nine-mile Creek. I went

Dr. Kellogg was led around for an hour by two guerrillas who kept cocked revolvers at his ears all the time. He expected to be killed, but made up his mind to please his captors, if possible. On their order he guided them to the best liquor-shops and stores, secured money for them, and set fire to the houses of his neighbors. He was finally released and told to go. He

---

in very cooly and asked the stable keeper if he had a good, swift buggy horse. He pointed out a horse to me and I walked in and unhitched the horse and took him out, when he, the stable boss, came out with a club and said, "What do you mean?" "I mean to swap horses." He began to show fight and I drew out a revolver that I carried through the Kaw River, but he didn't know it. I told him to change the harness and he complied. As soon as the horse was hitched to the buggy I jumped in and said, "The rebels are in Lawrence, and I want to get to Leavenworth. I'll bring your horse back."

I came on as fast as that horse could bring me from there to this city. I stopped at Col. Jennison's or Jim Brown's stable; they were both together then. I told him rapidly the story and asked for Gen. Ewing. He went post-haste to the fort for Gen. Ewing, telling the story up there. Gen. Ewing came in person to the Planter's House to see me.

I said to him that I had rode up on to the hill four miles from Lawrence, and that evidently the town was burned, for I saw it all on fire. I said to him the whole border was guarded with the exception of one place about ten miles south of Kansas City; that if he would press into the service three steamboats that lay at the wharf here and take his men to Kansas City he could intercept the entire gang.

He said that he thought that he could go across the country and intercept them better. So he started across the country by the way of De Soto, thinking that he could intercept them in that way. It was a long march, though a forced one, and he simply got behind them, and drove them out of the state, without harm to any of them.

In the middle or some time in the night of August 21 there came word from Lawrence that everything was burned up, with about 100 persons dead, without a coffin to bury them in. Early on the morning of the 22d every coffin in this town was taken, about 100 of them, in two wagon loads, and started for Lawrence. Gov. Carney, Nelson McCracken, L. T. Smith, and some others got together and made a donation of about $1500 in groceries and provisions, and started that to Lawrence.

Gov. Carney and myself, in his team, drove over. We found the town almost absolutely destroyed, most of the prominent men killed, and the stories of escape were wonderful. . . .

George W. Collamore was Mayor of the city. His house was surrounded, and, believing it was death to show himself, he was lowered into the well by his wife, and when the rebels had gone they found he was dead.

They went to my house and set it on fire. My wife pleaded with them, told them she was a widow, and it was all she had in the world, and she didn't want them to burn it up. Nellie, my daughter, who was little more than a year old, grabbed around the leg of one of the men and said: "You won't kill my papa, will you?"

There was an old colored woman who had two children, a little boy and girl. The little boy ran up to see the Free State Hotel burned, and one of the men grabbed and threw him into the flames.

Quantrell, as we knew him, lived there by the name of Charley Hart,

said the first breaths he drew after his release were worth one thousand dollars each.

One man saved his house and his life by payment of one thousand dollars. Another paid a thousand dollars for his life, but another guerrilla shot him. A woman wrote on a card in large letters the word "Southern" and nailed it above her door and saved her house. A young man and wife from Illinois were stopping at the Johnson House. He saw no chance to escape except to jump from a second-story window, which he did, just as two guerrillas came around the corner. They seized him and took him behind the building where they robbed and shot him.[10]

Robert Morrow and James Blood lived near Mount Oread, up which they went before the guards were placed, escaping all harm. Mrs. Morrow saved the houses of both families, putting out fires as often as they were set.

William Hazeltine owned a grocery store above which he lived. He did not see the guerrillas until they had filled the street in front of his store. His only chance of escape was by running out at the rear door, which he did, crossing Vermont street and aiming for a ravine to the west. He was shot at a dozen times, and at the edge of the ravine stumbled and fell. The

---

and made his personal headquarters at the Lawrence Hotel kept by Mr. Stone. Quantrell guarded the hotel, and had it surrounded. Quantrell had a long fit of sickness there, and was tenderly nursed by the Stone family. Some of his men killed the old gentleman.

I knew Quantrell quite well when he lived in Lawrence under the name of Charles Hart. I was going East at the time he was sick at the hotel. I visited him, and left him $10 to buy medicine with. He was known among us as a noted Abolitionist from Ohio. He planned raids into Missouri to steal negroes. There was a band formed, of which he was the leader, for that purpose. They made several raids into Missouri, and brought to Lawrence quite a number of slaves that were shipped on to Canada. Finally he made an arrangement for another raid into Missouri. Under the pretense of reconnoitering he went to a farm house near Independence, and selected the spot, told the man they were coming to steal his negroes that night. He said they were a gang of desperate Abolitionists from Lawrence. True to what he said, a band of fellows from Lawrence went there, and the farmer was well supplied with help. Four of them were badly wounded, and five of them escaped. From that hour Charley Hart became Quantrell, which was his real name, and soon became the leader of the most desperate outlaws in Western Missouri.

10 Letter of C. M. Chase to the *True Republican and Sentinel*, dated Lawrence, Kansas, August 22, 1863. The above instances, including the account of Dr. Kellogg, are given on his authority.

guerrillas supposed he fell from a shot and did not molest him further. He was unhurt and escaped.

The livery stable near the northeast corner of Winthrop and Massachusetts streets was owned by the Willis Brothers. It was one of the first buildings set on fire. Walter Willis and E. V. Banks started to Leavenworth before the guerrillas entered the city, and escaped. John Frawley, who worked at the stable, was shot and his body burned in the barn.

John Bergen was wounded and captured. He and six other prisoners were shot — all killed except Bergen, who was badly wounded and feigned death. This was discovered and a guerrilla shot at him, the ball grazing his head, which he dropped as though shot. His head was now partly under the body of a dead man. His mother came and began to wash his face, believing him dead, but he entreated her to leave him, as the guerrillas would return and kill him certainly if they discovered him to be alive.

A man named Winchell ran into the house of Dr. Charles Reynolds, where the ladies hurriedly attired him as a female, first having shaved off a bushy beard. A cap of ancient style was put on his head, and he was placed by a small table on which were spoons and medicine-bottles. A serious and acrid lady was appointed to fan him and revive his drooping spirits. When the ruffians arrived they were told that whatever they desired they might take, but were requested to be as easy and quiet as possible so as not to disturb "Poor Aunt Betsy." The remnant of the bristling beard caused some misgivings in the suspicious minds of the denizens of the Sni as to the genuineness of the sex assumed by "Aunt Betsy," but they did not investigate beyond furtive glances, and Mr. Winchell escaped with his life.

A sort of blind cellar east of the Johnson House proved a refuge for a dozen men hard pressed by ruffians. A woman first thought of hiding her husband there. It was outside a wall, and the dilapidated entrance gave no promise of the capacious cavern twenty feet back. Taking post in the vicinity, the lady directed fugitives to the underground retreat. Seeing their victims disappear in the patch of tall jimson weeds surrounding the cave, the ruffians demanded to know what became of them and were told they were lying concealed in the weeds. A cautious tramping failed to flush the game, when the woman was threatened with death if she did not reveal the hiding-place. But she bravely told them to shoot if they wanted to, which they did not do, and the men were saved.

The Rev. Michael Hummer had been driven from Topeka by a lawless combination of one A. A. Ward, the Topeka Town Company, and the notorious Edwards Brothers, border-ruffians, who were afterwards lynched for their crimes. Mr. Hummer was a Presbyterian minister of the hardy stock which settled the Shenandoah Valley, and after his outrageous treatment at Topeka, he settled in Lawrence. When the revelry of death was at its height he appeared in the streets, and, like a prophet of old, proclaimed himself a preacher and called on the guerrillas to desist "in the name of Jesus Christ." His boldness amazed the ruffians. He told them he was a Virginian and sympathized with the South, but condemned violence and murder under guise of civilized war. He saved a number of men from death. Finally the guerrillas warned him to get indoors or suffer the consequences. A poor German came at that instant sore beset and bleeding from wounds. Hummer threw himself between the monsters and their prey and was wounded and left for dead. The German was killed and his body burned to a shapeless mass by the fire of an adjacent building.[11]

The guerrillas at no time in Lawrence showed bravery or daring. Those who fought them fared best and usually escaped. Captain William A. Rankin and Lieutenant John K. Rankin, cousins, were at home on furlough. They had gone forth for a walk early in the morning and saw the guerrillas enter the town. They drew their revolvers and started home. Turning a corner, they saw two guerrillas trying to shoot a man in his dooryard. As they ran to the rescue four more bushmen rode up and all began firing. One ruffian aimed deliberately at Captain

[11] Mr. Hummer moved to Old Wyandotte, where he lived until his death. He often recounted to the author the dreadful experiences of that awful Friday in Lawrence.

Rankin and would have killed him had not the ball struck the Captain's revolver. Some of the guerrillas were wounded but none were killed. The Rankins soon had the field to themselves and escaped unhurt. And it was well for them that the bushwhackers left when they did, for their ammunition had given out.

Captain Wilder lived near the intersection of Winthrop and Kentucky streets. His house was of stone, the shutters were closed, and the curtains dropped. The guerrillas rode around this house several times, taking care to keep at a good distance, but they never once attempted to molest it.

The residence of a Mr. Allen was a large brick house on Kentucky street. When the guerrillas arrived there they found him in and armed with a pistol. Four guerrillas knocked roughly at his door and demanded admittance, threatening to kill all the inmates if resistance was offered, but making the usual promise that no one should be hurt if the door was opened and prompt surrender made. Mr. Allen was quite old, but full of courage and resolution. He told the guerrillas to come on in if they could get in, assuring them that he was good for at least six ruffians as soon as they might enter. The bushwhackers left and no others ever returned.

Lieutenant Ellis was in command of the soldiers stationed on the north side of the river, but boarded at the Eastern House, just across from the livery stable near the corner of Massachusetts and Winthrop streets. A ridiculous ordinance forbid one to be armed in the city, so he was without his pistols. When he looked from his window the street was full of cursing, raving bushmen on guard or riding swiftly in pursuit of any citizen who might show himself. The house was surrounded and escape seemed impossible. His only chance was in bold action. Dressed in his uniform he dashed into the street among them. He seized bridles and whirled horses about, dodged from one to another, ran when he could, and shielded himself from one guerrilla behind another. He reached the stable in a shower of pistol-balls, ran through the carriage room to the first tier of stalls, sprang to the top of a partition and into the loft, his pursuers firing at him all the time, killing the horse in the stall from which he went aloft. They ordered him to come down, assuring him that he would not be hurt if he surrendered. But he knew better. Arming himself with a piece of scantling he stood guard at the hole by which he had climbed up and dared any bushwhacker to show his head above the floor. None came. The barn was soon set on fire, and while the guerrillas were watching the upper exits he came down and slipped out of the rear door, from which he dodged from one cover to another until he reached the garden of Mrs. Leis across the alley west of the City Hotel. There he hid in the rank weeds and remained until the guerrillas left the city. He had the holes of seven balls in his clothes but was not wounded.

The foregoing comprise only some of the experiences of the people of Lawrence on that terrible day. Instances could be set out indefinitely, but enough has been given to show conclusively the actions of the guerrillas — that there was nothing soldierly in their course. It was atrocious murder, arson, robbery, pillage — inexcusable savagery.

CHAPTER XXX

VIII

A LITTLE before nine o'clock the lookout on Mount Oread descried the column of Union troops under Major Plumb far to the east as it emerged from the timber bordering Captain's creek. With hot haste he spurred down the steeps to notify the guerrilla chieftain that pursuers were hard upon the trail. Quantrill called together his captains, and it was soon decided to leave the city at once. Orders were sent out for the guerrillas to assemble just east of South Park. Captain Gregg was given twenty men with which to gather up stragglers and bring them out. He anticipated trouble, for many of the guerrillas were drunk and reckless. Calling Captain Gregg to the middle of Massachusetts street, Quantrill pointed to a large white house on the hill beyond the Wakarusa and said he would wait for him there one hour. Quantrill rode to the place of assembly and there formed and marched out the greater part of his command. They went directly south, crossing the Wakarusa at Blanton's bridge and rode up to the white house and dismounted to readjust their trappings and their plunder, of which every horse carried much.

Gregg called Jacob Rote, the boy forced to guide them into Lawrence, put a new suit on him, gave him a horse left by a guerrilla when a better one had been stolen in the city, and dismissed him. Early in the morning Gregg and Bledsoe were standing mounted on the bank of the river. Gregg saw a soldier on the north bank climb out on a leaning willow and take deliberate aim; the guerrilla supposed the distance too great for the range of a gun. But the ball whizzed by his breast and struck Bledsoe in the groin wounding him severely. Gregg got a heavy carriage of the city-hack variety and placed Bledsoe in it to take him back to Missouri. This hack he sent out with the advance.

The prisoners at the City Hotel had passed their time as best they could. Sentries tramped their beats about the building to keep them in and to keep bloodthirsty ruffians out, — calling for food and eating as they walked. Some of the prisoners paced the floor in terror and anxiety. Others sat and discussed the terrible blow which had fallen on the city. Early in the day a ruffian, now believed to have been Skaggs, took from Miss Lydia Stone a diamond ring which had been given to her by Quantrill after his recovery from a severe illness through which she had nursed him in the fall of 1860. She did not fancy the idea of losing this ring, and, noting the guerrilla carefully, described him to Quantrill, who swore it should be returned. In a short time the ruffian was brought up and forced to give back the ring, which he did with ill grace, muttering under his breath that she would be "d——d sorry for it." When the main body of the guerrillas had gone, Skaggs and one other drunken ruffian returned to the hotel and ordered the prisoners to come out, using very coarse and vulgar language in the order. The prisoners, supposing they must obey, crowded through the door to the south porch, but not all of them got out before the bushmen opened fire. The crowd surged back indoors, shouting, "They are shooting the prisoners." Most of the prisoners ran down the bank to the ferry. Captain Stone was mortally wounded by the guerrillas and died that day, and a peddler named Brown was wounded, but recovered.

Captain Gregg found the drunken stragglers extremely refractory. Some of them fired the gunshop just west of the camp, on the east side of Massachusetts street, owned by D. W. Palmer, who had escaped to that time. The proprietor and another citizen believed the guerrillas were gone and had come from hiding and were standing in the door as the last squad rode by. They were fired on and both wounded. The building was set on fire. The hands of the wounded men were tied together and they were flung into the burning house. The men struggled up and got to the front wall of the blazing shop. With whoops and cries of exultation the inhuman ruffians thrust them back with their revolvers. Amid their cries of joy Palmer again rose, the cords having been burned away from his arms. He raised his hands above his head, and as the flames wrapped him in a sheet of fire he sank back, on his face a look of indescribable agony. With yells of triumph and satisfaction the monsters mounted their plunder-laden horses and rode rejoicing on their way.

At the foot of Mount Oread, Captain Gregg found a drunken guerrilla trying to burn a small house. Two or three times he got the ruffian out at the gate, but he would return. The last time he went in he fell on the porch in a drunken stupor. Scattered about the yard were many greenback bills, and Gregg picked up a large roll of them, not noticing the denominations. This is all the plunder he secured that day and all he tried to get, and he did not pick up half the bills he saw, all of which had been dropped by his drunken companion, who had secured them by robbery. Time was precious, and he left the drunken wretch on the porch and rode away. The next day when he counted his money he found he had one hundred and ninety-nine one-dollar bills. The fellow he left on the porch followed and got to Missouri.

Skaggs would not be hurried by the party gathering stragglers. He was drunk and exultant. He stopped at the residence of Fred W. Read and as he entered the house he insinuatingly said, "I have come to make a call." Mrs. Read said, "I am not receiving calls." He said he would burn the house and demanded matches, which Mrs. Read refused to give him. He went into another room and found matches, and, laying his pistol on the piano, he began to strike them. When one was lighted Mrs. Read would immediately blow it out. This continued ten minutes, when he said, "You are the queerest woman I ever saw!" At this instant James Faxon came to the door, when Mrs. Read cried out, "Run for your life!" Faxon escaped, though pursued by Skaggs, who returned to the house in a fury and threatened to shoot Mrs. Read. As he was about to do this it occurred to him that his fellow-ruffians might all be gone, and he hurried out, saying as he mounted his horse: "I have staid here so long I fear I shall be killed!"

No praise can be too great for the women of Lawrence on that black day. With indomitable courage they faced the ruffians. With ready resources they concealed husbands, sons, soldiers, friends, and went forth to outwit the shaggy bushmen bent on murder. They threw themselves into the breach without counting the consequences. They fought fire, stood undaunted in the presence of death, seized and quenched lighted brands, clung desperately to the reins of plunging horses, and battled with ruffians and flames to save trapped and hidden husbands from burning in their own homes. Quantrill said the men of Lawrence were a set of cowards, but that the women were heroines. Let the people of Lawrence set up a stone in that city to the memory of the women who bore the burden of that horrible day. Let it be as strong, as graceful, in as fine proportion, and as enduring as their devotion, as their scorn of danger and death, as their interepid bravery, as their unfaltering courage, and as their undying fame.

William Speer, son of John Speer, finally got home, in company with his chum, the late Frank C. Montgomery. Mrs. Speer was greatly excited, weeping for her children, her hands and arms severely burned in saving her home from the torch. She gave William an old gun and told him to go and kill some of the guerrillas. On this mission he and Montgomery started forth. In the south part of town they hid behind a hedge as Skaggs came by just ahead of some soldiers and Indians who had crossed the river at the ferry. Young Speer poked his gun through the hedge and fired at Skaggs, hitting him in the shoulder and knocking him from his horse. As he fell, White Turkey, the Delaware, came up and said: "Him kill everybody; me kill

White Turkey, the Delaware

him," and shot him through the heart. The Delaware scalped the guerrilla and hurried on in the pursuit.[1]

---

[1] Larkin Milton Skaggs was descended from those hardy wilderness-breakers known in history as the "Long Hunters." They settled in Ken-

The last man killed was a Mr. Rothrock, a Dunkard minister, who lived some ten miles south of Lawrence. He lived a little way from the road, and a gang rode down to his house and ordered the women to cook them a breakfast. This was done. While eating they inquired of the women whom the old gentle-

tucky, in which state many of their descendants yet live and where Larkin M. Skaggs was born. He came to Missouri at an early day and settled in Cass county. He was a Baptist minister, and had it not been for the demoralization caused by slavery agitation he would have ended his days in usefulness and respectability. But he was one of the earliest border-ruffians. He was at the sacking of Lawrence, May 21, 1856, and at the sackings of Osawatomie, and Captain Ely Snyder made special efforts to meet him where a Sharps's rifle could be used.

Skaggs raged against his neighbors who favored the Union. Long before the Civil War he had quit the church and was a blustering, swearing, vulgar ruffian. One of his neighbors, D. P. Hougland, has written an article entitled ''Voting for Lincoln in Missouri in 1860,'' published in Volume IX, *Kansas Historical Collections*. There it is described how Larkin Skaggs came to Hougland's house to kill him in 1860. ''A man that was in the crowd when he started to come told me afterwards that Larkin said he didn't want a better job than killing that damned negro lover; and that his brother Willis caught him by the arms and told him he shouldn't go, but that others pulled him loose and said: 'Let him go; it will save a lot of trouble.' ''

The author knew many of the relatives of Skaggs in Kentucky, and in fact grew up near some of them, and knows that the family was a good one. No other member of it ever came to a bad end, so far as the author ever heard. And but for the awful conditions existing on the border Larkin M. Skaggs would have died in his own bed and in his church, a respected and useful member of society. The indignities to which his body was subjected were barbarous and wholly inexcusable, and never would have been permitted in Lawrence at any other time than immediately after the Massacre. No matter what his crimes, resentment should have stopped at death, and would have done so but for the excitement under which the people labored after that bloody and terrible day.

C. M. Chase, in the letter to his paper, from which quotations have already been made, says:

So we rode into town. The first sight attracting my attention was a negro rushing through the streets on horseback, dragging the dead body of a dead rebel, with a rope around his neck hitched to his saddle. A crowd was following pelting the rebel with stones.

There was an attempt later by the negroes to burn the body, which was not successful. The bones lay naked all winter in a ravine in the town, and negroes and boys sawed finger rings from some of them. No part of the body was ever given burial.

man was. He had no idea of the danger in which he stood, and remained at the house. When told that he was a minister, the guerrillas said: "Oh, we intend to kill all the d——d preachers," shot him several times, and rode away. He lived but a few minutes.

Two marriages resulted from incidents which occurred on that awful "Black Friday." A young man took refuge under a pig-pen, where he was found by a young lady, a stranger to him, after the guerrillas were gone. In a few months these young people were married.

A young man named Haseltine was captured very early in the morning and carried to a liquor shop in the rear part of which the proprietor lived. The guerrillas killed the liquor-seller, and the housemaid was forced to serve them with liquor. Unobserved she put the money from the cash-drawer into her pocket. She entertained the ruffians as well as her limited knowledge of liquors would admit, talking with brightness and animation all the while. When they drew their revolvers and took Haseltine to the street to kill him she rushed out and threw her arms around him, screaming and imploring the ruffians to spare her dear brother. She had won them by her courageous course in the shop and now they spared her "brother," a young man she had never seen before. The end was marriage.

———

Whatever can be said to the credit of any guerrilla in Lawrence should be set down. Not all of them were inhuman monsters, though many were. Even the worst were touched with pity sometimes and showed kindness. In many instances they offered to help remove furniture from buildings they fired. One bearded ruffian, bristling with deadly weapons, held the baby and entertained it by walking the floor and with "baby-talk" while Mrs. Fisher got him a lamp. Holding this babe touched his heart and he rode away at Mrs. Fisher's request to allow her to put out the fire he had helped to light. The building in which Mrs. Hoyt kept boarding-house was spared because she was a poor widow. General Holt protected H. S. Clarke and saved his life and dwelling. Because of the earnest pleading of the women, Doctor

Griswold's house was not burned. George Todd protected the prisoners on the way from the Eldridge House to the City Hotel, and he saved the life of Arthur Spicer, whom Quantrill had before spared. Quantrill kept faith with the prisoners and protected them by a strong guard at the City Hotel, though it seemed at one time before they left the Eldridge House that he did not intend to keep his word with them. He listened to Stevens, his former attorney, and stood by his stipulation. Every guerrilla the author ever talked to said that there were men in the command which went to Lawrence who were opposed to going there at all and did not favor the purpose of the raid. Two showed their pistols, full-loaded and free of powder-soot to prove that they had not fired a shot and they expressed their purpose not to fire one in Lawrence. Captain William H. Gregg, who a certain malignant, soured, and disgruntled old woman says gave the command to "Wheel left; kill every man, woman and child!" showed mercy many times that awful day and saved life more than once. He killed men in Lawrence, no doubt, but he never in the world gave such a command as malice attributes to him, and would have shot any guerrilla heard giving it. It has never been charged that the chastity of any woman was violated at Lawrence. Quantrill, inhuman as he was and as fond of fallen women as he is known to have been, made it a law in his band that the violation of chastity would be punished by death, and it is said this penalty was inflicted more than once. Perhaps those who sometimes spared life at Lawrence did not often spare it. Morgan T. Mattox says the only order he heard at Lawrence was to kill every man who could carry a gun. The Lawrence Massacre was atrocious savagery, bloodthirsty brutality, was fiendish, diabolical, but any credit due the guerrillas individually must be freely given. Some showed no mercy. Bill Gaw, Allen Parmer, and Dick Maddox are supposed to have killed more than any other three guerrillas. Peyton Long is said to have killed more citizens in Lawrence than any other guerrilla. The band of Bill Anderson did more killing than that of any other captain. Jesse James was not at Lawrence; he did not join the guerrillas until late the following fall. Frank James was as ferocious and merciless as a hyena. The Youngers did bloody work.

When the guerrillas were gone, the citizens came from their hiding-places. What a sight met their eyes! The city was in ruins. Where had stood blocks of buildings were cellars filled with burning timbers and smouldering merchandise. But two business houses remained on Massachusetts street. Dwellings were burned everywhere and lay now smoking ashheaps. Dead men lay in the streets, some half consumed by the fires, and others blackened masses of charred remains. Long rows of them had been dragged by devoted women through leaden hail into vacant lots away from burning buildings. Widows who, an hour before were happy wives, wailed in the desolate streets as they sought

Old Stone Building, Lawrene, Opposite Stone's Hotel

the stiffening corpses of their murdered husbands. Trails of blackening blood indicated where many a helpless victim ran in hope to find some haven of safety, when pursued by murderous wretches — vain hope, as his pale form, bloodstained and lifeless, would plainly show! Piercing screams rose on the smoke-laden air as some poor woman threw herself upon the dead body of husband or son sought and found in the ruins. Women moaned piteously and wrung their hands in despair as they went from corpse to corpse peering into death-white faces in search of loved ones now missing. Above all hung the clouds of black smoke like a funeral pall. Men called through the gloom for volunteers to assemble the dead and make their graves. Purged with fire, smitten with the sword, choked with dead, the mourners crying in the streets, plague and famine threatened, and terror, affliction and desolation descended on the city.[2]

---

[2] The dead numbered about one hundred and fifty, but as many bodies were consumed in the flames the exact number can never be known. Rev. Mr. Cordley, in his *History of Lawrence*, gives the following list:

25

It is but just that this account should close with the cry wrung from the heart of one who passed through it all, endured it all, and lost one son shot to death and one burned alive — still a kindly, just, patient, God-fearing man, and, as pioneer and

Names of seventeen recruits killed from a total of twenty-two:

Anderson, C.
Allen, Charles R.
Cooper, James F.
Green, John R
Griswold, Walter B. S.
Halderman, Aaron
Markle, David
Markle, Lewis
Markle, Samuel
Parker, Asbury
Parker, Isaac
Riggs, Charles F.
Speer, Robert
Watson, John
Waugh, William A.
Wilson, James
Woods, Andrew

Names of citizens killed:

Albach, George
Allen, E.
Alwes, ———
Anderson, John
Allison, D. C.
Argel, ———
Allen, Clay (col.)
Bell, Capt. Geo. W.
Bowers, Samuel
Brechtlesbauer, James
Brant, ———
Burt, George
Burns, Dennis,
Burns, Michael,
Carpenter, Judge Louis
Coates, George
Collamore, Gen. Geo. W.
Crane, John L.
Cloud, Charles
Cooper, James,
Coleman, L. D.
Cornell, ———
Dix, Ralph C.
Dix, Stephen H.
Dyre, Uncle Frank
Dulinsky, Sylvester
Ehles, August
Eldridge, James
Ellis, ——— (col.)
Evans, John
Engler, Carl
Englesman, ———
Fitch, Edward P.
Fillmore, Lemuel
Frawley, John
Frank, Joseph
Fritch, S. H.
Giebal, Anthony
Gentry, ———
Green, John
Gates, Levi
Gill, John
Griswold, Dr. J. F.
Griswold, Abner
Griswold, Watt
Gregg, ———
Hendrix, ———
Hay, Chester
H———, Cal
Holmes, Nathan
Johnson, M.
Johnson, Ben
Jones, Samuel
Kimball, Fred
Keefe, Pat. [Keith, Patrick?]
Klaus, William
Klaus, Fred
Kleffer, W. M. R.
Laurie, John
Laurie, William
Leonard, Christopher
Lambert, ———
Little, John
Limboch, Henry
Laner, Christian
Longley, Otis
Loomis, Rich.
Lowe, Joseph
McFarland, ———
McClellan, ———
McFadden, J.
Martin, R.
Murphy, Dennis
Makin, Michael
Martha, ———
Meeky, M.

commonwealth-builder, the noblest Roman of them all — John
Speer, the Covenanter: [3]

[3] Written for the *Globe-Democrat*, and published in that paper October 8, 1898. It was in response to an article written by Captain William
H. Gregg and published in the same paper.

Nathan, W.

Oldham, Anthony (col.)

Oehrle, ———

O'Neil, James

Palmer, Charles

Palmer, Daniel W.

Perine, James

Pope, George

Pollock, J.

Purington, David H.

Roach, ———

Reedmiller, A.

Reynolds, Samuel

Range, George

Range, Samuel

Speer, John M.

Snyder, Rev. S. S.

Stewart, Henry

Smith, Charles

Schwab, John

Sanger, George H.

Sargeant, G. H.

Stonestreet, Benj.

Stone, Nathan

Swan, L. L.

Thorpe, S. M .

Trask, Josiah C.

Turk, ———

Wise, Louis

Williamson, W. T.

Wood, James

Waugh, Addison

Zimmerman, John

Mr. G. Grovenor was employed in 1868 to remove the bodies of victims of the raid buried in the old cemetery, to the new cemetery, where a
monument was erected. Mr. Grovenor's statement and list of names appeared in the *Lawrence Journal*, June 1, 1895, and the author was furnished a list by Mr. Grovenor:

To the Editor of the Journal:

Presuming that many of your readers may be interested to know who
of the victims of the Quantrell raid are buried in the plat of ground
where the new monument has just been erected, and having the list of
names so far as is known I take pleasure in furnishing it. In all there
are fifty-three bodies buried in that plat, forty-seven of which were taken
from the "trench" in the old cemetery southwest of the University,
where they were buried the day following the raid, one W. M. R. Kliffler,
from a single grave in the same cemetery and five from the river bank
near the present canning factory.

The names of the forty-seven that were buried in the trench as taken
at the time by Mrs. Samuel Simpson and numbered in the order of their
burial, are as follows:

1. Richard Loomis,
2. M. Johnson,
3. Geo. Pope,
4. ——— Gentry,
5. Unknown,
6. Unknown,
7. John Wilson,
8. Soldier of fourteenth regiment,
9. Unknown,
10. Cal. H———,
11. Unknown,
12. Uncle Henry, colored,
13. Ben Johnson,
14. Charles Cloud,
15. Uncle Frank Dyre,
16. Benj. Stonestreet, colored,
17. Nathan Holmes,
18. ——— Gregg,
19. P. Cornell, colored,
20. E. Allen,
21. Charles Palmer,
22. Daniel Palmer,
23. John W. Laurie,
24. Wm. Laurie,

Wichita, Kan.

Special Correspondence of the *Globe-Democrat*.

I have read in your daily of the 20th ult., and the semi-weekly of the 23d, a statement of Capt. William H. Gregg, who claims to have been Quantrell's First Lieutenant in the Lawrence massacre, which I think ought to be replied to.

Every thing is magnified by this man. He counts forty tents of soldiers at the entrance to the town, and exultantly declares they were all killed. There were twenty-one boys in

John Speer, the Covenanter

tents, and three escaped. They were not soldiers. They were boys, so young that it was a common remark that Capt. Beam was gathering in all the infants who were before considered of ages unfit for service; they were called "Beam's Babes." They were not mustered into the service; and, perhaps, none of them could have been legally held without the consent of parents. They had not a single gun. But if forty tents had been full of such men, armed, Quantrell would not have entered the town. Quantrell knew, and undoubtedly informed his Lieutenant of that fact; and to kill those boys without a chance to surrender was as brutal a murder of the innocents as was ever committed by savages. Then, right

25.	Unknown,	37.	Joseph Frank,
26.	Unknown,	38.	—— Argel,
27.	Unknown,	39.	August Ehlis,
28.	Unknown,	40.	— — Lambert,
29.	John Green,	41.	Unknown,
30.	Samuel Markle,	42.	Thos. Murphy,
31.	Lewis Markle,	43.	Christopher Leonard,
32.	David Markle,	44.	—— Turk,
33.	Unknown,	45.	Chas. Allen,
34.	Unknown,	46.	C. S.
35.	L. D. Coleman,	47.	W. Nathan,
36.	Unknown,	48.	Unknown.

The remains of these bodies were taken up in the spring, as I remember, of '68, placed in boxes and numbered and removed to Oak Hill cemetery and buried in order, so that each body can be located. Six bodies originally buried in the "trench" had previously been removed by friends. The names of these are:

1.	John Gille	4.	Ralph Dix,
2.	Geo. Coates,	5.	Stephen Dix,
3.	John ——,	6.	Christopher Leonard.

The names of the five persons buried on the river bank I have never been able to learn, they are buried in the grave immediately back of the monument and on the north side of the walk.

after this scene of carnage, he describes their arrival at "a kind of ravine," which is the crossing of Massachusetts and Warren streets, and says: "Near that ravine was a collection of structures in part of boards and in part of hay. Those shacks were filled with household goods stolen from Jackson County by the Kansans on their raids into Missouri. There were feather-beds and all manner of household effects. There were pianos which had cost $1000 apiece. We didn't have cheap pianos in those days. The inhabitants of the shacks were mostly negroes who had been run off from their owners in Missouri. I recognized some from my own neighborhood. We went among the shacks touching matches to the hay."

This statement is entirely false. I passed that place going to and coming from my work every day, morning, noon and night; and no shacks were there, and nothing was burned. The only building near that place was a small stone building, one story high, which escaped fire. They then passed without firing John Dean's wagon shop, where Quantrell once worked, and the store of Gurdon Grovenor, on the east side of the street. The west side was fired a little south of Grovenor's. Two large furniture and undertaking establishments, Ridenour's and Baker's, on the east, and all else on both sides of the street in that block were burned. It is safe to say there never was a piano stolen from Missouri and brought to Lawrence. In the Union command under Lane was Capt. John G. Haskell, as quartermaster, and no such thing could have occurred without his knowledge and connivance. He never tolerated such a thing. The only band of suspicious characters was a small band, exclusively horsemen, called "Red Legs," which Gen. Blunt soon disbanded. They could not carry "thousand-dollar" pianos on horseback.

This man belittles the work of that day by pretending that they destroyed $150,000, "as much property that had belonged to Jackson County people as that belonging to the citizens of Lawrence." He tries to reduce the thefts to petty larceny. More than $80,000 — over half his estimate of Lawrence losses — were destroyed in two stores, Bullene's dry goods and Ridenour & Baker's groceries, etc. The official statement is $882,390.11, reported in hopes of relief by the government, state or national. These excluded notes, accounts, etc. John N. Edwards in "Shelby and His Men," says: "Every hotel, except the City Hotel, was burned. Other property valued at $2,000,000 was also fired and consumed." Hon. Hovey E. Lowman in his history, says: "They destroyed something near $2,000,000 of property, left eighty widows and 250 orphans, as the result of their four hours' work." This Lieutenant says:

"As we went along, he (Quantrell) fired to the left and I to the right." No being in sight was spared.

This man has the audacity to say: "We waged no war on women and children. If any women or children were ever hurt by Quantrell's men, it was accidental. I have always believed that most of the men killed at Lawrence were soldiers." There were no soldiers, except six to eight, absent on leave. I think I can name them: Capt. A. R. Banks, who surrendered the town as provost marshal; Andrew J. Shannon, ———— Hazeltine, John A. Rankin, William K. Rankin, Maj. J. B. Abbott and Capt. Frank B. Swift; the two latter resigned, and one man, whose name I can not remember. There was not a soldier killed.

Two weeks before a report came that Quantrell was preparing for a dash on Lawrence, and something near 400 men were rallied, and every preparation made for defense. No enemy appeared. It was a great expense to the town, and a great loss to farmers, who were just gathering in their crops. Everybody was disgusted with what was considered a false alarm. A lull of excitement pervaded all such as had never been experienced. Capt. Frank B. Swift was among the prisoners taken to the City Hotel; and Quantrell told him that the report he was coming was true; that he knew of our preparations, and waited till he knew all fear was over and the way clear. Quantrell knew there was not a soldier prepared for action, and the massacre of the town was contemplated. In cowardice and brutality, it had no parallel. No honorable Southern soldier ever recognized Quantrell's men as a part of the Confederate army.

The Kansas River was very high, and the ferry cable was cut by Quantrell's men as soon as they could reach it. There happened to be camped on the north side of the river sixteen brave soldiers, who immediately opened fire across the river whenever they could see a head. Quantrell then threatened to murder everybody, and Miss Lydia Stone, daughter of the landlord of the City Hotel, which Quantrell spared, went to the river bank, and called pleadingly to the soldiers to stop, or no person would be left alive.

This man, who now so unprovokedly harrows up the souls of the living over their innocent dead, says of the only man killed: "We lost but one man in Lawrence — Milt. Skaggs. The citizens shot him. Then one of them tied him to a horse and dragged him through the streets, until his body was naked. After that he was hung to the limb of a tree, and riddled with bullets and stoned. This is what we were told afterward by persons present.'' Now for a specimen on the retaliation theory; and then for Skaggs:

In April, 1855, the writer brought three prattling boys up the Missouri River through that state, aged, respectively, 11, 9 and 7 years. He never touched a dollar of Missouri property, nor lifted his hand in anger against any man in the state, nor can he recollect an unkindly word spoken by him or to him in Missouri. These innocent lads had never looked across the line of that state. As Skaggs reached the corner of New Hampshire and Henry streets, he met John, the oldest of these boys; demanded his money, and he handed up his pocketbook, saying he had but little, and was instantly shot down, wounded. Skaggs passed on. Three men fired a house; as the wounded boy lay within 10 feet of it, he implored them to move him, and not let him burn alive. One of them shot him dead. The fire went out.

John M. Speer,
Murdered by Skaggs

The second son, Robert, was burned in the ruins, whether dead or alive, God only knows. The third, William, was a prisoner, and only escaped death by giving his name as Smith. The men who captured him read a paper to see if any Smith was doomed to die. Dr. Moore, brother of Hon. H. L. Moore, heard a man in the ranks, whom he supposed to be Quantrell, give orders as to who should die, and he read Speer as among the doomed. After terrible abuse, and three attempts, William escaped. As Quantrell evacuated the town, Skaggs and two others rode back to the City Hotel, called out the landlord, Mr. Stone, and shot him dead. Stone was the man who had secreted Quantrell when the sheriff was after him for horse-stealing. Then they advanced toward Quantrell's command; but halted at the house of one of our best citizens, brutally treated his wife, holding her by the wrists while they fired the house; and then, when the smoke got thick, forcibly took her out of the house, so that she might not put the fire out, and robbed her of a pair of little gold armlets belonging to her dead babe.

Robert Speer,
Burned alive by the Guerrillas

Thence he struck out for the command, but ran up against some countrymen, who halted him. Just then the escaped boy appeared upon the scene with a loaded rifle he had found, and, telling his mother of the carnage and his escape, she said: "There is one of them — go and shoot him." As Skaggs attempted to escape, the boy fired, and the dust flew out from where the ball struck Skaggs on the shoulder-blade. Then White Turkey, a Delaware Indian, appeared, exclaiming: "Oh! he kill everybody! Me kill him!" and shot him through the heart, and he made one bound towards eternity,—

> With all his crimes broad blown,
> As flush as May; and how his audit stands,
> Who knows, save heaven, but in our circumstance
> And course of thought, 'tis heavy with him.

How do I know these facts about Skaggs? The second day after the massacre, Mr. John McFarland, of Franklin, met me in the street, and said: "I took the new coat which he had stolen off that man, and I think a pocketbook I got out of one of the pockets must be yours. It has some gold coin and jewelry in it, and papers in your name." I told him I had lost no pocketbook, nor jewelry, nor gold coin; but that Mr. Fred Read had, and I would go with him and introduce him. As I rang the bell Mrs. Read opened the door. She almost fainted. I told her it was Mr. McFarland, our neighbor, and there was no cause for alarm. Recovering, she exclaimed, "Where did you get that coat?" Mr. McFarland said, "I took it off the man that was killed." She said she had recognized it; but he had taken no jewelry from her, except a pair of gold armlets of her little babe, made greatly valuable to her because her only child was then dead. Mr. McFarland's brother, Thomas, shortly after made the same statement about the pocketbook, and I made the same reply. But a day or two after, as I was riding in a buggy, the thought came that Skaggs might be the man who murdered John, took his pocketbook and filled it up, and instantly turned the horses' heads toward my home, called my wife out, and told her of my thoughts. She said she would know it — a very beautiful portmonie, with an outer and inner clasp. We drove up to Mr. McFarland's door, and met him on his porch, Mrs. Speer telling him not to show it to her till she described it, which she did. He said, "It is yours," and went into the house and brought it out. It had papers in it, both in John's and my own hand-writing, and a $1 and $2 bill on the Lawrence Bank, the identical money surrendered to his murderer, and we still preserve it as a relic of that bloody event.

Now, another: Several of these men went into a house where an amiable lady was sitting alone in a lonely part of the city. They rummaged drawers, found infant's clothes, and in the most insulting manner told her of her condition, which she modestly and in agony confessed. They cursed and swore about "more abolitionists," and used her so roughly that her husband took her from the scenes of her sorrows to friends at Detroit, where, in nervous prostration, she died in childbirth. That will do. A good woman will almost die before she will reveal such scenes of shame. And the brutes who know of them, and know their own guilt, therefore feel safe in denial where no accusation is made.

These men shot Mr. Swan, his child in his arms, and his wife by his side. In the same manner they murdered Mr. Oehle, and that child was afterward the editor of the Frie Presse, the German paper of Lawrence. The parents could not speak English, and he said, "Nich verstay." They replied, "G—d d——n you; we'll make you verstay!" The mother grasped the infant as the father fell, and fled to my house, a mile away. When I returned, she sat among sympathizing ladies, swaying to and fro in a rocking chair, exclaiming in broken English: "My mon! My mon! They murder my mon!" They pursued Judge Carpenter, wounded, and when his wife and sister threw their bodies upon his to save him, they pulled the women's clothes and persons from him, and stuck their guns between them, and gave him two death shots. The merciful part of it is that they didn't shoot through the wife's and sister's bodies.

Our first schoolmaster, who had taught free state and pro-slavery parents' children alike, Mr. Edward Fitch, and never spoke of politics in school, was wantonly murdered in his home, and the house set on fire. The widowed wife succeeded in hauling the body from the flames. They cursed her and threw it back, and it was consumed. One of them discovered her looking at her husband's photograph, with her three little children around her. He grabbed it and cast it in the fire. Nobody could conceive the cause for this cruelty, till the mother said: "My little child had gotten a toy American flag, and had climbed upon the shed and placed it there." And they call that honor toward women and children.

So inconsiderate of women and children were these men that one of them violently grabbed her baby from the arms of Mrs. H. D. Fisher, and gave her her choice, with a revolver at her head, whether she would be shot or light a lamp to enable them to find her husband in the cellar to shoot him and burn him with the house. She lit the lamp. But her husband laid so closely in a trench by the cellar wall that they did not find him, but set with cocked guns to shoot him in any attempt to escape. Mrs. Fisher and Mrs. John Sugrue carried him out in a roll of carpet, and piled chairs, pots, kettles, etc., over him, and saved his life. "Truth is stranger than fiction" — and more horrible.

They went to the house of Dr. Griswold, called out the men, pledging the honor of soldiers that they would not hurt them. Expecting to be treated no worse at most than as prisoners, they went out, only to be shot down in the presence of their wives and children. There fell Dr. Griswold, Editor Trask, Senator Thorp & H. W. Baker, now, as then, one of the firm of Ridenour & Baker, shot through the lungs, left for dead, still living to tell all he knows of the horrors of that day. These are but specimens.

Now, to my own home. The mother, who knew not the fate of her boys, but believing it impossible that they would murder such children, clung to the house through all this. It was a mile from the heart of these scenes. About twenty men came up and set it on fire. One man showed her some sympathy by helping her as she was attempting to drag a heavy sofa from the flames. She asked him why that home should be burned over her and her little children. He said: "I will ask the Lieutenant," and he did, to which came the brutal response: "No; G—d d——n the abolitionists! Why should this house be saved?" That ended it. From the heartless manner in which Gregg rode over "Beam's babes," and "shot right and left with Quantrell," and from the fact that he did not shoot her and her poor little children, I suspect that that man must have been Quantrell's Second Lieutenant. But she did save the house after he left. All my other property was destroyed, as I expected. That was war. All else was demonism, murder, butchery.

In expiation of these crimes, this man says "the Kansans" went to Jackson County and robbed and burned the houses of two citizens, Messrs. Sanders and Crawford, and "took them to Blue Springs and killed them." He names no individual as engaged in it, and no such crime was ever traced to a Lawrence citizen. And for these alleged deaths they murdered 180 Lawrence people. He says the perpetrators of that deed "refused to let the women folks put on so much as a bonnet, although it was in the winter." And for this incivility, by unnamed persons, these avengers made eighty mothers widows and 250 innocent children orphans.

The statements about Quantrell having "a grievance" are all false. He was an all-around tough, and came to Lawrence as a better place for opportunities, dishonoring his parents by changing his name to Charley Hart. He belonged to a gang who stole negroes from Missouri and held them for the reward. He sneaked from Lawrence as a horse-thief. He never was an "abolitionist," nor did he come to Kansas with abolitionists. He came with Col. Torry, of Paola, Kan., an honest, upright man, but never an abolitionist. That story has been told with many variations, generally that the abolitionists robbed him and killed his father and brother, but he never had a father or brother in Kansas. That is like the fables told about the James boys and the Youngers to palliate their murders and bank and train robberies.

History of Gen. Lane "going out to a pond and getting under water all but the tip of his nose," is such contemptible "rot" as to make a person doubt whether he ever was with Quantrell. Three men captured Arthur Spicer, compelled him, with revolvers at his head, to mount a horse and lead them to Lane's house. There was not water enough in less than half a mile — the Kansas River — to cover Lane's toes, and to get there he would have had to pass in sight of Quantrell's forces.

"It is strange that men can't be brave enough to tell the truth. * * * Quantrell and his men went to Lawrence with h—ll in their necks, and raised h—ll after they got there," says this man. It took his mouth thirty-five years to get open. Time passes, and but few of the sufferers are alive. Then I was in the prime of manhood, and I have lived to be 81 years old before I heard the howl of the hyena around the graves of his victims. Baxter says every criminal but the hypocrite has been converted; the hypocrite never. Pollock did not live long enough to properly cauterize the hypocrite; but he made a pretty good stagger at it for a youth:

————————In the grave
The hypocrite had left his mask, and stood
In naked ugliness * * *
* * * of all the reprobate,
None seemed maturer for the flames of hell;
Where still his face, from ancient custom, wears
A holy air, which says to all that pass
Him by: I was a hypocrite on earth.

                                        JOHN SPEER.

CHAPTER XXXI

IX

LIEUTENANT-COLONEL C. S. CLARK, Ninth Kansas Volunteers, was in command of all the troops guarding the border south of Little Santa Fé. He was in command also of the stations of Aubry, Coldwater Grove, Rockville, and Trading Post. The force at each post consisted of two companies, but none of the companies were full, and few had more than fifty men each. The garrisons of the posts were Ninth Kansas troops. Headquarters of the border forces were at Coldwater Grove, Missouri, thirteen miles south of Aubry, and almost due east of Paola.[1]

Captain Pike notified Clark of the appearance of Quantrill on Grand river ten miles from the Kansas line, but did not notify him when Quantrill crossed the line into Kansas. Clark got his information of that event from Captain C. F. Coleman, stationed at Little Santa Fé, at three o'clock on the morning of the 21st. He took thirty men — all he had — and started towards Paola, getting into Johnson county, but after marching twelve miles he learned that Quantrill had gone through Gardner the night

---

[1] See *Rebellion Records*, Series I, Vol. XXII, p. 581, Report of Brig.-Gen. Thomas Ewing, Jr. The critics of Major Plumb insist, notwithstanding the fact that these *Records* have been published more than twenty years, that he was in command of the troops of the border at this time. Major Plumb belonged to the Eleventh Kansas, few of the troops of which were then stationed on or guarding the border. And Major Plumb never did command the Eleventh Kansas. Thomas Moonlight was its colonel. Plumb was promoted to lieutenant-colonel May 17, 1864. From the date of the promotion of Thomas Ewing, Jr., from colonel of the Eleventh Kansas to brigadier-general, March 13, 1863, to the promotion of Moonlight to be colonel, April 25, 1864, it was commanded by Moonlight as lieutenant-colonel, not having enough men to enable the officers to muster. See *Kansas Adjutant General's Report*, Eleventh Kansas.

before. Clark then marched back to Paola — why, no one ever could tell.

Captain Charles F. Coleman acted with vigor, courage and judgment. He sent couriers to Kansas City, Westport, and Olathe as soon as he knew that Quantrill had crossed the line, requesting the commander at Olathe to send couriers on west. He started at nine o'clock, p. m., with all the men he could muster — about eighty — and went to Aubry. He took all the men at that post and started on Quantrill's trail, having a total force of one hundred and eighty men. As the night was dark after ten o'clock, it was difficult to follow the guerrillas, and it was five in the morning before he arrived at Gardner — six hours behind Quantrill.

The first courier arrived at the headquarters of General Ewing in Kansas City at eleven-thirty p. m., and the second an hour later. Ewing was in Leavenworth and could not be reached. Major Plumb was chief-of-staff, and he acted promptly. But thirty men could be mustered in Kansas City, and before one o'clock he was on his way west along the Old Santa Fé Trail in search of Quantrill. The troops he had were infantry, but he mounted them on some heavy horses which had just arrived from Ohio and Indiana with which to mount the Eleventh Kansas (infantry), the order for which had been issued a short time before.

Lieutenant Cyrus Leland, Jr., was an aide on the staff of General Ewing and had been sent on the 20th to Black Jack, Douglas county, to inspect the militia company of Captain Jackson, which he found in good condition. On his return he got as far as Olathe, where he stopped for the night at the headquarters of the post. About midnight the long roll alarmed him and all the garrison. He found that a dispatch had arrived telling that Quantrill had crossed the line into Kansas, and he expressed the opinion that Olathe would not be

Lieut. Cyrus Leland, Jr.

molested as the guerrillas would have arrived before that time had that town been their destination. But the commander was uneasy, and none of the soldiers there slept again that night. About sunrise a column of troops was discovered approaching from the east, and in a few minutes it galloped into the public square. It was Major Plumb with his thirty men, and he had ridden nearly thirty miles in four hours. He had not been in the public square twenty minutes when a great column of black smoke rose against the western sky. Plumb saw it and said: "Quantrill is in Lawrence." He immediately started on, and Lieutenant Leland asked permission to go with him, which was granted.

Major Plumb did not follow the roads, but struck across the prairie. South of Captain's Creek Crossing he came into the road and found that many horsemen had gone on ahead of him. At the Blue-Jacket Crossing, on the Wakarusa, he came up with Captain Coleman. Here was observed a great cloud of dust south of Lawrence on the Fort Scott road and soon flames burst up from farm-houses. He knew that Quantrill was retreating from Lawrence, and he again left the trail and took to the prairies to come into the Old Santa Fé Trail ahead of the guerrillas.

When the guerrillas had left Lawrence Senator Lane rode into the town from the west. About a dozen farmers whom he had rallied were with him. He announced his intention to follow the bushwhackers and called for volunteers, and some twelve additional men got horses and joined him. These horses had been left by the guerrillas, and were worn out with the long march from Missouri. Riding out on Quantrill's trail, other farmers joined in the pursuit, and Lane put them all under the command of Lieutenant John K. Rankin. At the

General James H. Lane

little town of Brooklyn, on the Santa Fé Trail they came up with the guerrillas in the act of firing the dwelling of Thaddeus Prentice, and drove them through the village, forcing them to abandon the Santa Fé Trail as an avenue of escape. And no other houses were burned. Lane here counted his men and found that he had but thirty-five. These were mounted, some on mules, some on old brood-mares with colts following, some on the worn-out guerrilla horses and some on fairly good horses. Some had saddles, some had none. Some had squirrel-rifles, some had shot-guns, some had antiquated muskets, some had old pepper-box pistols, and half a dozen had corn-knives. Lane was mounted on an old clumsy dark-bay mare, with a blind-bridle and no saddle, but soon got a better mount. He was still arrayed in the costume secured after leaving home, and armed with a small pistol.

Lane directed Rankin to hang on the left flank of Quantrill, who was going south on the Fort Scott road, until Prairie City was reached, where he hoped to find a company of militia, when something might be done. He also sent back to Lawrence for any men, arms and ammunition that might be had there. Near Prairie City, George Wood, a farmer who lived near Black Jack, came up and said to Lane: "There are two hundred and fifty cavalry just over there." This was the force under Major Plumb and was in plain sight. Lane directed Wood to return to Major Plumb and inform him that Quantrill was about half a mile to the west going down the Fort Scott road, and that he would attack at once. When Wood started to return to Plumb's command, Lane ordered Rankin to attack Quantrill, and took his place at the head of the column. The men had no idea of military tactics and could not be made to act as a body. Lane

Col. John K. Rankin

got far in advance where he rode towards the enemy alone. He passed the mouth of a lane leading west. Two companies of Federal cavalry soon entered this lane. When Rankin arrived at the lane he discovered that but one man of all his force was keeping up with him. He directed this man to turn all the men into this lane as they came up and have them follow the cavalry.

Beyond the lane the road emerged upon a prairie, which was found covered with plunder flung away by the guerrillas on seeing the troops under Major Plumb. When Rankin came up he found one company deployed as skirmishers and saw the charge on the rear guard of the guerrillas which carried the troops beyond the farm of Josiah Fletcher, some two or three miles down the Fort Scott road, and to the Ottawa Crossing, where four guerrillas fell from their horses, two dead and two severely wounded. Fletcher's field had been made across the old road, and the new road passed around to the west. It was expected that Quantrill would make a stand at the angle in the road, which he did. Lieutenant Rankin told the commander of the company coming up in column to form and charge through the cornfield. Lane here came up with the troops and ordered a charge through the field. The captain of the company ordered his men to dismount and fire, which they did without effect. Quantrill had come back from the Crossing and formed at the angle in the road, and the aimless volley fired by the troops beyond the field gave him their exact position. He charged at once and drove Rankin's men from the corn into the ranks of the troops back of them.

The point where the guerrillas crossed Ottawa creek was about the center of Section 32, Township 15, Range 20, in Franklin county, and about six miles southwest of Baldwin.

J. C. Coffield, now of Iola, Kansas, was a private in Company H, Ninth Kansas. A part of the company was with Major Plumb, commanded by Lieutenant John M. Singer, now of Fairmount, Kansas.

When the company came in sight of Quantrill the horses of Coffield and a comrade named Chalmers were exhausted. Lieutenant Singer told them to secure fresh mounts if possible, giving receipts for horses taken. Coffield went to a farm-house, where he found a widow living. She had a very young horse, little more than a colt, in the stable. He explained to her the situation, and she told him to take her horse and it would be all right if he never returned it; it proved a good mount. Chalmers also secured a fresh horse. These two were mere boys and were constantly urging that they be allowed to try to kill or capture

Quantrill. Lieutenant Singer had considerable trouble to restrain them from a reckless course. They were everywhere and saw everything.

When Quantrill was forced out of Brooklyn by the appearance of Lane's men in pursuit, he abandoned the Santa Fé Trail for the Fort Scott road. At the suggestion of Captain Charles F. Coleman, Company D, Ninth Kansas, Major Plumb kept on the east side of the main stream of East Ottawa creek. The Fort Scott road ran on the west side, about midway between it and a small stream falling into it some distance below. Keeping down the east side was for the purpose of heading off Quantrill at the ford, a position of great natural strength, and where it was supposed a hundred men might make a successful stand against a thousand.

When Lane, who was following Quantrill down the Fort Scott road, asked for men, Captain Coleman was sent across the creek to aid him. When he left Plumb it was understood that the main command under Plumb would hurry on and endeavor to get to the ford and be ready to head Quantrill off. There Coleman would attack him in the rear, and it was hoped thus to destroy him.

Coleman was a brave and energetic officer. He charged Quantrill with such vigor with his few troops that the guerrilla command was brought to a halt near the ford. There Quantrill, not knowing that Plumb was supposed to be at the ford, turned and drove Coleman back up the road to a point beyond Fletcher's field. Coffield saw Quantrill at the head of his command riding recklessly, the bridle-reins on the saddle-horn, firing rapidly with revolvers in both hands.

When the guerrillas had secured fresh horses at Lawrence they made up a pack-train of the horses they had ridden into the city. Every horse that was supposed to be able to get back to Missouri was loaded with plunder taken from the stores and homes of Lawrence. Guerrillas were detailed to lead these horses, and their number made it appear to Coffield that there was a whole regiment of the invaders. At the Fletcher farm many of the pack-horses were abandoned, and the loads of others were reduced. The whole country there along the road was found

26

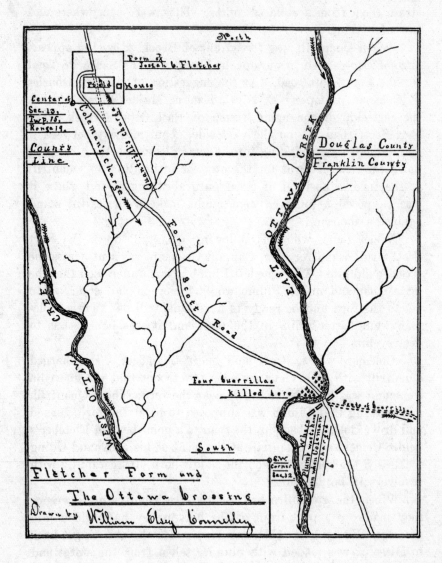

North

Farm of Joseph b. Fletcher

Field ☐ House

Center of
Sec. 13,
Twp. 15,
Range 19.

County
Line

Coleman's charge

Quantrill's Trail

Fort Scott Road

DOUGLAS COUNTY
FRANKLIN COUNTY

EAST OTTAWA CREEK

WEST OTTAWA CREEK

Four guerrillas
killed here

Route of Guerrillas

S.W.
Corner
Sec.32

Where Plumb's
men met Coleman's
charge

South

Fletcher Farm and
The Ottawa Crossing
Drawn by William Elsey Connelley

covered with goods flung away in preparation for the attack of Captain Coleman. This pack-train deceived Major Plumb as to the number of men Quantrill had.

When Coleman was driven back by Quantrill he found Major Plumb north of the field, pale and trembling. He supposed from the noise made in the charges of Coleman and Quantrill that a general engagement was on, and being unable to see clearly through the timber along the creek just what was being done, he had abandoned his intention to go on to the ford and had come across to the aid of Coleman, following the well-established principle in tactics that any officer must at once hurry to the aid of a command in battle with a superior force and in danger of destruction.

Coleman could scarcely restrain his anger when he saw Plumb above Fletcher's field, and it is said that he used sharp language in his inquiry as to why Major Plumb had not gone on to the ford as agreed, saying that the one opportunity to destroy the guerrillas had been lost. But Plumb's explanation convinced Coleman that the anxiety and solicitation of his commanding officer for the troops in his charge was genuine and that he was in the line of his duty in crossing over to the rescue.

Coffield and his comrade were constantly dashing up to the main guerrilla command and firing at Quantrill. One of them (they never knew which) shot one of the guerrillas from the column. He was a tall man with a long red mustache. The guerrillas seeing that his wound was mortal put him on a shelving rock below the road, out of sight, but the boys soon found him. He was in the last gasps of death, swearing at them and his luck with his last breath.

Having cleared the field Quantrill ordered Gregg to cut out sixty men and hold the rear. Gregg said sixty men were not enough, but Quantrill said he could have no more. Gregg had secured a flea-bitten gray mare at Lawrence, and she was suffering from the heaves. Quantrill told him to dismount and loosen the girths, and give her relief, which he did. He formed his sixty men in line across the road and held his position until Quantrill made the crossing at the ford, when he rode leisurely after the guerrilla command.

At this point many citizens came to Major Plumb's command, also Captain Jackson with his militia company from Black Jack. The horses of the cavalry were exhausted, some of them having fallen as they crossed the country from Blue-Jacket Crossing. All of them had traveled fifty miles without rest, and those of Captain Coleman had traveled more than seventy miles. Quantrill's men had secured fresh horses at Lawrence, and it was impossible for Major Plumb to do any effective work against them. The mistake of Plumb was in not placing his men on the horses of the farmers and militia that there met him.

Lieutenant Cyrus Leland, Jr., requested permission to form the militia and citizens into a body and press Quantrill. Major Plumb granted this permission, ordering him to form them into comapnies of fifty and follow the guerrillas as closely as possble.

When Leland appeared Gregg abandoned his position and went to the Ottawa Crossing. When he arrived there he could not see Quantrill, but when he got up out of the timber beyond the creek he saw that the command had left the road and taken to the prairie, holding a south-easterly course toward Paola and Missouri. Leland was close at his heels, finding the four guerrillas in the slough-grass at the crossing and killing the two wounded.

When Gregg reached the prairie he threw his men into two columns of thirty men each. These columns were formed in open order — the men fifty or sixty feet apart — a sort of rear skirmish line. They were thrown across the line of retreat, one column some four hundred feet in advance of the other, both fronting the command of Leland. When Leland's men came up the first line would hold its position as long as possible, then turn and retreat through the second line, taking a position about four hundred feet to the rear of it. The second line would then do as the first had done. This would be kept up until Major Plumb came in sight and Quantrill had the main command well ahead, when the guerrilla rear-guard would all gallop away, and, near the main body, form in the same manner, and repeat the former tactics. The Hesper and Black Jack militia, fairly armed and mounted, about fifty men, would charge on these rear columns, stand fire, and stand their ground when charged. But the citizens, being poorly armed and unused to war, would break when thrown against the guerrilla column, or when charged.

This was kept up all the afternoon. Sometimes the grapple was close. Once Leland forced Gregg into the main guerrilla command and hoped to hold it until Major Plumb came up, but when the entire force of guerrillas turned on him he was compelled to retire. Gregg told Quantrill that he would see that the rear-guard was not again driven up to the main body, and it was not while Gregg was in command, probably as much on account of exhaustion of the ammunition of the militia as any other cause. No more heroic effort to overhaul an enemy was ever made than that made by Leland that day.[2]

---

[2] This account was written from statements now in the Collection of the author, made by Captain Gregg. They agree with the *Gregg Manuscript*. After securing these statements Leland was interviewed, and his account agrees exactly with what Gregg says. Gregg had no knowledge of who was in command of the force pressing him all the afternoon, and always praised the persistence and courage of the commander. Gregg says he lost no men, but Leland says six or seven guerrillas were killed. Gregg says one man, James Thompson, of the main command was killed, his account, in the *Gregg Manuscript* being as follows:

We lost but one man killed, James Thompson; when struck he was entirely out of sight of the enemy. I distinctly heard the bullet strike him, though he was over a rise and out of sight of the enemy. I looked along my line to see if it was one of my men who had been hit. When I saw that all my men were in place, I looked at the main line and saw the man fall from his horse. I will ever remember the dull, indescribable sound made by a bullet when it strikes a man. While it cannot be described, when once heard it is never forgotten.

Leland was born in Sauk county, Wisconsin, June 15, 1841, and came with his father to Kansas in 1858, settling in Doniphan county, where he has lived to this time (1909). He has always been prominent in Kansas, and has held many positions of responsibility. He was a splendid soldier. The following is taken from Vol. X, p. 427, *Kansas Historical Collections*, where a brief biography of him appears:

Cyrus Leland, Jr., came to Kansas with his father's family in the spring of 1858, and located in Doniphan county. He was born in Sauk county, Wisconsin, June 15, 1841. He entered the Union army as a private soldier in August, 1861, being assigned to the Fourth Kansas. In 1862 the Third and Fourth regiments were consolidated, and became the Tenth Kansas. He was made a first lieutenant, and at Prairie Grove commanded his company, being then one of the youngest officers in the army. In 1863 he was detailed as aide-de-camp on the staff of General Ewing. In 1864, while still in the army, the people of Doniphan county elected him a member of the legislature of 1865. On the first of January, 1866, Mr. Leland opened a small store in Troy, which has greatly expanded, and is

At four o'clock Gregg was so hoarse from shouting commands to his men that he could not speak above a whisper, and he was nearly exhausted. He had eaten nothing for twenty-four hours. Soon after entering Lawrence a guerrilla came by with an arm-load of quart bottles of blackberry brandy and gave Gregg one. He broke the neck off the bottle against a post and drank the contents. He got nothing more that day until after dark.

When Gregg reported to Quantrill that he was incapacitated, Todd was sent out to command the rear-guard. All the afternoon Quantrill had been marching towards Paola over the high prairies and along the "divides" between Bull creek and the Marais des Cygnes. He avoided timber as much as possible. He knew that if he could keep his men in hand until night he could escape. Only one man faltered. Soon after Gregg was relieved Joab Perry broke from the ranks and galloped in a northeasterly direction, "Splendidly mounted, with six excellent Colt's pistols in his belt, his long golden hair flying back in the Kansas breeze." Gregg said to Jarrette:

" 'Let's kill him!'

" 'No,' said Jarrette, 'let him go. He will get it soon enough.'

"But he didn't. He got to Missouri alive. He was described by the comrade who first met him as the most woe-begone object he had ever beheld! He was on foot, with but one pistol, bareheaded, barefooted, with but little clothing on his person and that torn to shreds — his flesh terribly lacerated!"[3]

About sunset Leland could see Paola and could see Union soldiers there. He expected co-operation, and pressed the guerrilla rear-guard so closely that it was driven into the rear of the

still conducted by him. For twenty-one years he was chairman of the board of county commissioners of Doniphan county. For sixteen years he was a member of the Republican national committee. Under President Harrison he served four years as collector of internal revenue for Kansas, Oklahoma and Indian Territory, and under President McKinley he served four years as pension agent. He was a member of the house of representatives in 1865, 1903, 1905 and 1907. He married Miss Mattie Stout, at Troy, in 1868, by whom he had eight children, five of whom are still living. Mrs. Leland died in 1894. He has been in public life for forty-seven years.

3 *The Gregg Manuscript.*

main columns. This was on the hill west of Paola. Quantrill saw the persistency of the attack and knew the danger he was in, for he, too, saw the Union troops at Paola. He halted his men and turned them about-face and charged savagely up the hill to the aid of Todd. Leland held his ground against the whole guerrilla force for ten minutes, though he had at the time no more than fifty men.[4] But he could not hold it long enough for Plumb and his troops on their jaded horses to come up. The guerrillas broke his line and he had to fall back.

Quantrill turned his men and marched down a steep high bank to Bull creek. Then he turned north through the timber and in the darkness escaped further pursuit for the night.[5]

---

[4] *The Gregg Manuscript.*

[5] The alarm of the inhabitants was general far to the south and west of Quantrill's line of retreat. C. M. Chase, on his way from the Sac and Fox Agency, in Franklin county, to Lawrence, August 21, 1863, has preserved the best record of this state of terror, in a letter to the *True Republican and Sentinel,* as follows:

Yesterday we passed two little villages, Centropolis and Minneola, on opposite sides of the same grove and about a mile apart. As we reached the first place we found people in arms, and excited over a report that Lawrence had been burned by Quantrill, and that all the negroes in the place had been killed. Every one was disposed to prepare for defense, while but few inclined to credit the report. As we entered Minneola, we found more excitement. All who could shoulder a musket had gone towards Lawrence, leaving the aged, with women and children, in a terrible fright. We had not believed the report, but now it did begin to look serious. A messenger, from the scene of terror, had just rushed through the place alarming the country, and informing the people that "the last house in Lawrence was burned," that the bushwhackers numbering from three to ten hundred were returning on this very road, destroying everything in their way, that they had just destroyed Brooklyn, and were this very moment burning Baldwin City and murdering the people. Baldwin City was only five miles ahead, and was the place we were designing to stop at during the night. We were not positive which road Quantrill would prefer, and consequently were not positive which road to take ourselves. The General was in a "phix." He had important papers in his possession which would make him a dead man if he was taken. No time was to be lost. After a moments reflection, he put the horses into a quick gait, and turned to the left into a less traveled road, passing Willow Springs on the Santa Fe road. Everywhere we found people in the greatest state of alarm, men were arming themselves and rushing to and fro. Some hastening towards Lawrence and others in doubt what to do. Women, terrified, were moving children and household goods to the cornfields, and running about in the wildest confusion. Commotion, confusion, terror and vengeance, all blended into one indescribable feeling, were driving the people into hurried and indiscriminate activity. As no one knew positively Quantrill's destination, every one was momentarily expecting his habitation to be turned into a scene of fire and bloodshed. Through these scenes we

Plumb turned towards Paola. He was met on the west side of Bull creek by a scouting party sent out by Lieutenant-Colonel Clark under Jesse Parsons.   In the gathering night Parsons came near firing on the Union forces, supposing them to be guerrillas.

Neither Major Plumb nor any of his men were in condition to follow Quantrill further that night. Plumb had been in the saddle constantly for nineteen hours, as had some of his men.   They

had marched more than seventy miles without rest or food. Their horses were exhausted and most of them died in a day or two. Many had broken down on the march. The troops of Captain Coleman had been in their saddles more than twenty-four hours and had marched more than one hundred miles.[6] They had prevented the burning of many homes and murder of citizens after meeting the guerrillas south of Brooklyn.

At Paola the command devolved on Lieutenant-Colonel C. S. Clark, Ninth Kansas, a very incompetent officer. He failed to find the trail of Quantrill for some hours.

Major Preston B. Plumb, as U. S. Senator

6 Major Plumb was severely criticised by the Robinsons and others at Lawrence. But this criticism was unjust and was inspired by personal hatred. Plumb had been a member of the house of representatives which impeached Robinson as governor. No man could have done more than did Major Plumb with the same force in the same condition. Lane criticised Plumb for refusing to turn over the command of troops to him. But Lane could have done no more than Plumb did. Plumb had no right to turn over his command to any one except a superior officer, and he would have been court-martialed for giving up the command to a civilian.

passed till nine o'clock in the evening, when we reached a Dutch farm house, seven miles from Lawrence, and were gladly welcomed as lodgers for the night. From here we could distinguish the line of Quantrill's retreat for many miles, by the light of burning houses. The nearest light, was that of buildings a mile distant, belonging to a forehanded farmer who had just completed a large harvest. He had a fine two story brick house, and the finest barn buildings in the county, packed to overflowing, with large stacks of grain and hay adjoining. All was now in ashes.
    During the evening at the Dutch farm several interesting law questions arose. The Dutchman's boy had brought home from the pursuit a

When the guerrillas descended the steep bluff into Bull Creek Valley, Quantrill and Gregg rode together in advance of the column — some two hundred yards. They came to a lake or pond made by a dam across a draw, and fed by a spring. They rode into the pond, which was so deep that the water reached the sides of their horses. Neither had tasted water since ten o'clock — Gregg since daylight. They sat on their horses and dipped up water in their hats and drank it. While they were in this pond the column passed them. They came up with it at a house in the valley where there was a well of fine cold water. A man and two women were drawing water and giving each guerrilla a drink. They had two cups, one holding a pint and one holding a quart. The men of the command were through drinking when Quantrill and Gregg arrived at the well. Gregg was offered the small cup but asked for the large one and it full. It was given him, and, notwithstanding his drinking at the lake, he said no water ever tasted so sweet. It was then quite dark in the timber. The guerrillas were in worse plight than their pursuers, having been much longer on the march and having slept none the night before. The reaction from excitement had come. Only their desperate situation kept them up.

About a mile beyond the well, at what is now the Rock

fine black horse, taken from a bushwhacker. Another man came in and claimed it. He was the nearest man in the pursuit when the bushwhacker jumped from the horse and ran into the woods; but being more patriotic than avaricious, he rushed into the woods after her, while the boy seized the horse and brought him home. Who owned the horse, was the question at issue. Both admitted the spoils of war belonged to the victor — that, as Uncle Sam's men were not in the engagement, Uncle Sam had no direct interest in the spoils, and that capture was the ground of title. All this admitted, the boy on his side kept putting the question ''who caught the horse,'' which seemed to puzzle the claimant, and in the end defeated the claim. Another Dutchman who had been burned out came in to claim a gun the Dutch boy had brought home. A rebel in his haste, dropped the gun in the public road before the Dutchman's burning house, and the Dutchman claimed it on the ground of its being dropped near his house. Both questions were argued with great zeal; but the boy ''couldn't see it'' plain enough to give up the horse or gun.

In the morning, after an early breakfast, we drove over to the road leading to this once beautiful town. Every house, save two or three was a smouldering ruin All along the road was a continuous line of beautiful farms, well cultivated and ready for the harvester. Occasionally a man would be seen sitting among the ruins of his once happy home, seemingly, striving to realize the awful and sudden change, but few people, however, were anywhere to be seen.

Ford or Connor's Ford, on Bull creek, the guerrillas halted
and were permitted to dismount and rest one hour. This rest did
them little good. It was extremely difficult to rouse some of
them from sleep, and all were stiff and stupid. Very slow progress was made until daylight. About an hour after sunrise
the guerrillas crossed the line into Missouri, only two or three
miles from the point where they had entered Kansas.

There were many Missouri Homeguards living about Paola.
They had been forced to leave Missouri border counties because
of insufficient protection by the United States. Major Dean, of
Harrisonville, Mo., was at Paola when Major Plumb got there.
He requested permission to take two hundred Homeguards, who
had their own arms and horses, and pursue Quantrill; he said
he could assemble that number in an hour or two. And he insisted that he could cut off Quantrill and harrass him until the
regular troops could come up and finish him. Plumb feared
such a force might be destroyed and refused Major Dean, who
all the time insisted that Quantrill would go into camp in an
hour or two, which he did.

Sandy Lowe was another Missourian who asked permission
to seek Quantrill with Homeguards. He was captain of Company D, Cass county Homeguards, and he and his men had been
forced to leave Missouri. His wife had suffered robbery of herself and week-old babe at the hands of guerrillas and he had
sworn to kill some thirty of them whose names he had written
in his book kept for such small matters. He said he could
gather sixty of his men in an hour or two and overtake Quantrill at a camp he would make near Paola. Or, he would go to
the State-line and arrange to receive the guerrillas there. Major
Plumb refused to permit the Homeguards to go out alone, believing they would be annihilated by the guerrillas. Clark had
refused to allow them to go out before Plumb arrived at Paola.
Lowe became disgusted with Plumb and told him to go to h—l,
and left saying he would have nothing further to do with the
pursuit; but he changed his mind and did good service the following day.

In refusing Major Dean and Sandy Lowe permission to go
in pursuit of Quantrill independently of other troops being then

put in readiness to take the field Major Plumb was careful to inform them that he was no longer in command of any of the troops. The command of the troops that had been with him all day went to Lieutenant-Colonel C. S. Clark, the ranking officer, as soon as he (Plumb) arrived in Paola and reported to him. He doubted the ability of Dean and Lowe to muster as many men as they believed they could, and feared that, having permission to go out, they would go with whatever force they could gather — few men or many — and meet with disaster. Plumb told them that as the command had passed to Colonel Clark it would be impossible for him to give the desired permission, saying that Clark could, but he would advise against dividing the forces until all preparations then under way in Paola for the pursuit were completed. Colonel Clark had charge of these preparations and would assign positions to all troops that could be assembled in the town.

Dean and Lowe having been refused permission to go out before the arrival of Major Plumb, their only object in making application to him was to have him use his influence with Colonel Clark in behalf of their request. Major Plumb did right in refusing to secure them permission to go out at that time. He might have obtained their desires by going personally to Colonel Clark, but that officer expected to start out with his entire force in an hour or two, which he did, and independent bodies of troops operating ahead of him might have caused disaster. Whatever the errors of judgment of Major Plumb that day, he was right in this instance in withholding his approval.

Major Preston B. Plumb,
in Uniform

Clark started his men out of Paola about three o'clock a. m. on the 22d. All the Federal forces of the country adjacent were concentrating along the State-line. The Red Legs were at Aubry at daylight.[7] About sunrise some of the troops began to

7 No body of men ever gained such notoriety as the Red Legs. They were an efficient body of scouts organized by General Ewing and General

come up with the rear-guard of the guerrillas, who were worn out and could not march rapidly. Jesse Parsons, in command of some Cass county, Mo., troops was the first to come up with them. He captured three just before they crossed the State-line. These he turned over to a guard detailed by George H. Hoyt, who arrived at the moment. Hoyt shot one of them a few minutes later. Leland arrived in time to see him shot. He was just disgorging the plunder he had secured at Lawrence as Leland rode up. This loot consisted of marbles, jewsharps, mouth organs, toys, shoestrings, cheap buttons. Hoyt looked over the collection in astonishment, then drawing his pistol, said: "I

Blunt for desperate service along the border. In the letters of C. M. Chase from Kansas to the *True Republican and Sentinel*, Sycamore, Illinois, are found definitions of the terms in use on the border in 1863. Writing from Leavenworth, August 10th, he says:

Jayhawkers, Red Legs, and Bushwhackers are everyday terms in Kansas and Western Missouri. A Jayhawker is a Unionist who professes to rob, burn out and murder only rebels in arms against the government. A Red Leg is a Jayhawker originally distinguished by the uniform of red leggings. A Red Leg, however, is regarded as more purely an indiscriminate thief and murderer than the Jayhawker or Bushwhacker. A Bushwhacker is a rebel Jayhawker, or a rebel who bands with others for the purpose of preying upon the lives and property of Union citizens. They are all lawless and indiscriminate in their iniquities. Their occupation, unless crushed out speedily, will end in a system of highway robbery exceeding anything which has existed in any country. It excites the mind, destroys the moral sensibilities, creates a thirst for wild life and adventure which will, on the restoration of peace, find gratification in nothing but highway robbery.

Every thief who wanted to steal from the Missouri people counterfeited the uniform of the Red Legs and went forth to pillage. This gave the organization a bad name, and much of the plundering done along the border was attributed to them, when, in fact, they did little in that line themselves. There were some bad characters among them — very bad. But they were, generally, honest and patriotic men. They finally hunted down the men who falsely represented themselves to be Red Legs, and they killed every man they found wearing the uniform without authority. The uniform was that of a commissioned company officer, but which one is not now known, supplemented with red leggings, usually made from the red sheepskins used by shoemakers. There were about thirty of them. They received usually the salary of the commissioned officer whose uniform they were authorized to wear. Among them were the following:

George H. Hoyt, captain, the lawyer who defended John Brown at Charlestown, Virginia.

Theodore Bartles, whose brother, Jacob H. Bartles, was in the Sixth Kansas, and who founded Bartlesville, Oklahoma. Their father, Joseph A.

will just kill you for being a d——d fool,'' and shot the guerrilla dead. Hoyt shot the other guerrillas a few minutes later.
This done, Bartles gave chase, and a guerrilla, who, when he
found he could not escape, stood at bay to fight. He fired but
once, when a shot from Bartles killed him.

The main body of the guerrillas was then four miles from
the State-line in Missouri, at the head of a branch of Grand
river. They had dismounted in a little prairie surrounded by
timber, and could plainly see the State-line and the Federal
troops pouring across it. Quantrill stopped to allow his men to
get something to eat. A friendly citizen came into the camp and
told him of a force of Missouri troops in waiting for him just
over the divide to the east. Quantrill mounted his horse and

Bartles, moved to Quindaro from New Jersey in 1857, and built the famous
''Six Mile House'' on the Leavenworth road, six miles from Wyandotte
in the winter of 1860-61. This house was the headquarters of the Red
Legs. Theodore Bartles was the best pistol shot in the Red Legs company
and one of the best that ever fired a revolver. He was a better shot than
''Wild Bill.''

Charles R. Jennison.

William Hickok (Wild Bill), afterwards famous in frontier towns in
dealing with the desperate characters in the days of range cattle.

''Red'' Clark, of Emporia. He was the best spy General Ewing ever
had.

Jack Harvey, who was a brother of Fred Harvey, the famous ''Eeat-
ing House Man'' of the Santa Fé lines.

Harry Lee, of whom the author has learned nothing beyond the fact
that he had a broken nose.

Joseph Guilliford, a jeweler before the Civil War, in Wyandotte,
where he married a Miss Garrett, of the Wyandot tribe and niece of
Governor William Walker. He was killed in Phillip Hescher's saloon in
Wyandotte after the war by Russell Garrett, a cousin to his wife. The
late Sanford Haff of Muncie, Wyandotte county, married his widow.

Al Saviers. The author has learned nothing of him except that it
is said he is still living in Colorado. He lived in Wyandotte county before
the war in an old stone building at a cross-roads, three or four miles south
of Argentine, locally known as ''The Junction.'' This old building was
standing when the author was county clerk of Wyandotte county.

——— Alsup. Lived in Wyandotte county near Saviers. Nothing
much known of him.

''Sore-eyed Dan,'' a soldier of the Fifteenth Kansas; name not
remembered. Protested when Jennison shot and killed David Gregg, saying,
''By G—d that is the first time I ever saw a dog killed that had no

rode among his men ordering them to "saddle up." To this they replied that they would not do so until they had something to eat. He called attention to the Kansas troops crossing the State-line in plain view. "D——n the Kansans," they said. "We whipped them yesterday and can whip them today." "Yes," said Quantrill, "I know you can whip the Kansans, but what will you do with the twelve hundred Missouri troops just over the divide?"

"Well," said the men, "that is a horse of another color! We will saddle up."

When the guerrillas started on the march again many horses could not move. Gregg's mare was one; her ears fell down and her tongue protruded. Quantrill ordered him to dismount and

teeth," meaning that Gregg was old and helpless and could not fight. Nothing now remembered of him.

James Flood.

Jerry Malcom.

Charles Blunt, known as "One-eyed Blunt," as he had lost an eye. Was disloyal, but acted as a scout for Jennison.

——— Hawkins, of whom little is known except that he went to kill "Jeff Davis" once and did not have the nerve to shoot his Red Leg brother when he faced him.

Jack Hays — was at Independence when James P. Duke was robbed.

Walt Sinclair, was six feet tall, light complexion, a giant in strength, a horseman who had no superior, a killer, and had a record and a grave-yard. Was probably an associate of Quantrill at Lawrence in 1860.

John Blachley, son the the Presbyterian minister of Wyandotte, the first of his denomination who preached in that town.

"Jeff Davis." Captain Joseph Bloomington Swain, from New York State. Was mustered as captain of Company K, Fifteenth Kansas, October 10, 1863. "Jeff Davis" was a nickname, but how he acquired it is not now known.

W. S. Tough, who was proprietor of the horse market at the Kansas City Stock Yards for many years. In the series of letters written by C. M. Chase, already referred to and quoted from, appears the following concerning Captain Tough;

The name of Captain Tuft — or according to his own spelling, "Tough" — carries with it a degree of terror in Kansas of which people in peaceable society can have no conception. It reminds some of the loss of horses, some of the destruction of their homes, and some of the murder of their dearest friends.

Captain Tuft was born in Savannah, Ga., and at an early age moved to Baltimore. In 1860, at the age of twenty-one, he moved to Saint Joseph, Mo. His father helped him to a little capital, and he, with a

go into the brush, which he did, six men in like condition going with him. About one hundred guerrillas there left the main command and took to the brush.

The carriage containing the wounded was drawn into the brush and left, but the team was taken. It was Gregg's order that Bledsoe be carried away on a horse, but that was not done.

Quantrill, with his remaining force marched on and met the Missouri troops, not more in number than his own, and in the skirmish scattered his men and escaped into the brush.

When the Kansas troops arrived at the abandoned camp the Indians under White Turkey and Pelathe soon found the carriage containing the wounded. Three of the guerrillas began to plead for mercy, but Bledsoe said: "Stop it! We are not entitled to mercy! We spare none and do not expect to be

---

partner, invested in mules and wagons, and commenced freighting from St. Joe to Denver City. They prospered in business until the war broke out, when, for some reason or other, his mules were taken from him by a squad of Jayhawkers. He immediately goes to headquarters, at Leavenworth, for indemnification, but gets no satisfaction from Uncle Sam. He then determines to state his cause to the rebels, and crosses the river at Leavenworth, in search for rebel headquarters. He had proceeded but a half mile into the woods when he was confronted by five Bushwhackers, who ordered him to halt. Not inclining to obey the order, he put spurs to his horse, the consequence of which was he was shot down and left for dead. He recovered, however, and after a few weeks nursing, by some kind woman, in the woods, he was able to travel. Prior to this occurrence he had no particular interest in the fight, either one way or the other. But now he determined to go into the fight with all the force he possessed, not from any feelings of patriotism, but from pure motives of revenge. He swore eternal vengeance to the squad that shot him down, and to all others of that class. In Leavenworth and vicinity he raised seventy-five men and took to the woods. They were soon well mounted on rebel horses, and well disciplined for their ferocious work. He adopted a system of scouts, spies and disguises, and was very soon in the secret of the Bushwhackers' operations. In just one month from the time he took his men into the brush he had the unspeakable satisfaction of seeing the five who first assaulted him swinging from the same limb. He seemed to have been transformed into a demon, he said, and to take the wildest delight in seeing the "poor cusses gasping for breath." On another occasion, he, with a half dozen of his men, were passing a house and found a woman crying bitterly over her dead baby. He learned that the Bushwhackers had just been there inquiring of the woman of Captain Tuft's men. While she was answering their questions her child began to cry, and one of the fiends drew his revolver and shot it through the head. Tuft put himself on track and in a week killed five of the gang including the one who shot the child. At another time he found one of his scouts beside the road with his head blown open with powder. He immediately took three of his men to track out the enemy. Towards night, after riding thirty miles, they came suddenly on seven horsemen whom they took to be rebels. Feigning himself

spared!'' Then addressing the troops that had come up, he said: ''Just take us out of this trap and put us on our knees facing you and shoot us. We are not able to stand on our feet. Let us see you. Do not shoot us from behind.'' His request was granted. After the guerrillas were shot the Indians scalped them.

Gregg, with his six men, went some distance to a house and questioned the man found there, one Collins, who proved an old friend of his father. He provided a good breakfast and

a Bushwhacker, he gallops into their midst with, ''Halloo, boys! whar's Quantrill?'' Not knowing Tuft or his companions, they were at first very cautious in their answers. But being a very shrewd man, ''let on right smart,'' like a Bushwhacker. ''Here's a hoss,'' says he, ''I shot a d—d yankee off from not more nor an hour ago.'' After boasting of several yankee butcheries and house burnings he had performed since breakfast, one of the rebels ventured to crow a little over what *they* had done. They had caught one of Old Tuft's scouts in the morning, made some holes in him, loaded his ears up with powder, touched 'em off, and ''blowed his old mug to h—l.'' Instantly Tuft gave the order, and those seven men were biting the dust before they had time to cock a revolver. These were among the incidents he related. There were an infinite numbers of single murders, and lesser crimes he mentioned, but enough has been related to give an idea of the character of the man. He lived in the woods, plundered from armed rebels, burned their houses and killed the fighting population without scruple. His plunder was divided among his men, who would sell it and get pay for their service. They belonged to no military organization, but run an independent concern. By many Tuft is regarded as a pure horse-thief and murderer; others of a rabid, lawless nature, incline to wink at his crimes as long as his avowed purpose is to rob and murder rebels. It proves dangerous, however, to suspend the law and give such characters as Tuft discretionary license to rob and murder. Where there is a fine horse in the way, or a personal enemy, Tuft's discretion between Union and Secesh is not accurate. Jayhawking has run its race in Kansas; honest people are all on the side of the law; indiscriminate robbery is the result of the Jayhawker's license, and in many cases its friends have paid heavily towards its support. Tuft himself acknowledges the inevitable tendency of the practice. He says he has few regrets for the past; his victims have not yet appeared in his dreams, still he don't like the business, and has determined to lead a better life. Gen. Blunt, a few months ago, gave him a position on his staff as Chief of Scouts, with a pay of $250 per month. He is now under arrest for killing a man at Fort Scott; but if his story is true the man ought to have been killed, and his detention will be brief. He says I shall meet him again at Fort Scott. We shall see.

''Beauregard,'' Jack Bridges. Little is known of him. Is said to have been part Indian and to have been raised near the Shawnee Mission, in Johnson county, Kansas. After the war he sold W. H. Ryus, a prominent citizen of Wyandotte county, Kansas, a stone woman, of the Cardiff Giant variety, supposed to have been manufactured in Colorado, where Bridges said he discovered her while mining in a gravel-bar. The author saw this ''stone woman,'' and she was big enough, heavy enough, and ugly enough

stood guard while it was eaten. He provided a guard for the day while the guerrillas slept. At night he furnished a guide to the Little Blue in Jackson county, where Gregg arrived and was safely hidden.

General Ewing left Leavenworth about one o'clock in the afternoon of the 21st and went direct to the field, crossing the Kansas river at De Soto, where he was delayed five hours for want of boats. He did not get to Missouri until after dark on the 22d. William Mowdry was a lieutenant in some Kansas Militia company, which was in pursuit of the guerrillas. General Ewing and Senator James H. Lane met at the point where Quantrill had stopped first after crossing back into Missouri. Mowdry was present when they met. Lane denounced Ewing for his milk-and-water administration of the military affairs along the border. Ewing asked what he should do. Lane replied that he would be removed as soon as he (Lane) could get to Washington. Ewing begged hard for his official head. Lane agreed to make no complaint if Ewing would issue the order, which had been under consideration for some time, depopulating portions of some of the border counties of Missouri. Ewing agreed to do it, and he and Lane went to a cabin near-by. There they drew up Order No. 11. Ewing promulgated it as soon as

---

to have been worth the money Ryus paid for her. She was a very coarse job of woman-making.

Newt Morrison. A bad man. After the war he stole a horse from Joseph Guilliford, who captured him at the house of a Mrs. Green, in Kansas, just south of Westport, Mo., and put him in the Wyandotte county jail. On the following night he was lynched by hanging at the instance of Guilliford.

"Pickles." Samuel Wright. Had something to do with the Linn county troubles in Territorial days and some mention is made of him in the *History of Vernon County, Mo.* Was sentenced to a term in either the Missouri penitentiary or the State prison at Carlisle, Pa., by the notorious Judge Williams of Fort Scott. Was pardoned by President Lincoln. He was killed at the house of Mrs. Green by Joseph Guilliford, for resisting arrest, the night of the capture of Newt Morrison.

A man named Gladhart, Lawrence, was said to have been a member, also "Pony" Searl and John Salathiel, of the same place, but the author has not been able to confirm this.

The headquarters of the Red Legs were at the "Six Mile House," mentioned above.

he got back to his headquarters. When they came out of the cabin Mowdry heard Lane say to Ewing: "You are a dead dog if you fail to issue that order as agreed between us."[8]

Jesse Parsons had been ordered into camp near the place where Quantrill first stopped to rest after getting back to Missouri. From there he was engaged in riding down squads of guerrillas until about four o'clock in the afternoon, when he was ordered to take fifteen men and go to Paola and bring up more men and some supplies. He set out through the woods to go on the Missouri side of the line and look for guerrilla bands on the way. He came to a steep hill covered with timber through which the road ran; at the top of the hill there stood a fine large house, where the prairie began. The road ran north and south between the house and the timber, and the road by which Parsons ascended the hill came into the main road almost in front of the house. When he came in sight of the main road he saw fifteen guerrillas ride south on it and form in line, facing the house. Parsons motioned caution to his men, and formed in the edge of the timber a hundred feet from the guerrillas without attracting attention. He ordered a charge and fired his revolver. His men were at the guerrillas in a moment, and they broke and ran for the timber, every man for himself. Parsons wounded some of them, but killed none; he selected a guerrilla finely mounted on a splendid roan gelding and pressed him to the timber, firing three shots at him at a range of about ten feet, the last shot knocking the man from his horse. He ran on his hands and knees into the timber, but Parsons thinks he must have been mortally wounded. Where he fell Parsons found his pistols and a short gun, also six new hats crowded one on top of another, in which condition he had been wearing them all the way from Lawrence. Parsons saw that the fine horse was going to escape, and to prevent it, shot and

---

8 Mowdry repeated these things to Colonel E. F. Rogers of one of the Missouri Militia regiments, and Colonel Rogers told them to the author. He also got his knowledge of what Major Dean and Sandy Lowe said at Paola on the night of the 21st from Mowdry. Colonel Rogers lives in Kansas City, Mo., and was for many years a special examiner for the bureau of pensions. His home was in Cass county, Mo., and he saw much border service.

wounded him. He took the horse back to camp, where it was recognized as General Deitzler's fine cavalry horse which had been taken by the guerrillas from Lawrence. The horse was much valued by General Deitzler, and was a pacer with a fine record. Soon after getting to camp the horse died of the wound inflicted by Parsons.

Parsons was engaged some time in pursuing the guerrilla bands. Three or four days after crossing the line he was on the Sni Hills, Jackson county. One of his scouts discovered a band in a brushy hill, in numbers about equal to his own force. Parsons, with his men, crept to within a hundred feet of the camp before they were discovered. The guerrillas were just ready to eat dinner when fired on; they scattered, and three of them were killed. Some of them fired as they ran, but without effect.[9]

A short distance beyond the place where the guerrillas first camped after getting back into Missouri Lieutenant Cyrus Leland, Jr., found a guerrilla walking about a cabin with a woman. He surrendered. The woman claimed to be his wife, and he finally admitted that she was. He was dressed throughout in new clothes. He confessed at last that he had been to Lawrence, and that he had obtained his new clothes there. He was hung in his own home.

Leland, with a party, captured three of the guerrillas near Lone Jack, and hanged them all on one tree so high their feet could not be touched by a man riding under them. They posted this notice on the tree: "Don't cut them down!"

Gregg says that in the pursuit many guerrillas were killed.

It is well to close this account of the Lawrence Massacre with a quotation from the *Gregg Manuscript*:

"I blame Quantrill for some things in connection with the Lawrence raid. He told me, in support of his argument for the raid, that there was a great deal of money in Lawrence. 'And,' said he, 'I want to compensate the people who have divided their

---

9 Statement made by Jesse Parsons to the author, Chanute, Kansas, (Parsons's home), June 13, 1905. This statement is extensive, covering various subjects, and is valuable, as Parsons is a man of the highest standing and integrity.

last biscuit with us and are still willing to do so.' 'Well,' said
I, in reply, 'that is very laudable.'

" 'Now,' said Quantrill, 'my plan is that whatever money
may be gotten in Lawrence shall be divided among the men with
instructions to give to these people very liberally.'

"But after we returned, this pro rata division was never
mentioned. The truth is, that Quantrill tried to manage so that
Todd. and his men would get all the money. I presume, however, that Charles Higbee secured the largest sum that any one
man got in Lawrence. Immediately after our return to Missouri
he left for parts unknown to us at the time. It was reported
that he went to Canada. Soon after the close of the war we
heard of Higbee at Fort Worth, Texas, in the banking business,
in the eyes of the survivors of Quantrill's men and the people
of Missouri, a traitor."

Morgan Townley Mattox, long one of Quantrill's men, says
that one B. Wood or Woods got the same amount of money that
Higbee got and that both went to Canada.[10]

—o—

All the reports of officers of the Lawrence Massacre are to
be found in Series I, Vol. XXII, *Rebellion Records*, beginning
at page 572.

—o—

The account of Order No. 11 does not properly fall within
the scope of this work. It will be fully treated in a volume soon
to be written and published by the author of this book.

---

[10] Mattox made a long statement to the author, April 29 and 30, 1909,
at Bartlesville, Oklahoma, where he lives, covering all the operations of
Quantrill. Mattox was at Lawrence, but says nothing of what he did
there. His statement is very clear, for his memory is good, and he talks
well. Mattox is now a painter and is said to be a good citizen.

CHAPTER XXXII

THE guerrillas did little in Missouri in 1863, after the Lawrence Massacre. The enforcement of Order No. 11 left almost nothing in the country upon which they could subsist. The Federal forces harried them day and night. The pursuit was grim, merciless, relentless, and many of them were killed.

About the last of September a rendezvous was fixed where the men were to assemble for the march to Texas to spend the winter. This was the old rendezvous, the farm of Captain Perdee, on the Blackwater, in Johnson county, from which Quantrill started to Lawrence.

So closely guarded had been all the avenues of escape that Colonel Holt had not been able to leave Missouri, and he and a Colonel Robinson and a Captain Tucker, all of whom had spent the summer recruiting for Price's army, went to the place appointed and took their men. All the guerrilla captains obeyed the summons. About five hundred men assembled at the farm of Captain Perdee. Gregg says four hundred. Quantrill then bore a commission as colonel from some Confederate authority, perhaps General Sterling Price, possibly Thomas C. Reynolds, Confederate governor of Missouri. At the rendezvous was organized the First Regiment, First Brigade, Army of the South, and Quantrill as colonel was put in command.

Quantrill in Uniform of
Confederate Colonel

The guerrilla command left the farm of Captain Perdee October 2, at daylight, and marched to the Grand river, where it camped for the night. The second night it camped beyond the Osage. It passed twelve miles west of Carthage and crossed Shoal creek at the falls. It followed the trail leading west through a corner of the Seneca country to the Fort Scott and Fort Gibson road, which passed north and south through what is now Baxter Springs, Kansas. It was the intention to go south to Texas over this old trail and its extensions.

Perhaps Quantrill had planned to take Fort Baxter. Some two weeks before the Massacre two citizen mail carriers were wounded and captured by the guerrilla, Cy Gordon, ten miles south of the Springs. One of these was known as "Fatty," and he and Gordon had been roistering chums at Leavenworth, on account of which the mail carriers were set at liberty after being told that Quantrill and his men would take dinner with the garrison at the Springs in about ten days. "Fatty" reported this conversation at the post but no one would consider it seriously. At the time of the Massacre he was at the fort under treatment for his wounds. But Captain Gregg says Quantrill previously knew nothing of any fort or camp at Baxter Springs.

To the 4th of October the garrison consisted of one company of the Second Kansas Colored Infantry, commanded by Lieutenant R. E. Cook, and Company D, Third Wisconsin Cavalry, commanded by Lieutenant John Crites. Crites was in command of the post. Before the 4th Crites was summoned to Fort Scott, and Cook was left in command. On the 4th Lieutenant James B. Pond arrived from Fort Scott with a part of his company (C, Third Wisconsin) and took command of the post which was officially designated as Fort Blair, in honor of Lieutenant-Colonel Charles W. Blair, Fourteenth Kansas.

The fort consisted of some log cabins with a total frontage of about a hundred feet, facing east — towards Spring river. These constituted the "fort." Back of the fort, and of the same width, was a large space enclosed by embankments of earth thrown up against logs and about four feet high. The west wall of the enclosure had been torn out the day before the attack by order of Lieutenant Pond, who found the camp too small for all the troops. Pond's tent was two hundred yards west of the fort and the men were extending the embankments

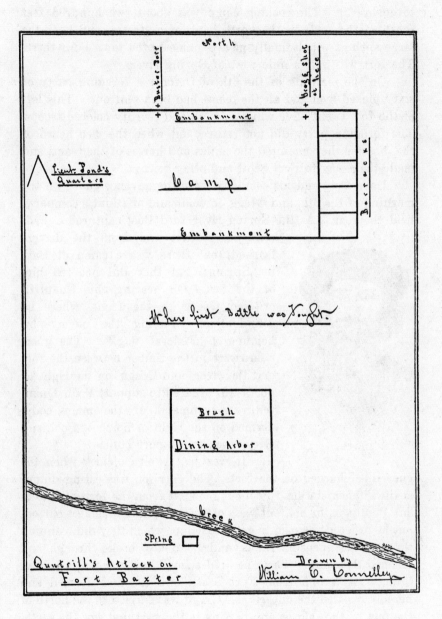

Quntrill's Attack on
Fort Baxter

Drawn by
William E. Connelley

to enclose it. The cooking camp was about two hundred feet south of the fort, on the north bank of a stream, and near the large springs which finally gave a name to the town built there. The fort was half a mile west of Spring river.

On the morning of the 6th of October a foraging party of sixty picked men and all the teams had been sent out. This left at the fort twenty-five white soldiers and seventy colored troops. The foraging party did not return, but when the men heard of the disaster they mounted the mules and horses of the teams and made their way to Fort Scott and other towns.

Dave Pool and his company were the advance-guard on the morning of the 6th, and Gregg, in command of Blunt's company, held the rear. At the Spring river ford Pool captured a Federal wagon-train and from the drivers learned that there was a camp at Baxter Springs, but they did not tell him of the fort. On hearing this Quantrill ordered Gregg to the front, where he found Pool "fooling the enemy by hoisting a Federal flag." The guerrillas were in the timber between the fort and the river, and Gregg, on the right or north was ordered to support Pool. Quantrill, in command of the main body, formed on the right or north of Pool, and Gregg was to support both.

Dave Pool

It was just twelve o'clock when the guerrillas charged on the fort. The garrison was eating dinner at the kitchen station. Pool cut them off from the fort. Lieutenant Pond was in his tent west of the camp and was also cut off, but he ordered the men to get into camp, which they did, running through the guerrilla ranks, and Pond also broke through and reached the camp. There he fired a small howitzer which he had brought with him from Fort Scott, and the men formed and fiercely resisted the guerrillas. Gregg was carried to the north of the fort by the charge, and passing to the west first saw the earthwork. He was shot at by a negro soldier who rose up from under the wall and who dodged back quickly. Gregg cocked his

pistol and waited five minutes for the negro to show himself
again, which he did not do. Seeing some men run southwest
from the camp and hide in the tall grass and willows along the
stream Gregg took two men and went there to capture them; and
he had secured a number, when bullets began to whiz past him,
and, looking around, saw nothing of Pool's men nor any of
the guerrillas. Gregg mounted his horse and rode northwest,
striking the Fort Gibson road at the crest of the ridge or elevation which extended from northeast to southwest north of the
fort. There he saw Quantrill in line confronting General Blunt
and his escort. Quantrill seems to have done nothing at the fort
and to have gone with three companies aimlessly out on the
prairie to the north where he by accident discovered Blunt. The
guerrillas had been repulsed at the fort and driven off, and the
Union forces had sustained small loss.

General Blunt had been successful in his operations in the
Southwest, and a new department had been made for him, with
headquarters at Fort Gibson, for which post he left Fort Scott
on the evening of the 4th. He had been at some pains to secure
a good band and a fine flag for his new post. His escort consisted of Company I, Third Wisconsin Cavalry, and Company A,
Fourteenth Kansas, about a hundred men. He had several wagons loaded with official documents and supplies. He arrived on
the prairie north of the post at Baxter Springs about noon of
the 6th in total ignorance of the presence of Quantrill in that
region — something for which he was severely criticised and
justly censured. He owed his final escape to his vanity, for he
had halted to arrange a gorgeous and impressive arrival at the
post — with colors flying and martial music by his fine band.
When he first saw Quantrill's column he supposed it to be a troop
sent out from the post to meet and greet him.

Quantrill formed his men east of the road and just north of
the crest of the ridge, and Blunt formed just west of the road
opposite and facing the guerrillas. There was a second line of
guerrillas in the woods to the rear. Blunt got only sixty-five
men into line. The lines were about two hundred yards apart.
Before a shot had been fired two of Blunt's men left the line
and started to run away, but were forced back by Major Cur-

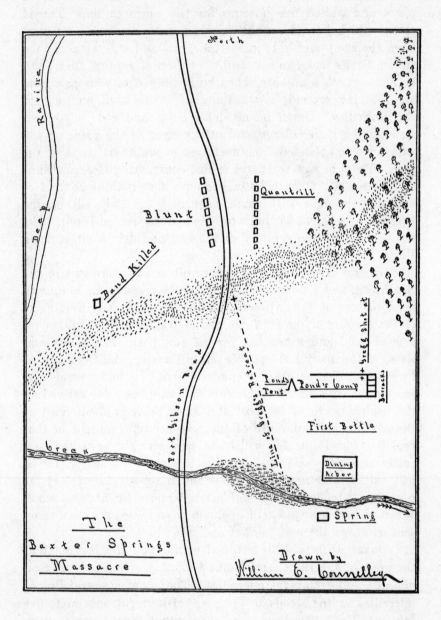

North

Deep Ravine

Blunt

Quantrill

Band Killed

Gregg shut at

Pond's Tent

Pond's Camp

Barracks

First Battle

Line of Gregg's Retreat

Fort Gibson Road

Creek

Dining Arbor

Spring

The

Baxter Springs

Massacre

Drawn by

William E. Connelley

tis. However, they were no more than back when they again broke away, eight more following them. Seeing this, Quantrill ordered a charge, when Company A, to a man, turned and fled. The Wisconsin troops stood until the guerillas were within twenty feet, when they turned to run away also. The guerrillas were among them instantly, and out of forty men, twenty-three were killed and six were wounded and left for dead. Major Henning, Third Wisconsin, ran through the guerrilla line and reached the fort, where he gave Pond the first intelligence of what was transpiring on the prairie beyond the elevation.

The charge of the guerrillas was soon a pursuit of fugitives, with whom it was every man for himself. Very few escaped. There was a deep ravine or wash in the prairie a quarter of a mile from the road, running south at an angle with it. There the greatest slaughter occurred, for many horses could not leap the ditch.

General Blunt and Major Curtis were passed by the first guerrilla line and closely beset by the second. Two gaps appeared in the first line, and Blunt told Curtis to try to escape through one and he would try the other. At the ravine, the horse of Curtis was, as it was gathering for the leap, shot in the hip, which caused it to tumble in, throwing Curtis, who was shot through the head a moment later. His horse scrambled out and ran wildly over the prairie. General Blunt got through the line, and his horse sprang over the ravine, but the rebound threw the General out of the saddle to the horse's neck, in which position he rode a mile or more. When well beyond the guerrillas he regained his seat in the saddle and rallied fifteen of his fleeing men, with which he advanced, checking the pursuit, but most of his men were strewn dead over the prairie. About sundown General Blunt came into the camp much crestfallen and mortified. He had sustained, at the hands of guerrillas, the severest reverse of his whole military career.

When General Blunt saw that he was to be charged by the enemy and was told that it was Quantrill's command in front of him he realized that he was in grave danger and that to flee with all speed was his only hope. He was riding in his carriage or ambulance in company with Mrs. Chester Thomas, of

Topeka, who was on the way to join her husband, then an army contractor at Fort Smith and Fort Gibson. Mrs. Thomas was but twenty-two and is said to have been a beautiful woman. There were always half a dozen splendid horses led saddled and ready for instant use in the general's escort. When he determined to escape, General Blunt put Mrs. Thomas on one of these led horses. There was no time for gallantry and delicate adjustments of garments. The saddle was an army tree of the McClellan model, and Mrs. Thomas was mounted astride. There was not even time to adjust the stirrups, and her feet were thrust through the straps above them. The General told her to cling to the saddle-horn for life. The horse proved a good one, and Mrs. Thomas rode from the dangerous field with fewer mishaps than Blunt, though, as she afterwards said, her clothing was in sad disorder in the wild ride for life, as she supposed. But she would have been in no danger had she remained on the battleground and been taken by the guerrillas. She would have suffered not a single indignity and would have been treated with respect and gallantry.

With General Blunt and Mrs. Thomas was Cyrus Leland, Senior, father of Lieutenant Cyrus Leland, Jr., who led the militia and citizens so bravely in the pursuit of Quantrill from Lawrence. Leland, Senior, was quarter-master of the Thirteenth Kansas, then stationed at Camden, Ark., and was on his way to join his regiment. He was splendidly mounted on a gray horse his son had gotten from General Ewing. Leland rode with General Blunt and Mrs. Thomas from the fatal field, his horse having to be held in to keep him from distancing those of his companions.[1]

Cyrus Leland, Sr.

In the band-wagon were fourteen musicians of the Brigade band, James O'Neale, correspondent of Frank Leslie's Weekly, Henry Pellage of Madison, Wis-

---

[1] Cyrus Leland, Senior, was born at Grafton, Massachusetts, in 1808. He graduated from Harvard College. The room he occupied there was afterwards jointly occupied by Hon. D. W. Wilder, now of Hiawatha, Kan-

consin, the driver, and a lad twelve years old, servant of the leader of the band. Seeing that the day was lost and the prisoners were being shot down, they attempted to escape in a southwesterly direction. William Bledsoe, a fat, jolly old guerrilla, approached them, demanding that they surrender, and was shot dead. Captain Gregg and George Todd saw Bledsoe killed and immediately gave chase, and when within fifty yards of the wagon the left front wheel came off the axle and the wagon fell, throwing the members of the band to the ground. They displayed handkerchiefs in token of surrender. The guerrillas demanded to know why they had not surrendered to Bledsoe, and shot them on the spot. The bodies were thrown in and under the wagon, which was set on fire and almost entirely consumed, several of the bodies being badly burned. The boy was not yet dead and succeeded in crawling some distance before he died, his clothes in flames. Gregg is of the opinion that the members of the band would not have been killed had Bledsoe not

---

sas, and the father of Kansas literature, and Charles F. Brown, the humorist ''Artemas Ward.'' Mr. Leland moved to Peoria, Illinois, in 1836. In 1839 he moved to Wisconsin, and in 1858 he moved to Doniphan county, Kansas, where he died about 1888. He was one of those hardy, intelligent and patriotic settlers to whom Kansas owes so much, and who laid so well the foundation of our famous commonwealth.

The horse on which he was mounted at the Baxter Springs Massacre was captured near Sedalia, Mo., by the escort of General Ewing in the pursuit of Shelby in October, 1863. On the 18th General Ewing and his escort arrived at Carthage. Before entering the town the advance-guard was fired on at a wooded creek-crossing. General Ewing was then riding the gray horse. Cyrus Leland, Jr., an aid on the General's staff, led up a dark horse and requested the general to ride it rather than the gray, saying that the gray would prove a conspicuous mark at night if it should turn out that there was to be a battle. The general changed to the dark horse, but there was no battle. At Carthage the horses were fed some wheat, which foundered the gray horse. General Ewing swapped the gray horse for a fine mare owned by Leland early in the morning before Leland knew the gray was foundered. This was intended for a joke on Leland, but he insisted on keeping the gray. He had him scarified around the hoofs and stood in water twenty-four hours, which effected a complete cure. He sent the horse to Troy, Kansas. His father wishing to return to his regiment rode the gray horse, and was mounted on him at Baxter Springs. He was compelled to abandon the horse that winter about fifty miles from Little Rock when hotly pursued by Confederate soldiers.

been shot, but all other guerrilla accounts say they would have been killed in any event.

The guerrillas feasted royally on the rations secured from Blunt's supply-train. And many of them became gloriously drunk on whiskey from the same source, among the latter being Riley Crawford, eldest son of Jeptha Crawford, who was shot in Jackson county by order of Penick. Mrs. Crawford brought her boys to Quantrill and told him to make soldiers of them that they might avenge their father's death. They did become desperadoes. After eating dinner near the dead soldiers, Riley Crawford, just as the mess was breaking up to get ready to fall into line for the march, stepped up to one of the dead of the band and struck him with a sword he had captured, saying, ''Get up, you Federal s—n of a b——h.'' And to the surprise of everybody and the consternation of young Crawford himself the man rose up and stood before him. He was not even wounded, but had feigned death, hoping thereby to escape; he now evidently supposed his feigning had been discovered and that he must be killed. Crawford drew a pistol and shot him dead.[2]

About this time two men rode almost into Quantrill's line. They were right on John Koger before they were observed, and one of them shot at Koger, breaking his collar-bone and making a dangerous wound. They wheeled and galloped away, followed by a shot from Koger.

Gregg says he never saw Quantrill under the influence of liquor until the day of the battle of Baxter Springs. He drank some of the captured whiskey and became drunk and talkative. He strutted around saying: ''By G—d, Shelby could not whip Blunt; neither could Marmaduke, but I whipped him.''

Gregg recalls that a man and woman escaped. They were riding in a buggy drawn by one horse. When Blunt's men broke over the prairie, they fled. The woman stood up in the buggy and whipped the horse while the man fired at the

---

[2] Riley Crawford was in Bill Anderson's band of guerrillas at the Centralia massacre. On the return of the guerrillas from North Missouri, Crawford was killed in Cooper county. He was not quite seventeen when killed. He is said to have been the youngest guerrilla in the brush. Major Edwards says that he was ambushed and fired on from a fence corner and fell from his horse dead.

approaching guerrillas. They came to the wash or ravine, and the woman forced the horse to jump over it, and so great was their speed that it could not be seen that the buggy had dragged at all; it had skimmed over as though on solid ground.[3]

Sergeant W. L. McKenzie, of Pond's company, killed two guerrillas. One was an officer and was killed after an exchange of eleven shots. McKenzie first killed the guerrilla's horse. He had one charge left, and with it killed his adversary. A woman and a child were shot, premeditatedly, it is claimed in the official reports, where it is also said that McKenzie killed the man who shot the child.[4] The husband of the woman who was wounded, and the father of the child which was shot, were both killed, the latter by a cousin. A teamster recognized in the guerrilla ranks a former acquaintance and friend, to whom he gave his revolver and surrendered, but the friend shot him and he died in thirty minutes. A negro saw in the advancing enemy his old master and ran to meet him with expressions of joy. But the master shot him through the heart and he rolled down the slope into the spring branch.

[3] *Gregg Manuscript.* Some of the language, in this incident is quoted almost as written by Gregg.

[4] In the library of the State Historical Society is preserved the pistol of McKenzie. The inscriptions with it state that he "killed Frank Fry and Bill Roder," and "Sergt. W. L. McKenzie, Third Wisconsin Cavalry, killed two bushwhackers and one horse with the six balls in this pistol, at Baxter Springs, Oct. 6, 1863."

Captain Gregg says he never knew any guerrillas named Frank Fry and Bill Roder. He does not dispute that McKenzie may have killed two men, but that they were guerrillas he does not believe.

The author knew McKenzie many years. He lived in Wyandotte county, Kansas, and was a prosperous farmer and substantial citizen. It was said that he bought his farm with money he got from the pockets of one of the guerrillas he killed. The author has inquired of him concerning this matter, but got neither denial nor affirmation, and he doubts the story. In the *History of Kansas* by Andreas it is said that some guerrilla officer had a duel with the saddler of Company D, Third Wisconsin. The saddler shot out his revolver at the officer, who was behind an oak tree, and rushed to his tent and got a carbine, but found it was not loaded. The guerrilla, finding himself alone, exclaimed, "Where in hell are my men?" and galloped away. This may be the foundation of the McKenzie story, for he was in youth a saddler.

The Federal loss was eighty killed and eighteen wounded.[5]
Among the killed was John Fry, known as "Pony Johnny," one
of the famous riders of the Pony Express across the plains to
California before the telegraph line was built.

While it was claimed that many guerrillas were killed, the official report made by Quantrill probably stated the exact loss, William Bledsoe killed and John Koger wounded, in the fight with
Blunt; and at the fort, Robert Ward and William Lotspeach killed;
wounded, Lieutenant Toothman and Private Thomas Hill.

F. Luther Wayman was at Baxter Springs under Quantrill,
and claims to have killed Major Curtis to get his horse and
holster-pistols; that Curtis waved his hand and revealed his

rank by his gauntlets when about half a
mile from the fort; that he rode up to
Curtis and shot at him several times, missing him; that then he shot him in the
temple and "tumbled him;" that Cole
Younger and Captain Jarrette then joined
him and they pursued twenty Federals
three miles, killing all but four.

Wayman further says that the guerrillas tied the body of Bledsoe on a horse
— across the saddle — and carried it until
the next day, when they buried it on a
beautiful hill in the Cherokee Nation, making a negro captured at Baxter dig the

Coleman Younger

grave.[6] A companion gave Wayman a pair of General Blunt's
pants; they were too large for him, but he wore them out.

---

[5] Summarized as follows in the report of Major Henning:

Maj. H. Z. Curtis; Lieut. A. W. Farr, Lieut. R. E. Cook,	3
Members of Brigade Band,	14
Clerks and orderlies,	6
Company A, Fourteenth Kansas,	18
Company I, Third Wisconsin,	23
Company C, Third Wisconsin, (In camp)	6
Citizens,	10
	80
Wounded,	18
Total,	98

[6] At the reunion of the guerrillas held at Independence, Mo.,

William E. Hopper, of the Wisconsin troops, was killed by Wayman, who, in searching the body, secured a packet of love letters from his sweetheart in Wisconsin. These letters were so chaste, so womanly, so just in sentiment to all soldiers that Wayman says he regretted having shot Hopper, and would have given the world to bring him back for his sweetheart. He shows a belt which he took from Hopper's body.[7]

When the guerrillas were assembled to continue the march and the men from Pool's company were missed, two messengers under a flag of truce were sent to the fort to inquire about them. In the official reports the bearers of the flag are said to have

August 20-21, 1909, the author inquired about this matter, and was told that the body of Bledsoe was carried away as Wayman says, but not on a horse. It was put in the ambulance in which John Koger was carried. Koger's wound rendered him unable to ride horseback, and he was taken away in Blunt's ambulance.

Captain William H. Gregg says they had no implements with which to dig a grave. Coming to an abandoned house, they found a small field or garden which had been ploughed. In this they scooped out a grave with boards and sticks. The body was buried there because Koger complained that it was beginning to smell. It was wrapped in blankets and buried in the shallow grave they were able to dig. The grave was on a considerable elevation north of a depression in a high ridge. The Fort Scott and Fort Gibson road ran through this depression. Gregg and party camped there as they went to Texas after the war was over. It was just south of this gap that Gregg chased the Federal officer, shooting him nine times without knocking him from the saddle.

The negro barber of Blunt was not killed by the guerrillas, and was taken with them to Texas, where he was made to act as barber for the band that winter.

7 Wayman lives now (1909) in Muskogee, Okla. The author saw him April 27, 1909, and had two long interviews with him. His claim to having killed Major Curtis is absurd, as the horse ran wildly on the prairie and no guerrilla got the pistols. And that three guerrillas killed sixteen of twenty Federals is not to be believed. The Federal troops acted in a manner cowardly enough, without doubt, in running off, as General Blunt says they did. But that three guerrillas should run twenty of them three miles, killing sixteen cannot be admitted as reasonable.

Wayman still believes that Quantrill had an elder brother murdered by Kansas men on the Cottonwood on the way to Pike's Peak. He became much offended at the author for saying such a thing could not have been, as Quantrill had no elder brother. He insists that other parties than Quantrill told him the same story, and that *that* makes it true.

28

claimed that Major Curtis was held a prisoner and that if the guerrillas captured and wounded were fairly treated, Major Curtis should not suffer harm.

Todd and Anderson both wanted to attack the fort after the massacre, but Quantrill would not consent, saying that they already had wounded men to carry and it was a long way to take them. The guerrillas marched away about five o'clock and went down the Fort Gibson road. They crossed the Arkansas river eighteen miles above Fort Gibson. Near this crossing they captured twelve Indian soldiers from Fort Gibson, and shot them down in cold blood after they had surrendered. In his official report Quantrill says he captured one hundred and fifty Federal Indians and negroes gathering ponies, and "brought none of them through" — all murdered after being captured.

So, in this year of 1863, of the innocent and helpless, Quantrill slew many. In the guilty blood-account laid upon his hands the scores ran high. Fire and death followed in his wake. Mourners went about desolate streets and cried in solitary highways. The oaks of the unfortunate land upon which he had flung and forced himself as champion and defender bore dead men — bitter and blasted fruit. Because of his inhuman deeds that domain was itself a blackened waste, a scourged and silent wilderness.

CHAPTER XXXIII

DISINTEGRATION OF THE QUANTRILL BAND

THE camp of General D. G. Cooper was six miles south of the Canadian. A little north of that river the guerrillas captured an Indian scout from Cooper's camp and another scout escaped. When the command had crossed the Canadian, Quantrill ordered the captured scout to ride to Cooper's camp with a dispatch telling of the approach of his force, but the scout refused to do it, saying that the guerrillas would follow and kill him. At a council of the captains, Gregg urged that a guard be sent with the scout, but the others said it was unnecessary, in which opinion Quantrill acquiesced. Guards were set about the camp and pickets placed on the north, but none on the south. There was little to eat in the camp, and after a meager meal the guerrillas went to sleep on the ground. Gregg had a foreboding that evil threatened, and he made his company sleep in line with their horses tied close by. The ambulance in which John Koger, wounded at Baxter, was carried, stood twenty yards north of Gregg's line and near the camp of Anderson, whose men slept sprawled in the grass and weeds without order. At daybreak a guard sounded an alarm, and in two minutes Gregg had his company mounted and riding forth to meet the enemy. Passing the ambulance, he saw Koger on his knees with two pistols leveled over the seat, and heard him call out "Des be d——d if you hadn't better stop. This is Quantrill." Colonel McIntosh, who was in command of the approaching Confederate force, heard Koger and tied a handkerchief on a weed-stalk and advanced, and a battle was averted. He had come to attack the guerrillas, thinking from the report of the Indian scout who had escaped them that they were Federal troops.

Quantrill stopped with his command at the camp of General Cooper, where he dated his report to General Price of the Baxter

Springs Massacre.[1] He soon continued his march southward, crossing the Red River at Colbert's Ferry, directly north of Sherman. He camped at Sherman a short time, and then established a permanent winter camp on Mineral creek, fifteen miles northwest of the city.

At the camp on Mineral creek dissensions arose and the disintegration of the guerrilla command began. Many causes contributed to this dissolution, the principal one being the growing power of Todd. The influence of Todd over the guerrillas increased because his heart was in the cause he was fighting for, as misguided and ineffectual as his services were. Quantrill fought from no principle, but for selfish purposes and as a result

---

[1] Vol. 22, Part I, Series I, page 700, *Rebellion Records*.

In this report he said he would soon prepare and submit a full report of his operations for the past summer. This he never did, as the disintegration of his band soon occupied all his time, and his appeals to Price and Shelby to aid him in his struggle to retain his place as nominal head of the guerrilla bands met with no response. On this account he became embittered towards both Price and Shelby and would never afterward have anything to do with either. He had a high opinion of the services he had rendered the Confederacy and hungered for official recognition and flattery. During the winter he discussed with W. L. Potter the chances of the success of the Confederacy, and said it was a failure. He came to despise the Confederate army officers. Had any opportunity offered at that time he would probably have acted towards the Confederacy as he had towards Kansas in the Morgan Walker raid.

The reply of General Price to the report of Quantrill is set out in Vol. 53, Series I, page 908, *Rebellion Records*, as follows:

Headquarters Price's Division,
Camp Bragg, Ark. Nov. 2, 1863.
Col. William C. Quantrill,
    Commanding Cavalry:

Colonel: I am desired by Major-General Price to acknowledge the receipt of your report of your march from the Missouri River to the Canadian, and that he takes pleasure in congratulating you and your gallant command upon the success attending it. General Price is very anxious that you prepare the report of your summer campaign, alluded to by you, at as early a date as practicable, and forward it without delay, more particularly so as he is desirous that your acts should appear in their true light before the world. In it he wishes you to incorporate particularly the treatment which the prisoners belonging to your company received from the Federal authorities; also the orders issued by General Blunt or other Federal officers regarding the disposition to be made of you or your men if taken or vanquished. He has been informed that orders of a most inhuman character were issued. Indeed, he has some eminating from those holding subordinate commands, but wants to have all the facts clearly portrayed,

of the condition his desperate life had placed him in. He cared nothing for the South or its cause, except as a means to his own selfish ends. When the supreme contest for leadership came the intensely earnest and devoted man won — as he always does. Quantrill felt his power slipping away from him and knew that it was going to Todd. He lost 'his bold independence of demeanor and action, and his attitude towards Todd became subservient, conciliatory, sometimes pitiably truculent, humble and imploring. He saw in Todd, long before it was apparent to others, his master and the master of the guerrillas.

There was at Lawrence a surfeit of blood — too much for even the bloodthirsty guerrillas, though they did not recognize it as such. Human blood appals men and becomes its own terror and avenger by remaining ever present and crying constant protest in the soul of the murderer. Who slays his fellow and sees life-blood spilled on the ground sleeps no more in peace. Like iron red from the furnace, sleeping or waking, that blood burns his soul day and night. The sight of it, the horror of it, are ever-present, gnawing, nauseous, corrosive, venomous, no matter what the outward appearance may indicate. The soul of the murderer is set on fires of hell, and the greatest punishment that can be inflicted on him is to let him live.

---

so that the Confederacy and the world may learn the murderous and uncivilized warfare which they themselves inaugurated, and thus be able to appreciate their cowardly shrieks and howls when with a just retaliation the same ''measure is meted out to them.'' He desires me to convey to you, and through you to your command, his high appreciation of the hardships you have so nobly endured and the gallant struggle you have made against despotism and the oppressions of our State, with the confident hope that success will soon crown our efforts.

I have the honor to remain, respectfully, your obedient servant.
MacLean,
Major and Assistant Adjutant-General.

At page 907, same volume, is a letter from General Price to Governor Thomas C. Reynolds, then at Marshall, Texas, referring in very complimentary terms to the report of Quantrill, a copy of which he enclosed. He praises Quantrill, his command, and his work, and asks that the command be attached to his (Price's) army. The conditions which developed among the guerrillas in the following winter caused all these plans to fall to the ground.

It is to be hoped that it will never be established that General Price approved the Lawrence Massacre, but his letters must speak for themselves.

Other causes are recorded in the *Gregg Manuscript*, here quoted:

Quantrill established his camp fifteen miles northwest from Sherman, Texas. It was there that the disintegration of Quantrill's command began. Pool, Jarrette, Younger, and Gregg, with some forty men, most of whom were old, tried, and true men, left Quantrill never to return. After the men scattered after the return from the Lawrence raid there was never again the unity of purpose which had animated the command up to that time. The enthusiastic initiative which had marked the career of the command to that date seemed to vanish in a day. Individual devotion seemed wanting. Not that the men did not obey orders readily and willingly and fight magnificently at every opportunity! They always did that! The condition existing at that time is indescribable. I could say truly that it was imperceptible. No difference whatever could be noticed; perhaps none existed; if so it was individual, — a feeling in the heart of which no man spoke to his comrade. I may liken this condition to the feeling which takes hold of men when the trail they have been following, broad and well-defined, emerges upon a barren plain and is lost in desert sands with no landmarks to be discovered. Differences between Captains were more frequent and marked by more feeling. Perhaps some of the reasons for these things can be discovered.

Among the men who volunteered to go with Lieutenant Gregg on the raid to Missouri City and Plattsburg were two of Todd's men, Fletch Taylor and James Little. Before these men were accepted they were told by Gregg that, in the event that money should be captured, it must be equally divided among the men, to which they agreed. When we captured Plattsburg, Taylor and Little captured six thousand dollars Government money. Being hard pressed after the taking of Plattsburg, Gregg made no demand on these men until the party had recrossed the Missouri River. When accosted by Gregg they positively refused to divide, and were severely censured by him for their course. Afterwards Gregg met Todd and Quantrill at the home of Mrs. David George and demanded that Taylor and Little be made to fulfill their agreement. Todd was mad because Gregg mentioned the matter, saying that these men had a right to all they got, no matter the agreement, and Quantrill acquiesced in Todd's view.

The remarks concerning the money secured at Lawrence, set down in a former chapter, may be now recalled by the reader; they have an application in this connection.

Soon after the arrival in Texas, Bill Anderson married, in Sherman, a Miss Bush Smith in defiance of the wishes of Quantrill, who desired that the wedding be postponed to days of peace. Anderson became hostile to Quantrill and left the camp on Mineral creek and with his company took up quarters in Sherman. Threats were made and guards were set in the town to prevent surprise by men from the country camp, and it was expected that Quantrill and Anderson would meet and one of them be killed, and that their bands would battle in the streets of Sherman.

The guerrillas began to rob and kill citizens of Texas.[2]   One Wise King, step-son of Colonel Alexander, led a party that robbed and murdered one Froman who lived about a mile northwest of Sherman, securing about three hundred dollars.

Colonel Alexander lived on a fine farm about two miles south of Sherman, and Jim Crow Chiles, John Ross, Fletch Taylor, and Andy Walker robbed and murdered him.

Major Butts lived on Red river north of Sherman, and the guerrillas robbed and murdered him.

The murdered men were Confederate soldiers, and Quan-

---

[2] At the reunion of the guerrillas at Independence, Mo., August 20-21, 1909, Sylvester Akers, who was with Quantrill, told the author that McCulloch ordered Quantrill to go to Jonnigan's (Jernigan's?) swamp, near McKinney, Texas, and arrest Federal guerrillas hiding there and robbing and murdering people in Texas. McCulloch insisted that these guerrillas should not be killed, but arrested and brought before him for trial. Quantrill said he would kill them if they fired on his men. Much correspondence passed back and forth on the matter and bad feeling was aroused. Quantrill finally went to arrest the guerrillas, but in doing so killed one or more of them. He captured but few. This still further widened the breach between him and McCulloch.

Now, there were no Federal guerrillas in Texas. Correspondence in the archives of the Confederacy at Washington show that there were many deserters from the Confederate army in Texas, and that General Kirby Smith wished McCulloch to have Quantrill capture or kill them. If captured they were to be forced back into the Confederate service. These were the men Akers calls Federal guerrillas, and he must have been told they were Federal guerrillas and made to believe they were to get him to take the field against them. McCulloch opposed the action of Smith in turning this matter over to Quantrill, and in his correspondence makes it plain that he considered Quantrill little better than a savage and his manner of waging war a disgrace to the Confederacy.

trill desired to have the murderers tried by court-martial and
shot, but Todd and Anderson protected them. The demoralization of the command was complete. Bands of the guerrillas committed robberies and murders in all the country adjacent to
Sherman and in the Chickasaw Nation. In Sherman they terrorized the people by riding recklessly through the streets yelling and firing their pistols right and left. They shot the steeples
of the churches full of holes, and they shot the lock off the door
of the postoffice. On Christmas Eve they rode their horses into
Ben. Christian's hotel and shot away the tassels and other orna-
ments on the cap worn by Mrs. Butts, widow of the murdered
man and mother-in-law of the proprietor. They constantly rode
their horses into grocery stores and there permitted them to tear
open flour-bags and eat the flour.[3]

The citizens complained of these things to General Henry
M. McCulloch (brother of General Ben. McCulloch), whose headquarters were at Bonham. Anderson got some intelligence of

Fletch Taylor

this proceeding, and, with the treachery
and baseness of character inherent in him,
went to Bonham with his men and had a
number of interviews with General
McCulloch in which he insisted that the
entire blame for the murders at Sherman
and all the prevailing conditions rested
with Quantrill. He also made it appear
that the horrible form of warfare adopted
by the guerrillas was due to the practices
of Quantrill. But he said nothing of his
own part in these matters. Fletch
Taylor, one of Todd's company, was with
Anderson, and he admitted that he had

---

[3] In addition to other authority I base this on the letter of W. L.
Potter to W. W. Scott, dated March 11, 1896, now in the Collection of
the author.

I was not at Sherman at the time. I was about 10 miles North East
in Grayson co was there a few days after it occurred The only Hotel
in the Town at that time was owned & managed by Ben christian, a friend
of W. C. Quantrill and all of his men, and every other confederate soldier.
He was as good a citizen as there was in Texas. He told me that the men
first got started at a House of their friends on Egg Nogg. they then got

killed Major Butts, but said that he had done so on Quantrill's order.

This was the last of March, 1864.

General McCulloch summoned Quantrill to headquarters, and the guerrilla chieftain appeared there accompanied by some of the men at the camp on Mineral creek. On his arrival Quantrill was placed under arrest, but was told that his parole would be accepted and that he would not be imprisoned before his trial. His pistols were taken from him and put on a bed in the general's room. General McCulloch then invited Quantrill to accompany him to dinner, but this the guerrilla chief declined to do, saying, "No, sir, I will not go to dinner. By G—d, I do not care a G—d d——n if I never taste another mouthful on this earth."

General McCulloch went to his dinner alone, leaving Quantrill in his office with two guards. On pretext of getting a drink of water he crossed the room and seized his pistols. Then he ordered the guards to lay down their guns, which they quickly did. Buckling on his belt, he walked out, locking the guards in and taking the door-key with him. At the foot of the stairs he encountered two more guards. These found the bandit's pistols in their faces as quick as a flash, with an order to drop their guns and step into the street, and they obeyed with alacrity. On getting to the street Quantrill shouted to his men to mount and get out of Bonham, as they were prisoners there. They were soon on their way to Colbert's Ferry with Quantrill at their head. Quantrill sent a courier ahead on a fleet horse to order Todd to break camp at once and meet him at the ferry with all the ammunition and what camp equipage he could carry. Colonel

hold of some Whiskey. & were like all other men on a christmas spree. soon became wild & full of Reckless fun. that the actors, had all benn at his Hotel before & naturally, they came there in their Frolick. Some two or more rode on the Porch in the Hall, & the Main reception room discharged their Revolvers in front of the Hotel. their Horses feet broke some few of the flooring in the Hall of the Hotel & they also done some damage to the furniture Mr christian said the Men were his Friends & would settle for whatever damage they done to him & all others, which was done in a few days afterwards

They also went to a Photographer in Town to get their Photographs & destroyed his instruments. all of which was paid for a few days after. as soon as they sobered up.

Martin's regiment was ordered to overhaul Quantrill and bring him back to Bonham dead or alive. Bill Anderson and his men joined in the pursuit. Todd obeyed the order of Quantrill and met him at Bois d' Arc creek just in time, for the chief was hard pressed. Todd formed his men in the timber at the ford and held Anderson, Fletch Taylor, and their men in check until Quantrill was well up towards the ferry. Many shots were exchanged and some on each side were wounded. Before the troops of Martin could come up Quantrill and Todd had crossed Red river and were out of the jurisdiction of General McCulloch.[4]

---

4 A number of guerrillas have told the author of this skirmish and the matters leading up to it. They do not wish to be quoted now, but if necessary will stand by their statement. The following quotation from the letter of W. L. Potter to W. W. Scott, not dated, but postmarked, Harrison, Ark., Feb. 19, 1896, in the Collection of the author, is also relied on as authority:

During the time that Quantrill was in camp, above Sherman Texas a citizen of Texas Named Major Butts was found Murdered several Miles above Sherman. his horse saddle & Bridle was found, the Horse nearly starved hitched to a tree, not far from his Body. Major Butt's Watch, & Pocket Book were missing. at first it was supposed that the Murder had been committed, by Indians, from the Nation It seems that Major Butts had been very active, in trying to have every able bodied Man in the county forced in the ranks of the confederate Army, & was also in favor of the able bodied citizens who were holding office throughout the country generally. And allmost every town was filled with stout Hearty able bodied Young Men. Either Wealthy Men or their sons. It Was Well known at that time, that Rich Men or their sons at that time Were either in the Quartermasters, Department. the Commissaries Department The transportation Department or some other Department. Simply to keep them out of the bullet department A Wealthy citizen & a Young man some 30 Yrs of age Named Alexander Held the office of Assessor of Taxes. Quantrill When he came up from Houston & San Antonio in March 1864. Received information from some of his men that led him to believe that one of his men a Lieutenant in his command had been concerned in the Killing of Major Butts. Quantrill immediately Placed him under arrest, sent a Dispatch to Gen Henry McCulloch at Bonham Fannin co Texas, who was then in command of the Northern sub District of Texas Informing McCulloch what he had done & asking him for authority to have him tried by a Court Martial. Some others were also Placed under arrest on some charge, while this correspondence was going on The Men Who Were Guarding the Prisoners gave them an opportunity to escape at night & they left camp with Horses & outfit Quantrill then ordered his men to form into line. Told them that if there was a Man in his Command that had been guilty of Robbing any Person While in Texas, that if they would come out and acknowledge their guilt & Promise that they Would Never again repeat it & that they were sorry for it, that they could remain in the command the same as ever & He would not Permit them to be punished for it. He also told them that if one of his Men, Was Guilty of committing

George Todd chose to cast his lot with Quantrill rather than with Anderson for the reason that he had obtained an ascendency over Quantrill and none over Anderson. Quantrill still had the confidence of the men, and through him Todd could command them.

Under the surface, however, Todd and Quantrill were bitter

any depredations on the Property of citizens of Texas, & if they did not acknowledge it then & there, & if it was afterwords Proved against one of them that they Were Guilty of Violating the Law. that he would not shelter them. but Would have them punished to the full extent of the Law, & he would also Expell them from his command Not One of them admitted their guilt. at the same time he told them. that if there was any Man or any Men in his Command, that did not like his style of commanding them, or if any of them wished to withdraw from his command. they could take their Horses, & Weapons and they were Welcome to leave and go where they pleased.

Bill Anderson & some eight or nine others Rode out of the ranks, told him that they were not Guilty of Violating any of the Laws of Texas. but they did not like his style of commanding them, & they Would quit his command They took their Property & rode out of camp — with His Permission This was the latter part of March 1864 I do not think they were ever on friendly terms again. The Lieutenant that Quantrill had under arrest, and that was Permitted to escape from the Guards went to Gen McCulloch, at Bonham Texas, told that he did kill Major Butts & that he did it by order of W C Quantrill I simply give the above as I heard it in Dallas Texas a few days after it all occurred.

Gen McCulloch, sent a dispatch to Quantrill's camp, informing him that he had Lieutenant T. a Prisoner at Bonham, and for Quantrill to come immediately to Bonham & bring all of his Witnesses along with him. that he McCullough. Would try him Lieutenant T. at Bonham Quantrill, With Nearly all of his Men but some eight or ten, Who Were left to keep camp along with George Todd Went to Bonham. Quantrill Went in the Court House to McCullough's office at His Head Quarters.

McCullough, informed Quantrill that Lieut T — acknowledged to the Killing of Major Butts. and claimed that he had killed him by order of Quantrill and that Quantrill could consider Himself a Prisoner and under Arrest. that he would accept his Parole & that he could remain at his Head Quarters, and that he would fare as Well, as he did, and invited him to go to the Hotel With him & take Dinner Quantrill replied. No sir. I will not. I consider this a strange way of doing business Gen McCullough I do not understand your manner of doing business Gen McCullough. I have preferred a criminal charge against one of My officers. I have Placed him under Guard as You Well Know. He made his Escape from my Camp, and now you place me under arrest. on his Word and undertake to try me for the crime that he acknowledges that he has committed No Sir. I will not go to Dinner. By God, I do not Care a God Dambd if I never taste another mouthful on this Earth.

Quantrill had taken off his belt & two Navy Revolvers & laid them on the bed in the office.

McCullough, went on to his Dinner left Quantrill sitting in his office With two Privates of Martins Texas Regiment With Guns in their hands standing Guard at the Door.

Quantrill rose from his seat to get a Drink of Water, Stepped to

towards each other. They were the only two guerrilla captains now left with the old organization, many members of which had left it. Gregg left under the following circumstances:

On the arrival of Quantrill's forces at Sherman, Texas, in November, 1863, Gregg found some of his Missouri friends with whom he stopped for two weeks, while the camp was being es-

---

Bed side and as Quick as the Lightnings flash he drew his Revolvers from their scabbard, threw them down on them cocked & his fingers on the triggers, ordered them to lay down their guns, & to step across the room, all of which they done as he ordered.

He then took the key out of the door opened it & put it in the Lock from the out side. He first buckled on his Belt. He stepped out & locked it with the two Guards inside. He sprang down the stairs like a flash Lightning. two other soldiers Were standing Guard there With his Revolvers in their faces he ordered them to throw down their guns, and to step out in the street they reluctantly obeyed the order.

His Men & Andersons at least Some of them were shaking hands & talking pleasantly across the street Quantrill Ordered his Men to Mount their Horses. Mount Your Horses Men We are all Prisoners here.

They gave a Yell & sprang in their Saddles, & Were soon on their Way to Colberts Ferry. col Martins Regiment was ordered after them to bring back Quantrill Dead or alive

His Regiment come in sight occasionally Many shots were exchanged. they skirmished to Red River Quantrill Dispatched one of his Men Who Was Mounted on one of the fleetest Race Mares in the West, to his old camp above Sherman With orders for Todd & all the rest of his Men to Meet him With all the Amunition that they could carry and meet him on the Sherman & Bonham rode.

Todd obeyed the order, and at the crossing of a creek. I think it is Bodark — there was heavy timber in the bottom stretching on each side of the creek. He met Bill Anderson & Fletcher Taylor, on the side next to Bonham Todd formed his men in the Timber & skirmishing commenced, Each side had one Man slightly Wounded. Anderson, Told Todd. that if they were not a Damb set of cowards, to come out of the Timber in the Open Prairie and fight him Like Men

Todd. replied you have the Most Men and if You are not a set of God Damb cowards, come in here and take us out. Each side knew better than to give the other any advantage of each other.

Todd was on the same road that he was ordered to come. it was some five Miles East of Sherman, on the Bonham Road, that he met Anderson. With some 12 or fourteen Men. He may have had more. He had some of col Martins Men with him at that time. at all events he out numbered Todd.

In the Mean time Quantrill had been compelled to abandon that Road. & Was slowly Retreating on the Road to colberts Ferry on Red River. a few Miles North of the Sherman & Bonham road. Todd heard the firing and Kept along the timber of the creek. "I now think it was Bodark creek. if not, it was a stream called caney"

Todd soon Joined Quantrill in his Retreat from Bonham

col Martin & his Men slowly followed Quantrill & his command to the Texas side of Red River. allways Keeping his Men, Numbering some several Hundred strong, Just beyond reach of the Deadly bullets and the deadly aim of the fearless Revolver fighters of Quantrill with Bill Ander-

tablished northwest of that town. Gregg, believing that disintegration was coming, determined to leave Quantrill and report to
Department headquarters for an assignment. Before leaving,
however, Gregg determined to go to Quantrill's camp and procure from him a leave of absence. On the way to camp Gregg
met Jarrette, Younger and others, who tried to dissuade him

---

son & his few Men in his advance leading his skirmishers all the Way.
(in advance of col Martin & leading his Men) At Red River, at colberts
Ferry, Quantrill crossed on the Indian Territory side, and beyond the
Jurisdiction of Gen Henry McCullough The Feather Bed General of the
Northern Sub District of Texas. A Brother of the Gallant Ben McCulloch and a General Who had nothing to Recommend him but the name
of his Gallant Brother Who fell in leading a charge of Texas cavalry at
the Pea Ridge. Battle also known as the Elk Horn Battle Field
    Quantrill formed his men at the ford waiting for Martin to make
his charge col Martin appeared on the Texas side. with a White Flag.
    P. S. Fletcher Taylor, is now at Joplin & a Wealthy Man. Made at
Lead Mining there since 1871, or 1872. I would rather his name would
not appear in connection with the Major Butts affair, & Especially to
have me as the authority for it I have gave you that from my own
knowledge. but from General Report at the time in Texas
    Quantrill met him in the Middle of the River, & held a consultation
with him. Quantrill told him that he did not Want to fight confederate
soldiers. and that he would not do so. Unless actually compelled to
    But if he Martin With his command undertook to follow him any
farther that him and his command would remain right Where they Were
and fight him as long as he had a Man left a live. With a catridge to
burst. and a Man left With strength to pull a trigger.
    col Martin, Stated that he had no Jurisdiction in the Indian Terri-
tory Neither had McCullough. and that he had no authority to follow
him any farther. and With his Regiment went back to Bonham & along
With Gen McCullough feasted on confederate Rations Until the collapse
of the so called confederate States of America in April 1865.
    When McCullough & his staff with several Ambulances well filled
with the Most Valuable confederate supplies, took the road through Dallas
to his home in Southern or in central Texas. What became of him after
that I never heard.
    I will hear state that the Messenger that Quantrill dispatched to
his old camp after George Todd & the rest of his command rode some
thirty or thirty five Miles. from the time he left Quantrill out side of
the Town of Bonham to 12 Miles above Sherman, up to the time he along
with Todd met Bill Anderson and had the skirmish in the creek bottom,
between Bonham & Sherman.
    After col Martin Went back to Bonham Quantrill Reported to Gen
Cooper Near Red River & also Near Boggy Depot, in the Indian Territory
in the choctaw Nation, and Proceeded with his command & made an attack
on Fort Smith, they did not succeed in capturing it.
    Much of this chapter is also substantiated by the statement now in
the Collection of the author made by H. Fuell, a negro, of Lawrence and
Topeka, Kansas. Fuell is a shoemaker. He was a slave, owned by Daniel
Brant at Osceola, Mo., who there sold him at auction to Colonel George
Douglas for $400. Douglas organized a company for the Confederacy
at Sarcoxie, one at Granby, one at Carthage, and one at Nevada — among

from going to Quantrill's camp, saying that Todd would kill him or have it done. But Gregg knowing the duty of a soldier and an officer argued that he would be liable to court martial if he should leave without permission, hence he went on to the camp, remaining two days and nights, when he sought an interview with Quantrill, the following conversation taking place between them:

Quantrill said to Gregg:

"You have been a good soldier and a good officer, and an honest man. I have no fault to find with you, but I think it best that you should go away. You have some enemies in camp."

At this time Quantrill did not know that Gregg had any intention of leaving.

Gregg replied to Quantrill:

"Who are those enemies?"

"Why, there are Taylor and Little, whom you denounced as thieves, and Barker don't like you first rate," said Quantrill.

"Well," said Gregg, "are not these men thieves?"

"Yes," said Quantrill, "they are."

"Now," replied Gregg, "you say that I have been a good soldier and officer and an honest man. Why do you want me to leave and the thieves to stay?"

Quantrill's answer was that Todd had been elected Captain of the Company and the men were under his influence. Then it was that Gregg informed Quantrill that he had come to the camp to get leave of absence that he might report to Department headquarters for assignment, telling Quantrill that he was going to Sherman that night, though he did not intend to do so. Quantrill wrote him a leave of absence good for ninety days, which surprised Gregg, as he believed that no leave was good for more than thirty days.

Gregg left camp on receipt of his order for leave, going out on the road to Sherman. Soon after leaving the camp, Todd, Little, Taylor, and Barker passed him, on their way, as they said, to Sherman. But Gregg suspected their purpose and stopped

the first troops organized in Missouri. With these troops he took his slaves to Texas. His son-in-law, "Clay" Cogswell, was with General Price. His son George was with General Shelby. He was accidentally killed after the war by the sudden turning of his horse, striking his gun against a fence, and shooting his head off. Douglas died four and a half miles south of Sherman, Texas, the last day of the war, and was buried in the cemetery at Sherman. Fuell made the shoes in which he was buried. During the war Fuell was at Sherman, and he saw Quantrill and his men in both the winters they spent there. He is an intelligent man and his statement is clear.

at the Halfway House, going on to Sherman the next morning. When he arrived there he hitched his horse in the north part of town. Walking down town, he saw Todd, Taylor, and Barker standing on the opposite side of the street earnestly engaged in conversation. Todd seemed very nervous. Gregg walked by without speaking, but kept close watch. Taylor afterwards said that Todd said to him and Barker:

"There goes that damned s— of a b——; now kill him."
Taylor says he replied to Todd:

"I will not kill Gregg. He is a Southern man, and he has been a good soldier and officer. If you want him killed you will have to kill him yourself."

Gregg walked on down town, remaining in the town some time, and he was not molested. Afterwards he mounted his horse and rode to Bonham, where he reported to Brigadier General McCulloch, showed his leave of absence, which the General said was of no use to him and that he was liable to arrest. Gregg said that he thought the leave was not good, and that he had reported on account of that belief. Gregg requested the proper leave, saying he wanted to report to General Smith for assignment. General McCulloch at once wrote out the proper leave, saying to Gregg that he commended him for his course. Gregg reported to General Smith, was sent to Shelby, who at once assigned him to Company I, Shanks' regiment; and Shelby soon afterwards appointed him Captain of Company H, Shanks' regiment, where he remained to the close of the war.

There was an early disagreement between Todd and Quantrill, and such characters never forgive. Todd. it is maintained, could not read or write, and with his father and brothers came from Canada to Westport before the war, and worked as stonemasons about Kansas City. When the Confederacy recognized Quantrill and his men by mustering them regularly into the service the third day after the battle of Independence, Todd wanted to be made first lieutenant, but Quantrill favored William Hallar, his first recruit, and Todd was defeated, though given the place of second lieutenant. This place was not satisfactory to him, and in a quarrel which followed, Quantrill ordered him to take his horse and outfit and leave camp, which he did, collecting a squad of men and fighting independently a few weeks. Then a reconciliation was effected, and Todd returned to Quantrill.[5]

---

[5] The letter of W. L. Potter to W. W. Scott, dated Harrison, Ark.,

These things rankled in the bosom of Todd more than in Quantrill. And Todd had avowed then to supplant his captain, and it will be remembered that Gregg says Quantrill told him that Todd had been elected captain of the company. This gave him the real power and left Quantrill to be content with his commission of colonel in some vague, indefinite regiment not in existence and to which Todd could claim to belong or not as might suit him best. When the company started back to Missouri in 1864 Quantrill was with it by the sufferance of Todd, which he realized and keenly felt.

About this time Todd began to boast of his superior prowess and courage, saying in the camp in Texas one day that he was not afraid of any man on the planet, when Quantrill said "How about me?" Todd, not being ready for an open rupture, said, "O, well, you are the only d——d man that I ever was afraid of." [6]

There was a more recent quarrel. Todd got drunk and became boisterous and disobedient in camp just before the summons to Bonham by General McCulloch. When he defied his chief Quantrill shot at him but missed, and ordered the men to shoot Todd. They did not want to kill Todd, and all ran down

<hr />

Jan. 22, 1896, has some account of this quarrel but is in error in saying that Todd was given no office. Otherwise the account agrees with what old guerrillas have told the author:

While in his camp above Sherman, Quantrill was allways friendly & pleasant with his men & often times joked with them. george Todd his Lieutenant, at one time was telling in a Joking maner, that he was not afraid of any man on the Planet Quantrill remarked in a very Pleasant manner how about me? Oh well you are the only Dambd man that I ever was afraid of. This heard my self

In 1862 in Jackson Co Mo in reorganizing Quantrill's command, on the Waters of the Blue There was an Election of officers & Geo Todd was a candidate for 1st Lieutenant he got beat then he run for 2nd Lieutenant & also got defeated He then declared to Quantrill that he would not stand camp guard or do duty as a Private. Quantrill listened to him, & replied verry coolley & Positively Verry well sir, take your Horse & out fit, & leave this camp. Todd, obeyed the order without further ceremony. But he soon gathered up a few recruits, & fought the Federals as before only on an independent manner & a smaller scale, they afterwards made up. Todd, was with the command during the Prairie Grove Battle, after which he took a few of his followers, & went back to Missouri, where he remained during the rest of the winter

6 Potter in his letter dated Jan. 22, 1896, says he heard this conversation himself.

the creek bank, except Barker, who remained by Quantrill, and both fired on Todd and missed. Todd shot at Barker and the ball cut his coat but did not hit him. Then the men interefered and stopped the fight. Quantrill claimed that he did not shoot with the intention of killing Todd, and peace was patched up between them.[7]

The final break came after the command got back to Missouri in the spring of 1864. Because of the action of General McCulloch and Anderson the trip was made earlier than usual. There was little food for man or beast in the country ridden through and all suffered. The streams were bank-full and the horses had to swim them bearing their riders. The guerrillas arrived, forty or fifty in the company, in Johnson county, Missouri, in bad condition. The Federal soldiers were ready for them and forced the fighting. All day the bushwhackers fled. There are two versions of what transpired in the evening. Gregg says:

Quantrill and Anderson had fallen out in Texas. Quantrill and Todd came to Missouri together, with forty or fifty men. Anderson came with forty or fifty more. Their hardships were many. They swam almost every stream from the Red River to the Missouri. Their horses were much worn, finding no grain on the way. Arriving in Johnson County, Missouri, they struck the enemy who were much stronger than they, — men hungry, bedrabbled, etc., horses worn out. So, it had to be a fight, and it was, and continuous through the county. Toward evening, when a considerable stretch of prairie lay before them, Quantrill and Todd became angered at each other and separated on the spot. Quantrill with eight or ten of his chosen followers, marched away, destined to do no more fighting in Missouri. Quantrill's power had all slipped away from him, and it all came about by reason of his favoritism for Todd. He trusted Todd and Todd betrayed the trust! Quantrill, with a few chosen friends, spent the summer in Howard County, Missouri, dormant, you might say. It really began to look as though Quantrill's military sun had set to rise no more forever!

Gregg was not present and reports only what he heard. The other story is that Quantrill left the command because of a

7 Told W. W. Scott by Ike Hall, Bob Hall, and Donny Pence at Samuels's Depot, Ky. Interview written by Scott, and now in the Collection of the author. What Barker is meant is not known by the author.

29

quarrel with Todd about a game of cards. They were playing seven-up for $100 a game. Quantrill accused Todd of renigging, and the bystanders said Quantrill was right. Quantrill, in reply to some defiant remark made by Todd, said he was not afraid of any man. Todd instantly flourished his cocked pistol in Quantrill's face and made him say he was afraid of him (Todd). It was thought Todd only sought an excuse to kill Quantrill, and Quantrill came to this belief. In any event, he could not remain longer with Todd. His humiliation was perfect, the triumph of his enemy and rival was complete. With bitterness and sadness he turned to go. His old horse alone remained his friend, and, mounting him, he rode into the gloom to be neglected, to be forgotten as a factor in the war — to become an outcast in Missouri.[8]

---

[8] There are two interviews in the Collection of the author of W. W. Scott with Ike Hall, Bob Hall and Donny Pence at Samuels's Depot, Kentucky, in which this version of the affair is asserted. The Halls and Pence were present and saw what they told Scott.

CHAPTER XXXIV

QUANTRILL had kidnapped Kate Clarke a year or more before his expulsion from the guerrilla band.[1] He now sought this mistress and went with her to the north side of the Missouri river, a region then less dangerous than that to the south. He took refuge in Howard county, where he and Miss Clarke lay concealed in the brush most of the time. Through James Little, John Barker, John Ross, David Hilton, and a few more who later left Todd and went to him, and through the families of Confederate soldiers, he kept in communication with those guerrillas who cared to hear from him.

When the Confederacy determined to send Price to invade Missouri in 1864 that general ordered all the guerrillas to go into North Missouri and terrorize that part of the state.

The order was sent to George Todd, who had, no doubt, let it be known at the Price headquarters that he had supplanted Quantrill and forced him out of the guerrilla band, making it

---

[1] Letter of Charles F. ("Fletch") Taylor to W. W. Scott in the Collection of the author, written at Joplin, Mo., some time in 1879, but not dated. In this letter it is said:

Kate Clarke, who keeps a fancy house in St. Louis now, and is a noted woman there, lived in Jackson County, and on the night Quantrill took her from home, he borrowed my gray mare for her to ride on, and from that time on he never did much fighting. He kept her that summer and that winter. We went South and he left her. The next summer he went back and got with her, and staid in the brush until he started to Kentucky, where he was killed.

What was the true name of this girl is not known. She pretended to have married Quantrill and took his name, "Clarke" — always assumed by him for sinister purposes in the last years of his life.

Other guerrillas admit this expulsion and his connection with Kate Clarke. It is stated in the *Gregg Manuscript* that he never fought again in Missouri. Quantrill's refuge in distress was always the company of fallen women.

plain that if any service should be required of the guerrillas in the future, requisition should be made to him. Captain John Chestnut bore the order, and he arrived at Todd's camp, near Judge Gray's, at Bone Hill, on the morning of the 8th of September.[2]

Bill Anderson raided through the northern counties along the Missouri river. He fought a militia force at Shaw's blacksmith shop, in Ray county, and operated as far east as Shelby county. About August 10th he arrived in Clay county with less than a dozen men. George Todd obeyed the orders of Price and crossed the Missouri at Sibley (the present crossing of the Santa Fé Railroad).[3]

Todd was in command of Quantrill's old company still, though little had been done by him during the summer. It was in the first week in September that he crossed the Missouri, and up to the 15th he and Thrailkill operated in portions of Clay, Platte, Clinton, Carroll and Ray; then they started east for Boone and Howard counties. Anderson was found in Howard. He and Quantrill made up their quarrel or arranged a truce for the campaign, as did Todd and Quantrill. It was decided that the combined guerrilla command should attack the Federal garrison at Fayette, the county-seat of Howard. The troops were stationed in a stockade north of the town, in the Female Academy building, and in the court-house. Quantrill advised against this attack and predicted defeat; he refused command of the troops, which was accepted by Bill Anderson. Quantrill had been able to rally but sixteen men, so low had he fallen in guerrilla estimation in the presence of Todd and Anderson. The guerrillas were badly defeated, as Quantrill had said they would be, and they lost eighteen killed and had forty-two wounded.[4]

Among the wounded was James Little, one of the staunch adherents of Quantrill, who took him from the field, telling Mattox that "Jimmy was shot *all to pieces.*" This attack was a

[2] So says the work of Major John N. Edwards.

[3] Some say they crossed by making their horses swim and carry them, as boats could not be had. But they probably crossed in skiffs, holding the bridles of their horses as they swam.

[4] According to Edwards, who is always unreliable.

humiliation to Quantrill. He was regarded with contempt by Todd and Anderson. He was upbraided by them for refusing the command and he was flouted with sinister remarks about "his sand being gone." There were contemptuous remarks about the military discipline of Kate Clarke. Pistols were clutched more than once, and their use was prevented by interference of some of the older guerrillas. Quantrill refused to have anything further to do with Todd or Anderson, and announced that General Price might look to them for his aid. They went on and perpetrated the Centralia Massacre. When they returned through Howard county they sent many jeering messages to Quantrill, telling him others besides him could annihilate Federal commands. When these were repeated to him he refused to cross the river with the retreating bushwhackers.[5]

---

[5] The Centralia Massacre and all the incidents of the guerrilla campaigns north of the Missouri river in the summer of 1864 will be treated in sketches of Todd and Anderson, in a separate volume, to be issued soon after this.

CHAPTER XXXV

QUANTRILL LEAVES MISSOURI

THE guerrillas crossed the Missouri river at Rocheport, October 5, 1864, to meet General Price, who was marching up the State on an invasion as absurd and preposterous as ever an army was sent on. There was never the remotest possibility that anything could be accomplished by it, and that the army did finally escape from the trap it made and set for itself was due solely to the iron command of Shelby.

From Centralia George Todd brought his company back to Bone Hill, near the line of Jackson and Lafayette counties, where he awaited the coming of General Price, joining Shelby's Division between Waverly and Lexington. Upon the appearance of the army of invasion Todd was directed to perform the service for which his knowledge of the country so well fitted him.

George Todd

He and his men, the old Quantrill band, scouted day and night. In this service he and two or three of his men met a Federal major and an equal number of men near the house of Dr. Graves, several miles east of Independence. The guerrillas wore Federal uniforms and pretended to be Union soldiers. When they had gained positions by the Federals, each guerrilla murdered his man, Todd shooting the major through the head. The major was magnificently mounted, and Todd took his horse.

The next day (October 22, 1864) the Confederate lines streamed out from Independence towards Kansas City and Westport. Todd took half a dozen of his men and went back to gain intelligence of the enemy following in the rear. He reached "the old Staples place" two and a half miles northeast of Independence. There the road ran along an elevation ending in a sort of point. Below this was a grassy glade or slough, where Todd told his men to stop while he looked about him. He was mounted on the splendid horse of the murdered major, and he was himself a fine figure. One of his men recalls how he rode out to the end of the elevation and halted to survey the country. From the slough he was outlined against the sky, seeming a statue of bronze. Suddenly a sharp report broke the stillness, and Todd pitched forward to the road, a dead man. A sharpshooter had taken advantage of the splendid mark. The ball struck Todd in the throat, just above the body, and shattered his neck. Mattox, one of his men, ran to him and dragged him to the slough, then galloped back for some conveyance for his dead captain. Securing an ambulance he took Todd to Independence and buried him, and there his grave may be seen to this day.

Quantrill took no part whatever in the invasion of Missouri by Price. He had come to regard General Price with bitterness, and for Shelby he had supreme contempt. He had appealed to both for aid to stand against the rising tide of Todd's popularity, but neither gave his cause attention. He was forced out of the guerrilla band and went into retirement cursing the Confederacy and its sponsors in Missouri. His every attempt at advancement had been thwarted at Richmond or at the headquarters of General Price.

C. W. Wright saw Quantrill in Howard county while Price was moving west about Boonville. Wright had been given permission to cross the river to see his family, and he met Quantrill in the road about half way from Arrow Rock to New Franklin. Quantrill inquired where he could stay all night. He was alone, seemed nervous and afraid, appeared to be skulking, timid, and at a loss what to do, and was taking no part in the war. Wright told him to go to the house of a man named Basket, which Quantrill did, and he remained there several days.[1]

---

[1] C. W. Wright was born near Frankfort, Ky., June 21, 1827. He moved to Missouri when a young man; was in Doniphan's Expedition, in the company of Captain Rodgers (Howard county) in the War with Mexico. Was in General Price's army from the organization to the surrender.

Now, with Todd dead, Anderson dead, the army of Price destroyed, and Shelby's command reduced to starving squads, Quantrill rejoiced. He saw his star rising again. This strange being believed he might yet save the Confederacy, not that he cared for the cause, but he was hungering for notoriety — fame — to achieve which end he would undertake any desperate chance. His plan was to take his old guerrilla band to Washington and assassinate President Lincoln, which, he reasoned, would so demoralize the Federal army that it could easily be conquered.[2]

The guerrillas did not follow Price and Shelby, but returned to Missouri. Sending Kate Clarke to St. Louis, Quantrill came to Jackson county and appointed a rendezvous at the farm of the widow Dupee, in Lafayette county.[3] This was about the 10th of November. The guerrillas were slow in assembling, and it was three or four weeks before enough had agreed to embark in the enterprise to warrant the departure.

The guerrillas all wore Federal uniforms, Quantrill that of a captain. They were to represent themselves as Federal soldiers all the time, and never admit their identity. Quantrill was provided with a captain's commission — said to have been taken from the dead body of a Federal Captain Clark, of Colorado troops; but this is not probable, for the guerrillas represented

Lives in Pettis county, Mo., but his postoffice is Iona, Benton county. The author had a long interview with him at Holden, Mo., at the reunion of the Mexican Veterans, Sept. 12, 1907.

[2] He told a few of his men that this was his purpose in leaving Missouri. He expected to reach Washington through Kentucky, Virginia, and Maryland. This claim has always been made, and on April 27, 1909, F. Luther Wayman, now living in Muskogee, Oklahoma, who served under Quantrill, told the author that his object in leaving Missouri was to go to Washington and assassinate President Lincoln. Another of Quantrill's men, M. T. Mattox, Bartlesville, Oklahoma, told the author that his understanding of the Kentucky campaign was that Quantrill did not believe his men would ever be permitted to surrender and he wanted to get them away from Missouri where they were known. This theory is not tenable, for if that had been his object he would have gone to Mexico with Price and Shelby.

[3] Mattox gives this farm as the rendezvous and this form of the name. It may have been *Dupree*.

themselves as a part of the Fourth Missouri Cavalry on detached duty to hunt guerrillas in Kentucky. There was no such regiment as the Fourth Missouri Cavalry.[4]

There were a number of places appointed for the rendezvous, and perhaps the last was at the Austin farm, three miles south of Lexington, Lafayette county, though "Babe" Hudspeth said the start was made from the Kimmel farm, six miles from Independence. Thirty-three guerrillas agreed to go to Kentucky with Quantrill. The following are believed to have been among the number: Ves Akers, Bill Gaw, Dick Burns, Dick Glasscock, Bill Noland, Ed Noland, Bill Robinson, John Barker, Jack Bishop, Payne Jones, Allen Parmer, John McCorkle, John Ross, Frank James, Clark Hockensmith, Bud Pence, Don Pence, Bill Hulse, Chat Renick, Bill Bassham, Jim Younger, Ike Hall, Bob Hall.[5]

---

[4] See Vol. XLIX, Series I, *Rebellion Records*, under references to Quantrill. It is repeatedly stated that he represented himself as Captain Clarke of the Fourth Missouri Cavalry. One such reference can be found at page 657 of Part I, said volume.

[5] Sylvester Akers gave the author, at Independence, Mo., August 21, 1909, the following roll of guerrillas who went to Kentucky with Quantrill: Sylvester Akers, Peyton Long, Allen Parmer, Chat Renick, Frank James, Dick Burns, Andy McGuire, Jim Williams, Tom Hall, George Hall, Dick Glasscock, Clark Hockensmith, R. M. Venable, Joe Gibson, Payne Jones, Jack Graham, Jim Little, Bill Bassham, John Barker, Henry Noland, Bill Noland, Tom Harris, George Wigginton, Tom Evans, Jim Younger.

He said it was not complete, but he could not recall any other names at the time. The Flannery boys did not go to Kentucky. By comparing the list of names in the text with this, most of the men who went to Kentucky may be identified.

Akers says that the object of Quantrill in going away from Missouri was to get to General Lee and surrender with him, being convinced that the Confederacy was near a collapse and that Lee would soon have to surrender. He was also of the opinion that neither he nor his men would be permitted to surrender in Missouri or the West. Akers says that a division of the men occurred at the Mississippi, a number of them abandoning the Kentucky trip and going to Texas. One of the brothers of Akers was among these, and Akers desired to go, but Quantrill said to him: "I got you into this war and I want to get you out of it. I want you to go with me." Akers went with him, and he says that the story that Quantrill intended to assassinate President Lincoln is absurd. Of all the guerrillas

Six others accompanied Quantrill to Pocahontas, Arkansas, where they turned toward Texas. Four of these were "Babe" Hudspeth, Rufus Hudspeth, John Koger, and Oll Shepherd.

It was about the middle of December, 1864, when Quantrill left Jackson county. Few incidents of the trip are preserved. The weather was very cold. The guerrillas crossed the Osage at Tuscumbia, county-seat of Miller county. There the first Federal force was encountered, encamped in a large hotel with a porch along the entire front. Quantrill said he was Captain Clarke of the Fourth Missouri, and asked to see the commander of the post, who was at a house on a hill, where he lived or boarded. Quantrill and "Babe" Hudspeth went to see him, and Quantrill talked with him several minutes, getting all the information he could about the Federal forces in the country. Then he covered the captain with a pistol and told him he was a prisoner, after which he was taken to the garrison and made to order his men out and surrender. There the guerrillas got themselves a good breakfast and fed their horses. The prisoners were paroled, except one, who was taken along as guide. All the arms and ammunition of the garrison were put into the

---

at the Independence reunion none would admit that Quantrill ever intended to assassinate Lincoln.

Akers said that it was not the original intention of Quantrill to go to Kentucky. He started from Missouri to Virginia to the army of Lee, and intended to go through Tennessee. At the Mississippi he was told that he would not be able to pass through the Federal lines in East Tennessee. Then he turned aside to go through Kentucky. This may all be true, but Quantrill's course in Kentucky would indicate that he did not wish to go on to Virginia, but desired to find a new field in which to rise as a guerrilla leader.

Akers was born in Floyd county, Kentucky, December 6, 1834, and with his father, Solomon Akers, came to Missouri in 1840, and settled in Jackson county. His mother was Matilda (Mead) Akers. The Akers and Mead families lived on Abbott's creek, Floyd county, Ky., (near where this author was born and brought up), and their descendants are there in numbers to this day. The Meads came from Scotland, and Rhodes Mead is said to have made the first "pegged" shoes ever made in Kentucky, the art of which he taught the author's father. These families are good ones, and they were divided in sentiment in the Civil War, members of them being found in both the Federal and Confederate armies, perhaps a majority of them fighting for the Union.

ferry-boat, which was pushed out amid stream, where they were thrown overboard.

Crossing the river, the guerrillas continued on their way south until late at night, when part of the command halted and some one called out "Quantrill, are you going to camp here?" As soon as the guide heard Quantrill addressed he put spurs to his horse and fled, and in the darkness was not followed. After his escape, the guerrillas pursued their journey, riding all night.

January 1, 1865, Quantrill crossed the Mississippi river at Pacific, a point fifteen miles above Memphis. Sometimes a survivor will speak of the point of crossing as the Devil's Elbow or the Devil's Bend. The course of the guerrillas avoided the large towns, and at several small posts rations and supplies were drawn from Federal stores.

CHAPTER XXXVI

ON SUNDAY, January 22, 1865, the guerrillas arrived at Hartford, county-seat of Ohio county, in the Green river country of Kentucky. There the usual false representation was made that they were a detachment of the Fourth Missouri Cavalry, deceiving the Federal officers at that place. They claimed to be going to the Ohio river over the Hawesville road, pretending to want a guide, and Lieutenant Barnett, an officer recruiting for the One Hundred and Twenty-fifth U. S. Colored Regiment, agreed to go with them in that capacity. W. B. Lawton, a soldier in an Indiana regiment, who was at Hartford on furlough to see his family, thought to get safe conduct back to his command, and went with them. Just after leaving town they were joined by W. Townsley, a discharged soldier of the Third Kentucky Cavalry. Three miles further on they rode into the timber and hung Townsley. Nine miles beyond they shot Lawton. They shot Barnett sixteen miles from Hartford.[1]

---

[1] Part I, Vol. XLIX, Series I, p. 657, *Rebellion Records*, where this is officially set out in a letter to General Burbridge. This refutes another of those boasting false stories told persistently for more than forty years by Frank James. According to James, the guerrillas through their bogus "Captain Clarke" asked for twenty-five men to assist them in running down the notorious bandit, "One-armed" Berry, and the men were detailed to go with them. Quantrill appointed a guerrilla to ride by each Federal soldier, and the second day out, on a signal from Quantrill, each guerrilla shot and killed his man, James killing Barnett. A German escaped, but was soon captured and hung, "because he was not a good Yankee," saying with his last breath, "Gentlemen, you are mistaken. I voted for Abe Lincoln." This story was printed in the *Cincinnati Enquirer*, in 1907, and reprinted in the *Topeka State Journal*, August, 26, 1907. It is printed in the sensational *Life and Adventures of Frank and Jesse James* by Dacus. Major Edwards got many of his exaggerated and false statements from Frank and Jesse James while they were in hiding for their highway robberies and murders, and it is no wonder that his book is wholly unreliable.

There is little that can be relied on as to the operations of the guerrilla band in Kentucky. The ruling passion of Quantrill returned, and he seems to have given up his intention to go to Washington and assassinate President Lincoln, if that was the object of his expedition. Murder and robbery became the object of life with him, as it had been in Kansas, Missouri, and Texas. On the 28th of February, 1865, a part of his band, in company with some of "One-armed" Berry's men, or those of Sue Mundy, plundered the town of Hickman, Kentucky, and burned a portion of it, even beating and shooting at women and children.[2] He had been forced to leave, for a time, the country about the headwaters of Green river, where he had many skirmishes with Federal forces. Monday, Jan. 28, 1865, he was three miles east of Chaplintown. On the 29th he was at Danville, where he stood the inhabitants in line while he plundered a store, robbed some citizens, and destroyed the telegraph office. There the guerrillas pretended to belong to the Fourth Missouri Cavalry. They left at eleven-fifteen a. m. on the Perryville pike.[3]

Captain J. H. Bridgewater pursued the guerrillas from Danville, and came up with them five miles west of Harrodsburg in the evening. He killed and captured twelve of the invincible heroes of Major Edwards and suffered no loss. Chat Renick was among the killed and the guerrillas distinguished themselves by a scramble to escape from the Kentucky militia under Bridgewater.[4]

Quantrill seems to have been operating with the notorious Kentucky robber and murderer, Jerome Clarke, known as Sue Mundy, who was later hanged at Louisville for his inhuman

---

[2] Part I, Vol. XLIX, Series I, p. 788, *Rebellion Records.*

[3] Part I, Vol. XLIX, Series I, pp. 17, 18, *Rebellion Records.* In the Collection of the author there is a communication from Alex Anderson to W. W. Scott, dated at Danville, Ky., July 10, 1888, giving a good account of the actions of the guerrillas in Danville, but concealing the robberies. Scott did not credit the statement, but it is substantially correct, with the above exception and the exact date. Chat Renick was recognized there.

[4] Part I, Vol. XLIX, Series I, p. 18, *Rebellion Records.*

crimes.[5] They were passing into Owen county, but the pursuit was close, Colonel Buckly reporting that he had chased them from Spencer county through Shelby county. February 1, 1865, Captain Searcy reported having chased the redoubtable guerrillas three miles on the road east of Chaplintown. On the 2d of February they burned the depot at Midway, Ky., on the retreat westward.[6] For several days the guerrillas were kept on the move by Captain Bridgewater, who pushed them hard and pursued them from town to town about Bradfordsville, Campbellsville, and other places. There is no account anywhere that these guerrillas, who have been held up as the bravest of the brave in Missouri, ever made a stand against the Kentucky troops, though these troops were only militia, and few in number. There is not any account of their having killed any of the militia. In fact, those heroic qualities so much dwelt on by Edwards and other Missourians completely vanished when the guerrillas got into Kentucky. A squad of raw militia could chase them from county to county. They thought only of saving their lives, and the swiftest runner became the best guerrilla. February 8, 1865, this band captured a wagon-train at New Market and three guards were killed and four captured. The prisoners were taken to Bradfordsville "where they were murdered by the guerrillas under Captain Clarke." The next morning at 2 o'clock Captain Bridgewater with a squad of militia came upon the guerrilla camp on the Little South Fork, west of Houstonville, killed four of them, captured thirty-five horses, and chased the others into the woods barefooted. The valiant "Captain Clarke" was glad to escape by running barefooted into the brush, though the snow was fresh and probably deep. None of Captain Bridgewater's company was even wounded.[7]

After this blow there is little or no record of the movements of the guerrillas. They seemed to dread this militia Captain Bridgewater, and to have gone back to the Mississippi, where they plundered Hickman, on the 28th of February, as before

5 Part I, Vol. XLIX, Series I, p. 626, *Rebellion Records*. Also Statements of guerrillas in Collection of the author.

6 Part I, Vol. XLIX, Series I, p. 635, *Rebellion Records*.

7 Part I, Vol. XLIX, Series I, p. 35, *Rebellion Records*.

stated. Probably only a portion of the band was at Hickman, and the leader there may have been Sue Mundy.

The guerrillas appeared in Spencer county, Ky., again in April; on the 13th Major Wilson, Captain Penn, and Captain Ed Terrill attacked a band under Quantrill and Marion near Bloomfield, and killed two and wounded three. One of Terrill's men shot and killed Marion.[8]

Some incidents of Quantrill's operations in Kentucky are preserved only in the memory of the survivors of the band. These can be given as received and perhaps out of the order of their occurrence; and no dates are preserved.

At one point in Kentucky the band camped a day or two with a Federal company. Peyton Long got drunk. In this condition he saw the horse of the captain and wanted it. The guard would not let him have it. When the captain came for his horse Long shot him and took the horse. The Federals tried to capture Long but Quantrill protected him, and to avoid fighting the guerrillas left the Federal camp.[9]

Peyton Long

In some accounts it is said that Allen Parmer shot the captain to get the horse. After the surrender Bill Robinson was tried and hung for this crime — of which he was innocent. But justice was done; Robinson was guilty of a thousand other crimes, for any of which he should have been hanged.[10]

---

8 Part I, Vol. XLIX, Series I, p. 512, *Rebellion Records.* There is a dispute as to whether Marion was killed by Terrill's men or Penn's men.

9 This incident gave rise to many newspaper stories. Those printed in later years were ridiculous. One version will be found in the *Globe-Democrat*, May 27, 1888.

10 Sylvester Akers told the author at the Independence reunion of the guerrillas, August 21, 1909, that it was Parmer who shot the Federal soldier to get his horse. Akers believes the murdered soldier was a private and not an officer. As Akers was on the ground, he had opportunity to know, and his statement settles it; Parmer shot the soldier to get his horse.

Akers says this occurred at Houstonville, Kentucky, and that Captain

Allen Parmer

Quantrill fell in with Sue Mundy soon after he arrived at Harrodsburg, and to Mundy he revealed his identity. They fought together in that region. In one of their skirmishes Jim Little was killed — the first of Quantrill's men to fall in the Kentucky expedition.

Peyton Long and Quantrill quarreled about the shooting of the Federal captain and were by the guerrillas prevented from shooting each other. To prevent a fight among themselves they separated from Sue Mundy, with whom Peyton Long remained and in whose command he was killed in a skirmish with Captain Bridgewater.

February 26, 1865, Quantrill was at the house of one Dawson, near Wakefield, Ky. Dawson's daughter Nannie requested him to write in her autograph album, and he wrote the following:[11]

> My horse is at the door,
> And the enemy I soon may see
> But before I go Miss Nannie
> Here's a double health to thee

Bridgewater came to take Parmer away. Quantrill did not want to give him up. Most of the men favored the surrender of Parmer, and they said to Quantrill: "Either give him up or kill him. If he is not given up or killed the object of our expedition will be thwarted." Quantrill chose to stand by Parmer, and when Bridgewater appeared he was told that Parmer would be protected. Bridgewater then said he would have to take the whole command to headquarters. At this point Quantrill told Bridgewater the truth as to the identity of himself and men. Captain Bridgewater had but few men, and Quantrill permitted him to depart.

[11] Quantrill had, at great trouble, made up these lines from Byron's poems for the edification of Annie Walker, daughter of Morgan Walker, soon after he entered on his guerrilla career. The leaf from Miss Dawson's album is in the Collection of the author. On it was written, by W. W. Scott, the following:

The only scrap of Quantrill's writing that I have been able to get anywhere after June, 1860. This his mother got from a young lady's album in Eastern Ky. in 1892 near Wakefield, Ky.

Here's a sigh to those who love me
And a smile to those who hate
And, whatever sky's above me
Here's a heart for every fate.

Though the cannons roar around me
Yet it still shall bear me on
Though dark clouds are above me
It hath springs which may be won.

In this verse as with the wine
The libation I would pour
Should be peace with thine and mine
And a health to thee and all *in door.*

Very respectfully your friend

Feb. 26, 1865. W. C. Q.

Quantrill was at the house of Jonathan Davis, judge of Spencer county, Ky. President Lincoln had been assassinated the night before. Quantrill and all his band were drunk. He apologized to the ladies, saying: "Excuse us, ladies. We are a little in our cups today. The grand-daddy of all the greenbacks, Abraham Lincoln, was shot in a theatre at Washington last night." Calling for glasses, they all drank, the cut-throat, "One-armed" Berry, pronouncing the following toast: "Here's to the death of Abraham Lincoln, hoping that his bones may serve in hell as a gridiron to fry Yankees on."

CHAPTER XXXVII

QUANTRILL THE FATALIST

QUANTRILL was a fatalist. In a letter to his mother he once expressed the belief that he was providentially spared and saved from death in the Pike's Peak region when his companions perished. In Kentucky premonition of his death came to him in a strange way.

At the battle of Independence, it will be remembered, Quantrill secured the magnificent brown horse of Buel and named him Charley. He rode this horse to the end of his career — at Lawrence, Baxter Springs, in Texas, in escaping from Bill Anderson at Bonham, on the expedition to Kentucky. This horse became a part of Quantrill, and the guerrillas believed he absorbed the nature of his master and became a guerrilla. He was said to be the best guard in the camp and sounded many an alarm that saved the guerrilla band. Once when Quantrill rode him to Clay county to visit Annie Walker Vaughan, the Federal soldiers found him and pressed him so hard that he believed his only hope of escape lay in abandoning his horse and running afoot into the woods. This he did, climbing a high rail fence into a thicket by the roadside. As he ran through the brush he heard a horse crashing after him and supposed a soldier was following. Turning at bay, he was surprised to see his own horse coming rapidly up to him. He mounted and made his escape. The horse had jumped the high fence and followed his master.

That this horse did absorb the nature of Quantrill through long service and association must be true. He became vicious. No one but Quantrill could control him. He would strike, bite, kick, and squeal if approached by others. It became necessary to tie him hard and fast to shoe him. A few days before Quantrill's death, one of the guerrillas, Jack Graham, was shoeing this horse. In paring the hoofs the guerrilla was using the old-fashioned instrument for that purpose pushed by the shoulder of the smith and called a buttress. In his vicious struggling the horse was hamstrung with this instrument, and disabled, ruined. When told of the accident and its result, Quantrill recoiled as though stricken with a pistol-ball, turned deathly pale, remained in deep silence for a time, then rose and said with firmness and deliberation, though with effort and suppressed emotion: "That means that my work is done. My career is run. Death is coming, and my end is near."

From that hour he was a changed man. He seemed only waiting. He expected death.[1]

The final hour was near. The lines were tightening. The pursuit became relentless. The Terror of the Kansas Border was no terror in Kentucky, but a cowering murderer skulking and hunted through thickets, along hedges, over hills, in the ploughed fields. Place to rest the sole of his foot was found not. Vengeance, grim, pitiless, followed him, rode by his side, stood before him as he snatched a morsel of food from some humble board. "Whatsoever a man soweth, that shall he also reap" is the law of the universe. In his last days Quantrill saw this judgment pending soon to be visited upon him by fate. And "God moves in a mysterious way." The instrument for the execution of the relentless decree was a boy with a story strange and romantic. In family and character he stood above Quantrill, but the difference was something of degree, motive, design, experience. Seeking to know what manner of man he might be, Quantrill's old companion was given the following:[2]

Shelbyville, Ky., Oct. 12th, 1888.

W. W. Scott, Esq.

Ed. Terrill was commissioned by Federal authority to fight guerrillas, and using his authority, bulldosed all the counties in

---

[1] Captain William H. Gregg told the author at the Independence reunion, August 21, 1909, that the accepted story of this horse was not correct in all respects. He says the horse belonged to Buel's quartermaster — not to Buel — that he himself got Buel's horse, an animal far inferior to the one Quantrill got. In the Lawrence Raid Quantrill did not ride this horse because of its lameness from having become graveled, but rode a fine horse a little lighter in color.

[2] Letter of R. T. Owen to W. W. Scott, date Shelbyville, Ky., Oct. 12, 1888, now in the Collection of the author.

this section. He first joined Capt. Jack Thompson's Company,
First Kentucky Confederate troops, and served the first year of
the war in Virginia. After the disbandment of that regiment,
in the spring of 1862, he joined the Confederate army in Tennessee (don't know the regiment), deserted and followed Jayhawking until regularly authorized by U. S. He and one of his Lieutenants, Harry Thompson, another Confederate deserter, in the
summer of 1865, arrested a Federal soldier named Johnson near
Bardstown, and brought him to this place, where he was guarded
by them for several days and then taken at night about a mile
from town, murdered and robbed, his body sunk in a creek,
where it was discovered a few days afterwards. Suspicion
pointed to Terrill and Thompson who were arrested, tried and
the jury hanging, they were confined in our county jail, from
which they made their escape.

Thompson was never heard from, but Terrill commenced
operations on a small scale and took in several small places, as
Taylorsville, Bloomfield, etc. With one of his men he rode into
this place one day about dark and the County Judge ordered out
a posse of citizens to arrest them, when, as the posse were proceeding to discharge their duty, Terrill rode up the main street
firing his pistol at every one in sight, one shot killing an old gentleman by the name of Redding, another wounding a young man
by the name of Randolph.

The posse fired at them, killing Baker, Terrill's uncle, who
was with him, and giving Terrill the wound from which he died.

As to Quantrill, he was killed, as you say, by Terrill's men,
but by whom. he was shot, I have never heard. He was killed in
Spencer County, near Bloomfield. I never heard of his having
been nearer here than the place where he was killed.

As to Terrill's reputation; he was very young when he
joined the army and his reputation was the worst imaginable and
his fighting qualities were only developed when under the influence of whisky; and his death was a great relief to his family, his
friends and his enemies. He had generally about twenty-five
men under him. Some few of the better men under him are living in or near Mt. Eden, Spencer County, Kentucky, and are
conducting themselves, as far as I know, as good citizens.

Terrill was from Harrisonville in this County and his family respectable people.

You may get a photograph of Terrill from J. W. Williams
of this place. He is not in his place of business to-day, but I
think he has a negative of him.

Yours respectfully,

R. T. Owen,

P. S. I knew Terrill well and saw him in Virginia, and after I was paroled. If I can give you any other information in regard to him, I will cheerfully do so.

R. T. Owen,

The letter of inquiry was handed me by Capt. J. N. Bell, P. M.

The following may also throw light on the nature of the command organized and placed under command of Captain Terrill:

From the *National Tribune*, April 10, 1904.

Editor National Tribune: In the National Tribune of December 10, 1903, I noticed an article from Geo. W. Bowers, New Philadelphia, Ohio, on the death of the mother of the infamous outlaw, Quantrill, in which appears a statement that he was mortally wounded by one of Gen. E. H. Hobson's command, and shortly afterwards died in a hospital at Louisville, Ky. I have not yet seen any correct accounts of the manner and by whom he was captured, as I understand it. In the month of February, 1865, Quantrill and his band were reported to be in the vicinity of Lebanon, Ky. By order of Gen. John M. Palmer, then in command of the department of Kentucky, I drew 100 guns, equipments and ammunition from the arsenal at Jeffersonville to equip 100 men from Park barracks, who were sent under a lieutenant to capture Quantrill and his band. This was a failure, of course, for when they got where he was, like the Irishman's flea, he "warn't there." There were so many rebel sympathizers there that he was posted as soon as a union soldier appeared; therefore, another kind of strategy had to be adopted.

Under instructions from General Palmer, I found a man who knew Quantrill in Kansas, who found thirty more men willing to undertake to capture him, dead or alive, as the necessity of the case might require. These scouts (all citizens, no soldiers) were instructed to be a band of guerrillas; to live off the community where they were scouting, and to assume the garb of genuine guerrillas, that they might gain the confidence of Quantrill and his band, and by that means capture him. This they were entirely successful in doing, and in the scrap which followed Quantrill was wounded in the back, much as Garfield was, three or four of his men killed, and as many more wounded.

Captain Terrill, who was in command of these scouts, reported May 10, 1865, at General Palmer's headquarters, with Quantrill in a wagon on a straw bed. He was sent to a hospital in the southwest part of the city, where he died about six weeks later, and the company was paid off and discharged on the above date. The names of the men comprising the company appear in my reports to the third auditor of the treasury for the months of April and May, 1865, signed by themselves, on their pay-roll. A copy is herewith enclosed. (Signed) J. M. Ridlon, First Lieutenant and Quartermaster Twenty-fifth Michigan, and A. A. Q. M., Headquarters, Department of Kentucky.

[The document which Lieutenant Ridlon sends us is a very interesting one. It is the roll-call of the thirty-one men who went as scouts on the expedition, and were employed in it from the 1st until May 10, 1865. The chief was Edwin Terrill. His lieutenants were John H. Thompson and Horace Allen. The chief received fifty dollars a month for his services, and the lieutenants thirty-five and thirty dollars, respectively. The document is a report of their services, and the expenditure of money on them, and is signed on honor by Lieutenant Ridlon, and vouched for by Gen. John M. Palmer, major-general commanding the Department of Kentucky—Editor *National Tribune*.] [2]

---

[2] Quoted from pp. 544-545, Vol. VIII, *Kansas Historical Collections*.

CHAPTER XXXVIII

THE LAST BATTLE

QUANTRIILL went up Salt river. On its waters, in the south part of Spencer county, there lived one James H. Wakefield, at whose house he made headquarters, remaining there little, for the dreaded Captain Bridgewater seemed always present. To Wakefield, Quantrill said he meant to go on to Virginia. He recruited some men to replace those lost at the hands of the vigilant militia captain. The people around Wakefield were principally Southern in sympathy, but some were for the old flag, and some were neutral. Wakefield stood neutral, but felt most interest in the Confederacy. Captain Edwin Terrill, then little more than nineteen, was the son of his neighbor of old of Mt. Eden and Harrisonville in Shelby county. The guerrilla chief had borrowed a horse of Miss Betty Russell to replace the old warhorse, Charley. This horse had not been in battle and knew not the odor of powder; had not heard the rush and roar of clashing arms.

Captain Terrill had been about thirty days armed and pursuing Quantrill. Early in May — on the morning of the 10th — a rainy morning, he was following a fresh cavalry trail on the road running north from Bloomfield to Taylorsville. Near noon, at the shop of a negro blacksmith, a halt was made to secure intelligence of the fugitive guerrillas. The sable Vulcan pointed to a great gate opening to the west and said a body of horsemen had just entered and gone toward the capacious barn of farmer Wakefield, the top only of which could be seen above the intervening elevation. The men of Captain Terrill went briskly up the lane, and, rising the swell, charged down upon the barn, unslinging carbines and getting pistols in hand. Coming in range, fire was opened and yells set up to terrify the Missourians.[1]

---

[1] Terrill had not to exceed thirty men, the full number of his com-

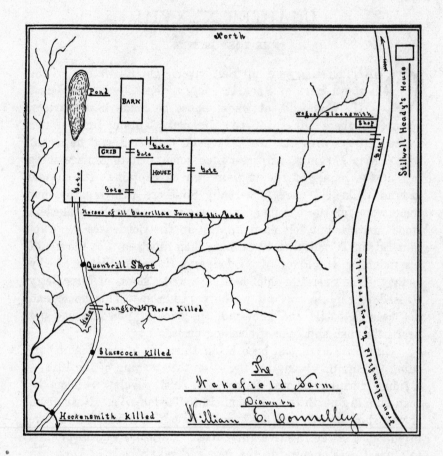

The guerrillas were surprised. Their horses were tied under the sheds about the barn, and some were eating hay from inside mangers. Most of the guerrillas were lying asleep in the fodder-loft. A few sought relaxation from tense times in a sham battle with cobs. Farmer Wakefield stood under a shed talking to Dick Glasscock. Hockensmith looked to the east and saw the Federal guerrillas coming full tilt down the slope. Shouts rose and firing began at that instant, and Hockensmith sounded the alarm, saying, "Here they come."

Terror and confusion seized the Missourians. They scrambled wildly for their horses, and those who were fortunate enough to mount, fled in a mad rout. No resistance was made, and no record is found that they even fired a single shot in the barn-lot. Some could not get their horses out in time to mount, and these concealed themselves in a pond there until the pursuit rolled by, then they dodged through shrubs and by fences and got into the woods. The iron hail, the indomitable courage, the invincible valor, the chivalric stand for the loved South raved about by Edwards in which one guerrilla was a match for twenty Federals, seemed sadly wanting that day when the Kentuckians swooped down on the alien guerrillas from the waters of the Blue and the Hills of the Sni.

Clark Hockensmith

Quantrill was sleeping in the hay-loft when the charge thundered down the slope. He clambered out and rushed to his horse, which reared madly and could not be mounted. When its wild plunging had secured its freedom from the guerrilla chief,

---

pany. Quantrill had about the same number, possibly not more than twenty-five. Some of the men of Marion were with him. In a letter to W. W. Scott, dated Clarinda, Iowa, Dec. 28, 1897, John Langford, one of Terrill's men, says Quantrill had twenty-one men — counted by the negro blacksmith.

At the Independence reunion, August 21, 1909, the author was told that Quantrill had started that morning to Louisville to surrender himself and men.

it galloped around the enclosure snorting with terror. Quantrill, seeing the situation to be desperate, followed his fleeing knights on foot. They had made their horses jump the gate at the southwest corner of the lot, and were running down a slight ridge in a sugar-orchard, Hockensmith and Glasscock in the rear. Quantrill called to them and they waited for him, firing back to check the pursuit. As Quantrill ran alongside Glasscock trying to mount behind, Glasscock's mare was shot in the hip and became unmanageable. Then Quantrill fired to check the pursuit while trying to mount behind Hockensmith. While running by Hockensmith he was hit in the back by a ball, which entered at the end of the left shoulder-blade, ranged down, struck the spine, and paralyzed him below his arms. He was shot once after he fell, the ball cutting off the index finger of his right hand.

Glasscock got a quarter of a mile after his mare was wounded, and was then shot. Hockensmith got four hundred yards beyond where Glasscock was shot, when he, too, was overtaken and killed in a branch or small creek crossing the sugar-grove.[2] Farmer Wakefield, being a non-combatant and having no thirst at all for military glory, ran at the first fire for the cover of his own good house, which, by dodging behind cribs and kennels, he happily reached uninjured.

When Quantrill was wounded, some of the victors jerked off his boots and perhaps others of his garments and made off with them. Others, less intent on loot, ran to the house for a blanket on which to bring him in, which they soon did, laying him on a lounge. Captain Terrill entered and talked with him. He repeated that he was Captain Clarke of the Fourth Missouri Cavalry. He did not wish to leave Wakefield's, and gave Captain Terrill his fine gold watch and $500 to allow him to remain. He promised an additional $500, saying that his men would get it for him.

By the military orders then existing, the life and property of Wakefield was forfeit for harboring the guerrillas. Captain

[2] Glasscock and Hockensmith were first buried at Smileytown. Afterwards Wakefield, at request of their people, removed the bodies to the cemetery at Bloomfield. Glasscock's horse was kept at Wakefield's until the owner, a widow, came and got it.

Terrill began to plunder the house, when Wakefield took him and his lieutenant aside, giving the captain $20 and the lieutenant $10, which, supplemented with a jug of whiskey, saved further depredations, and the hopeful command departed. It had performed a righteous and valuable service to the country. Through Captain Terrill's Federal guerrillas many a foul murder, many a crime cruel and inhuman to the last degree, many a sacked town blazing black in smoke and sunshine or rolling red against the midnight sky, the cries of many an orphan, the shrieks and wails of widows innumerable along the border found vengeance, satisfaction, something of restitution.

Captain Terrill and his desperate company gone, the family physician was summoned to the Wakefield home — a Doctor McClasky. He looked and felt and probed as is the wont of his kind. Then straightening the patient to as much comfort as a death-stricken man may have, he said to him that his hurt was mortal and of hope there was none — all of which Quantrill knew before his arrival.

Time for reflection had come for Quantrill. He stood on the shores of the dark river. What phantoms stood before him we may not know. The world was rolled back for him. He spoke of his mother and sister, saying that a Mrs. Olivia D. Cooper had of his $500 in gold which he hoped they might have. But ruling passions became strong in death. This request was broken. From his disordered mind mother and sister were banished. Kate Clarke — the kidnapped girl who had assumed his name without marriage — stood in their place and seized the gold. The priest that shrived him never heard their names.[3]

<hr/>

[3] In the Collection of the author are many clippings from newspapers detailing at length the last battle of Quantrill and his band. Some facts are found in them. W. W. Scott interviewed Wakefield, and that interview lies before the author as he writes. Wakefield, a kindly, truthful man, wrote Scott June 13, 1888, giving a commplete account of this affair, and the letter is set out here at length:

Wakefield, June 13th, 1888.

Mr. Scott:

In answer to your letter asking me to tell you all I know about Captain Quantrill's stay in Kentucky and his being fatally shot, I will say this:

In the spring of 1865, in March, I think, a man who went by the name of Captain Clarke, came to my place with a squad of men. I had

Dispute arose as to who had fired the shot which proved fatal to Quantrill. John Langford was one of Terrill's men. He afterwards moved to Clarinda, Iowa. There he came to believe that he had fired the shot. Some of his letters attempting to establish that claim are in the collection of the author. They do not establish it. Claim was made for Terrill, though it is not known that he sanctioned it. One account says Terrill

---

not been in the army on either side, but had been buying stock and forage for the Union troops at Louisville.

Captain Clarke treated us very well and behaved themselves so that we got to liking them. They came often to my place, but never stayed long at a time. After we got pretty well acquainted, Captain Clarke told his real name was Quantrill, but he did not want it known.

In the forenoon of the 10th of May, 1865, came to my place, hitched their horses in my barnyard, and as a hard rain came up, they went into the barn and under the shed. There was a roof from the barn out about fifteen feet all around. The Captain and some of the men were in the haymow asleep. Others sitting about talking, and some were having a sham battle with corn cobs. I was standing out at the edge of the shed talking with Glasscock, one of his men. The rain still falling fast. All at once Hockensmith looked up the slope toward the big road, and we saw a lot of horsemen galloping down toward us, unslinging their carbines and shooting, as they came. Hockensmith cried out "Here they come," and all scrambled for their horses, and hurried out the back corner of the barnyard past my house into the timber, by a bridle-path. Some of the horses got away, and the men ran out on foot or hid wherever they could. I think there were about fifteen or so of Quantrill's men; and may be fifty or more of the other fellows. They all kept shooting and running, but it was quick over. The attacking party was Ed Terrill and his Federal guerrillas. I heard pretty lively shooting down in the timber a couple of hundred yards beyond my house, and pretty soon some of Terrill's men came back for quilts to carry a wounded man up.

I went along down, and found Quantrill so badly wounded that he could neither sit or stand. They had taken his pistols and stripped off his boots. He was conscious, and they rolled him over on a blanket and carried him up to my house and laid him on the lounge. The men began to ransack my house, but I gave Terrill $20.00 and Taylor $10.00 and a jug of whiskey, and they let me alone. The first finger of Quantrill's right hand had been shot off, and he had been shot in the back about the shoulderblade; the ball striking his spine and paralyzing him all but his head and arms. He denied to Terrill that he was Quantrill, claiming that he was Captain Clarke of the Fourth Missouri Cavalry; and asked to be left at my house to die. He knew his fate if he admitted who he was.

Terrill first refused to leave him there, but knowing he was paralyzed, he finally consented; but said he would hold me accountable if he was missing when he came back. I promised to stand good for him as he had pledged me his word and honor that he would not let anyone take him away.

We sent for Dr. McClaskey, with whom he was acquainted with, and after he examined the wound, he said it was fatal.

That night some of Quantrill's men came and wanted to carry him away and hide him where he would be taken care of. But he refused to

sat on his horse during the fight, his leg thrown carelessly over the pommel of the saddle, unable to take a hand because of an injury to his arm a few days before, but encouraging his men with such chaste and choice phrases as "Give 'em hell, boys!" There is nothing to show conclusively who fired the fatal shot. It is said that Quantrill believed it was Terrill, and there is some reason to believe that Terrill did fire the shot which carried away his finger.[4]

In the gloom of night came some of the guerrillas to see their stricken chief. Among these was Frank James, who long

---

[4] On this point the letter of Thos. M. Yenowine is set out here:

Mt. Eden, Ky., Oct. 17, 1888.

W. W. Scott,
Sir:

Yours of the 9th to hand, and will answer your questions as far as I know. Joe Taylor and Ben Stevens reside near my office. Levi Cotton lives seven miles from here; C. A. Taylor in Davis County, Kentucky; John Langford lives somewhere in Illinois; no one knows. Ben Stevens told me no one knew who shot Quantrill. He helped to carry him to James Wakefield's house after he was wounded. On the following day they took him to Louisville, Ky., where he soon died after arriving. Terrill was from near this place and died in the City Hospital of Louisville, Ky., from an operation performed removing ball imbedded in the spine. He was a patient of mine and I had him sent there.

Any further information needed, I will cheerfully give.

Thos. M. Yenowine, P. M.

---

go, saying that he had pledged his word to stay, and if he did not, my property would be burned, and I would be held accountable. Besides he said he knew he had to die and did not want to be dragged around, and that Terrill had promised not to move him if he did not try to get away. Next night some more of his men came and insisted, but he refused.

Next day, Friday, Terrill came with twenty to twenty-five of his men, and putting some straw and things into a horse, farm, or spring wagon, took him away to Louisville; where I learned that he died about a month afterwards.

While he was lying wounded at our house, he told me again that his name was Quantrill and thanked us all for our kindness to him and his men. He told me of some money he wanted to leave for his mother and sister. But afterwards said he would write to me about it when he got to Louisville. He told me who had it and how much, but I never got any word from him about it.

I am sure he died at the Hospital in Louisville.

Spencer County, Kentucky.   James H. Wakefield.

P. S. Glasscock and Hockensmith were killed about a quarter of a mile from the same place that Quantrill was shot. They lost their lives trying to save their Captain, as his (Quantrill's) horse was wild and he could not mount, and they were trying to get Quantrill up behind one of them. He was in the act of mounting when shot. I had Hockensmith and Glasscock buried at Bloomfield, Nelson County, Kentucky.

afterwards told a story in Missouri to the effect that he was
wounded and could not be at the battle,
but was hidden away to nurse himself to
a recovery. How his wound could keep
him out of the fight, yet enable him to
ride by night to counsel rescue, it is hard
to see.

Frank James

The guerrillas wished to carry Quantrill away, but he would not go. He knew
his wound was mortal and told them so.
He had pledged his parole. Wakefield
had stood bail for him and his house
would be burned if he did not stay. No,
he would not go. He talked of the old
days of 1862 in Missouri. The later days
there seemed too black for discussion by a man in the presence
of death.

Citizens came to minister to him. Some of them watched
through the long hours of night. To one he is reported to have
said the accounts of his sacking of Lawrence were correct with
one exception — that if he had captured Senator James H. Lane
he intended to burn him at the stake in Jackson county, Missouri.[5]

Quantrill's men surrendered later. In an interview at
Samuels's Depot (now Wakefield, Ky.) with W. W. Scott, Bob
Hall said that sixteen men under Captain Henry Porter surrendered at Samuels's Depot, July 26, 1865, to Captain Young,
stationed at Bardstown. He gave the names of the following

---

[5] Letters of W. L. Davis and others, who spent the nights with Quantrill, are in the Collection of the author. Davis was postmaster at Paris,
Ky., when he wrote them. His father was Judge Jonathan Davis, of
Spencer county, and Quantrill prevented the guerrilla, Marion, from killing Judge Davis for not burning the court-house at his command. Davis
says Quantrill was a Freemason, an error. That ancient and honorable
order was never disgraced by his membership. Captain William H. Gregg
was a Freemason during his service under Quantrill, and he says that if
Quantrill was a Mason he never made himself known as such. It is not
impossible that Quantrill falsely represented himself a Freemason to secure
clemency when in extremity. He united with the Catholic church, something he could not have done had he been a Mason.

guerrillas who surrendered in that company: Bill Hulse, John Harris, John Ross, Ran Venable, Dave Hilton, Frank James, Bud Pence, Allen Parmer, Lee McMurtry, Ike Hall, Bob Hall, Payne Jones, Andy McGuire, Jim Lilly.

There must have been two more, but their names have not been found.[6]

---

[6] Memo of this interview is in the Collection of the author. It has no date but must have been made when Scott visited Samuels's Depot. On the sheet other matters are mentioned, among them, that a Captain Clarke of the Second Colorado had been killed and Quantrill took his commission.

CHAPTER XXXIX

DEATH

ON FRIDAY morning, May 12, 1865, Captain Terrill appeared at the Wakefield house with an old Conestoga wagon drawn by two mules. Into this he put a straw bed, upon which Quantrill was placed and covered comfortably. Terrill's men disposed themselves about the wagon as guards, and the cavalcade started to Louisville. The journey was slow, every consideration being shown the wounded guerrilla. Medical attention was secured at towns through which they passed.[1]

On the 13th day of May, Captain Terrill and his men reported at the headquarters of General John M. Palmer, in Louisville, with Quantrill.

Quantrill was taken to the hospital of the military prison in Louisville, where he lived until about four p. m., of the 6th of June, 1865, when he died, twenty-seven days after he was wounded.[2]

---

[1] In the Collection of the author is a letter from Mrs. Samuel N. Marshall, wife of Dr. S. N. Marshall, dated Jeffersontown, Jefferson county, Ky., Jan. 22, 1883. The letter is to W. W. Scott. In it the statement is made that Terrill stopped over night with Quantrill at Jeffersontown, and that Captain Terrill sent for Dr. Marshall and Dr. Lenteney, who treated the wounded man. The letter says the physicians found Quantrill's back broken, and the prisoner completely paralyzed below his arms. Dr. Marshall had but recently moved to Jeffersontown from Shelby county, Ky., where he had attended Quantrill professionally, and Quantrill recognized him and inquired if he was not the same physician, and Dr. Marshall said: "I am the man. I have moved here." Quantrill replied with an attempt at pleasantry, "So have I." Mrs. Marshall says there was a former Kansan then living in the town, and he recognized Quantrill as the same man he had known in Kansas before the war.

[2] There is no dispute as to the date of Quantrill's death. Other dates are not so clearly settled. Wakefield says the fight at his house was on the 10th of May. Official records seem obscure. The Louisville news-

In the first chapter of this book and the notes thereto will be found full proof of the identification of the grave of Quantrill and the removal of his bones to Canal Dover, Ohio.

The widow Ross, later Mrs. Harriet Lobb, of Independence,

---

papers seem to confirm the Wakefield date. Some extracts from the *Daily Union Press*, and other Louisville papers are given:

Saturday, May 13, 1865. *Quantrill.* — We learn from a gentleman who lives near Bloomfield, Kentucky, that Capt. Terrill came upon Quantrill, between Bloomfield and Taylorsville, on Wednesday [10th]. Captain Terrill and his men rushed on the guerrillas, when they broke and ran. They were closely pursued by the gallant Captain, who came upon Quantrill and shot him through the abdomen. He was carried to a farm-house close by, where he was on Thursday night. There is no hope of his recovery.

May 15, 1865. *Quantrill.* — The noted guerrilla who has been operating in Kentucky under the name of Quantrill, and whose capture we noticed Saturday, is in the Military Prison hospital. There is very little hope of his recovery, as his whole body is perfectly paralyzed.

May 16, 1865. We are informed that on the arrival of the guerrilla, who has assumed the name of Quantrill, at the barracks prison Saturday he was found to be in possession of a beautiful bouquet, to which was attached a card bearing the following inscription:
"Compliments of Miss Maggie Frederick and Sallie Lovell to Mr. Quantrill."
This was presented to the distinguished bandit, we suppose, as a testimonial of his valor. A strange way some people have of showing their loyalty.

June 7, 1865. *Quantrill Dead.* — The notorious guerrilla "Quantrill," calling himself William Clarke, Captain Fourth Missouri Cavalry, died in the Military Prison Hospital in this city yesterday evening at four o'clock. He was captured near Taylorsville, Ky., the 10th of last month, after being shot through the body.

Louisville Daily Courier, May 14, 1865.—Quantrill the notorious Kansas guerrilla, arrived in this city yesterday morning about 11 o'clock. He was conveyed in a country wagon on a bed of straw, and a few pillows, and guarded by Terrill's men disguised as guerrillas. He is wounded through the left breast, and it is thought he will die. All the honor of his capture is due to Captain Terrill and his company — "Terrill's guerrillas."

On Wednesday Terrill and his men surprised and charged on Quantrill's gang, five miles beyond Taylorsville, killing three of the outlaws and dispersing the remainder. They were also on the scent of Berry's guerrillas, and only one hour behind them when they received orders to report to the general commanding. Quantrill has been sailing under the name of Captain Clark and it is supposed by many that it is not the veritable Kansas outlaw, but we understand that Terrill and part of his company are intimately acquainted with him. One fact that strongly corroborates their assertions is that a picture of a young lady was found in his possession, which one of the parties recognized as Miss Hickman, who

Mo., visited Quantrill the day before he died. She reported that he died of neglect. It has been claimed that some of his men visited him, and this is probably true. They must have brought him or sent him the money he left with the priest for Kate Clarke, and for his monument.

And, so, the end came to Quantrill, the Jayhawker, the Border-Ruffian, the Bandit, the Guerrilla, the Freebooter, the Degenerate, the Depraved. Few men have achieved such notoriety. Of the Civil War in America he was the bloodiest man. Of the Border he was the Scourge and Terror. Idolized for his ferocious blood-madness, he forgot his mother. Embarked in savagery, he forswore his native land. Professing allegiance

---

resides within five miles of the Kansas line. Quantrill also stated that the three followers of his who were killed were from Missouri. The news of his capture will cause great joy throughout the Union. The inhuman outrages that he committed years ago, such as burning the town of Lawrence, etc., are still fresh in the memory of our people.

Louisville Daily Democrat, May 14, 1865.—Captain Terrill and his company arrived here yesterday from Taylorsville. They brought with them the guerrilla who bears the name of "Quantrill." It is not the Quantrill of Kansas notoriety, for we have been assured that he was at last accounts a colonel in rebel army under Price. This prisoner was shot through the body in a fight in a barn near Taylorsville on Wednesday last. Five others were killed on the spot by Terrill's men, but what their names were we could not ascertain. The prisoner brought down is confined in the military prison hospital and is said to be in a dying condition.

Louisville Daily Democrat, June 7, 1865.—It will be remembered that a guerrilla calling himself William Clark, captain in the Fourth Missouri Rebel cavalry, but generally supposed to be the infamous monster "Quantrill," was wounded and captured near Taylorsville, Ky., on the 10th ult., and placed in the military prison hospital in this city. He died of his wounds yesterday afternoon, about 4 o'clock.

Louisville Journal, June 7, 1865.—William Clark, alias Quantrill, captain Fourth Missouri cavalry, who was wounded and captured as a guerrilla, near Taylorsville, Ky., May 10, died in the military prison hospital in this city, yesterday evening about 4 o'clock. Magruder, who is lying in the same hospital, is very low and no hopes are entertained of his recovery.

John C. King, undertaker, coroner Third and Jefferson streets, Louisville, Ky., told W. W. Scott that he remembered seeing Quantrill brought to Louisville on a Sunday and passing his place of business in a wagon or ambulance on his way to the military prison hospital under escort. King afterwards furnished the Sisters of Charity a coffin for the same man, in June, and attended the burial. Memo. of this statement was made by Scott, and is now in the Collection of the author.

to an alien cause, he brought upon a fair land fire and sword, desolation and woe. To manifest a zeal he did not feel, he had recourse to slander, betrayed his companions and aided in their murder. With red hands he gave fair cities to torch and pillage, and reveled in the groans and cries of the helpless and innocent victims of his ruthless and inhuman crimes.

In the long days that Quantrill stood gazing into the valley of the Shadow of Death let us hope that remorse racked him, that repentance seized him, and that the ministrations of the church invoked by him were effective. For in his journey through this life there had stalked in his wake scenes

"Of maid,
Of mother, widow, sister, daughter, wife,
Stooping and weeping over senseless, cold,
Defaced, and mangled lumps of breathless earth,
Which had been husbands, fathers, brothers, sons,
And lovers, when the morning's sun arose."

And standing on the brink of eternity, in that hour of doom, his accounts were cast, and

"How his audit stands,
Who knows save Heaven!"

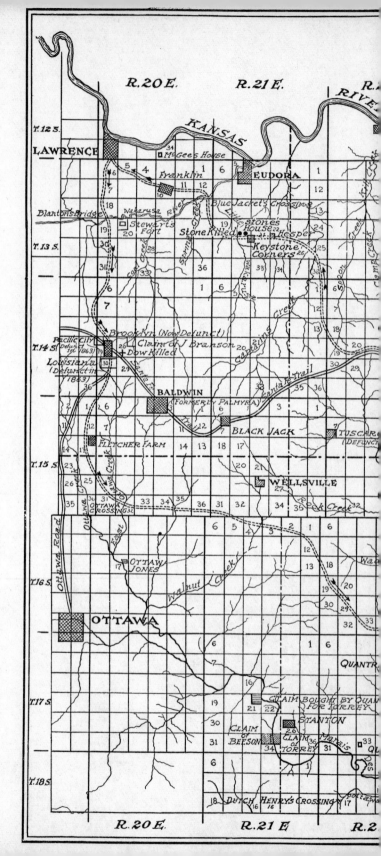

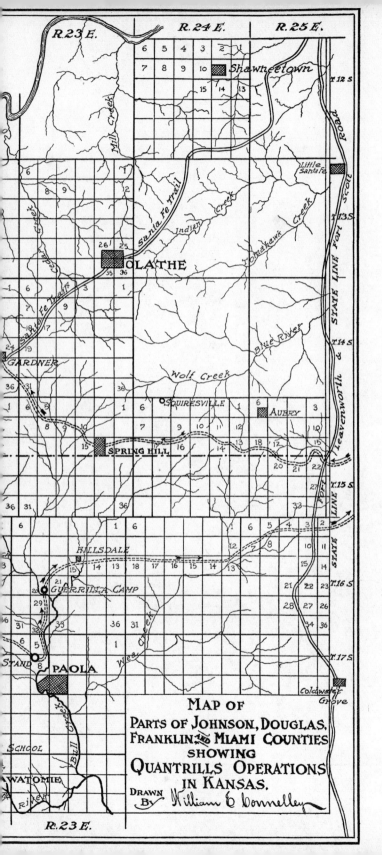

MAP OF
PARTS OF JOHNSON, DOUGLAS,
FRANKLIN AND MIAMI COUNTIES
SHOWING
QUANTRILLS OPERATIONS
IN KANSAS.

DRAWN BY William E Connelley

INDEX

33

trill went east to assassinate President Lincoln, 456.

Wear, Colonel: surprised at accuracy of Colonel Moonlight's artillery-shooting, 199; letter of Quantrill referred to, 232; Randlett met in Kansas City, 233; mentioned in report of Colonel Mitchell, 242.

Webb, Lieut. E. L.: where stationed, 312.

Webb, W. L.: author; work of referred to, 264.

Wheeler, Captain Holland: knew Quantrill as Charley Hart; Stone showed him Quantrill's true name in hotel register, 110; Quantrill's stealing from Delawares, 127; concerning Allen Pinks, 136.

Whitaker, ———: murdered at Aubry by Quantrill, 225.

White, Lieut. ———: in attack at Clark farm, 248.

White, E. W.: in Quantrill meeting at Paola, 150; sent to defend Quantrill, 185; went with Potter to Stanton, 187; went back to Paola with Quantrill, 189; attorney for Quantrill in *habeas corpus* proceedings, 191.

White, Major Frank J.: where stationed, 312.

White, Robert: in Quantrill meeting at Paola, 150; went to Stanton, 187; went to Paola with Quantrill, 189.

White Turkey: confronted Quantrill with proofs of stealing; made him sneak away, 127; portrait of; killed Skaggs, 381; trailed hack containing wounded guerrillas, 415.

Whitney house: Stone's hotel so called, 344.

Whittier, the poet: statement of concerning his poem, 23.

Wichita Eagle: mentioned, 355.

Wigfall, General Louis T.: interview of Quantrill described by, 279.

Wiggins, Phillip: killed by Quantrill at Olathe, 272.

Wigginton, George: went to Kentucky with Quantrill, 457.

Wild Bill: defeated in shooting contests by Theodore Bartles, 319; a Red Leg, 413.

Wilder, Captain: house of not molested, 376.

Wilder, D. W.: occupied at Harvard same room formerly had by Cyrus Leland, Sr., there, 428.

Wilder's Annals of Kansas: referred to, 271.

Wilkerson, T. R.: had store at Stanton, 183; Quantrill taken to store of, 184; Potter went to store of, 187.

Williams, Colonel: at sacking of Humboldt, 209.

Williams, Andrew: gave author information about Lawrence Massacre, 337.

Williams, Amanda: went to school to Quantrill, 87.

Williams, Daniel: saw Quantrill cut his name on watch, 112.

Williams, D. C.: one of the defenders of the Morgan Walker home, 156.

Williams, Elzena: went to school to Quantrill, 87.

Williams, H. H.: sheriff of Miami county; deputized Snyder to take Quantrill to Lawrence; betrayed Snyder, 185; said by Potter to have robbed first store looted in Missouri in Civil War, 190.

Williams, Jefferson: went to school to Quantrill, 87.

ERRATA

That Quantrill himself shot Dulinski, at Lawrence, is affirmed by Jacob Pike, who says that after he had passed Dulinski he fired back over his shoulder and killed him.

The location of the house of Rev. H. D. Fisher, as shown on the map is erroneous. It is a little further south and fronts east on Vermont street, but overlooks the park.

Judge C. D. Nichols, Topeka, has informed the author that the house of Barbara Freitchie is not now standing. It was torn down a few years since to give greater width to Carroll creek.—page 23.

In a recent article on the Baxter Springs Massacre published in the *Topeka Capital* it is said that Major Curtis "was unhorsed and captured, and was taken out and shot." The article is a good one.—p. 427.

Captain Holland Wheeler, of Lawrence, informs the author that John Dean shot Allen Pinks about nine o'clock at night. The moon shone brightly. Jacob Pike, also of Lawrence, saw Dean shoot Pinks, as he told the author, November 10, 1909.—p. 137.

Jacob Pike says the incident of the burning of the negro child by the guerrillas as told by Legate was on this wise: A guerrilla found in the Eldridge House a negro woman who had been his slave. Her child was torn from her arms and thrown into a room of the hotel and left to be burned alive. She was mounted on a horse and taken away by the captor. In the skirmishing she was shot in the left arm. She escaped before the guerrillas reached the State-line, and returned to Lawrence.—p. 372.

Concerning the escape of Mrs. Chester Thomas, at the Baxter Springs Massacre, there are conflicting statements. The text follows the account of Lieut. Cyrus Leland, Jr., who had it from his father, who was present. In the *Club Member*, May, 1907, there is an account of the escape very different from that given in the text, told by Charles A. Davis, Baraboo, Wis., who was present. There it is said that Mrs. Thomas was in a buggy with Davis, the buggy drawn by two horses. When the Union troops fled in a rout Davis had her lie down in the buggy. He got down on his knees and whipped the horses into a run and pressed them about three miles. Then Mrs. Thomas was put on a horse and taken back to Fort Scott.

In the *Gregg Manuscript* the escape of this buggy is noted, as is shown in the text, but the woman stood up in the buggy and whipped the horse to his highest speed while the soldier fired back at the guerrillas, and the buggy was drawn by one horse. Not being able to reconcile these accounts the author followed Leland. It may be that there is a confusion of the two accounts, for Davis says he mounted Mrs. Thomas astride a horse when his team stopped, and he mounted another, and they continued to flee.—p. 428.

As to the point where Major Plumb came up with Captain Coleman when following Quantrill's trail, the official reports are indefinite. The guerrilla lookout on Mount Oread saw both bodies of troops approaching and said they united south of the Wakarusa at or near the Blue-Jacket Crossing. The guerrillas then left Lawrence, going south to avoid the troops, hoping to strike the Santa Fe Trail and follow it in escaping from Kansas. A. J. Phillips told the author, at Lawrence, November 10, 1909, that Plumb came up with Coleman just south of the Blue Mound, which is two miles south and two miles west of the Crossing. Phillips was one of Coleman's force. It may have been scouting parties seen at the Crossing.—p. 398.